The Princeton Review®

Cracking the

ACT®

2016 Edition

By the Staff of the Princeton Review

PrincetonReview.com

Penguin
Random
House

The Princeton Review
24 Prime Parkway, Suite 201
Natick, MA 01760
E-mail: editorialsupport@review.com

Published in the United States by Penguin Random
House LLC, New York and in Canada by Random
House of Canada, a division of Penguin Random
House Ltd., Toronto.

ISBN: 978-1-101-88198-9
ebook ISBN: 978-1-101-88203-0
ISSN: 1059-101X

Editor: Sarah Litt
Production Editor: Liz Rutzel
Production Artist: Deborah A. Silvestrini

10   9   8   7   6   5   4   3   2   1

2016 Edition

Editorial
Rob Franek, Senior VP, Publisher
Casey Cornelius, VP Content Development
Mary Beth Garrick, Director of Production
Selena Coppock, Managing Editor
Meave Shelton, Senior Editor
Colleen Day, Editor
Sarah Litt, Editor
Aaron Riccio, Editor
Orion McBean, Editorial Assistant

Random House Publishing Team
Tom Russell, Publisher
Alison Stoltzfus, Publishing Manager
Melinda Ackell, Associate Managing Editor
Ellen Reed, Production Manager
Kristin Lindner, Production Supervisor
Andrea Lau, Designer

Acknowledgments

A test-preparation course is much more than clever techniques and powerful computer score reports; the reason our results are so great is that our teachers really care. A small group of Princeton Review instructors enthusiastically created a program to prepare students for the previous version of the ACT. We would like to thank John Cauman, Judy Moreland, Bill Lindsley, and Jim Reynolds for their commitment to the original ACT project.

The completion of this book would not have been possible without the help and dedication of several individuals. In particular, we would like to thank Melissa Hendrix and Jonathan Chiu, National Content Director for ACT.

Special thanks to Adam Robinson, who conceived of and perfected the Joe Bloggs approach to standardized tests and many other successful techniques used by The Princeton Review.

Contents

Register Your

1 Go to **PrincetonReview.com/cracking**

2 You'll see a welcome page where you can register your book using the following ISBN: 9781101881989

3 After placing this free order, you'll either be asked to log in or to answer a few simple questions in order to set up a new Princeton Review account.

4 Finally, click on the "Student Tools" tab located at the top of the screen. It may take an hour or two for your registration to go through, but after that, you're good to go.

If you are experiencing book problems (potential content errors), please contact EditorialSupport@review.com with the full title of the book, its ISBN number (located above), and the page number of the error. Experiencing technical issues? Please e-mail TPRStudentTech@review.com with the following information:

- your full name
- e-mail address used to register the book
- full book title and ISBN
- your computer OS (Mac or PC) and Internet browser (Firefox, Safari, Chrome, etc.)
- description of technical issue

Book Online!

Once you've registered, you can...

- Find any late-breaking information released about the ACT

- Read our special "ACT Insider" and get valuable advice about the college application process, including tips for writing a great essay and where to apply for financial aid

- Sort colleges by whatever you're looking for (such as Best Theater or Dorm), learn more about your top choices, and see how they all rank according to *The Best 380 Colleges*

- Check to see if there have been any corrections or updates to this edition

Look For These Icons Throughout The Book

 Proven Techniques

 Study Break

 Applied Strategies

 More Great Books

The **Princeton** Review®

Part I
Orientation

Chapter 1
Introduction to
the ACT

So you're taking the ACT. What will you need to do first? This chapter presents an overview of the ACT as a whole and discusses registration requirements, when to take the test, how to have your scores reported to colleges (or how not to), and the ways in which colleges use your scores.

THE ACT

The ACT is a standardized test used for college admissions. But you probably already knew that. In this book, we'll tell you all the things you didn't know about the ACT, all to show you how to crack the test and get your best score.

The ACT is traditionally a pencil-and-paper exam but is now given online as well. Usually taken on Saturday mornings, some states offer a special state-administration during the school day. Non-Saturday testing is available but only for students who live in remote areas or who can't test on Saturdays for religious reasons.

The ACT on Computer
Starting Spring 2016, the ACT exam will be offered on a computer at test centers along with the traditional pencil-and-paper version. Check with your local test center to see if the onlne version of the test is available. For more information, go to: www.act.org.

Where Does the ACT Come From?

The ACT is written by a nonprofit organization that used to call itself American College Testing but now just calls itself ACT. The company has been producing the ACT since 1959, introducing it as an alternative to the College Board's SAT. ACT also writes ACT Aspire, ACT Explore, and ACT Plan, which are tests you may have taken earlier in your academic career. The organization also provides a broad range of services to educational agencies and business institutions.

What Does the ACT Test?

The nice people who write the ACT—we'll refer to them as "ACT" from now on—describe it as an assessment of college readiness, "a curriculum- and standards-based educational and career planning tool that assesses students' academic readiness for college."

We at The Princeton Review have always been skeptical when any standardized test makes broad claims of what it can measure. In our opinion, a standardized test is just a measure of how well you take that test. Granted, ACT has spent an extraordinary amount of time analyzing data and providing the results of their research to various educational institutions and agencies. In fact, ACT has contributed to the development of the Common Core Standards Initiative, an educational reform that aligns diverse state curricula into national uniform standards.

Power Booking
If you were getting ready to take a history test, you'd study history. If you were preparing for a basketball game, you'd practice basketball. So if you're preparing for the ACT, study the ACT!

With all due respect to ACT and the various state and federal agencies working on the Common Core, we still think the ACT is just a measure of how well you take the ACT. Many factors other than mastery of the "curriculum-based" content determine your performance on a standardized test. That's why we'll teach you both the content you need as well as crucial test-taking strategies.

What's On the ACT?

The ACT consists of four multiple-choice, timed tests: English, Math, Reading, and Science, always given in that order. The ACT Plus Writing also includes an essay, with the Writing test given after the Science test. (ACT calls them tests, but we may also use the term "sections" in this book to avoid confusion.) In Parts II–VI, we'll thoroughly review the content and strategies you need for each test.

1. English Test (45 minutes—75 questions)

You will have 5 essays total with some words or phrases underlined. The essays will be situated on the left side of the page while on the right side of the page, you will be asked whether the underlined portion is correct as written or whether one of the three alternatives listed would be better. This is a test of grammar, punctuation, sentence structure, and rhetorical skills. Throughout each essay, commonly known as a passage, there will also be questions about overall organization and style or perhaps about how the writing could be revised or strengthened.

2. Math Test (60 minutes—60 questions)

These are the regular, multiple-choice math questions you've been doing all your life. The easier questions, which test basic math proficiency, *tend* to come first, but the folks at ACT can mix in easy, medium, and difficult problems throughout the Math test. A good third of the test covers pre-algebra and elementary algebra. Slightly less than a third covers intermediate algebra and coordinate geometry (graphing). Regular geometry accounts for less than a quarter of the questions, and there are four questions that cover trigonometry.

3. Reading Test (35 minutes—40 questions)

In this test, there will be four reading passages of about 800 words each—the average length of a *People* magazine article but maybe not as interesting. There is always one prose fiction passage, one social science passage, one humanities passage, and one natural science passage, and they are always in that order. After reading each passage, you have to answer 10 questions.

4. Science Test (35 minutes—40 questions)

No specific scientific knowledge is necessary for the Science test. You won't need to know the chemical makeup of hydrochloric acid or any formulas. Instead, you will be asked to understand scientific information presented in graphs, charts, tables, and research summaries, and you will have to make sense of one disagreement between two or three scientists. (Occasionally, there are more than three scientists.)

5. Optional Writing Test (40 minutes)

The ACT Plus Writing contains an "optional" writing test featuring a single essay. We recommend you take the "ACT Plus Writing," version of the test because many—if not most—schools require it. While on test day you may think you don't need it, you might later decide to apply to a school that requires a writing score. The last thing you want is to be forced into taking the whole ACT all over again…this time *with* the Writing test. The essay requires that you consider a socially relevant prompt and three perspectives on that prompt. Through a strangely intricate system of subscoring, your essay is graded, like the other sections, on a scale of 1–36. This score will NOT factor into your composite.

How Is the ACT Scored?

Scores for each of the four multiple-choice tests are reported on a scale of 1 to 36 (36 being the highest score possible). The four scores are averaged to yield your composite score, which is the score colleges and universities primarily use to determine admission. Next to each score is a percentile ranking. Percentile ranking refers to how you performed on the test relative to other people who took it at the same time. For instance, a percentile ranking of 87 indicates that you scored higher than 87 percent of the people who took the test, and the other 13 percent scored higher than you.

Closed Loop
The ACT tests how well you take the ACT.

Some of the scores have subcategories. English is broken down into Usage/Mechanics and Rhetorical Skills. In these subcategories, scores are reported on a scale of 1 to 18 (18 being the highest score possible). They are also reported as percentiles.

ACT will also give two cross-test scores called "STEM" (Science, Technology, Engineering, Mathematics) and "ELA" (English, Language Arts). Your STEM score is taken from your Math and Science scores. Your ELA score is taken from your English, Reading, and Writing scores (if you choose to take the Writing test). Neither score has any influence on your composite, nor, frankly, as far as we can tell, on your college admission.

On your score report, ACT also indicates if you met their "College Readiness Benchmark Scores:" 18 in English, 22 in Math, 21 in Reading, and 24 in Science. ACT maintains that these benchmarks can predict college "success," defined by a "50 percent or higher probability of earning a B or higher in the corresponding college course or courses." These scores and their meaning have been determined by ACT's own research and data, not by any studies done by colleges and universities themselves.

When Should You Take the ACT?

If you haven't already, go to **ACTStudent.org** and create your free ACT Web Account. You can register for tests, view your scores, and request score reports for colleges through this account. You can also view the specific test dates and centers for the upcoming academic year.

In the United States, U.S. Territories, and Canada, the ACT is given six times a year: September, October, December, February, April, and June. Internationally, the September test date is not offered, and the February administration is not available in New York.

Many states also offer an additional ACT as part of their state testing. Check with your high school to see if and when your state offers a special ACT. Your school will register you automatically for a state ACT. You must register yourself for all other administrations.

Traditionally, most students wait until the spring of their junior year to take the ACT. Many high schools still recommend spring of junior year because the content of the Math test includes topics some curricula do not cover before then. However, these topics appear in only a handful of questions, and many juniors take their first ACT in the fall or winter.

We recommend that you consider your own schedule when picking your test dates. Do you play a fall sport and carry a heavier load of extracurricular activities in the fall? Is winter a quiet time in between semesters? Do you act in the spring musical and plan to take several AP exams? Have you been dreaming of attending Big State University since you were a toddler and already plan to apply early decision? Let the answers to these questions determine your test dates. But we recommend taking your first test as early as your schedule allows.

How Many Times Should You Take the ACT?

For security reasons, ACT will not let you take the exam more than twelve times. But we certainly hope no one is dismayed by this restriction. There are certainly better things to do with your time on a Saturday morning, and we don't believe any college will accept "taking the ACT" as an extracurricular activity!

The Princeton Review recommends that you plan to take the ACT two to three times. If you achieve your goal score in your first administration, great. Take the money and run. On the other hand, if after three tests you have reason and motivation to take the ACT again, do it. On your first day of college, you will neither remember nor care how many times you had to take the ACT.

Does ACT "Super Score"?

The term "super score" or "super composite" is used by students, maybe even colleges, but not by ACT. ACT sends a separate score report for each test date and will send reports only for the dates you request. ACT does not combine scores from different test dates.

However, many schools (and the common application) will ask you to list the score and test date of your best English, best Math, best Reading, and best Science and then calculate a "super composite" based on these scores. Therefore, if you worry that some scores will rise as others fall when you take the ACT again, the "super composite" will reflect your best results.

The Princeton Review recommends strongly that you consult each school you're applying to. While ACT will send only the test dates you request, you should decide which and how many dates to send based on your scores and the school's guidelines about super scoring. Moreover, some schools require that you submit all test scores from every administration, and you should abide by any such requirements.

How Do You Register for the ACT?

Registration Tip #1
The registration includes ACT's survey on your grades and interests, but you are not required to answer these questions. To save time, you can provide only the required information, marked by an asterisk.

The fastest way to register is online, through your ACT Web Account. You can also obtain a registration packet at your high school guidance office, online at **ACTStudent.org/forms/stud_req**, or by writing or calling ACT at the address and phone number below.

> ACT Student Services
> 2727 Scott Blvd
> PO Box 414
> Iowa City, IA 52243-0414
> 319.337.1270

Registration Tip #2
If you take the December, April, or June test, sign up for the Test Information Release. Six to eight weeks after the test, you'll receive a copy of the test and your answers. This service costs an additional fee and is available only on these test dates. You can order the Test Information Release up to 3 months after the test date, but it's easier to order it at the time you register. It's a great tool to help you prepare for your next ACT.

Bookmark **ACTStudent.org**. You will start at this portal to view test dates, fees, and registration deadlines. You can also research the requirements and processes to apply for extended time or other accommodations. You will also start at ACTStudent.org to access your account to register, view your scores, and order score reports.

Check the site for the latest information about fees. The ACT Plus Writing costs more than the ACT (No Writing), but ACT also offers a fee waiver service. While you can choose four schools to send a score report to at no charge, there are fees for score reports sent to additional schools.

Test Security Changes

As part of the registration process, you have to upload or mail a photograph that will be printed on your admissions ticket. On test day, you have to bring the ticket and acceptable photo identification with you.

Standby testing is available, but you have to register in advance, usually before the prior Monday. Check ACTStudent.org for more information.

HOW TO PREPARE FOR THE ACT

The Princeton Review materials and test-taking techniques contained in this book should give you all the information you need to improve your score on the ACT. For more practice materials, The Princeton Review also publishes *1,460 Practice ACT Questions*, which includes six tests' worth of material.

Other popular coaching books contain several complete practice ACT exams. We strongly advise you *not* to waste your time taking these tests. In some cases, the questions in these books are not modeled on real ACT questions. Some of them cover material that is not even on the real ACT. Others give the impression that the ACT is much easier or more difficult than it really is. Taking the practice tests offered in these books could actually hurt your score.

One reason these coaching books do not use real ACT questions is that the folks at ACT won't let them. They have refused to let anyone (including us) license actual questions from old tests. You may have chosen our book because it contains full-length practice ACT exams. Rest assured that these tests are *modeled very closely after actual ACT exams*, with the proper balance of questions reflecting what the ACT actually tests.

More great titles by The Princeton Review
1,460 ACT Practice Questions offers the equivalent of 6 whole ACT practice tests.

Cynics might suggest that no one else can license ACT exams because ACT sells its own review book called *The Real ACT Prep Guide*. We think *The Real ACT Prep Guide* is well worth the price for the five real tests it contains (make sure you buy the third edition). We recommend that you either buy the book or ask your high school to send away to ACT for actual ACT tests. You can also buy real ACT tests on **ACT.org**. You should get a copy of *Preparing for the ACT Assessment* from your counselor. It's free, and it contains a complete, real ACT. The same test can be downloaded for free from ACT's website.

While we advise you to obtain these practice tests to further your preparation for the ACT, it is important that you use them properly. Many students like to think that they can prepare by simply taking test after test until they get the scores they want. Unfortunately, this doesn't work all that well. Why? Well, in many instances, repetitive test-taking only reinforces some of the bad test-taking habits that we address in this book. You should use practice tests for the following three key purposes:

- to build up familiarity with the exam
- to learn how to avoid the types of mistakes you are currently making
- to master our techniques and strategies so you can save time and earn more points

Do I Need to Prepare if I Have Good Grades?

Let's take the hypothetical case of Sid. Sid is valedictorian of his class, editor of the school paper, and the only teenager ever to win the Nobel Prize. To support his widowed mother, he sold more seeds from the back of comic books than any other person in recorded history. He speaks eight languages in addition to being able to communicate with dolphins and wolves. He has recommendations from Colin Powell *and* Bill Gates. So if Sid had a bad day when he took the ACT (the plane bringing him back from his Medal of Freedom award presentation was late), we are pretty sure that he is going to be just fine anyway. But Sid wants to ensure that when his colleges look at his ACT score, they see the same high-caliber student they see when they look at the rest of his application, so he carefully reviews the types of questions asked and learns some useful test-taking strategies.

I Have Lousy Grades in School. Is There Any Hope?

Let's take the case of Tom. Tom didn't do particularly well in high school. In fact, he has been on academic probation since kindergarten. He has caused four of his teachers to give up teaching as a profession, and he prides himself on his perfect homework record: He's never done any, not ever. But if Tom aces his ACT, a college might decide that he is actually a misunderstood genius and give him a full scholarship. Tom decides to learn as much as he can about the ACT.

Most of us, of course, fall between these two extremes. So is it important to prepare for the ACT?

If you were to look in the information bulletin of any of the colleges in which you are interested, we can pretty much guarantee that somewhere you would find the following paragraph:

> Many factors go into the acceptance of a student by a college. Test scores are *only one* of these factors. Grades in high school, extracurricular activities, essays, and recommendations are also important and may in some cases outweigh test scores.

> (2015 University of Anywhere Bulletin)

Truer words were never spoken. In our opinion, just about *every* other element in your application "package" is more important than your test scores. The Princeton Review (among other organizations) has been telling colleges for years that scores on the ACT or the SAT are pretty incomplete measures of a student's overall academic abilities. Some colleges have stopped looking at test scores entirely, and others are downplaying their importance.

So Why Should You Spend Any Time Preparing for the ACT?

Out of all the elements in your application "package," your ACT score is the easiest to change. The grades you've received up to now are written in stone. You aren't going to become captain of the football team or editor of the school paper overnight. Your essays will be only as good as you can write them, and recommendations are only as good as your teachers' memories of you.

On the contrary, in a few weeks you can substantially change your score on the ACT (and the way colleges look at your applications). The test does not pretend to measure analytic ability or intelligence. It measures your knowledge of specific skills such as grammar, algebra, and reading comprehension. Mostly, it measures how good you are at taking this test.

THE ACT VS. THE SAT

You may have to take the ACT anyway, but most of the schools in which you're interested also accept the SAT. We think the SAT is nowhere near as fair a test as the ACT. Whereas the ACT says it measures "achievement" (which we believe *can* be measured), the SAT says it measures "ability" (which we don't think can be measured at all; and if it can, the SAT sure isn't doing it).

More great titles by The Princeton Review
ACT or SAT? Choosing the Right Exam For You

What Exactly Are the Differences?

The SAT tends to be less time-pressured than the ACT. However, many of the questions on the SAT are trickier than those on the ACT. The SAT Verbal sections have a stronger emphasis on vocabulary than do the ACT English and Reading tests. The SAT Math section tests primarily algebra and plane geometry and includes no trigonometry at all.

Both tests include an Essay section, although ACT has made the Writing Test optional because some colleges require it, while others do not. ACT doesn't want to force students to take (and pay for) a test they don't need. The implication then is that many students can ignore the new Writing Test altogether, depending on what the schools to which they are applying require.

To find out if the schools in which you are interested require the ACT essay, visit the ACT Writing test page at **ACTstudent.org/writing,** or contact the schools directly.

While we are obviously not tremendously fond of the SAT, you should know that some students end up scoring substantially higher on the SAT than they do on the ACT and vice versa. It may be to your advantage to take a practice test for each one to see which is more likely to get you a better score.

The new SAT (or "redesigned SAT") will debut in March 2016. That test is coming much closer (some might say dangerously close!) to the ACT, though there will be some subtle differences. Stay tuned!

ADDITIONAL RESOURCES

Register your book to find a resource page we've created to track the upcoming changes to the ACT as this information is released by ACT, Inc. Visit **Princeton-Review.com/ACTChanges** to find out how these changes will (or won't) affect your test-taking experience and what additional preparation you may need. We've got you covered!

WHAT IS THE PRINCETON REVIEW?

The Princeton Review is the world's leading test-preparation and educational services company. We run courses at hundreds of locations worldwide and offer Web-based instruction at PrincetonReview.com. Our test-taking techniques and review strategies are unique and powerful. We developed them after studying all the real ACTs we could get our hands on and analyzed them with the most sophisticated software available. For more information about our programs and services, feel free to call us at **800-2Review**.

A FINAL THOUGHT BEFORE YOU BEGIN

The ACT does not measure intelligence, nor does it predict your ultimate success or failure as a human being. No matter how high or how low you score on this test initially, and no matter how much you may increase your score through preparation, you should *never* consider the score you receive on this or any other test a final judgment of your abilities.

Chapter 2
ACT Strategy

You will raise your ACT score by working smarter, not harder, and a smart test taker is a strategic test taker. You will target specific content to review, you will apply an effective and efficient approach, and you will employ common sense.

Each test on the ACT demands a specific approach, and even the most universal strategies vary in their applications. In Parts II–VI, we'll discuss these strategies in greater detail customized to English, Math, Reading, Science, and Writing.

THE BASIC APPROACH

The ACT test is different from the tests you take in school, so you need to approach it differently. The Princeton Review's strategies are not arbitrary. To be effective, ACT strategies have to be based on the ACT and not just any test.

You need to know how the ACT is scored and how it's constructed.

Scoring

When students and schools talk about ACT scores, they typically mean the composite score, a range of 1–36. The composite is an average of the four multiple-choice tests, each scored on the same 1–36 scale. Neither the Writing test score nor the combined English plus Writing score affect the composite.

The Composite

Whether you look at your score online or wait to get it in the mail, the biggest number on the page is always the composite. While admissions' offices will certainly see the individual scores of all five tests (and their subscores), schools will use the composite to evaluate your application, and that's why in the end it's the only one that matters.

The composite is an average. Add the scores for the English, Math, Reading, and Science tests, and divide the total by four. Do you add one test twice? Um, no. Do you omit one of the tests in the total? Er, no again. The four tests are weighted equally to calculate the composite. But do you need to bring up all four equally to raise your composite? Do you need to be a super star in all four tests? Should you focus more on your weakest tests than your strongest tests? No, no, and absolutely not. The best way to improve your composite is to shore up your weaknesses but exploit your strengths as much as possible.

> To lift the composite score as high as possible,
> maximize the scores of your strongest tests.

You don't need to be a rock star on all four tests. Identify two, maybe three tests, and focus on raising those scores as much as you can to raise your composite score. Work on your weakest scores to keep them from pulling you down. Are you strongest in English and Math, or maybe in English, Reading, and Science? Then work to raise those scores as high as you can. You shouldn't ignore your weaknesses, but recognize that the work you put in on your strengths will yield greater dividends. Think of it this way. If you had only one hour to devote to practice the week before the ACT, you would put that hour to your best subjects.

Structure

Let's review quickly the structure of the ACT. The five tests are always given in the same order.

English	Math	Reading	Science	Writing
45 minutes	60 minutes	35 minutes	35 minutes	40 minutes
75 questions	60 questions	40 questions	40 questions	1 Essay

Enemy #1: Time

How much time do you have per question on the Math test? You have just one minute, and that's generous compared with the time given per question on the English, Reading, and Science tests. But how often do you take a test in school with a minute or less per question? If you do at all, it's maybe on a multiple-choice quiz but probably not on a major exam or final. Time is your enemy on the ACT, and you have to use it wisely and be aware of how that time pressure can bring out your worst instincts as a test taker.

Enemy #2: Yourself

Many people struggle with test anxiety in school and on standardized tests. But there is something particularly evil about tests like the ACT and SAT. The skills you've been rewarded for throughout your academic career can easily work against you on the ACT. You've been taught since birth to follow directions, go in order, and finish everything. But that approach won't necessarily earn you your highest ACT score.

On the other hand, treating the ACT as a scary, alien beast can leave our brains blank and useless and can incite irrational, self-defeating behavior. When we pick up a No. 2 pencil, all of us tend to leave our common sense at the door. Test nerves and anxieties can make you misread a question, commit a careless error, see something that isn't there, blind you to what is there, talk you into a bad answer, and worst of all, convince you to spend good time after bad.

There is good news. You can—and will—crack the ACT. You will learn how to approach it differently than you would a test in school, and you won't let the test crack you.

ACT STRATEGIES

Personal Order of Difficulty (POOD)

If time is going to run out, would you rather it run out on the hardest questions or the easiest? Of course, you want it to run out on the questions you are less likely to get right.

You can easily fall into the trap of spending too much time on the hardest problems and either never getting to or rushing through the easiest. You shouldn't work in the order ACT provides just because it's in that order. Instead, find your own Personal Order of Difficulty (POOD).

Make smart decisions quickly for good reasons as you move through each test.

The Best Way to Bubble In

Work a page at a time, circling your answers right on the booklet. Transfer a page's worth of answers to the scantron at one time. It's better to stay focused on working questions rather than disrupt your concentration to find where you left off on the scantron. You'll be more accurate at both tasks. Do not wait to the end, however, to transfer all the answers of that test on your scantron. Go one page at a time on English and Math, a passage at a time on Reading and Science.

Letter of the Day (LOTD)

Just because you don't *work* a question doesn't mean you don't *answer* it. There is no penalty for wrong answers on the ACT, so you should never leave any blanks on your scantron. When you guess on Never questions, pick your favorite two-letter combo of answers and stick with it. For example, always choose A/F or C/H. If you're consistent, you're more likely to pick up more points.

Now

Does a question look okay? Do you know how to do it? Do it *Now*.

Later

Will this question take a long time to work? Leave it and come back to it *Later*. Circle the question number for easy reference to return.

Never

Test taker, know thyself. Know the topics that are your worst, and learn the signs that flash danger. Don't waste time on questions you should *Never* do. Instead, use more time to answer the Now and Later questions accurately.

Pacing

The ACT may be designed for you to run out of time, but you can't rush through it as fast as possible. All you'll do is make careless errors on easy questions you should get right and spend way too much time on difficult ones you're unlikely to get right. Let your (POOD) help determine your pacing. Go slowly enough to answer correctly all the Now questions but quickly enough to get to the number of Later questions you need to reach your goal score.

In Chapter 3, we'll teach you how to identify the number of questions you need to reach your goal score. You'll practice your pacing in practice tests, going slowly enough to avoid careless errors and quickly enough to reach your goal scores.

Process of Elimination (POE)

Multiple-choice tests offer one great advantage: They provide the correct answer right there on the page. Of course, they hide the correct answer amid 3–4 incorrect answers. It's often easier to spot the wrong answers than it is to identify the right ones, particularly when you apply a smart Process of Elimination (POE).

POE works differently on each test on the ACT, but it's a powerful strategy on all of them. For some question types, you'll always use POE rather than wasting time trying to figure out the answer on your own. For other questions, you'll use POE when you're stuck. ACT hides the correct answer behind wrong ones, but when you cross off just one or two wrong answers, the correct answer can become more obvious, sometimes jumping right off the page.

POOD, Pacing, and POE all work together to help you spend your time where it does the most good: on the questions you can and should get right.

Use Your Pencil
You own the test booklet, and you should write where and when it helps you. Use your pencil to literally cross off wrong answers on the page.

Be Ruthless

The worst mistake a test taker can make is to throw good time after bad. You read a question but don't understand it, so you read it again. And again. If you stare at it really hard, you know you're going to just *see* the answer. And you can't move on, because really, after spending all that time it would be a waste not to keep at it, right?

Wrong. You can't let one tough question drag you down, and you can't let your worst instincts tempt you into self-defeating behavior. Instead, the best way to improve your ACT score is to follow our advice.

- Use the techniques and strategies in the lessons to work efficiently and accurately through all your Now and Later questions.
- Know your Never questions, and use your LOTD.
- Know when to move on. Use POE, and guess from what's left.

In Parts II–VI, you'll learn how POOD, Pacing, and POE work on each test. In Chapter 3, we'll discuss in greater detail how to use your Pacing to hit your target scores.

Chapter 3
Score Goals

To hit your target score, you have to know how many raw points you need. Your goals and pacing for English, Math, Reading, and Science will vary depending on the test and your own individual strengths.

SCORE GRIDS

On each test of the ACT, the number of correct answers converts to a scaled score 1–36. ACT works hard to adjust the scale of each test at each administration as necessary to make all scaled scores comparable, smoothing out any differences in level of difficulty across test dates. There is thus no truth to any one test date being "easier" than the others, but you can expect to see slight variations in the scale from test to test.

This is the score grid from the free test ACT makes available on its website, **ACT.org**. We're going to use it to explain how to pick a target score and pace yourself.

Scale Score	English	Math	Reading	Science	Scale Score
36	75	59–60	40	40	36
35	73–74	57–58	39	39	35
34	71–72	55–56	38	38	34
33	70	54	—	37	33
32	69	53	37	—	32
31	68	52	36	36	31
30	67	50–51	35	35	30
29	66	49	34	34	29
28	64–65	47–48	33	33	28
27	62–63	45–46	32	31–32	27
26	60–61	43–44	31	30	26
25	58–59	41–42	30	28–29	25
24	56–57	38–40	29	26–27	24
23	53–55	36–37	27–28	24–25	23
22	51–52	34–35	26	23	22
21	48–50	33	25	21–22	21
20	45–47	31–32	23–24	19–20	20
19	42–44	29–30	22	17–18	19
18	40–41	27–28	20–21	16	18
17	38–39	24–26	19	14–15	17
16	35–37	19–23	18	13	16
15	33–34	15–18	16–17	12	15
14	30–32	12–14	14–15	11	14
13	29	10–11	13	10	13
12	27–28	8–9	11–12	9	12
11	25–26	6–7	9–10	8	11
10	23–24	5	8	7	10

PACING STRATEGIES

Focus on the number of questions you need to hit your goal scores.

English

For English, there is no order of difficulty of the passages or their questions. The most important thing is to finish, finding all the Now questions you can throughout the whole test.

Math

Spend more time to do fewer questions, and you'll raise your accuracy. Let's say your goal on Math is a 24. Find 24 under the scaled score column, and you'll see that you need 38–40 raw points. Take all 60 minutes and work 45 questions, using your Letter of the Day (LOTD) on 15 Never questions. You'll get most of the questions you work right, some wrong, and pick up a couple points on the LOTDs.

Look at this way: How many *more* questions do you need to answer correctly to move from a 24 to a 27? As few as five. Do you think you could find five careless errors on a practice test that you *should* have gotten right?

More great titles by The Princeton Review
English and Reading Workout for the ACT
and
Math and Science Workout for the ACT

Reading

When it comes to picking a pacing strategy for Reading, you have to practice extensively and figure out what works best for you.

Some students are slow but good readers. If you take 35 minutes to do fewer passages, you could get all of the questions right for each passage you do. Use your LOTD for the passages you don't work, and you should pick up a few additional points.

Other students could take hours to work each passage and never get all the questions right. But if you find all the questions you can do on many passages, using your LOTD on all those Never questions, you could hit your target score.

Which is better? There is no answer to that. True ACT score improvement will come with a willingness to experiment and analyze what works best for you.

Science

In the Science lessons, you'll learn how to identify your Now, Later, and Never passages.

Our advice is to be aggressive. Spend the time needed on the easiest passages first, but keep moving to get to your targeted raw score. Identify Never questions on Now Passages, and use your LOTD. Alternatively, find the Now questions on as many Later passages as you can get to.

PACING CHARTS

Revisit this page as you practice. Record your scores from practice. Set a goal of 1–3 points in your scaled score for the next practice test. Identify the number of questions you need to answer correctly to reach that goal. The score grids provided in Part VIII come with their specific scales. You can use those, or use the score grids in this chapter.

English Pacing

Scale Score	Raw Score	Scale Score	Raw Score	Scale Score	Raw Score
36	75	27	62–63	18	40–4
35	73–74	26	60–61	17	38–39
34	71–72	25	58–59	16	35–37
33	70	24	56–57	15	33–34
32	69	23	53–55	14	30–32
31	68	22	51–52	13	29
30	67	21	48–50	12	27–28
29	66	20	45–47	11	25–26
28	64–65	19	42–44	10	23–24

Remember that in English, your pacing goal is to finish.

Prior Score (if applicable): _____

Practice Test 1 Goal: _____   Practice Test 2 Goal: _____

# of Questions Needed: _____   # of Questions Needed: _____

Practice Test 1 Score: _____   Practice Test 2 Score: _____

Math Pacing

Scale Score	Raw Score	Scale Score	Raw Score	Scale Score	Raw Score
36	59–60	27	45–46	18	27–28
35	57–58	26	43–44	17	24–26
34	55–56	25	41–42	16	19–23
33	54	24	38–40	15	15–18
32	53	23	36–37	14	12–14
31	52	22	34–35	13	10–11
30	50–51	21	33	12	8–9
29	49	20	31–32	11	6–7
28	47–48	19	29–30	10	5

Our advice is to add 5 questions to your targeted raw score. You have a cushion to get a few wrong—nobody's perfect—and you're likely to pick up at least a few points from your LOTDs. Track your progress on practice tests to pinpoint your target score.

Prior Score (if applicable): _____

Practice Test 1 Goal: _____   Practice Test 2 Goal: _____

# of Questions Needed: _____   # of Questions Needed: _____

                                    +5   +5

= # of Questions to Work:_____   = # of Questions to Work:_____

Practice Test 1 Score: _____   Practice Test 2 Score: _____

Reading Pacing

Scale Score	Raw Score	Scale Score	Raw Score	Scale Score	Raw Score
36	40	27	32	18	20–21
35	39	26	31	17	19
34	38	25	30	16	18
33	—	24	29	15	16–17
32	37	23	27–28	14	14–15
31	36	22	26	13	13
30	35	21	25	12	11–12
29	34	20	23–24	11	9–10
28	33	19	22	10	8

Experiment with Reading by trying fewer passages, more time per passage and then adding more passages, more questions. Identify first how many questions you need.

Prior Score (if applicable): _____

Practice Test 1 Goal: _____   Practice Test 2 Goal: _____

# of Questions Needed: _____   # of Questions Needed: _____

How many passages to work: _____   How many passages to work: _____

Practice Test 1 Score: _____   Practice Test 2 Score: _____

Science Pacing

Scale Score	Raw Score	Scale Score	Raw Score	Scale Score	Raw Score
36	40	27	31–32	18	16
35	39	26	30	17	14–15
34	38	25	28–29	16	13
33	37	24	26–27	15	12
32	—	23	24–25	14	11
31	36	22	23	13	10
30	35	21	21–22	12	9
29	34	20	19–20	11	8
28	33	19	17–18	10	7

More great titles from The Princeton Review
Feeling confident? *ACT Elite 36* is designed specifically for advanced students who want to push themselves toward that perfect ACT score.

ACT Science tests may have either 6 or 7 passages.

Use this chart below to figure out how many passages to work.

Target Score	# of passages to attempt
< 20	4–5 passages
20–27	5–6 passages
> 27	6–7 passages

Prior Score (if applicable): _____

Practice Test 1 Goal: _____   Practice Test 2 Goal: _____

# of Questions Needed: _____   # of Questions Needed: _____

How many passages to work: _____   How many passages to work: _____

Practice Test 1 Score: _____   Practice Test 2 Score: _____

Chapter 4
Taking the ACT

Preparing yourself both mentally and physically to take the ACT is important. This chapter helps you learn exactly what you're in for, so you can plan ahead and be as comfortable as possible on test day. We not only talk about what to do but also what *not* to do.

PREPARING FOR THE ACT

The best way to prepare for any test is to find out exactly what is going to be on it. This book provides you with just that information. In the following chapters, you will find a comprehensive review of all the question types on the ACT, complete information on all the subjects covered by the ACT, and some powerful test-taking strategies developed specifically for the ACT.

To take full advantage of the review and techniques, you should practice on the tests in this book as well as on real ACT questions. We've already told you how to obtain copies of real ACT exams. Taking full practice exams allows you to chart your progress (with accurate scores for each test), gives you confidence in our techniques, and develops your stamina.

The Night Before the Test

Unless you are the kind of person who remains calm only by staying up all night to do last-minute studying, we recommend that you take the evening off. Go see a movie or read a good book (besides this one), and make sure you get to bed at a normal hour. No final, frantically memorized math formula or grammatical rule is going to make or break your score. A positive mental attitude comes from treating yourself decently. If you've prepared over the last several weeks or months, then you're ready.

If you haven't really prepared, there will be other opportunities to take the test, so get some rest and do the best you can. Remember, colleges will see only the score you choose to let them see. No *single* ACT is going to be crucial. We don't think night-before-the-test cramming is very effective. For example, we would not recommend that you try going through this book in one night.

On the Day of the Test

It's important that you eat a real breakfast, even if you normally don't. We find that about two-thirds of the way through the test, people who didn't eat something beforehand suddenly lose their will to live. Equally important: Bring a snack to the test center. You will get a break during which food is allowed. Some people spend the break out in the hallways comparing answers and getting upset when their answers don't match. Ignore the people around you, and eat your snack. Why assume they know any more than you do?

Don't Leave Home Without 'Em

Here are some items you'll want to have on test day.

- Admissions ticket
- Photo ID or letter of identification
- Plenty of sharpened No. 2 pencils
- A watch
- An acceptable calculator with new batteries

Warming Up

While you're having breakfast, do a couple of questions from an ACT on which you've already worked to get your mind going. You don't want to use the first test on the real exam to warm up. And please don't try a hard question you've never done before. If you miss it, your confidence will be diminished, and that's not something you want on the day of the test.

At the test center, you'll be asked to show some form of picture ID or provide a note from your school—on school stationery—describing what you look like. The time or time remaining is often *not* announced during the test sections, so you should also bring a reliable watch—not the beeping kind—and, of course, several No. 2 pencils, an eraser, and a calculator. Check **ACTStudent.org/faq** to see if your calculator model is permitted. If you haven't changed the batteries recently (or ever), you should do that before the test or bring a back-up calculator.

When you get into the actual room in which you'll be taking the exam, make sure you're comfortable. Is there enough light? Is your desk sturdy? Don't be afraid to speak up; after all, you're going to be spending three and a half hours at that desk. And it's not a bad idea to go to the bathroom *before* you get to the room. It's a long haul to that first break.

ZEN AND THE ART OF TEST TAKING

Once the exam begins, tune out the rest of the world. That girl with the annoying cough in the next row? You don't hear her. That guy who is fidgeting in the seat ahead of you? You don't see him. It's just you and the exam. Everything else should be a blur.

As soon as one test ends, erase it completely from your mind. It no longer exists. The only test that counts is the one you are taking right now. Even if you are upset about a particular test, erase it from your mind. If you are busy thinking about the last test, you cannot focus on the one on which you are currently working, and that's a surefire way to make costly mistakes. Most people aren't very good at assessing how they performed on a given section of the exam, especially while they're still taking it, so don't waste your time and energy trying.

Some Things to Remember

- Make sure you know where the test center is located and where you need to go once you are at the test center.
- Show up early; you can't show up right when the test is scheduled to begin and expect to get in.
- Lay out your pencils, calculator, watch, admission ticket, and photo identification the night before the test. The last thing you want to be doing on the morning of the test is running around looking for a calculator. Also, it's important to bring your own watch because there's no requirement that the room you're in needs to have a working clock.
- Bring a snack and a bottle of water just in case you get hungry. There's nothing worse than testing on an empty stomach.

Keep Your Answers to Yourself

Please don't let anyone cheat off you. Test companies have developed sophisticated anti-cheating measures that go way beyond having a proctor walk around the room. We know of one test company that gets seating charts of each testing room. Its computers scan the score sheets of people sitting in the immediate vicinity for correlations of wrong answer choices. Innocent and guilty are invited to take the exam over again, and their scores from the first exam are invalidated.

Beware of Misbubbling Your Answer Sheet

Probably the most painful kind of mistake you can make on the ACT is to bubble in choice (A) with your pencil when you really mean choice (B), or to have your answers be one question number off (perhaps because you skipped one question on the test but forgot to skip it on the answer sheet). Aargh! The proctor isn't allowed to let you change your answers after a section is over, so it is critical that you either catch yourself before a test section ends or—even better—that you don't make a mistake in the first place.

Write Now
Feel free to write all over your test booklet. Don't do computations in your head. Put them in the booklet; you paid for it. Go nuts!

We suggest to our students that they write down their answers in their test booklets. This way, whenever you finish a page of questions in the test booklet, you can transfer all your answers from that page in a group. We find that this method minimizes the possibility of misbubbling, and it also saves time. Of course, as you get near the end of a test, you should go back to bubbling question by question.

If you get back your ACT scores and they seem completely out of line, you can ask the ACT examiners to look over your answer sheet for what are called "gridding errors." If you want to, you can even be there while they look. If it is clear that there has been an error, ACT will change your score. An example of a gridding error would be a test in which, if you moved all the responses over by one, they would suddenly all be correct.

Should I Ever Cancel My Scores?

We recommend against canceling your scores, even if you feel you've done poorly. If you have registered as we recommended and not sent the scores to any colleges and possibly not to your high school, then the score you receive won't go anywhere unless you send it on later. There is no need to panic and cancel your score without knowing what it is if no one will ever see it. You never know—perhaps you did better than you think. Furthermore, if you've taken the ACT two or more times (something we heartily recommend), you can choose which score you want colleges to see when you request reports from ACT.

If you do decide to cancel your scores, ACT allows you to do it only at the test center itself. However, you can stop scores from reaching colleges if you call ACT by 12:00 P.M. (CST) on the *Thursday* following the test. The number to call is 319-337-1270.

Part II
How to
Crack the ACT
English Test

Chapter 5
Introduction to the ACT English Test

The English test is not a grammar test. It's also not a test of how well you write. In fact, it tests your editing skills: your ability to fix errors in grammar and punctuation and to improve the organization and style of five different passages. In this chapter, you'll learn the basic strategy of how to crack the passages and review the grammar you need to know.

WHAT'S ON THE ENGLISH TEST

Before we dive into the details of the content and strategy, let's review what the English test looks like. Remember, the five tests on the ACT are always given in the same order, and English is always first.

There are five prose passages on topics ranging from historical essays to personal narratives. Each passage is typically accompanied by 15 questions for a total of 75 questions that you must answer in 45 minutes. Portions of each passage are underlined, and you must decide if these are correct as written or if one of the other answers would fix or improve the selection. Other questions will ask you to add, cut, or reorder text, while still others will ask you to evaluate the passage as a whole.

WRITING

While the idea of English grammar makes most of us think of persnickety, picky rules long since outdated, English is actually a dynamic, adaptive language. We add new vocabulary all the time, and we let common usage influence and change many rules. Pick up a handful of style books, and you'll find very few rules that everyone agrees upon. This is actually good news for studying for the ACT: You're unlikely to see questions testing the most obscure or most disputed rules. However, few of us follow ALL of even the most basic, universally accepted rules when we speak, much less when we e-mail, text, or tweet.

The 4 C's: Complete, Consistent, Clear, and Concise

ACT test writers will never make you name a particular error. But with 75 questions, they can certainly test a lot of different rules—and yes, that's leaving out the obscure and debated rules. You would drive yourself crazy if you tried to learn, just for the ACT, all of the grammar you never knew in the first place. You're much better off with a common sense approach. We'll teach you the rules that show up the most often, and we'll show you how to crack the questions that test them. What about all the rest of the questions? That's where the 4 C's come in.

Good writing should be in **complete** sentences; everything should be **consistent**; the meaning should be **clear**. The best answer, free of any errors, will be the most **concise**. All of the rules we'll review fall under one or more of the 4 C's. But even when you can't identify what a question is testing, apply the 4 C's, and you'll be able to answer even the most difficult questions.

We'll explain in greater detail what the 4 C's mean in the grammar review and in the following lessons. But first, let's discuss your general strategies and overall approach to the English test.

HOW TO CRACK THE ENGLISH TEST

The Passages

As always on the ACT, time is your enemy. With only 45 minutes to review five passages and answer 75 questions, you can't read a passage in its entirety, and then go back to do the questions. For each passage, work the questions as you make your way through the passage. Read from the beginning until you get to an underlined selection, work that question, and then resume reading until the next underlined portion and the next question.

Steps 1 through 5 (below) demonstrate how to apply our Basic Approach to specific questions.

The Questions

Not all questions are created equally. In fact, ACT divides the questions on the English test into two categories: usage and mechanics and rhetorical skills. These designations will mean very little to you when you're taking the test. All questions are worth the same number of points, after all, and you'll crack most of the questions the same way, regardless of what ACT calls them. Many of the rhetorical skills questions, however, are on organization and style, and some take longer to answer than other questions. Since there is no order of difficulty of the passages or of the questions, all that matters is that you identify your *Now, Later, Never* questions and make sure you finish.

The best way to make sure you finish with as many correct answers as possible is to use our 5-step Basic Approach.

Step 1: Identify the Topic

For each underlined portion, finish the sentence, and then look at the answers. The answers are your clues to identifying what the question is testing. Let's start off with this first question.

Step
1

American <u>author Junot Díaz, was born in</u> the Dominican Republic.
1

1. **A.** NO CHANGE
   B. author, Junot Díaz
   C. author Junot Díaz
   D. author, Junot Díaz,

Do any of the words change? No. What is the only thing that does change? Commas. So what must be the topic of the question? Commas.

Always identify the topic of the question first. Pay attention to what changes versus what stays the same in the answers.

Step 2: Use POE

You may have chosen an answer for question 1 already. If you haven't, don't worry: We'll review all the rules of commas in the next lesson. But let's use question 1 to learn the next step, POE. To go from good to great on the English test, you can't just fix a question in your head and then find an answer that matches. Instead, after you've identified what's wrong, eliminate all the choices that do not fix the error.

For question 1, the comma after *Díaz* is unnecessary and should be deleted. Cross off the answers that leave it in, choices (A) and (D).

1. ~~A. NO CHANGE~~
   B. author, Junot Díaz
   C. author Junot Díaz
   ~~D. author, Junot Díaz,~~

Now compare the two that remain, choices (B) and (C). Do you need the comma after *author*? No, you don't need any commas, so choice (C) is the correct answer. Here's where you could have messed up if you didn't use POE: If you knew all along you didn't need any commas, you could have easily missed that new comma in choice (B) and chosen incorrectly. POE on English isn't optional or a backup when you're stuck. You have to first eliminate wrong answers, and then compare what's left.

Let's go on to the next step.

Step 3: Use the Context

Even though you may struggle with time on the English test, you can't skip the non-underlined text in between questions in order to save yourself a few minutes. Take a look at this next question.

After Díaz won the 2008 Pulitzer Prize, many college literary courses <u>will add his</u>[2] works to the curriculum.

2. F. NO CHANGE
   G. added
   H. were adding
   J. add

Don't forget to apply the first two steps. The verb in the answer choices is changing, specifically verb tense. How do you know which tense to use? Look at the beginning of the sentence: The phrase *After Díaz won* tells us we want past tense, so eliminate the choices that don't use past tense.

2. ~~F. NO CHANGE~~
   G. added
   H. were adding
   ~~J. add~~

This is the 4 C's in action, or at least two of them: Between choices (G) and (H), choice (G) is most *concise*. The correct tense has to be *consistent* with the clues in the non-underlined portion. Between two choices that are technically grammatically correct, the more *concise* choice wins.

Don't skip from question to question. The non-underlined text provides context you need.

Let's move on to the next step.

Step 4: Trust Your Ear, But Verify

For question 2, you may have never even considered choice (H) as serious competition for choice (G). It just sounds wrong, doesn't it? Well, it turned out you were right. In fact, your ear is pretty reliable at raising the alarm for outright errors and clunky, awkward phrasing.

You should, however, always verify what your ear signals by confirming the actual error. Steps 1 and 2 will help with that: Use the answers to identify the topic, and use POE heavily.

But remember to be careful for errors your ear *won't* catch. Using the answers to identify the topic will save you there as well.

Let's try another question.

One college class chose Díaz's *The Brief Wondrous Life of Oscar Wao* as their favorite book of the semester.
                                                    3

3. **A.** NO CHANGE
   B. it's favorite book
   C. they're favorite book
   D. its favorite book

That sounded pretty good to us, how about you? But before we circle NO CHANGE and go on our merry way, look at the answers to identify the topic and confirm there is no error. Only the pronoun changes, so the question is testing pronouns. We'll go over all the rules about pronouns in Chapter 7, so we'll just give a short explanation here. *Their* is a plural pronoun, but *class* is singular. Cross off choices (A) and (C)—choice (C) isn't even the right type of pronoun, plural or not. Since we need a possessive pronoun, cross off choice (B) as well. Choice (D) is the correct answer.

Let's move on to our last step.

Step **5**

Step 5: Don't Fix What Isn't Broken
Read the next question.

Among a generation of new American writers, Díaz has <u>emerged as one of the</u> freshest, most original voices.
₄

4. **F.** NO CHANGE
   G. been distinguished and deemed
   H. come on the scene as
   J. made a strong case to be called

Sounds okay, so go to Step 1, identify the topic. Remember that saved us with question 3. *Everything* seems to be changing in the answers for question 4: What the question is testing isn't obvious at all. You can't confirm what you can't identify, so leave "NO CHANGE," and apply the 4 C's.

Does one of the answers fix something you missed?

Does one of the answers make the sentence better by making it more concise?

If the answer to both questions is No for all three other answers, the correct answer is choice (A), NO CHANGE.

NO CHANGE *is* a legitimate answer choice. Don't make the mistake of assuming that all questions have an error that you just can't spot. If you use the five steps of our Basic Approach, you'll catch errors your ear would miss, and you'll confidently choose NO CHANGE when it's the correct answer.

Pace Yourself
Repeat Steps 1–5 as you make your way through all the questions on all five passages. Since there is no order of difficulty in the passages or questions, your pacing goal is to finish.

Goal Score
Use the pacing strategies and score grid on page 22 to find your goal score for each practice test and, eventually, the ACT.

GRAMMAR REVIEW

This is not an exhaustive review of English grammar. It is an overview of the most common rules tested on the English test. We focus on the rules that show up the most AND that we know you can easily identify. In the next two chapters, we'll teach you how to crack those questions on the ACT. For now, we'll introduce you to the terms and rules you need to know.

Verbs

What's wrong with the following sentences?

1. Ryan play soccer.

2. Mary and Allison practices every day.

3. Next week, the team traveled to play its bitter rival.

4. Shivani has became the star of the team.

If you read thoughtfully, your ear probably caught all of the verb errors in these sentences. Remember, your ear will pretty reliably raise the alarm with many errors you'll encounter on the English test. You don't always need to know why a sentence is wrong to get the right answer, but the more you know why, the more you can count on getting that question right the next time it appears, and every time after that. Know the likely errors for verbs.

Subject-Verb Agreement

First, know your terms. A *subject* is the performer of an action. A *verb* is an action, feeling, or state of being. Verbs have to be consistent with their subjects. Singular subjects take the singular form of the verb, and plural subjects take plural forms of the verb.

> ### The Rule
> Your ear can alert you to many, if not most, subject-verb agreement errors.
> **As a general rule, singular verbs end with *s* and plural verbs do not.**

*Ryan **plays** soccer.*

*Mary and Allison **practice** every day.*

Verb Tense

The tense of the verb changes with the time of the event.

Simple Tense

ACT tests your ability to choose from among the three simple tenses.

Past: *Last year, the team **finished** in last place.*

Present: *This year, the team **plays** a demanding schedule.*

Future: *Next week, the team **will travel** to play its bitter rival.*

Perfect Tenses

The perfect tenses provide additional ways to place an event in time. On the ACT, the perfect tenses appear less often than do the simple tenses.

Past perfect: *Before I went to the performance with Kelly, I **had** never **appreciated** ballet before.*

Use the past perfect to make clear the chronology of two events completed at a definite time in the past, one before the other.

Present perfect: *I **have lived** in Chicago for ten years. I **have read** all the* Harry Potter *books.*

Use the present perfect to describe an event that began in the past and continues into the present, or to describe an event that was completed at some indefinite time before the present.

Future perfect: *Jim **will have left** by the time I arrive.*

Use the future perfect to describe an event that will be completed at a definite later time.

Irregular Verbs

ACT tests heavily the correct past *participle* of irregular verbs. Participle refers to the form the verb takes when it's paired with the helping verb *to have* to form a perfect tense. For regular verbs, the simple past tense and the past participle are the same.

*I **called** you last night. I **have called** you several times today.*

For irregular verbs, the two are different.

*Shivani **became** the star of the team,* or *Shivani **has become** the star of the team.*

Here is a list of some common irregular verbs.

Infinitive	Simple Past	Past Participle
become	became	become
begin	began	begun
blow	blew	blown
break	broke	broken
bring	brought	brought
choose	chose	chosen
come	came	come
drink	drank	drunk
drive	drove	driven
eat	ate	eaten
fall	fell	fallen
fly	flew	flown
forbid	forbade	forbidden
forget	forgot	forgotten
forgive	forgave	forgiven
freeze	froze	frozen
get	got	gotten
give	gave	given
go	went	gone
grow	grew	grown
hide	hid	hidden
know	knew	known
lay	laid	laid
lead	led	led
lie	lay	lain

Infinitive	Simple Past	Past Participle
ride	rode	ridden
ring	rang	rung
rise	rose	risen
run	ran	run
see	saw	seen
shake	shook	shaken
sing	sang	sung
speak	spoke	spoken
spring	sprang	sprung
steal	stole	stolen
swim	swam	swum
take	took	taken
teach	taught	taught
tear	tore	torn
throw	threw	thrown
wear	wore	worn
write	wrote	written

Pronouns

What's wrong with the following sentences?

1. The team nominated their goalie the most valuable player.

2. My friends and me took the train downtown.

3. Her and I worked on the group project together.

4. The crowd pushed Cesar and I onto the stage.

Pronoun Agreement

First, know your terms. *Pronouns* take the place of nouns. Pronouns have to be consistent with the nouns they replace in number and in gender.

	Female	Male	Things
Singular	she, her, hers	he, him, his	it, its
Plural	they, them, their	they, them, their	they, them, their

*The team nominated **its** goalie the most valuable player.*

Pronoun Case

Pronouns also need to be consistent with the function they perform in a sentence. There are three different cases of pronouns: *subject*, *object*, and *possessive*.

	1st person	2nd person	3rd person
Subject	I, we	you	she, he, it, they
Object	me, us	you	her, him, it, them
Possessive	my, mine, our, ours	your	her, hers, his, its, their, theirs

*My friends and **I** took the train downtown.*

***She** and I worked on the group project together.*

*The crowd pushed Cesar and **me** onto the stage.*

Modifiers

What's wrong with these sentences?

1. No one took her warnings serious.

2. Blizzard is a charmingly energetically puppy.

3. Farid is more busy than Wesley is.

4. Lara was the beautifulest girl at the prom.

Adjectives and Adverbs

Adjectives modify nouns. *Adverbs* modify everything else, including verbs, adjectives, and other adverbs. Most adverbs are formed by adding *-ly* to the end of an adjective.

*No one took her warnings **seriously**.*

*Blizzard is a charmingly **energetic** puppy.*

Comparisons and Superlatives

For most adjectives, an *-er* at the end makes a comparison, and an *-est* makes a superlative. But some adjectives need instead the word *more* for a comparison and the word *most* for a superlative.

*Farid is **busier** than Wesley is.*

*Lara was the **most beautiful** girl at the prom.*

In the following chapters, we'll show you how these rules appear on the ACT and how to crack those questions. We'll also discuss some of the more difficult and challenging concepts that you may face.

Summary

- Identify what the question is testing by changes in the answer choices.

- Use POE heavily.

- Don't skip the non-underlined text: Use it for context.

- Trust your ear, but verify by the rules.

- NO CHANGE is a legitimate answer choice.

- Good writing should be complete, consistent, clear, and concise.

Chapter 6
Complete

The ACT English test contains a number of questions that test sentence structure and punctuation. This chapter discusses how to identify ideas as complete or incomplete and then explains how to punctuate different ideas. In addition to covering punctuation, the chapter also covers how to change ideas with the addition or removal of conjunctions.

COMPLETE AND INCOMPLETE IDEAS

Many questions on the English test involve sentence structure and punctuation. The correct structure and punctuation all depend on whether the ideas are complete or incomplete.

A complete idea can stand on its own, whether it's the entire sentence or just one part. Let's look at some examples.

1. *Amanda throws strikes.*
2. *Go Bears!*
3. *Who won the game?*
4. *The team celebrated after they won the game.*

Think of a complete idea as one part of a conversation. You don't have to say a lot to hold up one side of a conversation, but you can't leave your listener hanging. You have to finish your sentence. You can give commands, and you can ask questions too. Your listeners don't have to know what you're talking about: They just have to wait for you to finish to ask questions of their own. *What game are you asking me about? How did the team celebrate?*

In grammar terms, a complete idea must have a subject and a verb. Let's break down the examples above.

	Subject	Verb
1	*Amanda*	*throws*
2	*You* (understood)	*Go*
3	*Who*	*won*
4	*team* and *they*	*celebrated* and *won*

An incomplete idea can't stand on its own. Look at the following examples.

1. *The batter who hit second*
2. *Since you bought the hotdogs*
3. *To get a batter out*
4. *The team grabbed*

If anyone began a conversation with any of these, you would be waiting for the speaker to finish before you could speak. That's a sure sign all of the examples are incomplete: None of them are finished, and all would leave you hanging as a listener.

Now, in real life terms, we may think some of those examples could be fine as answers to these questions: *Who got the run? Why did you buy the sodas? Why did he pitch a fastball?* Remember, however, that in real life we don't always follow the conventional rules when we speak. So let's define an incomplete idea in grammatical terms.

An incomplete idea is always missing something, whether a subject and verb (example #3), the main idea (example #2), or the rest of an idea (examples #1 and #4). None of these could stand on its own, and each would need to link up with another idea to make a sentence. ACT tests heavily how to link ideas with punctuation and conjunctions, so let's see how that works.

STOP PUNCTUATION

Imagine two trucks heading toward a busy intersection, one from the south and one from the west. If there were no traffic signals at the intersection, the two trucks would crash. Writing is just like traffic, depending on punctuation to prevent ideas from crashing into each other.

Two complete ideas are like two trucks and need the strongest punctuation to separate them. All of the punctuation in the box below can come in between only two complete ideas.

STOP Punctuation

Period (.) Semicolon (;) Question mark (?) Exclamation mark (!)

Let's see how this works in a question.

Use the 4 C's:
Be *Concise.*

After the thumping music started. The
 bird began to dance.

1. **A.** NO CHANGE
   B. started, the bird began,
   C. started; the bird began
   D. started, the bird began

Here's How to Crack It

Begin with Step 1 of the Basic Approach you learned in Chapter 5. Use the differences and similarities in the answer choices to identify the topic. Whenever a question is testing Stop punctuation, use the Vertical Line Test. Draw a vertical line where the Stop punctuation is to help you determine if the ideas before and after the line are complete or incomplete.

After the thumping music started. The
 bird began to dance.

After the thumping music started is incomplete. *The bird began to dance* is complete.

Since Stop punctuation can come in between *only* two complete ideas, go to Step 2 and use POE. Eliminate all the answers that don't fix the error, and compare those that are left.

1. A. ~~NO CHANGE~~
   B. started, the bird began,
   C. ~~started; the bird began~~
   D. started, the bird began

Using Steps 3 and 4, we can use the context of the rest of the sentence to confirm that we don't need the second comma that choice (B) offers. Choice (D) is the correct answer.

———————○———————

GO PUNCTUATION

Let's go back to the traffic analogy. Imagine a road with a stop sign at every block. Those stop signs prevent accidents, but when rush hour hits, traffic backs up. Stop signs need to be used strategically, so that they don't cause more problems than they solve. Punctuation functions the same way: Use it to prevent accidents, but don't slow down ideas and make the sentence longer than necessary, or just plain incomprehensible.

A sentence is a complete idea, regardless of how many complete and incomplete ideas it's made up of, so it will always end with Stop punctuation. Within a sentence, use punctuation only to avoid an error or to make your meaning clear. Use Stop punctuation in between two complete ideas. Use a comma to slow down, but not stop, ideas. If you don't need to stop or slow down, don't use any punctuation. Keep traffic moving, and keep ideas flowing.

Here's another example.

———————○———————

I wondered how Snowball had learned to dance, and asked his trainer.
2

2. F. NO CHANGE
   G. to dance and asked his trainer.
   H. to dance; and asked his trainer.
   J. to dance. And asked his trainer.

Here's How to Crack It

Use the Vertical Line Test whenever you see Stop punctuation, either in the sentence as written or among the answer choices. When you draw your line in between *dance* and *and*, the first idea is complete, and the second idea is incomplete. Eliminate choices (H) and (J). There is no reason to slow down the ideas at all, so eliminate choice (F). The correct answer is choice (G). By the way, this question isn't testing whether you can start a sentence with *and*—that's a good example of an outdated rule few enforce anymore, so ACT doesn't test it. Choices (H) and (J) are wrong because the idea to the right of the Stop punctuation is incomplete.

Commas

Commas work like blinking yellow lights: They slow down but do not stop ideas. Since the goal is to be concise, use a comma only for a specific reason. On the ACT, there are only four reasons to use a comma.

Stop

A comma by itself can't come in between two complete ideas, but it can when it's paired with what we call FANBOYS: *for, and, nor, but, or, yet, so*. A comma plus any of these is the equivalent of Stop punctuation. These words also impact direction, which might influence the correct answer.

> *The music changed suddenly, but Snowball picked up the new beat.*

Draw a vertical line on either side of *but* to help break the sentence into separate ideas. *The music changed suddenly* is complete. *Snowball picked up the new beat* is complete.

For the record, all conjunctions link things, but coordinating conjunctions—that is, FANBOYS—specifically come in between two ideas and are never a part of either idea.

Go

A comma can link an incomplete idea to a complete idea, in either order.

> *After Snowball stopped dancing, the trainer gave the bird another treat.*

> *Snowball rocked out to Lady Gaga, oblivious to the growing crowd of fans.*

Lists

Use a comma to separate items on a list.

> *Snowball prefers songs with a regular, funky beat.*

Regular and *funky* are both describing *beat*. If you would say *regular and funky* then you can say *regular, funky*.

> *Snowball seems to like best the music of The Backstreet Boys, Lady Gaga, and Queen.*

Whenever you have three or more items on a list, always use a comma before the "and" preceding the final item. This is a rule that not everyone agrees on, but if you apply the 4 C's, the extra comma makes your meaning *Clear*. On the ACT, always use the comma before the "and."

Unnecessary Info

Use a pair of commas around unnecessary information.

> *Further research has shown that parrots, including cockatoos, can dance in perfect sync to music.*

If information is necessary to the sentence in either meaning or structure, don't use the commas. If the meaning would be exactly the same but the additional information makes the sentence more interesting, use a pair of commas—or a pair of dashes—around the information.

Try the next questions.

Many people point to dog dancing

competitions to argue that birds are not the only [3]

only animals that can dance. [3]

3. **A.** NO CHANGE
   B. argue, that birds are not the only animals,
   C. argue, that birds are not the only animals
   D. argue that birds are not the only animals,

Here's How to Crack It

The changes in the answers identify the topic of the question: commas. Remember, there are only four reasons to use a comma on the ACT, and if you can't name the reason you shouldn't use one. If you thought the sentence was fine, leave NO CHANGE, and confirm none of the answers fixed something you missed. Think of ACT's comma rules, and determine if any apply here. With neither STOP punctuation nor FANBOYS in play, it can't be two complete ideas or a list. If the Unnecessary Info rule is in play, choice (B) would mean that *that birds are not the only animals* isn't necessary, but the sentence would make no sense, so eliminate choice (B). The only other possible rule is GO, linking a complete idea to an incomplete idea. Neither choice (C) nor (D) offers a complete idea on one side of a comma, so eliminate both. The correct answer is choice (A), NO CHANGE.

For the Record
Semicolons can be used to separate items on a very complicated list, but ACT almost never tests this. Exclamation points and question marks show up only occasionally.

Scientists now believe that the ability to

mimic, which requires complex circuitry, for
———————————————————————————
                                            4
vocal learning, is necessary for an animal to

keep a synchronized beat.

4. **F.** NO CHANGE
   G. mimic, which requires complex circuitry
   H. mimic, which, requires complex circuitry
   J. mimic which requires complex circuitry

Here's How to Crack It

The changes in the answers identify the topic of the question: commas. By reading to the end of the sentence, you catch the comma that isn't underlined. Since the Unnecessary Info rule requires two commas, not three, check that rule first. The extra information is *which requires complex circuitry for vocal learning*, and thus the correct answer is choice (G).

COLONS AND SINGLE DASHES

Colons and single dashes are very specific pieces of punctuation, and they are very flexible. They can link a complete idea to either an incomplete idea or another complete idea. The complete idea must come first, and the second idea will be a definition, explanation, or list. Since they are always used with at least one complete idea, use the Vertical Line Test whenever they appear in and out of answer choices.

Let's see two examples.

Parrots don't respond well to genres with

the least noticeable upbeat; waltzes and salsa.
            ————————————————————————
                               5

5. **A.** NO CHANGE
   B. upbeat, waltzes, and salsa.
   C. upbeat: waltzes, and salsa.
   D. upbeat: waltzes and salsa.

Here's How to Crack It

Draw the vertical line in between *upbeat* and *waltzes*. The first idea is complete, but the second is incomplete. Eliminate choice (A). The list isn't *upbeat, waltzes, and salsa*, so eliminate choice (B). The list is only two things, so the comma in choice (C) is unnecessary. The correct answer is choice (D).

A waltz is particularly difficult—it
follows a three-beat pattern.

6. F. NO CHANGE
   G. difficult it follows a three-beat pattern.
   H. difficult, it follows a three-beat pattern.
   J. difficult, it follows, a three-beat pattern.

Here's How to Crack It
Draw the vertical line in between *difficult* and *it*. Both are complete ideas, so eliminate choices (G), (H), and (J). Choice (F) is correct.

Identical Punctuation
In question 6, a period, a semicolon, or a colon could have been used. Notice, however, that none of those appeared among the answer choices. ACT won't make you evaluate those subtle differences that might make one punctuation mark better than the others when they all perform essentially identical functions. Knowing which forms of punctuation are identical is a powerful POE tool. After all, you can't have two right answers, so if two or more choices are identical, they all must be wrong.

CONJUNCTIONS
Punctuation isn't the only way to link ideas. On some of the more difficult questions on sentence structure, you have to change the ideas by adding or deleting the conjunction.

Here are some of the more common conjunctions you may see.

> although, as, because, if, since, that, until, what,
> which, while, when, where, who, whom

Proper grammarians might object to calling *what, which, when, where, who,* and *whom* conjunctions, but the technical terms aren't important on the English test. It's not as if ACT makes you name any part of speech, and all that matters is that those words, when they are used in a sentence instead of a question, act just like conjunctions. They make an idea incomplete. (Look at how we used *when* in the next to last sentence in this paragraph!)

Add a conjunction to make an idea incomplete, or take one out to make the idea complete.

Let's see how this works in a few questions.

The African grey parrot, which also
        7
mimics human speech and therefore can

dance.

7. **A.** NO CHANGE
   B. parrot which
   C. parrot that
   D. parrot

Here's How to Crack It

If conjunctions change in the answer choices, it is likely testing Complete. When you read to the end of the sentence, you're left hanging, waiting for the main point about African grey parrots. The sentence is incomplete, and the only way to fix it is to take out the conjunction. Choice (D) is correct. It's no coincidence that it's the most concise.

Try another.

The videos of Snowball dancing have
        8
sparked a serious area of study, researchers

admit they appreciate the sheer entertainment

value.

8. **F.** NO CHANGE
   G. Although the videos of Snowball
   H. The videos appearing all over the Internet of Snowball
   J. Since the videos of Snowball

Here's How to Crack It

If it sounded fine to your ear, using the answers to identify the topic will help you spot something you missed or verify that NO CHANGE is correct. If conjunctions change in the answer choices, it is likely testing Complete. Check if the entire sentence makes a complete idea and that all ideas within are joined correctly. There are two complete ideas in the sentence, separated only by a comma. A comma alone is GO punctuation, so eliminate choices (F) and (H). You need a choice with a conjunction added to the first idea, making it incomplete. Conjunctions vary by direction, which we'll discuss in the next lesson. The two ideas show a contrast—*serious* and *entertainment*—so choice (G) is correct.

English Drill 1

Try an English passage on your own. Use the basic approach explained in Chapter 5. Answers are in Chapter 24.

Portraiture for the Common Man

Kehinde Wiley's paintings are powerfully disorienting for the way they blur the lines between new and old styles. Wiley paints large canvases that <u>watch</u> the many
₁

1. **A.** NO CHANGE
   B. color
   C. celebrate
   D. speak

<u>achievement's</u> of African-American men. His portrait of
₂

2. **F.** NO CHANGE
   G. achievements's
   H. achievements'
   J. achievements

<u>Ice-T,</u> the rapper and reality-TV star, draws from a nineteenth-
₃
century portrait of Napoleon. His striking portrayal of singer

3. **A.** NO CHANGE
   B. Ice-T
   C. Ice-T:
   D. Ice-T;

Michael Jackson <u>drawing</u> on the influence of Peter Paul
₄

4. **F.** NO CHANGE
   G. drawn
   H. draws
   J. while drawing

Rubens. <u>Although each of Wiley's subjects is famous, his</u>
₅
portraits cannot help but make his audience see them in new ways.

5. **A.** NO CHANGE
   B. Often painted in large dimensions,
   C. Born in 1977 in Los Angeles,
   D. Loved and adored by art critics,

In these paintings, Wiley uses very traditional techniques. Inspired by the Dutch masters, Wiley oversees a painting workshop: The ideas are his own, but the artisan assistants in his workshop aid in the <u>completion</u> of the paintings. This
₆
collaborative process allows for Wiley's vast output and allows him to impartially oversee the quality of the work. In addition,

6. **F.** NO CHANGE
   G. complete
   H. end with completing
   J. complete the end of

Wiley's assistants gather the raw materials and mix the paints,
₇

thereby making them a classical work from start to finish. This
₈
attention to detail and process made Wiley an art-world

celebrity in the time of life known as the early 20s. Wiley has
₉
forced art lovers to reconsider the relationship between the old

and the new. After all, paintings created by such profoundly

traditional means do not usually have the faces of contemporary

celebrities staring out of them.

Wiley's father was Nigerian, and Wiley did not meet him
₁₀
until a trip to Africa in his early 20s. Some of his most famous
₁₀

works of Harlem portray various, anonymous men Wiley has
₁₁

seen on the streets. In his more recent work, Wiley brings his
₁₂
classic style to the common people of Israel and the West

Indies. [13] To glorify people from oppressed cultures all over

---

7. A. NO CHANGE
   B. have gathered
   C. were gathering
   D. gathered

8. F. NO CHANGE
   G. it
   H. each
   J. each painting

9. A. NO CHANGE
   B. at the young age of being in his 20s.
   C. in his 20s.
   D. between the ages of 20 and 30.

10. Given that all the choices are true, which one most effectively introduces the paragraph?

   F. NO CHANGE
   G. Wiley grew up in South Central Los Angeles, but he made his name in Harlem.
   H. Although it was difficult financially for his mother, Wiley received the best art education money could buy.
   J. However, Wiley's focus is not exclusively on celebrities, and he is just as interested in "average" people.

11. The best placement for the underlined portion would be:

   A. where it is now.
   B. after the word *portray*.
   C. after the word *Wiley*.
   D. after the word *streets* (and before the period).

12. F. NO CHANGE
   G. its
   H. them
   J. their

13. At this point, the writer is considering adding the following true statement:

   His paintings were shown in the National Portrait Gallery in Washington, D.C., in 2008.

   Should the writer make this addition here?

   A. Yes, because it gives another instance of Wiley's popularity.
   B. Yes, because it demonstrates why Kehinde Wiley traveled abroad.
   C. No, because it strays from the paragraph's focus on Wiley's body of work.
   D. No, because it shifts the focus of the paragraph from the streets of Harlem to a museum in D.C.

the world, by depicting his subjects in the types of poses and
14
backgrounds usually reserved for royalty. He shows that even
those to whom history pays no attention can have their own
regal dignity.

Wiley's works can be seen in galleries all over the world
because the everyday appearance of those he portrays has an
15
almost universal appeal. Wiley may draw on the work of many
15
earlier artists, but his unique contribution is to show that art
need not be restricted to those who can afford to commission it,
or even those who are interested in viewing it.

14. **F.** NO CHANGE
   G. depicting
   H. by which Wiley depicted
   J. Wiley depicts

15. The writer is considering deleting the underlined portion
   (adjusting the punctuation as needed). Should the underlined portion be kept or deleted?

   A. Kept, because it gives additional information about how
   Wiley chooses his subjects.
   B. Kept, because it offers one idea for why Wiley's popular-
   ity is so far-reaching.
   C. Deleted, because it repeats other information given in the
   previous paragraph.
   D. Deleted, because it undermines claims made in the previ-
   ous paragraph about Wiley's importance.

Summary

- ACT writers like to test your knowledge of whether sentences are put together and punctuated correctly.

- A complete idea can stand on its own as a complete sentence even though it may be part of a longer sentence. An incomplete idea can't stand on its own as a complete sentence and must be appropriately linked to a complete idea.

- Stop punctuation includes a period, a semicolon, an exclamation mark, a question mark, and a comma plus FANBOYS. Stop punctuation can come in between only complete ideas.

- Go punctuation includes a comma and nothing at all. Go punctuation can link anything except for two complete ideas.

- Always put a comma before "and" at the end of a list with three or more items.

- Always put a pair of commas around unnecessary info.

- Colons and single dashes must follow a complete idea but can precede a complete or incomplete idea.

- Conjunctions make an idea incomplete.

Chapter 7
Consistent, Clear, and Concise

The key to an outstanding ACT English score is to focus on the topics that show up the most often *and* which are both easy to identify and simple to fix. In this chapter, we'll teach you how to crack questions on verbs, pronouns, apostrophes, and transitions. For each topic, following the rules makes good writing consistent, clear, and concise.

VERBS

A verb expresses an action, feeling, or state of being. The form of a verb depends on the number of the subject—singular or plural—the time of the event, and the presence of helping verbs. Whenever you spot the verb changing among the answer choices, use these three steps along with your Basic Approach.

1. Identify the subject. The verb must be consistent with its subject: Singular subject with a singular verb, and plural subject with a plural verb.
2. Check the tense. The tense must be consistent with the setting and the participle. Use the context of the non-underlined portion to determine if the verb should be past, present, or future.
3. Be concise. Pick the shortest answer free of any errors.

Here's an example.

Each of the first three taxis I saw <u>were too far away to hail.</u>

1. A. NO CHANGE
    B. are too far away
    C. is too far away
    D. was too far away

Here's How to Crack It

Use the changes in the answers to identify verbs as the topic ACT is testing. Both tense and number seem to be changing, so find the subject first. What was too far away? *Each* of the taxis. *Each* is singular, so eliminate the plural forms of the verb, choices (A) and (B). Now check the tense. *Saw* is past tense, so choose the past tense, choice (D).

Tricky Pronouns

Question 1 wasn't testing pronouns directly—the changes among the answer choices were verbs. To answer correctly, however, you had to know that the pronoun *each* is singular. The following pronouns are all singular.

anybody	either	nobody
anyone	everybody	somebody
each	everyone	someone

Your ear should reliably raise the alarm over a subject-verb agreement error, both for tricky pronouns and regular nouns. Consider the following examples.

*Somebody **love** me.*
*Everyone **like** ice cream.*
*Each **are** beautiful.*
*Nobody **do** it better.*

Your ear probably automatically fixed these.

*Somebody **loves** me.*
*Everyone **likes** ice cream.*
*Each **is** beautiful.*
*Nobody **does** it better.*

This is why your ear can frequently help you eliminate the wrong answers on verb questions. But remember Step 4 of the Basic Approach: Trust, but verify your ear. Confirm the error by making sure you have correctly identified the subject. Another way ACT can make identifying the subject difficult is with prepositional phrases, another trap in question 1.

Prepositional Phrases

Another way ACT made question 1 confusing was by burying the subject to the left of the prepositional phrase. *Each **of the first three taxis** I saw were too far away to hail.* Prepositions are little words that show a relationship between nouns. Some examples are *at, between, by, in, of, on, to,* and *with.* A prepositional phrase modifies—that is, describes—a noun. ACT will add prepositional phrases to distract you from the subject, so be on the lookout for them. Always look to the left of the preposition to find your subject. Try the following examples. Does the subject agree with its verb?

Only one of the dresses fit me.
A selection of fruit, cheese, and nuts were served at the party.
The argument between Pat and Ron sadden all of us.
The books on the table is due back to the library.

Cross out the prepositional phrases to find the subject and confirm the verb.

*Only **one** ~~of the dresses~~ **fits** me.*
*A **selection** ~~of fruit, cheese, and nuts~~ **was** served at the party.*
*The **argument** ~~between Pat and Ron~~ **saddens** all of us.*
*The **books** ~~on the table~~ **are** due back to the library.*

Irregular Verb Participles

ACT can make verb tense difficult as well. Most tense questions are straightforward choices of past, present, or future. However, ACT loves to test the correct past participle for irregular verbs.

Let's try another ACT question.

I <u>woken up</u> at 10:30 to find that my alarm clock had failed to go off.

2. **F.** NO CHANGE
   G. had woke up
   H. woke up
   J. waked up

Here's How to Crack It

The changes in the answers identify verbs as the topic. The subject, *I,* doesn't change the form, and all of the choices are in past tense. Use POE to get rid of all the wrong answers that do not use the correct form of the irregular verb, *to wake.* Use *woke* on its own but *woken* with *had* in front. Choice (H) is the only correct form.

Regular verbs follow a predictable pattern.

*Present: I **study** for the ACT every day.*
*Present perfect: I **have studied** for months.*
*Simple past: I **studied** all day yesterday.*
*Past perfect: I **had studied** for the SAT.*

Irregular verbs are the problem. While you can usually use your ear to find the correct participle, here is a small sample of some common irregular verbs. The *infinitive* is the form of the verb used with *to*; the simple past works on its own, without a helping verb; and the *past participle* works with a form of the helping verb *to have*.

*Infinitive: Jacob would like **to become** a biotech engineer.*
*Present perfect: Hannah **has become** a star swimmer.*
*Simple past: Samara **became** a voracious reader.*
*Past perfect: Jonah **had become** tired of practicing.*

Let's try another ACT question.

My boss was mad that I <u>had forgot to</u> ₃
<u>bring the report I had been preparing at home.</u> ₃

3. **A.** NO CHANGE
   B. had forgotten to bring the report that I had prepared at home.
   C. had forgotten to bring the report that had been prepared at home by me.
   D. had forgotten to bring the report I had been preparing at home.

Here's How to Crack It

The changes in the answer choices identify verbs as the topic, specifically past participles. Choice (A) incorrectly uses the simple past *forgot* with the helping verb *had*, so you can eliminate it right away. Choices (B), (C), and (D) all fix that error, so compare the differences among them. Choice (B) is the most concise, and neither choices (C) nor (D) fixed something choice (B) missed. Both just made the sentence longer, so the correct answer is choice (B).

> ## You Don't Have to Be Perfect
> The perfect tenses change the time of an event in subtle ways. You will never need to identify by name a particular tense on the ACT, nor choose between the present and present perfect. Choose the past perfect to establish an order of one event happening in the past before another.

Need a refresher on irregular verbs? Check out the table in Chapter 5.

Passive Voice

In question 3, choice (B) was the most concise in part because it uses the active voice. Choice (C) is passive, which makes the sentence much longer. Both active and passive voice are grammatically correct—they just describe one event in two different ways. Compare the following sentences:

Beatrice prepared the fine meal.

The fine meal was prepared by Beatrice.

Beatrice makes the meal in both sentences. Active voice preserves the performer of the action, *Beatrice,* as the subject. Passive voice promotes the receiver of the action, in this case *the meal,* to subject and changes the verb by adding the helping verb *was.*

How to Spot Passive Voice

Look for forms of the verb *to be* and the preposition *by.*

How to Crack It

Choose passive voice *only* when you're confident that the other three choices contain a grammatical error.

PRONOUNS

Pronouns take the place of nouns and make your writing more concise. On the ACT, several questions will test the correct usage of pronouns. Whenever you spot pronouns changing among the answers, use these two steps with your Basic Approach.

1. Find the original. The pronoun has to be consistent in number and gender with the noun it replaces and other related pronouns.
2. Check the case. Choose the correct pronoun based on its specific function in the sentence.

Let's try a few examples.

Revisit Chapter 5 for lists of different types of pronouns.

⎯⎯⎯⎯⎯⎯⎯○⎯⎯⎯⎯⎯⎯⎯

Have you ever had a day when you wished <u>you could have</u> just stayed in bed?
₄

4. **F.** NO CHANGE
   G. you could of
   H. one could of
   J. one could have

Here's How to Crack It

Nothing seems obviously wrong, so leave choice (F) and use the answers to see if you missed something. Pronouns and verbs are changing—sort of; *of* is not a verb, even if it sounds like *have*. Eliminate choices (G) and (H). The pronoun should be consistent with the *you* in the non-underlined portion, so eliminate choice (J). Choice (F) is correct.

⎯⎯⎯⎯⎯⎯⎯○⎯⎯⎯⎯⎯⎯⎯

Try another.

⎯⎯⎯⎯⎯⎯⎯○⎯⎯⎯⎯⎯⎯⎯

The taxi driver <u>who finally picked up my</u> ₅ <u>boss and I</u> wouldn't take credit cards.
₅

5. **A.** NO CHANGE
   B. whom finally picked up my boss and I
   C. who finally picked up my boss and me
   D. which finally picked up my boss and myself

Here's How to Crack It

The changes in the answers identify pronouns as the topic of the sentence. There are two pronouns in the underlined portion, so consider both and follow your two steps. *Taxi driver* is a person, and *which* is only used for things. *Myself* is correct only for emphasis (I myself don't know the answer) or when the subject and object are the same (I corrected myself). Cross off choice (D). Check the case for *who* and *I,* and don't worry—it's perfectly okay to check *I* first since everyone is scared of "who" versus "whom" (see "Who Versus Whom" below). For case, cross off everything except for the pronoun and the verb. *Picked up I* is incorrect because *I* is a subject pronoun, so eliminate choices (A) and (B). The correct choice is (C), and you didn't even have to worry about "who" and "whom." Now go learn about them so you don't have to depend on luck the next time.

Who Versus Whom

Who is the subject pronoun. *Whom* is the object pronoun. Why do they seem so hard to all of us? Very few movies and television shows use *whom* when it's needed, and most of us do the same in our regular conversations.

How to Crack It

Whenever you see *who* and *whom* tested on the ACT, try *he* and *him* in their place. If you would say *he called me,* you would say *who called me.* If you would say *I called him,* you would say *whom I called.* Don't worry about how the words flip: Just match your "m" pronouns and you'll be fine.

APOSTROPHES

Similar to pronouns, apostrophes make your writing more concise. They have two uses: possession and contraction.

Possession

To show possession with single nouns, add *'s*, and with plural nouns, add just the apostrophe. For tricky plurals that do not end in *s*, add *'s*.

Consider the following examples.

The new car of Peter = **Peter's** *new car*
The room of the girls = *the* **girls'** *room.*
The room of the men = *the* **men's** *room.*

To show possession with pronouns, never use apostrophes. Use the appropriate possessive pronoun.

His *car.*
Their *room.*
Its *door.*

Contractions

Whenever you see a pronoun with an apostrophe, it's (it is) a contraction, which means the apostrophe takes the place of at least one letter.

Consider the following examples.

It is important. = **It's** *important.*
They are happy to help. = **They're** *happy to help.*
Who is the leader of the group? = **Who's** *the leader of the group?*

Because these particular contractions sound the same as some possessive pronouns, these questions can be very tricky on the ACT. You can't use your ear—you have to know the above rules. Let's look at some sample ACT questions.

Pronouns Most Frequently Misused
The ACT test writers will sometimes try to confuse you by presenting both a possessive pronoun and the same pronoun in a contraction as answer choices. Do you know the difference between these words: *whose, who's; its, it's?*

I watched in dismay as my laptop was

crushed beneath the taxis wheels'.
—————————
       6

6. F. NO CHANGE
   G. taxis' wheels.
   H. taxi's wheels'.
   J. taxi's wheels.

Here's How to Crack It

The changes in the answer choices identify apostrophes as the topic. Use POE heavily with apostrophes: Eliminate all the answers that are wrong. If you just try to fix it in your head and find a match, you'll likely miss something. *Wheels* don't "possess" anything, so eliminate choices (F) and (H). There is only one taxi, so choose the singular, choice (J).

Its' screen was smashed to pieces.
—————————
   7

7. A. NO CHANGE
   B. Their screen
   C. It's screen
   D. Its screen

Here's How to Crack It

The changes in the answer choices identify apostrophes/pronouns as the topic. There is no such word as *its'*, so eliminate choice (A). The *laptop* (context from non-underlined portion in prior question) is singular, so eliminate choice (B). To determine if you need the possessive or a contraction, expand out to *it is*. *It is screen* makes no sense, so choose the possessive pronoun, choice (D).

TRANSITIONS

In Chapter 6, we used traffic as an analogy to explain punctuation. If good writing is like a pleasant drive, then transitions are road signs, preventing you from getting lost and helping you make important turns. Good transitions are consistent with the flow of ideas.

Many words can act as transitions. Some are specific to the context, where only one word will fit the precise meaning. But others are just slight variations, giving you directions: *turn around* or *keep going*. Here's a partial list.

Turn Around
although, but, despite, even though, however, nonetheless, nevertheless, or, yet

Keep Going
and, because, finally, furthermore, moreover, since, so, thus, therefore

---

Try an example.

I apologized for not having the report

ready, since she had told me the report wasn't
         ‾‾‾‾‾
           8

due for another week.

8. **F.** NO CHANGE
   G. even though she
   H. because she
   J. and she

Here's How to Crack It

The changes in the answer choices are transition words, but they are also FAN-BOYS and conjunctions. Before you consider direction, make sure the sentence is complete and that all ideas within the sentence are joined correctly. All are correct and complete, but the sentence doesn't make sense because the direction is wrong. It is a transitions question. The two ideas on either side of the transition word disagree, so choose a *turn around* word. Only choice (G) makes sense.

CONCISE

All the 4 C's are important on the ACT. They are your framework for understanding the topics that you can identify and your strategy to conquer the questions whose topics you can't identify. But concise isn't just a strategy or a tool used to understand certain grammar rules. Sometimes, ACT tests it directly.

Try the following examples.

Next, my boss was furious that I was late.
9

9. **A.** NO CHANGE
   B. My boss
   C. Then, my boss
   D. Next my boss

Here's How to Crack It

The changes in the answer choices identify transitions as the topic, with possibly commas as well. Use POE. The words *then* and *next* mean the same thing used in this context. If both could be right, both must be wrong. Eliminate choices (A) and (C). *Next* should have a comma after it because it's an introductory idea, so eliminate choice (D) also. The correct answer is choice (B) because you do not need a transition word here.

ACT will frequently test concise in a question concerning transitions. If you don't need a transition word for your sentence to be either complete or clear, don't use it. In the answer choices for question 9, note how *my boss* appeared in each, and one choice featured only *my boss* (and was correct). That is a reliable sign ACT is testing concise.

Try these additional questions.

---○---

I was already an hour and a half late for

work and not on time.
_____
10

10. **F.** NO CHANGE
  G. work, and behind schedule.
  H. work and delayed in getting the morning started.
  J. work.

Here's How to Crack It

The appearance of *work* in every choice and by itself in one identifies the topic as concise. Use POE and pay attention to the non-underlined portion of the sentence for context. The narrator has already established she's late, so all of the other choices are unnecessarily wordy. The correct answer is choice (J).

---○---

---○---

I had left the lights on the previous

evening, and my car wouldn't start. Many
                                    _____
                                        11
new cars have separate electrical boards for
_____
                  11
the lights, so the battery won't drain.
_____
                  11

11. **A.** NO CHANGE
  B. Batteries should be replaced every five years.
  C. I plan to buy a new car next year.
  D. DELETE the underlined portion.

Here's How to Crack It

The presence of DELETE is a sign the question might be testing concise, but it doesn't guarantee choice (D) is the answer. Read the answer choices through before making a decision. None of the other sentences add any useful info to the first sentence. Cross off the first three choices. In fact, the sentence *is* irrelevant to the passage, and Choice (D) is the correct answer.

There is no reliable pattern of how many times DELETE will be the correct answer on any given ACT. Always be biased toward DELETE. Unless deleting the underlined portion would create an error or drastically change the meaning, choose it.

---○---

English Drill 2

Try another English passage on your own. Answers are in Chapter 24.

A Tunnel to History

After school let out, my best friend and I, used to go to one
of the oldest parts of the city. From the little trail beside the
school, we'd climb down to the old railway tunnel that had

gone dark many years before that pitch darkness was terrifying
and mysterious. We would go down, staring into that darkened

tunnel, having our flashlights. We would leave our backpacks
at the edge of the tunnel, knowing that they would be good
landmarks when we re-emerged. As the throng of New Jersey

Turnpike traffic roared overhead, we would enter. [4]

But we were always looking for the traces of the history of
our city.

[1] When we first started going down into the tunnel, we

didn't do so with any specific purpose really we just liked
going to this place that everyone else was too scared to visit.
[2] Our history teacher directed us to some books at the public
library. [3] We learned that this railroad used to be a very busy
one, shipping goods from the western states to New York City.
[4] The long highway ramp that passed over the tunnel and
the whole area was actually pretty new: As recently as thirty
years ago, there had been no ramp at all. [5] What was now all
abandoned marshland had once been its own neighborhood,

1. A. NO CHANGE
   B. best friend, and I
   C. best friend and I
   D. best friend, and I—

2. F. NO CHANGE
   G. before, the
   H. before. The
   J. before, yet the

3. Which choice best conveys the idea that the narrator and
   his friend held their flashlights nervously?

   A. NO CHANGE
   B. clutching
   C. carrying
   D. donning

4. Which of the following true statements, if added here,
   would most effectively continue the narration of what happened during the summer walks the friends took?

   F. We were friends throughout most of middle school and
      high school.
   G. The tunnel was wide enough for two tracks, but it con-
      tained only one.
   H. Sometimes, we'd cast eerie shadows on the walls or listen
      to the echo of our voices in the long tunnels.
   J. Many rail lines have been shut down since the advent of
      trucking in the U.S.

5. A. NO CHANGE
   B. purpose real
   C. purpose: really,
   D. purposely: really,

6. F. NO CHANGE
   G. they're
   H. their
   J. it is

lined with streets and houses. [6] After a few aimless visits, though, we started to look more into the history of the area. ⁷

Being a teenager in New Jersey, history is everywhere.
8

Four centuries earlier our history teacher told us that our town
9
had been settled by Dutch traders. But the Lenape tribes had already been living there for many thousands of years. In fact, in the early seventeenth century, when the Dutch arrived, the

Lenape were one of the most powerful tribes in the region: an
10
area that spread from Delaware to Massachusetts to upstate New York. The tribe's influence is still with us. The Dutch

settlers were ruthless in the conquest of the region, which they
11
held on to many Lenape names, such as Manhattan, Raritan,

and Tappan. Lah-di-dah, the area looks so much different now,
12
but the Lenape influence is still undeniably there,

commemorated by the names.
13

7. For the sake of the logic and coherence of the paragraph, Sentence 6 should be placed:
   A. where it is now.
   B. before Sentence 1.
   C. before Sentence 2.
   D. before Sentence 4.

8. F. NO CHANGE
   G. Being raised in
   H. Raising a family
   J. Where I grew up

9. The writer wants to stress the amount of time that had passed since his city had first been settled by Europeans. Assuming that the capitalization would be adjusted as needed, where should the underlined portion be placed?
   A. Where it is now
   B. After the word *teacher*
   C. After the word *us*
   D. After the word *settled*

10. F. NO CHANGE
    G. region
    H. region;
    J. region is

11. A. NO CHANGE
    B. and
    C. but
    D. then

12. F. NO CHANGE
    G. Moving right along, the
    H. Meanwhile, the
    J. The

13. A. NO CHANGE
    B. commemorate
    C. commemorating
    D. in memoriam

This history lesson enriched our trips around the secret
corridors of the city because we began to feel all of our town's
historical layers at once. We became so enmeshed in the history

of our city that we were invited to give presentations, to our
fellow classmates and teachers. A little curiosity goes a long
way: You never know what you'll find in a place that people
have ignored for many years.

14. Which of the following alternatives to the underlined portion would NOT be acceptable?

F. hidden
G. lesser-known
H. classified
J. secluded

15. A. NO CHANGE
B. to: give presentations
C. to give: presentations
D. to give presentations

Summary

- Verbs, pronouns, apostrophes, and transitions are heavily tested on the ACT.

- All four are readily identifiable from changes in the answer choices, and all have relatively few rules to use to evaluate the question.

- The 4 C's can be applied to evaluate any question whose topic you can't identify. ACT also tests concise as its own topic.

- When working on a concise problem, be biased toward the answer choice that says DELETE, but do not assume it will be the correct answer all or even half the time.

Chapter 8
Rhetorical Skills

ACT categorizes the questions on the English test as either Rhetorical Skills or Usage and Mechanics. For most questions, the Basic Approach used to crack them is the same, regardless of how ACT labels them. Some questions, however, require a different approach. In this chapter, we'll teach you how to crack questions that ask for wrong answers, as well as questions on strategy and order.

EXCEPT/LEAST/NOT

You know a question is tricky when the right answer is wrong. That is, if the question asks you to identify the choice that is "NOT acceptable," you have to cross off three answers that work and choose the one that doesn't.

The EXCEPT/LEAST/NOT questions, or E/L/N for short, hide in plain sight, posing a challenge to spot. When most "questions" on the ACT feature only four answer choices, you could easily miss the presence of a bona fide question. Moreover, many of the topics on E/L/N will look familiar: Stop/Go punctuation and transition questions are two topics heavily tested in this format, so the four answers look pretty much the same way they always do.

> **For the Record**
> Not all EXCEPT/LEAST/NOT questions are Rhetorical Skills questions by ACT standards. Our argument is that when most of the "questions" are just four answer choices, the presence of a true question demands a different category and different approach.

POE provides your key to cracking these: Eliminate all choices that *could* work. Cross off the EXCEPT/LEAST/NOT word, and then use POE to cross off the answers that do work. NO CHANGE is almost never an option on these. Use the sentence as it is written as your standard of comparison for the answer choices. Let's try an example.

Be on the lookout for E/L/N questions: Expect as many as 3–4 *per passage.*

I gave my information to the director of

the animal shelter. She promised to contact
 ₁
me if any French Bulldogs came in.

1. Which of the following alternatives to the underlined portion would be NOT acceptable?

   A. shelter; she promised
   B. shelter, and she promised
   C. shelter, she promised
   D. shelter, who promised

Here's How to Crack It

Cross out NOT. Since the sentence used Stop punctuation, use POE to eliminate first all answers that are Stop punctuation, choices (A) and (B). Before you worry about choice (D), which changes the wording, focus on the remaining choice with the exact same wording as the original sentence. Remember that a comma alone can never be Stop Punctuation, so choice (C) is grammatically wrong—and therefore the correct answer here.

Word Choice and Idioms

Two of the most popular and challenging topics ACT tests are word choice and idioms, either in regular or E/L/N format. Word choice refers to selecting the precise word that fits with the context. An idiom is an expression that requires a specific preposition. Idioms follow no grammatical rules—they are what they are.

Both word choice and idioms will be easy to spot by the changes in the answers, but neither fits our standards for being easy to fix. While they tend to be fairly common words and expressions, you'll either know them or you won't. ACT rarely, if ever, repeats any words or idioms, so there is no way to prepare for the particular ones that will show up on your ACT. Use POE heavily with these, and don't let them drag you down in your pacing.

Try some more examples.

I remember well the day I first saw Wheezie at the animal shelter. In truth, I think Wheezie is the one who adopted me.
₂

2. Which of the following alternatives to the underlined word would be LEAST acceptable?

   F. selected
   G. assumed
   H. picked
   J. chose

Here's How to Crack It

Cross out LEAST. Use POE, trying each answer choice in place of *adopted*. Choices (F), (H), and (J) could all mean the same thing, but *assume* just doesn't work and is therefore the correct choice.

After an hour of play, chew toys, tennis balls, and stuffed animals were strewn around the living room.
₃

3. Which of the following alternatives to the underlined word would be LEAST acceptable?

   A. on
   B. throughout
   C. all over
   D. about

Here's How to Crack It

Cross out LEAST. This is testing an idiom, specifically which prepositions work with *strewn*. Use POE, trying each answer choice in place of *around*. Choices (B), (C), and (D) could all work with *strewn*, but *on* doesn't work and is therefore the correct choice.

STRATEGY QUESTIONS

Strategy questions come in many different forms, but they all revolve around the *purpose* of the text. Among the different types of Strategy questions, expect to see questions asking you to add and replace text, determine if text should be added or deleted, evaluate the impact on the passage if text is deleted, or judge the overall effect of the passage on the reader.

Let's see some examples.

Many dog owners turn to animal trainers when they find they can no longer control their pets. Most experts find that a poorly-trained dog has received plenty of affection but not enough discipline or exercise. [4]

4. Which of the following sentences provides new, specific guidelines about the proper training of a dog?

   F. Behavior that was cute in a twenty-pound puppy is alarming in a one hundred-pound adult dog.
   G. Would-be dog owners should consider their own lifestyles and the temperament of a specific breed before adopting the animal.
   H. Dogs should be walked at least three times a day and should never be given a treat without first obeying a command.
   J. Small children should never be left unsupervised with a dog.

Here's How to Crack It

Identify the purpose of the proposed text. According to the question, one of these choices *provides new, specific guidance about the proper training of a dog*. We don't even need to go back into the passage: Find an answer choice that fulfills the purpose. Choices (F), (G), and (J) all may be true, but they do not offer any *specific* information about training a dog. Only choice (H) does that, and it is our correct answer.

Try another.

Wheezie's puppy playfulness masked the steely determination of a true French bulldog, and she stubbornly resisted all the lessons from our obedience class. [5]

5. At this point, the writer is considering adding the following true statement:

> My nephews trained Blizzard, a black lab with a sweet dis-position, very easily.

Should the writer add this sentence here?

A. Yes, because it explains why the author felt so insecure about her dif-ficulties training her dog.
B. Yes, because it provides an important detail about another breed of dog.
C. No, because it doesn't explain how Blizzard was trained.
D. No, because it distracts the reader from the main point of this paragraph.

Here's How to Crack It

Whenever a strategy question asks if you should add or delete new text, evaluate the reasons in the answer choices carefully. The reason should correctly explain the purpose of the selected text. Here, choice (D) is correct because there is no reason to add text that is irrelevant to the topic.

Most puppy books no longer recommend
6
using newspapers to housebreak dogs. I
6
bought three safety gates to block off the kitchen from the rest of the house. I also brought home a crate, baby blankets to make it cozy, a stylish collar and matching leash, several bags of food, and of course, plenty of toys.

6. Given that all choices are true, which one provides the best opening to this paragraph?

F. NO CHANGE
G. When I was growing up, my family had an Irish Setter and four cats.
H. I made sure I had all the supplies we'd need before bringing Wheezie home.
J. Many people prefer cats as pets.

Here's How to Crack It

In many strategy questions, the purpose is to add a sentence to open or close a paragraph or tie two paragraphs together. Use the context of the paragraph, and read through to the end before deciding. Since the author mentions several things she's bought in preparation, choice (H) provides the best introduction to the paragraph.

ORDER

There are also several types of Order questions, but they all involve the correct placement of ideas. Some order questions will ask you to place correctly a modifier or additional text. Other questions will ask you to evaluate and possibly correct the order of sentences within a paragraph or the paragraphs themselves.

All order questions work best with POE. Ideas should be consistent and the meaning should be clear, but that meaning can be difficult to understand until ideas are in their proper place.

Let's look at a few examples.

French bulldogs can face a serious
<u>7</u>
number of health issues affecting the
respiratory system, knees, and eyesight.

7. The best placement for the underlined word would be:

   A. where it is now.
   B. before the word *French* (revising the capitalization accordingly).
   C. before the word *health*.
   D. before the word *respiratory*.

Here's How to Crack It

Use POE, trying the word in the places suggested by each answer choice. The best answer is choice (C) because it modifies health issues and therefore includes all three listed. "Serious" to mean "a lot of" is slang and thus appeals to your ear. But "large" is not a definition of serious, literally or figuratively, and none of the other definitions really apply to the figurative meaning of "large."

Order of Sentences

If there is a question on order of the sentences or placement of new text within a paragraph, all of the sentences in the passage will be numbered. NO CHANGE could be the answer to order of the sentences, but if you're reading along and get confused by a sudden shift in the action, that's a good sign the sentences are in fact out of order. Do not go back and reread, but instead wait until you get to the question.

Don't waste time trying to re-order all of the sentences yourself. Look for transition words that indicate an introduction, a conclusion, or a pair of sentences that should go back to back, and use POE.

Try an example.

———————————◯———————————

[4]

[1] He recommended an excellent specialist to perform the surgery. [2] When the day came, I drove to the hospital, dreading the moment I'd need to leave her behind. [3] While we waited for her to be admitted, Wheezie sensed something was wrong and curled on my lap, trembling. [4] My vet broke the bad news that Wheezie would have to have surgery to correct the problems in her nasal passage and vocal chords.

8. Which of the following order of sentences will make the paragraph most logical?
   F. NO CHANGE
   G. 2, 3, 1, 4
   H. 4, 3, 2, 1
   J. 4, 1, 2, 3

Here's How to Crack It

Use POE. The surgery isn't properly introduced until the end, which means sentence 4 should be the introduction. Eliminate choices (F) and (G), and determine if sentence 3 or 1 should be next. Sentence 1 makes more sense, so the answer is choice (J).

———————————◯———————————

Order of the Paragraphs

If there is a question on the order of the paragraphs, there will be a warning at the beginning of the passage, alerting you that the passages may or may not be in the correct order and identifying which question will ask about which paragraph.

Almost no one ever spots this warning. Treat these the same way you treat the order of the sentences. If you suddenly find yourself confused by an inexplicable shift in the action, check above the title if the warning is there. Alternatively, continue reading and working the questions and bet safely you'll encounter a question on the order of the paragraphs at the end of the passage.

AND IN THE END...

> Questions 9 and 10 ask about the passage as a whole.

Other than order of the paragraphs, two other questions routinely appear at the end and are always preceded by the announcement above.

Placement of New Info

The paragraphs will also be numbered for a question testing the placement of additional info.

---

9. Upon reviewing this essay and concluding some information has been left out, the writer composes the following sentence:

   > After a night spent winning the hearts of all of the attendants, Wheezie bounded out of the recovery room and into my waiting arms.

   This sentence should be:

   A. placed at the end of paragraph 4.
   B. placed at the end of paragraph 3.
   C. placed at the end of paragraph 2.
   D. placed at the end of paragraph 1.

Here's How to Crack It

Okay, so this is a little unfair: We didn't give you the entire passage, and only the correct paragraph (4) was numbered. But we couldn't leave you hanging about Wheezie's fate. Even with a little bit of cheating on our part, the new information is consistent with the rest of the information in that paragraph, and choice (A) is the correct answer.

———————◯———————

Grading the Passage

Questions at the end that ask you to evaluate the passage are another version of a strategy question. The question identifies the purpose of the passage and asks you to determine if the author succeeded. These are always at the end, so we waited to show you here.

———————◯———————

10. Suppose that one of the writer's goals has been to address the role obedience classes can play in the healthy development of dogs. Would this essay fulfill that goal?

    F. Yes, because the essay implies the writer and her dog benefited from obedience classes.
    G. Yes, because the essay indicates French Bulldogs are not easily trained.
    H. No, because the essay is focused on one anecdote about one dog.
    J. No, because the essay indicates the dog displayed aggressive and territorial behavior.

Here's How to Crack It

With all strategy questions, identify the purpose in the question. With questions that use a Yes/No format, connect the purpose in the question to the reasons given in the answer choices. Choice (H) is the correct answer.

———————◯———————

Rhetorical Skills Drill

In the drill below, you will find questions focusing only on Rhetorical Skills. Before you start, take a few moments to go back over the review material and techniques. Answers are in Chapter 24.

> The following paragraphs may or may not be in the most logical order. Each paragraph is numbered, and question 9 will ask you to choose where Paragraph 2 should most logically be placed.

[1]

The golden age of television means many things to many people, but to the small band of actors, writers, and directors who would rise to prominence in the late 50s and early 60s, without a doubt it meant the televisions shows such as

1

Playhouse 90, on which many of them worked for the first live time.

2

[2]

Despite the undeniable risks of live performances—or perhaps because of—the results rank among the greatest achievements in American entertainment. Many of its productions were later remade, both for television and film, including *Requiem for a Heavyweight, Judgment at Nuremberg,* and *Days of Wine and Roses.* 3 Many critics maintain none of the remakes could match the brilliance and electricity of the live performances displayed in *Playhouse 90.*

[3]

[1] Each week, a new "teleplay" was created from scratch—written, cast, rehearsed, and performed. [2] *Playhouse 90* was truly a remarkable training ground for the young talents. [3] Such future luminaries as Rod Serling, Sidney Lumet, Paddy Chayefsky, Marlon Brando, and Patricia Neal worked

1. Which of the following alternatives to the underlined word would be LEAST acceptable?
   A. fame
   B. projection
   C. stardom
   D. greatness

2. The best placement for the underlined word would be:
   F. where it is now.
   G. before the word *actors.*
   H. before the word *doubt.*
   J. before the word *television.*

3. The writer is considering deleting the preceding sentence. Should the sentence be kept or deleted?
   A. Kept, because it provides context for the reference to remakes in the next sentence.
   B. Kept, because it is crucial to understanding why *Playhouse 90* was a success.
   C. Deleted, because it does not match the objective tone of the essay.
   D. Deleted, because it contains information that has already been provided in the essay.

long hours reading scripts. [4] In some cases, when there
were problems with the censors, it would have to be created

twice. 5

[4]

Due to the frantic pace, accidents happened frequently.
David Niven once revealed that, during an early show, he
inadvertently locked his costume in his dressing room two
minutes before air time. As the announcer read the opening
credits, the sound of axes splintering the door to Niven's
dressing room could be heard in the background. 7

4. Which choice would most clearly indicate that the actors,
   writers, and directors became extremely skilled?

   F. memorizing their lines.
   G. honing their craft.
   H. constructing the set.
   J. skimming the want-ads.

5. Which of the following order of sentences will make the
   paragraph most logical?

   A. NO CHANGE
   B. 1, 2, 4, 3
   C. 2, 1, 4, 3
   D. 2, 3, 1, 4

6. Given that all choices are true, which one most effectively
   introduces this paragraph?

   F. NO CHANGE
   G. The ratings for *Playhouse 90* were unimpressive.
   H. Broadway has produced many famous actors as well.
   J. *Playhouse 90* ran on CBS from 1956 to 1961.

7. The writer is considering deleting the preceding sentence.
   If the writer were to make this deletion, the essay would
   primarily lose a statement that:

   A. explains the organization of the last paragraph.
   B. adds a much needed touch of humor to the essay.
   C. explains how one accident was resolved.
   D. adds nothing, since the information is provided elsewhere
       in the essay.

   Questions 8 and 9 ask about the preceding
   passage as a whole.

8. Suppose that one of the writer's goals had been to write a
   brief essay describing an influential program in television's
   history. Would this essay fulfill that goal?
   F. Yes, because it explains that many future stars underwent
       valuable training working on *Playhouse 90*.
   G. Yes, because it mentions that *Playhouse 90* had the
       greatest number of viewers in its time slot.
   H. No, because it fails to mention any future stars by name.
   J. No, because even though many future stars received their
       start on *Playhouse 90*, few ever returned to television.

9. For the sake of the logic and coherence of this essay, Paragraph 2 should be placed:

   A. where it is now.
   B. before Paragraph 1.
   C. after Paragraph 3.
   D. after Paragraph 4.

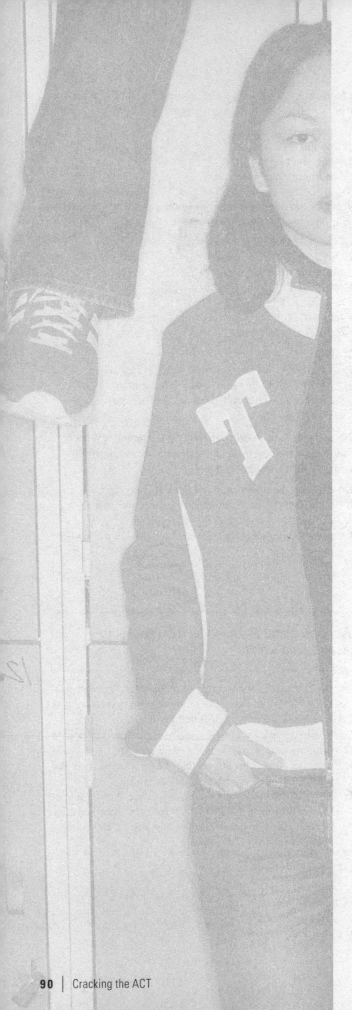

Summary

- o The official categories of Usage and Mechanics and Rhetorical Skills do not matter if you use the same approach to cracking them.

- o Questions that come with actual questions—not just answer choices—do need a different approach.

- o For EXCEPT/LEAST/NOT questions, cross off the E/L/N word and use POE.

- o Strategy questions all involve a purpose.

- o Order questions involve the correct placement of words, sentences, and paragraphs.

Part III
How to Crack the ACT Mathematics Test

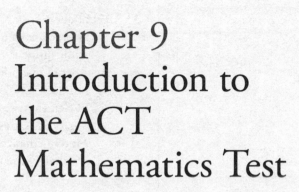

Chapter 9
Introduction to the ACT Mathematics Test

The second section of the ACT will always be the Math test. To perform your best, you'll need to become familiar with the structure and strategy of the ACT Math test. In this chapter, we discuss the types of questions you can expect to see and how you can use organizational strategy, estimation, and elimination skills to improve your Math score.

WHAT TO EXPECT ON THE MATH TEST

You will have 60 minutes to answer 60 multiple-choice questions based on "topics covered in typical high school classes." For those of you who aren't sure if you went to a typical high school, these questions break down into rather precise areas of knowledge.

The Math section usually breaks down into the following:

33 Algebra questions
- 14 pre-algebra questions based on math terminology (integers, prime numbers, and so on), basic number theory (rules of zero, order of operations and so on), and manipulation of fractions and decimals
- 10 elementary algebra questions based on inequalities, linear equations, ratios, percents, and averages
- 9 intermediate algebra questions based on exponents, roots, simultaneous equations, and quadratic equations

23 Geometry questions
- 14 plane geometry questions based on angles, lengths, triangles, quadrilaterals, circles, perimeter, area, and volume
- 9 coordinate geometry questions based on slope, distance, midpoint, parallel and perpendicular lines, points of intersection, and graphing

4 Trigonometry questions
- 4 questions based on basic sine, cosine, and tangent functions, trig identities, and graphing

What Not to Expect on the Math Test

The ACT does not provide any formulas at the beginning of the Math test. Before you panic, take a second look at the chart on the previous page. Because the ACT is so specific about the types of questions it expects you to answer, preparing to tackle ACT Math takes a few simple steps.

A NOTE ON CALCULATORS

Not all standardized tests allow calculators. Fortunately, ACT does. We're not about to give you the stodgy advice that you shouldn't use your calculator—quite the opposite, in fact. Your calculator can help to save a ton of time on operations that you may have forgotten how to do or that are easy to mess up. Adding fractions, multiplying decimals, doing operations with big numbers: Why not use a calculator on these? The place where you have to be really careful with your calculator, though, is on the easy ones. Let's see an example.

1. What is the value of $3x^2 + 5x - 7$ when $x = -1$?
   A. -15
   B. -9
   C. -1
   D. 5
   E. 15

Here's How to Crack It

If you've got your calculator handy, use it. This problem is pretty straightforward, but a calculator can help to put everything together. BUT, make sure you're treating the -1 with the respect it deserves. What you punch into your calculator should look something like this:

$$3(-1)^2 + 5(-1) - 7$$

When working with negative numbers or fractions, make doubly sure that you use parentheses. If not, a lot of weird stuff can happen, and unfortunately all of the weird, wrong stuff that can happen is reflected in the wrong answer choices. If you computed this equation and found -9, (B), you got the right answer. Well done. If not, try to go back and figure out where you made your calculator mistake.

Types of Calculators

Throughout the rest of the Math chapters, we discuss ways to solve calculator-friendly questions in an accurate and manageable way. Because TI-89 and TI-92 calculators are not allowed on the ACT, we will show you how to solve problems on the TI-83. If you don't plan to use a TI-83 on the test, we recommend you make sure your calculator is acceptable for use on the test and that it can do the following:

- handle positive, negative, and fractional exponents
- use parentheses
- graph simple functions
- convert fractions to decimals and vice versa
- change a linear equation into $y = mx + b$ form

> Use your calculator, but use it wisely. Be careful with negative numbers and fractions.

THE PRINCETON REVIEW APPROACH

Because the test is so predictable, the best way to prepare for ACT Math is with

- a thorough review of the very specific information and question types that come up repeatedly
- an understanding of The Princeton Review's test-taking strategies and techniques

In each Math chapter in this book, you'll find a mixture of review and technique, with a sprinkling of ACT-like problems. At the end of each chapter, there is a summary of the chapter and a drill designed to pinpoint your math test-taking strengths and weaknesses. In addition to working through the problems in this book, we strongly suggest you practice our techniques on some real ACT practice tests. Let's begin with some general strategies.

Order of Difficulty: Still Personal

The Math test is the only part of the ACT that is in Order of Difficulty (OOD). What this means is that the easier questions tend to be a bit earlier in the exam, and the harder questions are later. Usually, this means that question 1 is a freebie and question 60 is a doozy. None of the other tests have an OOD, unfortunately, so they are all about Personal Order of Difficulty (POOD). This OOD in and of itself is great to know when planning how you will attack this part of the ACT.

Now we all love easy questions, but hold on for a second. If you and I both get a B on a math test at school, is it necessarily because we got exactly the same questions right or wrong? Unfortunately, no. What makes for a hard question? Is it hard because it's a long word problem, or is it hard because it tests some arcane concept that your teacher went over for like five seconds? Only the very hardest questions will be both. So even on the Math test of the ACT, you still need to use your POOD. The things you might find easy or hard won't necessarily jibe with ACT's.

Now

Do the problems you're sure you can do quickly and accurately.

Later

If a problem looks time-consuming, save it for later. Do the Nows first.

Never.

Sometimes it's better to just walk away. If a problem has you totally stumped, answer with your Letter of the Day and move on.

Now, Later, Never

Hard questions take a long time. Easy ones take a short time. That's obvious, but as we've seen, the definition of an "Easy" question is a tough one to pin down. That's why you'll want to be careful trusting ACT's Order of Difficulty on the Math test. The no-brainer approach is to open the test booklet and work questions 1 through 60 in order, but you can get a lot of extra points by out-thinking this test. You'll have a lot easier time drawing your own road map for this test than letting ACT guide you.

Clearly, a lot of the easy questions will be right in the beginning, but they won't all be. This is why when you arrive at each question, you'll want to first determine whether it is a Now, Later, or Never question. Do the Now questions immediately: They're the freebies—the ones you know how to do and can do quickly and accurately. Skip any questions you think might take you a bit longer or which test unfamiliar concepts—save them for Later. Make sure you get all the points you can on the problems you know you can do, no matter what the question number.

Once you've done all the Now questions, go back to all the ones you left for Later. But here you should be careful as well. For both Now and Later questions, don't rush and make careless errors. On the other hand, don't get stuck on a particular problem. In a 60-minute exam, think of how much spending 5 minutes on a single problem can cost you!

Finally, there's no problem with leaving a few questions behind in the Never category. The good news here is that these problems are not necessarily totally lost. Fill them in with a Letter of the Day: Choose one pair of letters and bubble in all the blanks this way. For example, always bubble in A or F, B or G, etc. ACT doesn't have a guessing penalty, so there's nothing to lose, and you can even get lucky and score a few free points.

USE PROCESS OF ELIMINATION (POE)

Remember the major technique we introduced in Chapter 2: POE, or Process of Elimination. ACT doesn't take away points for wrong answers, so you should always guess, and POE can help you improve those chances of guessing. Don't make the mistake of thinking that POE is a strategy reserved only for English, Reading, and Science. Math has its own kind of POE, one facet of which we like to call Ballparking.

BALLPARK

You can frequently get rid of several answer choices in an ACT math problem without doing any complicated math. Narrow down the choices by estimating your answer. We call this Ballparking. Let's look at an example.

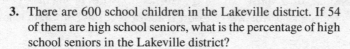

3. There are 600 school children in the Lakeville district. If 54 of them are high school seniors, what is the percentage of high school seniors in the Lakeville district?

   A. .9%
   B. 2.32%
   C. 9%
   D. 11%
   E. 90%

Here's How to Crack It

Before we do any serious math on this problem, let's see if we can get rid of some answer choices by Ballparking.

First, we need to figure out what percent 54 is of 600. It's pretty small, definitely way less than 50%, so we can eliminate (E) right off the bat. Now, think about easy percentages that you know—10 and 25%—and start from there. What's 10% of 600? Just move the decimal one place to the right to get it, and you'll find that 10% of 600 is 60. Therefore, if the number from the problem is 54, the answer must be less than 10%. Let's get rid of (D). Now, we know that 54 is pretty close to 60, so we want something close to 10% but slightly less, and the only possible answer is (C).

It may feel like we somehow cheated the system by doing the problem that way, but here's what ACT doesn't want you to know: The quick, easy way and the "real" way get you the same amount of points. Not all problems will be so easily ballparkable, but if you think before you start frantically figuring, you can usually eliminate at least an answer choice or two.

Cross Out the Crazy Answers
What's the average of 100 and 200?
~~A. 500~~
B. 150
~~C. a billion~~

WORD PROBLEMS

You've seen the breakdown of the topics that are tested on the ACT Math test. At a glance, it actually looks like the ACT should be kind of an easy test: You've definitely learned a lot of this stuff in school, a lot of it by the end of middle school. So what's the deal? Well, part of the deal is that ACT makes familiar stuff really unfamiliar by putting it into word problems. Word problems add some confusing steps that mask the often simple concepts trapped in the problems. Trap answers, partial answers, and weird phrasing abound in word problems. Is anyone else getting the feeling that this whole exam is about reading comprehension?

Word problems look a lot of different ways and test a lot of different math concepts, but if you keep these three steps in mind, you should be able to get started on most word problems.

We'll demonstrate these steps in action on the next page.

> When dealing with word problems on the ACT Math test
> 1. **Know the question.** Read the whole problem before calculating anything, and underline the actual question.
> 2. **Let the answers help.** Look for clues on how to solve and ways to use POE (Process of Elimination).
> 3. **Break the problem into bite-sized pieces.** When you read the problem a second time, calculate at each step necessary and watch out for tricky phrasing.

Let's try a problem.

8. Each member in a club had to choose an activity for a day of volunteer work. $\frac{1}{3}$ of the members chose to pick up trash. $\frac{1}{4}$ of the remaining members chose to paint fences. $\frac{5}{6}$ of the members still without tasks chose to clean school buses. The rest of the members chose to plant trees. If the club has 36 members, how many of the members chose to plant trees?

   F.   3
   G.   6
   H.   9
   J.   12
   K.   15

Here's How to Crack It

Step 1: Know the Question

This is actually a slightly tricky step on this one. First of all, the problem doesn't tell you until the very end that there are 36 students in this class. Without this piece of information, the fractions don't mean much of anything. Second, the question is asking for the number of members who chose to plant trees, and we're going to have to figure out a bunch of other things before we figure that out.

Step 2: Let the Answers Help

There aren't any crazy answers in this one, though if you noticed how much we're subtracting from 36, you're probably thinking that the answer will be one of the smaller numbers.

Step 3: Break the Problem Into Bite-Sized Pieces

The starting point of this word problem actually comes at the end: This club has 36 members. Once you've got that, work the problem sentence by sentence, and pay particular attention to the language of the problem.

$$\frac{1}{3}$$ of the members chose to pick up trash.

A nice easy way to start. There are 36 members, and $\frac{1}{3}$ of 36 is 12, so 12 members pick up trash.

$$\frac{1}{4}$$ of the remaining members chose to paint fences.

This is just like the last piece, except for one HUGE exception, which comes from the word *remaining*. First, we'll need to figure out how many remaining members there are from the first step. There are 36 total members and 12 of them are picking up trash, so there are 24 members remaining. $\frac{1}{4}$ of 24 is 6, so 6 members paint fences.

$$\frac{5}{6}$$ of the remaining members still without tasks chose to clean school buses.

There's that word remaining again. There were 24 members in the last step, but 6 of them chose to paint fences, so now there are 18 *remaining* members. $\frac{5}{6}$ of 18 is 15, so 15 members clean school buses.

The rest of the members chose to plant trees.

There were 18 members left over in the last step, and 15 of them chose to clean school buses, which means there must be 3 students left to plant trees. Choice (F) is the correct answer. Look at those other answers, then look at the numbers you were dealing with in the problem: What a mess of partial answers!

If it seems like this took kind of a long time to do, don't worry, they won't all take this long. Most of these steps will come naturally after a while, and you'll have a solid base with which to begin any ACT Math problem in such a way that enables you to get to the answer as efficiently as possible.

PACING

As you work through the following lessons, revisit your POOD. The more content you review and the more you practice, you may find more Now questions and fewer Never questions.

GOAL SCORE

Use the pacing strategies and score grid on page 23 to find your goal score for each practice test and, eventually, the ACT.

Summary

- On the ACT Math test, you have 60 minutes to attempt 60 questions. The questions fall into the following categories:
  - 33 Algebra questions (14 pre-algebra, 10 elementary algebra, 9 intermediate algebra)
  - 23 Geometry questions (14 plane geometry, 9 coordinate geometry)
  - 4 Trigonometry questions

- Use your Personal Order of Difficulty to determine if a question is for Now, Later, or Never.
  - Just because the Math test is technically in order of difficulty doesn't mean you need to do it in order.
  - Never leave any blanks! Fill in the Never questions with your Letter of the Day.

- Remember the basic approach for Word Problems.
  - **Know the question.** Read the problem all the way through and underline the question.
  - **Let the answers help.** Look for clues on how to solve. Use POE and Ballparking.
  - **Break the problem into bite-sized pieces.** Every problem has lots of information: Process each piece one at a time and be careful of tricky phrasing.

- Finally, use your calculator liberally but wisely!

Chapter 10
Fundamentals

A solid base in the fundamentals of the math tested on the ACT is essential to getting a good score. We'll see a number of strategies that will help to work around some of the more advanced concepts, but there's often no way to work around questions that test the fundamentals.

VOCABULARY

Calculators can solve a lot of problems, but Vocabulary is one aspect of the math with which a calculator can't help. Let's review some of the main terms.

A Note on Calculators

This chapter will deal mainly with concepts rather than operations. As mentioned in the previous chapter, we encourage you to use your calculator liberally but wisely. The operations discussed in this chapter will be those for which a calculator might be unhelpful or extra confusing.

Basics

Use the numbers below to answer questions 1 through 6 that follow. Check your answers against the Answer Key at the end of this chapter on page 122.

$$-81, -19, -9, -6, -\frac{1}{4}, -0.15, 0, 1.75, 2, 3, 12, 16, 81$$

1. List all the *positive numbers.* _____
2. List all the *negative integers.* _____
3. List all the *odd* integers. _____
4. List all the *even* integers. _____
5. List all the *positive, even* integers in *consecutive* order. _____
    _____
6. List all the numbers that are neither *positive* nor *negative.* _____
    _____

Now try these questions.

7. What is the *reciprocal* of $-\frac{1}{4}$? _____

8. What is the *opposite reciprocal* of 2? _____
9. When a number and its reciprocal are multiplied, what is the product?
    _____
10. How many times does 2 go into 15 evenly? _____
11. How much is left over? _____
12. What is 15 divided by 2? _____

Let's try it the other way. Use the following list of terms to answer questions 13 through 18.

> Number, Integer, Positive, Negative, Even, Odd,
> Consecutive, Reciprocal, Remainder

13. Which terms describe the number 6? _____

_____

14. Which terms describe the number $-\frac{1}{5}$? _____

_____

15. Which terms describe the number 0? _____

_____

16. When 14 is divided by 3, it has a _____ of 2.

17. The _____ of $-\frac{1}{4}$ is -4.

18. The numbers 2, 4, 6 are listed in _____ order, but the numbers 3, 1, 14 are not.

Factors and Multiples

Factors and multiples are all about numbers that are divisible by other numbers. Start with examples, and the definitions will become easier.

> Example
> - The factors of 10 are 1, 2, 5, 10.
> - The first four positive multiples of 10 are 10, 20, 30, 40.

A Good Rule of Thumb
- The factors of a number are always equivalent to that number or *smaller*.
- The multiples of a number are always equivalent to that number or *larger*.

1. List the factors of 12. _____

2. List the first four multiples of 12. _____

3. List the factors of 30. _____

4. List the first four multiples of 30. _____

5. Is 12 a multiple or factor of 24? _____

6. Is 8 one of the factors of 64? _____

7. What is the greatest common factor of 27 and 45? _____

8. What is the greatest common factor of 9 and 36? _____

9. What is the least common multiple of 9 and 12? _____

10. What is the least common multiple of 24 and 48? _____

Prime

A prime number is any number with only two distinct factors:
1 and itself.

1. What are the single digit prime numbers? _____

2. What is the only even prime number? _____

3. Is 1 a prime number? _____

The prime factorization of a number is the reduction of a number to its prime factors. Find the prime factorization of a number by using a factor tree. For example:

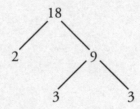

The prime factorization of 18 is $2 \times 3 \times 3$ or 2×3^2.

4. What is the prime factorization of 36?

5. What is the sum of all the prime factors of 36? _____

6. What is the product of all the distinct prime factors of 36? _____

ADVANCED TERMS

Real Numbers and Their Imaginary Friends

ACT uses the term "real" a lot, but it's usually only there to scare you. Sometimes, though, ACT will test it directly, so it's good to have at least a sense of what the term means.

1. How much would you like to earn in your eventual job? _____
2. How much scholarship money do you want from your eventual college? _____
3. What's the temperature in the Bahamas right now? (Ballpark it!) _____
4. How many slices of pizza could you eat in a single sitting? _____

Unless you have some interesting ideas about money and/or pizza, ALL of the numbers above are real. The only numbers that aren't real are imaginary—a negative number under an even root.

5. What is $\sqrt{1}$? _____
6. What is -1×-1? _____
7. What is $-1 \times -1 \times -1$? _____
8. What is $\sqrt{-1}$? _____
9. What real number could you square to get a product of -1? _____

That last question was a trick: There is no real number that you can square and get a negative product. The only way to get the square root (or any even root) of a negative number is to *imagine* it.

> $\sqrt{-1}$ is defined as the imaginary number *i*. All other imaginary numbers are something multiplied by *i*.

Rational Numbers and Their Irrational Friends

1. Write 0.5 as a fraction. _____
2. Write 3 as a fraction. _____
3. In the number 0.1666, what digit is coming next? _____
4. In the number, 0.191919, what digit is coming next? _____

> A *rational* number is any number that can be written as a fraction—that
> includes integers and repeating decimals. An *irrational* is a number
> that cannot be written as a fraction because it goes on unpredictably.
> *Both* types of numbers are *real*.

Love Your Calculator for Real, but Be Rational

Your calculator can be a really handy tool for problems dealing with imaginary and irrational numbers. If you have a Texas Instruments calculator, the second function of the decimal is i. Use this function to solve the following problems.

5. $(2 + i)(2 - i)$? _____
6. $(3 + i)^2$? _____

To determine if a number is rational or irrational, it can help to try to convert it into a fraction. In the MATH menu, the first item is >*Frac*. This will convert a decimal to a fraction if the number is rational. For each question below, after you have typed in the number provided hit ENTER, then MATH>ENTER>ENTER. Give the result in the blank and identify whether it is rational or irrational.

7. 0.375 _____
8. 0.16666666666 (until the end of the screen) _____
9. π _____
10. 0.479109801431 _____

Exponents

Exponents are a shorthand way of indicating that a number is multiplied by itself. The exponent tells you how many times (for example, $5^4 = 5 \times 5 \times 5 \times 5$). Exponents are tricky when you have to combine them in some way. Here's a great way to remember all the rules.

Remember MADSPM!

- When you *multiply* two numbers with common bases, *add* the exponents.
- When you *divide* two numbers with common bases, *subtract* the exponents.
- When you raise an exponential number to a *power*, *multiply* the exponents.

Basic Rules

1. $(x^2)(x^3)$

2. $\dfrac{x^4}{x^3}$

3. $(x^4)^3$

4. $2x^2 \times 6x^3$

5. $(2x^2)^3$

6. $\dfrac{9x^6}{3x^2}$

7. $\dfrac{(x^2)(x^5)}{x^4}$

Special Rules

Follow the basic rules to see how some of these special rules are derived.

1. $\dfrac{x^4}{x^4}$

2. x^0

3. $\dfrac{x^2}{x^5}$

4. x^{-3}

5. x^1

6. 1^{513}

7. 0^{619}

8. $(-2)^2$

9. $(-2)^3$

10. -2^2

11. $\left(\dfrac{1}{2}\right)^2$

12. $\left(\dfrac{2}{3}\right)^2$

Roots

You can add or subtract square roots only when the numbers under the square root sign are the same.

Example:

$$4\sqrt{x} + 2\sqrt{x} = 6\sqrt{x}$$

But $4\sqrt{x} + 2\sqrt{2x}$ can't be combined!

Multiplication and division are more flexible. Different values can be combined under the root, as long as the root has the same degree.

Example:

$$\left(\sqrt{x}\right)\left(\sqrt{y}\right) + \sqrt{xy}$$

$$\frac{\sqrt{x}}{\sqrt{y}} = \sqrt{\frac{x}{y}}$$

1. $\sqrt{x} + \sqrt{x} =$

2. $3\sqrt{x} + 5\sqrt{x} =$

3. $x\sqrt{3} + x\sqrt{5} =$

4. $\left(\sqrt{2x}\right)\left(\sqrt{y}\right) =$

5. $\left(\sqrt{x}\right)\left(\sqrt{xy}\right) =$

If ACT asks you to simplify exponents or roots with numbers instead of variables, use your calculator. But be extra careful with parentheses!

6. $4\sqrt{12} \times 2\sqrt{3} =$

7. $\dfrac{\sqrt{72}}{\sqrt{2}}$

8. $\left(\sqrt{529} - \sqrt{361}\right)^{\frac{1}{2}}$

Remember: The Answer Keys for the preceding drills can be found at the end of this chapter after the Summary page.

FUNDAMENTALS VOCABULARY DRILL

Absolute Value: _____

_____

Consecutive: _____

_____

Decimal: _____

_____

Difference: _____

_____

Digits: _____

_____

Distinct: _____

_____

Divisible: _____

_____

Even: _____

_____

Exponent/Power: _____

_____

Factor: _____

_____

Fraction: _____

_____

Greatest Common Factor: _____

_____

Imaginary: _____

_____

Integers: _____

_____

Irrational: _____

_____

Least Common Multiple: _____

_____

Multiple: _____

_____

Negative: _____

_____

Number: _____

_____

Odd: _____

_____

Opposite: _____

_____

Order of Operations: _____

_____

Positive: _____

_____

Prime: _____

_____

Product: _____

_____

Quotient: _____

_____

Real: _____

_____

Radical: _____

_____

Rational: _____

_____

Reciprocal: _____

_____

Remainder: _____

_____

Sum: _____

_____

GLOSSARY

Absolute Value:	The distance from zero on the number line
Consecutive:	In increasing order
Decimal:	A way of expressing a fraction in which numbers are divided by ten, hundred, thousand, and other powers of ten
Difference:	The result of subtraction
Digits:	The integers 0 through 9
Distinct:	Different
Divisible:	An integer can be divided by another integer evenly, with no fraction or decimal left over
Even:	Divisible by 2
Exponent/Power:	A number that indicates how many times to multiply a base by itself
Factor:	Integers that multiply together to make a given product
Fraction:	A way of expressing the division of numbers by stacking one over the other
Greatest Common Factor:	The largest factor common to two numbers
Imaginary:	The square (or any other even) root of a negative number
Integers:	All real numbers other than decimals or fractions
Irrational:	A number that can be expressed as a decimal but not a fraction
Least Common Multiple:	The smallest multiple common to two numbers
Multiple:	The product of an integer and another integer
Negative:	Less than 0
Number:	Everything
Odd:	NOT divisible by 2
Opposite:	Two numbers that have the same magnitude but are opposite in signs. That is, two numbers with the same distance from zero on the number line, but one is positive and the other negative.
Order of Operations:	Parentheses, Exponents, Multiplication, Division, Addition, Subtraction

Positive: Greater than 0

Prime: A number that has itself and 1 as its only factors

Product: The result of multiplication

Quotient: The result of division

Real: Zero, all positive and negative integers, fractions, decimals, and roots

Radical: Another word for the $\sqrt{}$ sign

Rational: A number that can be expressed as the ratio of two other numbers, making a fraction

Reciprocal: The inverse of a number—flip the numerator and denominator

Remainder: The number left over when a number is not divisible by another number

Sum: The result of addition

Fundamentals Drill

In the drill below, you will find questions focusing only on fundamental skills. Before you start, take a few moments to go back over the review material and techniques. Answers are in Chapter 24.

1. What is the product of the distinct prime factors of 54 ?

   A.   2
   B.   3
   C.   6
   D.   11
   E.   54

2. If x is the least odd prime number and y is the least positive integer multiple of 10, what is the difference between x and y ?

   F.   3
   G.   7
   H.   11
   J.   15
   K.   17

3. For all x and y, $(x^{-1}y^{-3})^{-2}(x^4y^7)^3 = ?$

   A. $x^{10}y^{15}$
   B. x^5y^{10}
   C. x^3y^4
   D. $x^{14}y^{27}$
   E. $x^{-6}y^{18}$

4. In the complex numbers, where $i^2 = -1$, which of the following is equal to the result of squaring the expression $(i + 4)$?

   F. $4i$
   G. $16i$
   H. $15 + 8i$
   J. $i + 16$
   K. $17 - 18i$

5. What is the least possible sum of three distinct prime numbers between 10 and 20 ?

   A.   30
   B.   39
   C.   41
   D.   45
   E.   60

Summary

o Learn the basics on the ACT Math test before you move on to more difficult concepts. The Fundamentals are the one thing on the ACT that you can't fake!

o Know your vocabulary. The Math test requires its own Reading Comprehension.

o Know your rules for 0.
  • 0 is an even number.
  • 0 is neither positive nor negative.
  • Anything multiplied by 0 is 0.
  • 0 raised to any power is 0.
  • Anything raised to the 0 power is 1.

o A number's factors are always *smaller than* or the *same as* that number.

o A number's multiples are always *larger than* or the *same as* that number.

o A prime number has only two distinct factors: 1 and itself.
  • 1 is NOT a prime number.
  • 2 is the only even prime number.

o Use your calculator well and wisely. A calculator is particularly helpful with
  • imaginary numbers (represented as i in problems)
  • square roots that don't contain variables (and often those that do)
  • converting decimals or other expressions into fractions
  • multiplying and dividing large numbers

o When combining numbers with exponents, remember MADSPM.

FUNDAMENTALS LESSON ANSWER KEY

Basics (page 106)
1. 1.75, 2, 3, 12, 16, 81
2. −81, −19, −9, −6
3. −81, −19, −9, 3, 81
4. −6, 0, 2, 12, 16
5. 2, 12, 16
6. 0
7. −4
8. $-\dfrac{1}{2}$
9. 1
10. 7
11. 1
12. 7 R 1 (7 *remainder* 1)
13. Number, Integer, Positive, Even
14. Number, Negative
15. Number, Integer, Even
16. Remainder
17. Reciprocal
18. Consecutive

Factors and Multiples (page 109)
1. 1, 2, 3, 4 , 6, 12
2. 12, 24, 36, 48
3. 1, 2, 3, 5, 6, 10, 15, 30
4. 30, 60, 90, 120
5. Factor
6. Yes
7. 9
8. 9
9. 36
10. 48

Prime (page 110)
1. 2, 3, 5, 7
2. 2
3. No, it does not have two *distinct* factors.
4. $2 \times 2 \times 3 \times 3$ or $2^2 \times 3^2$
5. 10 (2 + 2 + 3 + 3)
6. 6 (2 × 3)

Real Numbers and Their Imaginary Friends (page 111)

5. 1
6. 1
7. −1
8. No answer, or Imaginary
9. None

Rational Numbers and Their Irrational Friends (page 112)

1. $\dfrac{1}{2}$
2. $\dfrac{3}{1}$
3. 6
4. 1

Love Your Calculator for Real, but Be Rational (page 112)

5. 5
6. $8 + 6i$
7. $\dfrac{3}{8}$ Rational.
8. $\dfrac{1}{6}$ Rational.
9. No result. Irrational.
10. $\dfrac{479109801431}{10000000000000}$ Rational.

Basic Rules (page 113)

1. x^5
2. x^1, or x
3. x^{12}
4. $12x^5$. Don't forget the coefficients!
5. $8x^6$
6. $3x^4$
7. x^3

Special Rules (page 114)

1. x^0, or 1
2. 1

3. x^{-3}, or $\dfrac{1}{x^3}$

4. $\dfrac{1}{x^3}$

5. x
6. 1
7. 0
8. 4
9. −8
10. −4

11. $\dfrac{1}{4}$

12. $\dfrac{4}{9}$

Roots (page 115)

1. $2\sqrt{x}$

2. $8\sqrt{x}$

3. Can't be combined!

4. $\sqrt{2xy}$

5. $\sqrt{x^2 y} = x\sqrt{y}$

6. $8\sqrt{36} = 8(6) = 48$

7. $\sqrt{36} = 6$

8. $\left(\sqrt{529} - \sqrt{361}\right)^{\frac{1}{2}} = (23 - 19)^{\frac{1}{2}} = (4)^{\frac{1}{2}} = 2$

Chapter 11
No More Algebra

Once you have a solid foundation in basic operations and vocabulary, you are well-equipped to do a wide variety of problems. This chapter will look at some of the problems that test concepts you may have seen in Algebra classes, and it will show how to work around some of the toughest algebra problems.

ALGEBRA AND THE ACT

We've already seen in Chapter 10 some of the easier plug-and-chug algebra problems. Most questions that ACT considers "algebra" questions won't be so straightforward. ACT expects you to use algebra to solve word problems as well as plug-and-chug questions. Let's see how you can make this work in your favor.

HOW I LEARNED TO STOP WORRYING AND LOVE VARIABLES

Let's look at the following problem:

21. John has x red pencils and three times as many red pencils as blue pencils. If he has four more yellow pencils than blue pencils, then in terms of x, how many yellow pencils does John have?

   A. $x + 4$

   B. $x + 7$

   C. $\dfrac{x}{6}$

   D. $\dfrac{x + 12}{6}$

   E. $\dfrac{x + 12}{3}$

Let's think about the bigger picture for a second here. We're all familiar with these x values from algebra class, but what we often forget is that x is substituting for some real value. Equations use x because that value is an unknown. The variable x could be 5 or 105 or 0.36491. In fact, the ACT writers are asking you to create an expression that will answer this question to find what that "certain number" is. And they want you to make it even harder on yourself by forgetting that x is a number at all.

PLUGGING IN

If you had 1 dollar and you bought 2 pieces of candy at 25 cents apiece, how much change would you have? 50 cents, of course. If you had d dollars and bought p pieces of candy at c cents apiece, how much change would you have? Um, Letter of the Day.

Numbers are a lot easier to work with than variables. Therefore, when you see variables on the ACT, you can usually make things a lot easier on yourself by using numbers instead. Whenever there are variables in the answer choices or the problem, you can use Plugging In.

> Use Plugging In
>
> - when there are variables in the answer choices
> - when solving word problems or plug-and-chug questions
> - for questions of any difficulty level

Let's go back to question 21.

---○---

21. John has x red pencils and three times as many red pencils as blue pencils. If he has four more yellow pencils than blue pencils, then in terms of x, how many yellow pencils does John have?

   A. $x + 4$

   B. $x + 7$

   C. $\dfrac{x}{6}$

   D. $\dfrac{x + 12}{6}$

   E. $\dfrac{x + 12}{3}$

Make sure to keep your work organized when Plugging In. Always circle your target answer.

Here's How to Crack It

1. Know the Question. Underline "how many yellow pencils does John have?" We're not solving for x here; we need the number of yellow pencils. ACT just wants us to name the value "in terms of x."

2. Let the answers help. The answers help a lot here: Each contains the variable x, which means we can Plug In.

3. Break the problem into bite-sized pieces. We know we can Plug In. Let's take it step by step from there.

We want to make the math easy on ourselves, so let's say $x = 3$, so John has 3 red pencils. Now that we've dispensed with the variable, let's work the rest of the problem.

John has 3 red pencils and *three times as many red pencils as blue pencils*. He therefore must have 1 blue pencil. He has *four more yellow pencils than blue pencils*, so he must have 5 yellow pencils.

So now we can answer the question with what is called our *target answer*. The question asks *How many yellow pencils does John have?*, to which our answer is 5. Circle this answer on your paper. Let's go to the answer choices to see which one gives us our target. Remember, $x = 3$.

A.	$(3) + 4 = 7$	Not our target answer. Cross it off.
B.	$(3) + 7 = 10$	Not our target answer. Cross it off.
C.	$\dfrac{(3)}{6} = \dfrac{1}{2}$	Not our target answer. Cross it off.
D.	$\dfrac{(3) + 12}{6} = \dfrac{15}{6}$	Not our target answer. Cross it off.
E.	$\dfrac{(3) + 12}{3} = 5$	✔

Only (E) works, so this is our correct answer. Look how easy that was, and not a bit of algebra necessary! Let's try another.

17. For all $x \neq 3$, which of the following is equivalent to the expression $\dfrac{3x^2 - 7x - 6}{x - 3}$?

    A. $3x + 2$

    B. $3x - 2$

    C. $3(x - 2)$

    D. $3(x + 2)$

    E. $x^2 - 2$

Here's How to Crack It

This looks a lot more like a standard plug-and-chug than the last problem did, but remember, we can always Plug In when there are variables in the answer choices. This will be a tough problem to factor, so Plugging In will probably be your best bet, even if you're an ace with quadratic equations. The only thing the problem tells us is that $x \neq 3$, so let's say $x = 2$.

$$\frac{3(2)^2 - 7(2) - 6}{(2) - 3}$$

$$\frac{3(4) - 14 - 6}{-1}$$

$$\frac{-8}{-1} = 8$$

We now know that for the value we've chosen, the value of this expression is 8. That means **8** is our target answer. Let's plug our x value into the answer choices to find the one that matches the target.

    A. $3(2) + 2 = 8$ ✔   This matches our target answer, but when you Plug In, always check all 5 answers.

    B. $3(2) - 2 = 6 - 2 = 4$ Not our target answer. Cross it off.

    C. $3((2) - 2) = 3(0) = 0$ Not our target answer. Cross it off.

    D. $3((2) + 2) = 3(4) = 12$ Not our target answer. Cross it off.

    E. $(2)^2 - 2 = 2$ Not our target answer. Cross it off.

Only (A) worked, and it is the correct answer. So as we can see, Plugging In works for all kinds of algebra problems. Let's review what we've done so far.

What To Do When You Plug In

1. Identify the opportunity. Can you Plug In on this question?

2. Choose a good number. Make the math easy on yourself.

3. Find a target answer. Answer the question posed in the problem with your number, and circle your target answer.

4. Test all the answer choices. If two of them work, try a new number.

Let's try a tougher one.

───────────○───────────

36. In my dear Aunt Sally's math class, there are four exams. The first three exam scores are averaged, and the resulting score is averaged with the final exam score. If a, b, and c are the first three exam scores, and f is the final exam score, which of the following examples gives a student's final score in the class?

   F. $\dfrac{a+b+c}{3}+f$

   G. $\dfrac{a+b+c+3f}{6}$

   H. $\dfrac{a+b+c+f}{4}$

   J. $\dfrac{a+b+c+3f}{4}$

   K. $a+b+c+f$

Here's How to Crack It

This is a word problem, so remember the basic approach.

1. Know the question. Underline the question in this problem: *which of the following gives a student's final score in this class?*

2. Let the answers help. There are variables in each of these answer choices, which means we can Plug In, so these answers will help a lot. If you want to do a bit of POE, you might notice that the problem is asking for an average, so (K) can't work. Also, something funny will need to happen with the f variable, so you can eliminate (H).

3. Break the problem into bite-sized pieces. If you rush through this problem, it's very easy to mess up. Let's go piece by piece as we did in the earlier problem.

The first three exam scores are averaged.

There's no reason to give realistic exam scores here: We can pick whatever numbers we want, so let's use numbers that make the math easy. We know from this problem that the first three exam scores are represented by *a*, *b*, and *c*, so let's say *a = 2*, *b = 3*, and *c = 4*. The average of these three numbers can be found as follows: $\frac{2+3+4}{3} = \frac{9}{3} = 3$.

The resulting score is then averaged with the final score.

The resulting score is 3, and we need to plug in some final score, *f*. Let's use another easy number and say *f = 5*. In averaging these two numbers together, we find $\frac{3+5}{2} = \frac{8}{2} = 4$. Thus, we have our target answer: A student's final score with these exam scores will be 4.

Let's go to the answer choices and look for the one that matches the target. Remember, *a = 2*, *b = 3*, *c = 4*, and *f = 5*.

$$\text{F.} \quad \frac{2+3+4}{3} + 5 = \frac{9}{3} + 5 = 8 \qquad \textbf{X}$$

$$\text{G.} \quad \frac{2+3+4+3(5)}{6} = \frac{24}{6} = 4 \qquad \checkmark$$

$$\text{H.} \quad \frac{2+3+4+5}{4} = \frac{14}{4} = 3.5 \qquad \textbf{X}$$

$$\text{J.} \quad \frac{2+3+4+3(5)}{4} = \frac{24}{4} = 6 \qquad \textbf{X}$$

$$\text{K.} \quad 2+3+4+5 = 14 \qquad \textbf{X}$$

Choice (G) is the correct answer, and no tough algebra necessary!

Hidden Plug-Ins

Both of the above questions have had variables in the answer choices, which is a dead giveaway that we can Plug In. The good news is that that's not the only time. In any problem in which there are hypothetical values or values relative to each other, Plugging In will work. Let's have a look at a problem.

———————————○———————————

25. If $x - z = 6$ and $y = 3x - 2 - 3z$, then $y = ?$

    A.   2
    B.   4
    C. 14
    D. 16
    E. 18

Here's How to Crack It

There aren't any variables in the answer choices, but notice all values in the problem are defined relative to one another. Let's Plug In.

Using the first equation in the problem, let's make the numbers easy on ourselves and say $x = 8$ and $z = 2$. Using these values, let's find the value for the expression given in the problem: $y = 3(8) - 2 - 3(2) = 24 - 2 - 6 = 16$, choice (D).

It may feel like we just pulled these numbers out of thin air, but try any two numbers that work in the equation $x - z = 6$, and you'll find that it always works.

———————————○———————————

PLUGGING IN THE ANSWERS

So we've seen that Plugging In is a great strategy when there are variables in the question or the answers. How about when there aren't? Does that mean we have to go back to algebra? Of course not! On most problems on the ACT, there are a variety of ways to solve. Let's look at another one that helps to simplify the math in algebra-related problems.

2. If $600 were deposited in a bank account for one year and earned interest of $42, what was the interest rate?

    F. 6.26%
    G. 7.00%
    H. 8.00%
    J. 9.00%
    K. 9.50%

Before we get started cracking this problem, we should note a few things about it. First of all, there aren't any variables, but you get the feeling that you're going to have to put the $600 and the $42 in relationship to some other number by means of an algebraic expression. Then, notice that the problem is asking for a very specific number, the interest rate, and that the answer choices give possibilities for that specific number in ascending order. All of this taken together means that we can Plug In the Answers.

Plug In the Answers (PITA) when

- answer choices are numbers in ascending or descending order
- the question asks for a specific amount. Questions will usually be "what?" or "how many?"
- you get the urge to do algebra even when there are no variables in the problem

---

Let's see what this looks like.

———————————————○———————————————

2. If $600 were deposited in a bank account for one year and earned interest of $42, what was the interest rate?

    F. 6.26%
    G. 7.00%
    H. 8.00%
    J. 9.00%
    K. 9.50%

Here's How to Crack It

1. Know the question. As we've already identified, we need to find the *interest rate*.

2. Let the answers help. The way the answer choices are listed has already indicated that we'll be able to PITA on this problem, so we'll be using the answers a lot in this question.

3. Break the problem into bite-sized pieces. We're going to use the answer choices to walk through each step of the problem, working it in bite-sized pieces.

Because these answer choices are listed in ascending order, it will be best to start with the middle choice. That way, if it's too high or too low, we'll be able to use POE more efficiently.

Therefore, if we start with 8.00% as our interest rate, we can find what the annual interest on a $600 deposit would be by multiplying $600 × 0.08 = $48. Because the problem tells us that the deposit earned $42 of interest, we know choice (H) is too high, which also eliminates (J) and (K).

Let's try (G): You may find it helpful to keep your work organized in columns as shown below.

Interest Rate	Rate per $600	= $42?
F. 6.26%		
G. 7.00%	$42	Yes! ✔
H. 8.00%	$48	X
J. 9.00%		
K. 9.50%		

We haven't introduced any of our own numbers into this problem, so once we find the correct answer, we can stop. The correct answer is (G).

———————————————○———————————————

Let's try a harder one.

―――――――――――――――○―――――――――――――――

49. In a piggy bank, there are pennies, nickels, dimes, and quarters
     that total $2.17 in value. If there are 3 times as many pennies as
     there are dimes, 1 more dime than nickels, and 2 more quarters
     than dimes, then how many pennies are in the piggy bank?

     A. 12
     B. 15
     C. 18
     D. 21
     E. 24

Here's How to Crack It

1. Know the question. *How many pennies are in the bank?*

2. Let the answers help. There are no variables, but the very specific question
coupled with the numerical answers in ascending order gives a pretty good indication that we can PITA.

3. Break the problem into bite-sized pieces. Make sure you take your time
with this problem; you'll need to multiply the number of each coin by its
monetary value. In other words, don't forget that 1 nickel will count for 5 cents,
1 dime will count for 10 cents, and 1 quarter will count for 25 cents. As in the
previous problem, let's set up some columns to keep our work organized and begin
with (C).

Since ACT has already given us the answers, we will plug those answers in and work backwards. Each of the answers listed gives a possible value for the number of pennies. Using the information in the problem, we can work backwards from that number of pennies to find the number of nickels, dimes, and quarters. When the values for the number of coins adds up to $2.17, we know we're done.

If we begin with the assumption that there are 18 pennies, then there must be 6 dimes (*3 times as many pennies as there are dimes*). 6 dimes means 5 nickels (*1 more dime than nickels*) and 8 quarters (*2 more quarters than dimes*).

Now multiply the number of coins by the monetary value of each to see if they total $2.17.

	Pennies ($P)	Dimes ($D)	Nickels ($N)	Quarters ($Q)	Total = $2.17?
C.	18 ($0.18)	6 ($0.60)	5 ($0.25)	8 ($2.00)	Total = $3.03

That's too high, so not only is (C) incorrect, but so are (D) and (E). Cross them off, and try (B).

	Pennies ($P)	Dimes ($D)	Nickels ($N)	Quarters ($Q)	Total = $2.17?
A.	12 ($0.12)	4 ($0.40)	3 ($0.15)	6 ($1.50)	Total = $2.17 ✔
B.	15 ($0.15)	5 ($0.50)	4 ($0.20)	7 ($1.75)	Total = $2.60 X
C.	18 ($0.18)	6 ($0.60)	5 ($0.25)	8 ($2.00)	Total = $3.03 X
D.	21	Eliminated through POE			
E.	24	Eliminated through POE			

Only (A) works. No algebra necessary!

A NOTE ON PLUGGING IN AND PITA

Plugging In and PITA are not the only ways to solve these problems, and it may feel weird using these methods instead of trying to do these problems "the real way." You may have even found that you knew how to work with the variables in Plugging In problems or how to write the appropriate equations for the PITA problems. If you can do either of those things, you're already on your way to a great Math score.

But think about it this way. We've already said that ACT doesn't give any partial credit. So do you think doing it "the real way" gets you any extra points? It doesn't: On the ACT, a right answer is a right answer, no matter how you get it. "The real way" is great, but unfortunately, it's often a lot more complex and offers many more opportunities to make careless errors.

The biggest problem with doing things the real way, though, is that it essentially requires that you invent a new approach for every problem. Instead, notice what we've given you here: two strategies that will work toward getting you the right answer on any number of questions. You may have heard the saying, "Give a man a fish and you've fed him for a day, but teach a man to fish and you've fed him for a lifetime." Now, don't worry, our delusions of grandeur are not quite so extreme, but Plugging In and PITA are useful in a similar way. Rather than giving you a detailed description of how to create formulas and work through them for these problems that won't themselves ever appear on an ACT again, we're giving you a strategy that will help you to work through any number of similar problems in future ACTs.

Try these strategies on your own in the drill that concludes this chapter.

Need More Practice?
The Princeton Review's *Math and Science Workout for the ACT* has two more full-length Math tests.

Algebra Drill

For the answers to this drill, please go to Chapter 24.

1. What is the largest value of x that solves the equation $x^2 - 4x + 3 = 0$?

   A. 1
   B. 2
   C. 3
   D. 4
   E. 5

2. For all $\dfrac{x^2 + 6x - 27}{(x + 9)} = ?$

   F. $x + 9$
   G. $x - 3$
   H. $x + 3$
   J. $2x - 4$
   K. $2x + 3$

3. If 2 less than 3 times a certain number is the same as 4 more than the product of 5 and 3, what is the number?

   A. 7
   B. 10
   C. 11
   D. 14
   E. 15

4. A certain number of books are to be given away at a promotion. If $\dfrac{2}{5}$ of the books are distributed in the morning and $\dfrac{1}{3}$ of the remaining books are distributed in the afternoon, what fraction of the books remains to be distributed the next day?

   F. $\dfrac{1}{5}$
   G. $\dfrac{2}{5}$
   H. $\dfrac{1}{3}$
   J. $\dfrac{5}{7}$
   K. $\dfrac{8}{9}$

5. In the equation $a = \dfrac{3}{b}$, b is a positive, real number. As the value of b is increased so it becomes closer and closer to infinity, what happens to the value of a ?

   A. It remains constant.
   B. It gets closer and closer to zero.
   C. It gets closer and closer to one.
   D. It gets closer and closer to three.
   E. It gets closer and closer to infinity.

Summary

o Remember the basic approach for Word Problems:
  - Know the question.
  - Let the answers help.
  - Break the problem into bite-sized pieces.

o Use Plugging In when there are variables in the answer choices or the problem. Keep the following pointers in mind:
  - Choose numbers that make the math easy.
  - Try all the answer choices.
  - On more complex problems, keep your variables straight!

o Use Plugging In the Answers (PITA) when answer choices are listed in ascending or descending order and when the question is asking for a specific number. Keep the following pointers in mind:
  - Start with choice (C) or (H) to help with POE.
  - When you find the correct answer, STOP!

Chapter 12
Plane Geometry

The ACT test writers tell us there will be 23 geometry questions on the Math test, 14 of which supposedly cover plane geometry. It's better, however, to think of the topic breakdown in broader terms rather than these specific numbers. For one thing, many problems incorporate several concepts: You even need algebra to solve many geometry questions, so would the ACT test writers count a question like that in the algebra or plane geometry column?

What matters most is that you can identify the topics that can make a question Now, Later, or Never for you.

While ACT test writers occasionally may throw in a more advanced formula or complex shape, the majority of the questions test the basic rules on the basic shapes. This chapter will review a cross-section of those formulas and concepts and give you a strategic approach to apply those rules on the ACT.

CRACKING THE GEOMETRY ON THE ACT

Plug-and-chug geometry questions can have so much information in them that they feel like word problems. So treat them like word problems. Let's review the basic approach to word problems. We'll then add some points specific to geometry.

Step 1: Know the Question

Know the question. Read the whole problem before calculating anything, and underline the actual question.

Step 2: Let the Answers Help

Let the answers help. Look for clues on how to solve and ways to use POE (Process of Elimination).

Step 3: Break the Problem into Bite-Sized Pieces

Break the problem into bite-sized pieces. When you read the problem a second time, calculate at each step necessary and watch out for tricky phrasing.

For geometry questions, Step 3 has two specific additions:

> **Step 3a:** Write all the information given in the problem on the figure. If there is no figure, draw your own.
>
> **Step 3b:** Write down any formulas you need, and fill in any information you have.

Geometry BFFs: POE and Ballparking

Step 2 of the basic approach is particularly important to geometry questions. In the last few chapters, we've seen how POE and Ballparking can help to narrow down the answer choices when you're confused. Before you rush to calculate, Ballparking in particular will help you a ton on geometry problems because most figures are drawn to scale.

To Scale or Not to Scale?

That is the question. The ACT makes a big deal in the instructions about the fact that their figures are "NOT necessarily drawn to scale." Here's the thing, though: They usually are drawn to scale or at least enough to use them in broad strokes. Use Ballparking to eliminate answers that are too big or too small rather than to determine a precise value. Questions on angles and area especially lend themselves to Ballparking. The main place to be skeptical is on those problems that ask questions like, "Which of the following must be true?" Those are the ones whose figures can be purposely misleading.

In most other cases, if you know how to use the figures that are given (or how to draw your own), you can eliminate several wrong answers before doing any math at all. Let's see how this works.

How Big Is Angle *NLM*?

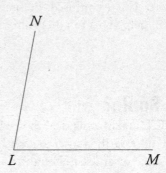

Obviously, you don't know exactly how big this angle is, but it would be easy to compare it with an angle whose measure you *do* know exactly. Let's compare it with a 90° angle.

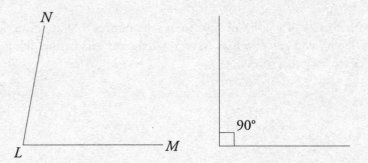

Angle *NLM* is clearly a bit less than 90°. Now look at the following problem, which asks about the same angle *NLM*.

1. In the figure below, O, N, and M are collinear. If the lengths of $\overline{ON}$ and $\overline{NL}$ are the same, the measure of angle LON is 30°, and angle LMN is 40°, what is the measure of angle NLM?

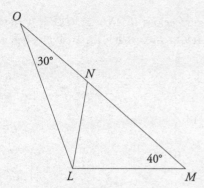

    A.   30°
    B.   80°
    C.   90°
    D. 110°
    E. 120°

Here's How to Crack It

Start with Step 1: Know the question. Underline *what is the measure of angle NLM?* and even mark the angle on your figure. You don't want to answer for the wrong angle. Now move to Step 2, and let's focus on eliminating answer choices that don't make sense. We've already decided that $\angle NLM$ is a little less than 90°, which means we can eliminate (C), (D), and (E). How much less than 90°? 30° is a third of 90°. Could $\angle NLM$ be that small? No way! The answer to this question must be (B).

In this case, it wasn't necessary to do any "real" geometry at all to get the question right, but it took about half the time. ACT has to give you credit for right answers no matter how you get them. Revenge is sweet. What's more, if you worked this problem the "real" way, you might have picked one of the other answers: As you can imagine, every answer choice gives some partial answer that you would've seen as you worked the problem.

Let's Do It Again

2. In the figure below, if $\overline{AB} = 27$, $\overline{CD} = 20$, and the area of triangle $ADC = 240$, what is the area of polygon $ABCD$?

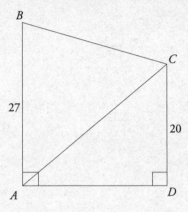

F. 420
G. 480
H. 540
J. 564
K. 1,128

Here's How to Crack It

Start with Step 1: Know the question. Underline *what is the area of polygon ABCD?* This polygon is not a conventional figure, but if we had to choose one figure that the polygon resembled, we might pick a rectangle. Try drawing a line at a right angle from the line segment $\overline{AB}$ so that it touches point C, thus creating a rectangle. It should look like the following:

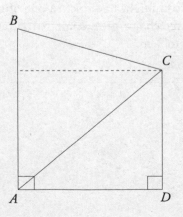

The area of polygon *ABCD* is equal to the area of the rectangle you've just formed, plus a little bit at the top. The problem tells you that the area of triangle *ADC* is 240. What is the area of the rectangle you just created? If you said 480, you are exactly right, whether you knew the geometric rules that applied or whether you just measured it with your eyes.

So the area of the rectangle is 480. Roughly speaking, then, what should the area of the polygon be? A little more. Let's look at the answer choices.

What Should I Do If There Is No Diagram?
Draw one! It's always easier to understand a problem when you can see it in front of you. If possible, draw your figure to scale so that you can estimate the answer as well.

Choices (F) and (G) are either less than or equal to 480; get rid of them. Choices (H) and (J) both seem possible; they are both a little more than 480; let's hold on to them. Choice (K) seems pretty crazy. We want more than 480, but 1,128 is ridiculous.

The answer to this question is (J). To get this final answer, you'll need to use a variety of area formulas, which we'll explore later in this chapter. For now, though, notice that your chances of guessing have increased from 20% to 50% with a little bit of quick thinking. Now what should you do? If you know how to do the problem, you do it. If you don't or if you are running out of time, you guess and move on.

However, even as we move in to the "real" geometry in the remainder of this chapter, don't forget:

> Always look for opportunities to Ballpark on geometry problems even if you know how to do them the "real" way.

GEOMETRY REVIEW

By using the diagrams ACT has so thoughtfully provided, and by making your own diagrams when they are not provided, you can often eliminate several of the answer choices. In some cases, you'll be able to eliminate every choice but one. Of course, you will also need to know the actual geometry concepts that ACT is testing. We've divided our review into the following four topics:

- Angles and lines
- Triangles
- Four-sided figures
- Circles

ANGLES AND LINES

Here is a line.

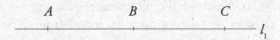

A line extends forever in either direction. This line, called l_1, has three points on it: *A*, *B*, and *C*. These three points are said to be **collinear** because they are all on the same line. The piece of the line in between points *A* and *B* is called a line **segment**. ACT will refer to it as segment *AB* or simply $\overline{AB}$. *A* and *B* are the **endpoints** of segment *AB*.

A line forms an angle of 180°. If that line is cut by another line, it divides that 180° into two pieces that together add up to 180°.

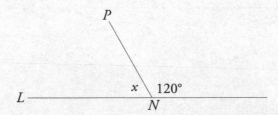

In the above diagram, what is the value of *x*? If you said 60°, you are correct. To find ∠*x*, just subtract 120° from 180°.

An angle can also be described by points on the lines that intersect to form the angle and the point of intersection itself, with the middle letter corresponding to the point of intersection. For example, in the previous diagram, $\angle x$ could also be described as $\angle LNP$. On the ACT, instead of writing out "angle LNP," they'll use math shorthand and put $\angle LNP$ instead. So "angle x" becomes $\angle x$.

If there are 180° above a line, there are also 180° below the line, for a total of 360°.

When two lines intersect, they form four angles, represented below by letters A, B, C, and D. $\angle A$ and $\angle B$ together form a straight line, so they add up to 180°.

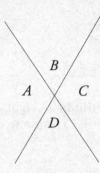

Angles that add up to 180° are called **supplementary** angles. $\angle A$ and $\angle C$ are opposite from each other and always equal each other, as are $\angle B$ and $\angle D$. Angles like these are called **vertical** angles.

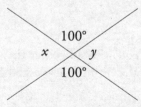

In the previous figure, what is the value of $\angle x$? If you said 80°, you're right. Together with the 100° angle, x forms a straight line. What is the value of $\angle y$? If you said 80°, you're right again. These two angles are vertical and must equal each other. The four angles together add up to 360°.

When two lines meet in such a way that 90° angles are formed, the lines are called **perpendicular**. The little box at the point of intersection of two lines below indicates that they are perpendicular. It stands to reason that all four of these angles have a value of 90°.

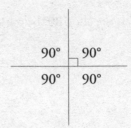

When two lines in the same plane are drawn so that they could extend into infinity without ever meeting, they are called **parallel**. In the figure below, l_1 is parallel to l_2. The symbol for parallel is | |.

When two parallel lines are cut by a third line, eight angles are formed, but in fact, there are really only two—a big one and a little one. Look at the diagram below.

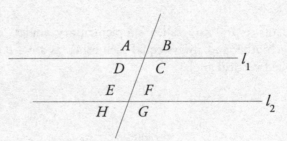

If $\angle A = 110°$, then $\angle B$ must equal 70° (together they form a straight line). $\angle D$ is vertical to $\angle B$, which means that it must also equal 70°. $\angle C$ is vertical to $\angle A$, so it must equal 110°.

The four angles $\angle E$, $\angle F$, $\angle G$, and $\angle H$ are in exactly the same proportion as the angles above. The little angles are both 70°. The big angles are both 110°.

Try the following problem.

1. In the figure below, line *L* is parallel to line *M*. Line *N* intersects both *L* and *M*, with angles *a*, *b*, *c*, *d*, *e*, *f*, *g*, and *h* as shown below. Which of the following lists includes all the angles that are supplementary to ∠*a* ?

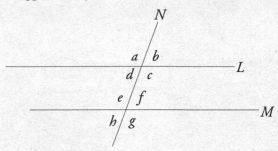

A. Angles *b*, *d*, *f*, and *h*
B. Angles *c*, *e*, and *g*
C. Angles *b*, *d*, and *c*
D. Angles *e*, *f*, *g*, and *h*
E. Angles *d*, *c*, *h*, and *g*

Here's How to Crack It

An angle is supplementary to another angle if the two angles together add up to 180°. Because ∠*a* is one of the eight angles formed by the intersection of a line with two parallel lines, we know that there are really only two angles: a big one and a little one. ∠*a* is a big one. Thus, only the small angles would be supplementary to it. Which angles are those? The correct answer is (A). By the way, if you think back to the last chapter and apply what you learned there, could you have Plugged In on this problem? Of course you could have. After all, there are variables in the answer choices. Sometimes it is easier to see the correct answer if you substitute real values for the angles instead of just looking at them as a series of variables. Just because a problem involves geometry doesn't mean that you can't Plug In on it.

N

a = 100° b = 80° *L*
d = 80°   c = 100°

e = 100° f = 80°   *M*
h = 80°   g = 100°

TRIANGLES

A triangle is a three-sided figure whose inside angles always add up to 180°. The largest angle of a triangle is always opposite its largest side. Thus, in triangle *XYZ* below, *XY* would be the largest side, followed by *YZ*, followed by *XZ*. On the ACT, "triangle *XYZ*" will be written as Δ*XYZ*.

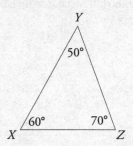

The ACT likes to ask about certain kinds of triangles in particular.

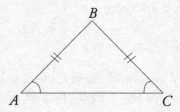

An **isosceles** triangle has two equal sides. The angles opposite those sides are also equal. In the isosceles triangle above, if ∠*A* = 50°, then so does ∠*C*. If $\overline{AB}$ = 6, then so does $\overline{BC}$.

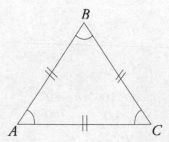

An **equilateral** triangle has three equal sides and three equal angles. Because the three equal angles must add up to 180°, all three angles of an equilateral triangle are always equal to 60°.

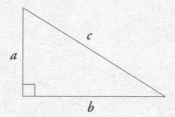

A **right triangle** has one inside angle that is equal to 90°. The longest side of a right triangle (the one opposite the 90° angle) is called the **hypotenuse.**

Pythagoras, a Greek mathematician, discovered that the sides of a right triangle are always in a particular proportion, which can be expressed by the formula $a^2 + b^2 = c^2$, where a and b are the shorter sides of the triangle, and c is the hypotenuse. This formula is called the **Pythagorean theorem**.

There are certain right triangles that the test writers at ACT find endlessly fascinating. Let's test out the Pythagorean theorem on the first of these.

$$3^2 + 4^2 = c^2$$
$$9 + 16 = 25$$
$$c^2 = 25, \text{ so } c = 5$$

The ACT writers adore the 3-4-5 triangle and use it frequently, along with its multiples, such as the 6-8-10 triangle and the 9-12-15 triangle. Of course, you can always use the Pythagorean theorem to figure out the third side of a right triangle, as long as you have the other two sides, but because ACT problems almost invariably use "triples" like the ones we've just mentioned, it makes sense just to memorize them.

The ACT has three commonly used right-triangle triples.

3-4-5 (and its multiples)

5-12-13 (and its multiples)

7-24-25 (not as common as the other two)

Pythagoras's *Other* Theorem

Pythagoras also developed a theory about the transmigration of souls. So far, this has not been proven, nor will it help you on this exam.

Don't Get Snared

- Is this a 3-4-5 triangle?

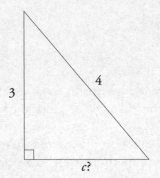

No, because the hypotenuse of a right triangle must be its *longest* side—the one opposite the 90° angle. In this case, we must use the Pythagorean theorem to discover side c: $3^2 + c^2 = 16$, so $c = \sqrt{7}$.

- Is this a 5-12-13 triangle?

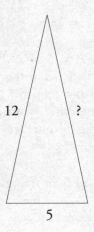

No, because the Pythagorean theorem—and triples—apply only to *right* triangles. We can't determine definitively the third side of this triangle based on the angles.

The Isosceles Right Triangle

As fond as the ACT test writers are of triples, they are even fonder of two other right triangles. The first is called the **isosceles right triangle**. The sides and angles of the isosceles right triangle are always in a particular proportion.

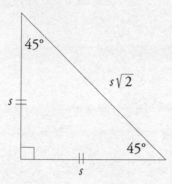

You could use the Pythagorean theorem to prove this (or you could just take our word for it). Whatever the value of the two equal sides of the isosceles right triangle, the hypotenuse is always equal to one of those sides times $\sqrt{2}$. Here are two examples.

> **Be on the Lookout . . .**
> for problems in which the application of the Pythagorean theorem is not obvious. For example, every rectangle contains two right triangles. That means that if you know the length and width of the rectangle, you also know the length of the diagonal, which is the hypotenuse of both triangles created by the diagonal.

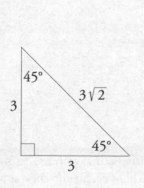

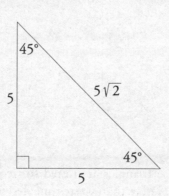

The 30-60-90 Triangle

The other right triangle tested frequently on the ACT is the **30-60-90 triangle**, which also always has the same proportions.

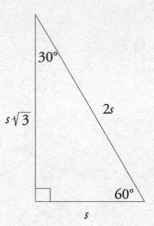

You can use the Pythagorean theorem to prove this (or you can just take our word for it). Whatever the value of the short side of the 30-60-90 triangle, the hypotenuse is always twice as large. The medium side is always equal to the short side times $\sqrt{3}$. Here are two examples.

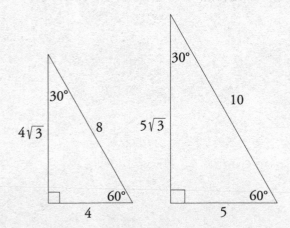

Because these triangles are tested so frequently, it makes sense to memorize the proportions, rather than waste time deriving them each time they appear.

Don't Get Snared

- In the isosceles right triangle below, are the sides equal to $3\sqrt{2}$?

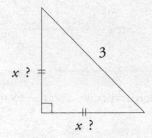

No. Remember, in an isosceles right triangle, hypotenuse = the side $\sqrt{2}$. In this case, $3 =$ the side $\sqrt{2}$. If we solve for the side, we get $\dfrac{3}{\sqrt{2}} =$ the side.

For arcane mathematical reasons, we are not supposed to leave a radical in the denominator, but we can multiply top and bottom by $\sqrt{2}$ to get $\dfrac{3\sqrt{2}}{2}$.

- In the right triangle below, is x equal to $4\sqrt{3}$?

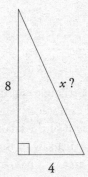

No. Even though it is one of ACT's favorites, you have to be careful not to see a 30-60-90 where none exists. In the triangle above, the short side is half of the *medium* side, not half of the hypotenuse. This is some sort of right triangle all right, but it is not a 30-60-90. The hypotenuse, in case you're curious, is really $4\sqrt{5}$.

Area

The **area** of a triangle can be found using the following formula:

$$\text{area} = \frac{\text{base} \times \text{height}}{2}$$

Height is measured as the perpendicular distance from the base of the triangle to its highest point.

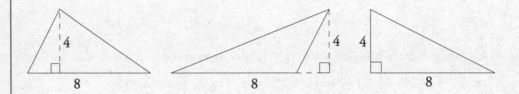

In all three of the above triangles, the area is

$$\frac{8 \times 4}{2} = 16$$

Don't Get Snared

- Sometimes the height of a triangle can be *outside* the triangle itself, as we just saw in the second example.
- In a right triangle, the height of the triangle can also be one of the sides of the triangle, as we just saw in the third example. However, be careful when finding the area of a *non-right* triangle. Simply because you know two sides of the triangle does not mean that you have the height of the triangle.

Similar Triangles

Two triangles are called similar if their angles have the same degree measures. This means their sides will be in proportion. For example, the two triangles below are similar.

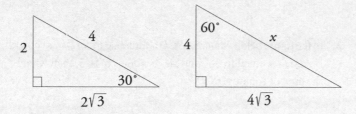

Because the sides of the two triangles are in the same proportion, you can find the missing side, x, by setting up a proportion equation.

$$\frac{\text{short leg}}{\text{hypotenuse}} \quad \overset{\text{small triangle}}{\frac{2}{4}} = \overset{\text{big triangle}}{\frac{4}{x}}$$

$$x = 8$$

ACT TRIANGLE PROBLEMS

In this chapter, we've pretty much given you all the basic triangle information you'll need to do the triangle problems on the ACT. The trick is that you'll have to use a lot of this information all at once. Let's have a look at a typical ACT triangle problem and see how to use the basic approach.

3. In the figure below, square *ABCD* is attached to △*ADE* as shown. If △*EAD* is equal to 30° and $\overline{AE}$ is equal to $4\sqrt{3}$, then what is the area of square *ABCD* ?

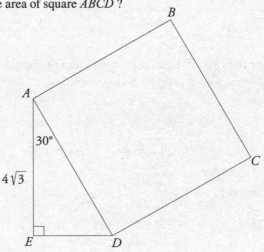

A. $8\sqrt{3}$
B. 16
C. 64
D. 72
E. $64\sqrt{2}$

Here's How to Crack It

Start with Step 1: Know the question. Underline *what is the area of square ABCD*? Move to Step 2: Look at the answers. We don't have any values for areas of other shapes within the figure, so there is nothing to Ballpark. But note the presence of $\sqrt{2}$ and $\sqrt{3}$ in the answers: They're an additional clue, if you haven't absorbed the info given, that either 30-60-90 and/or 45-45-90 triangles are in play.

The triangle in the figure is in fact a 30-60-90. Now move to Step 3: Break the problem into bite-sized pieces. Because angle *A* is the short angle, the side opposite that angle is equal to 4 and the hypotenuse is equal to 8. Now move on to Step 3a: Mark your figure with these values. Now move to Step 3b: Write down any formulas you need. The area for a square is s^2. Because that hypotenuse is also the side of the square, the area of the square must be 8 times 8, or 64. This is (C). If you forgot the ratio of the sides of a 30-60-90 triangle, go back and review it. You'll need it.

POE Pointers

If you didn't remember the ratio of the sides of a 30-60-90 triangle, could you have eliminated some answers using POE? Of course. Let's see if we can use the diagram to eliminate some answer choices.

The diagram tells us that $\overline{AE}$ has length $4\sqrt{3}$. Remember the important approximations we gave you earlier in the chapter? A good approximation for $\sqrt{3}$ is 1.7. So $4\sqrt{3}$ = approximately 6.8. We can now use this to estimate the sides of square $ABCD$. Just using your eyes, would you say that $\overline{AD}$ is longer or shorter than $\overline{AE}$? Of course it's a bit longer; it's the hypotenuse of $\triangle ADE$. You decide and write down what you think it might be. To find the area of the square, simply square whatever value you decided the side equaled. This is your answer.

Now all you have to do is see which of the answer choices still makes sense. Could the answer be (A)? $8\sqrt{3}$ equals roughly 13.6. Is this close to your answer? No way. Could the answer be (B), which is 16? Still much too small. Could the answer be (C), which is 64? Quite possibly. Could the answer be 72? It might be. Could the correct answer be $64\sqrt{2}$? An approximation of $\sqrt{2}$ = 1.4, so $64\sqrt{2}$ equals 89.6. This seems rather large. Thus, on this problem, by using POE we could eliminate (A), (B), and (E).

FOUR-SIDED FIGURES

**Your Friend
the Triangle**
Because a quadrilateral is
really just two triangles,
its interior angles must
measure twice those
of a triangle:
2(180) = 360.

The interior angles of any four-sided figure (also known as a quadrilateral) add up to 360°. The most common four-sided figures on the ACT are the rectangle and the square, with the parallelogram and the trapezoid coming in a far distant third and fourth.

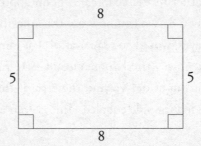

A **rectangle** is a four-sided figure whose four interior angles are each equal to 90°. The area of a rectangle is *base × height*. Therefore, the area of the rectangle above is 8 (*base*) × 5 (*height*) = 40. The perimeter of a rectangle is the sum of all four of its sides. The perimeter of the rectangle above is 8 + 8 + 5 + 5 = 26.

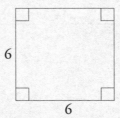

A **square** is a rectangle whose four sides are all equal in length. You can think of the area of a square, therefore, as **side squared**. The area of the above square is 6 (*base*) × 6 (*height*) = 36. The perimeter is 24, or 4*s*.

A **parallelogram** is a four-sided figure made up of two sets of parallel lines. We said earlier that when parallel lines are crossed by a third line, eight angles are formed but that in reality there are only two—the big one and the little one. In a parallelogram, 16 angles are formed, but there are still, in reality, only two.

The area of a parallelogram is also *base × height*, but because of the shape of the figure, the height of a parallelogram is not necessarily equal to one of its sides. Height is measured by a perpendicular line drawn from the base to the top of the figure. The area of the parallelogram above is $9 \times 5 = 45$.

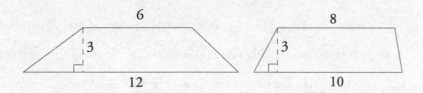

A **trapezoid** is a four-sided figure in which two sides are parallel. Both of the figures above are trapezoids. The area of a trapezoid is the *average of the two parallel sides × the height*, or $\frac{1}{2}$ (*base* 1 + *base* 2)(*height*), but on ACT problems involving trapezoids, there is almost always some easy way to find the area without knowing the formula (for example, by dividing the trapezoid into two triangles and a rectangle). In both trapezoids above, the area is 27.

Geometry Hint
If there isn't a figure, always draw your own.

D'oh, I'm in a Square!
To help you remember the area of a four-sided figure (a square, a rectangle, or a parallelogram), imagine that Bart and Homer Simpson are stuck inside of it. To get its area, just multiply **B**art times **H**omer, or (*b*)(*h*), or the base times the height.

CIRCLES

The distance from the center of a circle to any point on the circle is called the **radius**. The distance from one point on a circle through the center of the circle to another point on the circle is called the **diameter**. The diameter is always equal to twice the radius. In the circle on the left below, *AB* is called a **chord**. *CD* is called a **tangent** to the circle.

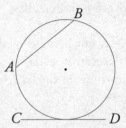 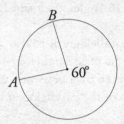

The curved portion of the right-hand circle between points *A* and *B* is called an **arc**. The angle formed by drawing lines from the center of the circle to points *A* and *B* is said to be **subtended** by the arc. There are 360° in a circle, so that if the angle we just mentioned equaled 60°, it would take up $\frac{60}{360}$ or $\frac{1}{6}$ of the degrees in the entire circle. It would also take up $\frac{1}{6}$ of the area of the circle and $\frac{1}{6}$ of the outer perimeter of the circle, called the **circumference**.

The formula for the **area** of a circle is πr^2.

The formula for the **circumference** is $2\pi r$.

In the circle below, if the radius is 4, then the area is 16π, and the circumference is 8π.

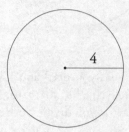

The key to circle problems on the ACT is to look for the word or phrase that tells you what to do. If you see the word *circumference*, immediately write down the formula for circumference, and plug in any numbers the problem has given you. By solving for whatever quantity is still unknown, you have probably already answered the problem. Another tip is to find the radius. The radius is the key to many circle problems.

1. If the area of a circle is 16 square meters, what is its radius in meters?

   A. $\dfrac{8}{\pi}$

   B. 12π

   C. $\dfrac{4\sqrt{\pi}}{\pi}$

   D. $\dfrac{16}{\pi}$

   E. $144\pi^2$

Here's How to Crack It

Step 1: Know the question. We need to solve for the radius. Step 2: Let the answers help. We don't have a figure, so there's nothing to Ballpark. But no figure? Step 3a: Draw your own.

Step 3b: Write down any formulas you need and fill in the information you have. Set the formula for area of a circle equal to $\pi r^2 = 16$. The problem is asking for the radius, so you have to solve for r. If you divide both sides by π, you get

$$r^2 = \frac{16}{\pi}$$

$$r = \sqrt{\frac{16}{\pi}}$$

$$= \frac{4}{\sqrt{\pi}}$$

$$= \frac{4\sqrt{\pi}}{\pi}$$

The correct answer is (C).

2. In the figure below, the circle with center O is inscribed inside square $ABCD$ as shown. If a side of the square measures 8 units, what is the area of the shaded region?

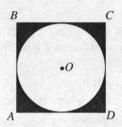

   F. $8 - 16\pi$
   G. 8π
   H. 16π
   J. $64 - 16\pi$
   K. 64π

Here's How to Crack It

Begin with Step 1, and underline *what is the area of the shaded region*? Step 2 brings us to the answers, and we see all of the answers have π in them. If no answer choice can be obviously eliminated via Ballparking move to Step 3. Break the problem into bite-sized pieces, but don't get hung up on "inscribed." Yes, that's an important term to know, but since we have the figure, it's irrelevant. Move to Step 3a and 3b: Mark the side of the square "8," and write down the formulas for the area of a circle and square: πr^2 and s^2.

Is there a formula for the shape made by the shaded region? Nope. We just need the basic formulas for the basic shapes. $8^2 = 64$, so we at least know the shaded region is less than 64, the area of the square. But what's the link between the square and the circle? The side of the square equals the diameter. So if the diameter is 8, then the radius must be 4. Use that in the area formula: $4^2 \pi = 16\pi$. Subtract the area of the circle from the area of the square, and we get (J).

FUN FACTS ABOUT FIGURES

Read and review the following facts you need to know about plane geometry.

Angle Facts

- There are 90° in a right angle.
- When two straight lines intersect, the angles opposite each other are equal.
- There are 180° in a straight line.
- Two lines are perpendicular when they meet at a 90° angle.
- The sign for perpendicular is ⊥.
- Bisect means to cut exactly in half.
- There are 180° in a triangle.
- There are 360° in any four-sided figure.

Triangle Facts

In any triangle

- The longest side is opposite the largest angle.
- The shortest side is opposite the smallest angle.
- All angles add up to 180°.
- Area = $\frac{1}{2}$ (base × height) = $\frac{1}{2}bh$
- The height is the perpendicular distance from the base to the opposite vertex.
- Perimeter is the sum of the sides.
- The third side of any triangle is always less than the sum and greater than the difference of the other two sides.

In an isosceles triangle

- Two sides are equal.
- The two angles opposite the equal sides are also equal.

In an equilateral triangle

- All three sides are equal.
- All angles are each equal to 60°.

Four-Sided Figure Facts

In a quadrilateral
- All four angles add up to 360°.

In a parallelogram
- Opposite sides are parallel and equal.
- Opposite angles are equal.
- Adjacent angles are supplementary (add up to 180°).
- Area = base × height = bh
- The height is the perpendicular distance from the base to the opposite side.

In a rhombus
- Opposite sides are parallel.
- Opposite angles are equal.
- Adjacent angles are supplementary (add up to 180°).
- All 4 sides are equal.
- Area = base × height = bh
- The height is the perpendicular distance from the base to the opposite side.
- The diagonals are perpendicular.

In a rectangle
- Rectangles are special parallelograms; thus, any fact about parallelograms also applies to rectangles.
- All 4 angles are each equal to 90°.
- Area = length × width = lw
- Perimeter = 2(length) + 2(width) = $2l + 2w$
- The diagonals are equal.

In a square
- Squares are special rectangles; thus, any fact about rectangles also applies to squares.
- All 4 sides are equal.
- Area = (side)^2 = s^2
- Perimeter = 4(side) = $4s$
- The diagonals are perpendicular.

Circle Facts

Circle
- There are 360° in a circle.

Radius (*r*)
- The distance from the center to any point on the edge of the circle.
- All radii in a circle are equal.

Diameter (*d*)
- The distance of a line that connects two points on the edge of the circle, passing through the center.
- The longest line in a circle.
- Equals twice the radius.

Chord
- Any line segment connecting two points on the edge of a circle.
- The longest chord is called the diameter.

Circumference (*C*)
- The distance around the outside of the circle.
- $C = 2\pi r = \pi d$

Arc
- Any part of the circumference.
- The length of an arc is proportional to the size of the interior angle.

Area
- The amount of space within the boundaries of the circle.
- $A = \pi r^2$

Sector
- Any part of the area formed by two radii and the outside of the circle.
- The area of a sector is proportional to the size of the interior angle.

Line Facts

Line

- A line has no width and extends infinitely in both directions.
- Any line measures 180°.
- A line that contains points A and B is called $\overleftrightarrow{AB}$ (line AB).
- If a figure on the ACT looks like a straight line, and that line looks like it contains a point, it does.

Ray

- A ray extends infinitely in one direction but has an endpoint.
- The degree measure of a ray is 180°.
- A ray with endpoint A that goes through point B is called $\overrightarrow{AB}$. Pay attention to the arrow above the points and the order they are given; those will determine the direction the ray is pointing!

Line Segment

- A line segment is a part of a line and has two endpoints.
- The degree measure of a line segment is 180°.
- A line segment, which has endpoints of A and B, is written as $\overline{AB}$.

Tangents

- Tangent means intersecting at one point. For example, a line tangent to a circle intersects exactly one point on the circumference of the circle. Two circles that touch at just one point are also tangent.
- A tangent line to a circle is always perpendicular to the radius drawn to that point of intersection.
- If $\overline{AB}$ intersects a circle at point T, then you would say, "$\overline{AB}$ is tangent to the circle at point T."

PLANE GEOMETRY FORMULAS

Here's a list of all the plane geometry formulas that could show up on the ACT. Memorize the formulas for perimeter/circumference, area, and volume for basic shapes. ACT usually provides the more advanced formulas if they are needed.

You won't be able to take any notes into the test with you, so it's a good idea to make sure you know these formulas by heart!

Circles

- Area: $A = \pi r^2$
- Circumference: $C = 2\pi r = \pi d$

Triangles

- Area: $A = \dfrac{1}{2}bh$

- Perimeter: P = sum of the sides

- Pythagorean theorem: $a^2 + b^2 = c^2$

SOHCAHTOA

- $\sin(\theta) = \dfrac{\text{opposite}}{\text{hypotenuse}}$

- $\cos(\theta) = \dfrac{\text{adjacent}}{\text{hypotenuse}}$

- $\tan(\theta) = \dfrac{\text{opposite}}{\text{adjacent}}$

- $\csc(\theta) = \dfrac{1}{\sin}$

- $\sec(\theta) = \dfrac{1}{\cos}$

- $\cot(\theta) = \dfrac{1}{\tan}$

Quadrilaterals

Parallelograms

- Area: $A = bh$
- Perimeter: P = sum of the sides

Rhombus

- Area: $A = bh$
- Perimeter: P = sum of the sides

Trapezoids

- Area: $A = \frac{1}{2}h\left(b_1 + b_2\right)$
- Perimeter: P = sum of the sides

Rectangles

- Area: $A = lw$
- Perimeter: $P = 2(l + w)$

Squares

- Area: $A = s^2$
- Perimeter: $P = 4s$

Polygons

- Sum of angles in an n-sided polygon: $(n-2)180°$
- Angle measure of each angle in a regular n-sided polygon:

$$\frac{(n-2)180°}{n}$$

3-D Figures

- Surface area of a rectangular solid: $S = 2(lw + lh + wh)$
- Surface area of a cube: $S = 6s^2$
- Surface area of a right circular cylinder: $S = 2\pi r^2 + 2\pi rh$
- Surface area of a sphere: $S = 4\pi r^2$
- Volume of a cube: $V = s^3$
- Volume of a rectangular solid: $V = lwh$
- Volume of a right circular cylinder: $V = \pi r^2 h$
- Volume of a sphere: $V = \frac{4\pi r^3}{3}$

GLOSSARY

Arc:	Any part of the circumference
Bisect:	To cut in half
Chord:	Any line segment connecting two points on the edge of a circle
Circumscribed:	Surrounded by a circle as small as possible
Collinear:	Lying on the same line
Congruent:	Equal in size
Diagonal (of a polygon):	A line segment connecting opposite vertices
Equilateral triangle:	All sides are equal and each angle measures 60°
Inscribed (angle in a circle):	An angle in a circle with its vertex on the circumference
Isosceles triangle:	A triangle with two equal sides
Parallel:	Two distinct lines that do not intersect
Perpendicular:	At a 90° angle
Plane:	A flat surface extending in all directions
Polygon:	A closed figure with two or more sides
Quadrilateral:	A four-sided figure
Regular polygon:	A figure with all equal sides and angles
Sector:	Any part of the area formed by two radii and the outside of the circle
Similar:	Equal angles and proportional sides
Surface area:	The sum of areas of each face of a figure
Tangent:	Intersecting at one point
Vertex/Vertices:	A corner point. For angles, it's where two rays meet. For figures, it's where two adjacent sides meet.

Geometry Drill

For the answers to this drill, please go to Chapter 24.

1. In $\triangle ABC$ below, $\angle A = \angle B$, and $\angle C$ is twice the measure of $\angle B$. What is the measure, in degrees, of $\angle A$?

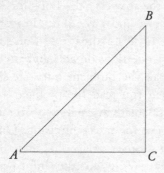

- **A.** 30
- **B.** 45
- **C.** 50
- **D.** 75
- **E.** 90

2. In the figure below, $l_1 \parallel l_2$. Which of the labeled angles must be equal to each other?

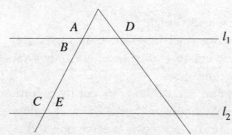

- **F.** A and C
- **G.** D and E
- **H.** A and B
- **J.** D and B
- **K.** C and B

3. In the figure below, right triangles ABC and ACD are drawn as shown below. If $\overline{AB} = 20$, $\overline{BC} = 15$, and $\overline{AD} = 7$, then $\overline{CD} = ?$

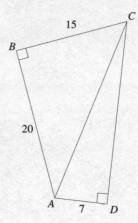

- **A.** 21
- **B.** 22
- **C.** 23
- **D.** 24
- **E.** 25

4. If the area of circle A is 16π, then what is the circumference of circle B if its radius is $\dfrac{1}{2}$ that of circle A ?

- **F.** 2π
- **G.** 4π
- **H.** 6π
- **J.** 8π
- **K.** 16π

5. In the figure below, $\overline{MO}$ is perpendicular to $\overline{LN}$, $\overline{LO}$ is equal to 4, $\overline{MO}$ is equal to $\overline{ON}$, and $\overline{LM}$ is equal to 6. What is $\overline{MN}$?

- **A.** $2\sqrt{10}$
- **B.** $3\sqrt{5}$
- **C.** $4\sqrt{5}$
- **D.** $3\sqrt{10}$
- **E.** $6\sqrt{4}$

Summary

o Use the basic approach.
  - **Step 1:** Know the question. Read the whole problem before calculating anything, and underline the actual question.
  - **Step 2:** Let the answers help. Look for clues on how to solve and ways to use Process of Elimination (POE). Ballparking works well on geometry questions on area and angles.
  - **Step 3:** Break the problem into bite-sized pieces. When you read the problem a second time, calculate at each step necessary and watch out for tricky phrasing. On geometry, this means
    o **Step 3a:** Write all the information given in the problem on the figure. If there is no figure, draw your own.
    o **Step 3b:** Write down any formulas you need and fill in any information you have.

o There are several things to know about angles and lines.
  - A line is a 180° angle.
  - When two lines intersect, four angles are formed, but in reality there are only two distinct measures.
  - When two parallel lines are cut by a third line, eight angles are formed, but in reality there are still only two (a large one and a small one).

o There are several things to know about triangles.
  - A triangle has three sides and three angles; the sum of the angles equals 180°.
  - An isosceles triangle has two equal sides and two equal angles opposite those sides.
  - An equilateral triangle has three equal sides and three equal angles; each angle equals 60°.
  - A right triangle has one 90° angle. In a right triangle problem, you can use the Pythagorean theorem to find the lengths of sides.
  - Some common right triangles are 3-4-5, 6-8-10, 5-12-13, and 7-24-25.
  - ACT test writers also like the isosceles right

triangle, in which the sides are always in the ratio $s:s:s\sqrt{2}$, and the 30-60-90 triangle, in which the sides are always in the ratio $s:s\sqrt{3}:2s$.

- Similar triangles have the same angle measurements and sides that are in the same proportion.

- The area of a triangle is equal to $\dfrac{(base \times height)}{2}$, with height measured perpendicular to the base.

o Four-sided objects are called quadrilaterals and have four angles, which add up to 360°. There are several important things to remember.
  - The area of a rectangle, a square, or a parallelogram can be found using the formula *base × height = area*, with height measured perpendicular to the base.
  - The perimeter of any object is the sum of the lengths of its sides.
  - The area of a trapezoid is equal to the average of the two bases times the height.

o For any circle problem, you need to know four basic things.
  - Radius
  - Diameter
  - Area (πr^2)
  - Circumference (πd or $2\pi r$)

o Don't forget that you can plug in on geometry questions that have variables in the answer choices.

Chapter 13
Word Problems

Now that you've refreshed some of the essential geometry concepts, we will see how to integrate those concepts with your test-taking strategy. In addition, we'll see some other Word Problem strategies that will help you to complete problems quickly and accurately.

PLUGGING IN: NOT JUST ALGEBRA

Remember what the main requirements are for a Plugging In problem. You need variables in the answer choices or question: That's it. It doesn't say anywhere that the problem needs to be a pure algebra problem. What is a pure algebra problem anyway? Don't forget: Part of what makes this test so hard is that ACT piles concept on top of concept in its problems. In other words, geometry problems often *are* algebra problems.

WORD PROBLEMS VS. PLUG-AND-CHUG QUESTIONS

We prefer a simple definition of a word problem: It has to tell a story. But as we discussed in Chapter 12, plug-and-chug geometry questions can have so much information in them that they feel like word problems. So treat them like word problems, and let's refresh the basic approach we discussed in Chapter 12.

Step 1: Know the Question
Know the question. Read the whole problem before calculating anything, and underline the actual question.

Step 2: Let the Answers Help
Let the answers help. Look for clues on how to solve and ways to use POE.

Step 3: Break the Problem into Bite-Sized Pieces
Break the problem into bite-sized pieces. When you read the problem a second time, calculate at each step necessary and watch out for tricky phrasing.

For geometry questions, Step 3 has two specific additions:

> **Step 3a:** Write all the information given in the problem on the figure. If there is no figure, draw your own.
>
> **Step 3b:** Write down any formulas you need and fill in any information you have.

Let's look at a short, straightforward example.

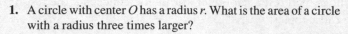

1. A circle with center O has a radius r. What is the area of a circle
    with a radius three times larger?

    A. $3\pi r$
    B. $9\pi r$
    C. $3\pi r^2$
    D. $6\pi r^2$
    E. $9\pi r^2$

Here's How to Crack It

Step 1: **Know the question.** We need to find the area of this new larger circle, not
the larger radius.

Step 2: **Let the answers help.** First of all, we're looking for the area, which means
something will have to be squared, so we can eliminate (A) and (B), which can't
be right. Now, notice that each of these answer choices has a variable in it. If
you're thinking Plugging In, you're thinking right.

Step 3: **Break the problem into bite-sized pieces.** Let's pick an easy value for r,
like $r = 2$.

Step 3a: **Write all the information given in the problem on the figure.** There's
no figure here, so draw 2 circles.

Step 3b: **Write down any formulas you need and fill in any information you
have**. The formula for the area of a circle that we'll need is $A = \pi r^2$.

If the original radius is 2, then the larger radius, which is three times larger, must
be 6. Therefore, the area of the larger circle must be $A = \pi(6)^2 = 36\pi$. We've got a
target answer, so let's try it in the answer choices. Remember, we've already eliminated (A) and (B).

    A. ~~$3\pi r$~~
    B. ~~$9\pi r$~~
    C. $3\pi(2)^2 = 12\pi$ X
    D. $6\pi(2)^2 = 24\pi$ X
    E. $9\pi(2)^2 = 36\pi$ ✔

Choice (E) is the correct answer. Have another look at those answer choices and
think of all the ways you could make mistakes on this problem. Plugging In saves
the day again by minimizing the possibility for algebra errors.

ARITHMETIC

When it comes to writing word problems, ACT test writers can draw on both algebra and geometry, as we've seen. But lots of word problems, and even some plug-and-chugs, will test a variety of arithmetic concepts. The rest of this chapter will review those topics.

PERCENTAGES, PROBABILITIES, AND RATIOS: DIDN'T WE JUST DO THIS?

Percentages, probabilities, and ratios can get mighty complex in your math classes at school. Do you want the good news or the bad news? Well, the bad news is that ratios, percentages, and probabilities will all appear on the ACT Math test, but the good news is that they're all testing the same basic concept: parts to wholes.

Let's say you're taking batting practice. You are thrown 100 pitches and hit 20 of them. Ignoring the fact that you're probably not ready for the MLB, let's put this into some math language. Once we get the basics down, we'll try some more advanced problems.

First, what percentage of the pitches did you hit? Well, that's easy on this one because we're dealing with 100. But you can always find percentages with this simple part-to-whole formula:

$$\frac{part}{whole} \times 100\%$$

Once we put the numbers in, we'll get this: $\frac{20}{100} \times 100\% = 0.2 \times 100\% = 20\%$. If you hit 20 of the 100 pitches, you hit 20% of them.

Next, what is the probability that you were to hit any given pitch? Remember, this is just a matter of parts to wholes, so we can find this probability as follows: $\frac{part}{whole} = \frac{hits}{pitches} = \frac{20}{100} = 0.2$. In other words, there's a 0.2, or $\frac{1}{5}$, probability you hit any given pitch during batting practice.

Ratios are a little different. Usually these will ask for the relationship of some part to some other part. If we're still using our batting practice statistics, we might want to know something like, what's the ratio of the pitches you hit to the pitches you missed?

Even though we're not dealing with the whole this time, we'll find the ratio the same way, but instead of $\dfrac{part}{whole}$, we'll use $\dfrac{part}{whole} = \dfrac{hits}{misses} = \dfrac{20}{80} = \dfrac{1}{4}$. The ratio of hits to misses is $\dfrac{1}{4}$, or 1 to 4, or 1:4.

If it feels like we just did the same thing three times, it was supposed to. As we've seen a few times already, just because things have different names doesn't mean that they are unrelated. Let's try some problems.

Percentages

1. At a restaurant, diners enjoy an "early bird" discount of 10% off their bills. If a diner orders a meal regularly priced at $18 and leaves a tip of 15% of the discounted meal (no tax), how much does he pay in total?

   A. $13.50
   B. $16.20
   C. $18.63
   D. $18.90
   E. $20.70

Here's How to Crack It

Step 1: **Know the question.** We want the price of the discounted meal plus tip.

Step 2: **Let the answers help.** We are reducing a number by 10%, then increasing it by 15%, so it's not likely that the final number will be much less or much greater than $18. Let's eliminate (A) and (E).

Step 3: **Break the problem into bite-sized pieces.**

First, we'll need to figure out what the discounted price of the meal is. There are a number of ways to do this, but if you find this $\dfrac{part}{whole}$ method useful, you could find the discount this way:

$$10\% = discount$$

$$\frac{10}{100} = \frac{discount}{\$18}$$

$$discount = \$1.80$$

The price of the discounted meal, then, is $18 − $1.80 = $16.20. Let's find the tip the same way.

$$15\% = tip$$

$$\frac{15}{100} = \frac{tip}{\$16.20}$$

$$tip = \$2.43$$

The price of the discounted meal plus tip, therefore, is $16.20 + $2.43 = $18.63. The correct answer is (C).

Another Way to Deal with Percents

A percentage is a fraction in which the denominator equals 100. In literal terms, the word *percent* means "divided by 100," so any time you see a percentage in an ACT question, you can punch it into your calculator quite easily. If a question asks for 40 percent of something, for instance, you can express the percentage as a fraction: $\frac{40}{100}$. Any time you are looking for a percent, you can use your calculator to find the decimal equivalent and multiply the result by 100. If four out of five dentists recommend a particular brand of toothpaste, you can quickly determine the percent of doctors who recommend it by typing $\frac{4}{5} \times 100$ and hitting the ENTER key. The resulting "80" just needs a percent sign tacked onto it. To properly translate all percent questions, it is helpful to have a decoding table for the various terms you'll come across.

English	Math Equivalent
percent	/100
of	multiplication (×)
what	variable (y, z)
is, are, were	=
what percent	$\frac{y}{100}$

Percentage Shortcuts

In the last problem, we could have saved a little time if we had realized that $\frac{1}{5} = 20$ percent. Therefore, $\frac{4}{5}$ would be 4×20 percent, or 80 percent. Below are some fractions and decimals whose percent equivalents you should know.

Another fast way to do percents is to move the decimal place. To find 10 percent of any number, move the decimal point of that number over one place to the left.

$$10\% \text{ of } 500 = 50$$

$$10\% \text{ of } 50 = 5$$

$$10\% \text{ of } 5 = .5$$

To find 1 percent of a number, move the decimal point of that number over two places to the left.

$$1\% \text{ of } 500 = 5$$

$$1\% \text{ of } 50 = .5$$

$$1\% \text{ of } 5 = .05$$

You can use a combination of these last two techniques to find even very complicated percentages by breaking them down into easy-to-find chunks.

- 20% of 500: 10% of 500 = 50, so 20% is twice 50, or 100.
- 30% of 70: 10% of 70 = 7, so 30% is three times 7, or 21.
- 32% of 400: 10% of 400 = 40, so 30% is three times 40, or 120.
- 1% of 400 = 4, so 2% is two times 4, or 8.

Therefore, 32 percent of 400 = 120 + 8 = 128.

> ### The Big Four: Fraction/Percent Equivalents You Should Know
>
> $$\frac{1}{5} = .2 = 20\%$$
>
> $$\frac{1}{4} = .25 = 25\%$$
>
> $$\frac{1}{3} = .\overline{33} = 33\frac{1}{3}\%$$
>
> $$\frac{1}{2} = .5 = 50\%$$

Let's have a look at another ACT percentage problem.

———————————◯———————————

2. When 15% of 40 is added to 5% of 260, the resulting number is:

F. 19
G. 40
H. 95
J. 180
K. 260

Here's How to Crack It

Let's try this one using the decoding table. Although this isn't really a word problem, that doesn't mean we shouldn't be careful and break it into bite-sized pieces.

First, 15% of 40. Remember, % translates to divide by 100, and "of" translates to multiplication. Therefore, we can rewrite 15% of 40 as $\frac{15}{100} \times 40$. Put this expression in your calculator to find that $\frac{15}{100} \times 40 = 6$.

Now, find 5% of 260. Use the same translations to find $\frac{5}{100} \times 260 = 13$. We've done the tough part, so let's substitute what we've found back into the problem: *When 6 is added to 13, the resulting number is*: Now that's a problem we can handle! 6 + 13 = 19, so the answer is (F).

———————————◯———————————

Probability

3. Herbie's practice bag contains 4 blue racquetballs, one red racquetball, and 6 green racquetballs. If he chooses a ball at random, which of the following is closest to the probability that the ball will NOT be green?

   A. 0.09
   B. 0.27
   C. 0.36
   D. 0.45
   E. 0.54

Here's How to Crack It

Step 1: **Know the question.** Make sure you read carefully! We want the probability that the chosen ball will NOT be green.

Step 2: **Let the answers help.** Green balls account for slightly more than half the number of balls in the bag, so the likelihood that the ball will NOT be green should be slightly less than half. That eliminates (A), (B), and (E). Not bad!

Step 3: **Break the problem into bite-sized pieces.** This is a pretty straightforward $\frac{part}{whole}$ problem: $\frac{part}{whole} = \frac{NOT\,green}{all} = \frac{5}{11}$. The only slight difficulty is that the answers are not listed as fractions, but it's nothing a calculator can't help. Find $5 \div 11 = 0.45$, choice (D).

Ratios

4. If the ratio of $2x$ to $5y$ is $\frac{1}{20}$, what is the ratio of x to y?

F. $\frac{1}{40}$

G. $\frac{1}{20}$

H. $\frac{1}{10}$

J. $\frac{1}{8}$

K. $\frac{1}{4}$

Here's How to Crack It

The difficulty of this problem is all in the setup. Just remember that you're comparing parts to wholes, and you'll be fine.

$$\frac{2x}{5y} = \frac{1}{20}$$

To isolate $\frac{x}{y}$ on the left side of this equation, let's multiply both sides of the equation by $\frac{5}{2}$.

$$\frac{5}{2} \times \frac{2x}{5y} = \frac{1}{20} \times \frac{5}{2}$$

$$\frac{x}{y} = \frac{5}{40}$$

$\frac{5}{40}$ reduces to $\frac{1}{8}$. The answer is (J).

If you got stuck on this one, look at those answer choices: You could've used PITA!

Let's see how ACT might test ratios in a word problem.

_____ ⌣ _____

5. If 3.7 inches of rain fell on Vancouver during the first 4 days of December, and the rain continues to fall at this pace for the rest of the month, approximately how many feet of rain will fall during December? (Note: The month of December has 31 days.)

   A.   2.4
   B.   3.7
   C.   9.5
   D.   28.7
   E.   114.7

Here's How to Crack It

Step 1: **Know the question.** It's in the last line: *how many feet of rain will fall in December?* But be careful: The value given in the problem is in inches. We're going to have to do some converting!

Step 2: **Let the answers help.** Since we know the problem is asking how many *feet* of rain will fall, and the problem tells us that 3.7 *inches* of rain will fall in 4 days, we can do some Ballparking. The number of inches will increase, but it will be reduced again when we convert it into feet. Choice (E) is definitely too big, and (D) probably is too.

Step 3: **Break the problem into bite-sized pieces.** There are going to be two main parts to this problem: First, we want to figure out how much rain will fall in 31 days, then we want to convert it to feet. We can do this by using ratios.

The ratio given in the problem is 3.7 inches every four days, or in math terms, $\frac{3.7 \text{ in}}{4 \text{ days}}$. The ratio will remain the same no matter how many days there are, so let's use this ratio to find how many inches of rain will fall in December.

$$\frac{3.7 \text{ in}}{4 \text{ days}} = \frac{? \text{ in}}{31 \text{ days}}$$

We can rearrange the terms to find

$$? \text{ in} = \frac{(3.7 \text{ in})(31 \text{ days})}{4 \text{ days}} = 28.675 \text{ in}$$

But we can't stop here! Remember, the problem is asking for a value in feet. (It's a good thing we did some early POE, isn't it?)

We'll use the same process, and this time we already know the ratio of inches to feet: $\dfrac{12 \text{ in}}{1 \text{ ft}}$. As we did above, let's use this ratio to find our answer.

$$\frac{12 \text{ in}}{1 \text{ ft}} = \frac{28.675 \text{ in}}{? \text{ ft}}$$

Rearrange the equation to find

$$? \text{ ft} = \frac{28.675 \text{ in}(1 \text{ ft})}{12 \text{ in}} \approx 2.4 \text{ ft, choice (A)}$$

AVERAGES

There are only three parts to any average question. Fortunately for you, the ACT must give you two of these parts, which are all you need to find the third. The average pie is an easy way to keep track of the information you get from questions dealing with averages. If you have the total, you can always divide by either the average or the number of things in the set (whichever you are given) to find the missing piece of the pie. Similarly, if you have the number of things and the average, you can multiply the two together to arrive at the total (the sum of all the items in the set).

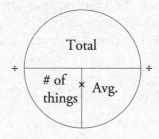

> Playing the Averages
>
> **Arithmetic mean**—just a fancy way of saying "average."
>
> **Median**—the one in the middle, like the median strip on the highway.
>
> **Mode**—you're looking for the element that appears most. Get it? MOde, MOst.

For example, if you want to find the average of 9, 12, and 6 using the average pie, you know you have 3 items with a total of 27. Dividing the total, 27, by the number of things, 3, will yield the average, 9. Your pie looks like this:

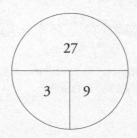

Although you probably could have done that without the average pie, more difficult average questions involve multiple calculations and lend themselves particularly well to using the pie. Let's take a look at one:

———————————◯———————————

3. Over 9 games, a baseball team had an average of 8 runs per game. If the average number of runs for the first 7 games was 6 runs per game and the same number of runs was scored in each of the last 2 games, how many runs did the team score during the last game?

   A.   5
   B.   15
   C.   26
   D.   30
   E.   46

The Missing Number
The ACT loves to leave out totals on average problems. You aren't done until you've found it.

Here's How to Crack It

Step 1: **Know the question.** *How many runs did the team score during the last game?*

Step 2: **Let the answers help.** Eliminate (A). Even though the average for the first 7 is higher than all 9, the runs scored in the last two games can't be that few. Similarly, (E) is probably too big. If you don't trust your sense of numbers and you're not comfortable Ballparking here, however, leave both. It's a complicated question on a more advanced topic.

Step 3: **Break the problem into bite-sized pieces.** Let's use bite-size pieces to put the information from the first line of this problem into our trusty average pie.

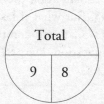

What is the sum of everything for these 9 games? 9 × 8, or 72.

Now let's put the information from the second line into the average equation.

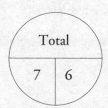

What is the sum of everything for these 7 games? 7×6, or 42.

If all 9 games added up to 72 and 7 of these games added up to 42, then the remaining 2 games added up to $72 - 42$, or 30. In case you are feeling smug about getting this far, the ACT writers made 30 the answer for (D).

But of course you know that they only want the runs they scored in the last game. Because the same number of runs was scored in each of the last two games, the answer is $\frac{30}{2}$ or 15, choice (B).

The Weighted Average

ACT writers have a particular fondness for "weighted average" problems. First, let's look at a regular unweighted average question.

> If Sally received a grade of 90 on a test last week and a grade of 100 on a test this week, what is her average for the two tests?

Piece of cake, right? The answer is 95. You added the scores and divided by 2. Now let's turn the same question into a weighted average question.

> If Sally's average for the entire year last year was 90 and her average for the entire year this year was 100, is her average for the two years combined equal to 95 ?

The answer is "not necessarily." If Sally took the same number of courses in both years, then yes, her average is 95. But what if last year she took 6 courses, while this year she took only 2 courses? Can you compare the two years equally? ACT likes to test your answer to this question. Here's an example.

---

1. The starting team of a baseball club has 9 members who have an average of 12 home runs apiece for the season. The second-string team for the baseball club has 7 members who have an average of 8 home runs apiece for the season. What is the average number of home runs for the starting team and the second-string team combined?

   A. 7.5
   B. 8
   C. 10
   D. 10.25
   E. 14.2

Here's How to Crack It

The ACT test writers want to see whether you spot this as a weighted average problem. If you thought the first-string team was exactly equivalent to the second-string team, then you merely had to take the average of the two averages, 12 and 8, to get 10. In weighted average problems, the ACT test writers always include the average of the two averages among the answer choices, and it is always wrong. 10 is choice (C). Cross off (C).

The two teams are not equivalent because there are different numbers of players on each team. To get the true average, we'll have to find the total number of home runs and divide by the total number of players. How do we do this? By going to the trusty average formula as usual. The first line of the problem says that the 9 members on the first team have an average of 12 runs apiece.

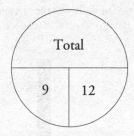

So the sum of everything is 9 × 12, or 108.

The second sentence says that the 7 members of the second team have an average of 8 runs each.

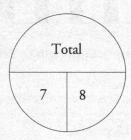

So the total is 7 × 8, or 56.

Now we can find the true average. Add all the runs scored by the first team to all the runs scored by the second team: 108 + 56 = 164. This is the true total. We divide it by the total number of players (9 + 7 = 16).

The answer is 10.25, or (D).

CHARTS AND GRAPHS

Since calculators were added to the arsenal you're allowed to bring with you when you take the ACT, more and more of the test has been composed of questions on which calculators are of little or no use, such as questions based on charts and graphs. On this type of question, your math skills aren't really being tested at all; what ACT is interested in is your ability to read a simple graph (not unlike on the Science Reasoning test, which we'll get to later in Part V). All of the questions we have seen in this format have been very direct. If you can read a simple graph, you can always get them right. What's most important on questions like these is paying attention to the labels on the information. Let's take a look at a graph.

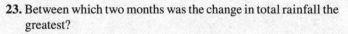

23. Between which two months was the change in total rainfall the greatest?

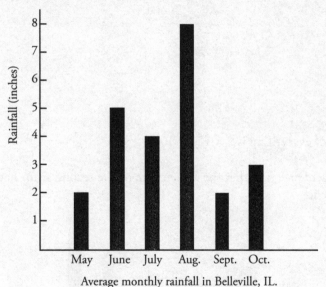

Average monthly rainfall in Belleville, IL.

   A.   May and June
   B.   June and July
   C.   July and August
   D.   August and September
   E.   September and October

Here's How to Crack It

The ACT test writers want to see if you can decipher the information presented in the graph. Before you read the question then, you need to take a look at the graph. What is measured here? It says on the bottom: *Average monthly rainfall in Belleville, IL.* You should look at the values along the left side and bottom of the graph as well. When you do, you'll see that the rain is measured in inches (left-hand side), and the measurements were made each month (bottom).

Now for the question. To determine which two months had the greatest change, we need to compare the change between each pair of months, discarding the smaller ones until we have only one left. The difference from May to June is about 3, and that's larger than June to July and September to October, so (B) and (E) are out. July to August is larger still, though, so (A) is out, leaving only (C) and (D). It should be pretty apparent that the August to September change is larger than the July to August change, though, so the correct answer must be (D).

Although most questions involving graphs on the Math test are this simple, you may see slightly more complicated variations. Here's another question based on the same bar graph.

24. Based on the information presented in the graph below, what is the approximate average monthly rainfall in Belleville, IL, for the period given?

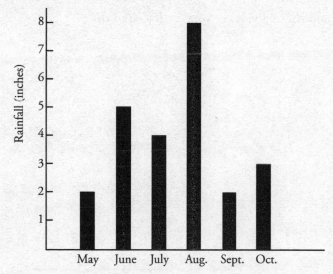

Average monthly rainfall in Belleville, IL.

    F. 2
    G. 3
    H. 4
    J. 5
    K. 8

Here's How to Crack It

As with the last question, the first thing you want to do is examine the graph and figure out what information is being given to you and how it is being presented. Because you already did that for this graph, we'll skip that step on this one.

This question combines graph reading with average calculation, so the next thing you'll have to do is estimate the rainfall for each month. Because the question uses the word *approximate*, you don't have to worry too much about making super-exact measurements of the heights of the bar graphs. Eyeballing it and rounding to the closest value given on the left-hand side will be good enough to get you the right answer. Do that now before you read the next sentence.

To us, it looks like about 2 inches fell in May and September, and around 3 fell in October. July saw about 4, June roughly 5, and August about 8. Your estimates should be the same as ours. If they're not, go back now and figure out why not. You probably need to be a little more careful in your estimating. Use another piece of paper as a guide if necessary (you can use your answer sheet in this manner when taking the real ACT).

Now it's just a matter of calculating the average. Find the total first.

$$2 + 2 + 3 + 4 + 5 + 8 = 24$$

There are 6 months, so divide the total by 6 to find the average.

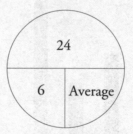

So the answer is 4, or (H).

COMBINATIONS: CAN YOU SLOT ME IN?

Combination problems ask you how many different ways a number of things could be chosen or combined. The rules for combination problems on the ACT are straightforward.

---

1. Figure out the number of slots you need to fill.
2. Fill in those slots.
3. Find the product.

Seem confusing? It's not. Let's look at an example. This is what most combination problems on the ACT will look like:

6. At the school cafeteria, students can choose from 3 different salads, 5 different main dishes, and 2 different desserts. If Isabel chooses one salad, one main dish, and one dessert for lunch, how many different lunches could she choose?

   F. 10
   G. 15
   H. 25
   J. 30
   K. 50

Here's How to Crack It

We've got three slots to fill here, one for each item: salad, main dish, dessert. And the number of possibilities for each is pretty clear. Set up the slots and take the product as your answer.

$$\underset{\text{Salad}}{\underline{\ 3\ }} \times \underset{\text{Main}}{\underline{\ 5\ }} \times \underset{\text{Dessert}}{\underline{\ 2\ }} = 30$$

The correct answer here is (J).

On a more difficult problem, you may run into a combination with more restricted elements. Just be sure to read the problem carefully before attempting it. If the question makes your head spin, leave it and return to it later, or pick your Letter of the Day and move on. For good measure, though, here's what one of those tougher ones might look like.

---

7. At the school cafeteria, 2 boys and 4 girls are forming a lunch line. If the boys must stand in the first and last places in line, how many different lines can be formed?

A. 2
B. 6
C. 48
D. 360
E. 720

Here's How to Crack It

These restrictions might make this problem seem daunting, but this is where the slot method is really helpful. We have six spots in line to fill, so draw six slots:

$$\underline{\quad}\ \ \underline{\quad}\ \ \underline{\quad}\ \ \underline{\quad}\ \ \underline{\quad}\ \ \underline{\quad}$$

It even looks like the line the boys and girls are standing in! Do the restricted spots first. The problem tells us that the two boys *must stand in the first and last places in line*. This means that either of the boys could stand in first place, and then the other boy will stand in last. This means that we have two options for the first place, but only one for the last.

$$\underline{\ 2\ }\ \ \underline{\quad}\ \ \underline{\quad}\ \ \underline{\quad}\ \ \underline{\quad}\ \ \underline{\ 1\ }$$

Now do the same with the unrestricted parts. Any of the four girls could stand in the second spot.

$$\underline{\ 2\ }\ \ \underline{\ 4\ }\ \ \underline{\quad}\ \ \underline{\quad}\ \ \underline{\quad}\ \ \underline{\ 1\ }$$

Now, since one of the girls is standing in the second spot, there are only three left to stand in the third spot, and so on, and so on.

$$\underline{\ 2\ }\ \ \underline{\ 4\ }\ \ \underline{\ 3\ }\ \ \underline{\ 2\ }\ \ \underline{\ 1\ }\ \ \underline{\ 1\ }$$

Now, as ever, just take the product, to find that the correct answer is (C), 48.

$$\underline{\ 2\ } \times \underline{\ 4\ } \times \underline{\ 3\ } \times \underline{\ 2\ } \times \underline{\ 1\ } \times \underline{\ 1\ } = 48$$

Let's try one more that tests a few things.

---

8. Elias has to select one shirt, one pair of pants, and one pair of shoes. If he selects at random from his 8 shirts, 4 pairs of pants, and 3 pairs of shoes, and all his shirts, pants, and shoes are different colors, what is the likelihood that he will select his red shirt, black pants, and brown shoes?

F. $\dfrac{1}{3}$

G. $\dfrac{1}{4}$

H. $\dfrac{1}{15}$

J. $\dfrac{1}{32}$

K. $\dfrac{1}{96}$

Here's How to Crack It

Step 1: **Know the question.** The problem is asking what the probability is that he will select this one group of clothes from all possible combinations of clothes.

Step 2: **Let the answers help.** The answers offer the important reminder that we're looking for a probability. We know that it will be only one arrangement out of a reasonably large number of them, so we should at least get rid of (F) and (G).

Step 3: **Break the problem into bite-sized pieces.** First, we should find the total number of possible combinations. Then, we can deal with the probability.

We have three slots to fill here, and we want to find the product of the three.

$$\underset{\text{Shirts}}{\underline{\quad 8 \quad}} \times \underset{\text{Pants}}{\underline{\quad 4 \quad}} \times \underset{\text{Shoes}}{\underline{\quad 3 \quad}} = 96 \text{ arrangements}$$

Of the 96 possible arrangements, an ensemble of red shirt, black pants, and brown shoes is only one. Therefore, we can go to our $\dfrac{part}{whole}$ ratio to find $\dfrac{part}{whole} = \dfrac{\text{red, black, brown}}{\text{ALL arrangements}} = \dfrac{1}{96}$, choice (K).

Word Problems Drill

For the answers to this drill, please go to Chapter 24.

1. The ratio of boys to girls at the Milwood School is 4 to 5. If there are a total of 27 children at the school, how many boys attend the Milwood School?

   A. 4
   B. 9
   C. 12
   D. 14
   E. 17

2. Linda computed the average of her six biology test scores by mistakenly adding the totals of five scores and dividing by five, giving her an average score of 88. When Linda realized her error, she recalculated and included the sixth test score of 82. What is the average of Linda's six biology tests?

   F. 82
   G. 85
   H. 86
   J. 87
   K. 88

3. In the process of milling grain, 3% of the original is lost because of spillage, and another 5% of the original is lost because of mildew. If the mill starts out with 490 tons of grain, how much (in tons) remains to be sold after milling?

   A. 425
   B. 426
   C. 420.5
   D. 440
   E. 450.8

4. A rectangular box has a base measuring a by a meters and height of b meters. Which of the following represents the surface area of the box?

   F. $6ab$
   G. a^2b
   H. $a^2 + 2ab$
   J. $2a(a + 2b)$
   K. $2(a^2 + b^2)$

5. In the word HAWKS, how many ways is it possible to rearrange the letters if none repeat and the letter W must go last?

   A. 5
   B. 15
   C. 24
   D. 120
   E. 650

Summary

o   Plugging In works on all kinds of problems, not just Algebra. Always look for opportunities to simplify the math by Plugging In!

o   Percentages and Probabilities are all based on a relationship of PART to WHOLE. Ratios are based on a relationship of PART to PART. Probabilities can be found by taking the part (the number of things that meet some given criteria) divided by the whole (all possibilities, including those that don't meet the criteria).

o   Percentages can typically be found by multiplying $\frac{part}{whole} \times 100\%$.

   • When dealing with percentages, remember to convert Math into English with the handy chart.

English	Math Equivalent
percent	/100
of	multiplication ($\times$)
what	variable (y, z)
is, are, were	=
what percent	$\dfrac{y}{100}$

   • Ratios are typically a relationship of one *part* to some other *part*.

o   On Combination problems
   1. Figure out the number of slots you need to fill.
   2. Fill in those slots.
   3. Find the product.

o   On Average problems, use the average pie.
   1. Divide the total by the number of things to find the average.
   2. Divide the total by the average to find the number of things.
   3. Multiply the number of things by the average to find the total.

Chapter 14
Graphing
and Coordinate
Geometry

We've covered most of what you'll need to get a great score on the ACT Math test. This chapter will give a brief overview of Coordinate Geometry. While it's not tested as heavily as Plane Geometry, Coordinate Geometry offers many fast plug-and-chug opportunities. Though we will be discussing the basic rules and formulas you need, we will always have an eye on how we can crack some of these problems more strategically as well.

COORDINATE GEOMETRY

As we saw in the first Math chapter, coordinate geometry will account for about 9 questions in any given exam. While ACT makes a big deal about how separate this is from plane geometry, the only major difference between the two is that you need more graph paper to do coordinate geometry. We'll cover the basics of graphing and its related functions, but don't forget, you know a lot of this stuff from the earlier geometry chapter already!

Graphing Inequalities

Here's a simple inequality:

$$3x + 5 > 11$$

As you know from reading the algebra chapter of this book, you solve an inequality the same way that you solve an equality. By subtracting 5 from both sides and then dividing both sides by 3, you get the expression

$$x > 2$$

This can be represented on a number line as shown below.

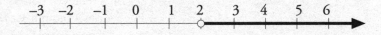

The open circle at 2 indicates that x can include every number greater than 2, but not 2 itself or anything less than 2.

If we had wanted to graph $x \geq 2$, the circle would have to be filled in, indicating that our graph includes 2 as well.

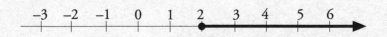

An ACT graphing problem might look like this.

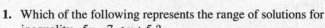

1. Which of the following represents the range of solutions for inequality $-5x - 7 < x + 5$?

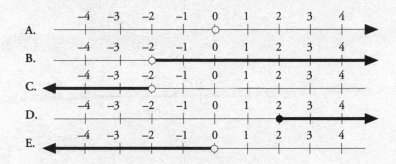

Here's How to Crack It

The ACT test writers want you first to simplify the inequality, and then figure out which of the answer choices represents a graph of the solution set of the inequality. To simplify, isolate x on one side of the inequality.

$$
\begin{array}{rl}
-5x - 7 & < x + 5 \\
-x & \phantom{<} -x \\
\hline
-6x - 7 & < 5 \\
+7 & \phantom{<} +7 \\
\hline
-6x & < 12
\end{array}
$$

Now divide both sides by -6. Remember that when you multiply or divide an inequality by a negative, the sign flips over.

$$
\frac{-6x}{-6} < \frac{12}{-6}
$$
$$
x > -2
$$

Which of the choices answers the question? If you selected (B), you're right.

Flip Flop
Remember that when you multiply or divide an inequality by a negative, the sign flips.

Graphing in Two Dimensions

More complicated graphing questions concern equations with two variables, usually designated x and y. These equations can be graphed on a Cartesian grid, which looks like this.

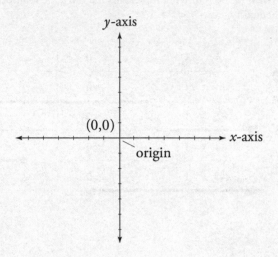

Every point (x,y) has a place on this grid. For example, the point A (3,4) can be found by counting over on the x-axis 3 places to the right of (0,0)—known as the **origin**—and then counting on the y-axis 4 places up from the origin, as shown below. Point B (5,–2) can be found by counting 5 places to the right on the x-axis and then down 2 places on the y-axis. Point C (–4,–1) can be found by counting 4 places to the left of the origin on the x-axis and then 1 place down on the y-axis.

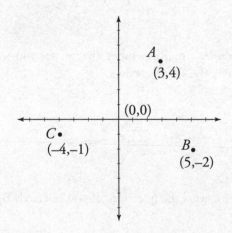

The grid is divided into four quadrants, which go counterclockwise.

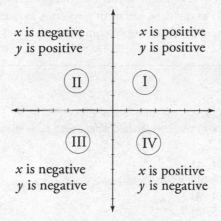

- In the first quadrant, *x* and *y* are both positive.
- In the second quadrant, *x* is negative but *y* is positive.
- In the third quadrant, *x* and *y* are both negative.
- In the fourth quadrant, *x* is positive but *y* is negative.

Note: This is when your graphing calculator (if you have one) will really get a chance to shine. Practice doing all the ACT coordinate geometry questions on your calculator now and you'll blow them away when you actually take the test.

Graphic Guesstimation

A few questions on the ACT might involve actual graphing, but it is more likely that you will be able to make use of graphing to *estimate* the answers to questions that the ACT test writers think are more complicated.

---

1. Point B (4,3) is the midpoint of line segment *AC*. If point *A* has coordinates (0,1), then what are the coordinates of point *C* ?

    A. (−4,−1)
    B. (4, 1)
    C. (4, 4)
    D. (8, 5)
    E. (8, 9)

Here's How to Crack It

You may or may not remember the midpoint formula: The ACT test writers expect you to use it to solve this problem. We'll go over it in a moment, along with the other formulas you'll need to solve coordinate geometry questions. However, it is worth noting that by drawing a rough graph of this problem, you can get the correct answer without the formula.

On your TI-83, you can plot independent points to see what the graph should look like. To do this, hit STAT and select option [1: Edit]. Enter the *x*- and *y*-coordinate points in the first two columns; use [L1] for your *x*-coordinates and [L2] for the *y*-coordinates. After you enter the endpoints of the line, hit [2nd] [Y=] to access the [STAT PLOT] menu. Select option [1: Plot1]. Change the [OFF] status to [ON] and hit GRAPH. You should now see the two points you entered. Now you can ballpark the answers based on where they are in the coordinate plane. Keep in mind that you can also plot all the points in the answers as well. Just be sure you keep track of all the *x*- and *y*-values. If you don't have a graphing calculator, use the grid we've provided on the next page.

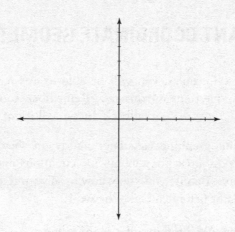

B is supposed to be the midpoint of a line segment *AC*. Draw a line through the two points you've just plotted and extend it upward until *B* is the midpoint of the line segment. It should look like this:

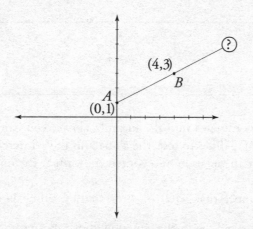

The place where you stopped drawing is the approximate location of point *C*. Now let's look at the answer choices to see if any of them are in the ballpark.

    A.   (−4,−1): These coordinates are in the wrong quadrant.
    B.   (4, 1): This point is way below where it should be.
    C.   (4, 4): This point does not extend enough to the right.
    D.   (8, 5): Definitely in the ballpark. Hold on to this answer choice.
    E.   (8, 9): Possible, although the *y*-coordinate seems a little high.

Which answer choice do you want to pick? If you said (D), you are right.

THE IMPORTANT COORDINATE GEOMETRY FORMULAS

By memorizing a few formulas, you will be able to answer virtually all of the coordinate geometry questions on this test. Remember, too, that in coordinate geometry you almost *always* have a fallback: Just graph it out.

And always keep your graphing calculator handy on these types of problems. Graphing calculators are great for solving line equations and giving you graphs you can use to ballpark. Be sure you know how to solve and graph an equation for a line on your calculator before you take the ACT.

The following formulas are listed in order of importance.

The Slope-Intercept Formula

$$y = mx + b$$

To find the x-intercept
Set *y* equal to zero, and solve for *x*.

By putting (x,y) coordinates into the formula above, you can find two pieces of information that ACT likes to test: the **slope** and the **y-intercept**. Most graphing calculators will put an equation into *y*-intercept form at the touch of a button.

The **slope** is a number that tells you how sharply a line is inclining, and it is equivalent to the variable *m* in the equation above. For example, in the equation $y = 3x + 4$, the number 3 (think of it as $\frac{3}{1}$) tells us that from any point on the line, we can find another point on the line by going up 3 and over to the right 1.

In the equation $y = -\frac{4}{5}x - 7$, the slope of $-\frac{4}{5}$ tells us that from any point on the line, we can find another point on the line by going up 4 and over 5 to the left.

The **y-intercept**, equivalent to the variable *b* in the equation above, is the point at which the line intercepts the *y*-axis. For example, in the equation $y = 3x + 4$, the line will strike the *y*-axis at a point 4 above the origin. In the equation $y = 2x - 7$, the line will strike the *y*-axis at a point 7 below the origin. A typical ACT $y = mx + b$ question might give you an equation in another form and ask you to find either the slope or the *y*-intercept. Simply put the equation into the form we've just shown you.

2. What is the slope of the line based on the equation
$5x - y = 7x + 6$?

F. −2
G. 0
H. 2
J. 6
K. −6

Here's How to Crack It

Isolate y on the left side of the equation. You can have your graphing calculator do this for you, or you can do it by hand by subtracting $5x$ from both sides.

$$
\begin{aligned}
5x - y &= 7x + 6 \\
-5x \qquad &\quad -5x \\
\hline
-y &= 2x + 6
\end{aligned}
$$

We aren't quite done. The format we want is $y = mx + b$, not $-y = mx + b$. Let's multiply both sides by −1.

$$(-1)(-y) = (2x + 6)(-1)$$
$$y = -2x - 6$$

The slope of this line is −2, so the answer is (A).

The Slope Formula

You can find the slope of a line, even if all you have are two points on that line, by using the slope formula.

The Slippery Slope
A line going from bottom left to upper right has a positive slope. A line going from top left to bottom right has a negative slope.

$$\text{slope} = \frac{\text{change in } y}{\text{change in } x} \quad \text{or} \quad \frac{y_2 - y_1}{x_2 - x_1}$$

Parallel Tracks

If two lines have the same slope, those lines are *parallel* to one another.

If two lines have opposite reciprocal slopes, those lines are *perpendicular* to one another.

So how about if the question on this page asked for the slope of a line parallel to the one given in the problem? How about perpendicular?

A *parallel* line would have a slope of $-\frac{1}{8}$.

A *perpendicular* line would have a slope of 8.

3. What is the slope of the straight line passing through the points (–2,5) and (6,4) ?

   A. $-\dfrac{1}{16}$

   B. $-\dfrac{1}{8}$

   C. $\dfrac{1}{5}$

   D. $\dfrac{2}{9}$

   E. $\dfrac{4}{9}$

Here's How to Crack It

Find the change in y and put it over the change in x. The change in y is the first y-coordinate minus the second y-coordinate. (It doesn't matter which point is first and which is second.) The change in x is the first x minus the second x.

$$\frac{y_2 - y_1}{x_2 - x_1} = \frac{5 - 4}{-2 - 6} = \frac{1}{-8}$$

The correct answer is (B).

If you take a look at the formula for finding slope, you'll see that the part on top ("change in *y*") is how much the line is rising (or falling, if the line points down and has a negative slope). That change in position on the *y*-axis is called the *rise*. The part on the bottom ("change in *x*") is how far along the *x*-axis you move and called the *run*. So the slope of a line is sometimes referred to as "rise over run."

In the question we just did, then, the rise was 1 and the run was −8, giving us the slope $-\frac{1}{8}$. Same answer, different terminology.

Midpoint Formula

If you have the two endpoints of a line segment, you can find the midpoint of the segment by using the midpoint formula.

$$(x[m], y[m]) = \left(\frac{x_1 + x_2}{2}, \frac{y_1 + y_2}{2}\right)$$

It looks much more intimidating than it really is.

To find the midpoint of a line, just take the *average* of the two *x*-coordinates and the *average* of the two *y*-coordinates. For example, the midpoint of the line segment formed by the coordinates (3,4) and (9,2) is just

$$\frac{(3+9)}{2} = 6 \text{ and } \frac{(4+2)}{2} = 3$$
$$\text{or } (6,3)$$

Remember the first midpoint problem we did? Here it is again.

1. Point *B* (4,3) is the midpoint of line segment *AC*. If point *A* has coordinates (0,1), then what are the coordinates of point *C* ?

   A. (−4,−1)
   B. (4, 1)
   C. (4, 4)
   D. (8, 5)
   E. (8, 9)

The Shortest Distance Between Two Points Is…a Calculator?

If you want to draw a line between two points on your TI-83, you can use the Line function. To access this, you'll want to press [2nd] [PRGM] to access the [DRAW] menu. From there, select option [2: Line]. The format of the line function is Line (X1, Y1, X2, Y2); for example, if you wanted to view the line that passes through the points (−2,5) and (6,4), you would enter Line (−2,5,6,4). Hit [ENTER] to see your line.

Here's How to Crack It

You'll remember that it was perfectly possible to solve this problem just by drawing a quick graph of what it ought to look like. However, to find the correct answer using the midpoint formula, we first have to realize that, in this case, we already *have* the midpoint. We are asked to find one of the endpoints.

The midpoint is (4,3). This represents the average of the two endpoints. The endpoint we know about is (0,1). Let's do the *x*-coordinate first. The average of the *x*-coordinates of the two endpoints equals the *x*-coordinate of the midpoint. So $\frac{(0+?)}{2} = 4$. What is the missing *x*-coordinate? 8. Now let's do the *y*-coordinate. $\frac{(1+?)}{2} = 3$. What is the missing *y*-coordinate? 5. The answer is (D).

If you had trouble following that last explanation, just remember that you already understood this problem (and got the answer) using graphing. Never be intimidated by formulas on the ACT. There is usually another way to do the problem.

The Distance Formula

We hate the distance formula. We keep forgetting it, and even when we remember it, we feel like fools for using it because there are much easier ways to find the distance between two points. We aren't even going to tell you what the distance formula is. If you need to know the distance between two points, you can always think of that distance as being the hypotenuse of a right triangle. Here's an example.

4. What is the distance between points *A* (2,2) and *B* (5,6) ?

  F. 3
  G. 4
  H. 5
  J. 6
  K. 7

Here's How to Crack It

Let's make a quick graph of what this ought to look like.

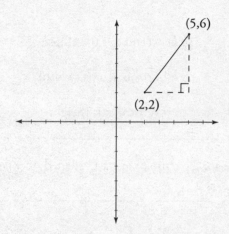

If we extend lines from the two points to form a right triangle under the line segment *AB*, we can use the Pythagorean theorem to get the distance between the two points. What is the length of the base of the triangle? It's 3. What is the length of the height of the triangle? It's 4. So what is the length of the hypotenuse? It's 5. Of course, as usual, it is one of the triples of which ACT is so fond. The answer is (H). You could also have popped the points into your calculator and had it calculate the distance for you.

Here's the distance formula if you must know (or know how to program into your calculator):
$$d = \sqrt{(x_2 - x_1)^2 + (y_2 - y_1)^2}$$
Isn't the triangle method so much easier?

Circles, Ellipses, and Parabolas, Oh My!

You should probably have a *vague* idea of what the equations for these figures look like; just remember that there are very few questions concerning these figures, and when they do come up, you can almost always figure them out by graphing.

The standard equation for a circle is shown below.

$$(x - h)^2 + (y - k)^2 = r^2$$

(h,k) = center of the circle

r = radius

The standard equation for an ellipse (just a squat-looking circle) is shown on the next page.

We include the ellipse formula because it has shown up on previous exams, but if you can't remember it, don't worry. It only shows up once in a blue moon, and you never need to reproduce it from memory.

$$\frac{(x-h)^2}{a^2} + \frac{(y-k)^2}{b^2} = 1$$

(h,k) = center of the ellipse

$2a$ = horizontal axis (width)

$2b$ = vertical axis (height)

The standard equation for a parabola (just a U-shaped line) is shown below.

$$y = x^2$$

5. If the equation $x^2 = 1 - y^2$ were graphed in the standard (x,y) coordinate plane, the graph would represent which of the following geometric figures?

    A. Square
    B. Straight line
    C. Circle
    D. Triangle
    E. Parabola

Graphing Circles on Your Calculator

To draw a circle on your TI-83, you first need to alter the Zoom settings. Press ZOOM and select option [5: ZSquare]. Next, hit 2nd PRGM to access the [DRAW] menu. Select option [9: Circle]. All you need to do is enter the coordinates of the circle's center and the value of its radius. If, for instance, you were trying to graph a circle with a center of (2,3) and a radius of 5, your screen would say the following: Circle (2,3,5). Hit ENTER to see the resulting graph. You can draw as many circles as you like. To clear the graph, you need to press 2nd [DRAW] and select option [1: ClrDraw].

Here's How to Crack It

If you're familiar with what the equations of the various elements in the answer choices are supposed to look like, you may be able to figure out the problem without graphing at all. (However, that's why you bought a graphing calculator in the first place....) Let's consider what we know about the equations of geometric figures. If an equation has only x and y, we know that the graph of the equation is a straight line. (Think back to the $y = mx + b$ problems we did earlier.) However, in this equation, both x and y are squared, so we can rule out (B). There is no equation for a square, so we can rule out (A). Similarly, there's no equation for a triangle, so (D) is out. If only one of the variables were squared, this might be a parabola, but in this problem both are squared, which means we can eliminate (E). We are left with (C).

Estimating Note

Of course, we could also just plug some numbers into the equation and plot them out on a homemade (x,y) axis in the scratchwork column of the test booklet. Let's try this on the grid below.

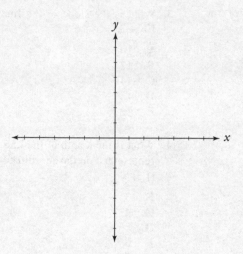

The easiest way to start is to let one of the variables equal 0. If $x = 0$, then y must equal 1. So one point of this equation is (0,1). If we let $y = 0$, then x must equal 1. So another point of this equation is (1,0). Plot out some other points of the equation. How about (–1,0) and (0,–1)? What kind of geometric figure do we appear to have? If you said a circle, you are correct.

Graphing and Coordinate Geometry Drill

For the answers to this drill, please go to Chapter 24.

1. Which of the following represents the solution of the inequality $-3x - 6 > 9$?

    A.

    B.

    C.

    D.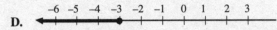

    E.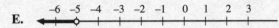

2. What is the midpoint of the line segment whose endpoints are represented on the coordinate axis by the points (3,5) and (−4,3) ?

    F. $(-2, -5)$

    G. $(-\frac{1}{2}, 4)$

    H. $(1, 8)$

    J. $(4, -\frac{1}{2})$

    K. $(3, 3)$

3. What is the slope of the line represented by the equation $10x + 2x = y + 6$?

    A. 10
    B. 12
    C. 14
    D. 15
    E. 16

4. What is the length of the line segment whose endpoints are represented on the coordinate axis by the points (−2,−1) and (1,3) ?

    F. 3
    G. 4
    H. 5
    J. 6
    K. 7

5. What is the slope of the line that contains the points (6,4) and (13,5) ?

    A. $-\frac{1}{8}$

    B. $-\frac{1}{9}$

    C. $\frac{1}{7}$

    D. 1

    E. 7

6. Which of the following gives the center point and radius of circle O, represented by the equation $(x - 3)^2 + (y + 2)^2 = 9$?

	Center	Radius
F.	(−3, 2)	3
G.	(−3, 2)	9
H.	(2, 3)	9
J.	(3, −2)	3
K.	(3, −2)	9

Summary

○ Coordinate geometry tests many of the same concepts you've seen elsewhere on the Math test.

○ If you are stuck on a coordinate geometry question, sketch a graph and draw in a few points.

○ Many coordinate geometry questions can be solved by putting them into the format $y + mx = b$, where m is the slope of the line and b is the y-intercept.

○ Review the midpoint equation.

$$\left(x[m], y[m]\right) = \frac{x_1 + x_2}{2}, \frac{y_1 + y_2}{2}$$

○ You can avoid using the confusing distance formula by drawing a right triangle and using the Pythagorean theorem.

○ Every once in a while, ACT asks a question based on the equations of circles, ellipses, and parabolas. If you need a very high score, it might help to memorize these equations, but remember, these questions can frequently be done by using graphing to estimate the correct answer.

Chapter 15
Trigonometry

We've covered most of what you'll need to get a great score on the ACT Math test. This chapter will give a brief overview of one of the more advanced topics covered on the exam: Trigonometry. Though we will be discussing the identities and rules you need, we will always have an eye on how we can crack some of these problems more strategically as well.

A NOTE ON ACT MATH "DIFFICULTY"

As we noted in the first Math chapter in this book, "difficulty" is kind of a weird thing on the ACT. Is a problem difficult because it tests an unfamiliar concept? Or is it difficult because it tests a very familiar concept in a long word problem? We've seen that Plugging In and PITA can make some of the toughest problems pretty easy, so this part of the exam is more about POOD than ever. In this chapter, we will review trigonometry. Trigonometry is one of the more advanced topics on the ACT, and ACT wants to make you think it and the other advanced topics are very difficult. Some of these questions *are* difficult, tapping some of the most advanced topics of algebra II. But as you will see with trigonometry, most if not all of these questions can be answered correctly with a smart approach. We will review the relevant concepts, but we will also keep an eye on how to use the strategies from earlier chapters.

TRIGONOMETRY

It's easy to get freaked out by the trigonometry on the ACT. But remember there are only four questions on any given exam that deal with trig. What this means is that if you haven't learned trig before, it's not worth your time to try to do it now. If you are familiar with trig, on the other hand, here are a few topics that might come up. And don't worry, in four questions, there's no way all of these topics can come up!

Finally, as ever, remember that you don't get bonus points for doing anything the "real" way on the ACT. Always be on the lookout to use some of the great new techniques you've learned in this book.

SOHCAHTOA

There are four trig questions on any given ACT Math test, and typically two of them will ask about very basic trig concepts, covered by the acronym SOHCAHTOA. If you've had trig before, you probably know this acronym like the back of your hand. If not, here's what it means:

$$\textbf{S}ine = \frac{\textbf{O}pposite}{\textbf{H}ypotenuse} \quad \textbf{C}osine = \frac{\textbf{A}djacent}{\textbf{H}ypotenuse} \quad \textbf{T}angent = \frac{\textbf{O}pposite}{\textbf{A}djacent}$$

Sine is Opposite over Hypotenuse. Cosine is Adjacent over Hypotenuse. Tangent is Opposite over Adjacent. So in the triangle below, the sine of angle θ [*theta*, a Greek letter] would be $\frac{4}{5}$. The cosine of angle θ would be $\frac{3}{5}$. The tangent of angle θ would be $\frac{4}{3}$.

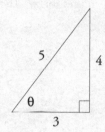

Sine, cosine, and tangent are often abbreviated as sin, cos, and tan, respectively.

The easier trig questions on this test involve the relationships between the sides of a right triangle. In the right triangle below, the angle x can be expressed in terms of the ratios of different sides of the triangle.

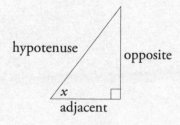

The **sine** of angle $x = \dfrac{\text{length of side opposite angle } x}{\text{length of hypotenuse}}$

The **cosine** of angle $x = \dfrac{\text{length of side adjacent angle } x}{\text{length of hypotenuse}}$

The **tangent** of angle $x = \dfrac{\text{length of side opposite angle } x}{\text{length of side adjacent angle } x}$

YOU'RE ALMOST DONE

There are three more relationships to memorize. They involve the reciprocals of the previous three.

$$\text{The cosecant} = \frac{1}{\text{sine}}$$
$$\text{The secant} = \frac{1}{\text{cosine}}$$
$$\text{The cotangent} = \frac{1}{\text{tangent}}$$

Let's try a few problems.

———————————◯———————————

31. What is $\sin \theta$, if $\tan \theta = \dfrac{4}{3}$?

    A. $\dfrac{3}{4}$

    B. $\dfrac{4}{5}$

    C. $\dfrac{5}{4}$

    D. $\dfrac{5}{3}$

    E. $\dfrac{7}{3}$

> **Helpful Trig Identities**
>
> $$\sin^2 \theta + \cos^2 \theta = 1$$
>
> $$\frac{\sin \theta}{\cos \theta} = \tan \theta$$

Here's How to Crack It

It helps to sketch out the right triangle and fill in the information we know.

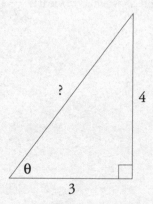

What kind of right triangle is this? That's right—a 3-4-5. Now, we need to know the sine of angle θ: opposite over hypotenuse, or $\dfrac{4}{5}$, which is (B).

———————————◯———————————

43. For all θ, $\dfrac{\cos \theta}{\sin^2 \theta + \cos^2 \theta} = ?$

    A. $\sin \theta$
    B. $\csc \theta$
    C. $\cot \theta$
    D. $\cos \theta$
    E. $\tan \theta$

Here's How to Crack It

Because $\sin^2 \theta + \cos^2 \theta$ always equals 1, $\dfrac{\cos \theta}{1} = \cos \theta$. The answer is (D).

50. In a right triangle shown below, sec θ is $\dfrac{25}{7}$. What is $\sin \theta$?

    F. $\dfrac{3}{25}$

    G. $\dfrac{5}{25}$

    H. $\dfrac{7}{25}$

    J. $\dfrac{24}{25}$

    K. $\dfrac{25}{7}$

Here's How to Crack It

The secant of any angle is the reciprocal of the cosine, which is just another way of saying that the cosine of angle θ is $\frac{7}{25}$.

Secant $\theta = \frac{1}{\cos\theta}$ so $\frac{1}{\cos\theta} = \frac{25}{7}$, which means that $\cos\theta = \frac{7}{25}$. Are you done? No! Cross off (H) because you know it's not the answer.

You need to find cosine, which is adjacent over hypotenuse. Let's sketch it.

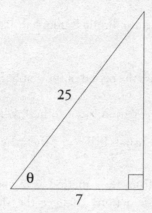

As you can see, we now have two sides of a right triangle. Can we find the third side? If you said this was one of the triples we told you about before, you are absolutely correct, although you also could have derived this by using the Pythagorean theorem. The third side must be 24. The question asks for sin θ; sine = opposite over hypotenuse, or $\frac{24}{25}$, which is (J).

ADVANCED TRIGONOMETRY

When graphing a trig function, such as sine, there are two important **coefficients**, A and B: A{*sin* (Bθ)}.

The two coefficients A and B govern the **amplitude** of the graph (how tall it is) and the **period** of the graph (how long it takes to get through a complete cycle), respectively. If there are no coefficients, then that means A = 1 and B = 1 and the graph is the same as what you'd get when you graph it on your calculator.

- Increases in A increase the amplitude of the graph. It's a direct relationship.

That means if A = 2, then the amplitude is doubled. If A = $\frac{1}{2}$, then the amplitude is cut in half.

- Increases in B decrease the period of the graph. It's an inverse relationship.

That means if B = 2, then the period is cut in half, which is to say the graph completes a full cycle faster than usual. If B = $\frac{1}{2}$, then the period is doubled.

You can add to or subtract from the function as a whole and also to or from the variable, but neither of those actions changes the shape of the graph, only its position and starting place.

Here's the graph of sin *x*. What are the amplitude and period?

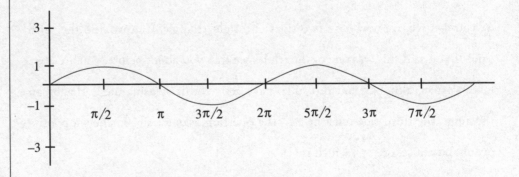

The simple function sin θ goes from –1 to 1 on the *y*-axis, so the amplitude is 1, while its period is 2π, which means that every 2π on the graph (as you go from side to side) it completes a full cycle. That's what you see in the graph above.

The graph below is also a sine function, but it's been changed. What is the function graphed here?

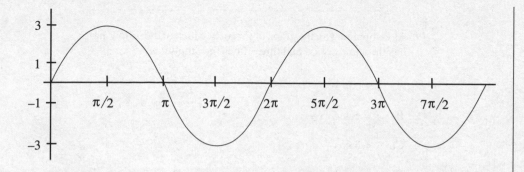

You have three things to check when looking at this graph: Is it sin or cos, is the period changed, and is the amplitude changed?

- This is a sin graph because it has a value of 0 at 0; cos has a value of 1 at 0.
- It makes a complete cycle in 2π, so the period isn't changed. In other words, B = 1.
- The amplitude is triple what it normally is, so A = 3. The function graphed, therefore, is 3 sin θ.

How about here?

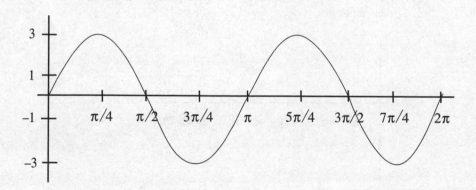

Once again, there are three things to check.

- This is a sin graph because it has a value of 0 at 0; cos has a value of 1 at 0.
- It makes a complete cycle in π, so the period has changed—it's half of what it usually is. B has an inverse effect, which means B = 2.
- The amplitude is triple what it normally is, so A = 3. The function graphed, therefore, is 3 sin 2θ.

Let's try some practice questions.

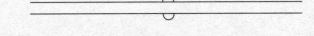

49. As compared with the graph of $y = \cos x$, which of the following has the same period and three times the amplitude?

   A. $y = \cos 3x$

   B. $y = \cos \dfrac{1}{2}(x + 3)$

   C. $y = 3 \cos \dfrac{1}{2}x$

   D. $y = 1 + 3 \cos x$

   E. $y = 3 + \cos x$

Here's How to Crack It

Recall that the coefficient on the outside of the function changes the amplitude, and the one on the inside changes the period. Because the question states that the period isn't changed, you can eliminate (A), (B), and (C). The amplitude is three times greater, you're told; because there's a direct relationship between (A) and amplitude, you want to have a 3 multiplying the outside of the function. That leaves only (D) as a possibility.

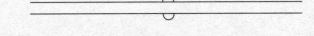

52. Which of the following equations describes the equation graphed below?

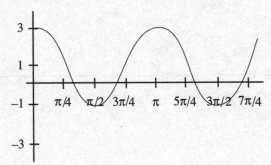

   F. $2 \cos x$
   G. $1 + 2 \cos x$
   H. $\cos 2x$
   J. $1 + \cos 2x$
   K. $1 + 2 \cos 2x$

Here's How to Crack It

At first it looks like this graph has an amplitude of 3, but if you look closer, you'll see that though the top value is 3, the bottom value is –1, which means that the whole graph has been shifted up. Because (F) and (H) don't add anything to the function (which is how you move a graph up and down), they're out. The period of this graph is half of what it usually is, so B = 2, which eliminates (G). Because the amplitude is changed also, you can eliminate (J). The answer is (K).

Trigonometry Drill

For the answers to this drill, please go to Chapter 24.

1. In $\triangle ABC$ below, the tan θ equals

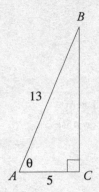

A. $\dfrac{5}{12}$

B. $\dfrac{12}{13}$

C. $\dfrac{17}{12}$

D. $\dfrac{12}{5}$

E. 3

2. If the cotangent of an angle θ is 1, then the tangent of angle θ is

F. −1
G. 0
H. 1
J. 2
K. 3

3. If $x + \sin^2\theta + \cos^2\theta = 4$, then $x = ?$

A. 1
B. 2
C. 3
D. 4
E. 5

Summary

o If you haven't had trigonometry in school, use your Letter of the Day on these trig problems. There are only 4!

o Remember SOHCAHTOA!

$$\text{sine} = \frac{\text{opposite}}{\text{hypotenuse}} \; ; \text{cosine} = \frac{\text{adjacent}}{\text{hypotenuse}} \; ;$$

$$\text{tangent} = \frac{\text{opposite}}{\text{adjacent}}$$

o For inverse functions, remember

$$\csc \theta = \frac{1}{\text{sine}} \qquad \sec \theta = \frac{1}{\text{cosine}}$$

$$\tan \theta = \frac{1}{\text{tangent}}$$

o Remember the special trig identities.

$$\sin^2 \theta + \cos^2 \theta = 1$$

$$\frac{\sin \theta}{\cos \theta} = \tan \theta$$

o For more advanced trig problems, remember A{*sin* (Bθ)}, where A represents the amplitude and B represents the period of the function. These are usually the easiest to see on the graph.

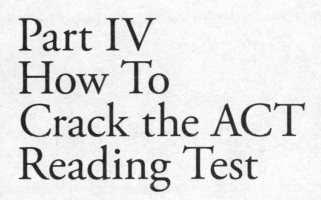

Part IV
How To
Crack the ACT
Reading Test

Chapter 16
Introduction to the ACT Reading Test

The ACT Reading test always comes third, after the Math test and before the Science test. Reading is a unique challenge on a timed standardized test: There are no rules and formulas to review, and the reading skills you've developed throughout your school career do not necessarily work as well on the ACT.

To maximize your score on the ACT Reading test, you need to develop reading skills specific to this test and learn how to use your time effectively.

We'll teach you how to work the passages in a personal order of difficulty that makes best use of the time allotted. We'll also teach you how to employ a strategic and efficient approach that will earn you your highest possible score.

WHAT'S ON THE READING TEST

On the Reading test, you have 35 minutes to work though 4 passages and a total of 40 questions. One of the passages will typically be split in two, with passages by different authors or from different works. The category, or genre, of the passages always appears in the same order: Prose Fiction (sometimes called Literary Narrative), Social Science, Humanities, and Natural Science. The passages are roughly the same length, 800–850 words, and each is followed by 10 questions.

Passage Content

Within the 4 categories, ACT selects excerpts from books and articles to create one long passage or two shorter passages. For each test, they choose 4 new passages, but the topics are always chosen from the same content areas.

Prose Fiction (aka, Literary Narrative)

The passages can be excerpts from novels or short stories, or even short stories in their entirety. While there are occasional uses of historical fiction, most passages are contemporary, emphasize diversity, and often center on family relationships.

Social Science

Topics are drawn from the fields of anthropology, archaeology, biography, business, economics, education, geography, history, political science, psychology, and sociology.

Humanities

These passages are nonfiction, but they are usually memoirs or personal essays that can read much like fiction. Topics include architecture, art, dance, ethics, film, language, literary criticism, music, philosophy, radio, television, and theater.

Natural Science

Content areas include anatomy, astronomy, biology, botany, chemistry, ecology, geology, medicine, meteorology, microbiology, natural history, physiology, physics, technology, and zoology.

The passages feature authors and topics that the ACT writers judge typical of the type of reading required in first-year college courses. And your goal, according to ACT, is to read the passages and answer questions that prove you understood both what was "directly stated" as well as what were the "implied meanings."

That's a pretty simple summary of the Reading test, but what is simple on paper can be more challenging in practice. In other words, the description from ACT doesn't really match the experience of trying to read 3,400 words and prove "your understanding" 40 times with a nub of a No. 2 pencil in your sweaty grip as you face a glaring proctor and a ticking clock.

Your reading comprehension skills and the challenge of the ACT format are intertwined. In Chapter 17, we'll teach you a Basic Approach that draws upon your skills to crack the Reading test. But first, let's pull both apart for further examination.

Reading Skills

For school, most of your reading is done with no time limits, at least theoretically. You have assignments of chapters, essays, and articles that you read, reread, highlight, and notate out of class. You may even make flash cards. In class, group discussions and even lectures from the teacher help you grasp the significance, meaning, and context of what you have read. You may need to "show your understanding" in a quiz, test, in-class essay, or paper, but you have had time to work with the text to develop a thorough understanding.

Outside of school, serious readers take time to process what they've read and form an opinion. As a college student, you'll be asked not only to read but also to think about what you've read and offer an opinion. Any professor will tell you that understanding takes thought, and thought usually takes time, more than 35 minutes.

When you take the ACT, you don't have the luxury of time. You can't read thoroughly, much less reread, highlight, notate, or make flashcards. There's certainly no group discussion to help elicit the meaning of each passage. So the first step in raising your score is to *stop treating the Reading test as a school assignment.* You need to read differently on the ACT, but you also need to know that a thorough, thoughtful grasp of the meaning isn't needed to answer the questions correctly.

In this section, we'll teach you how to read the passages and apply the Basic Approach to answer the questions correctly. But the next step in raising your scores is to apply your own personal order of difficulty to the order of the passages.

HOW TO CRACK THE READING TEST

Order the Passages

You shouldn't work the passages in the order ACT offers *just because they're in that order.* Always choose your own order, working first the passages that are easiest for you and leaving for last the most difficult. What if natural science is the easiest for you? If you did the four passages in the order ACT offers, you could easily run out of time before even getting to the natural science, or find yourself with so little time that you manage to answer correctly only half the number of questions you would have otherwise sailed through.

Now, Later, Never

When time is your enemy, as it is on the ACT, find and work Now the passages that are easiest for you. Leave for Later, or perhaps even Never, the passages that are the most difficult for you.

Every time you take an ACT, for practice and for real, pick your own order. In practice, you will likely build up a track record to determine your Personal Order of Difficulty (POOD). However, each ACT features all new passages, and certain characteristics may vary enough to affect the difficulty of a passage. Pay attention to the particulars of each test, and be willing to adapt your order for that day's test.

Under the Pacing section of this chapter, we'll help you decide if you should mark any passages as Never.

- **Your POOD**: categories and topics you like best
- **Paragraphs**: smaller and many are better than big and few
- **Questions**: the more line references, the better
- **Answers**: short are better than long

Let's discuss what each of these mean.

Your Personal Order of Difficulty (POOD)

The best way to determine which categories you work the best is through repeated practice tests followed by self-analysis. Regardless of where it is in your order, do you consistently do the best on social science? Do you usually prefer the prose fiction and humanities over the social science and natural science?

Before you've developed your POOD, identify your own likes and dislikes. For example, do you rarely read fiction outside of school? If so, then the prose fiction is unlikely to be a smart choice to do first. On the following pages, we've supplied brief excerpts of each category to give you an idea of what each is like.

Prose Fiction/Literary Narrative
On the fiction passages, facts typically matter less than do the setting, the atmosphere, and the relationships between characters. The plot and dialogue may even be secondary to the characters' thoughts and emotions, not all of which will be directly stated.

> Allen's grandmother was readying herself to leave. She was, in fact, putting the final touches on her makeup which, as always, looked to Allen as though someone had thrown it on her face with a shovel. As Mrs. Mandale placed her newly purchased bracelet
> 5 over her wrist, a look of troubled ambivalence came over her. "Perhaps this bracelet isn't right for me," she said. "I won't wear it."
>
> Waiting now for 30 minutes, Allen tried to be tolerant. "It is right for you," he said. "It matches your personality. Wear it." The bracelet was a remarkable illustration of poor taste. Its col-
> 10 ors were vulgar, and the structure lacked any sign of thoughtful design. The truth is, it did match his grandmother's personality. All that she did and enjoyed was tasteless and induced in Allen a quiet hopelessness.

The questions are more likely to involve identifying the implied meanings than what was directly stated.

1. Allen most likely encouraged his grandmother to wear her bracelet because he:

   A. found it colorful and approved of its appearance.
   B. found its appearance pathetic and wished his grandmother to look pretty.
   C. was impatient with his grandmother for spending time worrying about the bracelet.
   D. felt the bracelet matched his grandmother's bright personality.

If you like to read fiction for school assignments or for pleasure, you may find the prose fiction one of the easier passages. If you don't like to read fiction, you may find them unclear and confusing. Do the prose fiction later, or perhaps Never.

For the record, the answer is (C). Allen has been waiting and is trying "to be tolerant."

Social Science   Social science passages should remind you of the papers you write for school. The organization will flow logically with clear topic sentences and well-chosen transitions to develop the main idea. The author may have a point of view on the subject or may simply deliver informative facts in a neutral tone.

Religion is so fundamental a part of human existence that one might easily forget to ask how it started. Yet it had to start somewhere, and there had to be a time when human beings or their apelike ancestors did not entertain notions of the super-
5   natural. Hence the historian should want to probe the origins of religious belief.

It is doubtful that morality played a part in the beginnings of religious belief. Rather, religion is traceable to a far more fundamental human and animal characteristic. Storms, floods,
10   famine, and other adversities inspired *fear* in the hearts of primitive peoples as well they should have. Curiously, humankind early took the position that it might somehow subject such catastrophes to its control. Specifically, it believed it might control them by obedience and submission and by conforming its behavior to
15   their mandates. Worship, ritual, sacrifice of life, and property became means through which early peoples sought to cajole the powers and avoid the blights and miseries the peoples dreaded. As Petronius, in Lucretius's tradition remarked, "It was fear that first made the gods."

11.   According to the passage, natural disasters contributed to the development of religion by:

    A.   motivating human beings to acquire some command over their environment.
    B.   making human beings distinguish themselves from animals.
    C.   causing human beings to sacrifice their lives and goods.
    D.   providing a need for ritual and tradition.

12.   The author believes that the origins of religion:

    F.   are extremely easy to ascertain and understand.
    G.   should not be questioned by historians because religion is fundamental to civilized life.
    H.   are directly tied to apelike subhuman species.
    J.   should be the subject of serious historical inquiry.

The correct answer to 11 is (A), and the answer to 12 is (J).

Subscores
On your score report, ACT groups your performance on prose fiction and humanities under an Arts/Literature subscore and your performance on social science and natural science under a Social Studies/Science subscore. The subscores don't connect mathematically to the Reading score or the composite, but the groupings may help you think about your own order.

Humanities   Humanities passages are nonfiction, but because they are memoirs or personal essays, they can feel similar to the fiction passages. The narrative may use a more organic development instead of a linear one, and the tone will be more personal and perhaps more emotional than the more objective tones found in social and natural science.

> I grew up thinking I hated tomatoes. I used to describe the
> raw fruit as tasting like curdled water and preferred tomato sauce
> from a can. But it was not by accident that the tomato rapidly
> insinuated itself into the world's cuisines after 1492: it grows like
> 5 a weed, and wherever this weed took root, locals fell in love with
> it. To grow a bad tomato takes careful planning. Unfortunately,
> careful planning is exactly what the North American food industry
> has provided. It has carefully crafted tomatoes that can be hauled
> long distances and still look great, and the only casualty is taste.
> 10 And it has done so for so long now that most of us have forgot-
> ten, or never learned, what tomatoes are supposed to taste like.

> **24.** In the passage, the phrase "careful planning" (line 7) refers to the method of tomato cultivation that has:
>
> **F.** allowed the plant to grow like a weed.
> **G.** valued appearance and durability over taste.
> **H.** failed to make the fruit taste less like curdled water.
> **J.** made the narrator change his opinion of tomatoes.

The answer to 24 is (G).

Natural Science   Natural science passages feature a lot of details and sometimes very technical descriptions. Similar to the social science passage, the natural science passage features a linear organization with clear topic sentences and transitions to develop the main idea. The author may or may not have an opinion on the topic.

> It is further noteworthy that the terrestrial vertebrate's most
> significant muscles of movement are no longer located lateral
> to the vertebral column as they are in the fish but rather in ven-
> tral and dorsal relation to it. This trend in terrestrial evolution
> 5 is highly significant and means that the terrestrial vertebrate's
> principal movements are fore and back, not side to side. The
> trend is well documented in the whale, an aquatic animal whose
> ancestors are terrestrial quadrupeds. The whale, in other words,
> has "returned" to the sea secondarily after an ancestral stage on
> 10 the land. Unlike the fish, and in accordance with its ancestry, it
> propels itself by moving the tail up and down, not side to side.
> In a sense, the whale moves itself by bending up and down at
> the waist. Indeed, that very analogy is recalled by the mythical
> mermaid figure who seems to represent a humanlike line returned
> 15 to the water secondarily like the whale.

The questions usually track the text pretty closely and require you to make few inferences.

31. Which of the following best represents a general trend associated with mammalian evolution?

    A. Enhancement of bodily movement from right to left and left to right

    B. Minimization of muscle groups oriented lateral to the vertebral column

    C. The development of propulsive fins from paired limbs

    D. Secondary return to the sea

The answer to 31 is (B).

Order the Passages, Redux

As you take practice Reading tests, develop a consistent order that works for you, but always be willing to mix it up when you start each test, practice or real. The passages all run roughly the same number of words (800–850), and each features 10 questions followed by 4 answer choices. But the chosen topics, revealed in the blurb, and the way the passages, questions, and answers look can provide valuable clues that should make you reconsider that day's order.

Paragraphs

Which passage would you rather work, one with 8–10 medium-sized paragraphs or one with three huge paragraphs? The overall length is the same, but the size and number of the paragraphs influences how easily you can navigate the passage and retrieve answers as you work the questions.

Some fiction passages can feature too many paragraphs, with each paragraph an individual line of dialogue. Too many paragraphs can make it just as difficult to locate the right part of the passage to find answers.

Ideally, a passage should feature 8–10 paragraphs, with each paragraph made up of 5–15 lines.

Questions

The questions on the Reading test don't follow a chronological order of the passage, and not every question comes with a line reference. Line references (and paragraph references) are maps, pointing to the precise part of the passage to find the answer. You waste no time getting lost, hunting through the passage to find where to read. Therefore, a passage with only 1–2 line or paragraph reference questions will be more challenging than one that features 4, 5, 6, or more (8 is the most we've ever seen).

Need More Practice?
The Princeton Review's *English and Reading Workout for the ACT* has four more full-length Reading tests.

Answers

Compare the two "questions" and their answer choices below.

13. Blah blah blah blah:

    A. are caused primarily by humanity's overriding concern with acceptance and peace.
    B. are due in part to a faulty understanding of history.
    C. should make historians question the role of the individual in human affairs.
    D. should provoke historical inquiry into humanity's willingness to tolerate adversity.

14. Blah blah blah blah:

    F. more traditional.
    G. more formal.
    H. less rigid.
    J. less informative.

Which do you think is the easier question? Question 14, of course! Long answers usually answer harder questions, and short answers usually answer easier questions. A passage with lots of questions with short answers is a good sign.

Use Your Eye, Not Your Brain

Look at the passages to evaluate the paragraphs, line references, and answer choices. Don't thoughtfully ponder and consider each element, and don't read through the questions. Quickly check the blurb to see if you recognize the subject or author.

Use your eye to scan the paragraphs, look for numbers amidst the questions, and the length of answer choices. If you see lots of warning signs on what is typically your first passage, leave it for Later. If you see great paragraphs, line references, and lots of short answers on the passage you typically do third, consider bumping it up to second, maybe first. This should take no more than 1–2 seconds.

The Blurb
The blurb at the top of the passage will provide the title, author, copyright date, and publisher. The title may not make the subject clear, but it's always worth checking to see if it will or if you recognize the author.

Exercise: Pick Your Order

Put these passages in your own order: 1st, 2nd, 3rd, and 4th. We listed the number of paragraphs and questions with line references and short answers for the purpose of the exercise. This is not a hint that you need to be overly precise on a real test. You're looking for warning signs, a quick visual task.

Exercise I

Prose Fiction: _____

Unknown author and title, a ton of dialogue, over 20 paragraphs, many of them only one line, 2 line/paragraph references, and lots of long answers.

Social Science: _____

The title sounds technical, 6 paragraphs, 3 line/paragraph references, and 4 questions with short answers.

Humanities: _____

The title sounds deep, 9 paragraphs, 6 line/paragraph references, 1 question with short answers, and a dual passage.

Natural Science: _____

The title sounds kind of cool, 9 paragraphs, 4 line/paragraph references, and 4 questions with short answers.

Exercise II

Prose Fiction: _____

Familiar author, 7 paragraphs, 8 line/paragraph references, and 4 questions with short answers.

Social Science: _____

The title sounds sort of interesting, 6 paragraphs, 2 line/paragraph references, 2 questions with short answers, and a dual passage.

Humanities: _____

The title sounds sort of interesting, 11 paragraphs, 5 line/paragraph references, and 4 questions with short answers.

Natural Science: _____

The title sounds kind of dull, 9 paragraphs, 4 line/paragraph references, and 6 questions with short answers.

Order the Questions

In Chapter 17, we'll teach you the Basic Approach of how to attack the passage and the questions, and in that lesson we'll go into more depth about how you order the questions.

The only order you need to know now is the one to avoid: ACT's. The questions aren't in chronological order, nor are they in any order of difficulty from easiest to hardest. You shouldn't work the questions in the order given *just because ACT numbered them in order.*

Now Questions

Work the questions in an order that makes sense for you.

> Do Now questions that are easy to answer or easy to *find* the answer.

Easy to Answer   A question that is easy to answer often simply asks what the passage says, or as ACT puts it, what is directly stated. ACT in fact calls these "Referring questions," requiring the use of your "referral skills" (ACT's words, not ours) to find the right part of the passage. Referring questions don't require much reasoning; the answer will be waiting in black and white, and the correct answer will be barely paraphrased, if at all. Most answers are also relatively short: That's why you look for plenty of questions with short answers in picking your order of passages.

Easy to *Find* the Answer   A question with a line or a paragraph reference comes with a map, showing you where in the passage to find the answer. Some of these questions may be tough to answer, but as long as they come with line or paragraph references, they direct you where to read. Questions that come with a great lead word can also make finding the answer easy. Lead words are the nouns, phrases, and sometimes verbs that are specific to the passage. They're not the boilerplate language like "main idea" or "the passage characterizes."

Look at the following questions. All the lead words have been underlined.

11. Jeremy Bentham probably would have said that lawyers:

12. The author states that common law differs from civil law in that:

13. According to the passage, the integrative movement produced:

31. The main purpose of the passage is to:

35. Which of the following statements most accurately summarizes how the passage characterizes edema and hypoproteinemia?

> Lead words are words and phrases that can be found in the passage.
>
> Great lead words are proper nouns, unusual words, and dates.

Your eye can spot great lead words in the passage just by looking and without reading. They leap off the page. In Chapter 17, we'll teach you how to use lead words as part of the Basic Approach.

Later Questions

Later questions are both difficult to answer and difficult to find the answer, like Question 31 in the last set of examples. Most questions that are difficult to answer require reasoning skills to "show your understanding of statements with implied meaning."

Reasoning Questions   Reasoning questions require more thought than do Referring questions, so they do not qualify as "easy to answer." However, they are Later only if they don't come with a line or paragraph reference, which makes the answer easy to find.

In the description of the Reading test, ACT lists the various tasks that reasoning skills must be applied to.

- Determine main ideas
- Locate and interpret significant details
- Understand sequences of events
- Make comparisons
- Comprehend cause-effect relationships
- Determine the meaning of context-dependent words, phrases, and statements
- Draw generalizations
- Analyze the author's or narrator's voice and method

Any insight into the test writers' purpose and intent always benefits your preparation. However, you don't need to name the specific task when you come across it in a question. During the actual exam, identify questions as Now or Later, and don't forget that questions with a line or paragraph references are Now, regardless of the task assigned in the question.

Pace Yourself

It would be logical to assume that you must pace yourself to spend 8 minutes and 45 seconds on each passage. But to earn your best possible Reading score, you have to invest your time where it will do the most good and where its absence would create the most damage. To raise your score, you have to identify a pacing strategy that works for you.

> Focus on the number of questions that you need to answer correctly in order to earn your goal score.

Let's say you used 35 minutes to do all 4 passages, but because you had to hurry, you missed 2–3 questions per passage for a total of 10 wrong answers and therefore a raw score of 30. According to the score grid on page 24, 30 raw points would give you a scaled score of 25.

Letter of the Day (LOTD)
Just because you don't work on a passage doesn't mean you don't bubble in answers. Never leave any bubbles blank on the ACT. Bubble in your Letter of the Day for all the questions on your Never passages.

Let's say instead you used 35 minutes to do just 3 passages. With the extra time spent on your 3 best passages, you missed only 2 questions. And for that Never passage, you used your LOTD, choosing your favorite combination of answer choices to bubble in a nice straight line on the answer sheet. You picked up 2 correct answers, making your raw score 30, and your scaled score 25.

Which pacing strategy is better? Neither and both. Pacing strategies for Reading are just as personal as picking the order of the passages. You have to practice and find a pace that works for you. Some students are better off doing fewer passages, using the extra time per passage to answer most if not all questions correctly. Others find that even with all the time in the world, they'd never get all the questions right on one passage. They find the points they need across more passages, finding all the Now questions and guessing on the Never questions. Which type are you? That's what timed practice tests will help you discover.

One Sample Pacing Strategy
This is only one way to use the 35 minutes. This is a strategy for anyone working all 4 passages.

- First Passage: *11 minutes*
- Second Passage: *10 minutes*
- Third Passage: *8 minutes*
- Fourth Passage: *6 minutes*

Goal Score

Use the score grid on page 24 to find your goal score and determine how many raw points you need. This is the number of questions you need to answer correctly, whether by working them or lucky LOTD. A correct answer is a correct answer, no matter how you earn it.

Just as there is no one pacing strategy for all students, there is no one pace for all passages. In practice, try varying the amount of time you spend on each passage. Some students do best by dividing the 35 minutes equally over all the passages they do. Other students do best by spending more time on the first one or two passages and less on the remaining passages. Experiment in practice until you find a pacing strategy that works for you.

Be Flexible

Flexibility is key to your ACT success, particularly on the Reading test. Picking the order of the passages rests on your willingness to flip your order when you see that day's test. The passages, after all, are new on each test you see, and you have to look at what you've been given and adapt.

Similarly, you have to be flexible in your pacing. Focus on the number of raw points you need, and don't drown in one particular passage or get stuck on one tough question. Get out of a passage on which you've already spent too much time. Force yourself to guess on the question you've been rereading for minutes, use LOTD on any questions still left, and move on.

We're not saying this is easy. In fact, changing your own instinctual behavior is the hardest part of cracking the Reading test. Everyone has made the mistake of ignoring that voice that's screaming inside your head to move on, and we've all answered back, "But I know I'm almost there and if I take just a little more time, I know l can get it."

You may in fact get that question. But that one right answer likely cost you 2–3 others. And even worse, you had probably already narrowed it down to two answer choices. You were down to a fifty-fifty chance of getting it right, and instead you wasted more time to prove the one right answer.

In these chapters, we'll show you how to use that time more effectively to begin with and what to do when you're down to two. But both skills depend on the Process of Elimination, POE.

POE

POE is a powerful tool on a multiple-choice, standardized test. On the Reading test, you may find several Now questions easy to answer and be able to spot the right answer right away among the four choices. There will be plenty of tough Reasoning questions, however, whose answers aren't obvious, either in your own words or among the four choices. You can easily fall into the trap of rereading and rereading to figure out the answer. Wrong answers, however, can be more obvious to identify. After all, they are there to hide the right answer. In fact, if you can cross off all the wrong ones, the right answer will be waiting there for you. Even if you cross off only one or two, the right answer frequently becomes more obvious.

We'll spend more time with POE in the following chapters. For now, just remember that we started this lesson with a reminder that the first step in raising your ACT Reading score is to stop treating this test as if it's a reading assignment for school. You don't get extra points for knowing the answer before you look at the answer choices. You get a point for a correct answer, and you need to get to as many questions as possible in order to answer them. Use POE to escape the death spiral questions that will hold you back.

Process of Elimination
Each time you eliminate a wrong answer, you increase your chance of choosing the correct answer.

Summary

o   There are always 4 passages and 40 questions on the Reading test. One of these will be a 'Dual Passage,' that includes two shorter passages by different authors or from different works.

o   The passages are always in the same order: Prose Fiction/Literary Narrative, Social Science, Humanities, Natural Science.

o   Each passage has 10 questions.

o   The passages, including the Dual Passages, are all roughly the same length, between 800–850 words.

o   Follow your POOD to pick your own order of the passages.

o   Look for passages to do Now: categories and topics you like best or find easier.

o   Look for passages with 8–10 paragraphs of 5–15 lines.

o   Look for passages with lots of line references.

o   Look for passages with lots of questions with short answers.

o   Pace yourself. Find the number of questions you need to answer correctly in order to reach your goal score.

o   Be Flexible. Be ready to adapt your order, leave a tough passage, or guess on a tough question.

o   Use Process of Elimination to cross off wrong answers and save time.

Chapter 17
The 4-Step Basic Approach

To earn your highest possible score on the Reading test, you need an efficient and strategic approach to working the passages. In this chapter, we'll teach you how to work the passages, questions, and answers.

HOW TO CRACK THE READING TEST

The most efficient way to boost your Reading score is to pick your order of the passages and apply our 4-Step Basic Approach to the passages. Use the Basic Approach to enhance your reading skills and train them for specific use on the ACT.

> ### The 4-Step Basic Approach
>
> Step 1: **Preview.** Check the blurb and map the questions.
> Step 2: **Work the Passage.** Spend 2–3 minutes reading the passage.
> Step 3: **Work the Questions.** Use your POOD to find Now, Later, and Never Questions.
> Step 4: **Work the Answers.** Use POE.

Before we train you on each step in cracking the test the right way, let's talk about the temptations to attack the passages in the wrong way.

This Isn't School

In the Introduction, we discussed the reading skills you've spent your whole school career developing. You have been rewarded for your ability to develop a thorough, thoughtful grasp of the meaning and significance of the text. But in school, you have the benefit of time, not to mention the aid of your teachers' lectures, class discussions, and various tools to help you not only understand but also remember what you've read. You have none of those tools on the Reading test, but you walk into it with the instinct to approach the Reading test as if you do.

Where does that leave you on the ACT Reading test? You spend several minutes reading the passage, trying to understand the details and follow the author's main point. You furiously underline what you think may be important points that will be tested later in the questions. And when you hit a particularly confusing chunk of detailed text, what do you do? You read it again. And again. You worry you can't move on until you have solved this one detail. All the while, time is slipping by....

Now, onto the questions. Your first mistake is to do them in order. But as we told you in the Introduction, they are not in order of difficulty, nor chronologically. You confront main-idea questions before specific questions. You try to answer the questions all from memory. After all, you've spent so much time reading the passage, you don't have the time to go back to find or even confirm an answer. And when you do occasionally go back to read a specific part of the passage, you still don't see the answer. So you read the chunk of the passage again and again.

If you approach the Reading test this way, you will likely not earn the points you need to hit your goal score.

The Passage

You don't earn points from reading the passage. You earn points from answering the questions correctly. And you have no idea what the questions will ask. You're searching desperately through the passage, looking for conclusions and main points. You stumble on the details, rereading several times to master them. But how do you even know what details are important if you haven't seen the questions?

The Questions

When you answer the questions from memory, you will either face answer choices that all seem right, or you will fall right into ACT's trap, choosing an answer choice that sounds right with some familiar words, but which in reality doesn't match what the passage said.

The test writers at ACT know everyone is inclined to attack the Reading test this way. They write deceptive answer choices that will tempt you because that's what wrong answers have to do. If the right answer were surrounded by three ridiculous, obviously wrong answers, everyone would get a 36. Wrong answers have to sound temptingly right, and the easiest way to do that is to use noticeable terms out of the passage. You gratefully latch onto them the way a drowning person clutches a life preserver.

Pot Holes

If you're out driving and you hit a pot hole, do you back up and drive over it again? Rereading text you didn't understand is the literary equivalent of driving over and over the same pot hole.

THE 4-STEP BASIC APPROACH

The best way to beat the ACT system is to use a different one. The 4-Step Basic Approach will help you direct the bulk of your time to where you earn points, on the questions and answers. When you read the passage, you'll read knowing exactly what you're looking for.

Step 1: Preview

The first step involves two parts. First, check the blurb at the beginning of the passage to see if it offers any additional information. Ninety-nine percent of the time, all it will offer will be the title, author, copyright date, and publisher. There is even no guarantee that the title will convey the topic. But occasionally, the blurb will define an unfamiliar term, place a setting, or identify a character.

Passage III

HUMANITIES: This passage is adapted from the article "The Sculpture Revolution" by Michael Michalski (©1998 Geer Publishing).

True to form, this offers only the basic information.

The real value in Step 1 comes in the work you do with the questions.

Map the Questions

Take no more than 30 seconds to map the questions. Underline the lead words. Star any line or paragraph references.

Second Time Around
You'll check the blurb twice. Once when you're confirming your order and now as part of Step 1.

Lead Words

We introduced lead words in the Introduction. These are the specific words and phrases that you will find in the passage. They are not the boilerplate language of reading test questions like "main idea" or "author's purpose." They are usually nouns, phrases, or verbs.

Map the following questions that accompany the humanities passage. Even if a question has a line/paragraph reference, underline any lead words in the question.

21. The author expresses the idea that:

22. The information in lines 69–74 suggests that Quentin Bell believes that historians and critics:

23. Which of the following most accurately summarizes how the passage characterizes subjectivism's effect on Rodin?

24. According to the passage, academicism and mannerism:

25. Information in the fourth paragraph (lines 31–38) makes clear that the author believes that:

26. According to the passage, Renoir differs from Daleur in that:

27. According to the passage, Cézanne's work is characterized by:

28. Based on information in the sixth paragraph (lines 45–52), the author implies that:

29. In line 59, when the author uses the phrase "modern," he most nearly means sculpture that:

30. Which of the following statements would the author most likely agree with?

Your mapped questions should look like this:

21. The author expresses the idea that:

⭐ 22. The information in lines 69–74 suggests that <u>Quentin Bell</u> believes that <u>historians</u> and <u>critics</u>:

23. Which of the following most accurately summarizes how the passage characterizes <u>subjectivism's effect</u> on <u>Rodin</u>?

24. According to the passage, <u>academicism</u> and <u>mannerism</u>:

⭐ 25. Information in the fourth paragraph (lines 31–38) makes clear that the author believes that:

26. According to the passage, <u>Renoir differs from Daleur</u> in that:

27. According to the passage, <u>Cézanne's work</u> is characterized by:

⭐ 28. Based on information in the sixth paragraph (lines 45–52), the author implies that:

⭐ 29. In line 59, when the author uses the phrase "<u>modern</u>" he most nearly means <u>sculpture</u> that:

30. Which of the following statements would the author most likely agree with?

Two Birds, One Stone

Mapping the questions provides two key benefits. First, you've just identified (with stars) four questions that have easy-to-find answers. With all those great lead words, you have two more questions whose answers will be easy to find. Second, you have the main idea of the passage *before* you've read it. When you read the passage knowing what to look for, you *read actively*.

Read Actively

Reading actively means knowing in advance what you're going to read. You have the important details to look for, and you won't waste time on details that never appear in a question. Reading passively means walking into a dark cave, wandering in the dark trying to see what dangers or treasures await. Reading actively means walking into the cave with a flashlight and a map, looking for what you know is in there.

Look again at all the words you've underlined. They tell you what the passage will be about: modern sculpture, Renoir, Daleur, Cézanne, Rodin, and a bunch of "-isms" that you could safely guess concern art. There is also someone named Quentin Bell, historians, critics, and art. You're ready to move on to Step 2.

Step 2: Work the Passage

Your next step is to work the passage. Spend no more than 2–3 minutes. Look for and underline the lead words, underlining each time any appear more than once.

You're not reading to understand every word and detail. You'll read smaller selections in depth when you work the questions. If you can't finish in three minutes, don't worry about it. We'll discuss time management strategies later in the chapter.

Don't Back Up Over the Pot Hole

If you read something you don't understand, do not reread it. Just keep going, and worry about it later only if you have to.

Passage III

HUMANITIES: This passage is adapted from the article "The Sculpture Revolution" by Michael Michalski (©1998 Geer Publishing).

If we were to start fresh in the study of sculpture or any art, we might observe that the record is largely filled by works of relatively few great contributors. Next to the influences of these great geniuses, time periods themselves
5 are of little significance. The study of art and art history are properly directed to the achievements of outstanding individual artists, not the particular decades or centuries in which any may have worked.

Nonetheless, when we study art in historical perspective
10 we select a convenient frame of reference through which diverse styles and talents are to be compared. Hence we write of "movements" and attempt to understand each artist in terms of the one to which he "belongs." Movements have limited use, but we should not talk of realism, impressionism,
15 cubism, or surrealism as though they genuinely had lives of their own to which the artist was answerable. We regard the movement as the governing force and the artist as its servant. Yet it is well to remember that the movements do not necessarily present themselves in orderly chronological series, and
20 the individual artist frequently weaves her way into one and out of another over the course of a single career.

Great artists are not normally confined by the "movements" that others may name for them. Rather, they transcend the conventional structure working now in one style, then in
25 another, and later in a third. Picasso's work, for example, echoes many of the artistic movements, and other artists too, moving from one style through another. Indeed, artists are people, and any may decide to alter her style for no more complex a reason than that which makes most people want
30 to "try something new" once in a while.

In studying modern sculpture one is tempted to begin a history with Auguste Rodin (1840–1917), who was a contemporary of Paul Cézanne (1839–1906). Yet the two artists did not, in artistic terms, belong to the same period. Their
35 strategies and objectives differed. Although Rodin was surely a great artist, he did not do for sculpture what Cézanne did for painting. In fact, although Cézanne was a painter, he had a more lasting effect on sculpture than did Rodin.

Cézanne's work constitutes a reaction against impres-
40 sionism and the confusion he thought it created. He searched persistently for the "motif." Cézanne strived for clarity of form and was able to convert his personal perceptions into concrete, recognizable substance. He is justly considered to have offered the first glimmer of a new art—a new classicism.

45 Rodin was surely a great artist, but he was not an innovator as was Cézanne; prevailing tides of subjectivism came over him. Rodin's mission was to reinvest sculpture with the integrity it lost when Michelangelo died. Rodin succceded in this mission. His first true work, *The Age of Bronze* (1877),
50 marked the beginning of the end of academicism, mannerism, and decadence that had prevailed since Michelangelo's last sculpture, the *Rondanini Pietà*.

Yet it is largely Cézanne, not Rodin, who was artistic ancestor to Picasso, Gonzalez, Brancusi, Archipenko, Lipchitz,
55 and Laurens, and they are unquestionably the first lights in the "new art" of sculpture. This "new art," of course, is the sculpture we call "modern." It is modern because it breaks with tradition and draws little on that which preceded it.

When I speak of "modern" sculpture, I do not refer to
60 every sculptor nor even to every highly talented sculptor of our age. I do not exclude, necessarily, the sculptors of an earlier time. Modern sculpture, as far as I am concerned, is any that consciously casts tradition aside and seeks forms more suitable to the senses and values of its time. Renoir and
65 Daumier are, in this light, modern sculptors notwithstanding the earlier time at which they worked. Daleur and Carpeaux are not modern, although they belong chronologically to the recent era.

Professor Quentin Bell argues that historians and critics
70 name as "modern" those sculptors in whom they happen to be interested and that the term when abused in that way has no historical or artistic significance. That, I think, is not right. The problem is that Professor Bell thinks "modern" means "now," when in fact it means "new."

Your passage should look like this. If you couldn't find all the lead words to underline, don't worry. You can do those questions Later. But did you notice that there is nothing underlined in the second and third paragraphs? If you hadn't mapped the questions first, you would have likely wasted a lot of time on details that ACT doesn't seem to care about.

Passage III

HUMANITIES: This passage is adapted from the article "The Sculpture Revolution" by Michael Michalski (©1998 Geer Publishing).

If we were to start fresh in the study of sculpture or any art, we might observe that the record is largely filled by works of relatively few great contributors. Next to the influences of these great geniuses, time periods themselves
5 are of little significance. The study of art and art history are properly directed to the achievements of outstanding individual artists, not the particular decades or centuries in which any may have worked.

Nonetheless, when we study art in historical perspective
10 we select a convenient frame of reference through which diverse styles and talents are to be compared. Hence we write of "movements" and attempt to understand each artist in terms of the one to which he "belongs." Movements have limited use, but we should not talk of realism, impressionism,
15 cubism, or surrealism as though they genuinely had lives of their own to which the artist was answerable. We regard the movement as the governing force and the artist as its servant. Yet it is well to remember that the movements do not necessarily present themselves in orderly chronological series and
20 the individual artist frequently weaves her way into one and out of another over the course of a single career.

Great artists are not normally confined by the "movements" that others may name for them. Rather, they transcend the conventional structure working now in one style, then in
25 another, and later in a third. Picasso's work, for example, echoes many of the artistic movements, and other artists too, moving from one style through another. Indeed, artists are people, and any may decide to alter her style for no more complex a reason than that which makes most people want
30 to "try something new" once in a while.

In studying modern sculpture one is tempted to begin a history with Auguste Rodin (1840–1917), who was a contemporary of Paul Cézanne (1839–1906). Yet the two artists did not, in artistic terms, belong to the same period. Their
35 strategies and objectives differed. Although Rodin was surely a great artist, he did not do for sculpture what Cézanne did for painting. In fact, although Cézanne was a painter, he had a more lasting effect on sculpture than did Rodin.

Cézanne's work constitutes a reaction against impres-
40 sionism and the confusion he thought it created. He searched persistently for the "motif." Cézanne strived for clarity of form and was able to convert his personal perceptions into concrete, recognizable substance. He is justly considered to have offered the first glimmer of a new art—a new classicism.

45 Rodin was surely a great artist, but he was not an innovator as was Cézanne; prevailing tides of subjectivism came over him. Rodin's mission was to reinvest sculpture with the integrity it lost when Michelangelo died. Rodin succeeded in this mission. His first true work, *The Age of Bronze* (1877),
50 marked the beginning of the end of academicism, mannerism, and decadence that had prevailed since Michelangelo's last sculpture, the *Rondanini Pietà*.

Yet it is largely Cézanne, not Rodin, who was artistic ancestor to Picasso, Gonzalez, Brancusi, Archipenko, Lipchitz,
55 and Laurens, and they are unquestionably the first lights in the "new art" of sculpture. This "new art," of course, is the sculpture we call "modern." It is modern because it breaks with tradition and draws little on that which preceded it.

When I speak of "modern" sculpture, I do not refer to
60 every sculptor nor even to every highly talented sculptor of our age. I do not exclude, necessarily, the sculptors of an earlier time. Modern sculpture, as far as I am concerned, is any that consciously casts tradition aside and seeks forms more suitable to the senses and values of its time. Renoir and
65 Daumier are, in this light, modern sculptors notwithstanding the earlier time at which they worked. Daleur and Carpeaux are not modern, although they belong chronologically to the recent era.

Professor Quentin Bell argues that historians and critics
70 name as "modern" those sculptors in whom they happen to be interested and that the term when abused in that way has no historical or artistic significance. That, I think, is not right. The problem is that Professor Bell thinks "modern" means "now," when in fact it means "new."

Step 3: Work the Questions

As we told you in the Introduction, you can't do the questions in the order ACT gives you. Question 21 has no stars or lead words and poses what seems to be a Reasoning question. Thus, it's neither easy to answer, nor is the answer easy to find. Question 22 is a great question to start with, however. It has a star, and it's a Referral question, asking directly what is stated in the passage.

☆ **22.** The information in lines 69–74 suggests that <u>Quentin Bell</u> believes that <u>historians</u> and <u>critics</u>:

Here's How to Crack It

Make sure you understand what the question is asking. Now read what you need out of the passage to find the answer. The line reference points you to line 69, but you'll find your answer within a window of 5–10 lines of the line references. Read the last paragraph to see what Quentin Bell thinks about historians and critics.

Work the Questions

1. Pick your order of questions. Do Now questions that are easy to answer, easy to find the answer, or best of all, both.
2. Read the question to understand what it's asking.
3. Read what you need in the passage to find your answer. In general, read a window of 5–10 lines.

Step 4

Step 4: Work the Answers

Do you see the importance of making sure you understand the question? We care here what Quentin Bell thinks about historians and critics, not what the author thinks of them. But the question is a Referral question, asking what is directly stated. Lines 69–72 offer Bell's opinion. Now find the match in the answers.

> ### Work the Answers
> - If you can clearly identify the answer in the passage, look for its match among the answers.
> - If you aren't sure if an answer is right or wrong, leave it. You'll either find one better or three worse.
> - Cross off any choice that talks about something not found in your window.
> - If you're down to two, choose key words in the answer choices. See if you can locate them back in the passage, and determine if the answer choice matches what the passage says.

Here's How to Crack It

F. have no appreciation for the value of modern art.

Bell is critical of historians and critics, and value could refer to significance in the passage. This seems possible, so keep it.

G. abuse art and its history.

The passage states that the term is abused, not art and its history. This is a trap, and it's wrong. Cross it off.

H. should evaluate works of art on the basis of their merit without regard to the artist's fame.

There was nothing in the window about "fame." Cross it off.

J. attach the phrase "modern art" to those sculptors that intrigue them.

Attach the phrase is a good match for *name* as '*modern*' and *sculptors that intrigue them* is a good match for *in whom they happen to be interested*. This answer is better than (F), and it is correct.

Steps 3 and 4: Repeat

Look for all the Now questions, and repeat Steps 3 and 4. Make sure you understand what the question is asking. Read what you need to find your answer, usually a window of 5–10 lines. Work the answers, using POE until you find your answer.

———————————○———————————

Referral Questions

Referral questions are easy to answer because they ask what was directly stated in the passage. Read the question carefully to identify what it's asking. The passage directly states something about what? Once you find your window to read, read to find the answer. The correct answers to Referral questions are barely paraphrased and will match the text very closely.

> ### How to Spot Referral Questions
> - Questions that begin with *According to the passage*
> - Questions that ask what the passage or author states
> - Questions with short answers

If the answer to a Referral question is also easy to find, they are great Now questions. Look for Referral questions with line references or great lead words.

———————————○———————————

26. According to the passage, <u>Renoir differs from Daleur</u> in that:

    F. Daleur had no inspiration, while Renoir was tremendously inspired.

    G. Renoir's work was highly innovative, while Daleur's was not.

    H. Daleur was a sculptor, while Renoir was not.

    J. Renoir revered tradition, while Daleur did not.

       When I speak of "<u>modern</u>" <u>sculpture</u>, I do not refer to
60 every sculptor nor even to every highly talented sculptor of our
    age. I do not exclude, necessarily, the sculptors of an earlier
    time. <u>Modern sculpture</u>, as far as I am concerned, is any that
    consciously casts tradition aside and seeks forms more suitable
    to the senses and values of its time. <u>Renoir</u> and Daumier are,
65 in this light, modern sculptors notwithstanding the earlier time
    at which they worked. <u>Daleur</u> and Carpeaux are not modern,
    although they belong chronologically to the recent era.

Here's How to Crack It

Renoir and *Daleur* are great lead words, easy for your eye to spot in the eighth paragraph. On the real test, you'll have the passage on the left and all your mapped questions on the right page. For convenience's sake and to avoid flipping back to the passage, we're printing the window to read with the question.

Lines 64–66 state that *Renoir was a modern sculptor* and *Daleur* is not. But that same sentence mentions four artists *in this light*. What light? Any time you see *this*, *that*, or *such* in front of a noun, back up to read the first mention of that topic. *This light* is the author's definition of modern, given on lines 62–64.

Now work the answers. Cross off answers that don't state Renoir is modern and Daleur is not. *Innovative* in (G) is a good match for modern and is the correct answer. *Inspiration* in (F) doesn't match modern. Choice (H) is disproven by the passage. Choice (J) tempts with *tradition* but compare it to the text, and the author states modern sculpture *consciously casts tradition aside*.

———————◯———————

Try another Referral question with great lead words.

———————◯———————

27. According to the passage, Cézanne's work is characterized by:

    A. a return to subjectivism.
    B. a pointless search for form.
    C. excessively personal expressions.
    D. rejection of the impressionistic philosophy.

>   Cézanne's work constitutes a reaction against impres-
> 40 sionism and the confusion he thought it created. He searched
> persistently for the "motif." Cézanne strived for clarity of form
> and was able to convert his personal perceptions into concrete,
> recognizable substance. He is justly considered to have offered
> the first glimmer of a new art—a new classicism.

Here's How to Crack It

Cézanne appears first in the fourth paragraph, but the question is about *Cézanne's work*, which is in the fifth paragraph. Choice (D) matches *reaction against impressionism* and is the correct answer.

———————◯———————

Reasoning Questions

Reasoning questions require you to read between the lines. Instead of being directly stated, the correct answer is implied or suggested. In other words, look for the larger point that the author is making.

Reasoning questions aren't as easy to answer as Referral questions, but they're not *that* much harder. If they come with a line or paragraph reference or a great lead word, they should be done Now.

> ## How to Spot Reasoning Questions
> - Questions that use *infer, means, suggests,* or *implies*
> - Questions that ask about the purpose or function of part or all of the passage
> - Questions that ask what the author or a person written about in the passage would agree or disagree with
> - Questions that ask you to characterize or describe all or parts of the passage
> - Questions with long answers

☆ **25.** Information in the fourth paragraph (lines 31–38) makes clear that the author believes that:

    A. Rodin was more innovative than Cézanne.
    B. Cézanne was more innovative than Rodin.
    C. Modern art is more important than classical art.
    D. Cézanne tried to emulate impressionism.

       In studying <u>modern sculpture</u> one is tempted to begin a history with Auguste <u>Rodin</u> (1840–1917), who was a contemporary of Paul <u>Cézanne</u> (1839–1906). Yet the two artists did not, in artistic terms, belong to the same period. Their
35 strategies and objectives differed. Although <u>Rodin</u> was surely a great artist, he did not do for sculpture what <u>Cézanne</u> did for painting. In fact, although <u>Cézanne</u> was a painter, he had a more lasting effect on sculpture than did <u>Rodin</u>.

Here's How to Crack It

The question doesn't provide specific clues what to look for and instead asks what the author's point is in the fourth paragraph. The author is comparing the artists Cézanne and Rodin. The concluding sentence states that *Cézanne...had a more lasting effect on sculpture than did Rodin.* Choice (A) says the opposite. The paragraph does not mention either *classical art* or *impressionism,* so (C) and (D) can be eliminated. Choice (B) is a good paraphrase of the author's point and is the correct answer.

———————————○———————————

Work Now the Reasoning questions with line or paragraph references or great lead words. Use POE heavily as you work the answers.

———————————○———————————

☆ **28.** Based on information in the sixth paragraph (lines 45–52), the author implies that:
   F. mannerism reflects a lack of integrity.
   G. Rodin disliked the work of Michelangelo.
   H. Rodin embraced the notion of decadence.
   J. Rodin's work represented a shift in style different from the works of artists who preceded him.

45   <u>Rodin</u> was surely a great artist, but he was not an innovator as was <u>Cézanne</u>; prevailing tides of <u>subjectivism</u> came over him. <u>Rodin</u>'s mission was to reinvest sculpture with the integrity it lost when Michelangelo died. <u>Rodin</u> succeeded in this mission. His first true work, *The Age of Bronze* (1877), marked the be-
50   ginning of the end of <u>academicism</u>, <u>mannerism</u>, and decadence that had prevailed since Michelangelo's last sculpture, the *Rondanini Pietà*.

Here's How to Crack It

Use POE. Choices (F) and (H) use terms from the paragraph but garbles them. Rodin wanted to restore elements of sculpture that had changed since the death of Michelangelo, which means he respected Michelangelo's work, so (G) is not supported. The last sentence states that Rodin's work *marked the beginning of the end* and therefore represented something new, as is stated in (J), which is the correct answer.

———————————○———————————

☆ **29.** In line 59, when the author uses the phrase "modern," he most nearly means sculpture that:

   A. postdates the *Rondanini Pietà*.
   B. is not significantly tied to work that comes before it.
   C. shows no artistic merit.
   D. genuinely interests contemporary critics.

> When I speak of "modern" sculpture, I do not refer to every
> 60 sculptor nor even to every highly talented sculptor of our age. I do
> not exclude, necessarily, the sculptors of an earlier time. Modern
> sculpture, as far as I am concerned, is any that consciously casts
> tradition aside and seeks forms more suitable to the senses and
> values of its time. Renoir and Daumier are, in this light, modern
> 65 sculptors notwithstanding the earlier time at which they worked.
> Daleur and Carpeaux are not modern, although they belong
> chronologically to the recent era.

Here's How to Crack It

Use POE. The *Rondanini Pietà* is in the wrong window, so eliminate (A). Choice (B) is a good paraphrase of the art that *consciously casts tradition aside and seeks forms more suitable to the sense and values of its time,* and it is the correct answer. Choice (C) can't be proven by the passage; the author doesn't state that they have no worth at all. Choice (D) tempts with *contemporary* as a possible match for *modern* or *its time,* but *critics* are not in this window.

Later Questions

Once you have worked all the questions with line or paragraph references and great lead words, move to the Later questions. The answers to questions without a line or paragraph reference or any great lead words can be difficult to find, which is why you should do them Later. But the later you do them, the easier they become. You've either found them or you've narrowed down where to look. From the windows you've read closely to answer all the Now questions, you may have located lead words you missed when you worked the passage. And if you haven't, then they must be in the few paragraphs you haven't read since you worked the passage.

24. According to the passage, <u>academicism</u> and <u>mannerism</u>:

    F. were readily visible in *The Age of Bronze.*
    G. were partially manifest in the *Rondanini Pietà.*
    H. were styles that Rodin believed lacked integrity.
    J. were styles that Rodin wanted to restore into fashion.

45   <u>Rodin</u> was surely a great artist, but he was not an innovator as was <u>Cézanne</u>; prevailing tides of <u>subjectivism</u> came over him. <u>Rodin</u>'s mission was to reinvest sculpture with the integrity it lost when Michelangelo died. <u>Rodin</u> succeeded in this mission. His first true work, *The Age of Bronze* (1877), marked the be-
50 ginning of the end of <u>academicism</u>, <u>mannerism</u>, and decadence that had prevailed since Michelangelo's last sculpture, the *Rondanini Pietà.*

Here's How to Crack It

According to the passage means that this is a Referral question and should be easy to answer. The challenge, however, is finding the lead words. But you read this paragraph when you answered 28. Not only would you find *academicism* and *mannerism* if you missed them when you worked the passage, but you also know the paragraph well from working question 28. Use POE to eliminate choices that don't match your correct answer from 28. Choices (F), (G), and (J) all contradict both the passage and your previous answer. Choice (H) matches, and it is the correct answer.

Now move onto question 23. Because you worked it Later, the answer is easy to find.

23. Which of the following most accurately summarizes how the passage characterizes <u>subjectivism's effect</u> on <u>Rodin</u>?

    A. It ended his affiliation with mannerism.
    B. It caused him to lose his artistic integrity.
    C. It limited his ability to innovate.
    D. It caused him to become decadent.

Here's How to Crack It

You know this paragraph well by now, but *subjectivism* didn't play a major role in the points made for questions 28 and 24. Use POE to eliminate (B) and (D) because they don't match what you've learned about Rodin. You know Rodin didn't like *mannerism*, but check the part of the window that specifically discusses *subjectivism*. Lines 45–47 give *subjectivism* as the explanation of why Rodin *was not an innovator.* That matches (C) perfectly.

Last

Questions 24 and 23 showed how your work on each question builds your under-standing of the passage, making the Later questions easier to do than if you hadn't waited. The questions, after all, refer back to the same passage, so the answers should agree with each other. Some questions may ask about a relatively minor detail in the passage, but most should ask about important details, the ones that help the author make the main point.

Use what you've learned about the passage to answer last the questions that ask about the entire passage.

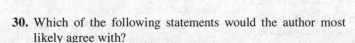

21. The author expresses the idea that:

   A. art should never be studied in terms of movements.
   B. art can be labeled as modern when it introduces a style that is different from those found in works that came earlier.
   C. lesser artists do not usually vary their styles.
   D. great artists are always nonconformists.

Here's How to Crack It

Question 29 helps the most with this question, but several questions echoed the theme of art making a break from the past. The correct answer is (B).

30. Which of the following statements would the author most likely agree with?

   F. Cézanne had greater influence on modern sculpture than did Rodin.
   G. Rodin made no significant contribution to modern sculpture.
   H. Daumier should not be considered a modern sculptor.
   J. Carpeaux should be considered a modern sculptor.

Here's How to Crack It

Questions 23, 24, 25, 26, 27, and 28 all help eliminate the wrong answers (G), (H), and (J), making (F) the correct answer.

THE 4-STEP BASIC APPROACH

Try a passage on your own. Give yourself up to 12 minutes, but don't worry if you go a little over. Use the passage on the next page to help you master the Basic Approach, and worry less about your speed. Later in the chapter and in the next, we'll discuss other strategies to help with time. The answers are given on the page following the passage.

The Basic Approach
1. Preview.
2. Work the Passage.
3. Work the Questions.
4. Work the Answers.

PROSE FICTION: This passage is adapted from the novel *Skyward* by Prakriti Basrai (©2012 by Prakriti Basrai).

Ever since I graduated from high school, I've worked at the company my father started, Singer Stations and Service, a gas station and car maintenance center that was the fulfillment of my father's American dream shortly after he arrived here in the late 1960s and that, if all goes according to plan, will pass to my grandsons and their grandsons in perpetuity, and which is already making its way into the twenty-first century with a Facebook page and a sophisticated iPhone app.

Our family name is still Singh, but in our small town, my father thought it would put a safer face on the business to change the name to Singer, a name which we've all unofficially adopted now that we're in the United States, as I suppose many of our more-established neighbors' ancestors must've done a few generations ago.

Also, Singer is just a nice name for a business: it's got a nice, musical ring to it, and the alliterative name of our gas station chain seems to churn up memories of great American businesses and the non-threatening pose that has been necessary to immigrant assimilation from the beginning. When drivers pull up to our pumps, they do so with the sense that we'll smile back at them, whistling while we work, operating the pumps like expert musicians, and it'll cost them a song (a line, I'm sure you can imagine, that is emblazoned proudly on all of our public signage). All of the credit for this name has always gone to my father, and I can believe that he was the one behind this smart change: He was always a good businessman, and he had that added penchant, almost a poetic sense for a clever, musical turn of phrase. My father has always loved his business, and although that love has been diluted as it has come through my generation and my son's, it's nothing that the standard narrative of Americanization and the decline of hard work can't explain, and which I have no interest in rehashing here. We've all had our challenges, regardless of age, so who says one generation has it tougher than the next, and frankly, who cares?

When I really think about it, though, I think my son, Ravneet, whom everyone calls Richie, might have it hardest. Even for our relatively small business, Richie's public-relations responsibilities are those of any of the international stations. He's always posting something new to the Internet or monitoring the price of gas all over the world at once. It doesn't hurt that the kid knows how to make a buck—my father marvels every day at what his grandson has been able to do with the family business. You'd think with all that's gone wrong with the economy in the last few years, Richie would've sold his Italian sports car, but the kid actually just bought another one.

Richie's success is undeniable, but sometimes I worry that he works too hard for all that he's got. It's nearly impossible to get him on the phone; he must work 80 hours a week, and he's spent more than one Thanksgiving Day stuck at the office balancing the books. My father at the very least had a family to come home to, and the saving grace of his religious observance forced him to take at least a day off every week. I was pulled neither to overwork nor underwork; I was always focused on maintaining what had been given to me. In later years, my mother told me secretly that she thought I actually had it worst of all—I had no burning desire to enter this business, but I didn't really have any other choice. I did well enough, and if I might've been brilliant at something else, I guess we'll never know.

Even so, I was Raman (The Gas Man) Singer's son, but I never quite shared his pioneer spirit at breaking new ground, nor his enviable belief that he did what he did because it had to be done. I did perfectly well at Singer Stations and Service. I wasn't the boss's lazy kid, and I worked just as hard as any of my employees making minimum wage. I stuck with it. When you look at it this way, I did just fine.

When I fully handed the business over to Richie five years ago, I knew right away that my life couldn't simply be over at the age of 50. As a result, at the urging of my college-aged daughter Geeta, I decided to try something I always wished that I had done. I enrolled in the business program at the State University, and before long, I realized that Geeta knew me better than I knew myself. I had fun like I never had before, and looking back, I came to see that the part of the business that always drew me in was learning: whether it was the stories of my co-workers or the inner workings of a small business that is trying to grow. Now that I'm done with school, I'm starting my own business. In fact, Geeta and I are starting one, and while I've left to her what exactly it is we're selling, I'm brimming with excitement to find out.

1. The passage can be best described as primarily:

   A. one business owner's questioning of the direction his business has taken after he handed the management over to his son.
   B. a son's elegant praise of his father's skill and determination in creating a family business.
   C. a personal narrative that describes one man's role within a business started by his father and passed down through generations.
   D. a story of the changes in American immigrant businesses in the twentieth century.

2. Which of the following actions affecting the family business does the narrator NOT attribute to his father?

   F. A sophisticated iPhone app
   G. The founding of Singer Stations and Service
   H. A change in the family's last name
   J. An alliterative name for the business

3. The narrator explicitly declines to take a firm stand on which of the following issues?

   A. The personal preferences he had that enabled him to succeed in business
   B. The quality of the name Singer Stations and Service
   C. Which generation has had the most difficult time in the world of business
   D. Whether the family should have kept the name Singh rather than Singer

4. According to the passage, what is the narrator's father's attitude toward words?

   F. He treats them like a poet would.
   G. He believes business names should be alliterative.
   H. A man should keep his mouth closed and his ears open.
   J. He believes that advertisers work in the business of deception.

5. As it is used in line 40, the word *hurt* most nearly means:

   A. impede success.
   B. injure.
   C. sting.
   D. cause a bruise.

6. What or who is the "saving grace" referred to in the passage?

   F. Singer Stations and Service
   G. The narrator's mother
   H. The narrator's daughter
   J. Religious piety

7. What does the narrator state is his mother's view of his role in Singer Stations and Service?

   A. In actuality, the credit for the business's name should go to him because he was the real artist.
   B. He had the worst time of any of his family members because he ran a business in which he did not have a passionate interest.
   C. His hard work, though less public than his son's, was crucial to the company's success at the time.
   D. He should be more grateful for his inheritance and not insist on changing professions.

8. According to the passage, who or what is "Raman (The Gas Man)"?

   F. Singer's main gas supplier
   G. The business's main competitor
   H. The narrator's son
   J. The narrator's father

9. According to the passage, the narrator's daughter knows the narrator better than he knows himself because:

   A. the company's new Internet presence emerged after he retired.
   B. she suggested that he go back to school, and he enjoyed doing so.
   C. Richie bought a second Italian sports car.
   D. the history of Singer Stations and Service is a history of the immigrant experience.

10. As it is used in line 73, the phrase *came to see* most nearly means:

   F. arrived at.
   G. realized.
   H. attended.
   J. visited.

Score and Analyze Your Performance

The correct answers are (C), (F), (C), (F), (A), (J), (B), (J), (B), and (G). (For detailed explanations, see Chapter 24.) How did you do? Were you able to finish in 12 minutes or less? If you struggled with time, identify what step took up the most time. Identify any questions that slowed you down. Did you make good choices of Now and Later questions? Did you use *enough* time? If you finished in less than 12 minutes but missed several questions, next time plan to slow down to give yourself enough time to evaluate the answers carefully. In Chapter 18, we'll work on skills to help you work the questions and answers with more speed and greater accuracy. But first, we'll finish this chapter with strategies to help you increase your speed working the passage.

BEAT THE CLOCK

When you struggle with time, there are several places within the Basic Approach that are eating up the minutes.

> **Pacing the Basic Approach**
> If you spend 10–11 minutes on your first passage, use your time wisely.
>
> Step 1: Preview. *30–60 seconds*
> Step 2: Work the Passage. *3 minutes*
> Steps 3 and 4: Work the Questions and Answers. *7 minutes*

Step 1: Preview

To move at the fastest speed when you preview, you can't read the questions. Let your eye *look* for lead words and numbers. Don't let your brain *read*.

Time yourself to see if you can preview the following blurb and questions in less than a minute.

Passage IV

NATURAL SCIENCE: This passage is adapted from the article "What Giotto Saw" by James Herndon (©2001 by Galaxy Press).

31. The author characterizes the comparison of the work of Sagdeev to that of Peale as:

32. The main point of the last paragraph (lines 43-48) is to show that Zdenek Sekanina:

33. In terms of their role in studying the rotational period, the 1920 photographs are described by the author as:

34. Lines 17–19 mainly emphasize what quality?

35. According to the passage, the nuclear surface of Halley's comet is believed to be:

36. As described in the passage, Giotto's camera was specifically programmed to:

37. As used in the passage, the word *resolution* (line 11) means:

38. The passage indicates that H. Use Keler:

39. Lines 25–28 are best summarized as describing a problem that:

40. According to the passage, the volume of Halley's comet is:

Step 2

Step 2: Work the Passage

This step should take no more than 3 minutes, and you should not be trying to read the passage thoroughly. Your only goal is to find as many of your lead words as you can and underline them.

Skimming, Scanning, and Reading

If we told you to skim the passage, would you know that means? If you do, great. If you don't, don't worry. *Skimming* is something many readers feel they're supposed to do on a timed test, but they don't know what it means and therefore can't do it.

Reading needs your brain on full power. You're reading words, and your brain is processing what they mean and drawing conclusions. Reading is watching the road, searching for directional signs, and glancing at the scenery, all for the purpose of trying to figure out where the road is leading.

Skimming means reading only a few words. When you work the passage, your brain can try to process key parts that build to the main idea, but you don't necessarily need to identify the main idea just yet. Working the questions and answers tells you the main idea and all the important details. Skimming is reading only the directional signs and ignoring the scenery.

Scanning needs very little of your brain. Use your eyes. Look, don't think, and don't try to process for understanding. Scanning is looking for Volkswagen Beetles in a game of Slug Bug.

When you're working the passage, you can skim or scan, but you shouldn't be reading. Read windows of text when you work the questions.

If you feel you can't turn your brain off when you work the passage, or you even skim and scan too slowly, then focus only on the first sentence of each paragraph. You may find fewer lead words, but you will give yourself more time to spend on working the questions and answers and can find the lead words then.

Time yourself to work the following passage, focusing only on the first sentence of each paragraph. We've actually made it impossible to do otherwise. Look for the lead words you underlined in Step 1 and underline any that you see.

Depending on where you're from, Slug Bug might be known as Punch Buggy.

Such relatively reliable insights as we have into the nature of Halley's comet's nucleus derive largely from the work done by the Giotto imaging team. Blah blah blah blah blah blah blah blah. Blah blah. Blah blah blah blah blah blah blah blah blah.
5 Blah blah blah. Blah blah blah blah blah blah blah blah blah. Blah blah blah blah blah blah blah blah blah. Blah blah blah blah blah blah blah blah blah.

Discernibility of detail varies at different points in the photograph. Blah blah blah blah blah blah blah blah. Blah blah. Blah
10 blah blah blah blah blah blah blah blah. Blah blah blah. Blah blah blah blah blah blah blah blah blah. Blah blah blah blah blah blah blah blah blah. Blah blah blah blah blah blah blah blah blah. Blah blah blah blah blah blah blah blah. Blah blah blah blah blah blah blah blah blah. Blah blah blah blah blah blah blah blah blah.

15 The Giotto photographs have allowed investigators to conclude that the surface of the nucleus is rough. Blah blah blah blah blah blah blah blah. Blah blah. Blah blah blah blah blah blah blah blah blah. Blah blah blah. Blah blah blah blah blah blah blah blah blah. Blah blah blah blah blah blah blah blah blah.
20 Blah blah blah blah blah blah blah blah blah. Blah blah blah blah blah blah blah blah blah.

On the other hand, the Giotto photographs reveal virtually nothing on the interior of the comet's nucleus or its rotational period. Blah blah blah blah blah blah blah blah. Blah blah. Blah
25 blah blah blah blah blah blah blah blah. Blah blah blah. Blah blah blah blah blah blah blah blah blah. Blah blah blah blah blah blah blah blah blah. Blah blah blah blah blah blah blah blah blah. Blah blah blah blah blah blah blah blah blah.

Moreover, the comet's overall dimensions were already
30 known to an approximation, and on this basis Rickman took the volume as 500–550 cubic centimeters. Blah blah blah blah blah blah blah blah. Blah blah. Blah blah blah blah blah blah blah blah blah. Blah blah blah. Blah blah blah blah blah blah blah blah. Blah blah blah blah blah blah blah blah blah. Blah
35 blah blah blah blah blah blah blah blah.

Using an analogous technique, R.Z. Sagdeev and colleagues arrived at a value of 0.2 to 1.5 grams per cubic centimeter. Blah blah blah blah blah blah blah blah. Blah blah. Blah blah blah blah blah blah blah blah blah. Blah blah. Blah blah blah blah blah
40 blah blah blah blah. Blah blah blah blah blah blah blah blah blah. Blah blah blah blah blah blah blah blah. Blah blah blah blah blah blah blah blah blah.

Finally, Zdenek Sekanina and Stephen M. Larson studied the rotational period by first processing images of 1920 photographs
45 in an attempt to improve the image of spiral dust features. Blah blah blah blah blah blah blah blah. Blah blah. Blah blah blah blah blah blah blah blah blah. Blah blah blah. Blah blah blah blah blah blah blah blah blah. Blah blah blah blah blah blah blah blah blah.

Let's see what you learned in less than three minutes.

Now Questions

You should have several Now questions.

- Questions 32, 34, 37, and 39 all have line references.
- Questions 31, 33, 35, 36, 38, and 40 all have lead words, great lead words in some.
- The lead words in 31 can be found in the first sentence of the sixth paragraph.
- The lead words in 33 can be found in the first sentence of the last paragraph.
- The lead words in 35 and 36 can be found in the first sentence of the first paragraph.
- The lead words in 40 can be found in the first sentence of the fifth paragraph.
- Nine of the ten questions have been located, and the great lead word in 38 should be easy to find easy to find when you're given the whole passage and not a lot of "blahs."

> **The Pencil Trick**
> When you have to look harder for a lead word, use your pencil to sweep each and every line from beginning to end. This will keep your brain from reading and let your eye look for the word.

The Passage

You also have a great outline of the passage. The topic sentences have drawn a map of the passage organization, and the transition words tell you how the paragraphs connect.

- What is the first paragraph about? The nucleus of Halley's Comet and the Giotto camera.
- The second paragraph? The details that the photographs show.
- The third? What scientists have learned from the photographs.
- How does the fourth paragraph relate to the third? *On the other hand* tells you that it is different from the third.
- How does the fifth paragraph relate to the fourth? *Moreover* tells you that they are similar.
- What is the sixth paragraph about? It's still on *volume*, which came up in the fifth paragraph.
- What is the last paragraph? It's the conclusion, which the transition word *Finally* makes clear.

Topic Sentences and Transition Words

Think of your own papers that you write for school. What does a good topic sentence do? It provides at worst an introduction to the paragraph and at best a summary of the paragraph's main idea. What follows will be the details that clarify or prove the main idea. And do you care about the details at Step 2? No, you'll focus on the details if and when there is a question on them.

Transition words are like great road signs. They show you the route, direct you to a detour, and get you back on the path of the main idea. When you *skim*, you're focusing on topic sentences and transition words.

In the next chapter, we'll cover more strategies for working the questions and answers. But now it's time to try another passage.

Look for Transition Words
Here are 15 transition words and/or phrases.

- *Despite*
- *However*
- *In spite of*
- *Nonetheless*
- *On the other hand*
- *But*
- *Rather*
- *Yet*
- *Ironically*
- *Notwithstanding*
- *Unfortunately*
- *On the contrary*
- *Therefore*
- *Hence*
- *Consequently*

Reading Drill 1

Use the Basic Approach on the following passage. Time yourself to complete in 8–10 minutes. Check your answers in Chapter 24.

Passage III

HUMANITIES: This passage is adapted from the article "The Buzz in Our Pockets" by Danielle Panizzi (©2013 by Telephony Biquarterly).

To the extent that it has a creator at all, the text message, or SMS (short message service), was created in the early 1980s by Friedhelm Hillebrand and Bernard Ghillebaert, who wanted to find a way to send data over the parts of phone lines that were
5 not being used in normal telephony. The first text messages were 160 characters long. Hillebrand suggested that "160 characters was sufficient to express most messages succinctly," citing typical postcard and Telex lengths.

Although this form might seem to limit the way we commu-
10 nicate, the text message is the most widely used data application in the world, with about 80% of all cellphone users (3.5 billion people) using the medium. Text messages are already a part of the cultural landscape: They are mentioned in rap and rock songs; they show up in billboards and advertisements selling just
15 about anything; and they've even cropped up in serious novels like Jonathan Franzen's *Freedom* and David Foster Wallace's *The Pale King*. Text messages, in fact, move the whole plot of Martin Scorsese's 2006 film *The Departed*, a critical success and eventual Oscar winner for Best Picture.

20 But the text message is more than a cultural fad. It's part of a broader shift in the way we connect with one another. Speaking on an actual telephone is basically defunct in 2013, not only for the economic reason that "time is money" and a text is quicker than a call, but also for a much older desire in all of us for
25 permanence. With a text message, we've got a record of all our communications, and although we may cast them off quickly, even the shortest text message requires more pre-thought than a verbalized remark: We can't go back to our recorded calls, but our texts live on our phones for as long as we choose to keep
30 them there. The text message has made even our most fleeting conversations permanent—and in this way, the text harkens back to one of the earliest modes of communication, even before the telephone: the letter.

Although America was a sprawling, disparate place even
35 before the War for Independence in the 1770s, its residents always felt the need to communicate with those farther and farther away. Ships carried people back and forth across the Atlantic Ocean, but they also carried correspondence, and we could even say that our very nation was founded in these written
40 communiqués: Much of what we know about that era comes

from these letters. One day, text messages may provide a similar record of our own moment.

But it would be naïve to say that these quick notes are anything like the voluminous correspondence of ages past. In
45 her recent monograph *Write Me a Letter,* Kari Fields wonders if the sophisticated concentration of that historical correspondence is even available to us anymore. Fields warns not only that we may have been "dumbed down" by our technologies but also that we may have lost one of the essential elements of the human
50 experience. "The content of our communication with each other ('I'll be late to work today'; 'I'll be home at 10'; or even, 'I love you') may be ultimately the same," Fields concedes, "but the real communication lives in the form—the tone, the unsteady hand on a particular word, the hasty erasures." Perhaps Fields herself
55 is missing the point: Naysayers have said that everything from the printing press, to the radio, to the movie screen, to Google, has compromised the way we think and understand. It makes no difference whether a letter takes a month by boat, two weeks by Pony Express, a few days by post, or a few seconds by email.
60 The medium, it seems safe to say, is not the message.

However, Fields is aware of all these earlier changes. She is as sophisticated a historian of these media as anyone working in the field today. We cannot deny that text messages and the Internet have isolated us from one another like never before. In
65 addition to placing us alone at our computers or on our phones, these new technologies also force us to spread our limited attention spans thinner and thinner. We may have to think about the texts messages we send, but we typically do so while looking at something else on the web, listening to music or podcasts,
70 or seconds before or after sending messages to someone else. It's not merely that our communications are getting shorter and shorter; it's that the time we have for real interactions has shrunk. All of these new devices are supposed to be time-savers, but what they've really given us is more time to use the devices,
75 to the point that a year without seeing a dear friend seems less daunting than a few hours without the phone.

Still, text messages may be our last, best surrogate for the intimacy of "real" communication. As Herberth Chacon observes in *I Like You...on Facebook*, "Whatever the limitations of this
80 new medium of communication, people are interacting on a day-to-day basis with more people than their ancestors might have met in a lifetime." Text messages have gained such currency because, for all their flaws, they do bring us together. After all, even if the words "I love you" are flashing up impersonally on
85 a screen—stripped of all tone and affection—the words are nice

to hear nonetheless, and even if our new definition of "friends" may not square with the old definition, it's nice to know there's a world out there that's paying attention to us.

1. The main idea of the passage is that:

   A. telephone conversations are defunct because they are so impermanent.
   B. telephones took the place of serious long-letter writing.
   C. text messages do not provide real interactions for the people who send them.
   D. text messaging is a popular medium whose social effects are debatable.

2. Based on the passage, with which of the following statements would Fields most likely agree?

   F. The frequent use of text messaging can limit people's other human experiences.
   G. Internet users lost their capacity for human experience when they started using Google.
   H. Text messages provide a quick, intimate way for people to communicate.
   J. Text messages force people to write more thoughtfully to one another.

3. How does the passage's author directly support her claim that the text message is more than a simple message?

   A. By citing examples from American culture in which text messaging plays a role
   B. By describing famous novels about the cultural role of texting in American society
   C. By listing the accomplishments of the two German men who created the medium of text messaging
   D. By showing that text messaging was initially limited to 160 characters

4. The passage's author most likely discusses the era before the War of Independence to:

   F. demonstrate how historical figures refused to use text-messaging technology.
   G. prompt the reader to do more research into the history of communication.
   H. give a fun digression in an otherwise dry discussion of communication media.
   J. show that forms of communication can provide historical records.

5. Which of the following people think or act in a way that is most similar to that of the naysayers described in the fifth paragraph (lines 43-60)?

   A. Scientists who see improvements in medicine as an improvement in the quality of life
   B. Sports journalists who say that a change in rules will destroy the integrity of a sport
   C. Novelists who prefer to write on computers rather than with pen and paper
   D. Historians who would prefer to read official documents rather than letters

6. According to the passage, of the following, who were the earliest contributors to the development of the medium of the text message?

   F. Fields and Chacon
   G. Scorsese and Franzen
   H. Franzen and Wallace
   J. Hillebrand and Ghillebaert

7. A character in a short story published in 1994 had this to say about text messages:

   Say what you will about the "decline of real interaction"—I've had plenty of them that would've felt a lot more real if they'd happened in a sentence or two rather than a two-hour phone conversation.

   Based on the passage, would Hillebrand agree or disagree with this statement?

   A. Disagree, because 160 characters proved to be an inadequate number of characters.
   B. Disagree, because he ultimately believed that most communication should occur by letter.
   C. Agree, because he felt that the telephone was no longer an effective communicator.
   D. Agree, because he thought that 160 characters was adequate to express most messages concisely.

8. Based on the passage, why might *The Departed* have been considered a film interested in contemporary issues?

   F. It made a recent communication medium, text messaging, central to its story.
   G. Its actors spoke in favor of text messaging, and the medium exploded in popularity after the film's release.
   H. It won an important award in honor of the quality of the filmmaking.
   J. It showed that letter writing was no longer a sufficient way to communicate.

9. Based on the passage, when the author cites the saying "time is money" (line 23), she most likely means that a text message:

   A. is an inexpensive way to send a message.
   B. keeps a long-lasting record of people's conversations.
   C. is a quick way for people to communicate.
   D. allows an intimacy that can otherwise take a long time to develop.

10. Based on the passage, Chacon suggests the number of people with whom people's ancestors might have had interactions in order to:

    F. state that the family unit is no longer as important as it once was.
    G. suggest that new media can connect people in new ways.
    H. imply that people in older times should have traveled more.
    J. encourage readers to explore what their ancestors said in letters.

Summary

- Use the 4-Step Basic Approach.

- Step 1: Preview. Check the blurb, and map the questions. Star line and paragraph references and underline lead words.

- Step 2: Work the Passage. Finish in 2–3 minutes. Look for and underline lead words. One option is to focus on only the first sentence of each paragraph.

- Step 3: Work the Questions. Do Now questions that are easy to answer or whose answers are easy to find. Read what you need in a window of 5–10 lines to find your answer. Save for Later questions that are both hard to find and hard to answer.

- Step 4: Work the Answers. Use POE to find your answer, particularly on Reasoning questions.

- Skim and scan when you work the passage.

- Read windows of text when you work the questions.

- Look for topic sentences and transition words.

Chapter 18
Advanced Reading Skills

In this lesson, we'll help you hone your skills to crack specific question types and the most challenging of difficult text. We'll also build on your mastery of the 4-Step Basic Approach by teaching you advanced POE (Process of Elimination) strategies.

LATER QUESTIONS

On the Reading test, some questions appear in unique formats that make them stand out among the Referral and Reasoning questions. These questions still require you to show your understanding of what is directly stated or what is implied. However, it's useful to have specific strategies to crack these.

Negatives

The test writers can throw a curveball at you when they ask a question in the negative using EXCEPT, LEAST, or NOT to twist the task. These questions are inherently tricky. What's right is wrong, and the right answer is the one that's wrong. Clear as a bell, isn't it?

No wonder it's so easy for your brain to trip all over itself. You may even start off trying to find the one choice that is false. But you somehow lose sight of the trap, and when you come across one of the answers in the passage, you think, "Eureka! This answer is true. I found it right here." Of course it's "right" in the passage: Two other answer choices are somewhere in the passage as well. It's the choice that isn't in the passage that is the "right" answer.

Here's a better approach. Let's take a look at a question after it has been previewed in Step 1.

> The 4-Step Basic Approach
> Step 1: **Preview.** Check the blurb, and map the questions. Underline lead words and star line or paragraph references.
> Step 2: **Work the Passage.** Spend 2–3 minutes reading the passage.
> Step 3: **Work the Questions.** Use your POOD to find Now, Later, and Never Questions.
> Step 4: **Work the Answers.** Use POE.

33. The passage mentions <u>transportation of bees by river</u> in all of the following <u>countries</u> EXCEPT:

    A. Scotland.
    B. France.
    C. Poland.
    D. Egypt.

When you map the questions, underline *transportation of bees by river* and *countries,* but don't underline or mark *EXCEPT.* Wait until you work the question to deal with the trick.

This is a Referral question. If the negative weren't there, it would be easy to answer. What country transports bees by river? But it wouldn't be easy to find the answer, since there is no line or paragraph reference, and none of these lead words qualify as great.

Occasionally, an EXCEPT question will come with a line or paragraph reference to help narrow down your search, but most times they don't. The answers can be scattered throughout the passage or grouped together in one paragraph.

That's why you should always do a negative question Later. By the time you get to it, you should be able to identify where in the passage you'll find at least some of the answers, or you will have narrowed down where to look.

When you do work this question, mark the EXCEPT so your eye can help your brain. You could double underline it. You can circle it and jot down two double exclamation points. You can cross it out altogether and write "True/False," or "T/F." Do whatever you need to keep yourself focused on the goal: Identify the one answer that is not like the others.

33. The passage mentions <u>transportation of bees by river</u> in all of the following <u>countries</u> <u>EXCEPT</u>:

   A. Scotland.
   B. France.
   C. Poland.
   D. Egypt.

For question 33, the answers happen to be grouped into the same paragraph, something you would have found easier to spot by using the great lead words in the answers. Always let the answers help in an EXCEPT question.

Now use POE. Locate the countries in the window of text, and read to find out which use rivers. When you find one, cross it off in the answers.

> In Scotland, after the best of the Lowland bloom is past, the bees are carried in carts to the Highlands and set free on the heather hills. In France, too, and in Poland, they are carried from pasture to pasture among orchards and fields in the same way and
> 5 along the rivers in barges to collect the honey of the delightful vegetation of the banks. In Egypt they are taken far up the Nile and floated slowly home again, gathering the honey-harvest of the various fields on the way, timing their movements in accord with the seasons. Were similar methods pursued in California,
> 10 the productive season would last nearly all the year.

The correct answer is choice (A). All four countries are listed, but only Scotland doesn't involve *rivers*.

Answer Choice Lead Words
In any type of question, lead words may be found in the answers instead of the question.

Negative questions can be more complicated when the question type itself is Reasoning instead of Referral.

Particularly difficult are questions that ask what is NOT answered by the passage. These essentially require four times the amount of work, since you have to look for four answers instead of just one. Sometimes, the question is asked but not answered, and in others, the topic may not arise at all, both of which can frustrate you and make you waste a lot of time, scouring the passage over and over. That's why Negative questions can be good candidates for Never. If you do work a negative question, always use POE. Cross off the ones that you know are true. If you're stuck between two, or even among three, don't waste that much more time before forcing yourself to guess and move on.

These next two questions would both be the last questions you do, and you would have gained a good grasp of the passage, even the details, by reading small windows as you worked the rest of the questions.

For the purposes of this exercise, don't worry about time. Read the excerpt of the passage, and use POE.

---

36. Which of the following questions is NOT answered by information given in the passage?

   F. How many bee ranches might be successfully established in the Sierra Mountains?
   G. What types of flowers attract bees?
   H. Where did the honeybees in the Sierra Mountains come from?
   J. How much honey is produced by bee-trees in the Sierra Mountains?

38. Which of the following statements is LEAST supported by the passage?

   F. The Sierra Mountains have the appropriate requirements to support bee ranching activities.
   G. Bees flourish in the Sierra Mountains in part because the area is not hospitable to traditional cattle ranching.
   H. The presence of bees in the Sierra Mountains prevents sheep from grazing in certain areas.
   J. Bee-ranching is an economically viable and environmentally sound enterprise.

The Sierra region is the largest of the three main divisions of the bee-lands of the State, and the most regularly varied in its subdivisions, owing to its gradual rise from the level of the Central Plain to the alpine summits. Up through the forest region,
5 to a height of about 9,000 feet above sea-level, there are ragged patches of manzanita and five or six species of ceanothus, called deer-brush or California lilac. These are the most important of all the honey-bearing bushes of the Sierra.

From swarms that escaped their owners in the lowlands,
10 the honey-bee is now generally distributed throughout the whole length of the Sierra, up to an elevation of 8,000 feet above sea-level. At this height they flourish without care, though the snow every winter is deep. Even higher than this, several bee-trees have been cut, which contained over 200 pounds of honey. Wild
15 bees and butterflies have been seen feeding at a height of 13,000 feet above the sea.

The destructive action of sheep has not been so general on the mountain pastures as on those of the great plain. Fortunately, neither sheep nor cattle care to feed on the manzanita, spiraea, or
20 adenostoma; these fine honey-bushes are too stiff and tall or grow in places too rough and inaccessible to be trodden under foot. Also the canyon walls and gorges, which form so considerable a part of the area of the range, while inaccessible to domestic sheep, are well fringed with honey-shrubs and contain thousands of lovely
25 bee-gardens, lying hidden in narrow side-canyons and recesses fenced with avalanche taluses, and on the top of flat, projecting headlands, where only bees would think to look for them.

The plow has not yet invaded the forest region to any appreciable extent, nor has it accomplished much in the foot-hills.
30 Thousands of bee-ranches might be established along the margin of the plain and up to a height of 4,000 feet, wherever water could be obtained. The climate at this elevation admits of the making of permanent homes, and by moving the hives to higher pastures as the lower pass out of bloom, the annual yield of honey would
35 be nearly doubled. The foot-hill pastures, as we have seen, fail about the end of May; those of the chaparral belt and lower forests are in full bloom in June, those of the upper and alpine region in July, August, and September.

Of all the upper flower fields of the Sierra, Shasta is the
40 most honeyful, and may yet surpass in fame the celebrated honey hills of Hybla and hearthy Hymettus. In this flowery wilderness the bees rove and revel, rejoicing in the bounty of the sun, clambering eagerly through bramble and hucklebloom, ringing the myriad bells of the manzanita, now humming aloft among
45 polleny willows and firs, now down on the ashy ground among gilias and buttercups, and anon plunging deep into snowy banks of cherry and buckthorn....

Here's How to Crack Them

Work questions 36 and 38 as your last questions. For 36, double underline, circle, or cross off the NOT when you work it. As you find the answers to the answer choices—that is, the answers to the questions in the answer choices—cross off that choice. Choice (F) is answered in lines 31–33. Choice (G) is answered in lines 7–8 and again in 18–22. Choice (H) is answered in line 31–33. Choice (J) is never answered, and it is therefore the correct answer.

Question 38 is less specific and less dependent on detail than is question 36. Remember, the answers to your questions should all agree with each other, at least in terms of reinforcing the main points. Double underline, circle, or cross off the LEAST, and use POE for any answer that doesn't reinforce the theme in the rest of the questions. Choice (H) is not supported by the passage and is therefore the correct answer. Choices (F) and (J) describe positive benefits of bees to the Sierra Mountains, and they would likely be the easiest choices to eliminate right away. Choice (G) is supported by lines 18–28.

Vocabulary in Context

In some Referral questions, you'll have to determine the meaning of a word or phrase as it's used in context. The level of the vocabulary can vary, and most of these questions use relatively common words, but their meaning in the passage can be figurative more than literal.

Don't Know the Word?

If the Vocabulary in Context question tests a more difficult word that you're familiar with, you can still try to read the context to see if you can come up with your own word that fits the meaning, and then use POE among the answers. But if you can't eliminate three choices, guess from what's left and move on. Similarly, if you are pressed for time and need to get to the next passage, mark this a Never. Choose your LOTD and move on.

You don't need to read a full window of 5–10 lines for Vocabulary in Context questions, but you do need to read at least the full sentence to determine the meaning in its context. Cross off the phrase, and try to substitute your own word. Then move to the answers, and use POE to eliminate choices that don't match your word. The correct answer has to be the *literal* definition of the meaning. Don't choose a word that could be used figuratively to convey the meaning.

Let's try an example.

The plow has not yet invaded the forest region to any ap-
30 preciable extent, nor has it accomplished much in the foot-hills.
Thousands of bee-ranches might be established along the margin
of the plain and up to a height of 4000 feet, wherever water could
be obtained. The climate at this elevation admits of the making
of permanent homes, and by moving the hives to higher pastures
35 as the lower pass out of bloom, the annual yield of honey would
be nearly doubled. The foot-hill pastures, as we have seen, fail
about the end of May; those of the chaparral belt and lower forests
are in full bloom in June, those of the upper and alpine region in
July, August, and September.

37. As it is used in lines 33–36, the phrase *admits of* most nearly
means:

  A. makes possible.
  B. grants permission.
  C. confesses guilt.
  D. leaves out.

Here's How to Crack It

Admits is a common word, but it has different definitions depending on the context. The phrase *admits of* may be a less common phrase, but if you cross it out and
read the sentence, you may come up with a word like "allows." Choice (A) works
the same way "allows" does, and it's the correct answer. Choice (B) is close, but
grants is a good example of a word that could be used figuratively to mean "allows." It doesn't literally mean "allows." And *permission* doesn't work for the literal
meaning at all. A climate can't literally *permit* anything. Choice (C) is tempting if
you don't use the context of the sentence, since *confessing guilt* is a correct definition of *admits* in another context.

Roman Numerals

Roman numeral questions show up on the Reading test very rarely. They can be
used in a Referral question or in a Reference question. They may come with line
references or great lead words, or they may not. Use those factors to determine
when to work the question, but in general, Roman numeral questions are good
choices for Later when you know the passage better.

When you do work a Roman numeral question, be efficient. Choose the easiest of the Roman numerals to look up in passage. Once you know yes or no, go to the answer choices and use POE. Look up only the Roman numerals that are still in the running among the answers.

Let's try an example.

———○———

They consider the lilies and roll into them, and, like lilies, they toil not for they are impelled by sun-power, as water-wheels by water-power; and when the one has plenty of high-pressure water, the other plenty of sunshine, they hum and quiver alike.
5 Sauntering in the Shasta bee-lands in the sun-days of summer, one may readily infer the time of day from the comparative energy of bee-movements alone—drowsy and moderate in the cool of the morning, increasing in energy with the ascending sun, and, at high noon, thrilling and quivering in wild ecstasy, then gradually
10 declining again to the stillness of night.

39. The passage describes the movement of the bees during the day as which of the following?

   I.   Drowsy and moderate
   II. Thrilling and quivering
   III. Cool and still

   A. I only
   B. III only
   C. II and III only
   D. I and II only

Here's How to Crack It

Work efficiently. Use the lead words in the Roman numerals to find them in the passage, beginning with I. *Drowsy* and *moderate* are used in lines 5–10 to describe the bees in the morning. Eliminate all choices without I, which leaves you with just II to review: I and III are not both in any choice. *Thrilling* and *quivering* are used in line 9 to describe the bees at high noon. Choice (D) is correct.

———○———

Dual Reading Passages

You may also see a "Dual Passage" in Reading. You've already seen passages like this in the Science: They give two separate passages with questions about each passage individually and then passages about both together.

As such, these passages require a slightly different approach. The passages require a bit more reading than the single passages, but they are also susceptible to more strategic thinking.

Here's the strategy we'll be using in this section:

1. **Preview.** Read the blurb, and map the questions as you would in a typical passage. Do a quick count of how many questions are asked about each passage.

2. **Work the Popular Passage.** If one passage has more questions than the other, work that one first. Take the questions that ask only about that passage and reorder them chronologically, reading through the passage as you do the questions.

3. **Work the Other Passage.** Before you jump to the questions that deal with both passages, work the other the same way you worked the first. Reorder the questions chronologically, and read through the passage as you answer the questions in the new chronological order.

4. **Work the Questions that Deal with Both Passages.** By this point, you've hopefully got a good sense of what unites the passages. Answer the questions that deal with both passages, and make sure that these answers agree with the others regarding each individual passage!

A NOTE ON THE GOLDEN THREAD

As you may have noticed, correct answers seem to repeat in a lot of ACT passages. It almost seems like sometimes if you get one answer, you can get three more with the same information. We call this phenomenon "The Golden Thread": some main idea or topic that threads through many of the answer choices.

On Dual Passages, it's more important than ever to find the Golden Thread. If you think about it, the questions that ask about both passages are really just variations on the theme, "What do these two passages have to do with each other?"

As you read through the two passages separately, try to answer this question even if only in a vague way. "What's the link between these two passages?" "Why are these passages on the same page together?" Any kinds of answers you can generate to these "Golden Thread"-type questions will help you down the line.

Here is what one of the passages will look like. Note how kindly ACT has separated the questions for you.

HUMANITIES: Passage A is adapted from the essay "From West Orange to Paris and Back" by Ashley C. Throckmorton. Passage B is adapted from the essay "Train Robberies and Magic" by Abigal Colorado Tintype.

Passage A

While it may be impossible to know when the history of the cinema properly begins, there is no question that it had its first real flowering in the late-nineteenth and early-twentieth centuries. The history of photography goes back much further—
5 to the 1830s at least—, but the history of cinema properly began when the technological advancements caught up with the theoretical advancements in photography. English photographer Eadweard Muybridge was the first to figure out how to take photographs in rapid enough succession as to produce the illusion
10 of movement. First created in 1877, his series of photographs of "animal locomotion" (a running horse in Muybridge's case) look like early film strips, as they seem to capture the horse's movement in minute intervals.

Around this same time, Thomas Edison invented one of
15 the most popular technologies of the century: the phonograph. In 1888, Edison wanted a visual component to add to the now near-universal phonograph, and he commissioned one of his lab assistants, William Dickson, to do so. Dickson incorporated the work of Muybridge and others into a series of mechanisms
20 that could both record motion-pictures and then play them back. The tangible result of this process was the Kinetoscope, which would, with internal battery power, "play" the pictures in rapid enough succession that they produced the illusion of continuous movement. Edison established a Kinetograph studio in West
25 Orange, NJ, where he and his assistants made short pieces for the Kinetoscope, usually portraying simple actions like kisses or individual dances. As the phonograph had before it, the Kinetoscope took the world by storm.

Inspired by Edison's invention, two French brothers, Au-
30 guste and Louis Lumière, sought to make it more available for public consumption. To that end, they invented the first commercially viable projector, the *cinématographe*, which made the single-viewer mechanism of the Kinetoscope available to many viewers at once. Where the Kinetoscope could weigh
35 more than 1,000 pounds, the *cinématographe* weighed only 20. As a result, the Lumières were able to shoot much larger scenes and did not require the stability of a particular studio as Edison had. Their most famous film, "The Arrival of a Train at La Ciotat Train Station," was just that, and while it may be dull
40 by contemporary standards, this simple 50-second film thrilled and amazed audiences.

Here, from the hands of nearly a half-century of inventors, was the birth of the cinema. We have them to thank when we go to the movies or even, one could argue, watch videos on our
45 computers and video-chat on our phones. Indeed, if we are able to suspend our disbelief for just a moment, we can put ourselves back in that early cinema moment. Watch the Lumière film of the arriving train in just the right mood, and it can fill you with the same wonder that overtook the original audiences.

Passage B

50 While the history of the cinema is inconceivable without the efforts of Thomas Edison and Lumière brothers, they in fact contributed little more than the invention of a technology. After all, when we think of the cultural force that the cinema has become, we do not refer to the miniature documentary curiosi-
55 ties of the Kinetoscope. Without this mechanism, the cinema would have been impossible, but Edison and the Lumières are no more responsible for the history of the cinema than a dairy farmer is responsible for a delicious milkshake.

The real birth of the cinema began in the early years of
60 the twentieth century. With the technology that had been given to him, a French magician named Georges Méliès started to experiment. As a magician, Méliès saw the new film cameras as working in his professional favor: He saw the cinema as producing illusions along the lines of those he created on the
65 stage. In the nearly 500 films he produced between 1896 and 1913, Méliès not only showed the artistic capabilities of "trick" cinema. He also created some of the first and most complex narrative films ever to be seen on screen: *A Trip to the Moon* (1902) was 14 minutes long and had 30 scenes.

70 Around this same time, a former Edison employee, the American Edwin S. Porter, was creating some narrative films of his own. Porter worked as a projectionist for the Edison company, where he would arrange fifteen-minute programs from a series of short films. This assembly no doubt inspired
75 Porter to think of how a narrative film could be assembled, and Porter was the first to see that scenes could be portrayed from multiple perspectives at once. Inspired by but departing from Méliès's theatrically staged narrative films, Porter found a new way, one that was only available in the cinema. In *The Great*
80 *Train Robbery* (1903), Porter used a technique that has since been dubbed parallel editing, which enabled him to tell the story of both the train robbers and the train passengers themselves in different places for much of the film's action, at what seemed to be the same time.

85 Therefore, while the contributions of Edison and the Lumières are indispensable, the cinema as we know it today began a few years later with Porter and Méliès. Indeed, the cinema has its cultural power today because of its *artistic* achievements, not merely its technological ones. Edison and Lumières may
90 have provided the canvas, but Porter and Méliès were the first to use that canvas to create real art.

21. According to information in the second paragraph (lines 14–28), the early film camera was related to the phonograph in that the camera was:

    A. conceived as a technology to accompany the sounds produced by the phonograph.
    B. designed to replace the phonograph within fifteen to twenty years.
    C. inspired by the work of Eadweard Muybridge, the inventor of the phonograph.
    D. limited by its weight and size in the same way that the phonograph was.

22. According to Throckmorton, the primary advantage of the *cinématographe* over the Kinetoscope was that the *cinématographe* was:

    F. invented in France, where inventors could take proper credit for their inventions.
    G. mobile in a way that the Kinetoscope was not and could therefore capture new subjects on film.
    H. able to shoot films that were as much as fifty seconds longer than Kinetoscope films.
    J. intimate for the viewer in a way that the Kinetoscope's large projections could not be.

23. The word "play" (line 20) is set off in quotation marks in order to signify that the:

    A. Kinetoscope was invented before movies were considered fun to watch.
    B. *cinématographe* was the first film technology to use electricity.
    C. films produced by the Kinetoscope were intended mainly for children.
    D. technology used still photographs to produce the illusion of motion.

24. According to Throckmorton, why do contemporary viewers have Edison and the Lumières "to thank" (line 43)?

    F. Edison and the Lumières created some of the first and most thrilling narrative films of the nineteenth century.
    G. Edison and the Lumières popularized the inventions of William Dickson and Eadweard Muybridge.
    H. Edison and the Lumières contributed to the invention of a technology that is now almost universally accessible.
    J. Edison and the Lumières contributed major parts to the invention of the computer and smartphone.

25. When Tintype states that Edison and the Lumières "provided the canvas" but that Méliès and Porter were the first "to create real art," (lines 89–91) she most nearly means that:

    A. the narrative innovations of Porter and Méliès would have been possible without the work of Edison and the Lumières.
    B. the narrative innovations of Porter and Méliès were less significant in the history of science than the work of Edison and the Lumières.
    C. the technological innovations of Edison and the Lumières were not supposed to be used to create narrative films.
    D. the technological innovations of Edison and the Lumières enabled the early cinematic achievements of Porter and Méliès.

26. According to Tintype, Porter and Méliès are the true inventors of the cinema because they:

    F. made the first blockbuster films that made significant amounts of money.
    G. proposed that films should be longer than a few seconds.
    H. introduced the artistic elements that made cinema a cultural force.
    J. predicted that films would one day be universally accessible.

27. Tintype compares Edison and the Lumières to "a dairy farmer" (lines 57–58) in order to suggest that:

    A. those who produce the raw material do not necessarily deserve credit for what is done with that raw material.
    B. people who cannot invent significant technologies should consider work in industries where they will be more useful.
    C. scientific innovators maximize their use of resources in order to produce things that people find interesting or necessary.
    D. some of the most interesting technological innovations come from those who work in the field of agriculture.

28. The accounts of Throckmorton and Tintype are similar in that they believe:

F. Porter and Méliès were the true inventors of the medium of film as a storytelling medium.

G. cinema's greatest achievements would not have been possible without the work of Edison and the Lumières.

H. the history of film would have been much different if the Lumières had perfected their camera before Edison perfected his.

J. Méliès's background in magic suited him especially well for work in the illusionistic medium of cinema.

29. What is the main component of Tintype's essay that is not addressed in Throckmorton's essay?

A. Technological innovation
B. Particular films
C. Camera size
D. Narrative storytelling

30. Throckmorton would most likely see *A Trip to the Moon* as:

F. a copy of a Lumière film produced ten years earlier.
G. superior to Porter's *Great Train Robbery*.
H. an extension of earlier technological innovations.
J. the subpar work of an amateur magician.

How to Work Through a Dual-Passage Reading Section

Step 1: Preview

As the blurb indicates, these passages are adapted from a couple of essays. It doesn't tell much more than that. Lead words include *early film camera*, *phonograph*, *cinématographe*, *kinetoscope*, *Edison*, *Lumière*, *Méliès*, *Porter*, and *A Trip to the Moon*.

Then, a quick count will show that there are more questions about Passage A than there are about Passage B. Let's do Passage A first!

Step 2: Work the Passage

Before you start reading, rearrange the questions chronologically. Use lead words where there aren't any line references. In this case, it looks like the questions will appear in roughly this order: 23, 21, 22, 24.

Read through the passage and stop as you come to the lines in each questions. The questions are in order, so you don't have to think too much about missing anything.

Use the techniques you've learned throughout these reading chapters! POE still applies like crazy, and bad answers are just as bad here as they are in any other passage.

Step 3: Work the Other Passage

Rinse and repeat! These questions will fall roughly into this order chronologically: 27, 25, 26. Work through these questions, always looking to eliminate bad answers.

Step 4: Work the Questions that Deal With Both Passages

By this point, you have hopefully noticed what unites these passages. Passage A sees Edison and the Lumières as the inventors of the cinema because they invented the cameras. Passage B sees Méliès and Porter as the inventors because they made it a narrative form.

Use your POOD as you answer the remaining questions!

Check your answers here:

21. A
22. G
23. D
24. H
25. D
26. H
27. A
28. G
29. D
30. H

CRITICAL READING

Your use of the 4-Step Basic Approach and your personal order of difficulty (POOD) of both passages and questions should by now make you feel more confident on the Reading test. But you also may still be struggling with time and feel that you just can't work fast enough to get to enough questions.

In Chapter 17, we discussed ways to use your time better when you preview and work the passage. But you may also be wasting time when you work the questions, reading and rereading the window of text, trying to figure out what it's saying. You may have eliminated two answers but when you're still not sure what the correct answer is, what do you do? You read the window yet again, desperate to figure out the meaning and answer the question in your own words.

We've all been there. Part of what makes standardized tests so evil is how they encourage us to listen to our worst instincts. You can't treat the Reading test as you would a school assignment, and you can't fall prey to your own panicked responses. You have to develop both strategies and skills specific to *this* test.

Critical Thinking

The key to better reading skills is to *think* better, which means to think critically. Getting lost in even a small window of text that makes no sense is like getting lost on unfamiliar roads. You don't stare down at the yellow line. You look around, looking for landmarks and road signs, trying to figure out where you are and where the road is going.

When you're lost in a tough section of text, use topic sentences and transitions as your landmarks and road signs. Don't try to understand every single word. Use the topic sentences to identify what the main point of the paragraph is. Look for transitions to see if points are on the same or different sides from each other.

Topic Sentences and Main Points

Think of how you write papers for school. A good topic sentence makes clear the main subject of the paragraph, and it may even provide the author's main point on the subject. The rest of the paragraph will be details or examples that explain that point, and it may also include a more explicit conclusion of the main point. If you don't understand the details, read the main point to know what they mean. Examples and details usually come right before or right after the main point. If you don't understand the details, read the sentence before or after to see if it gives you the main point. If you don't understand the main point, read the sentence before or after to see if the details explain it for you.

Let's see how this works. Read the following topic sentence.

> Studies of American middle and high school students have shown that there is considerable uncertainty among students about what behaviors count as cheating.

What's going to come next in the paragraph? It could be examples of the behaviors. It could be an explanation of why students are uncertain. It could even be a statement of a different study that contradicts this one. You would be safe anticipating any of those outcomes, but the anticipation is the key. Don't sit back and wait to see where the road is going. Lean forward and look for the fork in the road or the detour sign telling you to turn around. In other words, look for transitions.

Transitions

The first word or phrase after the topic sentence can tell you what direction you're heading.

Let's look at some choices for our cheating sentence.

If the next words were *In particular*, what does that tell you is coming next? Examples of the behavior.

If the next word were *However*, what does that tell you is coming next? A contradiction to this study.

Transitions play a key role in critical thinking. Look for transitions to announce additional points, contradictory points, cause and effect relationships, examples, or conclusions. Here are just a few common transitions.

Additional Points	Cause and Effect Relationships
And	Because
Also	Since
As well	So
In addition	
Furthermore	
Moreover	Examples
	For example
	In particular
Contradictory Points	Such as
Although	
But	
Even though	Conclusions
However	Consequently
Nevertheless	In other words
On the other hand	That is
Rather	Therefore
Yet	Thus

Modifiers

Nouns and verbs reliably give you the facts in a statement, but they don't necessarily provide the author's point. Look at the two adverbs in the prior sentence and see how they helped shape the point. *Reliably* means you can infer that nouns and verbs *almost always* give facts. *Necessarily* modifies the verb phrase *don't provide*. Without it, you could infer that nouns and verbs never give you the point. Adjectives and adverbs are just as useful as transitions, conveying the author's opinion on what would otherwise be a statement of fact.

Consider this sentence.

> Surprisingly, students do not consider sharing notes to be cheating.

The point of this sentence is that *sharing notes* is a form of *cheating*, and the author believes students should know this. If you removed *surprisingly* from the sentence, it's just a factual statement of what students think. On the Reading test, most Reasoning questions involve the author's opinion or main point, or as ACT puts it, "the implied meaning."

Try another.

> Students offered a refreshingly candid explanation for their behavior.

Refreshingly means that the author judged the admission as unexpected but welcome. *Candid* means the students were honest and open.

Translation

When you're struggling to make sense of a window of confusing text, look for transitions and modifiers to help you determine the main point. You may be in the thick of a body paragraph with the topic sentence in the rearview mirror. Instead of focusing on every single word, use the transitions and modifiers to get the general direction of points and the connections between them.

Let's look at a tough window to see how this works.

The strikingly tolerant attitudes demonstrated by the students toward cheating cannot be explained by mere immorality and laziness, but may rather point to a sobering conclusion that high-stakes tests have created a ruthless atmosphere in which
5   students are desperate to succeed at any cost.

Here's How to Crack It

Focus on the transitions and modifiers. *Strikingly* tells you that the author finds the students' tolerance of cheating noteworthy and unusual. The key verb phrase *cannot be explained* directs you away from what <u>is not</u> the cause and the transitions *but* and *rather* direct you to what <u>is</u> the cause. Even if you didn't understand all the vocabulary words, the transitions act as huge road signs that identify the most important part of the sentence. Students don't cheat because of *immorality* and *laziness* but because *high-stakes tests* have made things *ruthless* and *desperate*. Even just knowing which sentence, or which part of the sentence, to focus on will help, along with POE, to find the right answer.

ADVANCED POE SKILLS

When you're stuck on a confusing window of text, the best use of your time is spent working the answers. Reread your window, even to spot transitions and modifiers, in conjunction with working the answers.

In an ideal situation, you read a question, read the window of text looking for your answer, answer the question in your own words, and then work through the answer choices looking for the best match, using POE to get rid of those that don't.

But situations are seldom ideal on the Reading test. When you don't quite understand the window and therefore have no clue about the answer, go straight to working the answers.

The Art of Wrong Answers

If you worked for ACT, you'd have to sit in a cubicle all day writing test questions. The easy part of the job is writing the correct answer. You may even know that before you write the question. The harder part is coming up with three wrong answers. If you didn't write great wrong answers, everyone would get a 36. So you have to come up with temptingly wrong answers.

Let's take a look at some ways to make wrong answers.

Read the following question, correct answer, and text. We don't care about the right answer in this exercise, so you can read it before you read the window.

13. The main point of the fifth paragraph (lines 40–48) is that:

    A. cultural norms affect how students judge cheating behaviors.

40   The authors of one such study contend that differences between German students and the other students in the study regarding what constitutes cheating can be explained by differences in social norms. In particular, German students viewed passive cheating more as "helping others" or "cooperation" rather than
45 as unethical or immoral behavior. Costa Rican students also were more liberal than Americans in their views of passive cheating, also due to a cultural tendency toward cooperation rather than competition.

Our goal here is to examine *why* the three wrong answers are wrong.

    B. German students consider passive cheating to be unethical and immoral.

Look carefully at line 45. Choice (B) took tempting words out of the passage and garbled them. The passage disproves this answer.

> **C.** American students have a less liberal view of passive cheating than do Costa Rican students.

Since lines 45–48 say Costa Rican students are *more liberal than Americans*, (C) is true. But it's not the correct answer because it's not the main point of the paragraph.

> **D.** Russian students do not consider passive cheating to be unethical.

Russian students are not mentioned in this window and have instead been taken from a different window.

Answers can be wrong because they don't match what the passage says, because they answer the wrong question, or because they're not even found in the right window. But no matter how tempting or obvious wrong answers are, they are all easier to understand than 5–10 lines of text, simply because they're shorter. So when you're stuck on tough questions on tough windows, work backwards with the answers.

Work Backwards

Instead of rereading the window to try to determine the meaning, read the answer choices for their meaning. Then see if you can match each back into the passage.

> Read to understand the meaning of the answer choices instead of rereading the window.
>
> • Look for lead words or phrases in the answer choices.
> • Determine if the words match those found in the window.
> • Use POE to cross off choices that don't match the window.

Let's see how this works. Read the following question and window.

> The dictionary defines cheating as unfairly gaining advantage in a given situation by deliberately violating established rules. Cheating behaviors may include plagiarism, copying exam answers, using crib notes, obtaining test questions beforehand (all
> 5 active behaviors), as well as allowing others to copy from you, taking advantage of teacher scoring errors, and failing to report cheating (more passive behaviors). The definition of cheating is not under debate, but the way that students define their behavior, in relation to this definition, and how morally acceptable they
> 10 deem such behavior, is. In other words, there is a large variance regarding which behaviors students consider to be cheating.

13. It can reasonably be inferred that the author provides the dictionary definition of cheating (lines 1–2) in order to:

Take the answer choices one at a time. In each choice, we've put in bold a lead word or phrase in the answer. Can you match these words, or a paraphrased meaning of them, in the window of text?

A. argue that passive behaviors **are more morally acceptable** than active behaviors.

Morally acceptable appears in line 9, but the phrase isn't used to compare *passive* and *active behaviors*. Tempting, but wrong.

B. illustrate what behaviors will get students **expelled or suspended**.

Expelled and *suspended*, or any paraphrases of those words, don't appear anywhere in the window, so (B) can't be the right answer.

C. prove that students **deliberately violate established rules**.

Deliberately violating established rules appears in line 2, but it's used as part of the definition of cheating, not as proof of students' conduct. We've eliminated three answers, so (D) must be right. But always check all four answers to be sure the one you choose is better than the three you've eliminated.

D. show that students may not consider their own **behavior to be cheating**.

Students' *own behavior* is in the last sentence, and (D) matches well the point of that sentence.

Try another example. Choose your own words or phrases out of each answer to work backwards with. Does the passage match the answer?

Patterns of individual cheating behavior in different societies typically reflect their respective normative climates. Students recognize certain activities as cheating and may be able to pro-
60 vide justifications for their unethical behavior in some way. Yet cheating, when identified as such, is overall felt to be wrong. However, an eye-opening study of Russian university students' cheating behaviors by Yulia Poltorak reveals a different type of normative climate that is a unique part of the Communist legacy.
65 According to this study, cheating behavior in Soviet Russia was not only very widespread, but also widely accepted as an appropriate response to social conditions.

12. It can reasonably be inferred by information in the seventh paragraph (lines 57–67) that:

   F. cheating in Soviet Russia was widely rejected as an acceptable response.
   G. the cold climate in Russian classrooms motivated students to cheat.
   H. the normative climate that produced cheating in Soviet Russia may be explained by the role of the Communist legacy.
   J. students in Soviet Russia failed to provide justifications for their unethical behavior.

Here's How to Crack It

In (F), you could choose *widely rejected* and try to place it in line 66. The passage disproves this, stating that cheating is *widely accepted*, so cross off (F). Choice (G) misuses the word *climate*, but it also discusses *classrooms*, which are nowhere to be found in the passage. Eliminate it. Choice (H) offers *Communist legacy*, an easy lead word phrase to locate in the passage. Choice (H) could match lines 62–64, so keep it. Choice (J) offers *justifications for their unethical behavior*, words right out of the passage. But the passage doesn't state that Russian students *failed to provide* them. The correct answer is (H).

Reading Drill 2

Use the 4-Step Basic Approach on the following passage, and apply your advanced reading skills. Time yourself to complete in 8–10 minutes. Check your answers in Chapter 24.

Passage I

PROSE FICTION: This passage is taken from *The Heart Is a Lonely Hunter*, by Carson McCullers (© 1940 and 1967 by Carson McCullers).

The sun woke Mick early, although she had stayed out late the night before. It was too hot even to drink coffee for breakfast, so she had ice water with syrup in it and cold biscuits. She messed around the kitchen for a while and then went out
5 on the front porch to read the funnies. She had thought maybe Mister Singer would be reading the paper on the porch like he did most Sunday mornings. But Mister Singer was not there, and later on her dad said he came in the night before and had company in his room. She waited for Mister Singer a long
10 time. All the other boarders came down except him. Finally, she went back into the kitchen and took Ralph out of his high chair and put a clean dress on him and wiped off his face. Then when Bubber got home from Sunday School she was ready to take the kids out. She let Bubber ride in the wagon with Ralph
15 because he was barefooted and the hot sidewalk burned his feet. She pulled the wagon for about eight blocks until they came to the big, new house that was being built. The ladder was still propped against the edge of the roof, and she screwed up nerve and began to climb.

20 "You mind Ralph," she called back to Bubber. "Mind the gnats don't sit on his eyelids."

Five minutes later Mick stood up and held herself very straight. She spread out her arms like wings. This was the place where everyone wanted to stand. The very top. But if you lost
25 your grip and rolled off the edge it would kill you. All around were the roofs of other houses and the green top of trees. On the other side of town were the church steeples and the smokestacks from the mills. The sky was bright blue and hot as fire. The sun made everything on the ground either dizzy white or black.

30 She wanted to sing. All the songs she knew pushed up toward her throat, but there was no sound. One big boy who had got to the highest part of the roof last week let out a yell and then started hollering out a speech he had learned in High School—"Friends, Romans, Countrymen, Lend me your ears!"
35 There was something about getting to the very top that gave you a wild feeling and made you want to yell or sing or raise up your arms and fly.

She felt the soles of her tennis shoes slipping and eased herself down so that she straddled the peak of the roof. The house
40 was almost finished. It would be one of the largest buildings in the neighborhood—two stories, with very high ceilings and the steepest roof of any house she had ever seen. But soon the work would be all finished. The carpenters would leave and the kids would have to find another place to play.

45 She was by herself. No one was around and it was quiet and she could think for a while. She took from the pocket of her shorts the package of cigarettes she had bought the night before. She breathed in the smoke slowly. The cigarettes gave her a drunk feeling so that her head seemed heavy and loose
50 on her shoulders, but she had to finish it.

M.K.—That was what she would have written on everything when she was seventeen years old and very famous. She would ride back home in a red-and-white Packard automobile with her initials on the doors. She would have M.K. written in red
55 on her handkerchiefs and underclothes. Maybe she would be a great inventor. She would invent tiny little radios the size of a green pea that people would carry around and stick in their ears. Also flying machines people could fasten on their backs like knapsacks and go zipping all over the world. After that she
60 would be the first one to make a large tunnel through the world to China, and people would go down in big balloons. Those were the first things she would invent. They were already planned.

When Mick had finished half of the cigarette she smashed it dead and flipped the butt down slant on the roof. The she
65 leaned forward so that her head rested on her arms and began to hum to herself.

1. As it is used in line 18, the phrased *screwed up* most nearly means:

   A. lost.
   B. made a mistake.
   C. examined.
   D. gathered.

2. If the passage describes a typical Sunday, Mick then spends part of her Sundays:

   F. learning grammar from Mister Singer.
   G. cooking breakfast for her family.
   H. going to Sunday School.
   J. caring for her younger brothers.

3. Mick believes that the other children in the neighborhood:

    A. did not want to play with her.
    B. also liked to climb the roof.
    C. thought that Mick was crazy for climbing the rooftop.
    D. had more housework then she did.

4. The name of Mick's father is:

    F. Ralph.
    G. Bubber.
    H. Mister Singer.
    J. not mentioned in the passage.

5. It can be reasonably inferred that one of the reasons that Mick enjoyed being on the roof was that:

    A. she could enjoy some time alone.
    B. her friends did not believe that she could do it and she liked proving them wrong.
    C. she felt very athletic while climbing.
    D. she knew that she was the only one who could climb that high.

6. It is suggested that no sound came out of Mick's throat (line 31) because she:

    F. did not think she had a good singing voice.
    G. could not express all that she was feeling.
    H. was afraid of heights.
    J. did not want to scare her brothers by yelling too loudly.

7. It can be inferred from the passage that Mister Singer is:

    A. Mick's father.
    B. a boarder at Mick's house.
    C. a schoolteacher.
    D. a journalist.

8. All the following are included in the list of things Mick would like to invent EXCEPT:

    F. a miniature radio.
    G. a small flying machine.
    H. a big balloon.
    J. a tunnel through the earth.

9. The house that Mick climbs onto is:

    A. three stories tall.
    B. on a hill.
    C. unfinished.
    D. owned by a celebrity.

10. According to the passage, it can be reasonably inferred that Mick spent a great deal of time wishing:

    F. to be famous.
    G. to have children.
    H. to get good grades in school.
    J. to spend more time with her mother.

Summary

- Work special question types Later. They require more work than a typical question, and they will become easier to do the later you do them.

- Double underline, circle, or cross out negative words EXCEPT, LEAST, or NOT. Use POE to cross off answers that are found in the passage.

- For Vocabulary in Context questions, read the entire sentence. Cross off the word or phrase and come up with your own word. Use POE to eliminate answers that don't match your word.

- Work Roman numeral questions efficiently, using POE.

- Don't waste time on special question types if you can't eliminate three answers. Guess from the choices that are remaining and move on.

- Use topic sentences, transitions, and modifiers to help translate confusing windows of text.

- Work backwards with answer choices. Try to match the answer to the passage instead of the passage to the answer.

Part V
How to Crack the ACT Science Test

Chapter 19
Introduction to the ACT Science Test

The ACT Science test always comes fourth, after the Reading test and before the optional Writing test. Fatigue can negatively affect even the founding president of the I Heart Science Club. Even if the Science test were first, many students would find it the most intimidating and feel that they need to crack open their freshman bio textbooks. But this is not a test of science facts: It is instead a test of how well you look up and synthesize information from tables, graphs, illustrations, and passages.

To maximize your score on the Science test, you need to work the passages in a personal order of difficulty. We'll teach you how to order the passages, and we'll teach you how to employ a strategic and efficient approach that will earn you your highest possible score.

WHAT'S ON THE SCIENCE TEST

Remember when you had to study for that tough biology exam, memorizing dozens of facts about things like meiosis, mitosis, and mitochondria? When you sat down to take the test, you either knew the answers or you didn't. Well, that's not the case on the ACT Science test. Even though the word *science* appears in the title, this test doesn't look much like the tests you've taken in your high school science classes. Like the English and Reading tests, the Science test is passage-based, but most of the passages present the really important content in figures rather than in text.

The Format
You have 35 minutes to do 40 questions, split up among 6 or 7 passages.

On the Science test, you have 35 minutes to spend on 6 or 7 passages and a total of 40 questions. There are 3 types of passages, but unlike in the Reading test, the order of the passages will vary every time. We'll go into more detail about the 3 types of passages later in this chapter.

What Do You Need to Know?

For the topics of the passages, ACT pulls content from biology, chemistry, physics, and the Earth/space sciences such as astronomy, geology, and meteorology. While you won't be quizzed on specific facts, background familiarity with the topics certainly helps. If the passage is on genetics, you'll undoubtedly do better if you've recently finished that unit in school and know it cold. But the information you need in order to answer the questions is offered in the passage itself, most frequently presented in a table, graph, or illustration of some kind. The ACT Science test is an open-book test, and you do not need advanced knowledge of any science topic.

You may not need an encyclopedic knowledge of science facts. You *do* need good scientific reasoning skills, a personalized pacing strategy, and a smart, effective approach to working the passages. You also need to be flexible, ready to adapt your strategy or abandon a question you've already spent way too much time on: Guess, and move on. Of all the tests on the ACT, Science is the most time-sensitive. Even the biggest science geeks find themselves barely finishing.

Outside Knowledge

Most of the questions can be answered from the information presented in the passages or figures, but be prepared for 3 to 4 questions that require outside knowledge. The outside-knowledge questions are nothing to stress over, however. There is no way to predict what the outside-knowledge questions will be on the next ACT, so there is nothing you can do to prepare; you cannot, and *should not*, try to review everything you've never learned or already forgotten. Besides, the outside-knowledge questions tend to ask about fairly basic facts, commonly addressed in intro-level high school science courses.

For example, you may need to know that a honey badger is a mammal, or you may need to identify a chemical formula as bleach, or you may need to know where acid falls on the pH scale. In any case, remember that for the overwhelming number of questions, everything that you need to answer them is right there in front of you. Use the basic approach we'll teach you in Chapter 21, and you'll do just fine.

On ACT.org, ACT identifies the skills you need for this test: "interpretation, analysis, evaluation, reasoning, and problem solving." We can boil this down to a more concise list.

You need to be able to

- look up data and trends
- make predictions
- synthesize information

But before you learn how to work the passages, you need to learn how to order them. To understand the reasoning behind the method, it's helpful to know the 3 categories of passages.

The Passages

All of the passages fall within 3 categories. The order of the passages will vary on each test, but the distribution of types of passages is always the same. To pick your order, it's less important what the passage is called than what it looks like. But it is important to know that there are 3 categories of passages and to know their similarities and differences. ACT has very formal-sounding names for the categories, so we made up our own.

Charts and Graphs (aka Data Representation)

5 Questions Each These passages will *always* come with figures: it's their purpose in life. You'll see one or more charts, tables, graphs, or illustrations. Charts and Graphs passages are intended to test your ability to understand and interpret the information that's presented. There is a total of 15 questions.

Experiments (aka Research Summaries)

6 Questions Each These passages will *usually* come with figures. They're intended to describe several experiments, and they include more text than do the Charts and Graphs passages. But the results of the experiments are frequently presented in tables or in graphs, and you may have trouble distinguishing the Experiments passages from Charts and Graphs passages. That doesn't matter, however, because in Chapter 21 we'll teach you the basic approach that applies to both types of passages. You'll never need to identify one over the other when you're taking the test. For the record, however, Experiments passages come with more questions: a grand total of 18.

Fighting Scientists (aka Conflicting Viewpoints)

1 Passage, 7 Questions This passage *sometimes* comes with figures. Even when there are figures, however, the passage is fundamentally different from the Charts and Graphs passages and the Experiments passages. That means it also requires a different way to crack it, and we'll teach you how to do just that in Chapter 22. The Fighting Scientists passage involves much more reading than you'll need to do for the other 2 types. In fact, most of the Fighting Scientists passages will feel more like the passages on the Reading test, and you'll be able to use some of the skills you learned to crack the Reading test as you compare, contrast, and synthesize the different viewpoints.

When it comes to the topics, ACT may use arguments already resolved by the scientific community as well as more cutting-edge issues that are still contested. In either case, remind yourself again that the Science test is an open-book test, providing you the information you need to answer almost all the questions.

HOW TO CRACK THE SCIENCE TEST

Order the Passages

As always on the ACT, time is your enemy. With only 35 minutes to review 6 or 7 passages and answer 40 questions, you can't afford to spend too much time on the most difficult ones only to run out of time for the easiest. ACT doesn't present the passages in order of difficulty, but on every exam, some are easier than others, while some are truly tough. What would happen if on your ACT, the most difficult came first and the easiest last? If you did them in order, you could likely run out of time without a chance to correctly answer all the questions on the easiest passage.

That's why you can't do the passages in the order ACT picks—unless that happens to match your Personal Order of Difficulty (POOD). If time is going to run out, you want it to run out on the hardest passage, not the easiest.

Now, Later, Never

We're using the term "easier" only because we're grading the passages on a curve. "Easy" is a loaded term.

Therefore, it's more useful to think of the passages as those you'd do *Now*, those you'd do *Later*, and those you'd *Never* do.

Now Passages

Your goal with all the passages is to crack the main point. You don't necessarily need to know the topic, but you do need to spot the conclusions the content offers: trends, patterns, and relationships. You will spot the main point faster when those conclusions are presented in figures rather than in text. The easier the figures are to "read," the faster you'll crack the main point.

As we explained earlier, this is not a test of science knowledge. Instead, it's a test of your scientific reasoning skills. That means spotting the trends and patterns of variables and the relationships between figures and viewpoints.

The best passages to do Now have the most obvious patterns as well as a few other common characteristics.

Look for

- **Small graphs and tables:** A good Now passage can have only tables, only graphs, or both. Tables should be no more than 3–4 rows and columns, and graphs should have no more than 3–4 lines or curves.
- **Easy-to-spot consistent trends:** Look for graphs with all lines/curves heading in the same direction: all up, all down, or all flat.
- **Numbers in the figures:** To show a consistent trend, the figure has to feature numbers, not words or symbols.
- **Short answers:** Look for as many questions as possible with short answers, specifically answers with numbers and short relationship words like *increase* or *decrease*.

In Chapter 20, we'll show in greater detail how trends and patterns deliver the main point.

Personal Order of Difficulty (POOD)

There is one additional important characteristic you need to look for: topics you know. Even if the figures are really ugly and confusing, if a passage is on a topic you just finished in school and know cold, you'll get the main point of the passage quickly, and that's the goal of choosing a Now passage.

Pace Yourself

Unless you're shooting for a 27 or higher on the Science test, you're better off choosing at least one passage as Never. Take 35 minutes, and do fewer passages. You'll give yourself more time and increase your accuracy. As you steadily increase your scoring goals in practice, target the number of questions you need to reach your goal. The more aggressively you can move through the passages finding all the Now questions you can answer—no matter how difficult the passage may be— the better you'll score.

Goal Score

Use the pacing strategies and score grid on page 25 to find your goal score for each practice test and, eventually, the ACT.

Be Flexible

As we've mentioned before, to earn your best score on the ACT, you have to be flexible, and nowhere is this more true than on the Science test. The Science test

Patterns
Look for trends *within* a figure. Look for relationships *between* figures and viewpoints.

Letter of the Day (LOTD)
Just because you don't work on a passage doesn't mean you don't bubble in answers. Never leave any bubbles blank on the ACT. Bubble in your Letter of the Day for all the questions on your Never passages.

shows the greatest change in level of difficulty from one administration to the next. There is no way to predict how difficult the Science test will be, nor what the particular topics will be. Certainly, if you know more about the topic, you'll find even an ugly-looking passage more understandable. But that doesn't mean you're relying on luck. The Princeton Review's basic approach works regardless of what the topics are. The goal is to practice using the basic approach so that the particulars of the passage are irrelevant.

Hard Test = Generous Curve
Don't be scared of a hard Science test on any particular administration. Each test is curved against only the students who took that particular exam. If the Science test is hard, *everyone* will struggle with the hardest questions, and the curve will be more generous.

However, you have to fight your own instincts, or at least retrain them into those of a great test-taker. Always be prepared to adapt your order based on what you see, both in practice and on a real test. If you choose a passage that looked good and then find yourself struggling, leave it and find another. Ignore the voice in your head that says, "Well, I've put so much time into this incredibly hard passage already, all that time would be a waste if I didn't finish the passage." Nothing could be further from the truth. You're throwing away perfectly good time if you stick with a passage that you're just not grasping.

**1 Point Earned,
3 Points Lost**

Easy questions earn the same number of points as difficult questions. Don't waste time struggling with a hard question when you can move on and answer easy questions. You can always come back to the question if you have time.

You have to be just as strict with a tough question. When you're stumped, your first instinct may be to go back and read the passage or stare at the figure *again*, waiting for a flash of inspirational genius to suddenly make everything clear. Instead, focus on using POE to get rid of answers that can't be right. Even if you can cross off only one answer, guess from what's left and move on. If you stick with one tough question too long, you may be robbing yourself of 2–3 questions.

Process of Elimination (POE)

Just as in the other tests, POE is a powerful tool on the Science test. Particularly on tougher questions, use POE to eliminate wrong answers that are clearly contradicted by what you're looking at.

Let's see how POE works on the Science test.

POE

Each time you eliminate a wrong answer, you increase your chance of choosing the correct answer.

1. An epidemiologist claims that a patient infected with chicken pox faces the greatest risk of mortality for any of the diseases studied. Do the results of Experiment 1 support her claim?

   A. Yes; the percentage of fatal chicken pox infections is greater than the percentage of fatal rabies infections.

   B. Yes; the percentage of fatal chicken pox infections is less than the percentage of fatal rabies infections.

   C. No; the percentage of fatal chicken pox infections is greater than the percentage of fatal rabies infections.

   D. No; the percentage of fatal chicken pox infections is less than the percentage of fatal rabies infections.

Infection Severity Incidence for Four Diseases

chicken pox

0%   percentage of infections   100%

tuberculosis

0%   percentage of infections   100%

measles

0%   percentage of infections   100%

rabies

0%   percentage of infections   100%

Level of Severity

unapparent   mild   moderate   severe   fatal
                                  (nonfatal)

Here's How to Crack It

Don't waste time staring at the figure trying to look up the answer. Look at how descriptive the answer choices are: POE will be much faster. Ignore the "Yes" and "No," and focus on the reasons given. Do they accurately describe the figure? Choices (A) and (C) are disproven by the figure, so cross them off. The reason given in (B) and (D) is the opposite of the reason given in the other two, so both are proven by the figure. If you had no clue what *mortality* meant, you'd have a fifty-fifty chance of getting this right. If you do, you have to consider the claim and reason that chicken pox is less fatal than rabies and therefore poses less of a risk of mortality, i.e., death. The correct answer is (D).

Maybe you read the question, and a quick glance at the figure was all you needed to know the answer was "No." Great, cross off (A) and (B), and then compare what's different between (C) and (D). The point is to save time by looking at the answers and then the figure rather than staring at the figure and then the answers. The harder the figure, the more important POE is to your success.

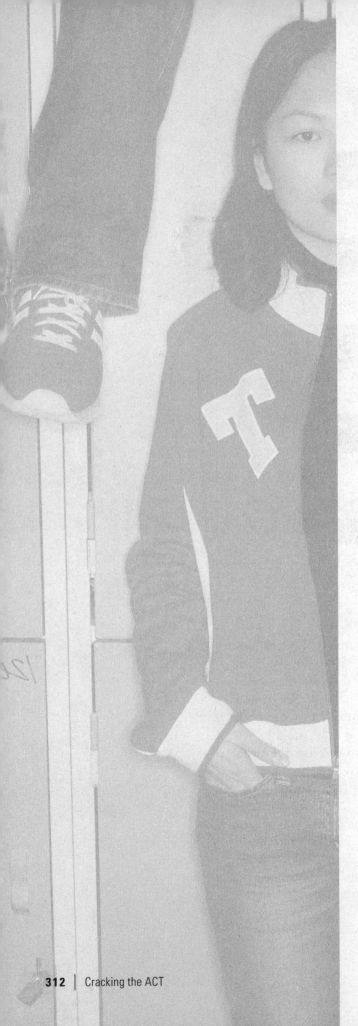

Summary

o   There are always 40 questions on the Science test. They are split up into Charts and Graphs, Experiments, and Fighting Scientists passages.

o   You don't need to know science content, but you do need good scientific reasoning skills.

o   Look for trends within figures and relationships between figures and viewpoints.

o   Order your passages. Use your POOD to look for topics you know a lot about. Look for Now passages, which feature small graphs and tables, easy-to-spot consistent trends, numbers instead of words or symbols, and short answers made up of numbers or short relationship words like *increase* or *lower*.

o   Pace yourself. Slow down and do fewer passages, but work up to your goal score by focusing on the number of points you need to earn your goal score.

o   Be flexible. Be ready to adapt your order, leave a tough passage, or guess on a tough question.

o   Use Process of Elimination to cross off wrong answers and save time.

Chapter 20
Scientific Reasoning Skills

You don't need to know science facts for the ACT. For the most part, the Science test is an open-book test, with the passages offering the content you need to answer nearly all the questions. According to ACT, you do need scientific reasoning skills. But all this really means is that you need some common sense. Science may seem intimidating, but it's based on a lot more common sense than you may think.

YOU KNOW MORE THAN YOU THINK

It's easy to feel very intimidated by the content and even the figures on the Science test. But all of science is built on common sense. The key to building good scientific reasoning skills is to realize you *already have* those skills. You use common sense every day to figure things out, to solve problems, to make conclusions. A scientist does the same. When you solve a problem, you think critically, and that's the basis of scientific reasoning.

How to Solve a Problem

Let's try an experiment. Say you put on a wool sweater and go out to dinner one night. At the restaurant you order some delectable shrimp for dinner and then a beautiful bowl of strawberries for dessert.

The next morning, you wake up covered in red, itchy hives. What caused them? Do you jump to the conclusion it was the sweater? What about the shrimp? A lot of people have allergies to shellfish. But so, too, do a lot of people have allergies to strawberries. How are you supposed to know which one caused your hives? How do you know any of these options are the only possible culprits?

Assumption = Guess

An assumption is nothing more than a guess, and a lazy one at that, if you are willing to believe the riddle has been solved. A guess doesn't cut it in the scientific world: only proof does.

You don't. That's the first rule of scientific reasoning: Make no assumptions. You can't assume it was the sweater, the shrimp, or the strawberries. But you have to prove it was one and only one of these, if any. So how do you set about finding out which one?

You design an experiment. You first need to narrow the list of suspects down to the sweater, shrimp, and strawberries. Begin with a baseline. You need to see what happens on a day with none of the possible causes in play to compare to the days with them. Wear a cotton T-shirt and eat cauliflower and cantaloupe. Do you still have hives? Then the three suspects have all been vindicated. But if your hives have cleared up, you've confirmed your first hypothesis that it was indeed the sweater, the shrimp, or the strawberries.

Hypothesis

A hypothesis is a theory. An assumption is a guess with no proof. A hypothesis is more advanced than that. It's a theory that tries to explain what happened, but it requires proof.

Now you have to figure out which one of the three caused your hives. We need a day with one, and one only, of the possibilities, or *variables*, in play. That's the second rule of scientific reasoning: Change one variable at a time. On one day wear the sweater, but skip the shrimp and strawberries. On another lose the sweater, and eat the shrimp but not the strawberries. On yet another replace the shrimp with the strawberries. On each day check for hives. The itchy red bumps *depend* on whatever *independent* variable is causing them.

That's all well and good. But what about everything else in your life? Notice we said you couldn't wear the sweater on the days you ate the shrimp and strawberries. But other than the sweater, *you have to wear the exact same clothes on the day you eat shrimp and on the day you eat strawberries*. It's not just what you wear. Everything else in your life has to be exactly the same. If on the day you wore the sweater, you worked out at the gym, but on the day you ate shrimp, you lay on your sofa all day watching television, how much would you know? Not much. Certainly not much of anything with proof, and proof is what it's all about in science. The third rule of scientific reasoning is that you have to keep all the other variables in the experiment the same as you vary one and only one independent variable. In the hives experiment, this means that in order to conclusively prove the cause, you have to keep everything else the same on each day that you change one and only one independent variable. Do the same things. Wear the same clothes (except the sweater). Eat the same things (except the shrimp and strawberries).

And that's it. If you follow these three rules, you'll know what causes your hives.

Trends

In our first example, we looked at a dependent variable, hives, that were present only when an independent variable was present. You've undoubtedly faced other situations in which different amounts of a variable seem to have an effect on another variable. The more you study, the better your grades. The more pints of ice cream you eat, the more pounds you gain. The more miles you run, the more pounds you lose.

Let's look at another situation. You sleep only 5 hours a night, staying up late and getting up early to study, but you're con-

sistently scoring in the high 70s on your daily math quizzes no matter how many hours you study. Suppose you had a hypothesis that if you slept more, your scores would improve. How would you design an experiment to test this? You already have a baseline of 5 hours and consistent scores in the high 70s. So beginning with the first night, you sleep longer, and then see how you score the next day. The next night, you sleep even longer, and check your quiz score the next day. Can you do anything else differently? No, you have to keep all the other variables in your life the same. Each day you eat the same things and study the same number of hours. You even track quiz scores in the same unit to eliminate any possibility that there is any other reason why your quiz scores improve.

To be organized, you record all your data in a simple table.

Table 1	
Hours of sleep	Quiz scores
5	78
6	83
7	88
8	93

Direct Proportion

As x increases, y increases. As x decreases, y decreases.

As the number of hours of sleep increases, your quiz score increases. In this experiment, the number of hours of sleep is the independent variable, and the quiz score is the dependent variable. You've established that your quiz score is ***directly*** proportional to the number of hours you sleep.

Let's look at another experiment. Suppose your hypothesis this time is that the more cups of coffee you drink, the fewer hours you sleep. How would you design the experiment? Same rules as always. First, you need a baseline. You need to get all the caffeine out of your system and cut your consumption down to 0 cups each day. You establish a consistent routine of the same diet, exercise, studying, sports practice, and so on. Then, without changing any of those variables, you begin drinking coffee again—same size cup each day—increasing the number of cups and measuring the number of hours you sleep the following night.

Once again, you record your findings in a table.

Table 2	
Cups of coffee	Hours of sleep
0	8
1	7
2	6
3	5

Inverse Proportion

As x increases, y decreases. As x decreases, y increases.

As the cups of coffee increase, the hours of sleep decrease. This time, the number of hours of sleep is the dependent variable, and the number of cups of coffee is the independent variable. You've established that the amount you sleep is ***inversely*** proportional to the amount of coffee you drink.

Many passages on the Science test feature passages whose main point is either a direct or inverse trend of the variables. In Chapter 19, we outlined characteristics of Now passages, for example, small tables and graphs with easy-to-spot consistent trends. When you look at the two tables above, the trend is pretty obvious from just a quick glance. You've already cracked the main point, and you will find all the questions that much easier to tackle as a result.

Graphs

Tables and graphs both show the trends of variables. Graphs are more visual, making the trends easier to spot.

If you graphed your data from Table 1, what would it look like?

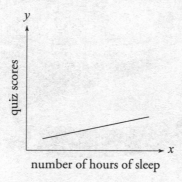

Remember that in math, the horizontal axis is always x: It's the independent variable. The vertical axis is always y: It's the dependent variable. Science follows the same rules. This graph shows you that as x increases, y increases. They have a direct relationship.

Let's stick with using math to understand the graphs on the Science test better. Think about slope. It's the change in y over the change in x. In this graph, the slope is positive. Direct relationships have positive slopes.

$$\text{Slope} = \frac{rise}{run}$$

$$\frac{y_2 - y_1}{x_2 - x_1}$$

Let's graph Table 2.

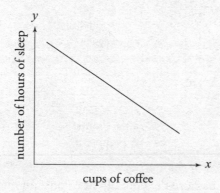

This graph shows you that as x increases, y decreases. They have an inverse relationship, and the slope is negative. Inverse relationships have negative slopes.

Positive and Negative Slope

Using your math skills in coordinate geometry is a great way to see how much graphs tell you. We already pointed out that direct relationships have positive slopes, as shown by the graph of Table 1, and inverse relationships have negative slopes, as shown by the graph of Table 2. But the size of the slope tells you even more.

Let's take a look at another real-life example. You're sweltering in the middle of a heat wave, so it's time to fill your above-ground pool.

You pull out your hose to start filling the pool. The water fills at a constant rate of 1 gallon per hour, and it takes several hours to fill it.

As the number of hours increases (independent variable), the volume of the water, in gallons, increases (dependent variable). The following graph shows the direct relationship.

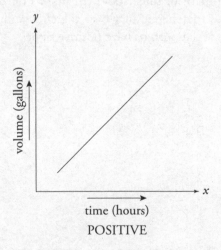

POSITIVE

The slope is positive 1 because the pool fills at a constant rate of 1 gallon per hour.

After a few days of enjoying your pool, the forecasts warn of an impending hurricane. For safety's sake, you have to drain the pool. You unplug the drain, and the water begins to flow out at the same 1 gallon per hour rate. The following graph shows the inverse relationship.

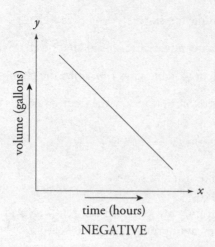

time (hours)

NEGATIVE

The slope is negative 1 because the pool drains at a constant rate of 1 gallon per hour.

It's very useful to spot a positive or negative slope on a graph in a Science passage. As we mentioned before, you've cracked the main point of the passage when you spot the relationship between the variables. But positive and negative linear graphs are not the only ones you'll see, and you'll also see different types of positive graphs and different types of negative graphs.

Let's dive back into the pool.

Flat Lines

At the last minute, the path of the hurricane heads out to sea and avoids landfall. In fact, your pool hasn't even finished draining when the storm changes direction. Now a new heat wave has descended, and you need to refill the pool. You turn your hose on and savor how great that water is going to feel at the end of a long, hot day. Unfortunately for you, you forget to replug the drain. Because you decide to spend the day in an air-conditioned movie theater, you don't even realize the pool isn't filling. Well, it is filling, but it is also draining at the exact same rate. Thus, the volume doesn't change.

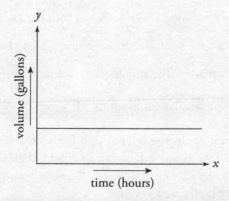

time (hours)

The slope of this line is 0 because the volume doesn't change. As time passes, the number of hours keeps increasing, but the change in time has no effect on the volume.

Think about the formula for slope: $\frac{y_2 - y_1}{x_2 - x_1}$. The change in y is divided by the change in x. The independent variable (x) can change all it wants—as time marches on—but if the dependent variable stays ***constant,*** the change between y values is 0. When 0 is in the numerator, that means the fraction equals 0.

Shallow Lines

Different rates will yield different slopes.

Once you replug the drain, your pool finishes refilling, and you spend several days floating in your pool, escaping the hot, humid weather.

Water, however, has a nasty habit of evaporating. But the rate of evaporation is far slower than the rate at which the pool empties when the drain is unplugged. Still, if you don't use the hose to refill the pool, the volume of water will decrease over a number of days. Let's take a look at what that graph would look like.

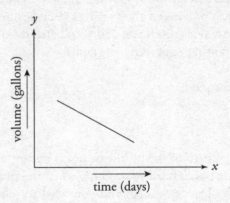

The slope is negative because as time increases, the volume decreases. Time and volume have an inverse relationship. But the effect that time has on volume is relatively small compared to the effects of an open drain.

Bring back the formula for slope: $\frac{y_2 - y_1}{x_2 - x_1}$. When the change in y is small compared to the change in x, you have a small numerator and a large denominator. Thus, you have a fraction smaller than 1. The smaller the fraction, the closer to parallel to the x-axis the line will be. In fact, it's approaching a flat line, or a slope of 0.

The slope tells you a lot about the relationship between the independent variable (time) and the dependent variable (volume), namely, that time has a very small effect on volume. If the effect were much less, the slope would be 0, which is to say that time would have no effect on volume.

Steep Lines

Back to the pool! You refill the pool to its full volume, but you decide it's time to rake around the pool with a deadly sharp rake. You swing a little wildly too close to the nylon pool and slice a huge gash in the side. Water starts gushing out, at a much faster rate than it empties when the drain is unplugged. Take a look at what the graph of your small accident looks like.

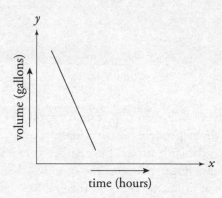

The slope is negative because as time increases, the volume of the water decreases. Time and volume have an inverse relationship. But compared to the rate of decrease when the drain is unplugged, the volume is decreasing at a faster rate. Compared to the rate of decrease from evaporation, the volume is decreasing at a *much* faster rate.

If you think about this with the formula of slope in mind, the change in y is very large, and the change in x very small. Therefore, the numerator is larger than the denominator, leaving a fraction greater than 1. The bigger the fraction, the closer to parallel to the y-axis the line will be. But the line will never be vertical. After all, time can't stand still, so there will always be a change in x. You know from your math review that the denominator can't be zero, so slope can't work if there is no change in x. Even if you had super powers to freeze time, the volume would freeze as well. So there is no way to have a change in y but no change in x.

Steep Line = Big Slope
When the independent variable has to change by only a small amount to have a huge effect on the dependent variable, the slope will be steep.

Curves

In Science passages, not all graphs will feature straight lines. Just as in real life, not all situations are linear.

The heat wave passes, and summer turns to fall. But you're not ready to give up the pool, even as the days turn crisp. You decide to install a heat pump to make it a heated pool. You turn the pump on, and it gradually heats the chilly water to a perfect 78°F. However, the heat pump malfunctions, and the temperature continues to rise, faster and faster, until soon it's over 100°F.

Luckily for you, you witnessed all this safely from outside the pool. But let's take a look at what the graph would look like.

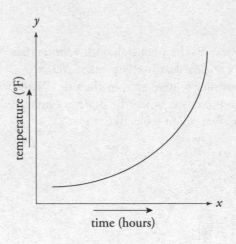

temperature (°F)

time (hours)

Curves = Exponential Change

When the dependent variable changes by a different amount every time the independent variable changes, the result will be a curved line.

The curve is obviously not linear, so slope doesn't apply. As the independent variable (time) increases, the dependent variable (temperature) increases, so the relationship between the variables is direct. But temperature increases ***exponentially*** faster, not in a constant, linear pattern. The amount that y changes with each change in x is different at different points on the graph.

Now let's think of this in math terms. What does the graph of $y = x^2$ look like? It's a parabola. Cut the parabola off at the origin and look only at the right half, and it will look just like the graph above.

TRENDS ON THE SCIENCE TEST

The key to cracking the Science test is to look for trends and patterns. Figures with consistent trends point to a Now passage because the figure has provided the main point of the passage—the relationship between the variables.

In the next chapter, we'll teach you a basic approach to cracking each passage, including passages that *don't* feature small tables and graphs with consistent trends. But we hope that this chapter has convinced you to look for passages featuring figures with consistent trends to do Now. You'll find even the hardest questions are easier to tackle when the figure tells you everything you need to know.

Look at each of the following figures. What are the relationships between the variables?

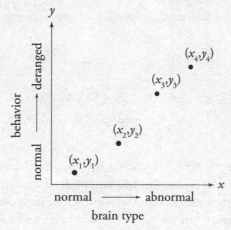

Dr. Frankenstein's Experiment

As the positive slope of the ordered pairs shows, it's a direct, linear relationship. The more abnormal the brain, the more deranged the behavior.

Try another.

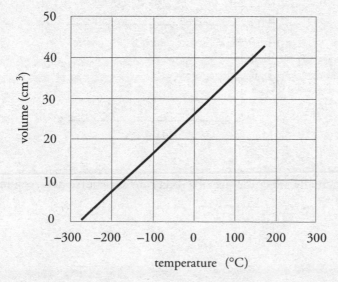

This, too, is a direct, linear relationship. As temperature increases, volume increases.

What about the next one?

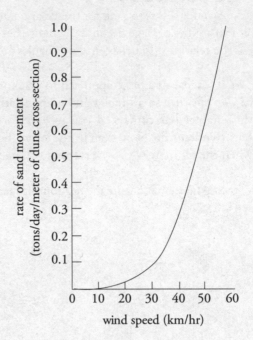

When the wind speed is 40 km/hr, what is the rate of sand movement? It's 0.3. When the wind speed is 50 km/hr, the rate of sand movement increases to 0.6, double the last reading even though the wind speed increased by only 10 km/hr. The relationship is direct, but the curve shows you it's an exponential relationship, not a linear one.

Try the next one.

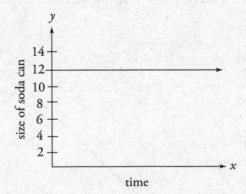

Does time actually affect the size of a soda can? Of course not. As a result, we get a flat line.

Try one more.

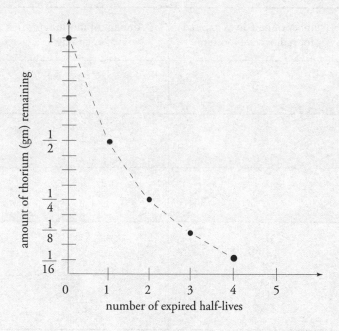

As the number of expired half-lives increases, the amount of thorium remaining decreases, so the two have an inverse relationship. But because the curve is headed downward, it's a negative relationship.

Do you need to know what "expired half-lives" and "thorium" are? No, you don't need to (but it's always helpful when you're familiar with the content). To answer the questions for this passage, everything you need to know comes from the relationships between the variables. The main point of the passage is just a summary of these relationships.

Tables

When we began this chapter, we showed you tables before switching to graphs. Everything we've discussed about graphs applies to tables. A table with consistent trends is just as helpful as a graph with consistent trends. The only difference is that tables are not as visual as graphs, so it's up to you to make them visual.

Look at the table below.

Number of half-lives expired for radioactive thorium	Amount of thorium (gm) remaining
0	1
1	$\frac{1}{2}$
2	$\frac{1}{4}$
3	$\frac{1}{8}$
4	$\frac{1}{16}$

This is the same information we saw in a graph. What direction is the number of half-lives headed? It's headed up. Draw an arrow to reflect the trend. What direction is the amount of thorium headed? It's headed down. Draw an arrow to reflect the trend. Your table should now look like this:

Number of half-lives expired for radioactive thorium	Amount of thorium (gm) remaining
0	1
1	$\frac{1}{2}$
2	$\frac{1}{4}$
3	$\frac{1}{8}$
4	$\frac{1}{16}$

↑ ↓

You've just gotten a preview of the next chapter. Marking the trends in a figure is the first step in the basic approach to cracking Science passages.

Inconsistent Trends and No Relationships

Wouldn't it be great if you saw only tables and graphs with consistent trends on the ACT? Yes, it would, but there will be uglier figures as well. Now that you know how powerful consistent trends are, you can actually use that knowledge even when there is no consistency. The absence of consistency tells its own story.

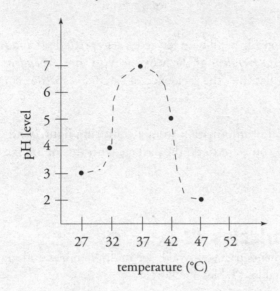

As temperature increases, what does pH do? It barely increases at first, then makes a sharp jump before an equally sharp fall to a point that is lower than where it began. You may have immediately identified this as a **bell curve**. Is a bell curve consistent?

A bell curve is certainly not as consistent as a straight line or even a curve that moves in a positive or negative direction. There is some consistency, however. It increases, then decreases. The problem is that we can't make a prediction of what it will do next. That's the real beauty of consistent lines and curves: We can predict what will happen off the figure. But with a bell curve, we can't determine whether it will repeat its trend or if it will steadily decrease.

What about the next graph? What story does it tell?

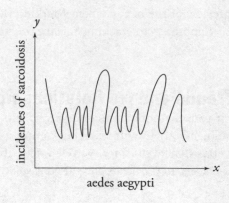

There is no relationship at all between aedes aegypti and sarcoidosis. The incidence of sarcoidosis is *independent* of the aedes aegypti, not *dependent*. And unlike the relationship in a flat line, the incidence of sarcoidosis is not constant. Instead, it fluctuates wildly.

That's a good deal of information from a confusing figure with two strange variables. But would you want to do the passage with this figure Now or Later? Definitely Later.

Multiple Variables

In many Experiments passages, you'll see multiple tables and graphs. Take a look at the following tables (Tables 3 and 4).

Table 3	
Length (m)	Resistance (Ω)
0.9	7.5
1.8	15.0
3.6	30.0

Table 3

Table 4	
Cross-sectional area (mm²)	Resistance (Ω)
0.8	35.0
1.6	18.0
3.2	7.5

Table 4

First, mark the trends within each figure. In Table 3, as length increases, resistance increases. Length is the independent variable, resistance is the dependent variable, and the two have a direct relationship. In Table 4, as cross-sectional area increases, resistance decreases, and the two have an inverse relationship. What's the relationship between the figures? Look at the variable they have in common: resistance.

In Experiments passages—as well as in scientific studies in real life—it's common to test different independent variables to measure their effect on the same dependent variable. But recall our second and third rules of scientific reasoning skills:

- **Change one variable at a time.** Vary each independent variable to see its effect on your dependent variable.
- **Keep all other variables the same.** Your other independent variables *and everything else* have to be the same as you vary one and only one independent variable.

When length is varied, can cross-sectional area vary at the same time? No, it has to stay the same, that is, constant. And when cross-sectional area is varied, length has to stay constant.

On the Science test, you are likely to see a question that tests your ability to spot the constants.

---

1. Based on the results shown in Table 3 and Table 4, the cross-sectional area used in the first experiment (resulting in Table 3), was most likely:
   A. 0.8 mm².
   B. 1.6 mm².
   C. 3.2 mm².
   D. 4.8 mm².

Here's How to Crack It

Find the link between the two tables by looking at the variable they have in common, resistance. Look for a value of resistance that is the same in both tables. In Table 3, resistance is 7.5 Ω when length is 0.9 m. In Table 4, resistance is 7.5 Ω when cross-sectional area is 3.2 mm². Thus, we know that as length was varied, cross-sectional area was held constant at 3.2 mm², and as cross-sectional area was varied, length was held constant at 0.9 m. The correct answer is (C).

Graphs can also have multiple variables. Take a look at the following graph.

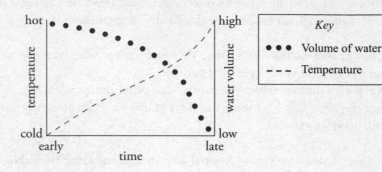

When there are multiple variables on a graph, you always need to be careful to look at the correct line and the correct axis. As time increases, temperature increases. As time increases, water volume decreases. Does that mean temperature and water volume have a relationship? Not directly, they don't. What's the variable they have in common? Time.

Try another question.

⎯⎯⎯⎯⎯⎯⎯⎯⎯○⎯⎯⎯⎯⎯⎯⎯⎯⎯

2. According to the figure above what was the temperature when water volume was at its highest?

    F. High
    G. Hot
    H. Low
    J. Cold

Here's How to Crack It

Find the link between the two axes by looking at the variable they have in common, time. Be sure to look at the correct curve on the correct axis. Water volume is the bubbled line, and when it's at its highest, the time on the x-axis is early. When time is early, look at the dashed line for the temperature. When it's early, the temperature is cold.

The correct answer is (J).

⎯⎯⎯⎯⎯⎯⎯⎯⎯○⎯⎯⎯⎯⎯⎯⎯⎯⎯

In the next lesson, we'll teach you how to use your scientific reasoning skills on ACT Science passages, which will feature plenty of tables and graphs with various trends and relationships.

Summary

- Scientific reasoning is based on common sense.

- The three rules of scientific reasoning skills are
  - Make no assumptions.
  - Change one variable at a time.
  - Keep all other variables the same.

- A hypothesis is a theory that needs proof to become a conclusion.

- An independent variable creates or causes an effect on a dependent variable.

- In a direct relationship, as x increases, y increases.

- Direct linear relationships on a graph have positive slopes.

- In an inverse relationship, as x increases, y decreases.

- Inverse linear relationships on a graph have negative slopes.

- A flat line means the dependent variable is constant, and the independent variable has no effect.

- A steep slope means the independent variable has a drastic effect on the dependent variable.

- A shallow slope means the independent variable has a slight effect on the dependent variable.

- When the dependent variable changes by different amounts every time the independent variable changes, the result is a curved line.

Chapter 21
The Basic Approach

To earn your highest possible score on the Science test, you need an efficient and strategic approach to working the passages. In this chapter, we'll teach you how to apply your scientific reasoning skills to quickly assess the content of the passage and figures and make your way methodically through the questions.

HOW TO CRACK THE SCIENCE TEST

The most efficient way to boost your Science score is to pick your order of the passages and apply our 3-Step Basic Approach to the Charts and Graphs passages and Experiments passages. Follow our smart, effective strategy to earn as many points as you can.

Step 1: Work the Figures

Take 10–30 seconds to review the figures. In the last chapter, we taught you how to look for and identify trends, patterns, and relationships. Your goal in Step 1 is to quickly identify the main point of the passage and the relationships between the variables that convey the main point. Consistent trends are the fastest to assess, but all trends and patterns tell a story. In Chapter 19, we gave you a way to spot the Now passages, which are chiefly characterized by consistent trends.

Now Passages

1. **Small tables and graphs:** No more than 3–4 curves on a graph, no more than 3–4 rows and columns on a table.
2. **Easy-to-spot consistent trends:** All lines headed in same direction, numbers in a table in easy-to-spot order.
3. **Numbers, not words or symbols:** Avoid tables and graphs with words or symbols.
4. **Short answers:** Numbers or trend words like *increase* and *decrease* or *higher* and *lower*.

Graphs

Graphs visually represent the relationship between the variables. When you work a graph, identify the relationship, and take note of the variables and their units.

Take a look at the graph on the next page.

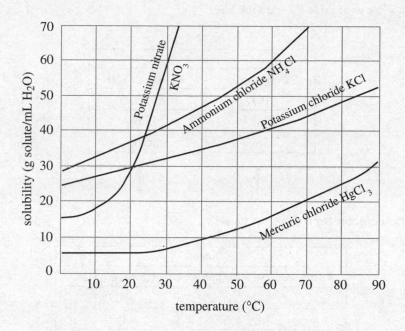

Figure 1

- Look at the direction of the curves: They are all headed up.
- Take note of the variables and their units. Temperature, in °C, is on the *x*-axis; solubility, in g solute/100 mL H_2O is on the *y*-axis.
- Identify the relationship. A positive slope means it's a direct relationship. As temperature increases, solubility increases.

Tables

For tables, you need to make the trends visual. Take a look at the table below.

Table 1	
Length (m)	Resistance (Ω)
0.9	7.5
1.8	15.0
3.6	30.0

- What is length doing? It's increasing. Mark it with an arrow.
- What is resistance doing? It's increasing. Mark it with an arrow.
- What are the units of the variables? m and Ω.
- Identify the relationship. Both variables move in the same direction, so it's a direct relationship.

Here's what your table should look like.

Table 1	
Length (m)	Resistance (Ω)
0.9	7.5
1.8	15.0
3.6	30.0

↑   ↑

Try another table from the same passage.

Table 2	
Cross-sectional area (mm²)	Resistance (Ω)
0.8	30.0
1.6	15.0
3.2	7.5

- What is the cross-sectional area doing? It's increasing. Mark it with an arrow.
- What is resistance doing? It's decreasing. Mark it with an arrow.
- What are the units of the variables? mm² and Ω.
- Identify the relationship. As the cross-sectional area increases, resistance decreases. It's an inverse relationship.

Here's what your table should look like.

Table 2	
Cross-sectional area (mm²)	Resistance (Ω)
0.8	30.0
1.6	15.0
3.2	7.5

↑   ↓

Last, identify the relationship between the tables. Each table has the variable **resistance** in common.

Step 2: Work the Questions
Once you've marked the figures, go straight to the questions.

Now, Later, Never

There is no set order of difficulty of these questions. Follow your Personal Order of Difficulty (POOD): If a question is fairly straightforward, do it Now. Most of the questions you consider straightforward will likely ask you to identify a trend, look up a value, or make a prediction. Now questions will have values or trend words like *increase* or *lower* in the answers. If a question strikes you as confusing or time-consuming, come back to it Later. Occasionally, you'll judge a question tough enough you may Never want to do it. Select your Letter of the Day (LOTD), and move on to the next passage. In Step 3, we'll address how smart use of Process of Elimination (POE) may eliminate the need for any Never questions on a Now passage. But for now, let's look at a sample Now question.

Acronyms Rule!
You've seen our favorite Princeton Review acronyms before and you'll see them again: POOD, LOTD, POE.

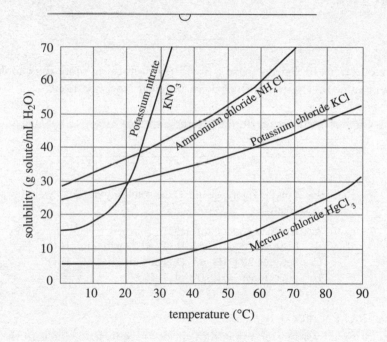

1. Based on the figure, as temperature increases, the solubility of $HgCl_3$:

    A. increases.
    B. decreases.
    C. increases, then decreases.
    D. decreases, then increases.

Here's How to Crack It

This question is asking you to identify a trend. You already cracked this question in Step 1, when you worked the figures and identified the trends. All the curves are headed up, so as temperature increases, the solubility of $HgCl_3$ increases. The correct answer is (A).

Try another.

---

2. According to Figure 1, KNO$_3$ and KCl have the same solubility at what temperature?

F. Between 0° and 10°
G. Between 10° and 20°
H. Between 20° and 30°
J. Between 30° and 40°

Here's How to Crack It

This question is asking you to look up a value in the figure. Find where KNO$_3$ and KCl have the same solubility. They have the same solubility when the lines intersect, at a solubility of 30 g/100 mL H$_2$O. Draw a line down to the *x*-axis to see what the temperature is when solubility is 30; it's just over 20°, so the correct answer is (H).

Many questions on Science passages will entail nothing more than looking up a trend or value in a figure. Both of these are great Now questions.

Let's try one more question from the same passage.

---

3. Based on the figure, at 100°C the solubility of HgCl$_3$ would most likely be:

A. less than 5 g/100 mL H$_2$O.
B. between 10 g/100 mL H$_2$O and 20 g/100 mL H$_2$O.
C. between 20 g/100 mL H$_2$O and 30 g/100 mL H$_2$O.
D. greater than 30 g/100 mL H$_2$O.

Here's How to Crack It

If a question cites a specific value, first check to see if that value is in the figure. If it's not, the question is asking you to make a prediction. Because the trend is consistent, you can predict what the curve will do. At 90°C, the solubility of HgCl$_3$ is already over 30 g/100 mL H$_2$O. Therefore, at 100°C, the solubility will be greater than 30 g/100 mL H$_2$O. The correct answer is (D).

Read If and Only When You Need To

On most of the questions, particularly on Now passages, you will be able to answer the questions based on the figures. Whether it's a Charts and Graphs passage or Experiments passage, waste no time reading any of the introduction, or in the case of the Experiments passages, the descriptions of each experiment/study. It's only when you can't answer a question from the figures, you should read.

Let's take a look at some questions from an Experiments passage. We've already marked the tables from this passage.

Passage III

The *resistance* of a material that obeys Ohm's Law can be calculated by setting up a potential difference at the ends of a wire made of that material and then measuring the current in the wire; the resistance is the ratio of potential difference to current. Because resistance is dependent on length and cross-sectional area, scientists created a standard measure, *resistivity*, which is the measure of how strongly a material opposes the flow of current. In the experiments below, scientists examined the factors affecting resistance in an Ohmic material that they invented.

Experiment 1

In their first experiment, scientists examined the relationship between the length of a wire and its resistance. The resistivity of the wires used in this experiment was 27.5 ρ, and the cross-sectional area of the wires was 3.2 mm^2.

Table 1	
Length (m)	Resistance (Ω)
0.9	7.5
1.8	15.0
3.6	30.0

↑   ↑

Experiment 2

In their second experiment, scientists examined the relationship between the cross-sectional area of a wire and its resistance. The resistivity of the wires used in this experiment was 27.5 ρ, and the length of the wires was 0.9 m. The results are shown in Table 2.

Table 2	
Cross-sectional area (mm^2)	Resistance (Ω)
0.8	30.0
1.6	15.0
3.2	7.5

↑   ↓

4. *Conductivity* measures a material's ability to conduct an electric current, and it is defined as the reciprocal of a material's ability to oppose the flow of electric current. If the scientists wanted to increase the conductivity of the material they invented, they would:

 F. increase the length.
 G. decrease the cross-sectional area.
 H. increase the resistivity.
 J. decrease the resistivity.

When to Read
Read if and only when you can't answer a question from the figures. If a question introduces a new term that you can't identify as one of the variables on the figures, look for information about that term in the introduction and/or experiments.

Here's How to Crack It
The question defines a new term, **conductivity,** and asks how the scientists would increase the conductivity of their specific material. As part of the definition, the question states that conductivity is the reciprocal of a material's ability to oppose the flow of current. The tables do not feature an obvious variable for this quality, so you have to read the introduction and studies.

In the introduction, the term **resistivity** is defined as a material's ability to oppose the flow of electric current. The question adds the information that conductivity is the reciprocal of resistivity. Therefore, to increase the conductivity, the scientists would decrease the resistivity. The correct answer is (J). Notice that (H) and (J) are exact opposites. Whenever there is only one pair of exact opposites, the correct answer is frequently one of the pair.

Step 3: Work the Answers
On more difficult questions, POE will be much faster and more effective than scouring the text or figures to find an answer. If the answers are wordy—that is, anything but a simple value or trend word like *increase* or *lower*—use POE. Read each answer choice, and eliminate any that are contradicted by the figures.

Let's try a question from a different passage.

The term *solubility* refers to the amount of a substance (solute) that will dissolve in a given amount of a liquid substance (solvent). The solubility of solids in water varies with temperature. The graph below displays the water solubility curves for four crystalline solids.

This passage refers to the graph on page 333.

6. A solution is *saturated* when the concentration of a solute is equal to the solubility at that temperature. If a saturated solution of potassium chloride (KCl) at 10°C were heated to 80°C, would the solution remain saturated?

   F. Yes, because solubility decreases with increasing temperature.
   G. Yes, because concentration decreases with increasing temperature.
   H. No, because solubility is unaffected by increasing temperature.
   J. No, because concentration is unaffected by increasing temperature.

Here's How to Crack It

The question defines a new term, *saturated*, identifies KCl as saturated at a given temperature, and asks if KCl will remain saturated at a new temperature. If you're familiar with the topic of saturation, you may already know whether it's yes or no. If so, cross off the two answers you know to be wrong, and examine the reasons given in the two remaining answers.

But if you didn't understand the new information and can't process what will happen at a new temperature, use POE on all four answers. Ignore the yes/no, and focus on the reasons given in each answer.

Choice (F) says that solubility will decrease with increasing temperature, but the figure disproves this. No matter what the new information in the question is, this cannot be the correct answer. Cross it off. Choice (G) brings in a new variable, *concentration*. Quickly check the introduction to see if concentration is defined. It's not, so you have to leave (G). You can't eliminate an answer about a variable that you know nothing about. You can eliminate (H), however, because the figure disproves the reason. Choice (J) revolves around concentration, so you have to keep that as well.

At worst, you have a fifty-fifty chance of getting this question right if you guessed from here and moved on. We can offer one extra tip to help sway you in your guess. Avoid an answer that provides either a value or describes a trend of an unknown variable if you have no proof of how that new variable will behave. Thus, between (G) and (J), the smart money is on (J), and it is the correct answer. Concentration is the number of grams of the substance per unit volume, and the concentration will not change with temperature.

POE and Pacing

POE is so powerful on Science, you should be able to eliminate at least one, sometimes two, wrong answers and therefore have fewer Never questions, particularly on a Now passage.

Depending on your pacing, you may try to reason between the remaining answers. Don't spend more than another minute. Even if you get the question right, spending too much time on one question will likely cost 2–3 questions later on.

THE 3-STEP BASIC APPROACH AND LATER PASSAGES

The 3-Step Basic Approach works on all passages with figures, not just the Now passages featuring consistent trends in tables and graphs.

Take a look using the 3-Step Basic Approach at a Later passage in the following section.

Step 1: Work the Figures

Some ACT passages will feature an illustration, a diagram, or tables and graphs with no consistent trends. Take 10–15 seconds to review the figure. When there are no consistent trends, a figure doesn't reveal the main point as readily. You'll learn the main point as you work the questions and answers. Spend the limited time devoted to Step 1 looking for any patterns or terms.

Try this figure.

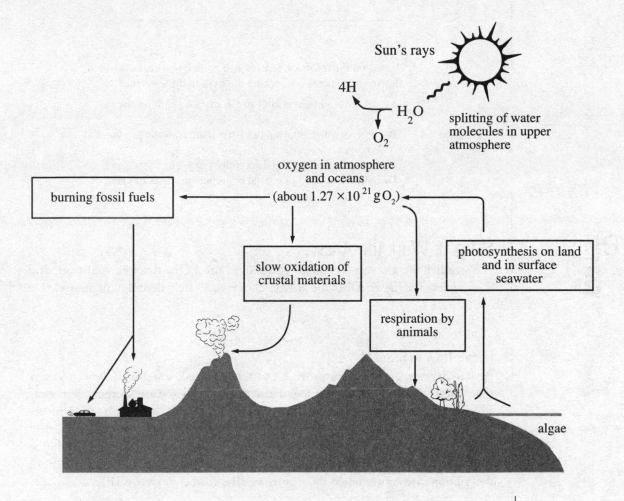

The terms **oxygen**, **fossil fuels**, **oxidation**, **respiration**, and **photosynthesis** all appear.

Step 2: Work the Questions

Even on Later passages, several questions will ask you to look something up in the figure. The more confusing the figure, however, the more likely you are to waste valuable time trying to figure everything out from staring at the figure, waiting for a flash of inspiration to hit. As we mentioned before, spend 10–15 seconds looking for any patterns or terms. Your time is better spent moving to Steps 2 and 3. Working the questions and answers will help you crack the main point of the passage.

Try a question.

---

13. Based on the information provided, which one of the following statements concerning the oxygen cycle is true?

A. Photosynthesis on land and in surface seawater uses up oxygen.

B. Photosynthesis on land and in surface seawater produces oxygen.

C. Respiration by animals produces oxygen.

D. Slow oxidation of crustal materials produces oxygen.

Step 3: Work the Answers

The wordier the answers, the more you should use POE. Read each answer, and then review the figure: Does the answer choice accurately describe the figure?

Here's How to Crack It

Pay attention to arrows. They provide a pattern that tells the story. Choice (A) says that photosynthesis uses oxygen, but the arrows lead toward oxygen, not away. Eliminate (A). Choice (B) is the exact opposite and matches the direction of the arrows. Keep it. Whenever there is only one pair of exact opposites, the correct answer is frequently one of the two opposites. Choices (C) and (D) both describe producing oxygen, but the arrows move away from oxygen, not toward it. Both descriptions are contradicted by the arrows. The correct answer is (B).

Basic Approach Drill 1

Use the Basic Approach on the passage below. For the answers to this drill, please go to Chapter 24.

The kinetic molecular theory provides new insights into the movement of molecules in liquids. It states that molecules are in constant motion and collide with one another. When the temperature of a liquid increases, there will be an increase in the movement of molecules and in the average kinetic energy. The figure below depicts the distribution of the kinetic energy of two volumetrically identical samples of water at different temperatures (T).

Water has attractive intermolecular forces that keep the molecules together. When enough heat is added to water, it will weaken these forces and allow some molecules to evaporate and escape the liquid as a gas. The activation energy (Ea) is the minimum energy necessary for molecules to escape the liquid and undergo a phase change.

Distribution of Kinetic Energy for Two Samples of Water

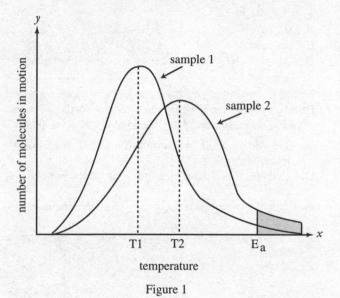

Figure 1

1. Which of the following statements best describes the changes observed in the graph?
   A. At T1, Sample 1 has a lower kinetic energy than does Sample 2.
   B. At T2, Sample 1 has a lower kinetic energy than does Sample 2.
   C. An increase in temperature leads to a decrease in kinetic energy.
   D. Water never undergoes a phase change.

2. Assume that water undergoes a phase change to a gas. Which of the following statements would be true?
   F. The attractive intermolecular forces of the escaping molecules are weak.
   G. The average kinetic energy of the water remains the same.
   H. The rate of movement of the gas molecules decreases.
   J. The gas will undergo no further phase changes.

3. Suppose a third sample of water is heated to a higher temperature than Sample 2. It is then found that a greater number of molecules escaped the liquid in Sample 3 than in Sample 2. Would these results be consistent with the results depicted in Figure 1 ?
   A. Yes, an increase in temperature leads to a decrease in the number of escaping molecules in the liquid.
   B. Yes, as the temperature increases, it leads to more molecules escaping the liquid.
   C. No, the temperature reading of Sample 2 would be five times as high as that of the third sample.
   D. No, the average kinetic energy of the water will decrease.

4. It can be inferred from the passage that when a substance undergoes a phase change from a liquid to a gas it will:
   F. evaporate.
   G. condense.
   H. disintegrate.
   J. remain the same.

5. Given the samples at T1 and T2, and the kinetic energies measured and shown in Figure 1, which temperature produces the highest single kinetic energy measurement?
   A. Both T1 and T2
   B. T2
   C. T1
   D. Neither T1 nor T2

Basic Approach Drill 2

Use the Basic Approach on the passage below. For the answers to this drill, please go to Chapter 24.

Amphibians are unique organisms that undergo drastic physical changes during the transformation from an immature organism into an adult form. This process, called metamorphosis, begins with the determination of cells at the tadpole stage. A study was conducted using tadpoles to determine the influence of thyroxine (a hormone) on metamorphosis.

As shown in the graph below, tadpoles were placed in solutions containing various concentrations of thyroxine. Increased levels of thyroxine correlated with increased rates of tail reabsorption and the appearance of adult characteristics such as lungs and hind legs.

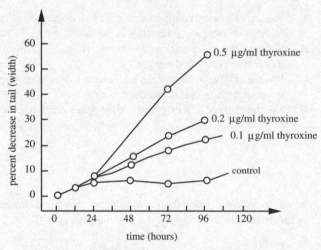

Decrease in tail width in relation to varying levels of thyroxine solutions

Figure 1

1. Suppose that a tadpole was immersed in a 0.3 μg/ml solution for 72 hours. What would be the expected approximate decrease in tail width?

   A. 22%
   B. 30%
   C. 41%
   D. 50%

2. Which of the following generalizations about tadpoles is supported by the results of the study?

   F. They will not undergo metamorphosis if they are not given thyroxine.
   G. Metamorphosis in a normal tadpole takes at least five days.
   H. The most rapid disappearance of the tail is associated with the immersion of tadpoles in the most dilute thyroxine solution.
   J. Temperature plays a major role in metamorphosis.

3. After four days, the tadpoles are checked for development. In all samples other than the control, which of the following concentrations of thyroxine would the tadpoles be likely to show the LEAST development?

   A. 0.5 μg/ml
   B. 0.2 μg/ml
   C. 0.1 μg/ml
   D. All of the tadpoles would show the same development.

4. Based on the information in the passage, which of the following would be a correct order of the stages of tadpole development?

   F. Tadpole → adult → reabsorption of tail → cell determination
   G. Tadpole → cell determination → reabsorption of tail → adult
   H. Tadpole → reabsorption of tail → cell determination → adult
   J. Cell determination → tadpole → adult → reabsorption of tail

5. According to Figure 1, immersing the tadpoles in solutions containing various concentrations of thyroxine does not begin to affect the rate of tadpole metamorphosis until when?

   A. No time at all; the thyroxine affects the rate of metamorphosis immediately.
   B. 0–12 hours after immersion
   C. 12–24 hours after immersion
   D. 24–36 hours after immersion

Basic Approach Drill 3

Use the Basic Approach on the passage below. For the answers to this drill, please go to Chapter 24.

Each element is arranged in the periodic table according to its atomic number, which represents the number of protons in the nucleus. In every neutrally charged atom, the number of electrons equals the number of protons. The table below lists some of the properties of row 2 elements in the periodic table. *Electronegativity* is a measure of the relative strength with which the atoms attract outer electrons. Within a row of the periodic table, the electronegativity tends to increase with increasing atomic number, due to the tighter bonding between protons and electrons. The highest value for electronegativity is 4.0.

Element	Atomic number	Atomic radius	Electro–negativity	Characteristic
Li	3	1.52	1.0	metal
Be	4	1.13	1.5	metal
B	5	0.88	2.0	non-metal
C	6	0.77	2.5	non-metal
N	7	0.70	3.0	non-metal
O	8	0.66	3.5	non-metal
F	9	0.64	4.0	non-metal

1. Which of the following graphs best represents the relationship between atomic number and atomic radius for row 2 elements?

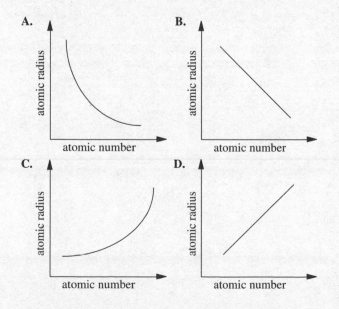

A.

B.

C.

D.

2. What conclusion could be appropriately drawn from the data regarding electronegativity in Table 1 ?

F. An element with high electronegativity has an even atomic number.

G. An element with high electronegativity will be a metal.

H. An element with high electronegativity will have little tendency to attract outer electrons.

J. An element with high electronegativity will be a non-metal.

3. What generalization can one make concerning the relationship between two properties of elements?

A. As the atomic radius decreases, the electronegativity decreases.

B. As the atomic radius decreases, the electronegativity increases.

C. All metals have higher electronegativity values than non-metals.

D. The atomic radius of F is larger than that of N.

4. Which of the following is true regarding the comparative electronegativity of fluorine (F) and lithium (Li)?

F. The electronegativity of F is greater than Li because F has fewer electrons in its outer shell.

G. The electronegativity of F is greater than Li because F electrons are more tightly bound.

H. The electronegativity of Li is greater than F because Li has a greater metallic character.

J. The electronegativity of F is greater than Li because Li has a greater metallic character.

5. Generally speaking, ionization energy follows the same trends as does electronegativity. Elements with a high electronegativity also have a high ionization energy. Which of the following is a correct order of elements with INCREASING ionization energies?

A. Li, N, F

B. F, N, Li

C. B, N, Be

D. Be, O, Li

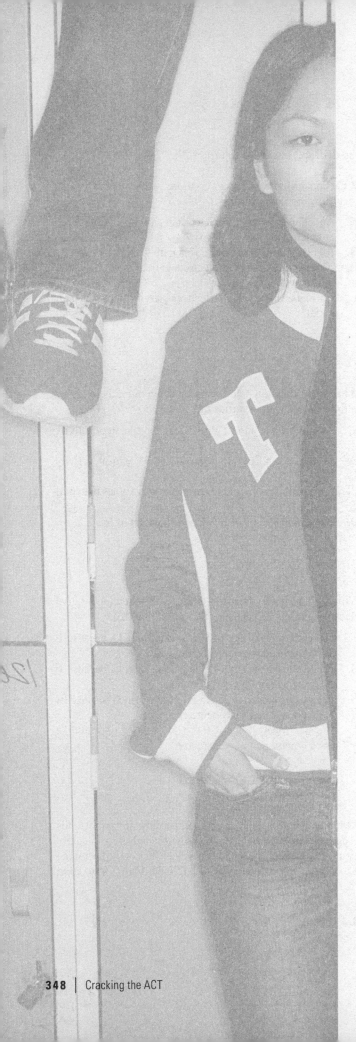

Summary

o All Charts and Graphs passages and most Experiments passages come with figures.

o Use the 3-Step Basic Approach on passages with figures.

Step 1. Work the Figures. Look at the trends and patterns in the figure to identify the relationship between the variables. Mark trends in tables with arrows.

Step 2. Work the Questions. Do Now the straightforward questions that involve looking up a trend or value on the figure or making a prediction of what a variable will do. Read if and only when you can't answer a question from the figures. Do Later any question that strikes you as more difficult or time-consuming.

Step 3. Work the Answers. For tougher questions, POE should help you eliminate at least one wrong answer if not three.

o Pace yourself. If you've eliminated at least one wrong answer, guess and move on to the next passage.

Chapter 22
Fighting Scientists

The third type of passage on the Science test is called "Fighting Scientists." Two, three, or possibly more conflicting views on a scientific phenomenon will be presented. Make a plan of the order in which you will read the scientists, and work one theory at a time before tackling the questions that require comparing and contrasting all of the theories.

Think of it as a debate. Each debater proposes a hypothesis and then supports that hypothesis with facts, opinions, and assumptions. The ACT test writers want you to evaluate and compare the arguments made by each debater, but they don't care who wins the debate. We don't care either, but we do want you to answer correctly seven questions about the debate. In order to do that, you must understand each viewpoint and how it agrees and disagrees with the others. Some questions will ask about just one theory, but most of the questions will ask you to compare and contrast two or more. That's a lot to keep track of. Wouldn't it be easier to navigate this passage if you had a plan?

FOLLOW A PLAN

The Fighting Scientists passage has a lot in common with the Reading test, and you might recognize some of the same strategies we taught you to employ for Reading. Remember when we asked you how you would fare if your boss assigned you the task of checking out an empty building? How well do you do when you don't know what you're looking for? Not very well. How well would you fare if you dived right into a passage on the Reading test if you didn't know what you're looking for? Right. So how can you succeed on the Fighting Scientists passage if you don't know what you're looking for?

Step 1: Preview

Your first task is to map the order in which you will read the scientists. Just as on the Reading test, you should look at the questions first. In the Fighting Scientists section, the questions help you determine which hypothesis to read and which questions to answer first.

Let's try this with the questions on the next page. Read each question, and mark it with a "1" if it asks about Hypothesis 1, a "2" if it asks about Hypothesis 2, and a "1 & 2" if it asks about both hypotheses.

1. Hypotheses 1 and 2 agree that the dinosaurs:

2. The basis of Hypothesis 1 is that a meteorite striking Earth was the primary cause of the dinosaurs' demise. Which of the following discoveries would best support this theory?

3. Suppose a geologist discovered that the fossilized bones of dinosaurs contained traces of radioactive iridium. How would this evidence influence the two hypotheses?

4. The authors of the two hypotheses would disagree over whether the extinction of the dinosaurs was:

5. If current climatic changes turn out to be as dramatic as those described by the author of Hypothesis 2, which of the following would he say is most likely to occur?

6. Studies have shown that climatic conditions are interdependent. As conditions become less favorable for life in one locale, they improve in another. If fossil evidence were found which showed that this happened at the K-T boundary, how would it affect Hypothesis 2?

7. Both Hypothesis 1 and 2 would be supported by evidence showing that:

You should have a "1 & 2" next to questions 1, 3, 4, and 7. Question 2 should have a "1" next to it, and questions 5 and 6 should have a "2" next to them. What does this tell us? We should read Hypothesis 2 first.

Step 2: One Side at a Time

In order to compare and contrast multiple hypotheses, you need to understand each viewpoint and how it agrees and disagrees with the others. Reading and working the questions for one scientist at a time will give you the firm grasp of each theory you need.

Once the questions have provided a map, read the introduction to identify the disagreement.

> Approximately 65 million years ago (at the boundary between the Cretaceous and Tertiary periods, known as the K-T boundary), the dinosaurs became extinct.

> Here are two of the hypotheses that have been presented to explain their disappearance.

What will the hypotheses debate? They will debate what caused the extinction of the dinosaurs.

Next, read Hypothesis 2. You don't need to comprehend everything in the passage or remember every point of fact or argumentation, and until you read the other hypothesis, you have no basis for comparison. You do need to grasp the argument each is making, so as you read Hypothesis 2, find and underline the scientist's main point.

Hypothesis 2

This event at the K-T boundary was neither sudden nor isolated. It was a consequence of minor shifts in the earth's weather that spanned the K-T boundary. Furthermore, its effect was not as sweeping as some have suggested. While the majority of dinosaurs disappeared, some were able to adapt to the changing world. We see their descendants every day—the birds.

Alterations in the earth's *jet stream* (a steady, powerful wind that blows from west to east, circling the globe) shifted rains away from the great shallow seas that extended across much of what is now North America. As these late-Cretaceous seas began to dry up, a chain reaction of extinctions was set into motion. First affected was plant life. Next, animals that fed on plants began dying off. Ultimately, the lack of prey caused the demise of the dinosaurs. It was the mobility of the winged dinosaurs that saved them, allowing them to move to more favorable locations as conditions in their ancestral homes deteriorated.

What Are They Fighting About?

Some of the scientific theories you'll read about in a Fighting Scientists passage were settled a long time ago. In reading a passage arguing that Earth is the center of the universe, you may think, "Wait, Earth is NOT the center of the solar system—why in the world are they arguing about this?" For the ACT, the arguments presented are what count. Even though an argument may have been disproved a long time ago, it's still possible to evaluate it scientifically, and that's all you're being asked to do on this test.

What is the main point of Hypothesis 2?

According to Hypothesis 2, the extinction of dinosaurs was caused by a chain reaction prompted by changes in the weather.

Your Underlined Version Should Look Like This

Hypothesis 2

<u>This event at the K-T boundary was neither sudden nor isolated. It was a consequence of minor shifts in the earth's weather that spanned the K-T boundary</u>. Furthermore, its effect was not as sweeping as some have suggested. While the majority of dinosaurs disappeared, some were able to adapt to the changing world. We see their descendants every day—the birds.

Alterations in the earth's *jet stream* (a steady, powerful wind that blows from west to east, circling the globe) shifted rains away from the great shallow seas that extended across much of what is now North America. As these late-Cretaceous seas began to dry up, a chain reaction of extinctions was set into motion. First affected was plant life. Next, animals that fed on plants began dying off. Ultimately, the lack of prey caused the demise of the dinosaurs. It was the mobility of the winged dinosaurs that saved them, allowing them to move to more favorable locations as conditions in their ancestral homes deteriorated.

Did you notice that we didn't underline the details of the theory in the second paragraph? It's not that they are unimportant, but until we dive into the questions, we don't know what to pay attention to other than the main point. As we work the questions for Hypothesis 2, we'll gain a deeper understanding of the details of the theory.

Without further ado, let's go to the questions about Hypothesis 2.

5. If current climatic changes turn out to be as dramatic as those described by the author of Hypothesis 2, which of the following would he say is most likely to occur?

    A. A rapid extinction of most of Earth's life, beginning with sea dwellers such as krill (a microscopic crustacean) and progressing through the food chain
    B. A gradual and complete extinction of Earth's life forms that moves through the food chain from the bottom up
    C. An extinction of most life forms on Earth that is gradual and simultaneous, affecting predators as well as prey at roughly the same rates
    D. A progressive extinction that begins with vegetation and eventually reaches to the top of the food chain, affecting most dramatically those life forms least suited to relocation

Here's How to Crack It

The main point of Hypothesis 2 is that changes in the weather prompted a chain reaction of extinctions through the food chain until the dinosaurs were affected. We need to look for an answer that would predict a similar result from today's climatic changes. Use POE as you make your way through the answer choices.

Choice (A) is tempting because it mentions a progression "through the food chain," but the word "rapid" contradicts the first sentence of Hypothesis 2: "The event at the K-T boundary was neither sudden nor isolated." Choice (B) looks good, until we go back to the passage to confirm it and see that some dinosaurs survived, those that evolved into birds. Because of the word "complete," we have to eliminate it. Choice (C) is out because of the word "simultaneous," which we know from evaluating (A) is contradicted by the passage. The answer must be (D), and it paraphrases nicely what we underlined as the main point.

6. Studies have shown that climatic conditions are interdependent. As conditions become less favorable for life in one locale, they improve in another. If fossil evidence were found which showed that this happened at the K-T boundary, how would it affect Hypothesis 2 ?

F. It would strengthen the hypothesis by supporting one of the argument's assumptions.

G. It would weaken the hypothesis, because the area of improving climatic conditions should have provided a means for the survival of the dinosaurs well into the Tertiary period.

H. It would weaken the hypothesis by introducing additional evidence that the author could not have anticipated.

J. It would have no bearing on the hypothesis because the mobility of the winged dinosaurs would render such shifts irrelevant.

Here's How to Crack It

We've learned a lot about Hypothesis 2. We read it and underlined the main point, and then we evaluated some of the nuances of the argument to eliminate wrong answers for question 5. When you consider the import of this new fossil evidence, you should draw upon the deeper understanding you've gained. The correct answer to question 5 reminded us that those *least* suited to relocation are more impacted by the changes in weather. The author stated explicitly that some dinosaurs survived and evolved into birds. Those two facts together allow us to realize this new evidence would make Hypothesis 2 more credible. Eliminate (G), (H), and (J), and select (F) as the correct answer.

Step 3: The Other Side

Now it's time to read Hypothesis 1, but we know more than we did before reading Hypothesis 2 and thus should read more proactively. When you read the second theory, you should look for and underline the following:

- the main idea

- how this hypothesis disagrees from the first

- how this hypothesis agrees with the first

Hypothesis 1

For many years, scientists have speculated about the cause of the extinction of the dinosaurs. Fossil records confirm that dinosaurs as well as other life forms were suddenly wiped out. The natural cause of extinction is the inability of an organism to adapt to environmental changes, yet the extinction of all life forms is unlikely. Chemical analysis of clay found from this era attributes the sweeping extinction of dinosaurs to the collision of a huge meteorite with Earth. These fossil records confirm the presence of a high concentration of iridium, a rare heavy metal that is abundant in meteorites. It is believed that a meteorite hit the earth and created a huge crater, which threw up a dust cloud that blocked the sun for several months. This event led first to the destruction of much plant life and eventually all other life forms that consumed plants and/or herbivores, including the dinosaurs.

Write, Write, Write
Underlining and taking notes in the margins helps you keep track of the differences between the scientists.

What is the main point? Hypothesis 1 believes a meteorite struck Earth and wiped out the dinosaurs.

How do the two hypotheses differ? Hypothesis 2 believes the extinction was gradual; Hypothesis 1 believes it was sudden.

How do they agree? Both hypotheses mention the food chain.

If you didn't come up with those points, look at the underlined portions of the passage below.

Hypothesis 1

For many years, scientists have speculated about the cause of the extinction of the dinosaurs. <u>Fossil records confirm that dinosaurs as well as other life forms were suddenly wiped out.</u> The natural cause of extinction is the inability of an organism to adapt to environmental changes, yet the extinction of all life forms is unlikely. <u>Chemical analysis of clay found from this era attributes the sweeping extinction of dinosaurs to the collision of a huge meteorite with Earth.</u> These fossil records confirm the presence of a high concentration of iridium, a rare heavy metal that is abundant in meteorites. It is believed that a meteorite hit the earth and created a huge crater, which threw up a dust cloud that blocked the sun for several months. <u>This event led first to the destruction of much plant life and eventually all other life forms that consumed plants and/or herbivores, including the dinosaurs.</u>

Fighting Scientists
In a Fighting Scientists passage, you're given two or more opinions about a scientific phenomenon. Your job is to identify the differences between or among the viewpoints and the information the scientists use to support their points of view.

Now let's do the one question on Hypothesis 1 before we tackle the questions on both.

---

2. The basis of Hypothesis 1 is that a meteorite striking Earth was the primary cause of the dinosaurs' demise. Which of the following discoveries would best support this theory?

F. The existence of radioactive substances in the soil

G. The presence of other rare metals common to meteorites in the clay beds of the ocean from that period

H. Fossil records of land-dwelling reptiles that roamed Earth for an additional 10 million years

J. Evidence of dramatic changes in sea levels 65 million years ago

Here's How to Crack It

What type of evidence would support Hypothesis 1? Any evidence that shows that dinosaurs were wiped out as a result of the impact of a meteorite. Would the presence of radioactive substances in the soil support Hypothesis 1? It could support the passage only if the radioactive elements were from meteorites (like iridium). Choice (F) did not specify that. Would the fact that some land-dwelling reptiles survived past this period support Hypothesis 1? No, so (H) is out. We can also get rid of (J) because it supports Hypothesis 2. What about (G)? What if other rare metals that are known to be found in meteorites were discovered? Would this support Hypothesis 1? Yes. The correct answer is (G).

Step 4: Compare and Contrast

We are now armed with a clear understanding of each hypothesis's main point, how the two differ, and how they agree.

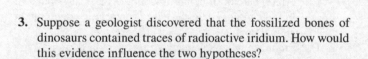

1. Hypothesis 1 and 2 agree that the dinosaurs:

    I.   vanished because of a meteorite impact with the earth.

    II.   became extinct due to disruptions in their food chain.

    III.   became extinct due to some external force other than predation.

    A.   I only
    B.   I and II only
    C.   II and III only
    D.   III only

Here's How to Crack It

We've already identified the area in which the two agree: the impact on the food chain. We can also eliminate choices that support only one of the theories. Statement 1 supports only Hypothesis 1, so it's out. Eliminate all answer choices with Statement 1, and we're left with (C) and (D) only. Because Statement II is in both answer choices, we know it must be correct. Of course, we'd identified the food chain as a point of agreement. Now let's check Statement III. Do both hypotheses state that dinosaurs became extinct because of some external force? Yes, so the correct answer is (C).

3. Suppose a geologist discovered that the fossilized bones of dinosaurs contained traces of radioactive iridium. How would this evidence influence the two hypotheses?

    A.   It would support both hypotheses.
    B.   It would support Hypothesis 2 and weaken Hypothesis 1.
    C.   It would support Hypothesis 1 and weaken Hypothesis 2.
    D.   It would not support Hypothesis 1 or Hypothesis 2.

Here's How to Crack It

Which of the hypotheses would be supported if a geologist found fossil bones that contained traces of radioactive iridium? Hypothesis 1, of course! The passage states that radioactive iridium is abundant in meteorites. If dinosaurs were exposed to the dust of meteorites, their bones would contain this metal. Hypothesis 2 didn't mention anything about iridium, so (C) is the correct answer.

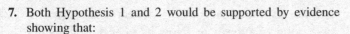

4. The authors of the two hypotheses would disagree over whether the extinction of the dinosaurs was:

   F. a natural process.
   G. rapid.
   H. the result of a disruption on the food chain of the late-Cretaceous period.
   J. preventable.

Here's How to Crack It
The two hypotheses disagreed about the cause of the extinction, but they also disagreed on the pace. Hypothesis 1 believed it was sudden, whereas Hypothesis 2 believed it was gradual. Thus, (G) is the correct answer. Be careful with (H)—that's an issue on which both *agree*.

7. Both Hypothesis 1 and 2 would be supported by evidence showing that:

   A. pterodactyls (winged dinosaurs) survived well into the Tertiary period, adapted to changes in the earth's environment, and eventually evolved into a non-dinosaur life form.
   B. blockage of the sun's rays by particles measurable only on the microscopic scale can still have a significant effect on rates of photosynthesis.
   C. even apparently minor degradation of the plant population in a given ecosystem can have far-reaching effects on the animal population within that ecosystem.
   D. iridium is extremely likely to remain trapped in an ocean's bed when that ocean dries up.

Here's How to Crack It
On what point do the hypotheses agree? Look for an answer choice that provides evidence about the food chain. Eliminate any answer choice that supports only one hypothesis. Choice (A) is out because Hypothesis 1 never mentioned relocation or winged dinosaurs. Choice (B) looks good because it mentions photosynthesis, so keep it. Choice (C) looks much better because it explicitly mentions the effects of plants on animals. Choice (D) is incorrect because Hypothesis 2 never mentioned iridium, and Hypothesis 1 never mentioned the ocean drying up. The test writers are trying to distract you with a switch, but you won't fall for it when you take the passages one at a time and learn each thoroughly before working the questions on both. The correct answer is (C).

Fighting Scientists Drill 1

How did the continents take on their current shape? Two differing views are presented below. For the answers to this drill, please go to Chapter 24.

Natural gas (a variable combination of methane and other heavier hydrocarbons) is extracted and brought to the surface from reservoirs located between 0 and 0.5 miles beneath the Earth's surface. Two scientists discuss the origin of natural gas in a particular undersea reservoir.

Scientist 1

All of the natural gas present in the reservoir was formed within the last 500 million years from the decay of organic matter. Natural gas formation began when the remains of marine organisms and terrestrial plants piled up on land and on the seafloor over a long period. Mud and other sediments then buried the accumulated plants and organisms. Deep beneath the surface, at depths greater than 10 miles, high temperatures and pressure converted the buried organic matter into natural gas over millions of years.

After its formation, the natural gas rises toward the surface. Some is dissipated into the air, but a significant amount is trapped under the specific geological formation overlaying the reservoir. Fossils from the plants and marine organisms that provided the organic matter can be found in rocks brought to the surface from locations in Earth's crust where natural gas forms.

Because of the unique geological conditions and time required for formation of such reservoirs, the Earth's crust contains only a small amount of natural gas formed in this manner.

Scientist 2

All of the natural gas present in the reservoir was formed by the action of microorganisms at depths from 2 to 10 miles beneath the surface of the Earth. The supply of natural gas has been in constant production since soon after the reservoir's formation. The production begins as various microorganisms digest buried organic material to produce simple, inorganic carbon compounds. Other microorganisms convert the carbon compounds and water into the hydrocarbons of natural gas.

After its formation, the natural gas rises and subsequently amasses in significant quantities in the reservoir. Many natural gas deposits can be found in deep rock layers, where the gas can be released by procedures such as *hydraulic fracturing*, the fracturing of rock by a pressurized liquid. A carbon-13 isotope, commonly linked to natural gas produced from microorganism involvement, is contained in the natural gas brought up to the reservoir.

Since natural gas is always forming and rising towards reservoirs such as this one, there is an infinite amount obtainable.

1. Based on Scientist 1's discussion, the natural gas reservoir would most likely be found at or near sites where:

   A. a body of water exists where none had existed in the past.
   B. a body of water had existed at some time in the past.
   C. microorganisms produce carbon compounds.
   D. carbon compounds produce microorganisms.

2. A natural gas reservoir has been found at a depth of 20 miles below Earth's surface. Is this information consistent with the position expressed by Scientist 1 ?

   F. No, because Scientist 1 indicates that natural gas forms at depths greater than 10 miles below Earth's surface.
   G. No, because Scientist 1 indicates that natural gas forms at depths between 2 and 10 miles beneath the Earth's surface.
   H. Yes, because Scientist 1 indicates that natural gas forms at depths greater than 10 miles beneath the Earth's surface.
   J. Yes, because Scientist 1 indicates that natural gas forms at depths between 2 and 10 miles beneath the Earth's surface.

3. Which scientist indicates that the natural gas found in the reservoir formed in the lower pressure environment?

   A. Scientist 1, because that scientist states that the natural gas formed at depths of more than 10 miles beneath Earth's surface.
   B. Scientist 1, because that scientist states that the natural gas formed at depths between 2 and 10 miles beneath Earth's surface.
   C. Scientist 2, because that scientist states that the natural gas formed at depths of more than 10 miles beneath Earth's surface.
   D. Scientist 2, because that scientist states that the natural gas formed at depths between 2 and 10 miles beneath Earth's surface.

4. Which of the following diagrams is most consistent with Scientist 2's description of the formation and migration of natural gas? (Note: Diagrams are not to scale.)

F.
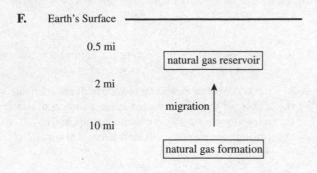

G.
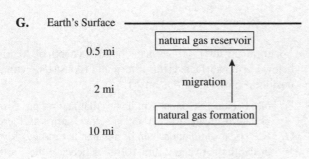

H.
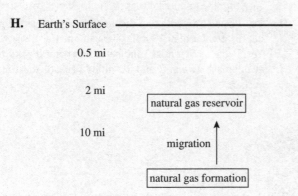

J.
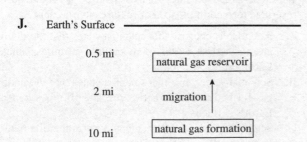

5. An experiment showed that natural gas can be formed through a reaction of carbon dioxide and water. Which scientist would most likely use this result to support his/her viewpoint?

A. Scientist 1, because it would demonstrate how, under high temperature and pressure, organic material can be converted into natural gas.

B. Scientist 1, because it would demonstrate a chemical reaction that microorganisms might carry out to convert organic material into natural gas.

C. Scientist 2, because it would demonstrate how, under high temperature and pressure, organic material can be can be converted into natural gas.

D. Scientist 2, because it would demonstrate a chemical reaction that microorganisms might carry out to convert organic material into natural gas.

6. Based on Scientist 2's discussion, which of the following statements describes two properties of natural gas that migrated to the reservoir in which it accumulated? The natural gas:

F. does not contain carbon-13 and is less dense than the material through which it migrates.

G. does not contain carbon-13 and is more dense than the material through which it migrates.

H. contains carbon-13 and is less dense than the material through which it migrates.

J. contains carbon-13 and is more dense than the material through which it migrates.

7. Based on Scientist 2's discussion, which of the following compounds is involved in the formation of natural gas?

   I. F_2
  II. KCl
 III. CO_2

A. I only
B. III only
C. I and II only
D. II and III only

Fighting Scientists Drill 2

How did life on Earth originate? Two differing views are presented. For the answers to this drill, please go to Chapter 24.

A professor placed 100 mL of Gas A at 25°C into a syringe. The syringe was then inserted into a rubber stopper placed in the top of an empty flask (see Figure 1). The escape of gas molecules from the syringe into the evacuated flask is known as *effusion*.

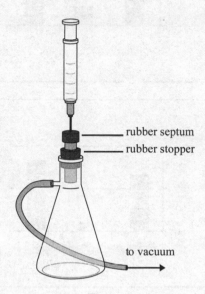

rubber septum

rubber stopper

to vacuum

Figure 1

After insertion of the syringe into the flask, the *total effusion time*, the time required for all 100 mL of the gas to effuse from the syringe into the flask, was measured and found to be 4 sec. The procedure was repeated with Gas B, which had a total effusion time of 16 sec.

Three students proposed explanations for why the total effusion time for the two gasses differed.

Student 1

Gas B effused more slowly than Gas A because it has greater *molecular mass* (the mass of each molecule) than Gas B. The temperature of a gas is a measure of the average kinetic energy of the molecules of that gas. If the temperature of each gas is the same, then the average kinetic energy of the molecules of both gasses is also equal. Since average kinetic energy depends on both the mass and the velocity of gas particles, gases with greater molecular masses travel with a smaller average velocity. Therefore, if two gases are at the same temperature, the gas with the greater molecular mass will effuse more slowly.

Student 2

Gas B effused more slowly than Gas A because it has greater *molecular volume* (the volume occupied by each molecule) than Gas A. Because of their greater molecular volume, fewer larger molecules are able to pass through the opening between the syringe and flask in a given period of time when compared to the number of smaller molecules that are able to pass through the opening in the same period of time. Therefore, if two gases are at the same temperature, the gas with the greater molecular volume will effuse more slowly.

Student 3

Gas B effused more slowly than Gas A because it has greater density than Gas A. Because Gas B has a greater density, its molecules are nearer one another than are the molecules of Gas A. The close proximity of the molecules of Gas B increases the likelihood of collisions, which slow the speed of the molecules. Therefore, if two gases are at the same temperature, the gas with the greater density will effuse more slowly.

Table 1 gives the molecular mass (in atomic mass units, amu), molecular volume (in cubic Angstroms (Å3), where 10 billion Å = 1 m), and density for several gases at 25°C.

Table 1			
Gas	Molecular mass (amu)	Molecular volume (Å3)	Density (kg/L)
Oxygen	32.00	52.86	1.429
Hydrogen	2.016	37.54	0.089
Xenon	131.3	42.12	5.894
Krypton	83.80	34.45	3.749
Helium	4.003	11.46	0.179
Fluorine	38.00	21.17	1.696

1. In the professor's experiment using Gas A, as the 4 seconds of measured effusion time elapsed, the volume of gas in the flask:

A. decreased only.
B. increased only.
C. decreased, then increased.
D. increased, then decreased.

2. Based on Student 1's explanation, which of the gases listed in Table 1 would effuse most quickly at 25°C ?

    F. Hydrogen
    G. Xenon
    H. Helium
    J. Fluorine

3. Suppose that the professor had also tested nitrogen gas and found that it had an effusion time of 9 seconds. Student 1 would claim that nitrogen:

    A. has a smaller molecular mass than Gas A but a greater molecular mass than Gas B.
    B. has a greater molecular mass than Gas A but a smaller molecular mass than Gas B.
    C. has a smaller molecular volume than Gas A but a greater molecular volume than Gas B.
    D. has a greater molecular volume than Gas A but a smaller molecular volume than Gas B.

4. Is the claim "At 25°C, xenon effuses more quickly than krypton" consistent with Student 2's explanation?

    F. No, because xenon has a larger molecular volume krypton.
    G. No, because xenon has a greater density than krypton.
    H. Yes, because xenon has a larger molecular volume than krypton.
    J. Yes, because xenon has a greater density than krypton.

5. Which of the following graphs of the relative effusion rates of oxygen, xenon, and krypton at 25°C is most consistent with Student 3's explanation?

A.

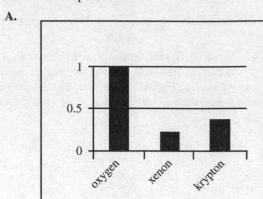

B.

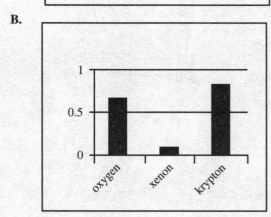

C.

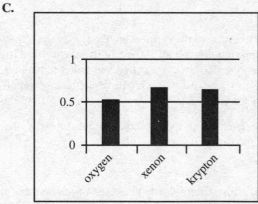

D.

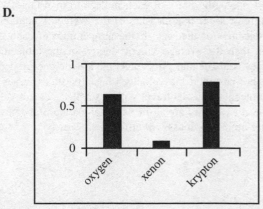

6. Suppose that Gas A had been hydrogen and Gas B had been helium. The results of the professor's experiment would have supported the explanation(s) provided by which student(s)?

   F. Student 1 only
   G. Student 2 only
   H. Students 1 and 2 only
   J. Students 1 and 3 only

7. Consider the data for carbon dioxide (a gas) at 25°C shown in the table below:

Molecular mass (amu)	Molecular volume (Å3)	Density (kg/L)
44.01	34.87	1.77

Which student(s), if any, would predict that carbon dioxide would have a shorter effusion time than krypton?

   A. Student 1 only
   B. Student 1 and 2 only
   C. Student 1 and 3 only
   D. Students 1, 2, and 3

Summary

o   In Fighting Scientists passages, two, three, or more scientists present their differing views on a scientific subject.

o   Don't pick a side. The ACT test writers want you to evaluate and compare the arguments presented, not decide which one is correct. Even if you know something about the topic, answer the questions using only what is presented in the passage.

o   First, use the questions to make a map of the order in which you will read the theories and answer questions on each, one at a time.

o   Leave the questions on more than one theory for last.

o   Don't forget to use your Letter of the Day if there are questions that you don't know how to do.

Part VI
How to Crack the ACT Writing Test

Chapter 23
Writing

The ACT includes an optional Writing Test. The Writing is optional because some schools want it, and some don't care either way. Unless you are 100% sure that everywhere you'll be applying doesn't need the Writing Test, we recommend that you sign up to take it when you take the ACT. You can't take the Writing on its own later if you find that you need it; you'd have to take the whole test again. Still, even though the task is kind of annoying, we've got some tips that will help you to get a great score.

THE OPTIONAL-ISH WRITING TEST

The ACT Writing Test is optional, but unfortunately, the "option" is not exactly yours. It's not whether you feel like taking an extra forty-minute section or not. Who would want to do that? Many of the schools you're applying to probably require the Writing Test. Even if you're not sure, we still recommend that you take the additional Test. We have two main reasons for saying so:

If you've purchased *ACT Elite 36* then you already know The Princeton Review's approach to cracking the Essay section. Feel free to use this as a refresher, and then go to page 386 to hone those finely tuned writing skills you're developing.

- First, many schools require that you take the Writing Test. You wouldn't want to have to take the entire test over again because you opted out of the Writing when you shouldn't have.
- Second, a Writing score can make your college application more attractive, even to those schools that don't require it. Your essay score will appear on every score report you send to colleges. Every school you apply to will see that you took the initiative to opt in for the Writing Test, which is a good thing. Think of it like Honors or AP classes. You don't have to take them, but it looks good if you do.

The biggest reason of all is that it's just not that hard to get a good score on the Writing test. An impressive score is an impressive score, optional or not.

ALRIGHT, YOU CONVINCED ME...NOW WHAT?

The ACT Writing Test consists of a single essay, which you are given 40 minutes to write. The big question will have to do with something ACT deems socially relevant. The question will not be relevant only for high-school students ("Are school uniforms the best, you guys?") nor so grandiose and abstract as to be basically unanswerable ("Is it always cruel to be kind in the right measure?").

A typical prompt will look something like this:

Education and the Workplace

Many colleges and universities have cut their humanities departments, and high schools have started to shift their attention much more definitively toward STEM (Science, Technology, Engineering, Mathematics) and away from ELA (English, Language Arts). Representatives from both school boards and government organizations suggest that the move toward STEM is necessary in helping students to participate in a meaningful way in the American workplace. Given the urgency of this debate for the future of education and society as a whole, it is worth examining the potential consequences of this shift in how students are educated in the United States.

Read and carefully consider these perspectives. Each suggests a particular way of thinking about the shift in American education.

Perspective One	Perspective Two	Perspective Three
ELA programs should be emphasized over STEM programs. Education is not merely a means to employment: ELA education helps students to live more meaningful lives. In addition, an exclusively STEM-based program cannot help but limit students' creativity and lead them to overemphasize the importance of money and other tangible gains.	ELA programs should be eradicated entirely, except to establish the basic literacy necessary to engage in the hard sciences, mathematics, and business. Reading and writing are activities that are best saved for the leisure of students who enjoy them.	ELA and STEM programs should always be in equal balance with one another. Both are necessary to providing a student with a well-rounded education. Moreover, equal emphasis will allow the fullest possible exposure to many subjects before students choose their majors and careers.

Essay Task

Write a unified, coherent essay in which you evaluate multiple perspectives on the issue of how schools should balance ELA and STEM subjects. In your essay, be sure to:

- analyze and evaluate the perspectives given
- state and develop your own perspective on the issue
- explain the relationship between your perspective and those given

Your perspective may be in full agreement with any of the others, in partial agreement, or wholly different. Whatever the case, support your ideas with logical reasoning and detailed, persuasive examples.

Here's How to Crack It

Your job is to write an essay in which you take some sort of position on the prompt, all while assessing the three perspectives provided in the boxes. ACT has hinted at the larger significance of the prompt, but you should also, if possible, give some indication of how you understand that significance.

This may be unlike essays you've written in your English classes. You're probably more used to answering some big question about a book or some ethical question. This time the question is, in a sense, already answered, so you need to be the moderator of the discussion. The idea behind such an exercise is that, in college, you will be required to take a variety of perspectives on some issue, assess those perspectives, and add your own. This is good practice: As you'll find in your college writing classes, essays are much less about coming up with the single correct answer than they are about *contributing to the conversation*.

Even if you have had to do something like this before, you probably haven't had to do it in 40 minutes. That's really not a lot of time, so throughout this chapter, we'll give you some tips for how to get a great score even with the time constraints.

A NOTE ON ARGUMENTS

You'll notice that ACT has placed a very explicit emphasis on the terms *argument* and *perspective*. These are terms that you assuredly already know, but the way these terms are used in everyday speech differs a lot from how they are used among English teachers and academics.

It's important to note that ACT is very careful to ask for your *perspective* rather than your *opinion*. That careful choice of language is there for your benefit. An argument can be a difficult thing to construct because it doesn't just take into account what you think: It requires a more complex understanding of the topic at hand.

The crucial thing about arguments is this:

> In order for a statement to be an *argument*, it must be possible to disagree with that statement.

Think about it this way. As you were reading the prompt above, you might have been thinking, "Great! I hate my English class!" or "Bummer! I hate my math class!" So you might think it would be good to center your essay on this kind of statement:

I don't like to read, so I like the idea of having to take fewer English classes.

That is an opinion, but it's not an argument. In order for it to be an argument, it would have to be possible to disagree with it. And go ahead and try to disagree with the italicized sentence. What could you say? "Yes, you do like to read!" or "No, you don't like the idea!" This isn't a real argument, and that's because the statement that started it (the italicized one) isn't a real argument itself.

The same goes for statements that are too large, like this one:

The question of how to balance ELA and STEM classes is an interesting one.

Or this one:

All three of the perspectives provided are interesting.

Think about what kinds of conversations these statements begin. How would you respond? Probably something along the lines of, "Um…yep" or "Okay." Not much of a conversation, is it? That's because it hasn't started with an *argument*.

If you can find a way to anchor your essay with some argument, some unique perspective of your own that can be defended and debated, you are already in the upper echelon of scorers. Although it may seem like a minor point, the quality of the *argument* at the center of your essay will go a long way to predicting your score.

WHAT THE GRADERS ARE GRADING

If you think you have a tough job writing an essay in only 40 minutes, have some sympathy for the graders. They have to grade each essay in a matter of minutes. Imagine how you would feel if you spent an entire day grading thousands of essays on the same topic. By essay number 50 or so, you probably wouldn't care much if a student used "except" instead of "accept."

ACT graders focus on the big picture. Your essay will be read by two graders, each of whom will assign it a series of four subscores, each from 1 to 6. Their scores will be combined and then scaled into a score of 1–36. The scores will be based on how closely the essay adheres to the standards outlined on the following page.

Given the complexity of this grading system, it's best to think about these graders as grading *holistically*. In other words, they grade the essay as a whole, rather than keeping tabs on every little success or failure within the essay itself. To give one simple example, if you've got a few misspellings in the essay, that won't hurt you that much, but if your grammar and spelling are so messy that the grader doesn't know what you're saying, your Language Use and Conventions score will suffer.

ACT Graders vs. English Teachers
The graders who grade for ACT aren't like your English teachers. They don't have the time to focus on the little details of each essay, and frankly, they don't care about your grade the way your English teacher does. So don't sweat the small stuff! Focus on the big picture for the ACT: strong argument, engagement with multiple perspectives, solid examples, and neatness.

According to the ACT guidelines, essay graders give scores in the following four categories.

1. **Ideas and Analysis:** Above all else, graders want to see that you can handle complex ideas. This essentially means how skilled you are at constructing an argument and assessing the arguments of others. You won't be graded on whether you pick the "right" answer (there isn't one). Instead, you'll be graded on how complex and sophisticated your answers are.

2. **Development and Support:** It's tough to make an argument without citing some examples. Graders want to see that you can justify the positions you're presenting in a given essay. This applies to how you assess the three given perspectives as well: Nothing damages your interlocutor's argument like a killer counterexample.

3. **Organization:** In order to make sure that your graders can see the complexity of your ideas and the quality of the support you provide for them, you need to make sure your essay is organized in a way that makes that easy. Your essay should be a vehicle to help your readers see how freakin' smart you are. If you don't organize the essay well or effectively, your readers won't be able to see your brilliance in its full and effervescent luminousness.

4. **Language Use and Conventions:** Writing is all about *communication*. If your use of the language is coated with grammatical errors and misspellings, your writing won't communicate the way that it should. Graders will forgive a few stray errors, but if your grammar and spelling get in the way of what you're trying to say, those mistakes could cost you.

HOW TO GET A GOOD SCORE

The way to get a good score on the Writing Test is to make the graders' job easy. Show that you understand the perspectives and can generate one of your own. Show that you can support your ideas with examples, real or hypothetical. Show that you can arrange your essay in a way that makes sense. Show that you can use the English language correctly. This may seem like a tall order, but in the next few pages, we'll talk about how to write an essay that is most pleasing to your graders.

Give the graders what they want! You may be a great writer, but the ACT graders are only concerned with a few very specific things.

It can be very intimidating to think that you have to keep all of this in mind as you write a 40-minute essay. It helps, though, if you remember that this essay is part of the ACT, and what do you typically have to do on the ACT? Fill in bubbles. Think of this essay as just another one of those bubbles: All the pieces should basically be in place before you even get to the test.

THE APPROACH

You may not know what the prompt will ask about, but you can at least go into the test with a consistent approach. You can approach each prompt the same way, and your essay can look very similar each time.

Just remember these four basic steps.

> **The Basic Approach for the Writing Test**
>
> 1. Work the Prompt.
> 2. Work the Perspectives.
> 3. Generate Your Own Perspective.
> 4. Consider Context.

In what follows, we'll use each of these steps to break down the given prompt.

Step 1: Work the Prompt

Let's have another look at the prompt.

> Many colleges and universities have cut their humanities departments, and high schools have begun to shift their attention much more definitively toward STEM (Science, Technology, Engineering, Mathematics) and away from ELA (English, Language Arts). Representatives from both school boards and government organizations suggest that the move toward STEM is necessary in helping students to participate in a meaningful way in the American workplace. Given the urgency of this debate for the future of education and potentially society at as whole, it is worth examining the potential consequences of this shift in how students are educated in the United States.

In order to work the prompt, we'll need to clarify a few things.

First, we should identify the major *terms* of the prompt. Give this a try.

_____

_____

_____

The answers you came up with are probably some version of these terms: *education, schools, STEM, ELA,* and *workplace.*

The next task is a little more complex. Figure out the central relationship in those terms, and identify the possible points of *tension* within those terms. In other words, what in the prompt requires you to weigh in? Why is this relationship still the subject of debate and not a done deal?

_____

_____

_____

This task is a little tougher, but it's essential. Try to pick two or three of the terms you identified as key, and write a sentence describing their relationship.

You may come up with something like this:

If schools *prepare students for the* workplace, *what should students be learning in schools?*

Or like this:

Schools *should weigh* ELA *and* STEM *differently depending on what those schools care about teaching.*

You may have come up with something different, and that's fine. The real test will come in the next step when you read the three perspectives provided. If those seem to address the central tension you've described, you're in good shape.

Step 2: Work the Perspectives

Typically, the three perspectives will be split: one *for*, one *against*, and one *in the middle*. Your job in Step 2 is to identify these perspectives, and to try to figure out what they have to say to each other.

> It doesn't matter whether you agree or disagree with the perspectives. Assess them *as arguments* first and foremost.

Let's have another look at the perspectives before we get started.

Perspective One	**Perspective Two**	**Perspective Three**
ELA programs should be emphasized over STEM programs. Education is not merely a means to employment: ELA education helps students to live more meaningful lives. In addition, an exclusively STEM-based program cannot help but limit students' creativity and lead them to overemphasize the importance of money and other tangible gains.	ELA programs should be eradicated entirely, except to establish the basic literacy necessary to engage in the hard sciences, mathematics, and business. Reading and writing are activities that are best saved for the leisure of students who enjoy them.	ELA and STEM programs should always be in equal balance with one another. Both are necessary to providing a student with a well-rounded education. Moreover, equal emphasis will allow the fullest possible exposure to many subjects before students choose their majors and careers.

Which perspective is *for* emphasizing STEM programs over ELA programs? What does this perspective consider? What does it overlook?

_____

_____

_____

Which perspective is *against* emphasizing STEM programs over ELA programs? What does this perspective consider? What does it overlook?

_____

_____

_____

Which perspective is *in the middle* on the question of emphasizing STEM programs over ELA programs? What does this perspective consider? What does it overlook?

_____

_____

_____

You may have come up with something like this:

For (Perspective 2): This perspective takes fully seriously the idea that education leads to employment, and as a result, it sees no value in ELA programs at all because those programs do not have any tangible benefits in the workplace. What this perspective misses, however, is that ELA could have some applicability to the world of work (in marketing, for instance, or in other creative spheres). Nor does it give any serious consideration to the idea that education could be good on its own.

Against (Perspective 1): This perspective is absolutely against the idea of allowing STEM programs to take over, even if those programs do lead to more employability. Perspective 1 says that education should be independent of the workplace and should be more about how to live life. What this perspective misses, however, is that de-emphasis of STEM programs is not practical in the contemporary world, which privileges STEM and technical knowledge. Perspective 1 also severs the link between education and employability too definitively: they must have something to do with each other!

In the middle (Perspective 3): This perspective is in favor of the status quo, which has STEM and ELA programs in equal balance with one another. It says that only a variety of exposure will allow students to find their niches within the workplace. What this perspective misses, however, is that if there is a link between education and employment, this variety is potentially irrelevant. It also overlooks the idea that there is a crisis in education, which is the whole impetus for the previous two ideas.

Your working of the perspectives may not look exactly like this, but that's okay. As long as you've identified where each perspective stands (*for, against,* or *in the middle*) and then identified at least one shortcoming of each perspective, you're in good shape for the next step: generating your own perspective.

Step 3: Generate Your Own Perspective

Now that you've outlined the prompt and the perspectives, it's time to generate your own. You'll draw from each of the perspectives, and you may side with one of them, but your perspective should have something unique about it.

> Come up with your own perspective! If you merely restate one of the three given perspectives, you won't be able to get into the highest scoring ranges.

Start by describing your perspective.

_____

_____

_____

Just so you have a sense of how to build this perspective, we've included one of our own. This is not to say that this perspective is correct—remember, there is no correct answer! It's just an effective argument that would generate a high score.

In my view, the question of how education and the workplace are related to each other misses the point. The cause and effect is wrong, and the very fact that we can ask this question shows that a significant change has already taken place. The prompt asks us to explain what the most effective link between school and workplace is, but that already presumes that there is a link between school and workplace, which is not necessarily universally true. Before we can answer the question of whether STEM programs should be emphasized over ELA programs, we should first wonder whether we'd like to proceed with this linkage between education and workplace. Understanding this linkage is essential because if we find that social prejudices are shaping education without seeming to do so, we will likely find that the potential for innovation and creativity shrinks, and all the technical knowledge in the world won't save us.

Now that you've generated your own perspective, check it against the perspectives already given.

How does your perspective compare to Perspective One?

_____

_____

_____

My perspective is probably closest to Perspective One, but it differs from Perspective One in that it refuses to engage in the question of employment. Perspective One is limited because, especially at the end, it tries to make a case for ELA as employable skills, which is not particularly viable.

How does your perspective compare to Perspective Two?

_____

_____

_____

My perspective is furthest from Perspective Two, though the disagreement is not so explicit as to say, "Perspective Two, you're wrong!" Instead, my perspective shows that Perspective Two is wrapped up in all kinds of assumptions and prejudices of which the author of Perspective Two is seemingly unaware.

How does your perspective compare to Perspective Three?

_____

_____

_____

My perspective has a different aim from that of Perspective Three. Perspective Three is interested in maintaining a balance, but only because he or she sees that balance as advantageous in determining one's eventual employment. In my view, Perspective Three is the worst of both worlds: it has a loose grip on the status quo while at the same time accepting premises that there is no good reason to accept.

If you were able to differentiate your view from all three perspectives while your view remained intact, congratulations! You're on your way to a great score! There's just one more thing…the bigger picture.

Step 4: Consider Context

As you build your argument, remember that the graders are looking to see a complex mind at work. Examples are important, but they mainly exist to help you structure and discuss your perspective and why you have that perspective. Examples can come from anywhere, but they should be reasonable, and they should have a clear application to your argument.

To start, list the examples you'll use to make your argument, and identify how they will help you make that argument. Try to come up with at least two.

_____

_____

_____

_____

I'm going to use one example that has a direct application to what's being discussed in the prompt: Albert Einstein. I'm going to use another that shows why the discussion may be irrelevant: the question of human happiness.

Now describe the order in which you'll discuss your examples and why.

_____

_____

_____

_____

I'm going to discuss the examples in the order I've given above. That way my essay will start by discussing the prompt directly and will then broaden out to show the larger question of which the prompt is part.

THE TEMPLATE

You've done a lot of pre-work, and now it's time to put it all in essay form. Remember, though, that you are taking a *standardized test,* so it will help you to be as *standardized* as possible in your presentation. If you come in knowing basically what your essay will look like, you'll have a much easier time saying all you need to say.

If you already know what your template will look like, great. The best essays always reveal something personal about the writer and his or her complex mind.

If you're not sure what your essay will look like, never fear! Below, we outline a basic template that will have space for all the good stuff you just did in your prewriting.

Introduction

A good introduction will lay out the terms of the *conversation* in which the writer is planning to participate. It will give the reader a preview of what is to come and will, hopefully, encourage the reader to keep reading. In roughly three to five sentences, try out the following:

1. Identify *why* the question posed in the prompt is important.
2. Present your perspective on the question posed in the prompt.
3. Preview how you intend to give support to your perspective.

Based on the pre-writing we did above, here is an example of an effective introduction.

"We want our students to have the best education possible." We've heard enough politicians say it to know that this idea is more or less a truth universally acknowledged. The problem comes when we start to think in a real way about what that "best" education could be. Recently, the rhetoric surrounding educational policy has been all about the importance of STEM programs—improving them, foregrounding them, and making them more attractive to all students. The idea motivating this rhetoric is economic. School is preparation for the workplace; therefore, students should become best educated in the subjects that will make them most employable. This seems like sound logic, but as I will show, both by citing some new examples and by showing the limitations of the three perspectives given in the prompt, this is not the only possible conclusion, nor even necessarily the best one. The more essential task, in my view, is to clarify what a "good education" is and, in a much larger sense, what we want from our lives.

This introduction is effective because it shows the broader context into which the prompt fits: that of education reform in the country as a whole. The introduction then goes on to show a potential problem with asking the question itself: the not-so-universal agreement on what a "good education" is. Then, the introduction is particularly effective at stating the essay's goal: to analyze the three perspectives, to show their limitations, and to show why a different question may get more squarely to the root of the problem.

Body Paragraphs

Body paragraphs provide your reader with the details and examples of your discussion. Try to generate one body paragraph for each example you discuss (usually two or three). Make sure that your body paragraphs do the following:

1. Provide a transition from the previous paragraph and a topic sentence that describes the new one.
2. Assess at least one of the perspectives given in the prompt as a way to strengthen your own perspective.
3. Use an example to develop your perspective or analyze one of the given perspectives.
4. Relate your discussion back to your position and the larger topic.

Based on the pre-writing exercises, here's an example of an effective body paragraph.

You may ask, then, which do I think is better? ELA or STEM? The idea that one would need to choose is part of the problem. Albert Einstein said, "Imagination is more important than knowledge." Now, you'd think that Einstein (the father of twentieth-century STEM, basically) would love the idea of turning all students into little scientists and mathematicians. What Einstein believed, and what his life showed, however, are far different. Einstein understood that all knowledge was valuable but that the imaginative things one does with that knowledge are even more valuable. One would be hard-pressed to find a great mind that was not richly educated across the subjects, from ELA to STEM and beyond. As a result, Perspectives One and Two both miss the point in suggesting the overemphasis of one subject group over another. As Einstein's example shows, what one learns is less important than how one applies that knowledge, and one's possibilities for breadth and imagination necessarily increase with the acquisition of many types of knowledge.

This is an effective body paragraph because it analyzes two or three perspectives given in the prompt. The paragraph gives an example, Albert Einstein, to show the limitations of both of those perspectives while supporting the author's own perspective.

The paragraph also contains an implied transition to the next paragraph, especially because the reader may now believe that if the author is neither *for* nor *against*, he or she must be *in the middle*. As we know from the introduction, however, this may not be the case, and we should read on to find out.

If you want to know what the author's next body paragraph says, good! That means we've got your interest. Think about some of the ways that has happened. What do you want to know? What questions have we left unanswered? What else do you want to contribute to the *conversation*?

Try your own paragraph. Even if our perspective doesn't match yours, try to think along with us here. You'll find it's a useful exercise: ACT Writing is not the place to express your deepest thoughts but to develop your most complex argument.

_____

_____

_____

_____

_____

What did you do well in that argument? What could you have improved? Do you need a third paragraph before you hit the conclusion?

_____

_____

_____

Conclusion

Even though you may be running out of time, it's important to write a conclusion. It gives your essay a completeness that it might not otherwise have. An effective conclusion will usually do the following:

1. Recap your discussion as it has related to the prompt and perspectives
2. Restate your perspective and arguments
3. Provide a final overarching thought on the topic

Here's an example of an effective conclusion.

In short, this prompt forces us to ask an even larger question. What is education? Is it job training? Is it life training? Education reform creates larger changes than many of us realize, and it therefore requires more reflection. While we are comfortable in the idea that education creates members of society, we should also see that society creates a certain type of education. Before we implement these changes, we need to be very certain what our goals are, especially in the very long term.

This conclusion is effective because it summarizes what the author has said without restating it outright. It also pushes the discussion toward a different, larger question, showing that the author has a broader understanding of what is going on in the prompt.

Now, here's the full essay in all its glory.

"We want our students to have the best education possible." We've heard enough politicians say it to know that this idea is more or less a truth universally acknowledged. The problem comes when we start to think in a real way about what that "best" education could be. Recently, the rhetoric surrounding educational policy has been all about the importance of STEM programs—improving them, foregrounding them, and making them more attractive to all students. The idea motivating this rhetoric is economic. School is preparation for the workplace; therefore, students should become best educated in the subjects that will make them most employable. This seems like sound logic, but as I will show, both by citing some new examples and by showing the limitations of the three perspectives given in the prompt, this not the only possible conclusion, nor even necessarily the best one. The more essential task, in my view, is to clarify what a "good education" is and, in a much larger sense, what we want from our lives.

You may ask, then, which do I think is better? ELA or STEM? The idea that one would need to choose is part of the problem. Albert Einstein said, "Imagination is more important than knowledge." Now, you'd think that Einstein (the father of twentieth-century STEM, basically) would love the idea of turning all students into little scientists and mathematicians. What Einstein believed, and what his life showed, however, are far different. Einstein understood that all knowledge was valuable but that the imaginative things one does with that knowledge are even more valuable. One would be hard-pressed to find a great mind that was not richly educated across the subjects, from ELA to STEM and beyond. As a result, Perspectives One and Two both miss the point in suggesting the overemphasis of one subject group over another. As Einstein's example shows, what one learns is less important than how one applies that knowledge, and one's possibilities for breadth and imagination necessarily increase with the acquisition of many types of knowledge.

This is not to say, however, that I find Perspective Three especially compelling either. While I do agree that there is some value in maintaining a balance between ELA and STEM subjects, Perspective Three's reasoning seems wildly misdirected. While it is to be hoped that all adults will be gainfully employed once they leave school, the idea that school should be all geared towards employability is disappointing. As Einstein's example shows, there is more to learning than employability, and even if STEM programs were somehow foregrounded, the lack of ELA programs would limit how imaginatively and creatively students could interpret their data. And let's not overlook the biggest problem of all: if all knowledge acquisition is geared toward how much money it can make us, then to what have we reduced the meaning of our lives? This rhetoric of schools as training sites can lead to only one place: five-year-olds who believe that the only purpose anyone could have on this earth is to get a good job and make money. Is that a world you'd want to live in? Consider yourself lucky to have the capacity to imagine such a world!

In short, this prompt forces us to ask an even larger question. What is education? Is it job training? Is it life training? Education reform creates larger changes than many of us realize, and it therefore requires more reflection. While we are comfortable in the idea that education creates members of society, we should also see that society creates a certain type of education. Before we implement these changes, we need to be very certain what our goals are, especially in the very long term.

A CONCLUSION OF OUR OWN

We know that this can seem like a lot to do in forty minutes, especially for something that won't count toward your composite. We can't help you with the composite part, but we can say this: The essay becomes easier with practice.

And now that you're an expert at the ACT Writing section, here are a few other things to keep in mind.

1. **Length.** ACT graders tend to reward longer essays. Make sure you get onto the second page and the third if possible. If your writing tends to be small, you may want to practice writing larger, especially because it will also make your essay a bit neater and easier to read. If your handwriting is large, make sure you write an extra page to compensate.

2. **Sentence structure.** Varying your sentence structure helps to improve the rhythm of your essay. If you write a really long sentence with lots of modifiers and dependent clauses, it sometimes helps to follow it with a shorter, more direct sentence. It really works. Don't try to be too fancy, though. The longer the sentence is, the more opportunity there is to confuse the reader or to make a grammatical mistake.

3. **Diction.** Diction refers to word choice. You certainly want to sprinkle some nice vocabulary words throughout your paper. But make sure to use and spell them correctly. If you're uncertain about the meaning or spelling of a word, it's best just to pick a different word. Using a big word incorrectly makes a worse impression than using a smaller word correctly.

4. **Neatness.** Make sure you indent each new paragraph. Align your essay using the lines on the paper. Don't go over the lines or write down the side of the page. Avoid messy cross-outs. Although the grader should not take these kinds of things into consideration when determining your grade, a neat, legible essay will be easier to read. Your grader will read hundreds, if not thousands of essays. A neat essay will make the grader happier.

PRACTICE ESSAY PROMPTS

Here are a few more sample essay prompts that you can use for practice. After you finish each essay, read it over—or better yet, have someone else read it—and see how well your essay conforms to the ACT's grading standards. When you practice writing the essay, it's best to limit your time to 40 minutes to experience how short the allotted time really is.

Prompt #1

Commercial Drones

One of the most exciting yet divisive technologies to become available to the public in the last few years is commercial drones. Commercial drones have been used by movie studios to cheaply and safely shoot action scenes for films. Scientists and researchers have used them in order to access the most restricted parts of the globe for observation. However, along with the beneficial uses of commercial drones come more detrimental ones. Several privacy concerns have surfaced over the use of commercial drones to spy on individuals, even on their personal property. Recently, a commercial drone interfered with the work of firefighter helicopters delivering water over a California forest fire. These events have prompted serious debate as to whether commercial drones should be regulated or restricted by the government and to what extent.

Read and carefully consider these perspectives. Each suggest a particular way of thinking about the manner in which the government should regulate commercial drone use.

Perspective One	Perspective Two	Perspective Three
The government can, and should, regulate the use of drones. If any behavior of an individual or business interferes with government and safety operations or violates the rights of an individual, that behavior is legally penalized. Drone use is no different.	Drones should absolutely be regulated when used for business purposes, as all aspects of business are regulated in this country. However, the regulation of personal drone use by private citizens seems to be an overreach of the government's power.	The very space that drones occupy implies that they should not be regulated: no one *owns* the sky. Just as an individual is free to take his boat into the ocean, so too should an individual or business be able to freely access the sky with a commercial drone.

Essay Task

Write a unified, coherent essay in which you evaluate multiple perspectives on the question of to what extent the government should regulate commercial drone use. In your essay, be sure to:

- analyze and evaluate the perspectives given
- state and develop your own perspective on the issue
- explain the relationship between your perspective and those given

Your perspective may be in full agreement with any of the others, in partial agreement, or wholly different. Whatever the case, support your ideas with logical reasoning and detailed, persuasive examples.

Prompt #2

Genetic Engineering

Since the 1970s, humans have directly altered the DNA of animals, plants, and bacteria to produce desired traits. Genetic engineering has been used by the medical industry to manufacture insulin for the treatment of diabetes. The agricultural industry has utilized genetic engineering to create pesticide-resistant crops, improve the health value of soybeans, and increase the size of cattle. If the scientific community generally sees genetic engineering as a massive step forward, why is there such widespread opposition to the practice? As the use of genetic engineering increases, it is important to examine the potential consequences of directly altering DNA.

Read and carefully consider these perspectives. Each suggests a particular way of thinking about genetic engineering.

Perspective One	Perspective Two	Perspective Three
Genetic engineering will have detrimental effects on the environment. Artificially strengthening particular organisms will upset the natural balance of ecosystems, with disastrous consequences.	Genetically modified organisms are superior to non-modified organisms in pest resistance, hardiness, and yield. Further genetic engineering of crops and livestock will help solve global food shortages.	Genetically modifying organisms is ultimately no different from the cross-breeding that farmers have been doing for thousands of years. While the technology has improved, it's still just combining favorable characteristics of organisms to produce a better plant.

Essay Task

Write a unified, coherent essay in which you evaluate multiple perspectives on the question of weighing the potential benefits versus consequences of genetic engineering. In your essay, be sure to:

- analyze and evaluate the perspectives given
- state and develop your own perspective on the issue
- explain the relationship between your perspective and those given

Your perspective may be in full agreement with any of the others, in partial agreement, or wholly different. Whatever the case, support your ideas with logical reasoning and detailed, persuasive examples.

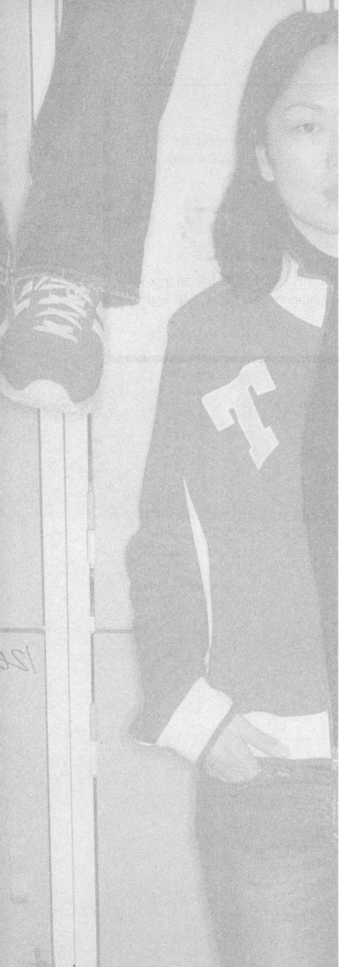

Summary: An Essay Checklist

Now look at your essays and see if you applied the strategies presented in this chapter.

- ○ The Introduction
  Did you
  - • start with a topic sentence that paraphrases or restates the central issue?
  - • clearly state your position on the issue?

- ○ Body Paragraph 1
  Did you
  - • start with a transition/topic sentence that discusses the opposing side of your argument?
  - • discuss the given perspective(s) that would support the opposing argument?
  - • give a specific example that could be used to support the perspective(s)?
  - • explain why you disagree with those perspectives?

- ○ Body Paragraph 2
  Did you
  - • start with a transition/topic sentence that discusses your position on the central issue?
  - • clearly explain your position including any of the given perspectives that support your position?
  - • give a clear example that supports your position?
  - • end the paragraph by restating your thesis?

- ○ Conclusion
  Did you
  - • restate your position on the issue?
  - • end with a flourish?

- ○ Overall
  Did you
  - • write neatly?
  - • avoid multiple spelling and grammar mistakes?
  - • try to vary your sentence structure?
  - • use a few impressive-sounding words?

Part VII
Drill
Answers and
Explanations

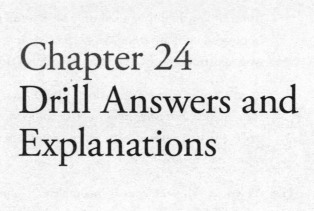

Chapter 24
Drill Answers and
Explanations

PART II: ENGLISH

English Drill 1 (Chapter 6)

1. **C** This sentence requires a word that will go with the non-underlined object, *the many achievements.* Choices (A), (B), and (D) do not work with this phrase. Only (C) can work with the non-underlined portions of the sentence, creating the phrase *large canvases that celebrate the many achievements.*

2. **J** Apostrophes should be used only to indicate possession or contractions. Since *achievements* is not in possession of anything, and *achievement is* would not work in the context, eliminate all choices with apostrophes: (F), (G), and (H). Only (J), containing no apostrophe, can work in the context.

3. **A** Since there is Stop punctuation in the answer choices, use the Vertical Line Test. The first part of the sentence, *His portrait of Ice-T,* is not a complete idea, so (C) and (D) can be eliminated. Choice (A) is the best answer because the comma sets off the unnecessary information that follows, *the rapper and reality-TV star.*

4. **H** As written, this sentence is incomplete, so eliminate (F). Choices (G) and (J) do not make the sentence complete, so those can also be eliminated. Only (H) creates a complete idea.

5. **A** Pay close attention to the non-underlined part of this sentence. The word *them* needs to refer back to a specific noun, and only (A) provides the appropriate one: *Wiley's subjects.* Choices (B), (C), and (D) do not make the meaning of the sentence clear.

6. **G** All four of the answer choices say essentially the same thing. In this case, choose the shortest one that makes the sentence complete, consistent, and clear. Choice (G) is the shortest, and it preserves the meaning of the sentence, so (G) is the best answer.

7. **A** The underlined portion of this sentence is part of a pair of activities: The non-underlined portion says *mix the paints,* so the underlined portion must match the verb tense of the word *mix.* Only (A), the original answer, does so.

8. **J** As written, this sentence contains an ambiguous pronoun. The word *them* could refer to *assistants, materials,* or *paints,* none of which would work in context, eliminating (F). Choices (G) and (H) are unclear. Only (J) is adequately specific and is therefore the correct answer.

9. **C** All four of the answer choices say essentially the same thing. In this case, choose the shortest one that makes the sentence complete, consistent, and clear. Choice (C) is the shortest, and it preserves the meaning of the sentence, so (C) is the best answer.

10. J Each sentence in this paragraph contains a description of Wiley's subjects: *various, anonymous men; common people; people from oppressed cultures;* and *those to whom history pays no attention.* Therefore, the first sentence must preview this theme of the "common" or "average" people whom Wiley paints. Choice (J) does so and is therefore the best answer. Choices (F), (G), and (H) are true statements about Wiley himself, but they do not fit with the focus of this paragraph.

11. D The underlined portion does not fit where it is now, eliminating (A). The phrase *portray of Harlem various, anonymous men* does not make sense, eliminating (B). The phrase *Wiley of Harlem* does not make sense in context because, in addition to being awkwardly phrased, this phrase assumes that Wiley is from Harlem, which is not supported by the passage, eliminating (C). Only (D) can work, as it correctly situates the underlined portion in the phrase *the streets of Harlem.*

12. F The *recent work* is that of Kehinde Wiley, so the only pronoun that can be substituted here is *his*, as in (F). Choices (G), (H), and (J) do not work in this context.

13. C Each sentence in this paragraph contains a description of Wiley's subjects: *various, anonymous men; common people; people from oppressed cultures;* and *those to whom history pays no attention.* It would therefore not make sense to include a sentence that lists a museum where Wiley's paintings have been been shown, eliminating (A) and (B). Choice (D) can also be eliminated because this paragraph is not exclusively about Harlem. Only (C) correctly states that the sentence should not be included and gives the appropriate reason.

14. J The sentence is not complete as written, which immediately eliminates (F). Choices (G) and (H) also create incomplete sentences, so those too can be eliminated. Only (J) creates a complete idea, so it is the best answer.

15. B This sentence states that *Wiley's works can be seen in galleries all over the world,* and the underlined portion offers one reason that Wiley's popularity is so broad. Therefore, there is no reason to delete the information, especially because it does not repeat or undermine earlier parts of the passage. Eliminate (C) and (D). The underlined portion does not contain information about Wiley's selection of subjects, so (A) can also be eliminated. Only (B) correctly states that the information should be kept and gives an appropriate reason.

English Drill 2 (Chapter 7)

1. C If you can't cite a reason to use a comma, don't use one. This particular comma separates the subject from its verb, so eliminate (A). Choice (B) adds a comma unnecessarily, so it can also be eliminated. Choice (D) uses a single dash, which requires a complete idea before it. *After school let out, my best friend and I* is not a complete idea, so (D) can be eliminated. Only (C), containing no punctuation, remains.

2. **H** Stop punctuation is used in the answer choices, so use the Vertical Line Test. The first part of the sentence, *From the little trail beside the school, we'd climb down to the old railway tunnel that had gone dark many years before,* is complete. The second part of the sentence, *that pitch darkness was terrifying and mysterious,* is also complete. These ideas must therefore be separated by Stop punctuation, which eliminates (F) and (G). Choice (J) contains Stop punctuation (comma + FANBOYS), but it introduces a contrast with the word *yet* that does not make sense in this context. Only (H) works.

3. **B** Identify the purpose stated in the question that the correct choice is supposed to fulfill. It asks for a word that indicates that the narrator and his friend held their flashlights *nervously*. Choices (A) and (C) are neutral and therefore do not contain any hint of this nervousness. Choice (D) does not make sense in this context. Only (B), *clutching*, fulfills the purpose.

4. **H** Pay close attention to the question, which asks for *what happened during the summer walks*. Only (H) continues the narration in an appropriate way. Choices (F), (G), and (J) break the narrative flow. Also, the word *Sometimes* in (H) provides the necessary contrast to the word *always* in the following sentence.

5. **C** Since there are colons in the answer choices, use the Vertical Line Test to start. The first part of the sentence (up to the word *purpose*) is complete, as is the second part of the sentence (from *really* onward). Therefore, Go punctuation cannot work, eliminating (A) and (B). Choice (D) changes the meaning, so it can also be eliminated. Choice (C) can work because a colon requires only a complete idea before it: The idea after it can be complete or incomplete.

6. **F** Choices (F), (G), and (H) sound the same, but make sure you are using the correct pronoun for the context. *They're* is a contraction of *they are*, which cannot work in this context, and *their* is a possessive pronoun, which also cannot work, eliminating (G) and (H). Choice (J) does not make sense in this context, so only (F) remains as the correct answer.

7. **C** The word *though* in Sentence 6 indicates a contrast with whatever sentence comes before it. Therefore, look for a sentence that contains *aimless visits* with which this sentence will contrast. Sentence 1 provides these *aimless visits,* stating that the narrator and his friend didn't go down into the tunnel *with any specific purpose.* Therefore, the sentence should go before Sentence 2, as suggested in (C).

8. **J** The subject of this sentence is *history*, so the modifier that comes before it should modify that word. Choices (F), (G), and (H) all create modifiers that describe the narrator or something other than history, so they can be eliminated. Only (J) provides an appropriate modifier for *history*.

9. **D** As written, this sentence suggests that the history teacher gave this bit of information to his students four hundred years earlier, which can't work, eliminating (A). *Four centuries earlier* must refer to something about the Dutch settlers, and only (D) provides a placement that will create the appropriate reference.

10. **F** There is Stop punctuation in the answers, so use the Vertical Line Test. The first part of the sentence, *In fact...region,* is complete, but the second part of the sentence, *an area...New York,* is incomplete. Stop punctuation cannot work, eliminating (H), but there must be some pause, eliminating (G). Choice (J) makes the sentence incomplete, so it too can be eliminated. Only (F) works because a colon can be used only after a complete idea but can be followed by either an incomplete or complete idea.

11. **C** This sentence is incomplete as written, so (A) can be eliminated. Choice (D) creates the same problem. Of the remaining two choices, (C) is better because it indicates a contrast between the *ruthless* behavior of the Dutch and the fact that they *held on to many Lenape names.*

12. **J** All answer choices contain the word *the.* Choices (F), (G), and (H) put some information before that word, but none of that information is necessary. Therefore, in order to make the sentence as concise as possible, (J) is the best answer.

13. **A** This part of the sentence describes the word *influence,* and (A) is appropriate because that influence is *commemorated by the names.* Choices (B), (C), and (D) cannot work in the context, so they can be eliminated.

14. **H** This sentence describes *corridors of the city* that are not well-known, and (F), (G), and (J) provide reasonable synonyms. Choice (H), *classified,* may be a synonym for secret, but it is not an appropriate synonym in this context. Choice (H) is therefore correct because it would NOT be acceptable.

15. **D** A colon must be preceded by a complete idea. Neither *we were invited to* nor *we were invited to give* are complete ideas, so (B) and (C) can be eliminated. Eliminate (A) because it inserts a comma where there is not a good reason to insert one. Only (D), containing no punctuation, remains and is the best answer.

Rhetorical Skills Drill (Chapter 8)

1. **B** Cross off LEAST, and use POE. *Fame, stardom,* and *greatness* can all work the same way as *prominence* in the context of the sentence. *Projection* does not mean the same thing and is the correct answer.

2. **J** Try out each answer choice. *Live television* is the intended meaning.

3. **A** Evaluate the reasons given in the answers. The reason given in (A) could be true, but you have to read through the third paragraph to be able to judge. That makes this a good question to do later. In fact, the proposed clause does provide necessary context for the information given in the second and third sentences of the second paragraph.

4. **G** Identify the purpose in the question. The correct choice must convey extreme skill. *Honing their craft* does just that, while all of the other choices contain no specific mention of skill.

5. **D** Use POE. Sentences 2 and 3 should go back to back, with sentence 3 providing a list of the *young talents* mentioned in sentence 2. Eliminate (B) and (C), and compare the difference between (A) and (D). Sentence 1 should precede sentence 4, so (D) is correct.

6. **F** Identify the purpose in the question. The correct choice must introduce the paragraph. Finish reading the paragraph, and then return to the question. Since the topic involves problems with the live broadcast, (F) is the best introduction.

7. **C** To crack this type of strategy question, use POE to consider which choice correctly describes the sentence to be deleted. Choice (C) is the best description.

8. **F** Identify the purpose in the question and connect to the best reason among the answers. Choices (G), (H), and (J) offer reasons that do not support the purpose well, nor describe the content of the essay accurately.

9. **D** If you didn't see the warning at the beginning of the passage, you may have found the flow of the essay jarring. Even if you didn't, always use POE with order of paragraph questions. Look for topic and concluding sentences to make the flow of ideas consistent. The topic sentence of paragraph 2 makes a good transition after the discussion of accidents in paragraph 4.

PART III: MATH

Fundamentals Drill (Chapter 10)

1. **C** You'll need to find the prime factorization of 54, so use a factor tree. In using this tree, you'll find the prime factorization of $54 = 6 \times 9 = (2 \times 3) \times (3 \times 3) = 2 \times 3^3$. The *distinct* prime factors of 54, therefore, are 2 and 3. The product of these two numbers is 6, (C). If you chose (E), you may have missed the word *distinct*! Read carefully!

2. **G** Take this problem in bite-size pieces. If x is the least odd prime number, x must be 3. If y is the least positive integer multiple of 10, y must be 10. The difference between these two numbers is therefore $10 - 3 = 7$, (G). If you selected (K), be careful, you may have thought that 20 was the first integer multiple of 10, but the first multiple of any number is that number itself!

3. **D** Remember MADSPM, and don't forget Order of Operations, or PEMDAS. Do the parentheses first, and remember, when you raise an exponent to a *power*, you *multiply* those exponents: $(x^{-1}y^{-3})^{-2}(x^4y^7)^3 = (x^2y^6)(x^{12}y^{21})$. Now, combine like terms, and remember, when you multiply numbers with exponents, you add those exponents to one another: $(x^2y^6)(x^{12}y^{21}) = x^{14}y^{27}$, (D).

4. **H** Although this problem involves an imaginary number, you can still use a traditional FOIL method to find the answer. You are asked to square the expression, so do so, and remember to multiply the First, Outer, Inner, and Last terms: $(i + 4)(i + 4) = i^2 + 8i + 16$. None of the answer choices look quite like this, but remember, $i^2 = -1$, so substitute this term: $i^2 + 8i + 16 = -1 + 8i + 16 = 8i + 15$, (H).

5. **C** The prime numbers between 10 and 20 are as follows: 11, 13, 17, 19. You want the *least* sum of three *distinct* numbers, so the only possible answer is 11 + 13 + 17 = 41, (C). If you chose (B), you may have missed the word *distinct*.

Algebra Drill (Chapter 11)

1. **C** This might look like a traditional plug-and-chug problem, but the problem is asking for a specific value, and the answer choices are all real numbers—a great indication that you can PITA! This time, the problem is asking for the *largest*, so start with (E). Does the equation work if $x = 5$? $5^2 - 4(5) + 3 = 25 - 20 + 3 \neq 0$. Eliminate (E). Try (D): $4^2 - 4(4) + 3 = 16 - 16 + 3 \neq 0$. Try (C): $3^2 - 4(3) + 3 = 9 - 12 + 3 = 0$. It works, and because you're using PITA, you can stop once you've found a correct answer. If you selected (A), be careful, this is the *smallest* value of x that solves the equation!

2. **G** There are variables in the answer choices, so let's Plug In. Let's say $x = 2$ and plug this in to the equation: $\dfrac{(2)^2 + 6(2) - 27}{(2 + 9)} = \dfrac{4 + 12 - 27}{11} = \dfrac{-11}{11} = -1$, which means your target answer is -1. Try $x = 2$ in the answer choices to see which one gives this target answer. Only (G) works.

3. **A** This problem is very confusingly worded, so let's make sure we use PITA to keep all the work manageable. We'll start with (C) and work out from there, so our number is 11. "2 less than 3 times 11" is $3(11) - 2 = 31$. "4 more than the product of 5 and 3" is $4 + (5 \times 3) = 19$. The problem tells us these numbers should be the same, and they're not here, so eliminate (C); you can also eliminate (D) and (E) because we know we need something smaller than 31. Try (B): 10. "2 less than 3 times 10" is $3(10) - 2 = 28$—still too big. You can actually stop here, because there's only one answer choice left, but let's check it just to be on the safe side. Try (A): 7. "2 less than 3 times 7" is $3(7) - 2 = 19$. Bingo! Choice (A) is the correct answer.

4. **G** There are no variables in this problem, but it deals with fractions of a "certain number," which means that this is a Hidden Plug-In. Let's plug something in for the number of books: It's usually a good idea to do some common multiple of the denominators, so let's say there are 30 books. $\dfrac{2}{5}$ of the books are distributed in the morning, which means $\dfrac{2}{5} \times 30 = 12$ books are distributed in the morning, leaving 18 books. $\dfrac{1}{3}$ of the remaining books are distributed in the afternoon, which means $\dfrac{1}{3} \times 18 = 6$ books are distributed in the afternoon, leaving 12 books. We're looking for the fraction of remaining books, so find $\dfrac{12}{30} = \dfrac{6}{15} = \dfrac{2}{5}$, (G).

5.　**B**　We need to find out what happens as b increases, and there's no easier way to do that than to try it out. Let's start with $b = 2$. If $b = 2$, $a = \dfrac{3}{2}$. We want to see what happens when b increases, so let's try $b = 3$. If $b = 3$, $a = \dfrac{3}{3} = 1$. Therefore, we can see even from these two numbers, that as b increases, a decreases, so we can eliminate (A), (D), and (E). Now, the remaining question is whether a gets closer to 1 or if it continues to get closer to 0. Try $b = 4$. If $b = 4$, $a = \dfrac{3}{4}$. It has continued decreasing past 1, so eliminate (C). Only (B) works.

Geometry Drill (Chapter 12)

1.　**B**　Although this is a geometry problem, it is asking for a specific value and giving a list of numerical answer choices as possibilities. This means you can use PITA. Start with (C). If $\angle A = 50$, then $\angle B = 50$, and because it is twice as large as $\angle B$, $\angle C = 100$. The sum of the three angles will then be $50 + 50 + 100 = 200$, which is too big, so you can eliminate (C), (D), and (E). Try (B). If $\angle A = 45$, then $\angle B = 45$, and because it is twice as large as $\angle B$, $\angle C = 90$. The sum of the three angles will then be $45 + 45 + 90 = 180$, which is exactly what you need, so the answer is (B).

2.　**F**　When two parallel lines are intersected by a third line, it creates two kinds of angles: BIG angles and small angles. All the BIG angles are equal, and all the small angles are equal. Because $\angle D$ is on a separate line, you don't know anything about it, so it can't possibly be correct, eliminating (G) and (J). The BIG angles, therefore, are A and C. The small angles are B and E. Only (F) matches like angles, so it is the only possible correct answer.

3.　**D**　Deal with the two right triangles separately. We already have the two legs of $\triangle ABC$, so use the Pythagorean theorem ($a^2 + b^2 = c^2$) to find the hypotenuse. In this case, $AB^2 + BC^2 = AC^2$, so $(20)^2 + (15)^2 = AC^2$, and $AC = 25$. Notice this is a special right triangle: It's a 3:4:5 with a multiplier of 5! Now that we have AC, we have two sides of the other right triangle and can find the third. This, too, is a special right triangle with sides 7:24:25, and since we have sides 7 and 25, the remaining side must be 24, or (D). If you don't spot these special right triangles, you can always use the Pythagorean theorem.

4.　**G**　If you have one piece of information about a circle, you can find everything else you need. The area of circle A is 16π, and because $A = \pi r^2$, the radius of circle A must be 4. If the radius of circle B is half that of circle A, then the radius of circle B must be 2. Then find the circumference of circle B, with $C = 2\pi r = 2\pi(2) = 4\pi$, (G).

5. **A**   Separate the triangles and take this problem in bite-size pieces. You know two sides of the left triangle, so find the third with the Pythagorean theorem: $LO^2 + MO^2 = LM^2$. Substitute the values you know: $(4)^2 + MO^2 = (6)^2$, and $MO = 2\sqrt{5}$. Then because we know MO is equal to ON, ON must also be equal to $2\sqrt{5}$. You can either use the Pythagorean theorem to find the third side, or note that this is a 45:45:90 triangle, which means its sides must be in a ratio of $x : x : x\sqrt{2}$, so the third side must be $2\sqrt{5} \times \sqrt{2} = 2\sqrt{10}$, (A).

Word Problems Drill (Chapter 13)

1. **C**   The question is asking for a specific number and offering a list of numerical answer choices as options. Use PITA! Start with (C). If there are 12 boys in the class, then there must be $27 - 12 = 15$ girls. The ratio of boys to girls is therefore 12:15, which, when divided by 3, reduces to 4:5—exactly what you need! Choice (C) is the answer.

2. **J**   Use an average pie to help Linda fix her mistake. She initially worked with only 5 items to get an average of 88. Multiply this average and this number of items to find the sum total of these five tests: $88 \times 5 = 440$. Now add the sixth score to the total to find a new total of 522. Divide this number by the correct number of things, 6, to find an average of 87, (J). You're welcome, Linda.

3. **E**   Read this problem carefully. Because both percentages are taken "of the original," add them together to find that 8% of the original amount is lost. Use the percentage translation to find how much is lost: *8% of 490 tons is how much?* In math terms, $\dfrac{8}{100} \times 490 = 39.2$ tons lost. The question asks for how much remains, so subtract $490 - 39.2 = 450.8$ tons, (E).

4. **J**   There's no figure in this problem, so draw one! This problem has variables in the answer choices, which is a dead giveaway that you can Plug In. Let's say $a = 2$ and $b = 3$. To find the surface area, simply find the area of all the surfaces, remember that there will be six in all. The surfaces will have areas of 4, 4, 6, 6, 6, and 6. Add them together to find $4 + 4 + 6 + 6 + 6 + 6 = 32$, your target answer. Go to the answer choices to find the one that matches this answer when $a = 2$ and $b = 3$. Choice (F) gives 36. Choice (G) gives 12. Choice (H) gives 16. Choice (J) gives 32. Choice (K) gives 26. Only (J) works!

5. **C** This problem is asking for arrangements, so start by creating the number of slots you will need:

_____ _____ _____ _____ _____

There is a restriction on the last in that only one letter, W, can go there, so fill this one in first:

_____ _____ _____ _____ __1__

Then, fill the rest in as normal, remembering that W is already taken, so there are only four letters left:

__4__ __3__ __2__ __1__ __1__

Now that you've got the slots filled in, go ahead and multiply the numbers to find the number of possible arrangements:

__4__ × __3__ × __2__ × __1__ × __1__ = 24 possible arrangements, (C).

Graphing and Coordinate Geometry Drill (Chapter 14)

1. **E** First, use POE to eliminate some answer choices. Since this is only a > sign, we can eliminate (B) and (D) right off the bat. Now, let's use Plugging In to narrow down the rest. First, let's try $x = -2$: $-3(-2) - 6 > 9$. This equation doesn't work, because 0 is NOT greater than 9, so eliminate any answer choices that include -2, leaving only (E).

2. **G** Use the midpoint formula with the two given points. The midpoint formula is $\left(\dfrac{x_1 + x_2}{2}, \dfrac{y_1 + y_2}{2} \right)$, so plug the points into the equation to find $\left(\dfrac{3 + (-4)}{2}, \dfrac{5 + 3}{2} \right)$, resulting in a midpoint of $\left(-\dfrac{1}{2}, 4 \right)$, (G).

3. **B** In order to find the slope, put this equation into slope-intercept form, or $y = mx + b$. Combine the x-terms, and subtract 6 from each side to find $12x - 6 = y$, in which the m term must be 12, (B).

4. **H** Plot your points on a graph, and use them to draw a right triangle. The triangle will rise 4 units and run 3 units, meaning the legs of the triangle will be 3 and 4. You can then use the Pythagorean theorem to find the third side, or if you notice this is a 3:4:5 Pythagorean triple, the third side of the triangle must be 5, (H).

5. **C** Use the slope formula, $\dfrac{rise}{run}$ or $\dfrac{y_2 - y_1}{x_2 - x_1}$ with the given points to find that the slope is equivalent to $\dfrac{5 - 4}{13 - 6} = \dfrac{1}{7}$, (C). If you selected (E), you may have switched the x- and y-terms!

6. J The circle formula is $(x - h)^2 + (y - k)^2 = r^2$, in which (h, k) is the center of the circle, and r is its radius. Since $r^2 = 9$, the radius of the circle must be 3, eliminating (G), (H), and (K). Then look at the first part of the equation, the $(x - 3)$ matches up without any manipulation with the $(x - h)$ part of the equation, so h must equal 3, eliminating (F). Only (J) is left, and we don't even need to solve for k!

Trigonometry Drill (Chapter 15)

1. D Use SOHCAHTOA to find that $\tan\theta = \dfrac{opp}{adj}$. Your first impulse here may be to solve for the unknown side, but take a close look at where the θ is. Its adjacent side is 5, meaning the tangent of that angle must have a denominator of 5. Only (D) has it, so it's the only answer that can work. If you *do* solve for the unknown side, remember your Pythagorean triples: this is a 5:12:13 triangle, so the unknown side must be 12.

2. H $\cot\theta$ is defined as $\dfrac{1}{\tan\theta}$. Therefore, because $\tan\theta = 1$, substitute to find $\cot\theta = \dfrac{1}{\tan\theta} = \dfrac{1}{1} = 1$. Only (H) works!

3. C Remember the special trig identity which states $\sin^2\theta + \cos^2\theta = 1$. Substitute this into the equation, $x + \sin^2\theta + \cos^2\theta = 4$ to find that $x + 1 = 4$, so x must be equal to 3. Choice (C) is the best answer.

PART IV: READING

Passage I: Prose Fiction (Chapter 17)

1. C The passage as a whole describes the narrator's father's business, the narrator's own time as head of the business, and his son's current achievements as head of the business. Choice (C) best summarizes this narrative movement. Choice (A) suggests that the narrator does not like the direction in which his son has taken the business, which is untrue. Choice (B) is partially correct, though it is not as complete as (C). Choice (D) is too general for this very personal narrative.

2. F In the first paragraph, the narrator refers to Singer Stations and Service as *the company my father started*, eliminating (G). In the second paragraph, the narrator states that *my father thought it would put a safer face on the business to change the name to Singer*, eliminating (H). In the middle of the third paragraph, the narrator refers back to the name of the station (which he calls *alliterative*), and he adds, *All of the credit for this name has always gone to my father, and I can believe that he was the one behind this smart change*, eliminating (J). Only (F) remains, and although the first paragraph cites *a sophisticated iPhone app*, there is NOT a clear indication that his father was responsible for it.

3. **C** The end of the third paragraph says the following: *We've all had our challenges, regardless of age, so who says one generation has it tougher than the next, and frankly, who cares?* Therefore, the narrator does not take a firm stand on whether *one generation has it tougher than the next*. This agrees with (C). The narrator takes a specific stand about (A) in the final paragraph and (B) and (D) in the second paragraph.

4. **F** The middle of the third paragraph says of the narrator's father, *he had that added penchant, almost a poetic sense, for a clever, musical turn of phrase.* This *poetic sense* agrees with (F). The other choices are not specifically supported in the passage.

5. **A** The sentence in which the word appears reads as follows: *It doesn't hurt that the kid knows how to make a buck.* In this sentence, the word *hurt* does not have its primary meaning of to cause harm to a person. It is used idiomatically in the phrase *It doesn't hurt*, which means something like *It helps*. Only (A) points toward this secondary, idiomatic meaning.

6. **J** The third sentence of the fifth paragraph reads as follows: *My father at the very least had a family to come home to, and the saving grace of his religious observance forced him to take at least a day off every week.* This sentence establishes a clear link between *saving grace* and *religious observance*, meaning that (J) is the best answer.

7. **B** The end of the fifth paragraph reads as follows: *In later years, my mother told me secretly that she thought I actually had it worst of all—I had no burning desire to enter this business, but I didn't really have any other choice.* This question asks for the narrator's mother's view, which appears only in these lines. Choice (B) gives a clear paraphrase of these lines. Choices (A) and (D) are not mentioned in the text, and although some words from the passage appear in (C), these reflect the narrator's view of himself, not his mother's view of him.

8. **J** The first line of the sixth paragraph reads, *Even so, I was Raman (The Gas Man) Singer's son.* Because the narrator is this man's son, the man in question must be the narrator's father, as in (J).

9. **B** The middle of the final paragraph states the following: *As a result, at the urging of my college-aged daughter Geeta, I decided to try something I always wished that I had done. I enrolled in the business program at the State University, and before long, I realized that Geeta knew me better than I knew myself. I had fun like I never had before.* Choice (B) paraphrases these lines. Choices (A), (C), and (D) may be true, but they do not answer the question regarding the narrator's daughter, nor the lines that the question indirectly references.

10. **G** The lines in which the phrase appears read as follows: *I had fun like I never had before, and looking back, I came to see that the part of the business that always drew me in was learning.* These lines do not have anything to do with coming or going to a place but have more to do with the secondary meaning of *come to see*, which is a synonym for *realize*, as in (G).

Reading Drill 1 (Chapter 17)

1. **D** While there are hints of (A), (B), and (C) in the passage, none can be called the main point. Each idea is mentioned in the passage, but the author is more interested in presenting many different perspectives. In other words, the author is interested in showing that texting's *social effects are debatable*, as (D) suggests.

2. **F** As the fourth paragraph states, *Fields warns not only that we may have been 'dumbed down' by our technologies but also that we may have lost one of the essential elements of the human experience. "The content of our communication with each other…may be ultimately the same," Fields concedes, "but the real communication lives in the form…."* Choice (F) essentially restates these lines, so it is reasonable to infer that Fields would agree with this choice. Google is mentioned in the paragraph on Fields, but she does not offer any ideas on it, eliminating (G). Choices (H) and (J) contradict the lines quoted above.

3. **A** In the second paragraph, the author claims, *Text messages are already a part of the cultural landscape.* She then goes on to offer many examples of places where the text message plays a role, as (A) suggests. Although she mentions two novels that discuss texting, she does not say that these novels are *about* texting, nor are novels the only examples given in this list, eliminating (B). Though (C) uses words from the first paragraph, it do not describe that paragraph accurately. Choice (D) may be true, but it does not answer the question.

4. **J** The fourth paragraph states, *we could even say that our very nation was founded in these written communiqués: much of what we know about that era comes from these letters.* This idea of providing a historical record is restated in (J), making this the correct answer. Choice (F) does not make sense, and (G) and (H) have no support in the text.

5. **B** Of the *naysayers*, the fourth paragraph states, *naysayers have said that everything from the printing press, to the radio, to the movie screen, to Google, has compromised the way we think and understand.* In other words, these *naysayers* speak out against any new technologies as impairing our ability to think. The sports journalists described in (B) provide the closest analogue, in that they warn against changes.

6. **J** According to the first paragraph, Hillebrand and Ghillebaert, (J), were early contributors to the creation of the text message *to the extent that it has a creator at all.* Scorsese is a filmmaker; Wallace and Franzen are novelists; and Fields and Chacon are media theorists.

7. **D** Hillebrand states, *160 characters was sufficient to express most messages succinctly.* Therefore, he would likely agree with the statement that prefers messages of *a sentence or two rather than…two-hour phone conversation[s],* thus eliminating (A) and (B). Hillebrand nowhere states that the phone is no longer an effective communicator, eliminating (C). Choice (D) correctly states that Hillebrand would agree and gives a paraphrase of his quotation.

8. **F** The last sentence of the second paragraph states, *Text messages, in fact, move the whole plot of Martin Scorsese's 2006 film* The Departed, *a critical success and eventual Oscar winner for Best Picture.* All we know about this film is that text messages play a central role in moving the plot, meaning that text messages must appear in the answer, eliminating (H) and (J). Choice (G) can also be eliminated because there is no support for the idea that *the medium exploded in popularity after the film's release.* Only (F) is supported by the passage.

9. **C** The second sentence of the third paragraph reads, *Speaking on an actual telephone is basically defunct in 2013, not only for the economic reason that "time is money" and a text is quicker than a call but also for a much older desire in all of us for permanence.* Only a portion of this sentence relates to "time is money": *the economic reason that "time is money" and a text is quicker than a call.* Choice (C) mentions this quickness, so it is the correct answer. Choice (A) is not discussed. Choice (B) is part of this sentence, but it is evidence that works against the idea that "time is money." Choice (D) is not discussed in this paragraph, and neither the author nor the later theorists argue that text messaging has any positive effects on *intimacy*.

10. **G** In the final paragraph, Chacon observes, *Whatever the limitations of this new medium of communication, people are interacting on a day-to-day basis with more people than their ancestors might have met in a lifetime.* The words *Whatever the limitations* suggest that Chacon is about to say something positive about *this new medium of communication*, the text message. Choices (F), (H), and (J) focus too much on *ancestors* and lose the main point of the passage and paragraph. Only (G) adequately paraphrases the quote.

Reading Drill 2 (Chapter 18)

1. **D** Let's look at how these words are used in context. On the last line of the first paragraph, Mick is wondering whether to climb the ladder, and the passage says that she *screwed up nerve and began to climb.* What word could we put in place of the words *screwed up*? Something like *found* or *gathered.* The choice that comes closest to this idea is (D).

2. **J** In the first paragraph, Mick does not find Mr. Singer, so (F) can be eliminated. She doesn't make breakfast for her family, so (G) can also be crossed off. Although the passage says that Bubber does go to Sunday School, it doesn't say that Mick does, so (H) won't be right either. The paragraph does, however, describe how she cares for her younger brothers; this makes (J) the best choice.

3. **B** In the third sentence of the third paragraph, Mick is on top of the roof and thinks to herself this is *where everybody wanted to stand.* This supports (B).

4. **J** In the first paragraph, we find that Mick cares for Ralph and Bubber, so they aren't her father. The first paragraph also states that her father tells Mick that Mr. Singer came in late the night before. Therefore, we can eliminate (F), (G), and (H), which leaves us with (J) as the answer.

5. **A** According to the fourth paragraph, other children also climbed the roof, so we can eliminate (D). Although (B) and (C) might be true, there isn't really any evidence in the paragraph to support them. Choice (A) has some support because the sixth paragraph tells us that Mick was finally somewhere *by herself. No one was around and it was quiet and she could think for a while.* This makes (A) the best answer.

6. **G** This is a good example of using POE to solve a problem. There is nothing in line 31 that tells us that Mick felt she had a poor singing voice or that she did not want to scare her brothers, so we can eliminate (F) and (J). While there is some reason from the first paragraph to believe that she was slightly afraid of climbing the ladder, we need to find an answer that has support in this particular line, which doesn't mention fear of heights. Therefore, we should avoid (H) as well. Even if it's not entirely clear what (G) is saying, we should pick it because we're sure that the others aren't correct.

7. **B** The first paragraph tells us that Mick *waited for Mister Singer a long time. All the other boarders came down….* This is evidence that Mr. Singer is a boarder in Mick's house.

8. **H** In the next-to-last paragraph of this passage, Mick dreams of inventing a tiny radio, a flying machine, and a tunnel through the earth. The passage mentions big balloons but doesn't state that Mick intends to invent them. This makes (H) the best choice.

9. **C** Toward the end of the first paragraph, it states that the house was being built, and the fifth paragraph says *soon the work would all be finished.* This tells us that the house is unfinished, so the answer is (C).

10. **F** The passage doesn't mention getting good grades in school or wanting to spend more time with parents, so (H) and (J) can be eliminated. Moreover, while Mick does care for her younger brothers, the passage doesn't actually state that she wants to have children of her own. This makes (G) not very promising either. In the seventh paragraph, Mick spends time thinking about what she would do when she was very famous. This makes (F) the most reasonable choice.

PART V: SCIENCE

Basic Approach Drill 1 (Chapter 21)

1. **B**   As you were reading the question, did you notice that (A) and (B) were the same except that the words "T1" and "T2" were switched? The answer choices are opposites, and one of them will probably be correct. Let's try (A) and (B) first. At T1, Sample 1 has a greater number of molecules in motion. The introduction clarifies that this corresponds to an increase in kinetic energy. The graph contradicts (A), so the answer appears to be (B). Now let's check the other two choices. Does an increase in temperature lead to a decrease in kinetic energy? No. The passage states that an increase in temperature leads to an increase in kinetic energy. So we can eliminate (C). Now let's look at (D). Is it true that water never undergoes a phase change? No; in fact, the text accompanying the graph says just the opposite. So we can eliminate (D). Also, remember to be cautious of extreme language such as "never." The correct answer is (B).

2. **F**   The question refers to the second paragraph, which mentions phase changes. What happens during a phase change? Two things happen: (1) Increased kinetic energy weakens the attractive intermolecular forces in the water, and (2) Some molecules escape the liquid as a gas. Now that we have reviewed this information, it's pretty easy to eliminate (G) and (H). Now let's look at (J). Did we read anything in the passage that told us about other phase changes? No. This answer is beyond the realm of the passage and can be eliminated. So the correct answer is (F), and again we've reached it by using POE.

3. **B**   The ACT test writers want to see if you can predict what will happen if you raise the temperature of water higher than that of Sample 2. What answer choices should you eliminate? Decide whether the correct answer should begin with a yes or a no. How do we do that? Just check the graph with the results for Samples 1 and 2. When you increase the temperature, will the sample have more or less kinetic energy? It will have more. That means we can rule out (D). We can eliminate (C) because the temperature reading of Sample 2 is lower than the third sample. Now compare (A) with (B) to see which one is correct. Does an increase in temperature lead to greater or fewer numbers of molecules escaping the liquid? Greater. Thus, the correct answer is (B).

4. **F**   The passage states that when a substance goes from the liquid to the gas phase, it will evaporate. When a substance has reached the temperature at which it undergoes the phase change, it will evaporate. That's how molecules will escape. Therefore, the answer is (F).

5. **C**   When you look at the figure, which line goes the highest? Which has the highest kinetic energy at any one point? Well, the curve for T1 goes higher than the curve for T2. T2 has the highest average kinetic energy, but that's not what this question asks us to find. Therefore, (A) and (B) can be eliminated. Choice (D) is a nonsensical answer choice. Choice (C) is the best answer.

Basic Approach Drill 2 (Chapter 21)

1. **B** Do we see a solution of thyroxine that is 0.3 µg/ml? No. The ACT test writers want you to "guess-timate" where 0.3 µg/ml would fall on the table. This value would have to lie somewhere between 0.2 µg/ml and 0.5 µg/ml. The question requires that you make a guess within the values given. What do we call this skill? Interpolation! Now if we move across the x-axis to the value of 72 hours, and we move up to the range of values between 0.2 µg/ml and 0.5 µg/ml, we see that the y-values range from about 23 percent to 37 percent. The only one that falls in that range is (B)—30 percent.

2. **G** Notice that they want to know what is true for tadpoles in general. Let's start with (F). This is a ridiculous answer choice. We know that all normal tadpoles undergo metamorphosis. If you're not sure, take a look at the graph. The control group in the graph represents normal tadpoles. They do have some decrease in tail width, although not a lot, in 120 hours or 5 days. (Notice that you needed to know that 5 days is the same as 120 hours.) Thus, (F) is incorrect. You can also rule out (H) because the figure clearly shows that high concentrations of thyroxine solutions lead to the greatest decrease in tail width. The passage doesn't mention anything about temperature, thus (J) is out. The correct answer is (G). We see that the control sample shows some reduction in tail size in 120 hours, so it must take longer for the process to be complete.

3. **C** You must realize that as the tadpole develops, the tail is reabsorbed—or it shrinks. The graph compares percent decrease in tail width to hours. At 96 hours (4 days), the tadpoles showing the lowest percent decrease in tail width would be the least developed. Therefore, the answer must be (C), the tadpoles in 0.1 µg/ml.

4. **G** Thyroxine affects the metamorphosis of the tadpole by influencing the process of cell determination from tadpole cells into mature adult cells. You don't have to understand this process—just realize that it occurs between tadpole and adult stages. Begin with (F), (G), and (H), because you need a tadpole to start the process. Using POE, the correct answer can be only (G).

5. **C** Take a look at the figure provided. When do the lines start to differentiate from one another (showing different rates of tail reabsorption)? We can see that by 24 hours, the tadpoles placed in the various thyroxine solutions have each had a larger percent of their tails reabsorbed than the tadpoles in the control group. Choice (D) can be eliminated. Now look between 0 and 24 hours. At 0 hours and at 12 hours, the percent decrease in tail width is the same for all the tadpoles. Therefore, the change in metamorphosis rate must occur between 12 and 24 hours, so (C) is correct.

Basic Approach Drill 3 (Chapter 21)

1. **A**   Finally, a question about drawing a graph! This question was easy because you only needed to look at the x- and y-axes. The atomic number of the elements was the independent variable, and the atomic radius was the dependent variable. What happens to the atomic radius as you increase the atomic number? It gets smaller. That means we can eliminate (C) and (D). Now we have to decide if it's a linear relationship or an exponential one. Just check the numbers. Notice that the numbers decrease by a smaller amount each time—so it's a curve, not a straight line. Thus, the correct answer is (A).

2. **J**   You should look at relationships between electronegativity and one of the other properties of elements. Let's start with (G) and (J). Why? They are opposites (the switch again), so they can't both be true. If an element has a high electronegativity, is it a metal or a non-metal? It's a non-metal, so eliminate (G). Now we can check the other answer choices. Must an element with a high electronegativity have an even or an odd atomic number? Let's check. If you look at the two highest electronegative elements, O and F, one is even and one is odd. So (F) is not true. As for (H), we know that elements with high electronegativity pull their outer electrons (the passage defines electronegativity as a measure of that strength). Therefore, we can eliminate (H). The correct answer is (J).

3. **B**   This question asks you to make a generalization about trends in the chart, with regard to the bigger picture. Let's take a moment to think about the answer choices. If we want to make generalizations about elements, would an answer that refers to specific elements be the correct one? Probably not. So we can probably eliminate (D). But let's look at (D) more closely to be sure. Is the atomic radius of F larger than that of N? No. Do all metals have high electronegativity values? No. Now notice that (A) and (B) state opposite trends. Use the chart to determine which is correct. As the atomic radius decreases, electronegativity increases. Thus, the correct answer is (B).

4. **G**   The first part is easy. Look at the chart to tell you which has a greater electronegativity, Li or F. F, of course! So we can get rid of (J). Now why is the electronegativity of F greater than that of Li? We have to choose between (F) and (G). Can you determine which one of these is correct by using the information in the chart? No. Go back to the introduction and skim for information about electronegativity. The passage says specifically that within a row of the periodic table, the electronegativity tends to increase with increasing atomic number, due to the tighter bonding between protons and electrons. It's not the number that's important, but rather how tightly bound they are. F has a higher atomic number than Li and more electrons than Li, therefore, F's electrons are more tightly bound than Li's. The best answer is (G).

5. **A**   You must take new information given in the question and apply it to the chart given in the passage. Fortunately, this is very easy. Be careful; the question asks for increasing order of ionization energies. Because it follows the same trend as electronegativity, just find the answer that lists elements with increasing electronegativities. The answer can only be (A).

Fighting Scientists Drill 1 (Chapter 22)

1. **A** Scientist 1 argues that natural gas formed where the *remains of marine organisms and terrestrial plants piled up on land and on the seafloor over a long period*. This indicates that the natural gas reservoir may have formed near the site of a past ocean, where the organic remnants of marine organisms could have been transformed into natural gas over a long period of time. Therefore, (A) is the correct answer. Choice (B) indicates that the natural gas reservoirs would be found near the site of a present day ocean, where none had existed in the past, leaving no time for the conversion process described by Scientist 1 to occur. Choice (C) is not mentioned by Scientist 1. Neither scientist's argument includes formation of microorganisms from non-living carbon sources, eliminating (D).

2. **H** Scientist 1 mentions that natural gas would have formed at depths greater than 10 miles below the Earth's surface. Natural gas formed 20 miles below the surface of the Earth is consistent with the mechanism described by Scientist 1. Therefore, (H) is the correct answer.

3. **D** Pressure will increase as the depth below the Earth's surface increases. Scientist 2 indicates that natural gas formed at depths of 2 to 10 miles below the surface. Scientist 1 indicates that natural gas formed at depths of more than 10 miles. As a result, Scientist 2, who indicates that natural gas formed at shallower depths, also indicates that natural gas formation occurred at lower pressures. Therefore, (D) is the correct answer.

4. **G** According to Scientist 2, natural gas formed at depths from 2 to 10 miles beneath the surface of the Earth. This eliminates (F) and (H), which depict natural gas as forming at depths of greater than 10 miles beneath the Earth's surface. The first paragraph of the passage explains that natural gas reservoirs are located between 0 and 0.5 miles beneath the Earth's surface. As this information precedes the discussion of the individual scientists' specific arguments, this information is not disputed and is acknowledged by both scientists, so Scientist 2's description should be consistent with this information. Only (G) depicts a natural gas reservoir located between 0 and 0.5 miles beneath Earth's surface.

5. **D** According to Scientist 2, *microorganisms convert the carbon compounds and water into the hydrocarbons of natural gas*. The reaction of carbon dioxide (CO_2), a carbon-containing compound, and water would be an example of such a reaction and would therefore support Scientist 2's argument that microorganisms convert organic material into natural gas. Thus, (D) is the correct answer.

6. **H** Scientist 2 states that carbon-13 is contained in the natural gas brought up to the reservoir, eliminating (F) and (G). In order for the gas to rise upward through the material in which it migrates, it must be less dense than that material, eliminating (J). Therefore, (H) is the correct answer.

7. **B** According to Scientist 2, *microorganisms convert the carbon compounds and water into the hydrocarbons of natural gas*. Carbon dioxide (CO_2) (III) is a carbon-containing compound and could be involved in the formation of natural gas as described by Scientist 2. Neither F_2 (I) nor KCl(II) are water or carbon compounds, eliminating (A), (C) and (D). Therefore, (B) is the correct answer.

Fighting Scientists Drill 2 (Chapter 22)

1. **B** This paragraph is about three students' explanations for effusion rates. In this passage, since the fighting scientists (in this case, fighting students) didn't perform the experiment for which they're offering competing explanations—the professor did—the question references the professor rather than the students. According to the passage, the time required for all 100 mL of the gas to effuse from the syringe into the empty flask was measured. As a result, the volume of gas in the flask continued to increase until all of the gas was emptied from the syringe. Therefore, the correct answer is (B).

2. **F** Student 1 proposes that gases with greater molecular masses diffuse more slowly. Therefore, gases with smaller molecular masses diffuse more quickly. Of the choices listed, hydrogen gas (2.016 amu) possesses the smallest molecular mass and will effuse most quickly. Thus, (F) is the correct answer.

3. **B** Student 1 proposes that gases with greater molecular masses diffuse more slowly. According to the results of the experiment, Gas A's total effusion time is 4 seconds, and Gas B's total effusion time is 16 seconds. The question states that nitrogen gas' effusion time is 9 seconds—longer than Gas A's total effusion time but shorter than Gas B's total effusion time. Consequently, nitrogen gas' molecular mass must be greater than Gas A's molecular mass and smaller than Gas B's molecular mass. Thus, (B) is the correct answer.

4. **F** According to Student 2, gases with greater molecular volumes effuse more slowly. Table 1 shows you that xenon's molecular volume is greater than krypton's. Based upon this, krypton should effuse more slowly than does xenon and contradicts the claim made in the question. Thus, (F) is the correct answer.

5. **A** Student 3 proposes that gases with greater densities effuse more slowly than gases with lesser densities. Table 1 says that xenon is denser than krypton and that krypton is denser than oxygen. Xenon, the densest gas, should therefore have the smallest relative effusion rate, while oxygen, the least dense gas, should have the greatest relative effusion rate. The relative effusion rate of krypton should be between the relative effusion rates of xenon and oxygen. Choice (A) correctly demonstrates this relationship between effusion rates.

6. **J** Student 1 proposes that gases with greater molecular *masses* diffuse more slowly than gases with smaller molecular masses. Student 2 proposes that gases with greater molecular *volumes* effuse more slowly than gases with smaller molecular volumes. Student 3 proposes that gases with greater *densities* effuse more slowly than gases with lesser densities. According to Table 1, helium's molecular mass and density is greater than hydrogen's, while hydrogen's molecular volume is greater than helium's. Students 1 and 3, then, would predict that helium would effuse more slowly;

Student 2 will predict that hydrogen will effuse more slowly. The professor's experiment finds that Gas B effuses more slowly than Gas A. If helium were Gas B and hydrogen were Gas A, then Student 1's prediction and Student 3's prediction would be consistent with the professor's finding, while Student 2's prediction would not be. Thus, (J) is the correct answer.

7. **C** Student 1 proposes that gases with greater molecular *masses* diffuse more slowly than gases with smaller molecular masses. Student 2 proposes that gases with greater molecular *volumes* effuse more slowly than gases with smaller molecular volumes. Student 3 proposes that gases with greater *densities* effuse more slowly than gases with lesser densities. According to the information provided in the table in the question and in Table 1, krypton's molecular mass and density are greater than carbon dioxide's, while carbon dioxide's molecular volume is greater than krypton's. Student 1 and Student 3 would predict that carbon dioxide effuses more quickly than krypton, yielding shorter effusion times for carbon dioxide. Student 2 would predict the opposite, that krypton would effuse more quickly than carbon dioxide, yielding shorter effusion times for krypton. Therefore, (C) is the correct answer.

Part VIII
The Princeton Review ACT Practice Exam 1

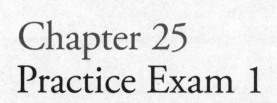

Chapter 25
Practice Exam 1

ACT Diagnostic Test Form

Use a No. 2 pencil only. Be sure each mark is dark and completely fills the intended oval. Completely erase any errors or stray marks.

1. YOUR NAME: _____
   (Print)   Last   First   M.I.

SIGNATURE: _____ DATE: _____ / _____ / _____

HOME ADDRESS: _____
   (Print)   Number and Street

_____
   City   State   Zip

E-MAIL: _____

PHONE NO.: _____
   (Print)

SCHOOL: _____

CLASS OF: _____

IMPORTANT: Please fill in these boxes exactly as shown on the back cover of your tests book.

2. TEST FORM

_____

3. TEST CODE

⓪	⓪	⓪	⓪
①	①	①	①
②	②	②	②
③	③	③	③
④	④	④	④
⑤	⑤	⑤	⑤
⑥	⑥	⑥	⑥
⑦	⑦	⑦	⑦
⑧	⑧	⑧	⑧
⑨	⑨	⑨	⑨

4. PHONE NUMBER

⓪	⓪	⓪	⓪	⓪	⓪	⓪
①	①	①	①	①	①	①
②	②	②	②	②	②	②
③	③	③	③	③	③	③
④	④	④	④	④	④	④
⑤	⑤	⑤	⑤	⑤	⑤	⑤
⑥	⑥	⑥	⑥	⑥	⑥	⑥
⑦	⑦	⑦	⑦	⑦	⑦	⑦
⑧	⑧	⑧	⑧	⑧	⑧	⑧
⑨	⑨	⑨	⑨	⑨	⑨	⑨

5. YOUR NAME

First 4 letters of last name				FIRST INIT	MID INIT
Ⓐ	Ⓐ	Ⓐ	Ⓐ	Ⓐ	Ⓐ
Ⓑ	Ⓑ	Ⓑ	Ⓑ	Ⓑ	Ⓑ
Ⓒ	Ⓒ	Ⓒ	Ⓒ	Ⓒ	Ⓒ
Ⓓ	Ⓓ	Ⓓ	Ⓓ	Ⓓ	Ⓓ
Ⓔ	Ⓔ	Ⓔ	Ⓔ	Ⓔ	Ⓔ
Ⓕ	Ⓕ	Ⓕ	Ⓕ	Ⓕ	Ⓕ
Ⓖ	Ⓖ	Ⓖ	Ⓖ	Ⓖ	Ⓖ
Ⓗ	Ⓗ	Ⓗ	Ⓗ	Ⓗ	Ⓗ
Ⓘ	Ⓘ	Ⓘ	Ⓘ	Ⓘ	Ⓘ
Ⓙ	Ⓙ	Ⓙ	Ⓙ	Ⓙ	Ⓙ
Ⓚ	Ⓚ	Ⓚ	Ⓚ	Ⓚ	Ⓚ
Ⓛ	Ⓛ	Ⓛ	Ⓛ	Ⓛ	Ⓛ
Ⓜ	Ⓜ	Ⓜ	Ⓜ	Ⓜ	Ⓜ
Ⓝ	Ⓝ	Ⓝ	Ⓝ	Ⓝ	Ⓝ
Ⓞ	Ⓞ	Ⓞ	Ⓞ	Ⓞ	Ⓞ
Ⓟ	Ⓟ	Ⓟ	Ⓟ	Ⓟ	Ⓟ
Ⓠ	Ⓠ	Ⓠ	Ⓠ	Ⓠ	Ⓠ
Ⓡ	Ⓡ	Ⓡ	Ⓡ	Ⓡ	Ⓡ
Ⓢ	Ⓢ	Ⓢ	Ⓢ	Ⓢ	Ⓢ
Ⓣ	Ⓣ	Ⓣ	Ⓣ	Ⓣ	Ⓣ
Ⓤ	Ⓤ	Ⓤ	Ⓤ	Ⓤ	Ⓤ
Ⓥ	Ⓥ	Ⓥ	Ⓥ	Ⓥ	Ⓥ
Ⓦ	Ⓦ	Ⓦ	Ⓦ	Ⓦ	Ⓦ
Ⓧ	Ⓧ	Ⓧ	Ⓧ	Ⓧ	Ⓧ
Ⓨ	Ⓨ	Ⓨ	Ⓨ	Ⓨ	Ⓨ
Ⓩ	Ⓩ	Ⓩ	Ⓩ	Ⓩ	Ⓩ

6. DATE OF BIRTH

MONTH	DAY		YEAR	
◯ JAN				
◯ FEB				
◯ MAR	⓪	⓪	⓪	⓪
◯ APR	①	①	①	①
◯ MAY	②	②	②	②
◯ JUN	③	③	③	③
◯ JUL		④	④	④
◯ AUG		⑤	⑤	⑤
◯ SEP		⑥	⑥	⑥
◯ OCT		⑦	⑦	⑦
◯ NOV		⑧	⑧	⑧
◯ DEC		⑨	⑨	⑨

7. SEX

◯ MALE
◯ FEMALE

8. OTHER

1 Ⓐ Ⓑ Ⓒ Ⓓ Ⓔ
2 Ⓐ Ⓑ Ⓒ Ⓓ Ⓔ
3 Ⓐ Ⓑ Ⓒ Ⓓ Ⓔ

OpScan iNSIGHT™ forms by Pearson NCS EM-255315-1:654321   Printed in U.S.A.

THIS PAGE INTENTIONALLY LEFT BLANK

The Princeton Review
Diagnostic ACT Form

Completely darken bubbles with a No. 2 pencil. If you make a mistake, be sure to erase mark completely. Erase all stray marks.

ENGLISH

1	Ⓐ	Ⓑ	Ⓒ	Ⓓ	21	Ⓐ	Ⓑ	Ⓒ	Ⓓ	41	Ⓐ	Ⓑ	Ⓒ	Ⓓ	61	Ⓐ	Ⓑ	Ⓒ	Ⓓ
2	Ⓕ	Ⓖ	Ⓗ	Ⓙ	22	Ⓕ	Ⓖ	Ⓗ	Ⓙ	42	Ⓕ	Ⓖ	Ⓗ	Ⓙ	62	Ⓕ	Ⓖ	Ⓗ	Ⓙ
3	Ⓐ	Ⓑ	Ⓒ	Ⓓ	23	Ⓐ	Ⓑ	Ⓒ	Ⓓ	43	Ⓐ	Ⓑ	Ⓒ	Ⓓ	63	Ⓐ	Ⓑ	Ⓒ	Ⓓ
4	Ⓕ	Ⓖ	Ⓗ	Ⓙ	24	Ⓕ	Ⓖ	Ⓗ	Ⓙ	44	Ⓕ	Ⓖ	Ⓗ	Ⓙ	64	Ⓕ	Ⓖ	Ⓗ	Ⓙ
5	Ⓐ	Ⓑ	Ⓒ	Ⓓ	25	Ⓐ	Ⓑ	Ⓒ	Ⓓ	45	Ⓐ	Ⓑ	Ⓒ	Ⓓ	65	Ⓐ	Ⓑ	Ⓒ	Ⓓ
6	Ⓕ	Ⓖ	Ⓗ	Ⓙ	26	Ⓕ	Ⓖ	Ⓗ	Ⓙ	46	Ⓕ	Ⓖ	Ⓗ	Ⓙ	66	Ⓕ	Ⓖ	Ⓗ	Ⓙ
7	Ⓐ	Ⓑ	Ⓒ	Ⓓ	27	Ⓐ	Ⓑ	Ⓒ	Ⓓ	47	Ⓐ	Ⓑ	Ⓒ	Ⓓ	67	Ⓐ	Ⓑ	Ⓒ	Ⓓ
8	Ⓕ	Ⓖ	Ⓗ	Ⓙ	28	Ⓕ	Ⓖ	Ⓗ	Ⓙ	48	Ⓕ	Ⓖ	Ⓗ	Ⓙ	68	Ⓕ	Ⓖ	Ⓗ	Ⓙ
9	Ⓐ	Ⓑ	Ⓒ	Ⓓ	29	Ⓐ	Ⓑ	Ⓒ	Ⓓ	49	Ⓐ	Ⓑ	Ⓒ	Ⓓ	69	Ⓐ	Ⓑ	Ⓒ	Ⓓ
10	Ⓕ	Ⓖ	Ⓗ	Ⓙ	30	Ⓕ	Ⓖ	Ⓗ	Ⓙ	50	Ⓕ	Ⓖ	Ⓗ	Ⓙ	70	Ⓕ	Ⓖ	Ⓗ	Ⓙ
11	Ⓐ	Ⓑ	Ⓒ	Ⓓ	31	Ⓐ	Ⓑ	Ⓒ	Ⓓ	51	Ⓐ	Ⓑ	Ⓒ	Ⓓ	71	Ⓐ	Ⓑ	Ⓒ	Ⓓ
12	Ⓕ	Ⓖ	Ⓗ	Ⓙ	32	Ⓕ	Ⓖ	Ⓗ	Ⓙ	52	Ⓕ	Ⓖ	Ⓗ	Ⓙ	72	Ⓕ	Ⓖ	Ⓗ	Ⓙ
13	Ⓐ	Ⓑ	Ⓒ	Ⓓ	33	Ⓐ	Ⓑ	Ⓒ	Ⓓ	53	Ⓐ	Ⓑ	Ⓒ	Ⓓ	73	Ⓐ	Ⓑ	Ⓒ	Ⓓ
14	Ⓕ	Ⓖ	Ⓗ	Ⓙ	34	Ⓕ	Ⓖ	Ⓗ	Ⓙ	54	Ⓕ	Ⓖ	Ⓗ	Ⓙ	74	Ⓕ	Ⓖ	Ⓗ	Ⓙ
15	Ⓐ	Ⓑ	Ⓒ	Ⓓ	35	Ⓐ	Ⓑ	Ⓒ	Ⓓ	55	Ⓐ	Ⓑ	Ⓒ	Ⓓ	75	Ⓐ	Ⓑ	Ⓒ	Ⓓ
16	Ⓕ	Ⓖ	Ⓗ	Ⓙ	36	Ⓕ	Ⓖ	Ⓗ	Ⓙ	56	Ⓕ	Ⓖ	Ⓗ	Ⓙ					
17	Ⓐ	Ⓑ	Ⓒ	Ⓓ	37	Ⓐ	Ⓑ	Ⓒ	Ⓓ	57	Ⓐ	Ⓑ	Ⓒ	Ⓓ					
18	Ⓕ	Ⓖ	Ⓗ	Ⓙ	38	Ⓕ	Ⓖ	Ⓗ	Ⓙ	58	Ⓕ	Ⓖ	Ⓗ	Ⓙ					
19	Ⓐ	Ⓑ	Ⓒ	Ⓓ	39	Ⓐ	Ⓑ	Ⓒ	Ⓓ	59	Ⓐ	Ⓑ	Ⓒ	Ⓓ					
20	Ⓕ	Ⓖ	Ⓗ	Ⓙ	40	Ⓕ	Ⓖ	Ⓗ	Ⓙ	60	Ⓕ	Ⓖ	Ⓗ	Ⓙ					

MATHEMATICS

1	Ⓐ	Ⓑ	Ⓒ	Ⓓ	Ⓔ	16	Ⓕ	Ⓖ	Ⓗ	Ⓙ	Ⓚ	31	Ⓐ	Ⓑ	Ⓒ	Ⓓ	Ⓔ	46	Ⓕ	Ⓖ	Ⓗ	Ⓙ	Ⓚ
2	Ⓕ	Ⓖ	Ⓗ	Ⓙ	Ⓚ	17	Ⓐ	Ⓑ	Ⓒ	Ⓓ	Ⓔ	32	Ⓕ	Ⓖ	Ⓗ	Ⓙ	Ⓚ	47	Ⓐ	Ⓑ	Ⓒ	Ⓓ	Ⓔ
3	Ⓐ	Ⓑ	Ⓒ	Ⓓ	Ⓔ	18	Ⓕ	Ⓖ	Ⓗ	Ⓙ	Ⓚ	33	Ⓐ	Ⓑ	Ⓒ	Ⓓ	Ⓔ	48	Ⓕ	Ⓖ	Ⓗ	Ⓙ	Ⓚ
4	Ⓕ	Ⓖ	Ⓗ	Ⓙ	Ⓚ	19	Ⓐ	Ⓑ	Ⓒ	Ⓓ	Ⓔ	34	Ⓕ	Ⓖ	Ⓗ	Ⓙ	Ⓚ	49	Ⓐ	Ⓑ	Ⓒ	Ⓓ	Ⓔ
5	Ⓐ	Ⓑ	Ⓒ	Ⓓ	Ⓔ	20	Ⓕ	Ⓖ	Ⓗ	Ⓙ	Ⓚ	35	Ⓐ	Ⓑ	Ⓒ	Ⓓ	Ⓔ	50	Ⓕ	Ⓖ	Ⓗ	Ⓙ	Ⓚ
6	Ⓕ	Ⓖ	Ⓗ	Ⓙ	Ⓚ	21	Ⓐ	Ⓑ	Ⓒ	Ⓓ	Ⓔ	36	Ⓕ	Ⓖ	Ⓗ	Ⓙ	Ⓚ	51	Ⓐ	Ⓑ	Ⓒ	Ⓓ	Ⓔ
7	Ⓐ	Ⓑ	Ⓒ	Ⓓ	Ⓔ	22	Ⓕ	Ⓖ	Ⓗ	Ⓙ	Ⓚ	37	Ⓐ	Ⓑ	Ⓒ	Ⓓ	Ⓔ	52	Ⓕ	Ⓖ	Ⓗ	Ⓙ	Ⓚ
8	Ⓕ	Ⓖ	Ⓗ	Ⓙ	Ⓚ	23	Ⓐ	Ⓑ	Ⓒ	Ⓓ	Ⓔ	38	Ⓕ	Ⓖ	Ⓗ	Ⓙ	Ⓚ	53	Ⓐ	Ⓑ	Ⓒ	Ⓓ	Ⓔ
9	Ⓐ	Ⓑ	Ⓒ	Ⓓ	Ⓔ	24	Ⓕ	Ⓖ	Ⓗ	Ⓙ	Ⓚ	39	Ⓐ	Ⓑ	Ⓒ	Ⓓ	Ⓔ	54	Ⓕ	Ⓖ	Ⓗ	Ⓙ	Ⓚ
10	Ⓕ	Ⓖ	Ⓗ	Ⓙ	Ⓚ	25	Ⓐ	Ⓑ	Ⓒ	Ⓓ	Ⓔ	40	Ⓕ	Ⓖ	Ⓗ	Ⓙ	Ⓚ	55	Ⓐ	Ⓑ	Ⓒ	Ⓓ	Ⓔ
11	Ⓐ	Ⓑ	Ⓒ	Ⓓ	Ⓔ	26	Ⓕ	Ⓖ	Ⓗ	Ⓙ	Ⓚ	41	Ⓐ	Ⓑ	Ⓒ	Ⓓ	Ⓔ	56	Ⓕ	Ⓖ	Ⓗ	Ⓙ	Ⓚ
12	Ⓕ	Ⓖ	Ⓗ	Ⓙ	Ⓚ	27	Ⓐ	Ⓑ	Ⓒ	Ⓓ	Ⓔ	42	Ⓕ	Ⓖ	Ⓗ	Ⓙ	Ⓚ	57	Ⓐ	Ⓑ	Ⓒ	Ⓓ	Ⓔ
13	Ⓐ	Ⓑ	Ⓒ	Ⓓ	Ⓔ	28	Ⓕ	Ⓖ	Ⓗ	Ⓙ	Ⓚ	43	Ⓐ	Ⓑ	Ⓒ	Ⓓ	Ⓔ	58	Ⓕ	Ⓖ	Ⓗ	Ⓙ	Ⓚ
14	Ⓕ	Ⓖ	Ⓗ	Ⓙ	Ⓚ	29	Ⓐ	Ⓑ	Ⓒ	Ⓓ	Ⓔ	44	Ⓕ	Ⓖ	Ⓗ	Ⓙ	Ⓚ	59	Ⓐ	Ⓑ	Ⓒ	Ⓓ	Ⓔ
15	Ⓐ	Ⓑ	Ⓒ	Ⓓ	Ⓔ	30	Ⓕ	Ⓖ	Ⓗ	Ⓙ	Ⓚ	45	Ⓐ	Ⓑ	Ⓒ	Ⓓ	Ⓔ	60	Ⓕ	Ⓖ	Ⓗ	Ⓙ	Ⓚ

The Princeton Review
Diagnostic ACT Form

READING

1 (A) (B) (C) (D)	11 (A) (B) (C) (D)	21 (A) (B) (C) (D)	31 (A) (B) (C) (D)
2 (F) (G) (H) (J)	12 (F) (G) (H) (J)	22 (F) (G) (H) (J)	32 (F) (G) (H) (J)
3 (A) (B) (C) (D)	13 (A) (B) (C) (D)	23 (A) (B) (C) (D)	33 (A) (B) (C) (D)
4 (F) (G) (H) (J)	14 (F) (G) (H) (J)	24 (F) (G) (H) (J)	34 (F) (G) (H) (J)
5 (A) (B) (C) (D)	15 (A) (B) (C) (D)	25 (A) (B) (C) (D)	35 (A) (B) (C) (D)
6 (F) (G) (H) (J)	16 (F) (G) (H) (J)	26 (F) (G) (H) (J)	36 (F) (G) (H) (J)
7 (A) (B) (C) (D)	17 (A) (B) (C) (D)	27 (A) (B) (C) (D)	37 (A) (B) (C) (D)
8 (F) (G) (H) (J)	18 (F) (G) (H) (J)	28 (F) (G) (H) (J)	38 (F) (G) (H) (J)
9 (A) (B) (C) (D)	19 (A) (B) (C) (D)	29 (A) (B) (C) (D)	39 (A) (B) (C) (D)
10 (F) (G) (H) (J)	20 (F) (G) (H) (J)	30 (F) (G) (H) (J)	40 (F) (G) (H) (J)

SCIENCE REASONING

1 (A) (B) (C) (D)	11 (A) (B) (C) (D)	21 (A) (B) (C) (D)	31 (A) (B) (C) (D)
2 (F) (G) (H) (J)	12 (F) (G) (H) (J)	22 (F) (G) (H) (J)	32 (F) (G) (H) (J)
3 (A) (B) (C) (D)	13 (A) (B) (C) (D)	23 (A) (B) (C) (D)	33 (A) (B) (C) (D)
4 (F) (G) (H) (J)	14 (F) (G) (H) (J)	24 (F) (G) (H) (J)	34 (F) (G) (H) (J)
5 (A) (B) (C) (D)	15 (A) (B) (C) (D)	25 (A) (B) (C) (D)	35 (A) (B) (C) (D)
6 (F) (G) (H) (J)	16 (F) (G) (H) (J)	26 (F) (G) (H) (J)	36 (F) (G) (H) (J)
7 (A) (B) (C) (D)	17 (A) (B) (C) (D)	27 (A) (B) (C) (D)	37 (A) (B) (C) (D)
8 (F) (G) (H) (J)	18 (F) (G) (H) (J)	28 (F) (G) (H) (J)	38 (F) (G) (H) (J)
9 (A) (B) (C) (D)	19 (A) (B) (C) (D)	29 (A) (B) (C) (D)	39 (A) (B) (C) (D)
10 (F) (G) (H) (J)	20 (F) (G) (H) (J)	30 (F) (G) (H) (J)	40 (F) (G) (H) (J)

I hereby certify that I have truthfully identified myself on this form. I accept the consequences of falsifying my identity.

_____
Your signature

_____
Today's date

The Princeton Review
Diagnostic ACT Form

ESSAY

Begin your essay on this side. If necessary, continue on the opposite side.

Continue on the opposite side if necessary.

The Princeton Review
Diagnostic ACT Form

Continued from previous page.

THIS PAGE INTENTIONALLY LEFT BLANK

ENGLISH TEST
45 Minutes—75 Questions

DIRECTIONS: In the five passages that follow, certain words and phrases are underlined and numbered. In the right-hand column, you will find alternatives for the underlined part. In most cases, you are to choose the one that best expresses the idea, makes the statement appropriate for standard written English, or is worded most consistently with the style and tone of the passage as a whole. If you think the original version is best, choose "NO CHANGE." In some cases, you will find in the right-hand column a question about the underlined part. You are to choose the best answer to the question.

You will also find questions about a section of the passage, or about the passage as a whole. These questions do not refer to an underlined portion of the passage, but rather are identified by a number or numbers in a box.

For each question, choose the alternative you consider best and fill in the corresponding oval on your answer document. Read each passage through once before you begin to answer the questions that accompany it. For many of the questions, you must read several sentences beyond the question to determine the answer. Be sure that you have read far enough ahead each time you choose an alternative.

PASSAGE I

I Am Iron Man

[1] The term "Iron Man" has many connotations, including references to a song, a comic book icon, even a movie. [2] Yet only one definition of the term truly lives up to its name: the Ironman Triathlon held annually in Hawaii a picturesque setting for a challenging race. [3] This grueling race demands amazing physical prowess and the ability to swim, bike, and run a marathon, all in less than 12 hours with no break. [4] Very few individuals are up to the task. ☐2

1. **A.** NO CHANGE
   B. Hawaii,
   C. Hawaii, being
   D. Hawaii, it is

2. If the writer were to delete Sentence 4, the essay would primarily lose details that:
   F. emphasize how difficult the race truly is.
   G. mourn how few athletes are able to visit Hawaii in order to compete in the race.
   H. highlight that most athletes prefer the run to the swimming or biking components of the race.
   J. suggest that women are not truly competitive in the race.

Otherwise, Gordon Haller is a notable exception. Growing up in the 1950s, Haller developed an interest in many sports categorized as endurance athletics, and welcomed their grueling physical demands. As he pursued a degree in physics he drove a

3. **A.** NO CHANGE
   B. As a result,
   C. In addition,
   D. However,

4. **F.** NO CHANGE
   G. athletics and welcomed their
   H. athletics, and welcomed there,
   J. athletics and, welcomed there

GO ON TO THE NEXT PAGE.

taxi to pay the bills, but competitive training <u>proved</u> his passion.
₅
So when he heard about the race in 1978, the first year it was
held, he immediately signed up.

The race <u>somewhat</u> originated in an amusing way. The
₆
members of two popular sports clubs, the Mid-Pacific Road

<u>Runners of Honolulu, and the Waikiki Swim Club</u> of Oahu, had
₇
a long-standing and good-natured debate going over who made
better athletes: runners or swimmers. However, some local

bikers thought both clubs were wrong, <u>while claiming</u> that they,
₈
in fact, deserved the title. Wanting to settle the dispute once and

for all, <u>when</u> they decided to combine three separate races
₉

<u>already held annually on the island</u> into one massive test of
₁₀
endurance. Thus, the Waikiki Roughwater Swim of 2.4 miles,
the Around-Oahu Bike race of 112 miles, and the Honolulu
Marathon of 26.2 miles were all combined to form the Ironman
Triathlon.

Haller was one of only fifteen competitors to show up that
February morning to start the race. He quickly scanned the few
pages of rules and instructions, <u>and while reading those pages</u> on
₁₁
the last page he discovered a sentence that would become the
race's famous slogan: "Swim 2.4 miles! Bike 112 miles! Run
26.2 miles! Brag for the rest of your life!" Haller took that to

---

5. **A.** NO CHANGE
   B. verified
   C. justified
   D. certified

6. The best placement for the underlined word would be:
   F. where it is now.
   G. before the word *in*.
   H. before the word *amusing* (changing *an* to *a*).
   J. before the word *way*.

7. **A.** NO CHANGE
   B. Runners, of Honolulu, and the Waikiki Swim Club
   C. Runners of Honolulu and the Waikiki Swim Club
   D. Runners, of Honolulu, and the Waikiki Swim Club,

8. **F.** NO CHANGE
   G. and while claiming
   H. they claimed
   J. claiming

9. **A.** NO CHANGE
   B. and
   C. where
   D. DELETE the underlined portion.

10. The best placement for the underlined phrase would be:
    F. where it is now.
    G. before the word *Wanting* (revising the capitalization accordingly).
    H. before the word *once*.
    J. after the word *endurance* (ending the sentence with a period).

11. **A.** NO CHANGE
    B. and
    C. and while perusing those pages
    D. and in those sheets of paper

GO ON TO THE NEXT PAGE.

heart, and at the end of the day, he <u>had became</u> the first Ironman
12

champion in history. 13

    In the approximately thirty years since that very first race, the Ironman has become a tradition in Hawaii and now boasts approximately 1,500 entrants every year. <u>The competitors</u> who
14
complete the race don't have to be the first across the finish line to claim success: just finishing is a victory unto itself.

12. **F.** NO CHANGE
    G. become
    H. became
    J. becamed

13. Which of the following true statements, if added here, would most effectively and specifically emphasize Haller's achievement as described in this essay?

    A. Twelve other people also finished the race that day.
    B. There were points in the race when Haller thought he couldn't possibly finish.
    C. No women raced this year, but that was soon to change.
    D. Haller's amazing physical strength had enabled him to do what no one else in the past had accomplished.

14. Which of the following alternatives to the underlined portion would be LEAST acceptable?

    F. The individuals
    G. That
    H. The athletes
    J. The people

> Question 15 asks about the preceding passage as a whole.

15. If the writer were to delete the final paragraph of this essay, the essay would primarily lose information that:

    A. discusses the level of interest the race attracts in the present day.
    B. describes the way the current race is different from the race that Haller ran in 1978.
    C. describes how the victors respond when they cross the finish line.
    D. explains why 1,500 people would be willing to compete in such a difficult race.

GO ON TO THE NEXT PAGE.

PASSAGE II

New Beginnings

[1]

As a junior in high school, I am very concerned about college. I'm trying to do everything right: when I keep my
<u>grades up</u>, participate in a few extracurricular activities, prepare
16
for standardized tests, even perform community service. I spend most days thinking about the <u>future hoping</u> that I'm on the right
17
path, I do my best at everything I can.

[2]

[1] I'm interested in a career in <u>nursing,</u> I decided to try to
18
secure a spot as a volunteer at the local hospital. [2] I accepted his offer immediately, thinking to myself that here <u>lies</u> all the
19
opportunities I could ever want! [3] It would be the best of both worlds: helping people while gaining valuable on-the-job experience! [4] So I put on a nice <u>pair of slacks, a blouse, and</u>
20
some comfortable shoes—don't all nurses wear comfortable shoes?—and went to visit the business office. [5] Fortunately, the hospital director was quite willing to let me help out, and he said I could start that summer as soon as I finished my finals. 21

[3]

The director gave me a brief tour of various departments as he told me about the primary focus of each, <u>an expert himself</u>
22
<u>in every facet of hospital administration,</u> until we stopped right
22
in front of the maternity ward. "This is where you're going to work," he said, ushering me through the brown double doors.

16. **F.** NO CHANGE
    G. I keep
    H. I am keeping
    J. I have kept

17. **A.** NO CHANGE
    B. future, hoping
    C. future. Hoping
    D. future praying

18. **F.** NO CHANGE
    G. nursing, therefore,
    H. nursing, so
    J. nursing, but

19. **A.** NO CHANGE
    B. lays
    C. lay
    D. lie

20. **F.** NO CHANGE
    G. pair, of slacks, a blouse,
    H. pair, of slacks, a blouse
    J. pair of slacks a blouse

21. For the sake of the logic and coherence of this paragraph, Sentence 2 should be placed:

    A. where it is now.
    B. after Sentence 3.
    C. after Sentence 4.
    D. after Sentence 5.

22. **F.** NO CHANGE
    G. expert, himself in every facet of hospital administration,
    H. expert, himself, in every facet of hospital administration
    J. expert himself in every facet of hospital administration

GO ON TO THE NEXT PAGE.

Walking into the ward, my ears were immediately overwhelmed. Women yelled and newborns wailed. Nurses rushed around to adjust medical instruments that screamed for attention. I felt

suspicious in the center of so much action and wondered if I had been too hasty in seeking out such a difficult service project.

[4]

Apparently my fear must have shown clearly on my face as I looked around because the director said, "Don't worry. You'll get used to the pace up here. You are going to help in the

nursery." With that, we walked down the busy hallway past the numerous delivery rooms and into the most peaceful room I've ever seen. The pastel colors provided a quiet backdrop to the humming of machines and soft coos of sleeping infants. A

whispering nurse, the one in charge of the nursery, welcomed me, thanked me for volunteering, and asked me to start folding

some baby blankets and placing it in the appropriate drawer. The director gave me a questioning look, which I returned with a

quiet nod. 29 I got right to work.

23. A. NO CHANGE
B. my ears immediately felt overwhelmed, women
C. I was overwhelmed by the sounds. Women
D. hearing and overwhelmed. Women

24. Which choice would be most consistent with the figurative description provided elsewhere in this paragraph?
F. NO CHANGE
G. besieged
H. weak
J. defenseless

25. Which of the following alternatives to the underlined portion would be LEAST acceptable?
A. face while
B. face when
C. face at the same time that
D. face since

26. Given that all the choices are true, which one provides the most vivid description of the hospital hallway?
F. NO CHANGE
G. down a hallway filled with bright blue and pink balloons, beautiful flowers, and jubilant fathers
H. past a nurses' station and a handful of expectant fathers
J. under the yellowing ceiling of the dated hospital

27. A. NO CHANGE
B. nurse the one in charge of the nursery,
C. nurse the one in charge of the nursery
D. nurse, the one in charge of the nursery

28. F. NO CHANGE
G. place them
H. placed them
J. placing these

29. If the writer were to delete the phrase "which I returned with a quiet nod" from the preceding sentence and end the sentence with a period, the sentence would primarily lose:
A. a detail that expresses the narrator's ease while in the nursery.
B. a specific description of the narrator's anger toward the director.
C. information that indicates the narrator will quit the hospital as soon as the director leaves.
D. nothing at all, because this information had already been provided earlier in the passage.

GO ON TO THE NEXT PAGE.

> Question 30 asks about the preceding passage as a whole.

30. Upon reviewing the essay and realizing that some key information has been left out, the writer composes the following sentence incorporating that information:

> Soon enough, I showed up for my first day at the hospital.

This sentence would most logically be placed before the first sentence in Paragraph:

F. 1.
G. 2.
H. 3.
J. 4.

PASSAGE III

Give a Snake a Break

Throughout much of history, snakes have had a reputation
for being more deadly then they actually are. Negative
associations abound: a "snake in the grass" is a seemingly
innocent person intent on causing harm. [32] A "snake charmer"
uses flattery to distract you from his shady intent. Nearly every

reference to a snake that is popular in modern society bears this
negative connotation. Despite this perception, the snake,

with its ugly, slimy appearance, is one of the most unjustly
maligned creatures on the planet.

31. A. NO CHANGE
B. a reputation for being more deadly than
C. a reputation as the most deadly than
D. the deadliest reputation then

32. Given that all the following statements are true, which one provides the most relevant information at this point in the essay?
F. "Snake oil" refers to fake medicine that promises impossible results.
G. Most snakes are passive creatures that will never cause you injury.
H. Snakes are carnivorous reptiles that can be found on every continent except Antarctica.
J. Pet snakes have becomes increasingly common over the last decade.

33. A. NO CHANGE
B. reference that is popular about a snake
C. famous reference they have about a snake
D. popular reference to a snake

34. F. NO CHANGE
G. who's
H. sporting it's
J. with its'

GO ON TO THE NEXT PAGE.

Snakes are only rarely dangerous to humans. Their fangs, so
$\overline{35}$
intimidating when the snakes are hissing, are designed not to

attack people but to hold small prey; small rodents, birds, insects,
$\overline{36}$
etc. Only exceptionally large snakes, like pythons or anacondas,

pose a real threat. Most of the time, the typical snake you

encounter in your backyard is more afraid of you than you are of

it and will gladly avoid any contact with you.

Poisonous snakes—such as rattlesnakes, vipers, and

cobras—are most frightening to people, but they attack if they
$\overline{37}$
are only provoked. While certainly venomous, these snakes pose
$\overline{37}$
a threat mainly to smaller animals. Of the 5 million snake bites

that occur each year to humans around the world, only about

2.5 percent prove fatal. ☐38 Prompt treatment with one of the

available antivenoms do much to ensure the victim's survival.
$\overline{39}$
Although you may get an infection at the wound site, you can be

effectively treated, seeing as you are still shaken from the
$\overline{40}$
encounter, you will survive.

Why put up with snakes at all? Even if they don't normally

kill humans, most people still considering them a nuisance and
$\overline{41}$
avoiding them like the plague. Individuals who dislike snakes for
$\overline{41}$
this reason do not appreciate the great service snakes do for

humanity. The typical diet of a snake includes small rodents like

rats, mice, gophers, and prairie dogs, as well as lizards, birds,

fish, and insects. We may not like snakes, if they were
$\overline{42}$
mysteriously wiped out of existence, however, we would be

virtually overrun with other vermin that would spread disease and

filth.

35. **A.** NO CHANGE
    B. fangs being
    C. fangs, so they are
    D. fangs, they are

36. **F.** NO CHANGE
    G. prey,
    H. prey:
    J. prey

37. **A.** NO CHANGE
    B. they will provoke and attack them.
    C. they will attack humans only if provoked.
    D. if provoked, they will attack them.

38. The writer is considering deleting the preceding sentence from
    this paragraph. If the writer made this deletion, the paragraph
    would primarily lose:

    F. scientific proof that snakes are too dangerous to coexist
    with humans.
    G. an example of the various locations where most fatalities
    take place.
    H. a specific statistic to support a previous claim.
    J. excessive detail that distracts the reader from the broader
    message of the passage.

39. **A.** NO CHANGE
    B. can do much
    C. are able to do much
    D. have much ability

40. **F.** NO CHANGE
    G. but because
    H. and even if
    J. however

41. **A.** NO CHANGE
    B. consider them a nuisance and avoid
    C. considering them a nuisance and avoid
    D. considered them a nuisance to avoid

42. **F.** NO CHANGE
    G. snake's if they
    H. snakes, they
    J. snakes; if they

GO ON TO THE NEXT PAGE.

So, next time you hear about someone putting down snakes, stand up for our legless friends. These snakes in the grass help us more than we might think.
43
43

43. The writer wants to provide a sentence here that will tie the conclusion of the essay to its beginning. Which choice does that best?

   A. NO CHANGE
   B. Snakes make excellent pets.
   C. Let's reduce the incidence of snake bites around the world.
   D. Wouldn't you rather see a snake in your yard than a rat?

Questions 44 and 45 ask about the preceding passage as a whole.

---

44. The writer is considering deleting the last sentence of the first paragraph of the essay. If the writer were to make this deletion, the essay would primarily lose a statement that:

   F. adds a bit of sarcasm to a rather humorous introduction.
   G. identifies the overall point of the entire passage.
   H. summarizes the list of examples previously provided by the author.
   J. provides a list of animals more useful than the snake.

45. Suppose the writer's goal had been to write an essay focusing on the various ways in which humans were threatened by snakes. Would this essay fulfill that goal?

   A. Yes, because the author gives specific statistical evidence that proves snake bites happen around the world.
   B. Yes, because the essay focuses on many of the negative stereotypes associated with snakes.
   C. No, because the essay primarily focuses on the fact that snakes are not harmful to humans.
   D. No, because the essay points out that snakes feed primarily on rodents and other small animals.

PASSAGE IV

Zora Neale Hurston, Independent Woman

Zora Neale Hurston proves to be a study in contrasts: a black writer reaching a white audience, a woman struggling in a man's profession, an independent thinker living in a conformist era. Now, almost 50 years since her death, her hard work and
46
fabulous novels still have much to teach the modern audience.

46. Which of the following alternatives to the underlined portion would be LEAST acceptable?

   F. Presently,
   G. Currently,
   H. Instantly,
   J. At the present,

She overcame the challenges she faced and demonstrated that
47
perseverance makes anything possible.

47. Which of the following alternatives to the underlined portion would be LEAST acceptable?

   A. faced, and in so doing,
   B. faced and, thus,
   C. faced that
   D. faced, an action that

GO ON TO THE NEXT PAGE.

Hurston ascribed much of her deeply individualistic
personality to the experience of growing up in Eatonville,

Florida. The town was unique in that it was particularly hot in
the summer, but mild at other times of the year. Hurston always
said growing up in a community totally separate from the larger

white society allowed her a freedom that independence not
available to everyone in the south.

[1] Hurston began her undergraduate studies at Howard
University, but her obvious intelligence and talent soon earned
her a scholarship to Barnard College in New York City. [2]

Moving north in the 1920s thrust her into the midst of the
Harlem Renaissance, a black cultural movement that spawned

exceptional achievements in literature, books, poems, and plays,
art, and music. [3] Interacting with the likes of Langston
Hughes, W.E.B. DuBois, Billie Holiday, and Duke Ellington,
Hurston developed her skills as a writer and published numerous

short stories and poems. 55 [4] The most influential work that
came to define her career grew out of her attempt to capture the
black experience. [5] That novel, called *Their Eyes Were
Watching God*, traced three generations of a family living in

48. F. NO CHANGE
    G. personally individualistic
    H. freely independent
    J. truly egotistical

49. Given that all the choices are true, which one most effectively
    identifies why Eatonville has a history unlike any other city
    in the United States?

    A. NO CHANGE
    B. a fairly representative small town, founded in the mid-
       nineteenth century.
    C. the first all-black town to be incorporated in the country.
    D. not yet in existence at the start of the Civil War.

50. F. NO CHANGE
    G. and was
    H. it featured
    J. and

51. A. NO CHANGE
    B. intelligence, and talent
    C. intelligence, and talent,
    D. intelligence and talent,

52. F. NO CHANGE
    G. 1920s, thrust
    H. 1920s, thrust,
    J. 1920s; thrust

53. A. NO CHANGE
    B. literature, written records of stories once transmitted orally,
    C. literature, which includes all forms of written expression,
    D. literature,

54. F. NO CHANGE
    G. developed up
    H. develops up
    J. develops

55. At this point, the writer is considering adding the following
    true statement:

    > Billie Holiday's music evokes such feeling and melan-
    > choly that it's no wonder she became so popular.

    Should the writer add this sentence here?

    A. Yes, because it provides an interesting detail about one of
       the other Harlem Renaissance artists.
    B. Yes, because music was an important influence on Hur-
       ston's work.
    C. No, because it doesn't clearly identify which of Billie
       Holiday's songs were popular.
    D. No, because it distracts the reader from the main point of
       this paragraph.

GO ON TO THE NEXT PAGE.

Eatonville. [6] Her interesting representation of the southern
dialect caused her Harlem Renaissance contemporaries to belittle
the work for what they saw as its propagation of inaccurate

stereotypes. [7] Hurston, however, remained true to it, convinced
that the accuracy of her representation would ultimately prevail over

the political pressures her peers sought to inflict upon her. 58

History has shown that Hurston was right. However, modern
critics admire her authentic and skillful representation of the
language as well as her realistic portrayal of daily life in the
early twentieth century. She is universally applauded, as one of
the best writers of her era, ranked with Toni Morrison, Maya
Angelou, and Alice Walker as one of the most important African-
American writers of all time.

56. Which choice would most clearly indicate that the dialect referenced in the passage was a realistic representation of the actual way language was spoken in Eatonville?

   F. NO CHANGE
   G. unusual
   H. authentic
   J. fascinating

57. **A.** NO CHANGE
   B. her project,
   C. that thing,
   D. which,

58. The writer has decided to divide this paragraph into two. The best place to add the new paragraph break would be at the beginning of Sentence:

   F. 4, because it would indicate that Hurston's writing was most strongly influenced by Langston Hughes.
   G. 4, because it would signal the essay's shift in focus to one of Hurston's novels.
   H. 5, because all the remaining sentences in the paragraph provide a detailed summary of the plot of Hurston's novel.
   J. 5, because it would indicate that the essay is now going to focus on social conditions in Eatonville.

59. **A.** NO CHANGE
   B. Modern
   C. Thus, modern
   D. In addition, modern

60. **F.** NO CHANGE
   G. applauded as one of the best writers of her era and
   H. applauded as one of the best writers of her era
   J. applauded, as one of the best writers of her era, she is

PASSAGE V

Jimmy Carter, Humanitarian

[1]

Everyone has heard of Jimmy Carter. As president of the
United States from 1977 to 1981. He oversaw a particularly
turbulent time in American history. Americans taken hostage in
the Middle East, serious inflation woes, major gasoline shortages
around the country, and a tenuous relationship with a potential

61. **A.** NO CHANGE
   B. 1981 but he
   C. 1981, and he
   D. 1981, he

GO ON TO THE NEXT PAGE.

enemy—the Soviet Union—are hardly the stuff of pleasant
memories.
<u>62</u>

[2]

Yet even though Carter <u>held Americas most,</u> powerful office,
<u>63</u>

he will probably be remembered more for the work <u>he</u> has done
<u>64</u>
since he left the White House. His record on humanitarian issues
around the world sets him apart as a caring, dedicated person

who wants to see the <u>underprivileged, those of low economic</u>
<u>65</u>
<u>or social status,</u> benefit from the great wealth, power, and
<u>65</u>
generosity of this country.

[3]

One of the major issues Carter has focused on throughout his
career is peace in the Middle East. He <u>questioned</u> a national
<u>66</u>
energy policy designed to reduce American dependence long

before it was popular to do so <u>on foreign oil</u> and brokered a
<u>67</u>
peace treaty between Israel and Egypt. Likewise, he was among
the first to insist publicly on basic human rights for everyone

around the <u>world, founding</u> a nonprofit organization, The Carter
<u>68</u>
Center, to work toward that end. In his opinion, this includes
extending modern health care to developing nations in order to

contain disease and improve quality of life around the <u>world, in</u>
<u>69</u>
<u>many different countries.</u>
<u>69</u>

---

62. **F.** NO CHANGE
    G. enemy the Soviet Union—
    H. enemy the Soviet Union
    J. enemy—the Soviet Union

63. **A.** NO CHANGE
    B. held America's most,
    C. held America's most
    D. held Americas, most

64. **F.** NO CHANGE
    G. himself
    H. him
    J. itself

65. **A.** NO CHANGE
    B. underprivileged, who may not have many resources,
    C. underprivileged
    D. underprivileged, who have less than others in society,

66. **F.** NO CHANGE
    G. promoted
    H. purchased
    J. rejected

67. The best placement for the underlined portion would be:
    A. where it is now.
    B. after the word *designed.*
    C. after the word *dependence.*
    D. after the word *was.*

68. Which of the following alternatives to the underlined portion
    would NOT be acceptable?
    F. world, and he found
    G. world, and he founded
    H. world, so he founded
    J. world and founded

69. **A.** NO CHANGE
    B. world.
    C. world, both east and west of the United States.
    D. world, including countries on every continent except Ant-
    arctica.

GO ON TO THE NEXT PAGE.

[4]

[1] Carter works actively to improve the standard of living at home here in the United States as well. [2] He and his wife Roslyn are enthusiastic supporters of Habitat for Humanity. [3] This volunteer-based organization devotes itself to building affordable but quality housing for those who otherwise might not be able to buy a home. [4] However, Carter does not focus abroad all his efforts. [5] Community workers come together on their own free time to construct, paint, and landscape simple homes, working side-by-side with the families that will occupy the residences. 72

[5]

For all these reasons, Carter deserves respect for dedicating his career to public service. Everyone can agree for his impressive philanthropy and acknowledge his obvious devotion to all of humanity.

70. **F.** NO CHANGE
    G. at home, not just abroad,
    H. at home, within the area over which he was president,
    J. at home,

71. **A.** NO CHANGE
    B. focus all his efforts abroad.
    C. focus all abroad his efforts.
    D. focus all his abroad efforts.

72. For the sake of the logic and coherence of this paragraph, Sentence 4 should be placed:

    F. where it is now.
    G. before Sentence 1.
    H. after Sentence 2.
    J. after Sentence 5.

73. **A.** NO CHANGE
    B. agree to
    C. agree by
    D. agree with

74. Which choice would best help this sentence to summarize key points made in the essay?

    F. NO CHANGE
    G. he should have been president for a second term.
    H. he has the right to express his opinions as much as any other American.
    J. he clearly didn't want the hostages to be harmed.

    Question 75 asks about the preceding passage as a whole.

75. Upon reviewing notes for this essay, the writer comes across the following true statement:

    Habitat does more than build houses: it builds communities.

    If the writer were to use this sentence, the most logical place to add it would be at the end of Paragraph:

    A. 1
    B. 2
    C. 3
    D. 4

END OF TEST 1

STOP! DO NOT TURN THE PAGE UNTIL TOLD TO DO SO.

MATHEMATICS TEST

60 Minutes—60 Questions

DIRECTIONS: Solve each problem, choose the correct answer, and then darken the corresponding oval on your answer sheet.

Do not linger over problems that take too much time. Solve as many as you can; then return to the others in the time you have left for this test.

You are permitted to use a calculator on this test. You may use your calculator for any problems you choose,

but some of the problems may best be done without using a calculator.

Note: Unless otherwise stated, all of the following should be assumed:

1. Illustrative figures are NOT necessarily drawn to scale.
2. Geometric figures lie in a plane.
3. The word *line* indicates a straight line.
4. The word *average* indicates arithmetic mean.

---

1. On a level field, a telephone pole 24 feet tall casts a shadow 6 feet long, and at the same time of day, another nearby telephone pole casts a shadow 18 feet long. How many feet tall is the second telephone pole?

   A. 6
   B. 12
   C. 24
   D. 36
   E. 72

2. The membership fees for WebFilms consist of a monthly charge of $14 and a one-time new-member fee of $16. Sherwood made a credit card payment of $100 to pay his WebFilms fees for a certain number of months, including the new-member fee. How many months of membership did Sherwood include in his credit card payment?

   F. 4
   G. 6
   H. 7
   J. 12
   K. 14

3. If $y = -6$, what is the value of $\dfrac{y^2 - 4}{y - 2}$?

   A. -8
   B. -4
   C. 4
   D. 9
   E. 28

DO YOUR FIGURING HERE.

GO ON TO THE NEXT PAGE.

4. A school offered its students an optional field trip. If 15 or fewer students went on the field trip, the charge for each student would be $11.50. If more than 15 students chose to go on the field trip, the charge for each student would be $10.25. 18 students opted to go on the tour, but each pre-paid $11.50. The students agreed to put the extra amount toward dinner on the trip. How much total money will be put toward dinner on the trip?

   F. $12.50
   G. $14.75
   H. $21.75
   J. $22.50
   K. $33.00

DO YOUR FIGURING HERE.

5. A 16-piece orchestra wants to choose one of its members to speak at performances. They decide that this member CANNOT be one of the 4 soloists in the group. What is the probability that Itzhak, who is NOT a soloist, will be chosen as the speaker?

   A. 0

   B. $\dfrac{1}{16}$

   C. $\dfrac{1}{12}$

   D. $\dfrac{1}{4}$

   E. $\dfrac{1}{3}$

6. What is the perimeter, in feet, of a rectangle with width 8 feet and length 17 feet?

   F. 25
   G. 34
   H. 50
   J. 136
   K. 272

7. Passes to the Renaissance Faire cost $9 when purchased online and $12 when purchased in person. The group sponsoring the fair would like to make at least $4,000 from sales of passes. If 240 passes were sold online, what is the minimum number of tickets that must be sold in person in order for the group to meet its goal?

   A. 153
   B. 154
   C. 290
   D. 334
   E. 445

GO ON TO THE NEXT PAGE.

DO YOUR FIGURING HERE.

8. For what value of q is the equation $\frac{9}{q} = \frac{6}{10}$ true?

   F. 3
   G. 5
   H. 13
   J. 15
   K. 19

9. If $-9(y - 13) = 16$, then $y = ?$

   A. $-\frac{133}{9}$
   B. $-\frac{29}{9}$
   C. $\frac{16}{9}$
   D. $\frac{1}{3}$
   E. $\frac{101}{9}$

10. In the figure below, F, G, H, and J are collinear. $\overline{FG}$, $\overline{GK}$, and $\overline{HK}$ are line segments of equivalent length, and the measure of $\angle JHK$ is 120°. What is the degree measure of $\angle GFK$?

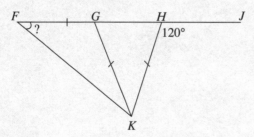

   F. 30°
   G. 45°
   H. 60°
   J. 120°
   K. 150°

11. If $f(x) = 7x^2 - 9x + 4$, then $f(-3) = ?$

   A. −32
   B. −2
   C. 32
   D. 40
   E. 94

GO ON TO THE NEXT PAGE.

12. What is the least common multiple of 25, 16, and 40 ?

    F.   27
    G.   32
    H.   320
    J.   400
    K. 16,000

DO YOUR FIGURING HERE.

13. While working on a problem on his calculator, Tex had meant to multiply a number by 3, but he accidentally divided the number by 3. Which of the following calculations could Tex then do to the result on the screen in order to obtain the result he originally wanted?

    A. Multiply by 3
    B. Multiply by 9
    C. Divide by 3
    D. Divide by 9
    E. Add the original number

14. The 8-sided figure below is divided into 12 congruent isosceles right triangles. The total area of the 12 triangles is 96 square centimeters. What is the perimeter, in centimeters, of the figure?

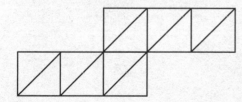

    F.   8
    G. $20 + 4\sqrt{2}$
    H. 48
    J. $40 + 8\sqrt{2}$
    K. 56

15. In $\triangle XYZ$, $\angle Y$ is a right angle and $\angle Z$ measures less than 52°. Which of the following phrases best describes the measure of $\angle X$?

    A. Greater than 38°
    B. Equal to 38°
    C. Equal to 45°
    D. Equal to 142°
    E. Less than 38°

GO ON TO THE NEXT PAGE.

16. Among the following arithmetic operations, which could the emoticon ☺ represent given that the equation $(8 ☺ 2)^3 - (4 ☺ 1)^2 = 48$ is true?

    I. Subtraction
    II. Multiplication
    III. Division

F. I only
G. III only
H. II and III only
J. I and III only
K. I, II, and III

17. Which of the following equations represents the linear relation shown in the standard (x,y) coordinate plane below?

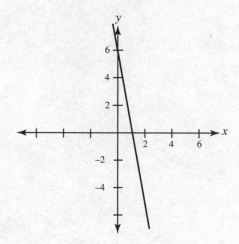

A. $y = -5x$
B. $y = -6x$
C. $y = -2x + 2$
D. $y = -5x + 6$
E. $y = -2x + 6$

18. An integer, x, is subtracted from 6. That difference is then multiplied by 3. This product is 15 more than half the original integer. Which of the following equations represents this relationship?

F. $3(6 - x) = \dfrac{x}{2} + 15$

G. $3(6 - x) + 15 = \dfrac{x}{2}$

H. $3(6 - x) = 15 - \dfrac{x}{2}$

J. $x - 6 \times 3 = \dfrac{15}{2}$

K. $6 + 3 = \dfrac{x}{2} + 15$

GO ON TO THE NEXT PAGE.

DO YOUR FIGURING HERE.

19. The employees of two factories, X and Y, are comparing their respective production records. Factory X has already produced 18,000 units and can produce 120 units per day. Factory Y has produced only 14,500 units but can produce 155 units per day. If d represents the number of days (that is, days during which each factory is producing its maximum number of units), which of the following equations could be solved to determine the number of days until X's total production equals Y's total production?

A. $18,000 + 120d = 14,500 + 155d$
B. $18,000 + 155d = 14,500 + 120d$
C. $(18,000 + 120)d = (14,500 + 155)d$
D. $(120 + 155)d = 18,000 - 14,500$
E. $(120 + 155)d = 18,000 + 14,500$

20. A ramp used to access the side entrance to the DPC Candy Store, which is located 7 meters above the ground, covers 24 meters along the level ground from the edge of the building. How many meters long is the ramp?

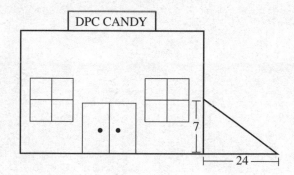

F. 13
G. 14
H. 17
J. 23
K. 25

21. The expression $9(y + 3) - 2(4y - 4)$ is equivalent to:

A. $y - 1$
B. $y + 15$
C. $y + 18$
D. $y + 23$
E. $y + 35$

22. If $a + 3b = 27$ and $a - 3b = 9$, then $b = ?$

F. 3
G. 9
H. 14
J. 18
K. 36

GO ON TO THE NEXT PAGE.

23. When $(2x + 4)^2$ is written in the format $ax^2 + bx + c$, where a, b, and c are integers, what is the value of $a + b - c$?

A. –20
B. 4
C. 20
D. 32
E. 36

24. What is the area, in square meters, of the figure below?

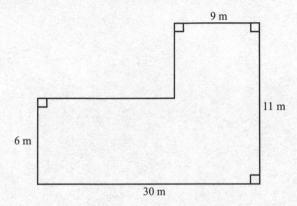

F. 336
G. 330
H. 225
J. 82
K. 56

25. The table below gives the values of two functions, g and h, for various values of x. One of the functions expresses a relationship that can be expressed by the formula $a + bx$, where a and b are real number coefficients. What is the value of that function for $x = 0$?

x	$g(x)$	$h(x)$
–3	4	
–2	2	3
–1	1	6
0		
1	1	
2		15
3		18

A. 0
B. 0.5
C. 1
D. 2
E. 9

GO ON TO THE NEXT PAGE.

26. What is the slope of the line represented by the equation $10y - 16x = 13$?

    F. -16

    G. $\dfrac{13}{10}$

    H. $\dfrac{8}{5}$

    J. 10

    K. 16

27. What is the sum of the 2 solutions of the equation $x^2 + 5x - 24 = 0$?

    A. -24
    B. -8
    C. -5
    D. 0
    E. 5

28. Two similar triangles have perimeters in the ratio 5:6. The sides of the larger triangle measure 12 in, 7 in, and 5 in. What is the perimeter, in inches, of the smaller triangle?

    F. 18
    G. 20
    H. 22
    J. 24
    K. 32

29. In early November in Winnipeg, Manitoba, the temperatures for each of nine consecutive days were –9°C, 3°C, –7°C, 2°C, 5°C, 1°C, 0°C, –8°C, and –7°C. What was the median of the temperatures for these nine days in early November?

    A. –7°C
    B. 0°C
    C. 1.5°C
    D. 3°C
    E. 5°C

DO YOUR FIGURING HERE.

GO ON TO THE NEXT PAGE.

30. When asked the price, in dollars, of his fancy calculator, Albert responded, "If you take the square root of the price, then add $\frac{3}{8}$ the price, the result is 66." What is the price, in dollars, of Albert's calculator?

    F. 169
    G. 144
    H. 121
    J. 13
    K. 12

DO YOUR FIGURING HERE.

31. The kinetic energy, KE, of an object travelling at v velocity can be modeled by the equation $KE = \frac{1}{2}mv^2$, where m is the mass of the object. If an object is moving at a velocity of 9, and it has a kinetic energy of 120, about how great is the object's mass?

    A. Between 0 and 1
    B. Between 1 and 2
    C. Between 2 and 3
    D. 6
    E. 13

32. Let x, y, and z be distinct positive integers. What is the fourth term of the geometric sequence below?

    $$2xz, \ 2x^2yz, \ 2x^3y^2z, \ \ldots$$

    F. $2x^2yz$
    G. $2x^4y^3z$
    H. $2x^3yz^2$
    J. $4x^3y^2z$
    K. $4x^4y^3z^2$

GO ON TO THE NEXT PAGE.

DO YOUR FIGURING HERE.

Use the following information to answer questions 33–35.

A recent survey of book critics asked 30 critics how many stars out of a possible 5 they gave to a recent novel from a popular author. The 30 critics' responses are summarized by the histogram below.

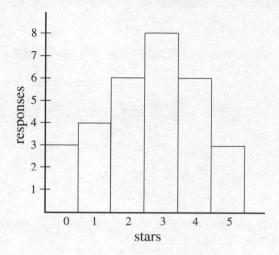

33. What fraction of the critics gave the book a one-star review?

A. $\dfrac{1}{2}$

B. $\dfrac{3}{8}$

C. $\dfrac{17}{50}$

D. $\dfrac{3}{10}$

E. $\dfrac{2}{15}$

34. The group that took the survey wants to show the data in a circle graph (pie chart). What should be the measure of the central angle of the portion for one-star reviews?

F. 15°
G. 24°
H. 30°
J. 48°
K. 60°

GO ON TO THE NEXT PAGE.

35. To the nearest hundredth, what is the average star review for the 30 reviews?

A. 2.00
B. 2.33
C. 2.50
D. 2.63
E. 3.00

DO YOUR FIGURING HERE.

---

36. For all $x > 8$, $\dfrac{(x^2 + 7x + 12)(x - 2)}{(x^2 + 2x - 8)(x + 3)} = ?$

F. $\dfrac{-3(x-2)}{(x+3)}$

G. $\dfrac{-2(x-2)}{(x+3)}$

H. $\dfrac{(x-2)}{(x+2)}$

J. $\dfrac{11}{4}$

K. 1

37. A rock band, The Young Sohcahtoans, is trying to design a T-shirt logo. The measurements they have chosen are represented on the figure below. The angle to the right of the logo "TYS" has a degree measure of 35°, and the side of the figure has a measure of 10 in. Which of the following expressions gives the measure, in inches, of the diagonal top side of the figure?

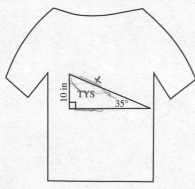

A. 10 tan 35°

B. 10 cos 35°

C. 10 sin 35°

D. $\dfrac{10}{\sin 35°}$

E. $\dfrac{10}{\cos 35°}$

$\dfrac{1}{\sin} = \csc$

$\dfrac{1}{\cos} = \sec$

$\dfrac{1}{\tan} = \cot$

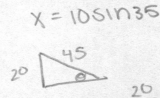

$\sin 35 = \dfrac{x}{10}$

$x = 10 \sin 35$

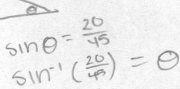

$\tan 30 = \dfrac{x}{10}$

$\sin \theta = \dfrac{20}{45}$

$\sin^{-1}\left(\dfrac{20}{45}\right) = \theta$

GO ON TO THE NEXT PAGE.

38. The endpoints of the diameter of a circle O are A and C. In the standard (x,y) coordinate plane, A is at $(4,3)$ and C is at $(-9,-2)$. What is the y-coordinate of the center of the circle?

F. -5

G. $-\dfrac{5}{2}$

H. $\dfrac{1}{2}$

J. 1

K. 2

DO YOUR FIGURING HERE.

39. On a sonar map in the standard (x,y) coordinate plane, the Yellow Submarine and the Sandwich Submarine are located at the points $(-7,4)$ and $(-2,6)$, respectively. Each unit on the map represents an actual distance of 5 nautical miles. Which of the following is closest to the distance, in nautical miles, between the two submarines?

A. 5
B. 19
C. 27
D. 30
E. 67

40. All of the following statements about rational and/or irrational numbers must be true EXCEPT:

F. the sum of any two rational numbers is rational.
G. the product of any two rational numbers is rational.
H. the sum of any two irrational numbers is irrational.
J. the product of a rational and an irrational number may be rational or irrational.
K. the product of any two irrational numbers is irrational.

41. For the imaginary number i, which of the following is a possible value of i^n if n is an integer less than 5 ?

A. 0
B. -1
C. -2
D. -3
E. -4

GO ON TO THE NEXT PAGE.

42. The table below gives the values of $f(x)$ for selected values of x in the function $f(x) = (x + 4)^2 - 1$, where x and y are both real numbers.

x	$f(x)$
−7	8
−5	0
−3	0
−1	8
0	15
1	24

For the equation above, which of the following values of x gives the greatest value of $f(x)$?

F. −4
G. −5
H. −6
J. −7
K. −8

43. The volume of the right circular cylinder shown below is 64π cubic inches. If its height is 4 in., what is its radius in inches?

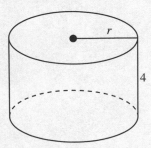

A. 2
B. 4
C. 8
D. 10
E. 16

DO YOUR FIGURING HERE.

44. Line segments $\overline{GH}$, $\overline{JK}$, and $\overline{LM}$ are parallel and intersect line segments $\overline{FL}$ and $\overline{FM}$ as shown in the figure below. The ratio of the perimeter of $\triangle FJK$ to the perimeter of $\triangle FLM$ is 3:5, and the ratio of $\overline{FH}$ to $\overline{FM}$ is 1:5. What is the ratio of $\overline{GJ}$ to $\overline{FG}$?

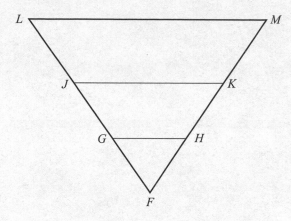

F. 1:5
G. 1:3
H. 1:2
J. 2:1
K. 5:3

45. Avi is trying to draw a map of his most recent bike ride. He chose to place Market Street on the x-axis and Broad Street on the y-axis. He rode 60 m at an angle of 60° relative to Market Street, then rode 100 m at an angle of 45° relative to Market Street, and finally rode 35 m directly north on Broad Street. How many meters north of Market Street did Avi ride?

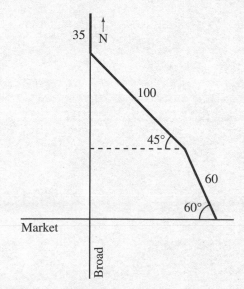

A. 35
B. 115
C. 195
D. $50\sqrt{2} + 30\sqrt{3}$
E. $35 + 50\sqrt{2} + 30\sqrt{3}$

GO ON TO THE NEXT PAGE.

46. In the standard (x,y) coordinate plane, what is the area of the circle $(x - 3)^2 + (y + 2)^2 = 25$?

   F. 5π
   G. 10π
   H. 25π
   J. 125π
   K. 225π

DO YOUR FIGURING HERE.

47. In the standard (x,y) coordinate plane below, the base of a right triangle lies along the x-axis and is bisected by the y-axis. The vertex of the angle opposite the base is on the graph of the parabolic function $f(x) = 2x^2 - 4$. Let b represent any value of x such that $-\sqrt{2} < x < 0$. Which of the following is an expression in terms of b for the area, in square coordinate units, of any such right triangle?

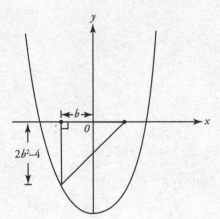

   A. $4b^4 - 16b^2 + 16$
   B. $4b^3 - 8b$
   C. $2b^3 - 4b$
   D. $2b^2 + b - 4$
   E. $b^2 - 4b + 4$

48. Which of the following expressions must be an even integer if x is an integer?

   F. $x + 5$

   G. $\dfrac{x}{4}$

   H. x^4

   J. $4x$

   K. 5^x

49. Which of the following ranges of consecutive integers contains the value of the expression $\log_9(9^{\frac{7}{3}})$?

   A. 0 and 1
   B. 1 and 2
   C. 2 and 3
   D. 5 and 6
   E. 7 and 8

GO ON TO THE NEXT PAGE.

Use the following information to answer questions 50–52.

The employees at Belinda's Paint Store are having a competition to see who can create the most new accounts over a period from January to June in a certain year. Data is missing because one of the employees began to erase it from the white board, thinking that the competition was over. The numbers in the chart below have been confirmed with the assistant manager's personal records.

Employee	Month					
	Jan.	Feb.	Mar.	Apr.	May	June
Don	64					
Maura	31	25		27	29	24
Cameron	23	19	22	17	20	22
Belinda	78	92	83	86		90

50. Which of the following is closest to the percent decrease in Cameron's new accounts from January to February?

F. 4.0%
G. 17.4%
H. 19.4%
J. 20.0%
K. 21.1%

51. At the beginning of the year, Maura wanted to average 30 new accounts per month for the first four months of the year. How many new accounts did she need to create in March in order to reach this goal?

A. 25
B. 27
C. 29
D. 31
E. 37

52. Additional records are uncovered that show that Don's sales decreased 5% each month from January to May because his responsibilities in the store mounted and he could not seek out new accounts as frequently. Which of the following is closest to the number of new accounts Don created in May?

F. 44
G. 52
H. 56
J. 72
K. 84

GO ON TO THE NEXT PAGE.

53. The amplitude of the trigonometric function shown below is defined as the average of the absolute values of the maximum value of $f(x)$ and the minimum value of $f(x)$. The trigonometric function graphed below can be described by the equation $f(x) = a \sin(bx + c)$, where a, b, and c are real numbers. Which of the following values describes the amplitude of this function?

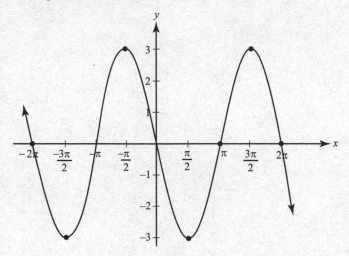

A. 1
B. 2
C. 3
D. π
E. 2π

54. A group of die-hard baseball fans has purchased a house that gives them a direct view of home plate, although their view of the rest of the field is largely impeded by the outfield wall. The house is 30 meters tall, and their angle of vision from the top of the building to home plate has a tangent of $\frac{7}{6}$. What is the horizontal distance, in meters, from home plate to the closest wall of the fans' house?

DO YOUR FIGURING HERE.

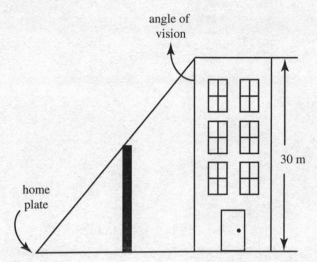

angle of vision

30 m

home plate

F. 35.0
G. 32.0
H. 25.7
J. 5.0
K. 4.3

55. Given the equation $|y^2 - 11| - 2 = 0$, which of the following is a solution but NOT a rational number?

A. $11\sqrt{13}$

B. $4\sqrt{13}$

C. $2\sqrt{13}$

D. $\sqrt{13}$

E. 3

GO ON TO THE NEXT PAGE.

DO YOUR FIGURING HERE.

56. Below is the graph that a specialty automobile manufacturer uses to plot the speed tests done on his new cars. The speed is recorded in units of $\frac{m}{s}$ and is conducted for a period of 9 seconds. A certain order of 3 of the following 6 actions describes the results of the speed test depicted in the graph below. Which order is it?

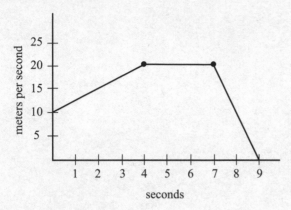

I.   Constant speed for 1 second
II. Constant speed for 3 seconds
III. Speed increase for 4 seconds
IV. Speed increase for 9 seconds
V.   Speed decrease for 2 seconds
VI. Speed decrease for 7 seconds

F. IV, II, VI
G. III, II, V
H. I, III, V
J. III, I, VI
K. V, I, II

57. As shown in the figure below, a compass has marks for every 10° and "North" and "South" are the endpoints of a line segment. If the point of the needle of this compass travels 42 mm as it moves in a clockwise direction from "East" to "North," how long is the needle to the nearest tenth of a millimeter?

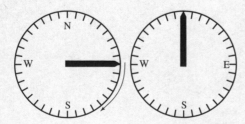

A.   6.7
B.   8.9
C.   13.4
D.   14.0
E.   17.8

GO ON TO THE NEXT PAGE.

58. For θ, an angle whose measure is between 270° and 360°, $\cos\theta = \dfrac{12}{13}$. Which of the following equals tan θ ?

F. $-\dfrac{5}{12}$

G. $-\dfrac{5}{13}$

H. $\dfrac{5}{13}$

J. $\dfrac{12}{5}$

K. $\dfrac{12}{13}$

DO YOUR FIGURING HERE.

59. Consider all positive integer values a and b such that the product $ab = 8$. For how many values does there exist a positive integer c that satisfies both $2^a = c$ and $c^b = 256$?

A. Infinitely many
B. 6
C. 4
D. 2
E. 0

60. A sphere is inscribed in a cube with a diagonal of $3\sqrt{3}$ ft. In feet, what is the diameter of the sphere?

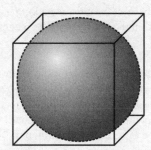

F. $3\sqrt{2}$

G. 2

H. $2\sqrt{2}$

J. 3

K. $3\sqrt{3}$

END OF TEST 2

STOP! DO NOT TURN THE PAGE UNTIL TOLD TO DO SO.

DO NOT RETURN TO A PREVIOUS TEST.

READING TEST

35 Minutes—40 Questions

DIRECTIONS: There are four passages in this test. Each passage is followed by several questions. After reading a passage, choose the best answer to each question and fill in the corresponding oval on your answer document. You may refer to the passages as often as necessary.

Passage I

PROSE FICTION: This passage is adapted from the novel *A Well-Worn Jacket* by Antonia Duke (© 2008 by Antonia Duke).

Monique was enjoying this afternoon more than she had anticipated. Often, the tryouts for the spring musical tested the limits of her patience and nerves, with one hopeful girl after the next taking turns strutting onto the tarnished wooden stage,
5 delivering a competent but uninspired version of some Rodgers & Hammerstein number, and then being politely excused by Mrs. Dominguez as the next name on the list was called.

However, this was to be Monique's third straight year in the musical, and the confidence that her seniority afforded her
10 around the more nervous newcomers allowed her to bask in the radiance of her own poise.

She had already sung her audition song an hour ago, commencing the day's ceremonies. This year, Monique used "God Bless the Child," a choice she found to be quite sophisticated
15 since Billie Holiday's version of it was familiar mostly to adults, and even then, mostly to adults of the previous generation. More importantly, it required a reserved performance, which Monique felt showcased her maturity, especially because most of the other auditioners chose songs that would show their enthusiasm, even
20 if it meant their technical mastery would not be on full display.

Normally, the first audition slot was dreaded by most. Mrs. Dominguez would ask if anyone wanted to volunteer to "get it over with," but no one would make a sound. Then, she would call the first name off her list and the room would drop into an
25 uncomfortably solemn silence as the first student walked nervously up to the stage. Monique often imagined during those moments that she was witness to a death-row inmate taking his inexorable march toward a quick curtain.

But not this year. Monique had decided to make a show
30 of her own self-confidence by volunteering to go first. Such a defiantly fearless act, she had figured, would probably instill even more fear into her competition because they would realize that Monique had something they clearly lacked. Mrs. Dominguez had seemed neither surprised nor charmed by Monique's
35 decision to go first. Although she was annoyed by Monique's escalating arrogance, she also acknowledged that Monique was

one of the more talented actors and was probably correct in assuming herself a shoo-in.

At this late stage of the afternoon, Monique felt like a mon-
40 arch, sitting in the back of the auditorium with her royal court of friends and admirers. They took care to sit far enough away from Mrs. Dominguez that they would not be caught in the act of belittling the other students' auditions.

To Monique, the endless parade of aspirants who sang their
45 hearts out for three minutes each were like jesters performing for her amusement. As Mrs. Dominguez read Esperanza Solito's name off her list, Monique and her entourage prepared themselves for a special treat.

Esperanza was one of the most awkward students at Thorn-
50 ton High. Her caramel-colored face was usually hidden behind thick tortoise shell glasses. Her wavy black hair exploded off her scalp like a snapshot of an atom bomb. She wore clothing that looked like it had spent years in a musty attic. Understanding her debased position on the social totem pole, Esperanza scur-
55 ried through the high school's hallways with her eyes looking narrowly at the back of the person walking in front of her, trying to disappear within the herd lest she be recognized by any malicious onlookers as easy prey.

Esperanza had been sitting alone in the front row, paying little
60 attention to the other auditions, working on geometry homework until her name was called. Shuffling her feet toward the center of the stage, Esperanza did not look up until she was there, and even then looked only at Mrs. Dominguez.

"Whenever you're ready," Mrs. Dominguez said politely,
65 sensing the potential for this audition to devolve into a painful target of ridicule.

As Esperanza began the opening notes to "The Star Spangled Banner," Monique and her friends looked at each other in total disbelief. Clearly, they thought, Esperanza had no theater
70 pedigree, or she would never stoop to singing such a trite, formulaic song. Standing perfectly still, Esperanza moved methodically through the tune with little flair or emotion. However, the

GO ON TO THE NEXT PAGE.

expectant smiles of mockery were quickly vanishing from the faces of all who listened.

75   Anticipating a tentative, mousy voice that would befit such a quirky presence as Esperanza's, the audience instead heard an unusually smooth, rich tone with full command of the multiple registers that the national anthem's melody requires. At the climactic "rocket's red glare," Esperanza's voice filled the room with
80 a calm resonance that forced one's heart to lift within one's chest as though some reluctant patriotism was determined to find its way out. The final phrase of the song, so often soaked in vibrato by melodramatic singers, was gently performed, with a touch that felt like a mother tucking in her baby to sleep.

85   Although Monique was loath to admit it and Esperanza was reluctant to want it, Esperanza had just set herself apart from the herd.

1. It can reasonably be inferred from the passage that Monique believed the song she chose for her audition:

A. would be the most inspiring Rodgers & Hammerstein number she could choose.
B. was the most sophisticated song in Billie Holiday's repertoire.
C. would likely be more recognizable to Monique's parents than to her friends.
D. would allow Monique to more effectively showcase her enthusiasm.

2. The passage initially portrays Monique and her friends as:

F. concerned and nervous.
G. confused and surprised.
H. friendly and inclusive.
J. aloof and disparaging.

3. According to the narrator, what did Esperanza do prior to singing "The Star Spangled Banner"?

A. Looked only at Mrs. Dominguez
B. Walked confidently up to the stage
C. Watched the other auditions carefully
D. Finished her geometry homework

4. The main purpose of the statement in line 29 is to:

F. inform the reader that students' fears of going first were largely a thing of the past.
G. present reasons for why this year's audition was the strangest yet.
H. suggest that Monique's imagination no longer involved the same imagery.
J. offer a contrast created by Monique's choice of audition slot.

5. It can be reasonably inferred from the passage that Esperanza Solito:

A. was teased more than anyone else at her school.
B. was not sitting near Monique and her friends during the auditions.
C. had her audition immediately after Monique's audition.
D. had previously explained her stage fright to Mrs. Dominguez.

6. According to the passage, Monique figured that volunteering to perform "God Bless the Child" as the first audition of the day would:

F. bolster her confidence in her performance.
G. make the other auditioners feel they could not compete with her.
H. guarantee her a part in the play.
J. impress and charm Mrs. Dominguez.

7. According to the passage, when Esperanza Solito got to the climax of "The Star Spangled Banner," she:

A. raised her voice to emphasize the lines.
B. demonstrated her patriotism.
C. had a sudden bout of nerves.
D. could be heard throughout the auditorium.

8. The passage states that Mrs. Dominguez suspected Esperanza's audition could be:

F. vulnerable to ridicule.
G. one of the most awkward.
H. a special treat.
J. neither surprising nor charming.

9. Which of the following details is used in the passage to describe how Monique and her friends responded to hearing Esperanza's audition?

A. Their decision to sit comfortably behind Mrs. Dominguez
B. Their preconceived notions about Esperanza's voice
C. Their fading facial expressions of mockery
D. Their fondness for patriotic songs

10. The passage most strongly suggests that Esperanza's choice of audition material was:

F. good for a mousy voice.
G. often partly sung with vibrato.
H. an impressive, original choice.
J. something Monique's friends had anticipated.

GO ON TO THE NEXT PAGE.

Passage II

SOCIAL SCIENCE: This passage is adapted from the article "Information Stupor-highway" by Cal Jergenson (© 2005 by Cal Jergenson).

Think about a remote control. Something so simple in function is seemingly capable of invisible magic to most of us. Only those with an engineering and electronics background probably have any real idea of *why* a remote control works. The rest of us
5 just assume it *should*. And the longer a given technology exists, the more we take it for granted.

Consider for a moment a split screen showing modern remote control users versus the first remote control users: the original users would be cautiously aiming the remote directly at
10 the television, reading the names of the buttons to find the right one, and deliberately pressing the button with a force that adds nothing to the effectiveness of the device. The modern users would be reclined on a sofa, pointing the remote any which way, and instinctively feeling for the button they desired, intuiting its
15 size, shape, and position on the remote.

Humans are known for being handy with tools, so it is no surprise that we get so comfortable with our technology. However, as we become increasingly comfortable with how to *use* new technologies, we become less aware of how they *work*.
20 Most people who use modern technology know nothing of its underlying science. They have spent neither mental nor financial resources on its development. And yet, rather than be humbled by its ingenuity, we consumers often become unfairly demanding of what our technology should do for us.

25 Many of the landmark inventions of the twentieth century followed predictable trajectories: initial versions of each technology (television, video games, computers, portable phones, etc.) succeeded in wowing the general public. Then these wondrous novelties quickly became commonplace. Soon the focus of
30 consumer attitudes toward these inventions changed from awed gratitude to discriminating preference.

Televisions needed to be bigger and have a higher resolution. Video games needed to be more realistic. Computers needed to be more powerful yet smaller in size. Cell phones needed to be
35 smaller yet capable of performing other tasks such as taking pictures, accessing the Internet, and even playing movies.

For children of the last twenty years born into this modern life, these technological marvels seem like elements of the periodic table: a given ingredient that is simply part of the universe.
40 Younger generations don't even try to conceive of life without modern conveniences. They do not appreciate the unprecedented technology that is in their possession; rather, they complain about the ways in which it fails to live up to ideal expectations.

"The videos that my phone can record are too pixelated."
45 "My digital video recorder at home doesn't allow me to program it from my computer at work." "It's taking too long for this interactive map to display on my portable GPS." "My robotic vacuum cleaner never manages to get the crumbs out of the cracks between the tiles."

50 If it sounds as though we're never satisfied, we aren't. Of course, our fussy complaints do actually motivate engineers to continually refine their products. After all, at the root of our tool-making instinct is the notion that "there must be a better way." Thus, the shortcomings of any current version of technology are
55 pinned on the limitations of its designers, and the expectation is that someone, somewhere is working on how to make the existing product even better.

The most dangerous extension of this mindset is its effect on our outlook on solving global climate problems. The firmly
60 substantiated problem of global warming threatens to quickly render the planet Earth inhospitable to most humans.

The solution? If you ask most people, you will hear that the solution resides in creating more efficient versions of our current technologies and devising alternative forms of energy
65 than those that burn fossil fuels.

Blindly confident that the creativity of human problem-solvers can wriggle us out of any dilemma, most people feel guiltless in continuing to live their lives with the assumption that someone else is working on these problems.

70 Unfortunately, having no real scientific perspective on the problems to be solved or the complexity of global weather patterns, most people are unduly optimistic about humanity's ability to think its way out of this problem. In a culture completely spoiled by the idea that technology can achieve whatever
75 goal it is tasked to perform, the idea that a global climate crisis may be beyond the reach of a clever technological solution is unthinkable.

Hence the idea that we, as a culture, may need to reexamine our lifestyles and consumer habits is too alien to take seriously.
80 In contemporary society, the leaders who are most able to communicate the state of the world do not dare suggest to the public the unpopular ideas that "times will be rough," "sacrifices must be made," or "we may have to take some steps backwards."

As a result, the human race will continue defiantly with the
85 status quo and, ultimately, blame technology when problems arise. At that point, we'll all be searching for the "rewind" button on the remote control.

GO ON TO THE NEXT PAGE.

11. The passage states that original users of remote controls likely did all of the following EXCEPT:
    A. use more strength pressing the button than is necessary.
    B. aim the remote directly at the television.
    C. feel instinctively for the desired button.
    D. read the names of the buttons carefully.

12. In the passage, the author answers all of the following questions EXCEPT:
    F. How do most people think the global climate crisis should be solved?
    G. What was the most significant invention of the twentieth century?
    H. What idea underlies humanity's tool-making instinct?
    J. How do consumer attitudes about new technology change?

13. The descriptions offered by the author in the second paragraph (lines 7–15) are used to illustrate the concept that:
    A. consumer behavior toward new forms of technology changes over time.
    B. modern humans do not pay enough attention to instructions.
    C. the first consumers of new technology used new devices with ease and comfort.
    D. remote controls have become far more effective over the years.

14. The principal tone of the passage can best be described as:
    F. nostalgic.
    G. critical.
    H. sympathetic.
    J. frightened.

15. As it is used in line 79, the word *alien* most nearly means:
    A. extraterrestrial.
    B. repetitive.
    C. unusual.
    D. hilarious.

16. The author uses the statement "these technological marvels seem like elements of the periodic table" (lines 38–39) most nearly to mean that:
    F. children learn technology while they learn chemistry.
    G. consumers regard many technological inventions as unremarkable.
    H. space exploration gives us most of our technology.
    J. consumers complain when modern conveniences break down.

17. The phrase *the status quo* (line 85) most likely refers to:
    A. reexamining the scope and complexity of technology.
    B. making sacrifices to combat the global climate crisis.
    C. blaming technology for the problems we encounter.
    D. our current pattern of lifestyles and consumer habits.

18. One form of consumer behavior the author describes is a discriminating preference for:
    F. less realistic video games.
    G. needing to understand technology.
    H. more powerful computers.
    J. wanting to make sacrifices.

19. Among the following quotations from the passage, the one that best summarizes what the author sees as a potential danger is:
    A. "the shortcomings of any current version of technology" (line 54).
    B. "devising alternative forms of energy" (line 64).
    C. "the complexity of global weather patterns" (lines 71–72).
    D. "our outlook on solving global climate problems" (line 59).

20. The last paragraph differs from the first paragraph in that in the last paragraph the author:
    F. makes a prediction rather than making an observation.
    G. refutes a scientific theory.
    H. quotes experts to support his opinions.
    J. uses the word "we" instead of "I."

GO ON TO THE NEXT PAGE.

Passage III

HUMANITIES: The following passage is adapted from the article "Conquering Jazz" by Patrick Tyrrell (© 2006 by Patrick Tyrrell).

From the time I started playing instruments, I have been intrigued and slightly mystified by the world of jazz. I'm not talking about adventurous, atonal, confusing jazz that normal music listeners have a hard time following. I'm talking about the lively,
5 accessible, beautiful jazz that came of age in the swinging 1920s and 1930s: the simultaneously hip and regal symphonic swing of Duke Ellington and Count Basie; the carnival of contrapuntal melodies that inexplicably harmonize with each other in New Orleans' jazz; the buoyant, atmosphere-touching saxophone solos
10 of Charlie Parker and the young John Coltrane.

The one thing I had always heard about jazz but could never accept was that jazz was an improvised form of music. How could this be?

The trademark of beautiful jazz is the complexity of the
15 music. All the instrumentalists are capable of dizzying arrays of notes and rhythms. The soloists find seemingly impossible transitions from one phrase to the next that are so perfect one would think they had spent weeks trying to devise *just* the right route to conduct safe passage. To think they spontaneously craft
20 these ideas seems preposterous.

My first nervous jabs into the world of jazz came during college. I was in a rock band, but my fellow guitarist and bandmate, Victor, also played in a jazz ensemble. At our practices, I would sometimes show off a new chord I had just "invented" only to
25 have him calmly and confidently name it, "Oh, you mean C-sharp diminished?" Often, in between our band's simplistic rock songs, I would look over and see him playing chord shapes on his guitar I had never seen before. Were we playing the same instrument?

Of course, rock music, as well as most early classical mu-
30 sic, operates within a much simpler harmonic world than does jazz. There are 12 tones in Western music: A-flat, A, B-flat, B, C, D-flat, D, E-flat, E, F, G-flat, and G. There are major chords, which sound happy, and minor chords, which sound sad. Essentially, rock music requires only that you learn the major and
35 minor chord for each of the 12 tones. If you do, you can play 99 percent of all the popular radio songs from the 1950s onward.

Jazz uses the same twelve tones as do rock and classical, but it employs a much more robust variety of chords. Major sevenths, augmented fifths, flat ninths, and diminished chords all add to
40 the depth and detail of the music. These often bizarre-sounding chords toss in subtle hints of chaos and imbalance, adding a worldly imperfection to otherwise standard chord values. Jazz starts sounding better the older you get, just as candy starts tasting too sweet and a bit of bitterness makes for a more appealing flavor.

45 For the most part, Victor's elliptical personality prevented him from ever giving me straightforward explanations when I asked him to divulge the "magician's secrets" of jazz. But I did learn that jazz is only *partly* improvised. The musicians aren't inventing the structure of songs spontaneously, just the specific
50 details and embellishments. A sheet of jazz music doesn't look like a sheet of classical music. There aren't notes all over the page dictating the "ideas." There are just chord names spaced out over time, dictating the "topic of conversation."

There's a legendary book in the jazz world known as "The
55 Real Book." It's a collection of a few hundred classic songs. Open it up in any room full of jazz musicians, and they could play in synchrony for a week. For years, I wanted my own copy, but I had always been too afraid to buy it, afraid that I wouldn't know how to use the book once I had it. Then, at age 30, more
60 than a decade since Victor and I had gone our separate ways, I bought myself a copy. I resolved to learn how to play all the chords on guitar and piano. For the next few months, I quietly plucked away at these strange, new combinations. F-sharp minor-7 flat-5? Each chord was a cryptic message I had to decode and
65 then understand. It felt like being dropped off alone in a country where I didn't speak the language.

But I made progress. Chords that initially took me twenty seconds to figure out started to take only a few. My left hand was becoming comfortable in its role of supplying my right hand
70 with a steady bass line. Meanwhile, to my amazement, my right hand began to improvise melodies that sounded undeniably *jazzy*.

It seemed like the hard work of figuring out the exotic jazz chords had sent new melodic understanding straight to my hand, bypassing my brain entirely. I felt like a witness to performances
75 by detached hands; I couldn't believe that I was the one creating these sounds. I'm sure this feeling will not last, but for now I'm enjoying the rare and miraculous feeling of improvising music that I still consider beyond my abilities.

21. Which chord, if any, does the author eventually conclude is the most confusing jazz chord to play?

   A. The passage does not indicate any such chord.
   B. C-sharp diminished
   C. Major sevenths
   D. F-sharp minor-7 flat-5

GO ON TO THE NEXT PAGE.

22. As it is used in line 47, "magician's secrets" most nearly means:

    F. information on how to play jazz.
    G. forbidden bits of knowledge.
    H. instances of harmless trickery.
    J. the true nature of a private person.

23. As portrayed by the author, Victor responds to the author's *invented* chord with what is best described as:

    A. amazement.
    B. jealousy.
    C. confusion.
    D. nonchalance.

24. The author states that "The Real Book" was something he explored for a few:

    F. years.
    G. months.
    H. weeks.
    J. days.

25. The details in lines 40–44 primarily scrvc to suggest the:

    A. aspects of jazz's complexity that more mature listeners enjoy.
    B. lack of depth and detail found in rock and classical music.
    C. confusion and awkwardness of standard jazz chord values.
    D. unpleasantly bitter taste of candy that develops with age.

26. In the context of the passage, the author's statement in lines 68–71 most nearly means that:

    F. he was so overworked that his hands could still move, but his thoughts were turned off.
    G. he had accidentally trained his hands to resist being controlled by his brain.
    H. it was easier to decode the exotic jazz chords by pointing at them with his hands.
    J. his hand was capable of playing music that his mind was incapable of fully comprehending.

27. The author implies that F-sharp minor-7 flat-5 is an example of a chord that he:

    A. had little trouble decoding now that he had "The Real Book."
    B. had previously only seen during his travels abroad.
    C. knew how to play on guitar but not on a piano.
    D. initially found confusing and struggled to understand.

28. The passage supports which one of the following conclusions about Victor?

    F. He played music with the author until the author turned 30 years old.
    G. He gave his copy of "The Real Book" to the author as a gift.
    H. He was at one time a member of multiple musical groups.
    J. He invented a chord and named it C-sharp diminished.

29. The passage is best described as being told from the point of view of someone who is:

    A. reviewing the chain of events that led to his career in jazz.
    B. discussing reasons why jazz is less complicated than it seems.
    C. relating his impressions of jazz music and his attempts to play it.
    D. highlighting an important friendship that he had in college.

30. Assessing his early and later experiences with "The Real Book," the author most strongly implies that it was:

    F. pleasantly strange to begin with but annoyingly familiar by the end.
    G. initially difficult to decipher, but ultimately manageable following diligent practice.
    H. almost impossible to understand because its pages didn't look like sheets of classical music.
    J. very useful as a learning tool, but not useful for more profound study.

GO ON TO THE NEXT PAGE.

Passage IV

NATURAL SCIENCE: This passage is adapted from the article "Fair-Weather Warning" by Julia Mittlebury (© 2007 by Julia Mittlebury).

Could the sun be causing epidemics? Take cholera, for example, an often fatal disease caused by the bacterium *Vibrio cholerae* (*V. cholerae*). Every so often, coastal areas suffer massive outbreaks of cholera due to infected food or water. Where
5 do these outbreaks come from?

The bacterium that causes cholera is found in areas that contain the copepod, a certain type of crustacean. The copepod depends on zooplankton for nourishment, and these zooplankton in turn depend on phytoplankton for their nourishment. Phyto-
10 plankton use photosynthesis to feed on sunlight. Although one might need to go to the bottom of the food chain, the evidence shows that an increase in sunlight might mean an increase in the potential for cholera.

Interested in this correlation, Rita Calwell and her fellow
15 researchers at the University of Maryland are studying ways to use satellite measurements of sea temperatures, sea height, and chlorophyll concentrations in order to predict when conditions favoring a cholera outbreak are more likely. As sea temperatures rise, photosynthetic organisms such as phytoplankton become
20 more abundant. As sea levels rise, the phytoplankton, zooplankton, copepods, and, by extension, the cholera bacterium are all brought closer to the shore. This increases the likelihood of food and water contamination.

By monitoring the cholera food chain in reverse, Calwell and
25 her colleagues believe they can predict the emergence of cholera 4 to 6 weeks in advance. Calwell's model predicted the rate of infection during one recent cholera outbreak in Bangladesh with 95 percent accuracy. Unfortunately, because this field of study is so new and its insights are so speculative, local public health
30 officials have not yet begun to base any preventative measures on these satellite-based forecasts.

Just up the road from Calwell and the University of Maryland, Kenneth Linthicum is leading similar efforts at the NASA Goddard Space Flight Centre in Greenbelt, Maryland. He has
35 designed a model to analyze the spread of Rift Valley fever, a mosquito-spread virus that killed about 100,000 animals and 90,000 people back in December 1997.

Scientists observed that prior to the outbreak, the equatorial region of the Indian Ocean saw a half-degree increase in surface
40 temperature. Although half a degree sounds like only a slight difference, the temperature of an ocean does not change easily. Warmer ocean water in this region corresponds with strong and prolonged rains, increased cloud cover, and warmer air over equatorial parts of Africa. These characteristics favor the pro-
45 liferation of mosquitoes and help keep them alive long enough for the virus to become easily transmittable.

In September 2007, Linthicum and his team became alerted to similar environmental changes. Over the next few months, they warned local health officials in Kenya, Somalia, and Tanzania that
50 conditions were ripe for a mosquito-based outbreak. As a result, only 300 lives were lost, an almost miraculous improvement from the devastation of the 1997 outbreak. While it is impossible to know if this outbreak would have been as far-reaching as that of 1997, it seems likely that the advance warning succeeded in
55 saving thousands, if not tens of thousands, of lives.

Similarly, a study by David Rogers at Oxford University has helped to predict outbreaks of sleeping sickness, a parasitic disease caused by West African tsetse flies. Here, Rogers first calibrated regional levels of photosynthesis to the size of a vein
60 in the wings of the flies. The vein size is a good measure of how numerous and robust the tsetse fly population is. Today, by reading the photosynthetic levels from satellite data, even researchers outside of West Africa can predict potential epidemics in the region.

65 This type of research is encouraging to many in the disease prevention field, because traditional methods involve slow, costly research. The newfound ability to cull massive amounts of meteorological data from satellites and to run that data through computer models has been much more efficient.

70 The goal of these models is to study the relationships between disease data and climate data. However, to do so requires decades', if not centuries', worth of high quality data to identify correlating factors with accuracy. Currently, the climatic data is much more reliable than the disease data. Nevertheless, excite-
75 ment about the potential usefulness of satellite-based predictions is persuading health agencies to compile and integrate their disease data more efficiently to give easier access to those trying to discover climate-disease links.

It may still take a good deal of time and energy before this
80 technology is ready for practical application. Critics claim that the number of variables underlying the spread of disease are too numerous and varied for a climate-based approach ever to be reliable. Fluctuations in the immunity of local populations, human and animal migrations, and the resistance to drugs used
85 to commonly treat certain diseases could confuse climate-based models. Advocates respond, though, that these non-climatic factors can similarly be incorporated into their research as long as the relevant data is collected, and the resulting models will have even better accuracy.

GO ON TO THE NEXT PAGE.

31. According to Calwell, scientists may be able to predict cholera outbreaks more than a month in advance by:

   A. noticing increased activity in a known food chain.
   B. using accurate climatic models derived from weather in Bangladesh.
   C. measuring the decline of zooplankton with falling sea temperatures.
   D finding connections between chlorophyll levels and diseased marine life.

32. According to the passage, levels of sunlight can influence cholera because:

   F. phytoplankton feed on sunlight and contaminate the water.
   G. the *V. cholerae* bacterium increases its photosynthetic rate.
   H. sunlight promotes the growth of organisms upon which copepods depend.
   J. many epidemics are caused by direct, prolonged exposure to sunlight.

33. According to the passage, the use of satellite data has aided the attempts of Oxford University researchers to predict outbreaks of sleeping sickness by providing information about:

   A. the number of West African parasites.
   B. which areas globally have the most photosynthesis.
   C. the health and number of tsetse flies.
   D. which flies have the biggest veins.

34. The passage states that Linthicum is conducting similar efforts to Calwell's in that Linthicum:

   F. studies the climatic triggers of cholera.
   G. works at the University of Maryland.
   H. managed to save thousands of lives in 2007.
   J. uses satellite data to build predictive models.

35. According to the passage, the use of satellite data to predict potential epidemics is encouraging because:

   A. computer number-crunching is quicker and less expensive than traditional research methods.
   B. it allows scientists to control the photosynthetic levels in West Africa.
   C. satellites do not make the same mathematical errors that human forecasters often do.
   D. there is already a large supply of long-term disease data available from satellites.

36. As it is used in line 44, the word *favor* most nearly means:

   F. errand.
   G. task.
   H. promote.
   J. request.

37. It can reasonably be inferred that the phrase *similar environmental changes* (line 48) refers to:

   A. the beginning of the rainy season in Kenya.
   B. the amount of bacteria circulating in the jet stream.
   C. the proliferation of mosquitoes throughout central Africa.
   D. warmer ocean water influencing rain and cloud cover.

38. The passage states that climatic satellite data has helped to do all of the following EXCEPT:

   F. measure sea height.
   G. predict tsetse fly populations.
   H. forecast disease outbreaks.
   J. raise the ocean temperature.

39. The phrase *confuse climate-based models* (line 85–86) refers directly to the fact that:

   A. current models do not account for non-climate related factors.
   B. drug resistance sometimes results in disorientation.
   C. epidemics sometimes vanish more quickly than they arise.
   D. researchers are not used to non-climate data.

40. It can reasonably be inferred from the passage that the information about the use of satellite-based data is presented primarily to:

   F. demonstrate the various kinds of data that must be collected.
   G. analyze the data's potential use in disease-prevention.
   H. illustrate how few scientists do on-the-ground research.
   J. show how West African tsetse fly populations have been predicted.

END OF TEST 3

STOP! DO NOT TURN THE PAGE UNTIL TOLD TO DO SO.

DO NOT RETURN TO A PREVIOUS TEST.

SCIENCE TEST

35 Minutes—40 Questions

DIRECTIONS: There are seven passages in this test. Each passage is followed by several questions. After reading a passage, choose the best answer to each question and fill in the corresponding oval on your answer document. You may refer to the passages as often as necessary.

You are NOT permitted to use a calculator on this test.

Passage I

Two ways to measure the quality of soil are *bulk density* and the *soil organic matter test*, SOM (a measure of the active organic content). High quality soil provides structure to plants and moves water and nutrients, so plants grow in larger quantities, leading to higher crop yields at harvest.

Bulk density is measured as the dry weight of a sample of soil divided by the volume of the sample. A bulk density measure above 1.33 g/cm³ negatively affects soil quality. Figure 1 shows the bulk density levels for 5 different years at Fields A and B.

Table 1 shows how soil quality varies with SOM. Table 2 shows the average SOM at the end of each of the 5 years.

Table 1	
SOM	Soil quality rating
<0.25	poor
0.25 to 0.50	fair
0.51 to 0.75	good
>0.75	excellent

Table 2	
Field	Average SOM
A	0.89
B	0.28

Figure 2 shows the total crop yield at each field at the end of the 5 years.

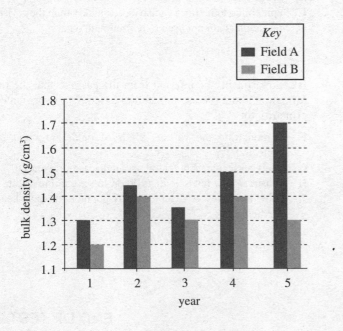

Figure 1

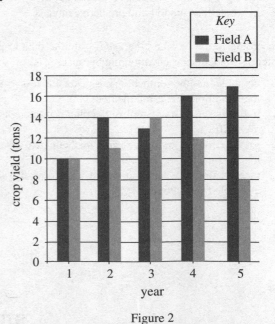

Figure 2

GO ON TO THE NEXT PAGE.

1. Which set of data best supports the claim that Field A has *lower* soil quality than Field B ?

   A. Figure 1
   B. Figure 2
   C. Table 1
   D. Table 2

2. If 8 tons or fewer in crop yields were considered a failed harvest, in which year and in which field would there have been a failed harvest?

   F. Field A in Year 1
   G. Field A in Year 3
   H. Field B in Year 4
   J. Field B in Year 5

3. Suppose a new crop rotation for Field B included legumes and other deep-rooted and high-residue crops. The SOM of this field will most likely change in which of the following ways? The SOM will:

   A. decrease, because soil quality is likely to increase.
   B. decrease, because soil quality is likely to decrease.
   C. increase, because soil quality is likely to increase.
   D. increase, because soil quality is likely to decrease.

4. Based on Figures 1 and 2, consider the average bulk density and the average crop yields for Fields A and B over the study period. Which site had the lower average crop yield, and which site had the higher average bulk density?

	Lower crop yield	Higher bulk density
F.	Field A	Field A
G.	Field B	Field B
H.	Field A	Field B
J.	Field B	Field A

5. As soil quality improves, the number of earthworms increases. Students hypothesized that more earthworms would be found in Field B. Are the data presented in Table 2 consistent with this hypothesis?

   A. Yes; based on SOM, Field B had a soil quality rating of fair, and Field A had a soil quality rating of poor.
   B. Yes; based on SOM, Field B had a soil quality rating of excellent, and Field A had a soil quality rating of fair.
   C. No; based on SOM, Field B had a soil quality rating of poor, and Field A had a soil quality rating of fair.
   D. No; based on SOM, Field B had a soil quality rating of fair, and Field A had a soil quality rating of excellent.

GO ON TO THE NEXT PAGE.

Passage II

Ferric oxide (Fe_2O_3) is more commonly known as rust. This is produced in a reaction between iron, a common metal, and water, H_2O.

$$2Fe + 3 H_2O \longrightarrow Fe_2O_3 + 3H_2$$

Table 1 shows the amount of Fe_2O_3 produced over time from 15 g Fe submerged in different liquids: 100 mL distilled water, a salt solution made from dissolving 20 g of salt in 100 mL of distilled water, and a sugar solution made from dissolving 20 g of sugar in 100 mL of distilled water.

Table 1				
Solution	g Fe_2O_3 produced			
	Day 2	Day 4	Day 6	Day 8
Distilled water	0.34	0.40	0.59	0.72
Salt solution	0.56	0.81	1.23	1.84
Sugar solution	0.00	0.05	0.11	0.19

The distilled water trial was repeated four times, but for each trial, a total volume of 100 mL of water was buffered to different pH levels.

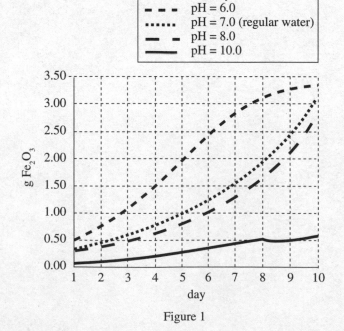

Key
- - - pH = 6.0
...... pH = 7.0 (regular water)
– – pH = 8.0
— pH = 10.0

Figure 1

6. Based on Table 1, if the amount of Fe_2O_3 produced on Day 9 had been measured for the salt solution, it would most likely have been:

F. less than 0.56 g.
G. between 0.59 g and 0.72 g.
H. between 1.23 g and 1.84 g.
J. greater than 1.84 g.

7. In the experiments shown in Table 1 and Figure 1, by measuring the rate at which Fe_2O_3 was formed every day, the experimenters could also measure the rate at which:

A. H_2O was produced.
B. H_2 was produced.
C. Fe was produced.
D. FeO was produced.

8. Consider the amount of Fe_2O_3 produced by the salt solution on Day 2. Based on Table 1 and Figure 1, the water buffered to pH = 10.0 produced approximately the same amount of Fe_2O_3 on which of the following days?

F. Day 1
G. Day 3
H. Day 6
J. Day 10

9. According to Table 1, what was the amount of Fe_2O_3 produced by the sugar solution from the time the amount was measured on Day 6 until the time the amount was measured on Day 8 ?
A. 0.08 g
B. 0.11 g
C. 0.19 g
D. 0.30 g

GO ON TO THE NEXT PAGE.

10. Based on Table 1, which graph best shows how the amount of Fe_2O_3 produced by the sugar solution changes over time?

F.

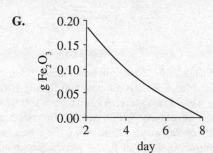

G.

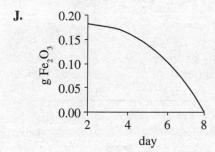

H.

J.

Passage III

Some physics students conducted experiments to study forces and springs. They used several identical springs attached to the bottom of a level platform, shown below in Figure 1.

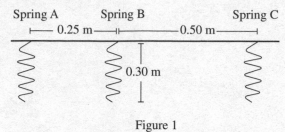

Figure 1

The length of each spring was 0.30 m when there were no weights attached. The springs had identical spring constants. When weights were attached, the length of the springs increased as the force of the weights stretched the springs downward. The length the springs stretched was proportional to the force of the weight.

Experiment 1

The students attached different weights to two springs at once. When the springs stopped oscillating and came to a rest, the students measured their length. In Trial 1, a 10.0 N weight was attached to Spring A and Spring B, which were attached 0.25 m apart on the board. In Trial 2, a 15.0 N weight was attached to Spring A and Spring B. In Trial 3, a 20.0 N weight was attached to Spring A and Spring B. The effects of the weights on Springs A and B for the three trials are shown below in Figure 2.

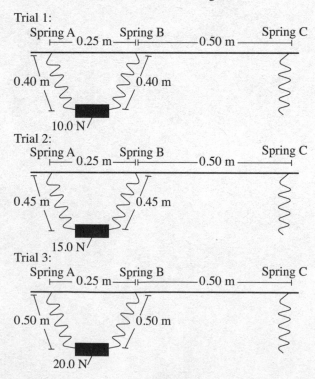

Figure 2

Experiment 2

The students attached a 0.25 m board with a high friction surface to Spring B and Spring C (see Figure 3). The students then placed a 5.0 N weight at different locations along the board. Because of the high friction surface, the weights stayed in place when the board was at an angle.

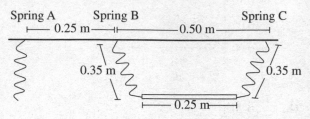

Figure 3

In each of these 3 trials, a 5.0 N weight was placed at various distances along the board from the attachment with Spring B (see Figure 4). In Trial 4, the weight was placed so its center was 0.075 m along the board from the attachment with Spring B. In Trial 5, the weight was placed so its center was 0.125 m along the board from the attachment with Spring B. In Trial 6, the weight was placed so its center was 0.200 m along the board from the attachment with Spring B. The effects of the weight position on the lengths of Springs B and C for the 3 trials are also shown in Figure 4.

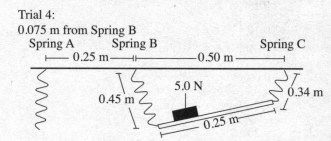

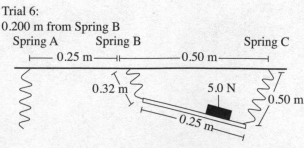

Figure 4

GO ON TO THE NEXT PAGE.

11. In a new study, suppose the students had placed a 10.0 N weight on Spring A only. Which of the following drawings most likely represents the results of this experiment?

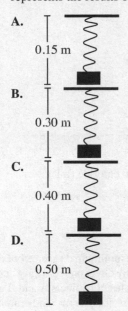

A. 0.15 m

B. 0.30 m

C. 0.40 m

D. 0.50 m

12. In Experiment 2, as the distance between the 5.0 N weight and the attachment of the board to Spring B increased, the force exerted on Spring B:

F. increased only.
G. decreased only.
H. increased, then decreased.
J. decreased, then increased.

13. Which of the following statements is most likely the reason that the students used identical springs in Trials 1–3 ?

A. To ensure that the springs stretched similarly when a weight was attached
B. To ensure that the springs did not share the weight evenly
C. To compensate for the effects of oscillation on the results of the experiment
D. To compensate for the weight of the board exerted on each of the springs

14. Based on the results of Trials 1 and 5, the weight of the board used in Experiment 2 was:

F. 0 N.
G. 2.5 N.
H. 5.0 N.
J. 10.0 N.

15. In which of the following trials in Experiment 2, if any, was the force exerted by the weight and the board equally distributed between Springs B and C ?

A. Trial 4
B. Trial 5
C. Trial 6
D. None of the trials

16. Assume that when a spring is stretched from its normal length, it stores the energy to return to its normal state as potential energy. Assume also that the greater the force of the weight stretching the spring, the more the spring will stretch. Was the potential energy stored by Spring C higher in Trial 5 or Trial 6 ?

F. In Trial 5, because the force of the weight on Spring C was greater in Trial 5.
G. In Trial 5, because the force of the weight on Spring C was less in Trial 5.
H. In Trial 6, because the force of the weight on Spring C was greater in Trial 6.
J. In Trial 6, because the force of the weight on Spring C was less in Trial 6.

GO ON TO THE NEXT PAGE.

Passage IV

Sodium chloride, or salt, is used to de-ice roads and sidewalks during the winter because it lowers the freezing point of water. Water with sodium chloride freezes at a lower temperature than water alone, so putting sodium chloride on icy sidewalks and roads can cause the ice to melt. Sodium chloride is highly effective as a de-icer and is given a *de-icer proof* of 100. Distilled water is ineffective as a de-icer and is given a de-icer proof of 0.

Different proportions of sodium chloride and distilled water were combined to create mixtures with de-icer proofs between 0 and 100.

Table 1		
De-icer proof	Volume of distilled water	Volume of sodium chloride
100	0 mL	50 mL
80	10 mL	40 mL
60	20 mL	30 mL
40	30 mL	20 mL
20	40 mL	10 mL
0	50 mL	0 mL

Experiment 1

A 125-g cube of ice, frozen from distilled water, was submerged in 500-mL of each de-icing mixture listed in Table 1. After 300 seconds, the portion of the cube that had not been melted was removed and weighed. The de-icing rate was calculated by determining the weight of ice melted per second. By doing this, it was possible to determine de-icer proof for a solution based on the rate at which ice was melted.

Experiment 2

The addition of magnesium chloride to a de-icer changes its de-icer proof. Different amounts of magnesium chloride were added to 500-mL samples of sodium chloride. Each de-icing mixture was tested under the same conditions as Experiment 1 and the measured de-icing rate was used to calculate the de-icer proof. The results are shown in Figure 1.

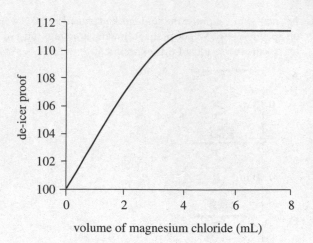

Figure 1

Experiment 3

The *temperature rating* (TR) is the minimum de-icer proof of a de-icing solution for a de-icer to have any effect on ice. 125-g cubes of ice were submerged in 500-mL samples of De-icers A and B and the samples were then placed in freezers at different temperatures. Table 2 shows the de-icer proof determined for each de-icer at each freezer temperature and the known TR for that temperature.

Table 2			
Freezer temperature	TR	Proof of:	
		De-icer A	De-icer B
−10°C	24.1	90.3	70.1
−25°C	36.9	78.9	64.9
−50°C	49.7	68.8	59.7
−75°C	52.3	56.6	51.7

17. Suppose a trial had been performed in Experiment 3 with a freezer temperature of −30°C. At this temperature, which of the following sets of proofs would most likely have been determined for De-icer A and De-icer B ?

	De-icer A	De-icer B
A.	68.8	59.7
B.	70.1	70.5
C.	75.5	61.8
D.	78.9	64.9

GO ON TO THE NEXT PAGE.

18. Based on Table 1, if 1 mL distilled water were added to 4 mL sodium chloride, the proof of this mixture would be:

    F. 4.
    G. 8.
    H. 40.
    J. 80.

19. Based on Experiment 3, as temperature decreases, the minimum proof for a de-icer to be effective:

    A. increases only.
    B. decreases only.
    C. increases, then decreases.
    D. decreases, then increases.

20. Which of the following expressions is equal to the proof for each de-icer mixture listed in Table 1 ?

    F. $\dfrac{\text{volume of sodium chloride}}{\text{volume of water}} \times 100$

    G. $\dfrac{\text{volume of water}}{\text{volume of sodium chloride}} \times 100$

    H. $\dfrac{\text{volume of sodium chloride}}{(\text{volume of water} + \text{volume of sodium chloride})} \times 100$

    J. $\dfrac{\text{volume of water}}{(\text{volume of water} + \text{volume of sodium chloride})} \times 100$

21. Based on Table 1 and Experiment 2, if 6 mL magnesium chloride were added to a mixture of 10 mL distilled water and 40 mL sodium chloride, the proof of the resulting de-icer would most likely be:

    A. less than 60.
    B. between 60 and 80.
    C. between 80 and 112.
    D. greater than 112.

22. Which of the two de-icers from Experiment 3 would be better to use to melt ice if the temperature were between –10°C and –75°C ?

    F. De-icer A, because its proof was lower than the TR at each temperature tested.
    G. De-icer A, because its proof was higher than the TR at each temperature tested.
    H. De-icer B, because its proof was lower than the TR at each temperature tested.
    J. De-icer B, because its proof was higher than the TR at each temperature tested.

GO ON TO THE NEXT PAGE.

Passage V

Comets originate from regions of our solar system that are very far from the sun. The comets are formed from debris thrown from objects in the solar system: They have a nucleus of ice surrounded by dust and frozen gases. When comets are pulled into the earth's atmosphere by gravitational forces and become visible, they are called *meteors*. Meteors become visible about 50 to 85 km above the surface of Earth as air friction causes them to glow. Most meteors vaporize completely before they come within 50 km of the surface of Earth.

The Small Comet debate centers on whether dark spots and streaks seen in images of the Earth's atmosphere are due to random technological noise or a constant rain of comets composed of ice. Recently, images were taken by two instruments, UVA and VIS, which are located in a satellite orbiting in Earth's magnetosphere. UVA and VIS take pictures of the aurora borealis phenomenon, which occurs in the magnetosphere. The UVA and VIS technologies provide images of energy, which cannot be seen by the human eye.

The pictures taken by VIS and UVA both show dark spots and streaks. Scientists debate whether these spots and streaks are due to a natural incident, such as small comets entering the atmosphere, or random technological noise. The layers of Earth's atmosphere are shown in Figure 1.

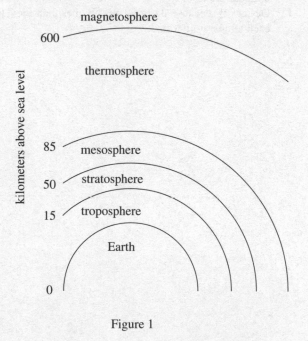

Figure 1

Two scientists debate whether there is a constant rain of comets burning up in Earth's magnetosphere.

Scientist 1

Small comets are pulled into Earth's atmosphere by gravitational effects and burn up in the magnetosphere. They are about 20 to 30 feet in diameter and burn up in the magnetosphere because they are much smaller than the comets that become meteors. Comets with larger radii will burn up in portions of the atmosphere much closer to Earth. About 30,000 small comets enter the Earth's magnetosphere every day. The dark spots and streaks on UVA and VIS images occur when the small comets begin to boil in the magnetosphere, releasing krypton and argon and creating gaseous H_2O, which interacts with hydroxyl, OH^-, radicals. Images taken by these instruments at different points in time show the same frequency of dark spots and streaks and give conclusive evidence in favor of the Small Comet theory. If the spots and streaks were due to random technological noise, then the frequency of their appearance would fluctuate.

Scientist 2

The dark spots and streaks in the UVA and VIS images are due to technological noise, not small comets. If the Small Comet Theory were true, and 20 small comets bombarded Earth's atmosphere per minute, there would be a visible bright object at least twice every five minutes. This is because, as objects enter the Earth's mesosphere, they burn up, creating large clouds of ice particles. As the ice particles vaporize, they have a brightness in the sky approximately equal to that of Venus. Because comets rarely enter Earth's atmosphere, such bright flashes are rare occurrences, far less than two times every five minutes, so the Small Comet theory cannot be correct. Further, since comets originate from regions of space beyond the orbit of the farthest planet, they contain argon and krypton. If the Small Comet theory were true and Earth were bombarded by 30,000 comets per day, there would be 500 times as much krypton in the atmosphere as there actually is.

23. According to Scientist 2, which of the following planets in our solar system is most likely the closest to the region of space where comets originate?

A. Jupiter
B. Venus
C. Neptune
D. Saturn

24. Based on Scientist 1's viewpoint, a comet that burns up in the thermosphere would have a diameter of:

F. 5–10 ft.
G. 10–20 ft.
H. 20–30 ft.
J. greater than 30 ft.

25. Which of the following generalizations about small comets is most consistent with Scientist 1's viewpoint?

A. No small comet ever becomes a meteor.
B. Some small comets become meteors.
C. Small comets become meteors twice every five minutes.
D. All small comets become meteors.

26. During the *Perseids*, an annual meteor shower, more than 1 object burning up in the atmosphere is visible per minute. According to the information provided, Scientist 2 would classify the Perseids as:

F. typical comet frequency in the magnetosphere.
G. unusual comet frequency in the magnetosphere.
H. typical meteor frequency in the mesosphere.
J. unusual meteor frequency in the mesosphere.

27. Given the information about Earth's atmosphere and Scientist 1's viewpoint, which of the following altitudes would most likely NOT be an altitude at which small comets burn up?

A. 750 km
B. 700 km
C. 650 km
D. 550 km

28. Suppose a study of the dark holes and streaks in the UVA and VIS images revealed krypton levels in the atmosphere 500 times greater than normal levels. How would the findings of this study most likely affect the scientists' viewpoints, if at all?

F. It would strengthen Scientist 1's viewpoint only.
G. It would strengthen Scientist 2's viewpoint only.
H. It would weaken both Scientists' viewpoints.
J. It would have no effect on either Scientist's viewpoint.

29. Scientist 1 would most likely suggest enhanced imaging technology that can take pictures of objects in the atmosphere be used to look at what region of the atmosphere to search for small comets?

A. The region between 15 km above sea level and 50 km above sea level
B. The region between 50 km above sea level and 85 km above sea level
C. The region between 85 km above sea level and 600 km above sea level
D. The region between above 600 km above sea level

GO ON TO THE NEXT PAGE.

Passage VI

A cotton fiber is composed of one very long cell with two cell walls. During a 2-week period of cell life called elongation, cotton fibers grow 3 to 6 cm. The level of hydrogen peroxide in cotton fiber cells during elongation is very high. Scientists wanted to study whether the level of hydrogen peroxide affected the length of the cotton fiber.

The amount of hydrogen peroxide is controlled by an enzyme called *superoxide dismutase* (SOD). This enzyme turns superoxide into hydrogen peroxide. Four identical lines of cotton fiber plants were created. Each line was able to express only one of three types of superoxide dismutase. The gene for SOD1 was incorporated into L1, the gene for SOD2 was incorporated into L2, and the gene for SOD3 was incorporated into L3.

Experiment

Five cotton plants of each line were grown in nutrient solution until cotton fibers completed the elongation period. The average length of cotton fibers and the average concentration of hydrogen peroxide were determined. This information is shown in Table 1.

Table 1			
	At the end of elongation period:		
Line	Average elongation period length (days)	Average amount of hydrogen peroxide (μmol/mg)	Average cotton fiber length (cm)
L1	8	2.1	3.6
L2	4	0.2	1.4
L3	20	5.6	5.9
L4	12	2.3	4.5

Next, because the scientists had determined the average elongation period, they measured the amount of hydrogen peroxide and the length of the cotton fibers halfway through their elongation period. This information is shown in Table 2.

Table 2			
	At the midpoint of elongation period:		
Line	Day of elongation period	Average amount of hydrogen peroxide (μmol/mg)	Average cotton fiber length (cm)
L1	4	4.1	2.7
L2	2	5.3	1.0
L3	10	12.4	2.0
L4	6	8.7	3.2

Finally, the scientists measured the amount of hydrogen peroxide and the length of cotton fibers on the first day of the elongation period. This information is shown in Table 3.

Table 3			
	On the first day of elongation period:		
Line	Day of elongation period	Average amount of hydrogen peroxide (μmol/mg)	Average cotton fiber length (cm)
L1	1	1.2	0.2
L2	1	6.0	0.5
L3	1	5.7	0.1
L4	1	1.9	0.2

30. For L2, as the elongation period moved from the first day to the end, the amount of hydrogen peroxide:
   F.   increased only.
   G.   decreased only.
   H.   increased, then decreased.
   J.   decreased, then increased.

31. Which of the following is a dependent variable in the experiment?
   A.   The point in time during the elongation period
   B.   The type of superoxide dismutase the plant could express
   C.   The length of the cotton fiber
   D.   The type of cotton plant

32. A cotton fiber is one very long cell with two cell walls. A cotton fiber is a special kind of what type of cell?
   F.   Prokaryotic
   G.   Animal
   H.   Plant
   J.   Bacterial

33. One plant had an average cotton fiber length of 0.5 cm, and the average amount of hydrogen peroxide in its fibers was 5.9 μmol/mg. Which of the following most likely describes this plant?
   A.   It was from L1 and at the end of its elongation period.
   B.   It was from L1 and at the midpoint of its elongation period.
   C.   It was from L2 and at the beginning of its elongation period.
   D.   It was from L2 and at the end of its elongation period.

GO ON TO THE NEXT PAGE.

34. The scientists used one of the four lines of cotton plants as a control. Which line was most likely the control?

    F. L1
    G. L2
    H. L3
    J. L4

35. Suppose the data for all the plants were plotted on a graph with the time of the elongation period on the x-axis and the average length of the cotton fiber on the y-axis. Suppose also that the best-fit line for these data was determined. Which of the following would most likely characterize the slope of this line?

    A. The line would have a positive slope.
    B. The line would have a negative slope.
    C. The line would have a slope equal to zero.
    D. The line would have no slope, because the line would be vertical.

GO ON TO THE NEXT PAGE.

Passage VII

Convection is a heat transfer process caused by moving liquid or gas currents from a hot region to a cold region. As a liquid or gas cools, it gets more dense. An example of a convection process is a cup of hot coffee: the liquid toward the top is cooled by the air, so it becomes more dense and sinks to the bottom of the cup; the hotter liquid toward the bottom of the cup is less dense, so it rises toward the top. See Figure 1, below.

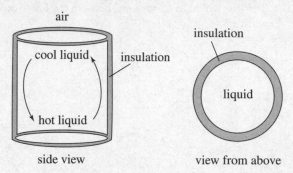

side view   view from above

Figure 1

The temperature of the liquid at the hot end of the insulated system is higher than the temperature at the cool end of the system. The difference (ΔT) between the hot liquid at the bottom and the cold liquid at the top changes depending on the starting temperature of the system. Table 1 gives ΔT for 500 mL of water in an insulated container with a height of 6.0 cm and a cross-sectional area of 4.0 cm^2 when the container is heated to different temperatures.

Table 1	
Heated temperature (°C)	ΔT (°C)
80	1
100	4
120	10
140	19

Figure 2 shows how ΔT changes with cross-sectional area for 500 mL of 100°C water in a container with a height of 6.0 cm. Figure 3 shows how ΔT changes with height for 500 mL 100°C water in a container with a cross-sectional area of 4.0 cm^2.

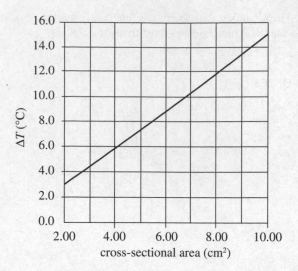

Figure 2

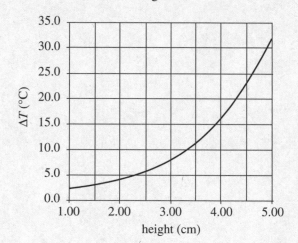

Figure 3

36. System 1 and System 2 are two convection systems. Based on Figure 2, if System 1 were the same height as System 2, but had two times the cross-sectional area and the systems were heated to the same temperature, the ratio of ΔT for System 1 to ΔT for System 2 would be:

   F. 1:1
   G. 1:2
   H. 2:1
   J. 3:1

GO ON TO THE NEXT PAGE.

37. For the systems described in the passage, if the containers were metal containers rather than insulated containers, heat would be transferred from the water to the container by which of the following heat transfer processes?

    I. Convection
    II. Conduction
    III. Radiation

A. I only
B. II only
C. I and III only
D. I and II only

38. Which of the following systems, if all were heated to the same temperature, would have the greatest ΔT ?

F.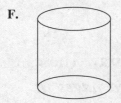

G.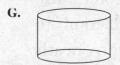

H.

J.

39. Based on the information in Table 1, if an insulated container of 500 mL of water with a height of 6.0 cm and a cross-sectional area of 4.0 cm² were heated to 120°C, which of the following pairs could represent the temperatures of the liquid at the top and bottom ends of the container?

	Bottom end	Top/Exposed to air end
A.	140°C	120°C
B.	140°C	110°C
C.	115°C	115°C
D.	120°C	110°C

40. The data in the passage supports the hypothesis that ΔT increases as which of the following increases?

F. Amount of insulation
G. Volume of liquid
H. Radius of the container
J. Air temperature

END OF TEST 4

STOP! DO NOT RETURN TO ANY OTHER TEST.

DIRECTIONS

This is a test of your writing skills. You will have forty (40) minutes to write an essay. Before you begin planning and writing your essay, read the writing prompt carefully to understand exactly what you are being asked to do. Your essay will be evaluated on the evidence it provides of your ability to express judgments by taking a position on the issue in the writing prompt; to maintain a focus on the topic throughout your essay; to develop a position by using logical reasoning and by supporting your ideas; to organize ideas in a logical way; and to use language clearly and effectively according to the conventions of standard written English.

You may use the unlined pages in this test booklet to plan your essay. These pages will not be scored. *You must write your essay on the lined pages in the answer folder.* Your writing on those lined pages will be scored. You may not need all the lined pages, but to ensure you have enough room to finish, do NOT skip lines. You may write corrections or additions neatly between the lines of your essay, but do NOT write in the margins of the lined pages. *Illegible essays cannot be scored, so you must write (or print) clearly.*

If you finish before time is called, you may review your work. Lay your pencil down immediately when time is called.

DO NOT OPEN THIS BOOK UNTIL YOU ARE TOLD TO DO SO.

ACT Assessment Writing Test Prompt

Globalization

Improved travel and communication networks have the potential to transform the world population into a single, global society. We can now travel across the globe in a matter of hours. The internet enables us to spread ideas and share cultural norms instantly. Many of the products we use every day are produced on the other side of the world. Globalization can be seen as beneficial, but is generally thought of as a more complicated issue. Given the accelerating pace of globalization, what are the implications it could have for humanity?

Read and carefully consider these perspectives. Each suggests a particular way of thinking about increasing globalization.

Perspective One	Perspective Two	Perspective Three
As the development of a single world culture becomes a real possibility, we risk losing the diversity that makes life interesting. As people become more similar, the unique elements that identify various cultures will be lost in global melting pot.	The ability to cheaply ship goods across the planet makes necessities and luxuries more affordable to all. Increased product affordability leads to an increase in the quality of life for millions of people globally.	Globalization brings greater interaction between countries, which could lead to more conflict. The more we interact with other cultures, the more our differences and disagreements will be emphasized. It would be better for cultures to be more isolated from one another in order to exist harmoniously.

Essay Task

Write a unified, coherent essay in which you evaluate multiple perspectives on the question of the implications increased globalization may have on humanity. In your essay, be sure to:

- analyze and evaluate the perspectives given
- state and develop your own perspective on the issue
- explain the relationship between your perspective and those given

Your perspective may be in full agreement with any of the others, in partial agreement, or wholly different. Whatever the case, support your ideas with logical reasoning and detailed, persuasive examples.

Chapter 26
Practice Exam 1:
Answers
and Explanations

	English			Math			Reading			Science	
1. B	39. B	1. E	31. C	1. C	21. A	1. A	21. C
2. F	40. H	2. G	32. G	2. J	22. F	2. J	22. G
3. D	41. B	3. B	33. E	3. A	23. D	3. C	23. C
4. G	42. J	4. J	34. J	4. J	24. G	4. J	24. J
5. A	43. A	5. C	35. D	5. B	25. A	5. D	25. A
6. H	44. G	6. H	36. K	6. G	26. J	6. J	26. J
7. C	45. C	7. B	37. D	7. D	27. D	7. B	27. D
8. J	46. H	8. J	38. H	8. F	28. H	8. J	28. F
9. D	47. C	9. E	39. C	9. C	29. C	9. A	29. D
10. F	48. F	10. F	40. K	10. G	30. G	10. F	30. G
11. B	49. C	11. E	41. B	11. C	31. A	11. D	31. C
12. H	50. J	12. J	42. K	12. G	32. H	12. G	32. H
13. D	51. A	13. B	43. B	13. A	33. C	13. A	33. C
14. G	52. F	14. K	44. J	14. G	34. J	14. H	34. J
15. A	53. D	15. A	45. E	15. C	35. A	15. B	35. A
16. G	54. F	16. G	46. H	16. G	36. H	16. H	36. H
17. C	55. D	17. D	47. C	17. D	37. D	17. C	37. B
18. H	56. H	18. F	48. J	18. H	38. J	18. J	38. F
19. C	57. B	19. A	49. C	19. D	39. A	19. A	39. D
20. F	58. G	20. K	50. G	20. F	40. G	20. H	40. H
21. D	59. B	21. E	51. E				
22. F	60. G	22. F	52. G				
23. C	61. D	23. B	53. C				
24. G	62. F	24. H	54. F				
25. D	63. C	25. E	55. D				
26. G	64. F	26. H	56. G				
27. A	65. C	27. C	57. B				
28. G	66. G	28. G	58. F				
29. A	67. C	29. B	59. C				
30. H	68. F	30. G	60. J				
31. B	69. B						
32. F	70. J						
33. D	71. B						
34. F	72. G						
35. A	73. D						
36. H	74. F						
37. C	75. D						
38. H							

ENGLISH TEST

1. **B** This sentence needs a comma after the complete idea and before the incomplete one. This brief pause clarifies that the incomplete idea is modifying Hawaii. Choices (C) and (D) introduce additional words that are unnecessary or create an error.

2. **F** In Sentence 4, the writer provides additional support for how difficult the race is. If deleted, the passage would lose this emphasis, as (F) describes. Choices (G), (H), and (J) all introduce extraneous details that have not been provided by the passage.

3. **D** This sentence requires a contrast to the previous paragraph. Only (D) provides that with *however*.

4. **G** As written, this sentence incorrectly places a comma after the word *athletics*, which is not needed since an incomplete idea follows. This eliminates (F) and (H). Choice (J) is not correct because it places a comma after the word *and*, and it uses the incorrect pronoun *there* to refer to sports' *physical demands*, which requires the possessive.

5. **A** This sentence is correct as written because *proved* as it is used means *became*. All the other options are synonyms of a different definition of *proved* and thus change the intended meaning of the sentence.

6. **H** The word *somewhat* is referring to the *amusing way* in which the race started. Therefore, *somewhat* needs to be before the word *amusing* to correctly modify it, (H).

7. **C** This sentence is providing the names of two sports clubs and the island on which they functioned. There is no need to separate anything here with a comma because it is a list of only two items, so that eliminates (A), (B), and (D). Only (C) correctly removes the commas.

8. **J** *Claiming* describes the bikers and does not require a conjunction, eliminating (F) and (G). Choice (H) would create a comma splice.

9. **D** The phrase before the comma is incomplete, and the word *when* introduces a second incomplete idea, leaving the sentence without any complete ideas. Therefore, the only possible answer is to delete the underlined portion, (D).

10. **F** The underlined phrase refers to the three separate races that were eventually combined into the single race of the Triathlon. Therefore, it should remain where it is now, (F).

11. **B** As written, the underlined section is redundant because it references the pages he is reading, although they were just mentioned a few words before. This redundancy can be eliminated by selecting (B).

12. **H** You can never join the helping verb *had* with the simple past tense *became*. This eliminates (F). Choice (G) is the present tense of the verb, and (J) is the incorrect form of the past tense, so both of those can be eliminated as well. Only (H) provides the correct form of the simple past tense.

13. **D**   Only (D) points out Haller's great achievement of winning the first Ironman. Choices (A) and (C) detract from his achievement by focusing on other competitors, and (B) discusses a moment of doubt Haller has.

14. **G**   Choices (F), (H), and (J) all provide specific, plural phrases that could represent the competitors to whom the sentence is referring. Choice (G) is a singular, ambiguous *that*, so it cannot refer to the competitors.

15. **A**   The final paragraph discusses how many compete in the race today, as well as how popular the race has become since its inception. This most closely aligns with (A).

16. **G**   The underlined portion is incorrect as written because the *when* makes the second part of the sentence incomplete. Therefore, (F) can be eliminated. Whenever there is a list, all the elements of that list must be parallel. None of the other items in the sentence as written end in *-ing*, so that eliminates (H). Nor are any of them in the past tense, which eliminates (J). Only (G) matches the others, and thus must be the correct answer.

17. **C**   As written, this sentence contains two complete ideas with no punctuation in between. This is incorrect, so eliminate (A). Simply adding a comma does not fix the problem, so (B) cannot be correct. Changing *hoping* to *praying* does not help either, so (D) cannot be correct. Only (C), which separates the sentence into two by introducing a period, offers a viable solution.

18. **H**   A conjunction is needed to join the two halves of the sentence together, eliminating (F) and (G) (note: *therefore* is an adverb, not a conjunction). *But* is not the right conjunction to use because the two clauses do not disagree with each other. That eliminates (J). The only answer left is (H).

19. **C**   This is a tricky question, but POE can help. Scanning the answer choices shows that this question is testing verb forms. Check the subject that goes with the underlined verb and see that all the opportunities is plural, so (A) and (B) can be eliminated since they are singular forms. Choices (C) and (D) appear to be testing whether a form of *to lie* or *to lay* is needed. Since the opportunities are simply resting or residing in the offer, a form of *to lie* is needed. The really sneaky part of this question, though, is that the verb that's being tested is part of an indirect quotation, as is signaled by the phrase *I thought to myself that*. When indirect quotation is used to relate a sentence with a present tense verb, the verb is shifted to past tense. For example, Emily said, "We need to get blueberries" would shift in an indirect quotation to Emily said that we needed to get blueberries. That means that the past tense form of *to lie* is needed, and the past tense of *to lie* is lay. Eliminate (D) and choose (C).

20. **F**   In a list, there should be a comma after every item, including the one before the *and*. The first item in this list is *a nice pair of slacks*, so the first comma is needed after that expression but nowhere inside of it. This eliminates all the answers except (F).

21. **D**   Sentence 2 refers to the narrator's acceptance of the volunteer position. This must logically follow the sentence that contains the director's offer of the position, Sentence 5.

22. **F** The phrase *an expert himself in every facet of hospital administration* is an additional descriptive detail that is not essential to the sentence. Therefore, it should have a comma on both sides of it. The correct answer is (F).

23. **C** The phrase preceding the comma at the beginning of this sentence must refer to the first noun following the phrase. As written, that noun is *my ears*, which cannot be correct because ears do not walk anywhere. Only (C) corrects the misplaced modifier by making *I* the subject.

24. **G** In an earlier sentence in this paragraph, the narrator describes herself as *overwhelmed* by all the noise in the hospital. Therefore, as the sounds continue, she becomes more overwhelmed, or *besieged*, as in (G).

25. **D** The underlined section of the sentence refers to how the narrator's face revealed her fear at the same time that she looked around the ward. Choice (D) changes this meaning, so it is therefore the LEAST acceptable option.

26. **G** This question calls for a vivid description of the hallway. Only (G) provides this, by giving specific details about all the family members and colorful decorations. Choice (F) just describes the hallway as busy, which is not particularly vivid. Choices (H) and (J) don't specifically refer to the hallway at all.

27. **A** The phrase *the one in charge of the nursery* provides an extra detail that is not essential to the meaning of the sentence. As such, it needs to be set off by commas on both sides. Only (A) gives us this option.

28. **G** The pronoun *it* should be referring to the blankets. However, *it* is singular, so (F) can be eliminated. *Them* is the appropriate pronoun to use, so (J) can be eliminated as well. Finally, *placing* doesn't match *start* as it needs to. Therefore, (H) can be eliminated, and (G) must be the answer.

29. **A** The final paragraph expresses the narrator's comfort in the nursery, especially as compared with the maternity ward. Therefore, when she gives the hospital director a nod, she is acknowledging the fact that she enjoys the new atmosphere. This most closely aligns with (A). At no point in the passage does the narrator express anger or the intention to quit, so (B) and (C) cannot be correct. Finally, nowhere else in the passage is the narrator nodding, so (D) can be eliminated as well.

30. **H** This new information acts as an introduction to the narrator's first day working at the hospital. This most logically should be inserted at the beginning of Paragraph 3, in which the actual activities of her first day are described.

31. **B** In this sentence, the author is making a comparison between the reputation snakes have and the reputation they deserve. Such a comparison will always be separated by the word *than*, which eliminates (A) and (D). Choice (C) can be eliminated because it changes the meaning of the sentence to imply that snakes have the deadliest reputation, which was not stated.

32. **F** At this point in the essay, the author is identifying numerous negative associations related to the snake. Only (F) adds to this list. Choices (G), (H), and (J) do not contain anything particularly negative in their portrayals of the snake.

33. **D** As written, the phrase *that is popular* refers to *a snake*, which is incorrect. The phrase should refer to the *reference*. The only choice which provides this concisely is (D).

34. **F** Choice (G) contains the word *who's*, which is the contraction for *who is* and is inappropriate in this sentence. Choice (H) contains the word *it's*, a contraction for *it is* and likewise inappropriate. Choice (J) contains the word *its'*, which is never correct. The only remaining answer is (F).

35. **A** This sentence is correct as written. The phrase following *fangs* is an unnecessary descriptive piece added to the sentence, which should be set off with commas. It is not necessary to introduce any additional words, because that would make the sentence a run-on.

36. **H** The word *prey* is followed by a list of the items that fall into this category. A colon is needed before such a list, which makes (H) correct.

37. **C** As written, the phrase *they are provoked* is ambiguous. Does it refer to the snakes or the people? Only (C) clarifies this ambiguity in a concise way.

38. **H** The statistic quoted acts as support for the preceding sentence, arguing that snakes normally do not pose much threat to humans. Therefore, (H) is the correct response.

39. **B** The underlined phrase needs a verb consistent with the singular subject of *Prompt treatment*. Only (B) is consistent and concise.

40. **H** As underlined, the transition in this sentence is neither parallel nor logical because the second half of the sentence is a separate idea that does not follow from the first. Only (H) provides a parallel transition.

41. **B** As written, this sentence is not a complete thought. It needs verbs, and without helping verbs like *was* or *is*, the words *considering* and *avoiding* can't stand alone. Choices (A) and (C) don't fix the problem. Choice (D) incorrectly changes the sentence to past tense, as well as combines two clauses. Only (B) gives two present tense verbs, "consider" and "avoid," to fix the fragment in the original sentence.

42. **J** As written, this sentence has complete ideas joined incorrectly. Two complete thoughts cannot be joined by a comma, which eliminates (F) and (H). Nor can two complete thoughts have no punctuation between them, so (G) must also be incorrect. Only (J) correctly uses a semicolon between the two thoughts.

43. **A** The opening paragraph referred to all the common derogatory phrases associated with snakes. Therefore, since (A) refers to the *snake in the grass* referenced in that paragraph, it would achieve the writer's aim of referencing the opening paragraph. All the other choices refer to items mentioned elsewhere in the passage, not in the first paragraph.

44. **G** The final sentence of the first paragraph refers to the snake as *unjustly maligned* despite its *ugly, slimy appearance*. The essay goes on to describe some of the misconceptions people have about snakes. Therefore, this sentence sets up the main idea of the passage as a whole, as (G) suggests.

45. **C** Choice (C) is correct because the author takes a positive view of snakes: They do not hurt humans to the degree commonly believed, and they help society by keeping the population of undesirable rodents and other pests in check.

46. **H** The underlined portion needs a word to indicate the present day. All the choices do this except (H), which changes the meaning.

47. **C** Choice (C) changes the meaning to indicate that the challenges showed anything was possible, whereas the original meaning of the sentence indicates that Hurston's perseverance is what made anything possible. Therefore, (C) is not acceptable.

48. **F** The underlined portion is correct as is because it is the only choice that accurately reflects Hurston as an individualistic person, in keeping with the description of her provided in the previous paragraph. All the other choices change the meaning of the phrase in ways not supported by the passage.

49. **C** This question calls for something historical in nature that makes Eatonville unique. Only (C) provides this. Choice (A) doesn't make the town unique, as many cities share a similar climate. Likewise, (B) and (D) discuss the town's founding but do not indicate that the town is different from any other community founded in the same era.

50. **J** This sentence needs a simple conjunction to join the two items listed, *freedom* and *independence*. For this reason, (J) is the answer. Choice (F) makes no sense in the context of the sentence because what follows *that* is not a separate clause. Choice (G) incorrectly introduces an unnecessary verb. Choice (H) makes the sentence two complete ideas linked incorrectly.

51. **A** The underlined portion is correct as written, (A). This list of two items is essential to the meaning of the sentence, so it should not be set off with commas. Only information that could be removed without altering the meaning requires commas.

52. **F** This sentence is correct as written. Choices (G) and (H) introduce a comma into the sentence that incorrectly separates the subject from the verb. Choice (J) incorrectly introduces a semicolon, which can be used only to connect two complete thoughts.

53. **D** The correct choice is (D) because it correctly eliminates the redundancy in the underlined passage. The term *literature* means *books, poems, and plays*, so there is no need to repeat it, as (A) does. The same applies to (B) and (C), so they are likewise incorrect.

54. **F** This sentence needs a verb in the past tense. This eliminates (H) and (J). Choice (G) cannot be correct because *developed* does not require a preposition to follow it. Therefore, the correct answer must be (F).

55. **D** This additional information relating to Billie Holiday is not relevant at this point in a passage dedicated to Hurston. It provides interesting but superfluous detail, which most closely aligns with (D).

56. **H** This question wants a word that indicates the novel accurately reflects the actual dialect spoken. Choice (H) does this because if something is authentic, it is true to the original. Choices (F), (G), and (J) positively comment on the dialect, but tell us nothing about how accurate it is.

57. **B** As written, the underlined *it* is ambiguous. The sentence needs to clearly identify what *it* is referring to. This eliminates both (A) and (C). Choice (D) cannot work, because *which* does not refer to Hurston's work. Therefore, (B) must be correct.

58. **G** Sentence 4 identifies one of Hurston's novels, and the following sentences provide additional information about the plot of that novel and the critical reception it received. Choice (G) most closely aligns with this summary. Choice (F) is incorrect because nothing in the remaining sentences indicates one specific influence. Choice (H) is incorrect because only one of the subsequent sentences provides a plot detail. Finally, (J) is incorrect because the remaining sentences focus on the novel, not Eatonville specifically.

59. **B** As written, the underlined portion is incorrect because the transition it uses indicates the sentence disagrees with the one that came before it. Therefore, (A) can be eliminated. However, (C) and (D) are incorrect as well because there is no direct cause and effect relationship between the two sentences. Choice (B) is the best choice because no transition is necessary at all.

60. **G** The phrase *as one of the best writers of her era* is essential to the meaning of the sentence, which means it cannot be set off by commas. It does, however, need an *and* after it to join the two halves of the sentence together. Thus, (G) must be correct.

61. **D** As written, this sentence is incomplete and cannot be ended with a period. This eliminates choice (A). There is also no need to introduce a conjunction because that does not fix the problem. Therefore, the correct answer must be (D).

62. **F** The phrase *Soviet Union* is extra information that is not essential to the meaning of the sentence. As such, it should have a dash on both sides of it, which only (F) provides.

63. **C** The word *Americas* is being used as a possessive because it owns the *powerful office* that follows. Therefore, it should have an apostrophe before the *s*. This eliminates (A) and (D). The phrase *most powerful* is modifying the word *office* and does not need a comma. Therefore, (C) must be correct.

64. **F** The underlined portion is correct as written. A pronoun in the subject case is needed here because it is the subject of the verb in the idea that follows.

65. **C** The phrase *underprivileged* indicates that these individuals are not as fortunate as others in a given society. As such, it would be redundant to specify this again. Only (C) eliminates this redundancy.

66. **G** This sentence indicates that Carter supported a national energy policy. Only (G) aligns with this information.

67. **C** The phrase *on foreign oil* refers to what America depended upon. Therefore, it should be as close as possible to the word *dependence*, (C).

68. **F** All the answer choices refer to the creation of the Carter Center. However, (F) changes the meaning to imply that Carter discovered the Center, rather than started it.

69. **B** The phrase *around the world* already refers to many different countries, so it would be redundant to specify those countries. Therefore, the correct answer is (B).

70. **J** The first words in this phrase, *at home*, indicate that Carter works within the United States. There is no need to identify this again, making the sentence redundant. Therefore, the correct answer is (J).

71. **B** As written, the placement of *abroad* incorrectly modifies the verb *focus*, which changes the intended meaning of the sentence. The word *abroad* refers to where Carter expends his efforts, (B).

72. **G** Sentence 4 functions as a transition between the previous paragraph and this paragraph. As such it should come first, as (G) suggests.

73. **D** The correct preposition needs to be *with* in order to maintain the intended meaning of the sentence: someone concurring with Carter. Choices (A) and (C) use prepositions that never work with *agree*. Choice (B) changes the meaning to taking on an obligation.

74. **F** This essay intends to identify some of the positive humanitarian goals Carter has sought to achieve in his career. Choice (F) most closely aligns with this goal. Choices (G) and (J) focus on his politics while ignoring his humanitarian interests, so they can be eliminated. Choice (H) comments on a right as an American, which has nothing to do with the rest of the passage.

75. **D** The new sentence references Habitat for Humanity, which was discussed in Paragraph 4. Therefore, it would most logically be added to the end of that paragraph, (D).

MATHEMATICS TEST

1. **E** Set up a proportion with the information you have and the information you are looking for:

$$\frac{\text{height}}{\text{length of shadow}} = \frac{24\,\text{ft}}{6\,\text{ft}} = \frac{x\,\text{ft}}{18\,\text{ft}}$$

Do the cross-multiplication to find that $x = 72$ feet, (E).

2. **G** Remember that Sherwood's $100 payment covers both his one-time new-member fee and a few months of a membership. Since the new-member fee is $16, this means that Sherwood put $100 − $16 = $84 toward his monthly fees. Since each month costs $14, Sherwood paid for $84 ÷ $14 = 6 months of membership.

3. **B** Although this looks like a problem in which you'll need to factor, you actually can just plug in the y value: $\dfrac{y^2 - 4}{y - 2} = \dfrac{(-6)^2 - 4}{(-6) - 2} = \dfrac{(36) - 4}{-8} = \dfrac{32}{-8} = -4$.

4. **J** Because the group ended up with more than 15 students, they overpaid. Figure out the total amount they should have paid and subtract it from the amount that they did pay: (18)($11.50) − (18)($10.25) = $22.50.

5. **C** When you are finding a probability, you need to figure out a basic part/whole relationship. In this case, there are 16 members in the orchestra, but only 12 of them are eligible to become speakers, so the "whole" (the denominator) must be 12. If you selected (B), you forgot to omit the 4 soloists. The likelihood that Itzhak would be chosen for this person is therefore $\dfrac{1}{12}$, because he represents one possibility out of the twelve eligible for the speaker position.

6. **H** In order to find the perimeter of a rectangle, remember that there are four sides. In this case, the four sides add up as follows: 8 ft + 8 ft + 17 ft + 17 ft = 50 ft. If you selected (F), you may have added only two sides of the rectangle, and if you selected (J), be careful—this is the area!

7. **B** Work slowly through this problem. The group has sold 240 passes online at $9 each. This means that they have already made (240)($9) = $2,160. In order to reach their goal, they will need $4,000 − $2,160 = $1,840. Since the question asks how many in-person tickets they will need to sell, you can approximate how many tickets will get them $1,840 by dividing: $1,840 ÷ $12 = 153.333. Since there is no such thing as 0.333 tickets, you have to round up to get 154 tickets, (B).

8. **J** Do basic cross-multiplication here. $\dfrac{9}{q} = \dfrac{6}{10}$ becomes (9)(10) = 6q, so $q = \dfrac{(9)(10)}{6} = \dfrac{90}{6} = 15$.

9. **E** Make sure you keep all your negative signs straight and distribute properly. The original equation is −9(y − 13) = 16. First, distribute the (−9) to find (−9y + 117) = 16. Subtract the 117 from both sides to find (−9y) = −101. Divide each side by the (−9) to find y = 11.2 = $\dfrac{101}{9}$.

10. **F** Because Points F, G, H, and J are collinear, you can figure out ∠GHK by subtracting 180° − ∠JHK = 180° − 120° = 60°. Segments $\overline{GK}$ and $\overline{HK}$ are equivalent, so angles ∠GHK and ∠HGK are congruent, and ∠HGK = 60°. Again because they are collinear, ∠HGK + ∠FGK = 180°, so ∠FGK = 120°. Isolate this triangle to find ∠GFK. Because of the two congruent sides, ∠GFK ≅ ∠GKF, so ∠FGK + ∠GFK + ∠GKF = ∠FGK + 2(∠GFK) = 120° + 2(∠GFK) = 180°, and ∠GFK = 30°.

11.   E   To find the answer, substitute (–3) for x throughout the equation $f(x) = 7x^2 – 9x + 4$. Once you've done this, you will find the following: $7(–3)^2 – 9(–3) + 4 = 7(9) + 27 + 4 = 63 + 27 + 4 = 94$. If you chose any of the other answers, you may not have distributed the negative properly.

12.   J   Use the answer choices, and work backwards. Find the smallest number that divides evenly by 16, 25, and 40. This is 400: $400 ÷ 16 = 25$; $400 ÷ 25 = 16$; and $400 ÷ 40 = 10$. If you selected (K), be careful—this is a common multiple of all three numbers, but it is not the *least* common multiple.

13.   B   In order to cancel the original mistake, Tex will need to multiply by 3. Then to get the number he wants, he will need to multiply by another 3. In total, he will be multiplying by 9, as in (B).

14.   K   There are 12 triangles, and the area of the whole figure is 96 cm², so each of the triangles has an area of 8 cm². Because each of the triangles is right isosceles, the base and height of each triangle are equivalent, so to find the length of each of these, use the area formula: $A = \dfrac{1}{2} = bh = \dfrac{1}{2}b^2$. Solve for b: $b = \sqrt{2A}$. The area of each triangle is 8, so you can find the base: $b = \sqrt{2A} = \sqrt{2(8)} = \sqrt{16} = 4$. You don't need to find the hypotenuse of the triangle because this problem asks for the perimeter of the figure, so count up the sides (there are 14) to find that the perimeter is 56 cm.

15.   A   The sum of the measures of all angles in a triangle is 180°. $\angle Y$ is described as a right angle, which means its measure is 90°. The other two angles, therefore, will have to add up to 90° to complete the 180° in the triangle. If $\angle Z$ measures less than 52°, then $\angle X$ must be *greater* than $90° – 52° = 38°$. It cannot be *equal* to this value [as in (B)], because $\angle Z$ is described as *less than* 52°.

16.   G   Try the different operations listed. You will find that the only operation that makes the statement true is division. Replace all the emoticons with division signs: $(8 ÷ 2)^3 – (4 ÷ 1)^2 = (4)^3 – (4)^2 = 64 – 16 = 48$.

17.   D   First, identify a point on the graph. The easiest place to start is with the intercepts. The x-intercept is unclear, but the y-intercept passes through (0,6), eliminating (A), (B), and (C). Between the latter two choices, you can solve for the x-intercept to find that in (D), $x = \dfrac{6}{5}$, and in (E), $x = 3$. Although the exact x-intercept is unclear on the graph, it is definitely less than 2, so you can eliminate (E).

18.   F   Translate the English in this problem into the math of the answer choices. The problem reads, "An integer, x, is subtracted from 6. That difference is then multiplied by 3." This translates into the following: $(6 – x) \cdot 3$ or $3(6 – x)$. The second part of the problem reads, "This product is 15 more than half the original integer." Therefore, $3(6 – x)$ will equal "15 more than half the original integer": $15 + \dfrac{1}{2}x$ or $\dfrac{1}{2}x + 15$. Therefore, $3(6 – x) = \dfrac{1}{2}x + 15$.

19.   **A**   Find the total production of each company after d days. Factory X starts with 18,000 units and can produce 120 units per day, so its production after d days will be 18,000 + 120d. Factory Y starts with only 14,500 units, but it can produce 155 units per day, so its production after d days will be 14,500 + 155d. Since you are looking for the number of days after which the total production of each factory will be equal, set the two equations equal to one another: 18,000 + 120d = 14,500 + 155d.

20.   **K**   Use the Pythagorean theorem to find the length of the hypotenuse: $a^2 + b^2 = c^2$, where c is the hypotenuse. $c = \sqrt{a^2 + b^2} = \sqrt{7^2 + 24^2} = \sqrt{625}$ = 25. Note that this is 7:24:25, a Pythagorean triple. If you remember a few of the basic triples, you can save yourself a lot of figuring.

21.   **E**   Make sure you are distributing properly: $9(y + 3) - 2(4y - 4) = 9y + 27 - 8y + 8 = y + 35$.

22.   **F**   Set up a system of equations to find a:

$$
\begin{array}{r}
(\quad a + 3b = 27) \\
+ (\quad a - 3b = 9) \\
\hline
2a = 36
\end{array}
$$

If $2a = 36$, then $a = 18$. Use this value to find the value of b:

$18 - 3b = 9$

$3b = 18 - 9$

$3b = 9$

$b = 3$

23.   **B**   Make sure you FOIL the equation properly: $(2x + 4)^2 = 4x^2 + 8x + 8x + 16 = 4x^2 + 16x + 16$. In this case, $a = 4$, $b = 16$, and $c = 16$, so $a + b - c = 4 + 16 - 16 = 4$. If you selected (C), you may have forgotten to FOIL. If you selected (E), you may done $a + b + c$ rather than $a + b - c$.

24.   **H**   Split the figure into two rectangles and find the area of each. See the figure below:

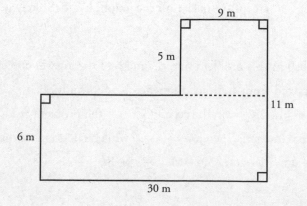

The smaller rectangle has sides of length 9 and 5, so its area by the formula $A = lw$ is 45. The larger rectangle has sides 30 and 6, so by the same formula, its area is 180. Add the two areas together to get $180 + 45 = 225$. If you selected (J), be careful—this is the perimeter.

25. **E** Look carefully at the values for each function. If a function can be graphed as $ax + b$, it is a linear function, and it will increase at constant increments. Function g decreases then increases in value. In fact, note the symmetry—this is a parabolic function and can be graphed according to $ax^2 + bx + c$. Note that all the values in h increase by 3, so this is the function you want to work with. Since $h(-1) = 6$, $h(0)$ must equal 9.

26. **H** Put the equation into the slope-intercept form, $y = mx + b$. The m in this equation is the slope of the line. From the equation given, $10y - 16x = 13$, isolate the y term to get $10y = 16x + 13$, and divide through by 10 to get $y = \frac{16}{10}x + \frac{13}{10}$. Reduce to $y = \frac{8}{5}x + \frac{13}{10}$. The m term in this equation is $\frac{8}{5}$.

27. **C** First, simplify the expression: $x^2 + 5x - 24 = (x + 8)(x - 3)$. Now that you have the two expressions, find the solutions by setting each quantity equal to 0. If $x + 8 = 0$, then $x = -8$. If $x - 3 = 0$, then $x = 3$. Now find the sum of the solutions: $-8 + 3 = -5$. If you selected (E), you may have simplified correctly but found the roots incorrectly. If you selected (A), you found the product, not the sum.

28. **G** The perimeter of the larger triangle is 12 in. + 7 in. + 5 in. = 24 in. Since you know the ratio of the perimeters, you do not have to find each side of the smaller triangle; you can set up the following ratio:

$$\frac{5}{6} = \frac{x}{24}$$

$$\frac{5(24)}{6} = x$$

$$x = 20 \text{ in}$$

29. **B** To find the median of a list of numbers, those numbers must be listed in order. Make sure you rearrange the numbers given before you find the median. If you didn't rearrange the numbers, you may have picked (E). When you rearrange the numbers in this list, they are in this order: $-9°C$, $-8°C$, $-7°C$, $-7°C$, $0°C$, $1°C$, $2°C$, $3°C$, $5°C$. $0°C$ is the median. If you selected (A), be careful—this is the mode.

30. **G** You can set up an equation to find the price of the calculator. If we call the price of the calculator x, then the equation will look like this: $\sqrt{x} + \left(\frac{3}{8}\right)x = 66$. A simpler tactic is to try out the answer choices to see which works in this equation. You will find this to be 144: $\sqrt{144} + \left(\frac{3}{8}\right)144 = 66$.

31. **C** You need to solve for m in the equation given. The equation as written is $KE = \frac{1}{2}mv^2$. Once you've solved for m, the equation should look like this: $m = \frac{2KE}{v^2}$. Once you have this equation, substitute the values from the problem: $m = \frac{2KE}{v^2} - \frac{2(120)}{9^2} = \frac{240}{81} \approx 2.97$, between 2 and 3. If you selected (B), you may have forgotten to apply the $\frac{1}{2}$.

32. **G** A geometric sequence is a pattern of multiplication in which each term is multiplied by a common ratio to determine the next term in the sequence. The first term $2xz$ is multiplied by xy to become the second term $2x^2yz$. This second term is multiplied again by xy to become $2x^3y^2z$. Multiply this term by xy to find the answer: $2x^4y^3z$. Note: Process of Elimination may be more effective here. Throughout the sequence given, neither 2 nor the z has changed, so you can eliminate (H), (J), and (K). The exponents have increased, not decreased, so you can eliminate (F).

33. **E** Use the histogram. Four critics gave the book a one-star review. There are thirty total critics, so the relationship you need is $\frac{4}{30} = \frac{2}{15}$.

34. **J** There are 360° in a circle, and, as the histogram shows, one-star reviews make up $\frac{2}{15}$ of all the reviews. As a result, the one-star reviews will make up $\frac{2}{15}$ of the whole circle: $\frac{2}{15} \times 360° = 48°$.

35. **D** Make sure you count every review. There are thirty of them, and the sum of the thirty reviews is 79. To find the average, divide $\frac{79}{30}$ to get 2.63, rounded to the nearest hundredth.

36. **K** Simplify the expression by factoring.

$$\frac{(x^2+7x+12)(x-2)}{(x^2+2x-8)(x+3)} = \frac{(x+3)(x+4)(x-2)}{(x+4)(x-2)(x+3)} = \frac{(x+4)(x-2)(x+3)}{(x+4)(x-2)(x+3)} = 1$$

37. **D** The logo in the T-shirt is a right triangle. You are given the 35° angle, so you need to determine which side you have and which side you need to find relative to this angle. On the figure, you have the 10-inch side, which is *opposite* this angle. You're looking for the top diagonal side of the triangle, which in this case is the *hypotenuse* of the triangle. Sine is the function that requires *opposite* and *hypotenuse* by the following formula: $\sin\theta = \frac{opp}{hyp}$. By this equation, $hyp = \frac{opp}{\sin\theta}$ and the top side = $\frac{10}{\sin 35°}$.

38. **H** The center of the circle will be the midpoint of the diameter. Use the midpoint formula to find the midpoint of the points (4,3) and (−9,−2): $\left(\frac{x_1 + x_2}{2}, \frac{y_1 + y_2}{2}\right)$. Insert the points to find $\left(\frac{4+(-9)}{2}, \frac{3+(-2)}{2}\right)$. If you selected (J), be careful—you may have forgotten to divide by 2, and if you selected (G), you mixed up the x- and y-coordinates.

39. **C** Use the distance formula to find the distance between the two points (–7,4) and (–2,6): $d = \sqrt{(x_2 - x_1)^2 + (y_2 - y_1)^2} = \sqrt{(-7 - (-2))^2 + (4 - 6)^2} = \sqrt{(-5)^2 + (-2)^2} = \sqrt{29}$.

This value is approximately 5.385, but if you selected choice (A), you didn't complete the problem. Every unit on the map is equal to 5 nautical miles, and the problem is asking for the value in nautical miles. Multiply 5.385 by 5 nautical miles to find 26.92 nautical miles, which is closest to (C).

40. **K** On a "must be" question, the relationships must be true in all cases. If there is one case in which a relationship is not true, that answer choice is incorrect. Because this is an EXCEPT question, the incorrect relationship will be the correct answer. Choice (K) is often true, but not always. If you multiply $\sqrt{2}$, an irrational number, by itself, you get a rational number: 4.

41. **B** Because i is defined as the square root of negative one ($\sqrt{-1}$), its range of possibility when raised to certain powers is limited. $i = \sqrt{-1}$, $i^2 = -1$, $i^3 = -\sqrt{-1}$, $i^4 = 1$. If you continue the pattern, you will find that these are the only possible values for i raised to any power (including negative powers). Choice (B) is the only answer choice that lists one of these values.

42. **K** Note the symmetry in the chart. The equation given shows that this graph is a parabola, but even if you haven't made that deduction, the values in the chart show a general trend in the data. When x is –3 and –5, $y = 0$; when x is –1 and –7, $y = 8$. According to this data, you can infer that values less than –7 and greater than –1 will be greater than 8. Therefore, –8 will have a greater value than the others listed in the answer choices. If you have trouble reading the chart, you can always try out the values in the equation and see which gives you the greatest $f(x)$.

43. **B** The formula for the volume of a right circular cylinder is $V = \pi r^2 h$. This question asks for the radius and gives V and h, so solve the equation for r: $r = \sqrt{\dfrac{V}{\pi h}}$. Substitute the values that you know to find r: $r = \sqrt{\dfrac{64\pi}{\pi(4)}} = \sqrt{16} = 4$. If you selected (E), you may have forgotten to take the square root of the radius. If you selected (C), you may have forgotten to include the height in your calculation.

44. **J** First, consider the relationships that you know. The ratio of the perimeter of $\triangle FJK$ to $\triangle FLM$ is 3:5, and the ratio of $\overline{FH}$ to $\overline{FM}$ is 1:5. Because all triangles share $\angle F$ and the lines are parallel, the three triangles are similar, which means all their sides—and therefore the perimeters—are proportional. From the proportions given, you can determine that the ratio of $\triangle FGH$ to $\triangle FJK$ to $\triangle FLM$ is 1:3:5; therefore, the ratio of $\overline{FG}$ to $\overline{FJ}$ to $\overline{FL}$ is also 1:3:5. Based on this ratio, you can substitute values for each of the segments to figure out the ratio of $\overline{GJ}$ to $\overline{FG}$. You can say that $\overline{FG} = 1$, $\overline{FJ} = 3$, and $\overline{FL} = 5$. This enables you to calculate $\overline{GJ} = \overline{FJ} - \overline{FG} = 3 - 1 = 2$. The ratio of $\overline{GJ}$ to $\overline{FG}$ is therefore 2:1. If you selected (H), make sure you read the question carefully—you may have switched the segments.

45.   **E**   You need to find the distance along the *y*-axis that Avi traveled in total. Isolate each part of Avi's ride. Note that each of these legs can be made into the hypotenuse of a right triangle. The first part of the ride creates a special 30-60-90 triangle, and the second part of the trip creates a special 45-45-90 triangle. See the figures below:

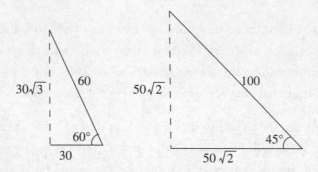

Therefore, the vertical height of the first part of the ride is $30\sqrt{3}$, and the vertical height of the second part of the ride is $50\sqrt{2}$. Don't forget to add the 35 m he rode along Broad St. at the end, to get a full vertical distance of $35 + 50\sqrt{2} + 30\sqrt{3}$. Choice (C) is the amount of the actual ride—read carefully; you just want the distance he traveled along the *y*-axis.

46.   **H**   The formula for a circle to which this problem is referring is $(x - h)^2 + (y - k)^2 = r^2$. In other words, the 25 in the equation $(x - 3)^2 + (y + 2)^2 = 25$ is the r^2. If $r^2 = 25$, then $r = 5$. With the radius, you can find the area of the circle with the basic formula $A = \pi r^2$. In this problem, since $r = 5$, the area will be $A = \pi(5)^2 = 25\pi$.

47.   **C**   Nearly everything you need is written on the figure. The only real piece of information you need from the text of the problem is that the *y*-axis bisects the base of the triangle. This tells you that the base of this triangle is $2b$. The height, according to the figure, is $2b^2 - 4$. With the base and height, you have all you need to find the area of the triangle with the standard formula $A = \frac{1}{2}bh$. Substitute the expressions to find $A = \frac{1}{2}(2b)(2b^2 - 4) = (b)(2b^2 - 4) = 2b^3 - 4b$. If you selected (B), you may have forgotten to divide by two.

48.   **J**   Because of the words "must be," the expression given must produce an even number in every instance. If you can find one instance in which an expression produces an odd number, you can eliminate that expression and answer choice. Since *x* can be any integer, there are many combinations you can try. In (F), *x* could be 4, in which case $x + 5 = 4 + 5 = 9$, which is not even. In (G), *x* could be 1, which would make $\frac{x}{4} = \frac{1}{4}$, which is not even (nor is it an integer). If $x = 1$, (H) gives

$x^4 = 1$, which is not even; in (K), 5 raised to any integer power will always be odd. Only (J) generates an even number with every integer. This is because the product of an even number multiplied by either an even or an odd number will always be even.

49. **C** First, bring the exponent to the front of the expression: $\log_9(9^{\frac{7}{3}}) = \frac{7}{3}\log_9 9$. Once you're done, you can simplify the log portion of the expression. By the rules of logarithms, $\log_9 9$ can be rewritten as either $9^x = 9$ or $\frac{\log_9}{\log_9}$. As both expressions show, $\log_9 9 = 1$, which means you're left with $\frac{7}{3}$, between 2 and 3.

50. **G** In order to find the percent change, use the formula: % change $= \frac{\textit{difference}}{\textit{original}} \times 100\%$. In this case, Cameron's sales decreased from 23 to 19. In other words, he started at 23 (the original number), and he decreased to 19 (a difference of 4). Therefore, % change $= \frac{4}{23} \times 100 \approx 17.4\%$. If you selected (K), you may have calculated the increase from 19 to 23 rather than the decrease from 23 to 19.

51. **E** Maura wanted an average of 30 new accounts over the course of 4 months. This means that over the course of these four months, she had to create a total of 120 new accounts. Write this in an equation: Total = Jan. + Feb. + Mar. + Apr. Substitute what you know. 120 = 31 + 25 + Mar. + 27. The total accounts needed in March will therefore be 120 − 31 − 25 − 27 = 37.

52. **G** Don had 64 sales in January, and this value decreased by 5% each month. Do the calculations as follows, and don't round until you're done. February accounts = (64) − (0.05)(64) = 60.8. March accounts = (60.8) − (0.05)(60.8) = 57.76. April accounts = (57.76) − (0.05)(57.76) = 54.872. May accounts = (54.872) − (54.872)(0.05) = 52.1284 ≈ 52 accounts.

53. **C** You can disregard the long equation of the function given in the problem. All you need to answer this question is the graph. As the problem says, the amplitude of this function is the "average of the absolute values" of the minimum and maximum values of $f(x)$. Pull this information from the graph. The graph goes up to $y = 3$ and down to $y = -3$. Take the average of the absolute values of these: $\frac{|3| + |-3|}{2} = 3$. If you selected (E), be careful—this is the period.

54. **F** Start with the tangent relationship. The problem says that the tangent of the angle of vision is $\frac{7}{6}$. From SOHCAHTOA, you know that the tangent relationship is defined as $\tan\theta = \frac{opp}{adj}$, or, in terms of this problem, the tangent of the angle of vision is $\frac{\text{horizontal distance}}{\text{height of the building}}$. Set up a propor-

tion: $\dfrac{7}{6} = \dfrac{\text{horizontal distance}}{\text{height of the building}}$. Fill in what you know: $\dfrac{7}{6} = \dfrac{\text{horizontal distance}}{30}$. Cross-multiply to

find that the horizontal distance from home plate to the building is 35 m. If you selected (H), you

may have found the opposite relationship.

55. **D** If you selected (E), be careful—3 is a solution to this equation, but it is rational. This question asks for a solution that is NOT rational. To find the solutions, solve the equation for y. First, isolate the absolute value expression $|y^2 - 11| = 2$. Remember as you're solving this equation that you will have to create two different equations as you're removing the absolute value sign: $y^2 - 11 = 2$ and $y^2 - 11 = -2$. Solve each of these equations to find that $y^2 = 13$ and $y^2 = 9$, so $y = \pm 3$ and $y = \pm\sqrt{13}$. The irrational solutions are $\pm\sqrt{13}$.

56. **G** A positive slope indicates a speed increase; a 0 slope indicates a constant speed; a negative slope indicates a speed decrease. The speed increases for 4 seconds, remains constant for 3 seconds, then decreases to 0 over 2 seconds. This is best described by (G). Note, if you're not sure how to read the graph, recall that the problem says the entire test takes 9 seconds. Therefore, whether speeds are increasing or decreasing, the times during which they do so will have to add to 9 seconds.

57. **B** Because the compass is a circle, it has a degree measure of 360°. "East" starts at 90° from "North," so the point of the needle will need to travel 270° to get back to "North" in a clockwise direction. In other words, the point of the needle will have to travel across $\dfrac{3}{4}$ of the circle as it goes from "East" to "North" in a clockwise direction. The problem states that the point of the needle travels 42 mm, so if you apply the ratio to this problem, you can say that 42 mm is $\dfrac{3}{4}$ of the circumference of the circle. Use this to find the full circumference: $42 = \dfrac{3}{4}C$ and $C = 56$ mm. Use this value to find the length of the needle, which is just the radius of this circle: $C = 2\pi r$. Solve the equation for r to find its value: $r = \dfrac{C}{2\pi} = \dfrac{56\,\text{mm}}{2\pi} \approx 8.9$.

58. **F** From 270° to 360°, the cosine function has a range of values from 0 to 1. In other words, it is always positive. Sine, by contrast, has a range of values from −1 to 0—it's always negative. Because the problem is asking for a tangent value from 270° to 360°, you know it must be negative because $\tan\theta = \dfrac{\sin\theta}{\cos\theta}$. Therefore, you can eliminate (H), (J), and (K). Then, because $\cos\theta = \dfrac{12}{13}$, the adjacent side, opposite side, and hypotenuse relative to the angle θ form the Pythagorean triple 5:12:13, respectively. $\tan\theta = \dfrac{opp}{adj}$, and within the range from 270° to 360°, tangent is negative, so $\tan\theta = -\dfrac{5}{12}$.

59. **C** Since you need a and b such that $ab = 8$, your four possible pairs are $a = 1$, $b = 8$; $a = 2$, $b = 4$; $a = 4$, $b = 2$; $a = 8$, $b = 1$. Keep your work organized as you figure:

a	b	2^a	c	c^b
1	8	2	2	256
2	4	4	4	256
4	2	16	16	256
8	1	256	256	256

As this small chart demonstrates, there are four values of c that work in both expressions. If you selected (D), you may have forgotten that both $a = 1$, $b = 8$ and $a = 8$, $b = 1$ are distinct and valid pairs.

60. **J** The formula for the length of the diagonal of a rectangular prism is $a^2 + b^2 + c^2 = d^2$ where a, b, and c represent the edges of the rectangular prism, and d represents its diagonal. In the case of a cube, $a = b = c$, so the equation can be rewritten as follows: $3a^2 = d^2$. In this problem, $d = 3\sqrt{3}$, so $3a^2 = (3\sqrt{3})^2$. Therefore, $3a^2 = (9)(3)$ and $a = 3$. Therefore, the length of the edge of this cube is 3. Look at the figure—you can see from the figure that the length of the diameter of the sphere is equivalent to the length from one side of the figure to another, an edge. The diameter of the sphere is equivalent to an edge of the cube, so the diameter is 3, (J).

READING TEST

1. **C** Choice (C) is correct because the third paragraph states that "God Bless the Child" was *familiar mostly to adults*. Because of this, it is more likely that the song would be familiar to Monique's parents, who must be adults, than it would be to her friends, who are presumably high school students and not yet adults. Choice (A) is incorrect because the passage never identifies "God Bless the Child" as a Rodgers & Hammerstein number. Choice (B) is incorrect because the passage does not support the extreme claim that "God Bless the Child" is the *most* sophisticated Billie Holiday song. Choice (D) is incorrect because Monique's song choice is presented as a contrast to the overly enthusiastic choices of her peers.

2. **J** Choice (J) is correct because the passage initially describes Monique and her friends as aloof (they isolate themselves in the auditorium and Monique acts like a monarch with a royal court) and disparaging (they belittle the other students during their auditions). Choice (F) is incorrect because, although the passage describes that most students are nervous about going first, this does not describe how Monique and her friends are presented. Choice (G) is incorrect because, although Monique and her friends react to Esperanza's song choice with *disbelief*, that is not how they are initially portrayed in the passage. Choice (H) is incorrect because Monique and her friends are portrayed as being unfriendly and excluding.

3. **A** Choice (A) is correct because the passage states that Esperanza did not look up until she got to center stage and then *looked only at Mrs. Dominguez*. Choice (B) is incorrect because the passage says she shuffled her feet on her walk to the stage, which is not a confident stride. Choice (C) is incorrect because the passage states she was *paying little attention to the other auditions*. Choice (D) is incorrect because the passage only states that she was *working* on her geometry homework, not that she finished it.

4. **J** The question is asking for the rhetorical effect of the statement *But not this year*. The previous paragraph establishes that students generally dread the first audition slot and relates the tense manner in which Monique used to view the first slot. The paragraph that follows this phrase explains that Monique had decided to embrace the first slot as a means of surprising her peers. Choice (J) is correct because it identifies the statement in question as a contrast between the status quo and Monique's surprising decision. Choice (F) is incorrect because the passage provides no evidence that most students have resolved their fears of going first, only that Monique has. Choice (G) is incorrect because the passage never establishes the extreme claim that this year's audition was the *strangest yet*. Choice (H) is incorrect because the passage does not go on to describe any different imagery Monique associates with the uncomfortable first slot but rather to say she is no longer uncomfortable with it at all.

5. **B** The passage describes in the sixth paragraph that Monique and her friends are *sitting at the back of the auditorium*. In the ninth paragraph, the passage states that *Esperanza had been sitting alone in the first row*. Together, these facts justify (B). Choice (A) is incorrect because it makes the extreme claim that Esperanza is the *most* teased student, for which there is no evidence in the passage. Choice (C) is incorrect because the passage does not say that Monique and Esperanza auditioned consecutively, and the seventh paragraph implies that there was *an endless parade* of students who auditioned in between them. Choice (D) is incorrect because, although Mrs. Dominguez was sensitive to possible ridicule meeting Esperanza's audition, there is no evidence of a conversation taking place beforehand.

6. **G** Choice (G) is correct because the passage states that Monique figured going first would *instill fear into her competition because they would realize that Monique had something they clearly lacked*. Choice (F) is incorrect because, although going first is evidence of Monique's self-confidence, the passage does not say Monique chose to go first to increase her self-confidence. Choices (H) and (J) are incorrect because Monique's stated motivation for going first is to intimidate her rivals, not to increase her chances of getting a part or to gain any favor with Mrs. Dominguez.

7. **D** The passage states that at the *climactic* moment of "rockets' red glare," *Esperanza's voice filled the room with a calm resonance*. This makes (D) correct. Choice (A) is incorrect because it is not supported in the passage. Choice (B) is incorrect because while the passage states that her version of the song caused the people in the room to feel *some reluctant patriotism*, it does not suggest that Esperanza was patriotic herself. Choice (C) is incorrect because the passage contradicts it by saying that Esperanza was *calm*.

8. **F**   When Mrs. Dominguez tells Esperanza she can begin to audition, the passage states that Mrs. Dominguez was *sensing the potential for the audition to devolve into a painful target of ridicule*. This makes (F) correct. Choice (G) is incorrect because this is how Esperanza is described in relation to Thornton High. Choice (H) is incorrect because this is what is anticipated by Monique and her friends. Choice (J) is incorrect because this relates to how Mrs. Dominguez viewed Monique's decision to audition first.

9. **C**   Choice (C) is correct because the passage states that once Esperanza was moving *methodically through the tune, the expectant smiles of mockery were quickly vanishing from the faces of all who listened*. Choice (A) is incorrect because the decision of where to sit was based on wanting to make comments about all the auditions and came before Esperanza's audition. Choice (B) is incorrect because their preconceived notions are described prior to Esparanza's audition, not as a reaction to the audition. Choice (D) is incorrect because the passage states that Monique and her friends were critical of Esperanza's song choice and even the resulting patriotism they felt is described as *reluctant*.

10. **G**   Esperanza sings "The Star Spangled Banner" for her audition. The twelfth paragraph explains that *the final phrase of the song* is *often soaked in vibrato*. This makes (G) correct. Choice (F) is incorrect because the passage states that Monique and her friends anticipated a "mousy" voice from Esperanza but says nothing about "The Star Spangled Banner" being well suited to that type of voice. Choice (H) is incorrect because, although Esperanza's performance is ultimately impressive, the passage says that the song is *trite* and *formulaic*. Choice (J) is incorrect because when Esperanza begins singing her song, *Monique and her friends looked at each other in total disbelief*.

11. **C**   The third paragraph asks the reader to consider a contrast between an original user of a remote and a modern user. Choices (A), (B), and (D) are details provided to describe the original user. Choice (C) is a detail provided to describe the modern user. Hence, (C) is correct.

12. **G**   Choice (G) is correct because the author lists several important inventions of the twentieth century but does not identify any of them as the *most significant*. Choice (F) is incorrect because the author states that most people think the solution is new clean energy technology. Choice (H) is incorrect because the author attributes the root of tool-making to the mindset of *There's got to be a better way*. Choice (J) is incorrect because the author describes how consumers go from *awed gratitude to discriminating preference*.

13. **A**   The point that an example is used to illustrate is often found right before the example. In this case, the end of the first paragraph states that *the longer a given technology exists, the more we take it for granted*. The comparison between different users of remote controls is designed to illustrate this idea. Choice (A) best summarizes this concept and so is correct. Choice (B) is incorrect because the author never stresses a need to read instructions. Choice (C) is incorrect because modern users are described as using remote controls with ease and comfort. Choice (D) is incorrect because, while likely true, there is no support in the passage for the idea that remote controls have become *far more effective* than they were.

14. **G** The passage focuses on the technology around us that often goes unappreciated, ultimately warning us that our unrealistic faith in technology may lead us into global climate trouble. Words and phrases like *spoiled*, *unduly optimistic*, and *unfairly demanding* indicate the author's attitude that most modern humans are somewhat in the wrong. Choice (G) is the safest match for this tone, which makes it the correct answer. Choice (F) is incorrect, because although the passage does look backward in time at certain spots, it is primarily focused on how the present is rather than a wish to return to the past. Choice (H) is incorrect because the author seems to be calling attention to the *dangerous extension of our mindset*, rather than sympathizing with it. Choice (J) is incorrect because the majority of the passage does not indicate the author's fear. The various references to shock and awe for new technology indicate amazement but not fright. The possible doomsday scenario toward the end of the passage does sound scary, but it functions only to demonstrate that modern humans have some problematic attitudes toward technology.

15. **C** The context for this sentence explains that, because we are spoiled by technology, we typically believe it can fix any problem. The notion that we might need to fix ourselves is unthinkable. Choice (C) is the correct answer because it best expresses that the suggestion that we need to change our own habits would be *unlike* our normal assumptions about technology. Choice (A) is incorrect because *extraterrestrial* literally means "not from Earth," and the context does not suggest the idea is *that* exotic. Choice (B) is incorrect because the passage indicates this idea is seldom heard within our culture, so the notion that it is a repetitive idea is not supported. Choice (D) is incorrect because, although we do not take the idea in question seriously, it is because we are not accustomed to hearing the idea, not because the idea itself is funny.

16. **G** The point of this paragraph is that children born into a society that already possesses impressive technology do not tend to appreciate how impressive it is that this technology is human-made. They accept it as a given, much as one accepts the elements of the periodic table as the given substances found in the universe. Choice (G) is correct because it best expresses this idea. Choice (F) is incorrect because the passage does not suggest that children are literally learning about technology side-by-side as they learn about the periodic table. Choice (H) is incorrect because the reference to the *universe* does not provide any support for such an extreme claim as *most technology* comes from space exploration. Choice (J) is incorrect because it confuses the point of this paragraph, which is that children tend *not* to be impressed by the technology around them.

17. **D** The penultimate paragraph discusses how people in our culture assume that technology will solve our problems and do not want to hear about needing to change or reassess our lifestyles. Because leaders are too afraid to tell the public otherwise, the final paragraph says that we will continue as we have been. Hence, (D) is correct. Choice (A) is incorrect because it misses the correct meaning of the phrase, and *scope* and *complexity* were discussed in relation to assessing the global climate problem, not technology. Choice (B) is incorrect because this describes specifically what the passage explains we will *not* be doing. Making sacrifices would mean *changing* the status quo. Choice (C) is incorrect because the passage is saying that if we ever find ourselves

in a disastrous situation as a result of maintaining our current lifestyles and habits, *then* we would blame technology. This would be a result of following the status quo but not the idea to which the phrase itself refers.

18. **H** *Discriminating preference* is used at the end of the seventh paragraph to foreshadow the ever-evolving demands of consumers for new technology. The eighth paragraph lists some of them. The passage states that *computers needed to become more powerful.* This makes (H) correct. Choice (F) is incorrect because the fifth paragraph contradicts that idea. Choice (G) is incorrect because the passage repeatedly suggests that most users of technology are happily oblivious to *how* it works. Choice (J) is incorrect because the second-to-last paragraph portrays this idea as something the public does not want to hear.

19. **D** The first half of the passage discusses the modern mindset toward technology. Then it says that the *most dangerous extension of this mindset* is how it relates to our ability to solve global climate problems. The second half of the passage explains why our attitude toward technology may worsen the situation. Choice (D) is correct because it precisely identifies the reason the author finds our overconfidence in technology to be potentially dangerous. Choice (A) is incorrect because this phrase refers to the flaws we consumers find with existing technology that we hope will be fixed. This is not directly relevant to the global warming problem with which the author associates the most danger. Choices (B) and (C) are incorrect because they refer to things that indirectly relate to the author's central concern. However, the author does not consider *devising new forms of energy* or *the complexity of global weather* to be dangerous in and of themselves.

20. **F** The passage ends with a severe prediction that humanity may ruin its habitat, all the while blaming technology for failing to rescue it. This makes (F) correct. Choice (G) is incorrect because the last paragraph does not contain any refutation of a theory. Choice (H) is incorrect because the last paragraph does not include an expert opinion. Choice (J) is incorrect because both paragraphs use "we."

21. **A** Choice (A) is correct because, although the author discusses having great difficulty and confusion in learning jazz chords, he does not ever identify one that is *most* confusing. Choices (B), (C), and (D) are incorrect because none of the chords are ever identified as the *most* confusing chords.

22. **F** In the context of the passage as a whole, the author discusses Victor as a source of knowledge about jazz. The author states he did not get *straightforward explanations* from Victor but that he *did learn* some things. Choice (F) is correct because, given the context of the passage, it refers to the most likely subject matter the author would be trying to get from Victor. Choice (G) is incorrect because the idea that knowledge about jazz would be *forbidden* is too strong. There is no evidence that the author was being purposefully excluded from learning about jazz. Choice (H) is incorrect because there is no context to support the idea that the author was asking about literal magic tricks. Choice (J) is incorrect because there is no context to support the idea that the author was trying to learn more about Victor as a person, nor does the passage ever describe Victor as *private.*

23. **D** Upon seeing the author's *invented* chord, Victor *calmly* informs the author of the chord's proper name. Choice (D) is correct because *nonchalance* indicates a relaxed, unimpressed manner, which is how Victor responds. Choice (A) is incorrect because Victor would not be amazed by a chord for which he already knows the technical name. Choice (B) is incorrect because Victor would not be jealous that the author could play a chord that was already familiar to Victor. Choice (C) is incorrect because Victor does not show confusion; he shows immediate recognition of what chord the author is playing.

24. **G** In the eighth paragraph, the author states that *for the next few months, I quietly plucked away* at the music found in "The Real Book." Hence, (G) is correct, and (F), (H), and (J) are incorrect.

25. **A** The passage describes the more complex chord types of jazz and describes the effects of using them as introducing *subtle hints of chaos and imbalance, adding a worldly imperfection*, and becoming more enjoyable as one's age starts making things like candy taste too sweet and "imperfections" like bitterness make *for a more appealing flavor*. Choice (A) provides the best summary for these ideas. Choice (B) is incorrect because the description of jazz's complexity is not intended to be a critical comment about fundamental flaws in rock and classical music. Just because jazz's unique chords add *detail and depth to the music*, that doesn't mean the author thinks that other styles of music necessarily lack detail and depth. Choice (C) is incorrect because the passage does not specify anything about the confusion and awkwardness of *standard jazz chord values*; it describes what elements jazz chords add to *standard chord values*. Choice (D) is incorrect because the context explains that candy starts tasting unpleasantly *sweet* the older one gets.

26. **J** The end of the passage describes the author beginning to develop an ability to play jazz, but his newfound ability is still mentally surprising. Choice (J) summarizes this context best and is therefore correct. Choice (F) is incorrect because the passage does not support the idea that the author was *overworked*. Choice (G) is incorrect because, although the author is surprised by what his hands can do musically, there is no context to support that the author is actually losing the ability to *control* his hands. Choice (H) is incorrect because there is no information to support the idea that the author *pointing* at chords was part of his learning process.

27. **D** Choice (D) is correct because the eighth paragraph describes the author's initial attempts to work through the *strange, new combinations* he found in "The Real Book." He mentions F-sharp minor-7 flat-5 while speaking of chords that he *had to decode and then understand*. Choice (A) is incorrect because the context of this paragraph suggests that the author did indeed have some trouble with these unfamiliar chords. Choice (B) is incorrect because the remark about not knowing the language of a foreign country has no literal relation to this specific chord or the author's previous travels (about which we know nothing). Choice (C) is incorrect because the passage provides no evidence that the author knew how to play this chord on guitar.

28. **H** The fifth paragraph identifies Victor as a member of the author's rock band as well as a member of a jazz ensemble. This makes (H) correct. Choice (F) is incorrect because the passage states that at age 30, it had been *over a decade* since the author and Victor had gone their separate ways. Choice (G) is incorrect because the passage states that the author bought his own copy of "The Real Book." Choice (J) is incorrect because the passage does not say that Victor invented this chord, rather that he told the author the name of the chord the author presumed to have invented.

29. **C** The passage begins with the author's love for jazz. It transitions into his own experiences learning how to play jazz and culminates with his early successes in doing so. Choice (C) is correct because it encompasses the various points of focus throughout the passage. Choice (A) is incorrect because the passage only occasionally refers to a chain of events and never establishes that the author has a jazz career. Choice (B) is incorrect because the author does not try to show that jazz is uncomplicated; he describes the hard work he put into learning its complexity. Choice (D) is incorrect because the central focus of the passage is the author's learning of jazz. Although the author's friendship with Victor relates to jazz, it is not the central focus of the author's discussion.

30. **G** In the last few paragraphs, the author describes the process by which he struggled to learn jazz. He begins by seeing jazz as *a cryptic message to decode* but later describes himself as *becoming comfortable* and possessing a *new melodic understanding*. These details make (G) correct. Choice (F) is incorrect because the author never says that the book becomes *annoyingly familiar* by the end. Choice (H) is incorrect because the author identifies a difference between jazz sheet music and classical sheet music, but this detail does not enter his discussion of his experiences with "The Real Book." Choice (J) is incorrect because the author has not suggested that he has moved on to other learning tools or more profound study.

31. **A** The third and fourth paragraphs discuss Calwell's work. Paragraph 4 explains that *by monitoring the cholera food chain in reverse*, Calwell is able to make predictions. This makes (A) correct. Choice (B) is incorrect because, while climatic models were used to predict an outbreak in Bangladesh, these models were derived from Oceanic data, not land-based measurements. Choice (C) is incorrect because, in addition to being too narrow a description of Calwell's method, the decline of zooplankton and falling sea temperatures would each suggest a reduced risk of a potential cholera outbreak. Choice (D) is incorrect because, while the passage states that cholera is found in areas that contain copepod, the passage never suggests that this marine life is diseased.

32. **H** The first few paragraphs explain the food chain that allows the cholera bacterium to grow. The bacterium grows around copepods, which feed on zooplankton, which feed on phytoplankton, which feed on sunlight. Hence, sunlight influences cholera by influencing the food chain on which the cholera bacterium depends. This makes (H) correct. Choice (F) is incorrect because the passage never says that phytoplankton *contaminate* the water. Choice (G) is incorrect because the passage does not state that *V. cholerae* uses photosynthesis at all. Choice (J) is incorrect because there is no support for this broad generalization about sunlight causing many epidemics. The first sentence of the passage is a rhetorical question, and the way in which the passage describes sunlight facilitating outbreaks has nothing to do with *direct, prolonged exposure*.

33. **C**   The eighth paragraph explains that researchers at Oxford *calibrated regional levels of photosynthesis to the size of a vein in the wings of the flies*. The vein size measures *how numerous and robust the tsetse fly population is*. Therefore, the satellite data that measures photosynthesis is used to tell researchers how big the veins of tsetse flies are and hence how strong and prevalent their population is. This makes (C) correct. Choice (A) is incorrect because the passage does not say that the satellite data can be used to determine the total number of *parasites* in West Africa. Choice (B) is incorrect because measuring photosynthesis is done to gauge the size of tsetse fly populations in West Africa, not to find the global area with the *most* photosynthesis. Choice (D) is incorrect because the point of the data is not to find the flies with the biggest veins but to estimate the size of veins in tsetse flies.

34. **J**   The passage as a whole is presenting ways in which satellite data is being used to predict disease outbreaks, and both Calwell and Linthicum are offered as examples of those efforts. Hence, (J) is correct. Choice (F) is incorrect because Linthicum is studying Rift Valley fever, not cholera. Choice (G) is incorrect because Linthicum works at NASA in Greenbelt, Maryland. Choice (H) is incorrect because this does not indicate a similarity between Linthicum and Calwell since the passage never indicates that Calwell may have saved thousands of lives.

35. **A**   The ninth paragraph states that satellite data is more efficient than the traditional method of doing research for the reasons discussed in (A). Thus, (A) is correct. Choice (B) is incorrect because the passage does not indicate that scientists can *control* photosynthetic levels, just that they can measure them. Choice (C) is incorrect because the passage does not discuss the types of *mathematical errors* that human forecasters make. Choice (D) is incorrect because the tenth paragraph contradicts this idea by indicating there is not a lot of reliable disease data available.

36. **H**   The context of this word discusses conditions that would encourage or help mosquito populations to grow. *Promote* means to encourage or help, so (H) is correct. Choices (F) and (G) are incorrect because the weather is not performing an *errand* or a *task* for the mosquitoes. Similarly, (J) is incorrect because weather conditions would not *request* the growth of mosquito populations. The three incorrect answer choices relate more to the sense of *doing someone a favor* than to how the word is used in this context.

37. **D**   The sixth paragraph explains the weather conditions that facilitate the growth and spread of mosquito populations, which include increased rain, more clouds, and warmer air. The environmental changes Linthicum is studying are those that would precede a growth in mosquito populations. Hence, (D) is correct. Choice (A) is incorrect because the beginning of the rainy season in Kenya is not identified as the precursor to mosquito population growth. Choice (B) is incorrect because the passage never mentions bacteria in the jet stream. Choice (C) is incorrect because the environmental changes Linthicum is monitoring are those that precede mosquito population growth, not the population growth itself.

38. **J** While it is true that satellite data has *measured* increases in ocean temperature, the passage never suggests or states that satellite data has actually *helped to* raise the ocean temperature. For this reason, (J) is correct. Choice (F) is incorrect because it is mentioned in the Calwell research. Choice (G) is incorrect because it is mentioned as part of the Oxford study. Choice (H) is incorrect because it is mentioned several times throughout the passage and represents the main point of the passage.

39. **A** The context for this phrase is that fluctuations in certain variables would make climate-based models inaccurate predictors. The variables are labeled as *non-climatic factors* in the following sentence. This makes (A) the correct answer. Choice (B) is incorrect because there is no discussion of the effects of drug resistance. Choice (C) is incorrect because it does not address the source of confusion, which is a failure to incorporate certain variables into the model. Choice (D) is incorrect because it implies—without any textual evidence—that researchers are unfamiliar with non-climate data although the passage suggests only that they are not currently using it in their models.

40. **G** With the examples of Calwell, Linthicum, and Rogers, the author presents researchers who are using satellite-based data to predict disease outbreaks. The passage ends by assessing the value of these efforts. This makes (G) the correct answer. Choice (F) is incorrect because the passage does not itemize which satellite data *must* be collected, nor is the type of data the primary focus. Choice (H) is incorrect because the author does not stress that a small number of scientists do research by traditional methods. Choice (J) is incorrect because it is too narrow a purpose for an author who also discussed applications relating to predicting cholera and Rift Valley fever.

SCIENCE TEST

1. **A** Higher bulk density means lower soil quality. Figure 1 shows that Field A consistently has a higher bulk density, so (A) is the correct answer. Table 1 does not contain any information about Field A or B, eliminating (C). Figure 2 and Table 2 show that the crop yields and average soil organic matter (SOM) for Field A are higher, which goes against what the question looks to prove, eliminating (B) and (D).

2. **J** Figure 2 shows that Field B had a harvest of approximately 8 tons in Year 5. Of the values given in the figure, this is the only one that has a harvest less than or equal to 8 tons, thus making it a failed harvest.

3. **C** Table 1 shows that as the SOM increases, the soil quality increases. Eliminate (A) and (D) because both show an inverse, rather than a direct, relationship. With the new information provided in the question, you can infer that legumes and *deep-rooted and high-residue crops* will increase the amount of organic matter in the soil, and thus lead to an increase in the SOM rating. Only (C) provides this relationship.

4. **J** Figure 1 shows that Field A had a higher bulk density every year; therefore, regardless of the actual values, it can be assumed that the average bulk density was higher for Field A. Figure 2 shows that Field B had the lower crop yield in every year but Year 3. Therefore, it can be assumed that Field B has a lower average crop yield than Field A. The only choice that is correct for both parts of the question is (J).

5. **D** Use Table 1 to judge the average SOM for Field A and Field B given in Table 2. Field A's average SOM of 0.89 rates as excellent, and Field B's average SOM of 0.28 rates as fair. This means the hypothesis is not consistent with the data presented, so the correct answer is (D).

6. **J** Based on Table 1, the salt solution increased the amount of rust every day. On Day 8, the sample had 1.84 g of rust, so on Day 9 the amount of rust would likely be higher than 1.84 g, (J).

7. **B** The formula shows that when rust is produced, H_2 is also produced, so (B) is the only possible correct answer.

8. **J** Table 1 shows that the salt solution produced 0.56 g Fe_2O_3 on Day 2. Figure 1 shows that the water buffered to pH = 10.0 had less than 0.50 g Fe_2O_3 until Day 8, so the only correct answer is (J).

9. **A** Table 1 shows that the sugar solution produced 0.11 g Fe_2O_3 by Day 6 and 0.19 g by Day 8. The amount produced from Day 6 to Day 8, then, would have been 0.19 − 0.11 = 0.08 g.

10. **F** Table 1 shows that the sugar solution had 0.00 g Fe_2O_3 on Day 2 and shows a steady increase. Choices (G) and (J) show the amount of Fe_2O_3 produced decreasing as time passes, so they cannot be correct. Choice (H) shows a big increase in Fe_2O_3 between Day 2 and Day 6, then a small increase between Day 6 and Day 8. Table 1 shows that the biggest increase in Fe_2O_3 was between Day 6 and Day 8, 0.08 g, so (H) cannot be correct. Only (F) shows 0.00 g on Day 1 and steady increases in g Fe_2O_3 produced, so this must be the correct answer.

11. **D** Based on Experiment 1, shown in Figure 2, you can see that a 10.0 N weight shared between two springs caused Spring A to stretch to 0.40 m, so a 10.0 N weight on Spring A alone must cause it to stretch further. Choice (D) is the best answer.

12. **G** Based on Experiment 2, shown in Figure 4, you can see that as the weight moved farther from Spring B, Spring B stretched less as the force on Spring B decreased. Choice (G) is the correct answer.

13. **A** Because the students were attaching weights to two springs at once in Trials 1–3, it was important to use identical springs so that the effects on each spring would be the same. If they had used different springs, there would be no way of determining the relationship between the length of the spring and the weight. Choice (A) best describes this reason. Choice (B) does not make much sense for the same reasons, so it should be eliminated. Choice (D) must be eliminated because it discusses the weight of the board, which is not used in Trials 1–3. Choice (C) discusses oscillation, which is only mentioned in the passage to state that the students waited until oscillation ceased before measuring. Once you are left with (A) and (C), choice (A) is the better answer.

14. **H**   Experiment 2, Trial 5 shows the 5.0 N weight at exactly the midpoint of the board, and the springs stretched to 0.40 m. Experiment 1, Trial 1 has springs stretched to 0.40 m and a weight of 10.0 N. So the board in Experiment 3 must weigh 10.0 N – 5.0 N = 5.0 N, (H).

15. **B**   Experiment 2, Trial 5 is the only trial in Experiment 2 for which the springs are stretched the same amount, (B).

16. **H**   If potential energy is highest when the springs are stretched the most, then the correct answer must be the trial for which the spring was stretched the most, so you can eliminate (F) and (G) right away. Now, you need to find the answer that gives the correct reason for this phenomenon. Spring C was stretched the most because the force of the weight was greater, (H).

17. **C**   Table 2 shows that the proofs for both de-icers decrease as temperature decreases, so you know that the proof at –30°C for each de-icer must be *less than* the proof at –25°C and *greater than* the proof at –50°C. Knowing this, you can eliminate (A) right away because the proofs are the same as the proofs at –50°C. You can eliminate (D) because the proofs are the same as the proofs at –25°C. Choice (B) shows the proof for De-icer B greater than the proof for De-icer A, but Table 2 shows that De-icer A always has a greater proof than De-icer B, so (B) cannot be correct. This leaves (C) as the correct answer.

18. **J**   Table 1 shows that when 10 mL of distilled water is added to 40 mL of sodium chloride, the de-icer proof is 80. The de-icer proof changes based on the relative proportions of distilled water and sodium chloride. Choices (F) and (G) can be eliminated because proofs that small must be from de-icers that have almost all water. Because the proportion of water to sodium chloride is the same as in the problem, (J) is the correct answer.

19. **A**   The passage states that TR is the minimum proof for a de-icer to be effective at a particular temperature. Table 2 shows that as temperature decreases, TR increases only, so (A) is the correct answer.

20. **H**   Use the values from Table 1 to test the formulas in the different answer choices. When the volume of water is 0 and the volume of sodium chloride is 50, the de-icer proof is 100. Choice (F) would be undefined, so leave it for now. Choices (G) and (J) do not work, yielding a de-icer proof of 0, so cross them off. Choice (H) works, yielding a de-icer proof of 100, so keep it. Try the second row of values on the two remaining choices. When the volume of water is 10 and the volume of sodium chloride is 40, the de-icer proof is 80. These values work with (H) but not (J).

21. **C**   Table 1 shows that a mixture of 10 mL of distilled water and 40 mL of sodium chloride produces a de-icer proof of 80. Figure 1 shows that adding magnesium chloride increases the proof of a 100 proof de-icer. But no matter how much magnesium chloride is added, the proof never goes above 112. Eliminate (A) and (B) because they indicate that the proof would decrease and (D) because it indicates that the proof would exceed 112. The correct answer is (C).

22. **G** The passage states that TR is the minimum proof for a de-icer to be effective, so the better de-icer will be one that has a proof higher than the TR for each temperature. Eliminate (F) and (H). Based on Table 2, only De-icer A had a proof higher than the TR for each temperature, so (G) is the correct answer.

23. **C** Scientist 2 says that small comets originate from regions of the solar system beyond the farthest planet's (Neptune's) orbit, (C).

24. **J** Scientist 1 says that small comets have a diameter of 20–30 feet and burn up in the magnetosphere. Since larger comets burn up in the parts of the atmosphere closer to the earth, a comet that burns up in the thermosphere must have a diameter of greater than 30 feet, (J).

25. **A** Scientist 1 states that small comets are too small to be meteors. Scientist 1 also states that small comets burn up in the magnetosphere, but the passage says that meteors burn up between 50 and 85 km above Earth's surface, in the mesosphere. The correct choice, therefore, is that no small comet ever becomes a meteor, (A).

26. **J** The passage states that visible objects burning up in the atmosphere are called meteors, so you should eliminate choices that do not call the objects meteors, (F) and (G). Second, Scientist 2 tells you that meteors are seen "far less" often than twice every five minutes, so to see bright objects every minute is not typical, eliminating choice (H). This leaves the correct answer, (J).

27. **D** Scientist 1 says that all small comets burn up in the magnetosphere. Figure 1 shows the magnetosphere is above 600 km, so the answer is (D). The other values given in the answer choices represent altitudes in or above the magnetosphere.

28. **F** Scientist 1's viewpoint is that the dark spots are not mere noise; a change in the atmospheric conditions around these spots would support that viewpoint. Scientist 1 also states that the comets release krypton as they burn up, so the discovery of krypton around the spots confirms Scientist 1's viewpoint, (F). The other choices can be eliminated because none state that Scientist 1's viewpoint was strengthened.

29. **D** Scientist 1 states that small comets all burn up in the magnetosphere. According to this hypothesis, only enhanced imaging technology that could take pictures of the magnetosphere would be useful for seeing small comets. Therefore, only enhanced imaging technology that could record data above 600 km above sea level would be effective, (D).

30. **G** In Tables 1, 2, and 3, the amount of hydrogen peroxide decreases consistently from the first day (Table 3) to the end of the elongation period (Table 1), (G).

31. **C** The dependent variable of the experiment is a variable that the experimenter is not intentionally manipulating or changing (which is the independent variable) or controlling (control groups or variables); it's the variable that the experimenter is trying to understand or predict. In this experiment, the experimenter manipulated the type of plant, the type of superoxide dismutase, and the

point in time that measurements were taken. The length of the cotton fiber was neither intentionally changed nor controlled (represented as L1, L2, and L3). The introduction indicates that the *scientists wanted to study whether the level of hydrogen peroxide affected the length of the cotton fiber.* Choice (C) is the correct answer.

32. **H** Only plant cells have cell walls, so the correct answer is (H). Choice (F), *prokaryotic*, refers to unicellular life forms without a membrane-bound nucleus; cotton plants are not unicellular, so (F) cannot be correct. Choice (G), *animal cells*, do not have cell walls, so this choice can be eliminated. Choice (J), *bacteria*, are also unicellular and cotton plants are not bacteria, so (J) cannot be correct. In addition, you could use "cotton" as the clue; because of the answer choices, *plant* is the best approximation of what cotton is.

33. **C** Take the information given, length of cotton fiber and amount of hydrogen peroxide, and find the most similar line and point in time. The correct answer is (C), L2 at the beginning of its elongation period.

34. **J** The only cotton plant line which did not have its genetic structure altered was L4, so this was the control.

35. **A** The *x*-axis will move in a positive direction, so determine how the average lengths change. For all the data, the lengths increase with increasing elongation periods. Thus, you can conclude that the line will have a positive slope, (A).

36. **H** Figure 2 shows that as cross-sectional area increases, ΔT increases. If System 1 has a larger cross-sectional area than System 2, it must have a larger ΔT, so eliminate (F) and (G). The question tells you that System 1 has twice the cross-sectional area of System 2, so choice (H) is the correct answer. A quick check of Figure 2 confirms this: When cross-sectional area is 4 cm^2, ΔT is 6°C, and when cross-sectional area is 8 cm^2, ΔT is 12°C.

37. **B** Based on the definition given in the passage, convection would not transfer heat from the water to the metal containers. This eliminates all choices except for (B).

38. **F** Figure 2 shows that ΔT increases with cross-sectional area. Figure 3 shows that ΔT increases with height. In particular, Figures 2 and 3 show that height affects ΔT more than cross-sectional area. Although (H) has the greatest cross-sectional area, (F) and (G) have much greater height. Since (G) has a smaller height, the system with the greater ΔT is (F). Choice (F) is the best answer because it has larger values for both than any other choice.

39. **D** Table 1 shows that for water in the setup described, ΔT should be 10°C. Find the differences in temperature in the answer choices given. Choice (A) has a difference of 20°C. Choice (B) has a difference of 30°C. Choice (C) has a difference of 0°C. Only (D) has the appropriate ΔT of 10°C.

40.   **H**   The passage gives relationships between ΔT and only three variables: cross-sectional area, length, and starting temperature. None of these are possible choices, but radius is linked to cross-sectional area. As radius increases, area increases. Figure 2 shows that as cross-sectional area increases, ΔT increases, so the correct answer is choice (H). Insulation, amount of liquid, and air temperature are not discussed as being related to ΔT in the passage.

WRITING TEST

To grade your essay, see the Essay Checklist on the following page. The following is an example of a top-scoring essay for the prompt given in this test. Note that it's not perfect, but it still follows an organized outline and has a strong introductory paragraph, a concluding paragraph, and transitions throughout.

It's a Small World, after all.

Not only is this an awesome ride at Disneyland, but it's also the reality of the world we live in today. Borders are disappearing, commerce is expanding internationally, and our world is getting smaller. Improved travel and communication have brought people together from all walks of life, and globalization has the potential to solve many of the problems we face today. As people begin to learn more about each other and the backgrounds from which we all come, tolerance will increase and war will decrease.

Some believe that globalization will ultimately result in our world's unique cultures losing elements key to their identities. Perspective 1 discusses the possibility that as cultures combine, the resulting melting pot will lack the character of our current world societies. While globalization definitely introduces cultures to new foods, clothing, and ideas, there is no danger of complete homogenization. In fact, the spread of ideas increases diversity, exposing people in different parts of the world to things they otherwise wouldn't have known about, without necessarily removing the current ideas. Bringing crepes to the United States doesn't mean we stop eating cheeseburgers, just as bringing Old Navy to India does not mean residents of New Delhi will stop wearing saris. While these are fairly superficial examples, they make a clear point that simply introducing a new idea doesn't preclude people from also keeping the old idea. On a bigger scale, more problems can be solved as ideas and innovations spread from culture to culture. The lack of clean water in Africa is a major crisis, and inventors world-wide, from Italy to Peru to the United States, are working on innovations that will help improve the situation. Without the spread of ideas brought forth by globalization, there would be no hope for those suffering from a lack of clean water.

Perspective 3 argues that increased interaction will result in increased tensions between cultures. While this may be true in some circumstances, the overall effect of those cultural interactions would be a positive one. A lack of knowledge about a culture can often result in false impressions, fear and distrust, and unhelpful stereotypes. Someone without a good working knowledge of another culture might assume stereotypes are true, and think all Swiss are punctual and boring while all Germans love cars and beer. In reality, a culture is not defined by how it's stereotyped, and one benefit of globalization is an increased knowledge of other cultures. High school and college student exchange programs, international corporations, and even social media allow individuals from different cultures to meet and get to know each other, fostering a richer sense of global community with more authentic interactions.

As our global population grows and spreads, there will be problems that arise. However, by taking advantage of the opportunities to learn more about each other and share resources, globalization can also help solve some of those same problems.

WRITING TEST

Essay Checklist

1. The Introduction
   Did you
   - o start with a topic sentence that paraphrases or restates the prompt?
   - o clearly state your position on the issue?

2. Body Paragraph 1
   Did you
   - o start with a transition/topic sentence that discusses the opposing side of the argument?
   - o give an example of a reason that one might agree with the opposing side of the argument?
   - o clearly state that the opposing side of the argument is wrong or flawed?
   - o show what is wrong with the opposing side's example or position?

3. Body Paragraphs 2 and 3
   Did you
   - o start with a transition/topic sentence that discusses your position on the prompt?
   - o give one example or reason to support your position?
   - o show the grader how your example supports your position?
   - o end the paragraph by restating your thesis?

4. Conclusion
   Did you
   - o restate your position on the issue?
   - o end with a flourish?

5. Overall
   Did you
   - o write neatly?
   - o avoid multiple spelling and grammar mistakes?
   - o try to vary your sentence structure?
   - o use a few impressive-sounding words?

SCORING YOUR PRACTICE EXAM

Step A

Count the number of correct answers for each section and record the number in the space provided for your raw score on the Score Conversion Worksheet below.

Step B

Using the Score Conversion Chart on the next page, convert your raw scores on each section to scaled scores. Then compute your composite ACT score by averaging the four subject scores. Add them up and divide by four. Don't worry about the essay score; it is not included in your composite score.

Score Conversion Worksheet		
Section	Raw Score	Scaled Score
1	_____/75	_____
2	_____/60	_____
3	_____/40	_____
4	_____/40	_____

SCORE CONVERSION CHART

Scaled Score	Raw Scores			
	Test 1 English	Test 2 Math	Test 3 Reading	Test 4 Science
36	75	59–60	40	39–40
35	72–74	57–58	---	38
34	71	56	39	37
33	70	54–55	38	---
32	69	53	37	36
31	68	51–52	---	35
30	66–67	50	36	34
29	65	49	35	33
28	64	47–48	34	32
27	62–63	45–46	33	31
26	60–61	42–44	32	29–30
25	58–59	40–41	31	27–28
24	56–57	38–39	30	26
23	53–55	35–37	29	24–25
22	51–52	33–34	27–28	22–23
21	47–50	32	26	20–21
20	44–46	30–31	24–25	18–19
19	41–43	28–29	22–23	17
18	39–40	26–27	21	15–16
17	37–38	22–25	19–20	14
16	34–36	18–21	17–18	13
15	31–33	14–17	15–16	12
14	29–30	10–13	13–14	11
13	27–28	08–09	11–12	10
12	25–26	07	09–10	09
11	23–24	05–06	08	08
10	20–22	04	06–07	07
09	17–19	---	---	05–06
08	15–16	03	05	04
07	12–14	---	04	---
06	10–11	02	03	03
05	07–09	---	---	02
04	06	01	02	---
03	04–05	---	---	01
02	02–03	---	01	---
01	00–01	00	00	00

Part IX
The Princeton
Review ACT
Practice Exam 2

Chapter 27
Practice Exam 2

ACT Diagnostic Test Form

1. YOUR NAME: _____
(Print) Last First M.I.

SIGNATURE: _____ **DATE:** _____ / _____ / _____

HOME ADDRESS: _____
(Print) Number and Street

_____
City State Zip

E-MAIL: _____

PHONE NO.: _____
(Print)

SCHOOL: _____

CLASS OF: _____

IMPORTANT: Please fill in these boxes exactly as shown on the back cover of your tests book.

2. TEST FORM

_____

3. TEST CODE

⓪	⓪	⓪	⓪
①	①	①	①
②	②	②	②
③	③	③	③
④	④	④	④
⑤	⑤	⑤	⑤
⑥	⑥	⑥	⑥
⑦	⑦	⑦	⑦
⑧	⑧	⑧	⑧
⑨	⑨	⑨	⑨

4. PHONE NUMBER

⓪	⓪	⓪	⓪	⓪	⓪	⓪
①	①	①	①	①	①	①
②	②	②	②	②	②	②
③	③	③	③	③	③	③
④	④	④	④	④	④	④
⑤	⑤	⑤	⑤	⑤	⑤	⑤
⑥	⑥	⑥	⑥	⑥	⑥	⑥
⑦	⑦	⑦	⑦	⑦	⑦	⑦
⑧	⑧	⑧	⑧	⑧	⑧	⑧
⑨	⑨	⑨	⑨	⑨	⑨	⑨

5. YOUR NAME

First 4 letters of last name | FIRST INIT | MID INIT

				FIRST INIT	MID INIT
Ⓐ	Ⓐ	Ⓐ	Ⓐ	Ⓐ	Ⓐ
Ⓑ	Ⓑ	Ⓑ	Ⓑ	Ⓑ	Ⓑ
Ⓒ	Ⓒ	Ⓒ	Ⓒ	Ⓒ	Ⓒ
Ⓓ	Ⓓ	Ⓓ	Ⓓ	Ⓓ	Ⓓ
Ⓔ	Ⓔ	Ⓔ	Ⓔ	Ⓔ	Ⓔ
Ⓕ	Ⓕ	Ⓕ	Ⓕ	Ⓕ	Ⓕ
Ⓖ	Ⓖ	Ⓖ	Ⓖ	Ⓖ	Ⓖ
Ⓗ	Ⓗ	Ⓗ	Ⓗ	Ⓗ	Ⓗ
Ⓘ	Ⓘ	Ⓘ	Ⓘ	Ⓘ	Ⓘ
Ⓙ	Ⓙ	Ⓙ	Ⓙ	Ⓙ	Ⓙ
Ⓚ	Ⓚ	Ⓚ	Ⓚ	Ⓚ	Ⓚ
Ⓛ	Ⓛ	Ⓛ	Ⓛ	Ⓛ	Ⓛ
Ⓜ	Ⓜ	Ⓜ	Ⓜ	Ⓜ	Ⓜ
Ⓝ	Ⓝ	Ⓝ	Ⓝ	Ⓝ	Ⓝ
Ⓞ	Ⓞ	Ⓞ	Ⓞ	Ⓞ	Ⓞ
Ⓟ	Ⓟ	Ⓟ	Ⓟ	Ⓟ	Ⓟ
Ⓠ	Ⓠ	Ⓠ	Ⓠ	Ⓠ	Ⓠ
Ⓡ	Ⓡ	Ⓡ	Ⓡ	Ⓡ	Ⓡ
Ⓢ	Ⓢ	Ⓢ	Ⓢ	Ⓢ	Ⓢ
Ⓣ	Ⓣ	Ⓣ	Ⓣ	Ⓣ	Ⓣ
Ⓤ	Ⓤ	Ⓤ	Ⓤ	Ⓤ	Ⓤ
Ⓥ	Ⓥ	Ⓥ	Ⓥ	Ⓥ	Ⓥ
Ⓦ	Ⓦ	Ⓦ	Ⓦ	Ⓦ	Ⓦ
Ⓧ	Ⓧ	Ⓧ	Ⓧ	Ⓧ	Ⓧ
Ⓨ	Ⓨ	Ⓨ	Ⓨ	Ⓨ	Ⓨ
Ⓩ	Ⓩ	Ⓩ	Ⓩ	Ⓩ	Ⓩ

6. DATE OF BIRTH

MONTH	DAY		YEAR	
⚬ JAN				
⚬ FEB				
⚬ MAR	⓪	⓪	⓪	⓪
⚬ APR	①	①	①	①
⚬ MAY	②	②	②	②
⚬ JUN	③	③	③	③
⚬ JUL		④	④	④
⚬ AUG		⑤	⑤	⑤
⚬ SEP		⑥	⑥	⑥
⚬ OCT		⑦	⑦	⑦
⚬ NOV		⑧	⑧	⑧
⚬ DEC		⑨	⑨	⑨

7. SEX

⚬ MALE
⚬ FEMALE

8. OTHER

1 Ⓐ Ⓑ Ⓒ Ⓓ Ⓔ
2 Ⓐ Ⓑ Ⓒ Ⓓ Ⓔ
3 Ⓐ Ⓑ Ⓒ Ⓓ Ⓔ

THIS PAGE INTENTIONALLY LEFT BLANK

The Princeton Review
Diagnostic ACT Form

Completely darken bubbles with a No. 2 pencil. If you make a mistake, be sure to erase mark completely. Erase all stray marks.

ENGLISH

#					#					#					#				
1	A	B	C	D	21	A	B	C	D	41	A	B	C	D	61	A	B	C	D
2	F	G	H	J	22	F	G	H	J	42	F	G	H	J	62	F	G	H	J
3	A	B	C	D	23	A	B	C	D	43	A	B	C	D	63	A	B	C	D
4	F	G	H	J	24	F	G	H	J	44	F	G	H	J	64	F	G	H	J
5	A	B	C	D	25	A	B	C	D	45	A	B	C	D	65	A	B	C	D
6	F	G	H	J	26	F	G	H	J	46	F	G	H	J	66	F	G	H	J
7	A	B	C	D	27	A	B	C	D	47	A	B	C	D	67	A	B	C	D
8	F	G	H	J	28	F	G	H	J	48	F	G	H	J	68	F	G	H	J
9	A	B	C	D	29	A	B	C	D	49	A	B	C	D	69	A	B	C	D
10	F	G	H	J	30	F	G	H	J	50	F	G	H	J	70	F	G	H	J
11	A	B	C	D	31	A	B	C	D	51	A	B	C	D	71	A	B	C	D
12	F	G	H	J	32	F	G	H	J	52	F	G	H	J	72	F	G	H	J
13	A	B	C	D	33	A	B	C	D	53	A	B	C	D	73	A	B	C	D
14	F	G	H	J	34	F	G	H	J	54	F	G	H	J	74	F	G	H	J
15	A	B	C	D	35	A	B	C	D	55	A	B	C	D	75	A	B	C	D
16	F	G	H	J	36	F	G	H	J	56	F	G	H	J					
17	A	B	C	D	37	A	B	C	D	57	A	B	C	D					
18	F	G	H	J	38	F	G	H	J	58	F	G	H	J					
19	A	B	C	D	39	A	B	C	D	59	A	B	C	D					
20	F	G	H	J	40	F	G	H	J	60	F	G	H	J					

MATHEMATICS

#						#						#						#					
1	A	B	C	D	E	16	F	G	H	J	K	31	A	B	C	D	E	46	F	G	H	J	K
2	F	G	H	J	K	17	A	B	C	D	E	32	F	G	H	J	K	47	A	B	C	D	E
3	A	B	C	D	E	18	F	G	H	J	K	33	A	B	C	D	E	48	F	G	H	J	K
4	F	G	H	J	K	19	A	B	C	D	E	34	F	G	H	J	K	49	A	B	C	D	E
5	A	B	C	D	E	20	F	G	H	J	K	35	A	B	C	D	E	50	F	G	H	J	K
6	F	G	H	J	K	21	A	B	C	D	E	36	F	G	H	J	K	51	A	B	C	D	E
7	A	B	C	D	E	22	F	G	H	J	K	37	A	B	C	D	E	52	F	G	H	J	K
8	F	G	H	J	K	23	A	B	C	D	E	38	F	G	H	J	K	53	A	B	C	D	E
9	A	B	C	D	E	24	F	G	H	J	K	39	A	B	C	D	E	54	F	G	H	J	K
10	F	G	H	J	K	25	A	B	C	D	E	40	F	G	H	J	K	55	A	B	C	D	E
11	A	B	C	D	E	26	F	G	H	J	K	41	A	B	C	D	E	56	F	G	H	J	K
12	F	G	H	J	K	27	A	B	C	D	E	42	F	G	H	J	K	57	A	B	C	D	E
13	A	B	C	D	E	28	F	G	H	J	K	43	A	B	C	D	E	58	F	G	H	J	K
14	F	G	H	J	K	29	A	B	C	D	E	44	F	G	H	J	K	59	A	B	C	D	E
15	A	B	C	D	E	30	F	G	H	J	K	45	A	B	C	D	E	60	F	G	H	J	K

The Princeton Review
Diagnostic ACT Form

READING

1 (A)	(B)	(C)	(D)	11 (A)	(B)	(C)	(D)	21 (A)	(B)	(C)	(D)	31 (A)	(B)	(C)	(D)
2 (F)	(G)	(H)	(J)	12 (F)	(G)	(H)	(J)	22 (F)	(G)	(H)	(J)	32 (F)	(G)	(H)	(J)
3 (A)	(B)	(C)	(D)	13 (A)	(B)	(C)	(D)	23 (A)	(B)	(C)	(D)	33 (A)	(B)	(C)	(D)
4 (F)	(G)	(H)	(J)	14 (F)	(G)	(H)	(J)	24 (F)	(G)	(H)	(J)	34 (F)	(G)	(H)	(J)
5 (A)	(B)	(C)	(D)	15 (A)	(B)	(C)	(D)	25 (A)	(B)	(C)	(D)	35 (A)	(B)	(C)	(D)
6 (F)	(G)	(H)	(J)	16 (F)	(G)	(H)	(J)	26 (F)	(G)	(H)	(J)	36 (F)	(G)	(H)	(J)
7 (A)	(B)	(C)	(D)	17 (A)	(B)	(C)	(D)	27 (A)	(B)	(C)	(D)	37 (A)	(B)	(C)	(D)
8 (F)	(G)	(H)	(J)	18 (F)	(G)	(H)	(J)	28 (F)	(G)	(H)	(J)	38 (F)	(G)	(H)	(J)
9 (A)	(B)	(C)	(D)	19 (A)	(B)	(C)	(D)	29 (A)	(B)	(C)	(D)	39 (A)	(B)	(C)	(D)
10 (F)	(G)	(H)	(J)	20 (F)	(G)	(H)	(J)	30 (F)	(G)	(H)	(J)	40 (F)	(G)	(H)	(J)

SCIENCE REASONING

1 (A)	(B)	(C)	(D)	11 (A)	(B)	(C)	(D)	21 (A)	(B)	(C)	(D)	31 (A)	(B)	(C)	(D)
2 (F)	(G)	(H)	(J)	12 (F)	(G)	(H)	(J)	22 (F)	(G)	(H)	(J)	32 (F)	(G)	(H)	(J)
3 (A)	(B)	(C)	(D)	13 (A)	(B)	(C)	(D)	23 (A)	(B)	(C)	(D)	33 (A)	(B)	(C)	(D)
4 (F)	(G)	(H)	(J)	14 (F)	(G)	(H)	(J)	24 (F)	(G)	(H)	(J)	34 (F)	(G)	(H)	(J)
5 (A)	(B)	(C)	(D)	15 (A)	(B)	(C)	(D)	25 (A)	(B)	(C)	(D)	35 (A)	(B)	(C)	(D)
6 (F)	(G)	(H)	(J)	16 (F)	(G)	(H)	(J)	26 (F)	(G)	(H)	(J)	36 (F)	(G)	(H)	(J)
7 (A)	(B)	(C)	(D)	17 (A)	(B)	(C)	(D)	27 (A)	(B)	(C)	(D)	37 (A)	(B)	(C)	(D)
8 (F)	(G)	(H)	(J)	18 (F)	(G)	(H)	(J)	28 (F)	(G)	(H)	(J)	38 (F)	(G)	(H)	(J)
9 (A)	(B)	(C)	(D)	19 (A)	(B)	(C)	(D)	29 (A)	(B)	(C)	(D)	39 (A)	(B)	(C)	(D)
10 (F)	(G)	(H)	(J)	20 (F)	(G)	(H)	(J)	30 (F)	(G)	(H)	(J)	40 (F)	(G)	(H)	(J)

The Princeton Review
Diagnostic ACT Form

ESSAY

Begin your essay on this side. If necessary, continue on the opposite side.

Continue on the opposite side if necessary.

The Princeton Review
Diagnostic ACT Form

Continued from previous page.

_____

_____

_____

_____

_____

_____

_____

_____

_____

_____

_____

_____

_____

_____

_____

_____

_____

_____

_____

_____

_____

_____

_____

**PLEASE PRINT
YOUR INITIALS**

First	Middle	Last

THIS PAGE INTENTIONALLY LEFT BLANK

ENGLISH TEST

45 Minutes—75 Questions

DIRECTIONS: In the five passages that follow, certain words and phrases are underlined and numbered. In the right-hand column, you will find alternatives for each underlined part. In most cases, you are to choose the one that best expresses the idea, makes the statement appropriate for standard written English, or is worded most consistently with the style and tone of the passage as a whole. If you think the original version is best, choose "NO CHANGE." In some cases, you will find in the right-hand column a question about the underlined part of the passage. You are to choose the best answer to the question.

You will also find questions about a section of the passage or the passage as a whole. These questions do not refer to an underlined portion of the passage, but rather are identified by a number or numbers in a box.

For each question, choose the alternative you consider best and blacken the corresponding oval on your answer document. Read each passage through once before you begin to answer the questions that accompany it. For many of the questions, you must read several sentences beyond the question to determine the answer. Be sure that you have read far enough ahead each time you choose an alternative.

PASSAGE I

Crocheting Makes a Good Hobby

Crocheting is the art of making fabric by twisting yarn or thread with a hook. Although many associate it by older women,
₁

crocheting can be a fun hobby for people of both genders and all
₂
ages. Once you start crocheting, you won't be able to put down

the hook; you'll have a hobby for life. ☐3

1. **A.** NO CHANGE
   B. to
   C. by
   D. with

2. **F.** NO CHANGE
   G. for people of both genders, masculine and feminine,
   H. for male and female people of both genders
   J. for people of both genders, both males and females,

3. At this point, the author is considering adding the following true statement:

   > Irish nuns helped save lives with crocheting when they used it as a way to make a living during the Great Irish Potato Famine of 1846.

   Should the writer add this sentence here?

   A. Yes, because it is essential to know when crocheting became internationally prominent and how it did so.
   B. Yes, because the reference to the Great Irish Potato Famine demonstrates that the author is conscious of historical events.
   C. No, because the reference to the Great Irish Potato Famine is not relevant to the main topic of this essay.
   D. No, because many people who left Ireland in 1846 brought crocheting with them to the United States and Australia.

GO ON TO THE NEXT PAGE.

Time-honored and easily <u>taught</u> to all, crocheting is an easy

₄

hobby to pick up. Instructional books are readily available, and

once you've learned a few basic <u>stitches. Picking</u> up the more

₅

advanced ones is a snap. Once you learn how to crochet, you can

<u>purchase store-bought books that detail crocheting patterns</u> that

₆

tell you exactly how to make the projects that interest you. Even

if you want to try several projects, the supplies required for

<u>it's</u> completion are minimal; all you need are a crochet hook,

₇

yarn, and a pair of scissors. You don't need to worry about

making a big investment, either; fifteen dollars will buy you no

<u>fewer than</u> three starter kits!

₈

[1] As you grow more proficient, you can expand your

supplies by purchasing hooks of different <u>types</u> to vary the

₉

size of your stitches. [2] Crochet hooks are available in all

<u>sizes, ranging,</u> from very small to very large, with everything in

₁₀

between. [3] Some are so big that you need to use two strands of

yarn. [4] Other hooks are very tiny, so small that you must use

thread. [5] These hooks are suitable for making smaller, more

delicate things such as lace doilies, tablecloths, and bedspreads.

[6] These hooks make big stitches, so you can finish a project

with them very quickly. [7] It is best to start with hooks that are

medium in size; these are the easiest to manipulate and require

only one strand of yarn. ☐11

4. **F.** NO CHANGE
   G. teaches
   H. taughted
   J. teached

5. **A.** NO CHANGE
   B. stitches; picking
   C. stitches, picking
   D. stitches since picking

6. **F.** NO CHANGE
   G. buy books and other pamphlets at craft and book stores detailing certain specific patterns
   H. buy pattern books
   J. acquire store-bought pattern books

7. **A.** NO CHANGE
   B. its
   C. its'
   D. their

8. **F.** NO CHANGE
   G. fewer then
   H. less than
   J. less then

9. **A.** NO CHANGE
   B. types;
   C. types:
   D. types,

10. **F.** NO CHANGE
    G. sizes, ranging
    H. sizes; ranging
    J. sizes ranging,

11. For the sake of the logic and coherence of this paragraph, Sentence 6 should be placed:

    A. where it is now.
    B. after Sentence 1.
    C. after Sentence 3.
    D. after Sentence 7.

GO ON TO THE NEXT PAGE.

Because it seems like there are a million hooks to keep
track of, crocheting makes a good hobby because it requires only
time and patience, not attention or tremendous investment. You
can crochet while watching television, listening to music, or
visiting with other people. It is fun and relaxing and allows you
to express your creative side in an easy way. Also, you
have finished a project, you have a cherished keepsake. Whether

you have made an afghan to keep you warm on cold winter
nights or a lace tablecloth to add a touch of elegance to your
dining room, your creation is sure to be cherished for a long time
to come.

12. Given that all the choices are true, which one provides the most effective transition from the preceding paragraph to this one?
   F. NO CHANGE
   G. Because it can take a long time to finish a project,
   H. With such a simple and inexpensive set of materials,
   J. No longer a field dominated primarily by older women,

13. A. NO CHANGE
    B. Also, finally you
    C. Also, despite the fact you
    D. Also, once you

14. F. NO CHANGE
    G. at
    H. of
    J. within

Question 15 asks about the preceding passage as a whole.

---

15. Suppose the writer's goal had been to write an essay that demonstrates the commercial potential of crocheting. Would this essay successfully accomplish that goal?

    A. Yes, because it gives examples of end products of crocheting and shows the different kinds of materials needed to produce a wide range of products.
    B. Yes, because it discusses the supplies necessary to create crocheted products, and it shows the usefulness of many of them during the cold winter months.
    C. No, because it does not mention the market value of crocheted products or how one might go about selling them.
    D. No, because it describes other industries and hobbies that would be more commercially successful.

PASSAGE II

Seurat's Masterpiece

[1] How can I describe the wonder I felt the first time I saw my favorite painting, Georges Seurat's *A Sunday on La Grande Jatte*? [2] I had admired the work for years in art books, but I never thought I saw the actual painting, which was housed in Chicago, many miles from where I lived. [3] I finally got my

16. F. NO CHANGE
    G. would see
    H. had seen
    J. was seeing

GO ON TO THE NEXT PAGE.

chance to when I met someone else who loved the painting as
17
much as I did. [4] We both had three days off at the same time,

so we decided to make a road trip to Chicago so we could see

the painting in all it's grandeur. [5] We packed our bags,
18

jumped in the car, and headed on our way toward Chicago. 20
19

[1] The first thing that struck me as we entered the room

where the painting was displayed; was the size of the painting.
21
[2] A common size for canvases is 24 by 36 inches. [3] It was

enormous! [4] It covered a large part of an even larger wall. [5]

The painting's size amazed me since it was painted with dots, a

technique called pointillism. [6] To create a painting of such

magnitude using this technique seemed an almost impossible

task. [7] Seurat had done it, though, and had made it look easy! 23
22

17. **A.** NO CHANGE
  B. at the moment
  C. just to
  D. DELETE the underlined portion.

18. **F.** NO CHANGE
  G. our
  H. its
  J. its'

19. **A.** NO CHANGE
  B. jumped in the car, and had headed
  C. jumped in the car, and head
  D. had jumped in the car, and headed

20. Upon reviewing this paragraph and noticing that some information has been left out, the writer composes the following
sentence, incorporating the information:

> Her name was Lisa; she lived in my dorm, and a mutual
> friend had introduced us to each other, knowing how
> much both of us loved art.

For the sake of the logic of this paragraph, this sentence should
be placed after Sentence:

  F. 2.
  G. 3.
  H. 4.
  J. 5.

21. **A.** NO CHANGE
  B. displayed:
  C. displayed,
  D. displayed

22. **F.** NO CHANGE
  G. task and difficult to complete.
  H. task, difficult to complete.
  J. task, overwhelming in its difficulty.

23. Which of the following sentences is LEAST relevant to the
development of this paragraph and therefore could be deleted?

  A. Sentence 2
  B. Sentence 4
  C. Sentence 5
  D. Sentence 6

GO ON TO THE NEXT PAGE.

Even more impressive, however, was the beauty of the
painting. Viewed from a distance, the colors looked muted,
capturing the idyllic mood of a summer day in the park.

When I approached the painting, though, its colors exploded into
myriad hues, illustrating the artist's skill in combining colors to
create a mood. Even the parts of the painting that appeared white
from a distance were vibrantly multicolored when viewed up
close. 26 The effect was incredible;

he sat and stared at the painting in wonder for a good portion of

the afternoon. 28

My friend and I saw many other sights, on our trip to
Chicago, but the best part by far was being able to see our favorite
work of art. The image is forever imprinted in my mind

24. Given that all of the choices are accurate, which provides the most effective and logical transition from the preceding paragraph to this one?

   F. NO CHANGE
   G. One thing that struck me was
   H. Many art critics have written about
   J. The debate rages on over

25. Which of the following alternatives to the underlined portion would NOT be acceptable?

   A. As I approached the painting, though,
   B. However, as I approached the painting,
   C. I approached the painting, though,
   D. However, when I approached the painting,

26. If the writer were to delete the phrase "from a distance" from the preceding sentence, the paragraph would primarily lose:

   F. an essential point explaining the author's love of the painting.
   G. the first part of the contrast in this sentence, which the author uses to describe viewing the painting.
   H. a further indication of the length of the road trip taken by the author and her friend.
   J. nothing, because the information provided by this phrase is stated more clearly elsewhere in the paragraph.

27. A. NO CHANGE
   B. one
   C. they
   D. we

28. At this point, the writer is considering adding the following true statement:

> The Art Institute of Chicago contains many other famous paintings, among them Edvard Munch's *The Scream* and Grant Wood's *American Gothic*.

Should the writer make this addition here?

   F. Yes, because it gives additional details essential to understanding the collection at the museum.
   G. Yes, because it demonstrates a contrast between the author's favorite painting and those in this sentence.
   H. No, because it provides information that is not relevant at this point in the paragraph and essay.
   J. No, because it is contradicted by other information presented in this essay.

29. A. NO CHANGE
   B. sights, which
   C. sights;
   D. sights

GO ON TO THE NEXT PAGE.

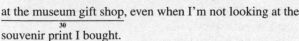

at the museum gift shop, even when I'm not looking at the
_____
             30
souvenir print I bought.

30. The best placement for the underlined portion would be:

    F. where it is now.
    G. after the word *image*.
    H. after the word *looking*.
    J. after the word *bought* (ending the sentence with a period).

PASSAGE III

The Language of Cats

Many people believe that language is the domain of human beings. However, cats have developed an intricate language not
                          _____
                                  31
for each other, but for the human beings who

have adopted them as pets.
_____
    32

31. A. NO CHANGE
    B. developed, an intricate language
    C. developed an intricate language,
    D. developed; an intricate language

32. Which choice would most clearly and effectively express the ownership relationship between humans and cats?

    F. NO CHANGE
    G. like to have cats around.
    H. often have dogs as well.
    J. are naturally inclined to like cats.

When communicating with each other, cats' "talk" is a
                            _____
                                    33
complex system of nonverbal signals. In particular, their tails,
_____
    33

33. A. NO CHANGE
    B. a complicated system of nonverbal signals is used by cats to "talk."
    C. cats "talk" with a complex system of nonverbal signals.
    D. "talking" is done by them with a system of complex nonverbal signals.

rather than any kind of "speech," provide cats' chief means of
                                  _____
                                        34
expression. They also use physical contact to express their feelings. With other cats, cats will use their voices only to express pain. 35

34. F. NO CHANGE
    G. having provided
    H. has provided
    J. were provided by

35. If the preceding sentence were deleted, the essay would primarily lose:

    A. a redundant point made elsewhere in the essay.
    B. another description of the ways in which cats communicate nonverbally.
    C. an exception to the general trend described in this paragraph.
    D. a brief summary of the information contained in the essay up to this point.

Next, incredibly, all of that changes when a human walks
_____
    36
into the room. Cats use a wide range of vocal expressions when they communicate with a person, from affectionate meows to

36. F. NO CHANGE
    G. (Do NOT begin new paragraph) Incredibly,
    H. (Begin new paragraph) Next incredibly,
    J. (Begin new paragraph) Incredibly,

GO ON TO THE NEXT PAGE.

menacing hisses. Since cats verbal expressions are not used to
                           ────────────────────
                                   37

communicate with other cats, it is logical and reasonable
                                    ─────────────────────
                                             38
to conclude that cats developed this "language" expressly to
communicate with their human owners.

This fact is demonstrated more clear since observing
                                ─────────────
                                      39
households that have only one cat. An only cat is usually very
vocal, since the only creature around with whom the cat can
communicate is its owner. Cats with other feline companions,
though, are much quieter. If they want to have a conversation, they
need only go to their fellow cats and communicate in their natural
way. 40

Since cats learned to meow for the sole purpose of
communicating with human beings, owners should take the time
to learn what their different meows mean. If an owner
knows, to name just a few examples, which meow means the cat is
─────
  41
hungry, which means the cat wants to be petted, and which means
the cat wants to have a little "conversation," the bond between cat
and owner will grow deeper. 42 Certainly, after a time, owners
will see that communicating with their pets, not just cats, is every
bit as important to forging good relationships

as to communicate with other humans. Once, as an owner,
──────────────
       43
you know that the cat is not just

37. **A.** NO CHANGE
    B. cat's verbal expressions
    C. cats' verbal expressions
    D. cats verbal expressions,

38. **F.** NO CHANGE
    G. logical and well-reasoned
    H. logical to a startling degree
    J. logical

39. **A.** NO CHANGE
    B. clear when
    C. clearly since
    D. clearly when

40. At this point, the writer is considering adding the following
    true statement:

    > On the other hand, the natural way for most birds to
    > communicate is vocally, by way of the "bird song."

    Should the writer add this sentence here?

    F. Yes, because it shows that cats are truly unique in com-
    municating nonverbally.
    G. Yes, because it adds a relevant and enlightening detail
    about another animal.
    H. No, because it basically repeats information given earlier
    in the essay.
    J. No, because it does not contribute to the development of
    this paragraph and the essay as a whole.

41. **A.** NO CHANGE
    B. knows, to,
    C. knows to,
    D. knows to

42. If the writer wanted to emphasize that cats communicate vo-
    cally with their owners to express a large number of different
    emotions in addition to those listed in the previous sentence,
    which of the following true statements should be added at this
    point?

    F. Many animals communicate hunger similarly to cats.
    G. Cats will tell their owners when they feel pain, sadness,
    irritation, or love.
    H. Cats communicate these emotions differently to other cats.
    J. Humans have the easiest time communicating with other
    mammals.

43. **A.** NO CHANGE
    B. as being communicative
    C. as communicating
    D. through communicating

GO ON TO THE NEXT PAGE.

making senseless noises without any rhyme or reason but is
_____
                            44
making an attempt to communicate, you can make an effort to

communicate back. After all, your cat isn't meowing just for the

sake of making noise; however, cats are less communicative than
                      _____
                                              45
many other animals.
_____
        45

44. F. NO CHANGE
   G. making senseless noises
   H. senselessly making noises with no thought involved
   J. making senseless noises, having no idea what they mean,

45. Which choice would best summarize the main point the essay makes about cats' communication with their human owners?

   A. NO CHANGE
   B. rather, there's a good chance your cat is trying to tell you something.
   C. instead, your cat is probably trying to communicate with other cats by meowing.
   D. on the other hand, it is better to have more than one cat so they can undergo a natural development.

PASSAGE IV

Visiting Mackinac Island

Visiting Mackinac (pronounced "Mackinaw") Island is like

taking a step back to the past in time. Victorian
_____
               46

houses' and a fort dating back to the War of 1812 surround the
_____
  47
historic downtown, where horses and buggies still pull

passengers down the road.

The only way to get to Mackinac Island is by boat or private
                                              ____
                                               48
plane, and you may not bring your car. Automobiles are

outlawed on the little, isolated, Michigan, island, so visitors can
                       _____
                                    49

see the sights only by horse, carriage, or by riding a bicycle, or
                                          _____
                                                    50
on foot. Luckily, the island is small enough that cars are not

necessary, Mackinac measures only a mile and a half in
_____
          51
diameter.

46. F. NO CHANGE
   G. moving in a past-related direction
   H. going back to the past, not the future,
   J. stepping back

47. A. NO CHANGE
   B. house's
   C. houses
   D. houses,

48. F. NO CHANGE
   G. your sweet self over to
   H. yourself on down to
   J. over to

49. A. NO CHANGE
   B. isolated Michigan island
   C. isolated Michigan island,
   D. isolated, Michigan, island

50. F. NO CHANGE
   G. by bicycle,
   H. riding on a bicycle,
   J. bicycle,

51. A. NO CHANGE
   B. necessary, furthermore, Mackinac
   C. necessary. Mackinac
   D. necessary Mackinac

GO ON TO THE NEXT PAGE.

There are many things to see while visiting Mackinac Island. The majestic Grand Hotel is a popular tourist spot, as are the governor's mansion and Arch Rock, a towering limestone arch formed naturally by water erosion. 52 Fort Mackinac, where they still set off cannons every hour, is also a popular place to visit. Visible from parts of the island are Mackinac Bridge—the longest suspension bridge ever built—and a picturesque old lighthouse.

Shopping is also a favorite pastime on Mackinac Island. The island's biggest industry is tourism, 53 For the island's many

tourists, the most popular item of sale on Mackinac Island is
                                     ——
                                     54

fudge. The downtown streets are lined with fudge shops, where
                                                          ———
                                                           55
tourists can watch fudge of all different flavors being made before lining up to buy some for themselves. These fudge shops

are so numerous and abundant that the local residents have even
      ————————————
            56

developed a special nickname for these tourists: I call the
                                                 ————
                                                  57
tourists "fudgies."

Apart from sightseeing and shopping, Mackinac Island is a great place to just sit back and relax. In the summer, a gentle lake breeze floats through the air, when it creates a beautiful,
                                     ——————————
                                          58
temperate climate. It is peaceful to sit in the city park and watch the ferries and private boats float into the harbor. The privacy of

52. If the writer were to delete the phrase "formed naturally by water erosion" (placing a period after the word *arch*), this sentence would primarily lose:

    F. a detail describing the unique formation of the Arch Rock.

    G. factual information concerning the geological formations of the tourist attractions on Mackinac Island.

    H. a contrast to the governor's mansion, which was constructed by human hands.

    J. nothing; this information is detailed elsewhere in this paragraph.

53. Given that all the following are true, which one, if added here at the end of this sentence, would provide the most effective transition to the topic discussed in the sentence that follows?

    A. so there are many souvenir stores, T-shirt shops, and candy and ice cream parlors.

    B. so Mackinac Island has not been negatively affected by outsourcing.

    C. which is a big change from the island's eighteenth-century use in the fur trade.

    D. but it's not a tourist attraction like many others with theme parks and chain restaurants.

54. **F.** NO CHANGE

    G. for selling

    H. for sale

    J. of selling

55. Which of the following alternatives to the underlined portion would NOT be acceptable?

    A. which

    B. so

    C. and

    D. in which

56. **F.** NO CHANGE

    G. abundantly numerous

    H. numerous

    J. of an abundance truly numerous

57. **A.** NO CHANGE

    B. one calls

    C. it calls

    D. they call

58. **F.** NO CHANGE

    G. creating

    H. once it creates

    J. as if it had created

GO ON TO THE NEXT PAGE.

the island's environs certainly <u>don't give</u> it the hustle-bustle
₅₉
quality of a city, but the relaxing atmosphere makes Mackinac

Island the perfect place to visit to get away from the hectic pace

of everyday life.

59. **A.** NO CHANGE
B. isn't giving
C. hasn't given
D. doesn't give

Question 60 asks about the preceding passage as a whole.

---

60. Suppose the writer had intended to write an essay on the difficulty the residents of Mackinac Island have had prohibiting automobile traffic from the historic island. Would this essay have successfully fulfilled that goal?

F. Yes, because the automobile has become such an essential part of American tourist travel that the residents are clearly threatened.

G. Yes, because this essay discusses the fact that automobiles are outlawed and goes on to detail many of the reasons this was possible.

H. No, because the essay focuses instead on other aspects of Mackinac Island, mentioning automobiles in only one part of the passage.

J. No, because this essay describes the ways the residents of Mackinac Island have sought to bring automobiles back to the island, not to outlaw them.

PASSAGE V

Fun with Karaoke

[1]

[1] Karaoke is one of the most popular forms of
entertainment in the world. [2] What defies understanding,
though, is why so many ordinary people insist on getting up on
stage in public, humiliating themselves in front of both their
<u>friends; and peers.</u> [3] Whether practiced at home, in a
₆₁
restaurant, or at a party, karaoke is a form of entertainment

<u>that provides</u> people with a great time and a positive feeling. [4]
₆₂
It is understandable that people would enjoy singing in the

61. **A.** NO CHANGE
B. friends and peers.
C. friends, and peers.
D. friends and, peers.

62. Which of the following alternatives to the underlined portion would NOT be acceptable?

F. that has provided
G. , providing
H. , that is, providing
J. that having provided

GO ON TO THE NEXT PAGE.

privacy of their homes. [5] There are many different ways to respond to this question. ☐ 63

[2]

Looking more closely, and you'll see a main reason for karaoke's success is its glitz and glamour. Karaoke provides people with a moment when they are more than just everyday folks—they are stars. Even though their performances may be heard only in dimly lit bars or busy restaurants, but karaoke singers are still performing as if in a true concert with such

concert-hall staples, as microphones, lights, and applause. Even though the singers' voices are not spectacular, the audience

has known that it's all for fun and responds anyway. And in the

end, everyone would like to be a rock star. Karaoke is as close as many people will get to fame and stardom, but this is not the only reason for its enduring popularity.

[3]

There is another, more obvious reason why karaoke is so popular and singing in public is such fun. The average person allows his or her singing to be heard only in the shower or in the car as the radio plays. Karaoke, by contrast, allows the average person the opportunity to share that ordinarily solitary

experience with other people. In lieu of how good or bad their voices are, people can experience the sheer joy of music with

63. For the sake of logic and coherence, Sentence 2 should be placed:
   A. where it is now.
   B. after Sentence 3.
   C. after Sentence 4.
   D. after Sentence 5.

64. F. NO CHANGE
    G. Having looked
    H. To look
    J. Look

65. A. NO CHANGE
    B. restaurants which
    C. restaurants,
    D. restaurants but

66. F. NO CHANGE
    G. staples:
    H. staples
    J. staples;

67. A. NO CHANGE
    B. is knowing
    C. knew
    D. knows

68. Given that all the choices are true, which one would most effectively conclude this paragraph while leading into the main focus of the next paragraph?
    F. NO CHANGE
    G. This is why AudioSynTrac and Numark Electronics were so successful in debuting the first sing-along tapes and equipment back in the 1970s.
    H. Japan's lasting influence on karaoke is obvious all the way down to its name—the Japanese word karaoke translates roughly to "empty orchestra."
    J. Singing in front of people is more fun for many people than singing in the shower or in the car.

69. A. NO CHANGE
    B. furthermore,
    C. moreover,
    D. as a result,

70. F. NO CHANGE
    G. Regardless of
    H. However
    J. Because of

GO ON TO THE NEXT PAGE.

others, whose singing is mostly a private affair as well, through
$\overline{71}$
karaoke.

[4]

The effect karaoke has on people may also provide an

explanation for its popularity: It helps bring people who are

ordinarily shy out of their shells. [72] Karaoke helps them

overcome stage fright, build their self-confidence, and conquer

their fears. The singers may feel nervous or silly if they first take
$\overline{73}$
the stage, but when the audience breaks out into applause, the

singers are sure to feel rewarded.

[5]

Whatever the reason, karaoke continues to grow in

popularity. Last year, karaoke made no less than $7 billion in
$\overline{74}$
profit in Japan. Many dismiss it as a fad, but as long as karaoke

is fun and leaves people feeling good, it will not disappear.

71. **A.** NO CHANGE
    B. who
    C. whom
    D. who's

72. If the writer were to delete the clause "who are ordinarily shy" from the preceding sentence, the essay would primarily lose:

    F. a detail that explains why karaoke is so popular in the international community.
    G. a detail meant to indicate that karaoke is popular among those not normally inclined to sing in public.
    H. information that emphasizes the possible psychological benefits of karaoke for the chronically shy.
    J. an indication that karaoke may be used at some future time to help singers overcome stage fright.

73. **A.** NO CHANGE
    B. when
    C. unless
    D. where

74. **F.** NO CHANGE
    G. lesser than
    H. fewer then
    J. few than

> Question 75 asks about the preceding passage as a whole.

75. Upon reviewing notes for this essay, the writer comes across some information and composes the following sentence incorporating that information:

    > While different regions of the United States prefer different artists, the most popular karaoke requests are invariably for country artists, varying from the modern Carrie Underwood to the classic Johnny Cash.

    For the sake of the logic and coherence of this essay, this sentence should be:

    A. placed at the end of Paragraph 3.
    B. placed at the end of Paragraph 4.
    C. placed at the end of Paragraph 5.
    D. NOT added to the essay at all.

END OF TEST 1

STOP! DO NOT TURN THE PAGE UNTIL TOLD TO DO SO.

MATHEMATICS TEST

60 Minutes—60 Questions

DIRECTIONS: Solve each problem, choose the correct answer, and then darken the corresponding oval on your answer sheet.

Do not linger over problems that take too much time. Solve as many as you can; then return to the others in the time you have left for this test.

You are permitted to use a calculator on this test. You may use your calculator for any problems you choose, but some of the problems may best be done without using a calculator.

Note: Unless otherwise stated, all of the following should be assumed:

1. Illustrative figures are NOT necessarily drawn to scale.
2. Geometric figures lie in a plane.
3. The word *line* indicates a straight line.
4. The word *average* indicates arithmetic mean.

---

1. Point *X* is located at –15 on the real number line. If point *Y* is located at –11, what is the midpoint of line segment *XY* ?

    A. –13
    B. –4
    C. –2
    D. 2
    E. 13

DO YOUR FIGURING HERE.

2. Given triangle *CDE* (shown below) with a right angle at point *E*, what is the length of leg *DE* ?

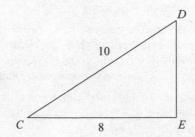

    F. $\sqrt{2}$
    G. 2
    H. 6
    J. $\sqrt{164}$
    K. 16

GO ON TO THE NEXT PAGE.

3. Lucy is studying her ant farm. She needs to approximate the number of ants in the population, and she realizes that the number of ants, N, is close to 50 more than double the volume of the ant farm, V. Which of the formulas below expresses that approximation?

A. $N \approx \dfrac{1}{2}V + 50$

B. $N \approx \dfrac{1}{2}(V + 50)$

C. $N \approx 2V + 50$

D. $N \approx 2(V + 50)$

E. $N \approx V^2 + 50$

DO YOUR FIGURING HERE.

4. Lisa has 5 fiction books and 7 nonfiction books on a table by her front door. As she rushes out the door one day, she takes a book at random. What is the probability that the book she takes is fiction?

F. $\dfrac{1}{5}$

G. $\dfrac{5}{7}$

H. $\dfrac{1}{12}$

J. $\dfrac{5}{12}$

K. $\dfrac{7}{12}$

5. In the spring semester of her math class, Katie's test scores were 108, 81, 79, 99, 85, and 82. What was her average test score in the spring semester?

A. 534
B. 108
C. 89
D. 84
E. 80

GO ON TO THE NEXT PAGE.

6. Given parallel lines *l* and *m*, which of the following choices lists a pair of angles that must be congruent?

DO YOUR FIGURING HERE.

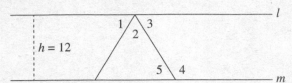

F.   ∠1 and ∠2
G.   ∠1 and ∠3
H.   ∠2 and ∠3
J.   ∠2 and ∠5
K.   ∠3 and ∠5

7. Gregor works as a political intern and receives a monthly paycheck. He spends 20% of his paycheck on rent and deposits the remainder into a savings account. If his deposit is $3,200, how much does he receive as his monthly pay?

A. $ 4,000
B. $ 5,760
C. $ 7,200
D. $ 8,000
E. $17,000

8. Given parallelogram *ABCD* below and parallelogram *EFGH* (not shown) are similar, which of the following statements must be true about the two shapes?

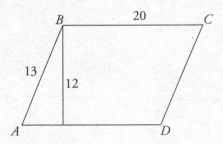

F.   Their areas are equal.
G.   Their perimeters are equal.
H.   Side *AB* is congruent to side *EF*.
J.   Diagonal *AC* is congruent to diagonal *EG*.
K.   Their corresponding angles are congruent.

9. A size 8 dress that usually sells for $60 is on sale for 30% off. Victoria has a store credit card that entitles her to an additional 10% off the reduced price of any item in the store. Excluding sales tax, what is the price Victoria pays for the dress?

A. $22.20
B. $24.75
C. $34.00
D. $36.00
E. $37.80

GO ON TO THE NEXT PAGE.

DO YOUR FIGURING HERE.

10. Erin and Amy are playing poker. At a certain point in the game, Erin has 3 more chips than Amy. On the next hand, Erin wins 4 chips from Amy. Now how many more chips does Erin have than Amy?

    F.   1
    G.   4
    H.   7
    J.   11
    K.   14

11. If $y = 4$, then $|1 - y| = ?$

    A.   −5
    B.   −3
    C.   3
    D.   4
    E.   5

12. $(3a + 2b)(a - b^2)$ is equivalent to:

    F. $4a + b^2$
    G. $3a^2 - 2b^3$
    H. $3a^2 + 2ab + 2b^3$
    J. $3a^2 - 3ab^2 + a^2b^2$
    K. $3a^2 - 3ab^2 + 2ab - 2b^3$

13. For all real values of y, $3 - 2(4 - y) = ?$

    A. $-2y - 9$
    B. $-2y + 8$
    C. $-2y - 1$
    D. $2y - 5$
    E. $2y + 11$

14. Which of the following is equivalent to $(y^3)^8$?

    F. y^{11}
    G. y^{24}
    H. $8y^3$
    J. $8y^{11}$
    K. $24y$

15. If the first day of the year is a Monday, what is the 260th day?

    A.   Monday
    B.   Tuesday
    C.   Wednesday
    D.   Thursday
    E.   Friday

GO ON TO THE NEXT PAGE.

16. If a square has an area of 64 square units, what is the area of the largest circle that can be inscribed inside the square?

   F. 4π
   G. 8π
   H. 16π
   J.   64
   K. 64π

DO YOUR FIGURING HERE.

17. What is the product of the solutions of the expression $x^2 - 5x - 14 = 0$?

   A. -14
   B. -2
   C.   0
   D.   5
   E.   7

18. Factoring the polynomial $x^{12} - 9$ reveals a number of factors for the expression. Which of these is NOT one of the possible factors?

   F. $x^6 + 3$
   G. $x^{12} - 9$
   H. $x^3 + \sqrt{3}$
   J. $x^3 - \sqrt{3}$
   K. $x - \sqrt{3}$

19. What is the value of $\dfrac{2x + 4}{3x}$ when $x = \dfrac{1}{6}$?

   A. $4\dfrac{1}{3}$

   B.   2

   C. $\dfrac{26}{3}$

   D.   12

   E.   24

20. If you drive 60 miles at 90 miles an hour, how many minutes will the trip take you?

   F.   15
   G.   30
   H.   40
   J.   60
   K.   90

GO ON TO THE NEXT PAGE.

DO YOUR FIGURING HERE.

21. The area of a trapezoid is found by multiplying the height by the average of the bases: $A = \frac{1}{2}h(b_1 + b_2)$. Given the side measurements below, what is the area, in square inches, of the trapezoid?

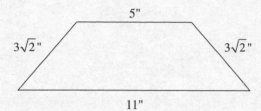

A. $15\sqrt{2}$
B. 22
C. 24
D. $24\sqrt{2}$
E. $30\sqrt{2}$

22. If $x = -\frac{2}{3}$ and $x = \frac{1}{4}$ are the roots of the quadratic equation $ax^2 + bx + c = 0$, then which of the following could represent the two factors of $ax^2 + bx + c$?

F. $(3x + 2)$ and $(4x - 1)$
G. $(3x + 1)$ and $(4x - 2)$
H. $(3x - 1)$ and $(4x + 2)$
J. $(3x - 2)$ and $(4x + 1)$
K. $(3x - 2)$ and $(4x - 1)$

23. In the rhombus below, diagonal $AC = 6$ and diagonal $BD = 8$. What is the length of each of the four sides?

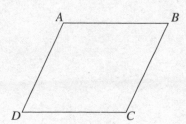

A. $\sqrt{7}$
B. $\sqrt{14}$
C. 5
D. 7
E. 10

GO ON TO THE NEXT PAGE.

DO YOUR FIGURING HERE.

24. A rectangular rug has an area of 80 square feet, and its width is exactly 2 feet shorter than its length. What is the length, in feet, of the rug?

F. 8
G. 10
H. 16
J. 18
K. 36

25. In the Cartesian plane, a line runs through points (1,–5) and (5,10). Which of the following represents the slope of that line?

A. $\dfrac{4}{15}$

B. $\dfrac{4}{5}$

C. 1

D. $\dfrac{5}{4}$

E. $\dfrac{15}{4}$

26. The equation of a circle in the standard (x,y) coordinate plane is given by the equation $(x + 5)^2 + (y - 5)^2 = 5$. What is the center of the circle?

F. $(-\sqrt{5}, \sqrt{5})$
G. $(-5, \quad 5)$
H. $(\sqrt{5}, -\sqrt{5})$
J. $(5, \quad -5)$
K. $(5, \quad 5)$

27. The graph below shows the function $f(x)$ in the coordinate plane. Which of the following choices best describes the *domain* of this function?

(Note: The domain is defined as the set of all values of x for which a function is defined.)

A. {0, 1, 2, 3, 4}
B. {0, 1, 2}
C. $\{x: 0 < x < 2\}$
D. $\{x: 0 < x < 4\}$
E. All real values of x

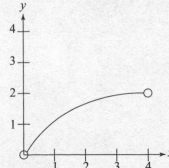

GO ON TO THE NEXT PAGE.

28. Amber decides to graph her office and the nearest coffee shop in the standard (x,y) plane. If her office is at point $(-1,-5)$ and the coffee shop is at point $(3,3)$, what are the coordinates of the point exactly halfway between those of her office and the shop? (You may assume Amber is able to walk a straight line between them.)

F. $(1,-1)$
G. $(1, 4)$
H. $(2,-1)$
J. $(2, 4)$
K. $(2, 0)$

DO YOUR FIGURING HERE.

29. For a chemistry class, Sanjay is doing an experiment that involves periodically heating a container of liquid. The graph below shows the temperature of the liquid at different times during the experiment. What is the average rate of change of temperature (in degrees Celsius per minute) during the times in which Sanjay is applying heat to this container?

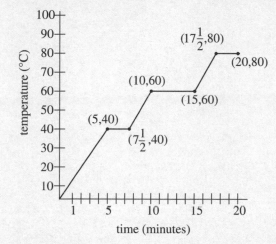

A. 4
B. 5
C. 8
D. 10
E. 20

30. If $\dfrac{a^x}{a^y} = a^5$, for $a \neq 0$, which of the following statements must be true?

F. $x \neq 0$ and $y \neq 0$

G. $x + y = 5$

H. $x - y = 5$

J. $xy - 5$

K. $\dfrac{x}{y} = 5$

GO ON TO THE NEXT PAGE.

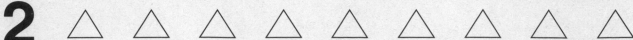
31. What is the slope of the line given by the equation $8 = 3y - 5x$?

    A. -5

    B. $-\dfrac{5}{3}$

    C. $-\dfrac{3}{5}$

    D. $\dfrac{3}{5}$

    E. $\dfrac{5}{3}$

DO YOUR FIGURING HERE.

32. When adding fractions, a useful first step is to find the least common denominator (LCD) of the fractions. What is the LCD for these fractions?

$$\frac{2}{3^2 \times 5}, \frac{13}{5^2 \times 7 \times 11}, \frac{2}{3 \times 11^3}$$

    F. $3 \times 5 \times 7 \times 11$
    G. $3^2 \times 5^2 \times 7 \times 11$
    H. $3^2 \times 5^2 \times 11^3$
    J. $3^2 \times 5^2 \times 7 \times 11^3$
    K. $3^3 \times 5^3 \times 7 \times 11^4$

33. $\dfrac{1}{4} \times \dfrac{2}{5} \times \dfrac{3}{6} \times \dfrac{4}{7} \times \dfrac{5}{8} \times \dfrac{6}{9} \times \dfrac{7}{10} = ?$

    A. $\dfrac{1}{720}$

    B. $\dfrac{1}{360}$

    C. $\dfrac{1}{120}$

    D. $\dfrac{27}{49}$

    E. 1

GO ON TO THE NEXT PAGE.

DO YOUR FIGURING HERE.

34. Dave is in Pikeston and needs to go to Danville, which is about 110 miles due south of Pikeston. From Danville, he'll head east to Rocketville, about 200 miles from Danville. As he sets out on his trip, a plane takes off from the Pikeston airport and flies directly to Rocketville. Approximately how far, in miles, does the plane fly?

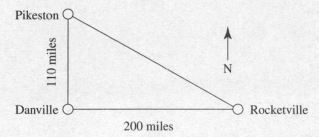

F. 310

G. $\sqrt{310}$

H. $\sqrt{27,900}$

J. $\sqrt{30,000}$

K. $\sqrt{52,100}$

35. The figure below is a pentagon (5-sided figure). Suppose a second pentagon were overlaid on this pentagon. At most, the two figures could have how many points of intersection?

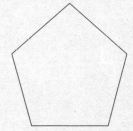

A. 1
B. 2
C. 5
D. 10
E. Infinitely many

36. MicroCorp will hold its annual company picnic next week and will assign planning duties to 3 of its employees. One person selected will reserve a venue, another will arrange catering, and a third will plan activities. There are 10 employees eligible to fulfill these duties, and no employee can be assigned more than one duty. How many different ways are there for duties to be assigned to employees?

F. 7^3

G. 9^3

H. 10^3

J. $9 \times 8 \times 7$

K. $10 \times 9 \times 8$

GO ON TO THE NEXT PAGE.

37. In the (x,y) coordinate plane below, points $P\,(6,2)$ and $Q\,(1,4)$ are two vertices of $\triangle PQR$. If $\angle PQR$ is a right angle, then which of the following could be the coordinates of R ?

DO YOUR FIGURING HERE.

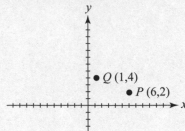

  A. (4,–3)
  B. (3, 0)
  C. (2, 1)
  D. (2, 4)
  E. (3, 9)

38. If $y = 0.25(100 - y)$, then what is the value of y ?

  F. 200
  G. 75
  H. 25
  J. 20
  K. 18

39. If $0° \le x \le 180°$ and $4\cos^2 x = 1$, then $x = $?

  A. 0°
  B. 60°
  C. 90°
  D. 150°
  E. 180°

40. Danielle's living room is a rectangle with the dimensions 16 feet by 18 feet. If she partially covers the bare floor with a circular throw rug with a diameter of 12 feet, what is the approximate area of bare floor, in square feet, that remains exposed?

(Note: Assume the rug lies completely flat and does not touch any wall.)

  F. 113
  G. 144
  H. 175
  J. 288
  K. Cannot be determined without knowing the exact position of the rug

GO ON TO THE NEXT PAGE.

41. In the standard (x,y) coordinate plane, which of the following is the equation of the line perpendicular to the line $y = -2x + 2$ and that passes through the point $(0,-3)$?

A. $y = -2x - 3$

B. $y = -\dfrac{1}{2}x + 2$

C. $y = \dfrac{1}{2}x - 3$

D. $y = \dfrac{1}{2}x + 2$

E. $y = 2x - 3$

42. In the figure given below, what is $\sin \theta$?

F. $\dfrac{1}{2}$

G. $\dfrac{\sqrt{3}}{3}$

H. $\dfrac{\sqrt{3}}{2}$

J. 1

K. $\sqrt{3}$

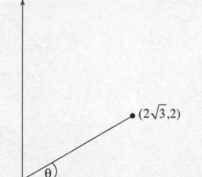

43. If $a = 5$ and $b = -\dfrac{1}{4}$, which of the following expressions will be the greatest?

A. $a + b$
B. $a - b$
C. $a \times b$
D. $a \div b$
E. $|a \times b|$

GO ON TO THE NEXT PAGE.

DO YOUR FIGURING HERE.

44. When $\dfrac{x}{3} - 1 = -\dfrac{13}{12}$, which of the following must be true?

   F. $-12 < x < -3$
   G. $-3 < x < 0$
   H. $0 < x < 3$
   J. $3 < x < 4$
   K. $4 < x$

45. Which choice below is the complete solution set of $|2z - 3| \geq 7$?

   A. $z \geq 5$
   B. $z \leq -2$ or $z \geq 5$
   C. $-5 \leq z \leq 5$
   D. $z \leq -6$ or $z \geq 2$
   E. $z \leq -5$ or $z \geq 2$

46. Which trigonometric function (where defined) is equivalent to

$\dfrac{\sin^2 x}{\cos x \tan x}$?

   F. $\dfrac{\cos x}{\sin^2 x}$

   G. $\dfrac{1}{\cos x}$

   H. $\sin x$

   J. $\dfrac{1}{\sin x}$

   K. $\dfrac{1}{\sin^2 x}$

GO ON TO THE NEXT PAGE.

47. When $a \neq b$, the expression $\dfrac{ax - bx}{4a - 4b} < 0$. Which of the following describes the complete set of x values that make this inequality true?

A. $x = -4$ only

B. $x = 4$ only

C. $x = -\dfrac{1}{4}$ only

D. $x < 0$

E. $x > 0$

48. The volume of a cone, which is derived by treating it as a pyramid with infinitely many lateral faces, is given by the formula $V = \dfrac{1}{3}\pi r^2 h$, where r is the radius of the base, and h is the height. If the radius is halved and the height is doubled, what will be the ratio of the new volume to the old volume?

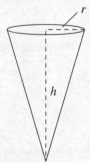

F. 4:1
G. 2:1
H. 1:1
J. 1:2
K. 1:4

GO ON TO THE NEXT PAGE.

DO YOUR FIGURING HERE.

49. Al bikes a trail to the top of a hill and back down. He bikes up the hill in m minutes, then returns twice as quickly downhill on the same trail. What is the total time, in hours, that Al spends biking up the hill and back down?

A. $\dfrac{m}{60}$

B. $\dfrac{m}{40}$

C. $\dfrac{m}{30}$

D. $\dfrac{3m}{2}$

E. $2m$

50. Pippin the guinea pig is running on her wheel when, due to a manufacturing error, the wheel breaks free of its axis. Pippin remains in her wheel, running in a straight line until the wheel has rotated exactly 15 times. If the diameter of the wheel is 10 inches, how many inches has the wheel rolled?

F. 75

G. 150

H. 75π

J. 150π

K. $1,500\pi$

51. A circle is inscribed in a square, as shown below. If x is the distance from the center of the circle to a vertex of the square, then what is the length of the radius of the circle, in terms of x ?

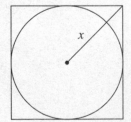

A. $2x$

B. $x\sqrt{2}$

C. x

D. $\dfrac{x\sqrt{2}}{2}$

E. Cannot be determined from the information given

GO ON TO THE NEXT PAGE.

52. A function is defined for x and y such that
$f_{(x,y)} = -2xy + y + x - 4$. So, for $x = 2$ and $y = 3$,
$f_{(2,3)} = -2 \times 2 \times 3 + 3 + 2 - 4 = -12 + 1 = -11$. If x and y
are to be chosen such that $f_{(x,y)} = f_{(y,x)}$, then which of
the following restrictions must be placed on x and y ?

F. $x > 0$ and $y > 0$

G. $x < 0$ and $y < 0$

H. $x = y$

J. $xy < 0$

K. No restrictions are needed.

DO YOUR FIGURING HERE.

53. A pipe of radius 4 feet sends water to two smaller pipes of equal
size. If each of the smaller pipes allows exactly half as much
water to flow as the larger pipe, what is the radius of one of
the smaller pipes?

A. 2

B. 2π

C. $2\sqrt{2}$

D. $4\sqrt{2}$

E. $2\pi\sqrt{2}$

54. The cross-sectional view of a tent is shown below. If the
tent is 6 feet wide at its base, then which of the following
expressions could be used to calculate the height of the tent,
in feet?

F. $\dfrac{3}{\tan 80°}$

G. $3\tan 40°$

H. $\dfrac{3}{\tan 40°}$

J. $6\tan 40°$

K. $3\tan 80°$

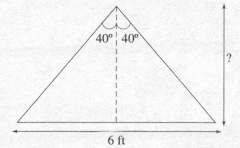

GO ON TO THE NEXT PAGE.

55. Two girls walk home from school. Starting from school, Susan walks north 2 blocks and then west 8 blocks, while Cindy walks east 3 blocks and then south 1 block. Approximately how many blocks apart are the girls' homes?

    A. 7.1
    B. 10.4
    C. 11.4
    D. 12.7
    E. 16.0

DO YOUR FIGURING HERE.

56. For all integer values of a and b such that $a > 0$ and $b < 0$, which of the following must also be an integer?

    F. 3^{a+b}

    G. 3^{a-b}

    H. 3^{ab}

    J. 3^{-a}

    K. $3^{\frac{a}{b}}$

57. If x and y are real numbers and $0 < x < y < \dfrac{y}{x}$, which of the following gives the set of all values which $\dfrac{y}{x}$ could have?

    A.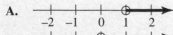

    B.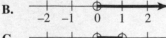

    C.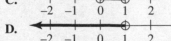

    D.

    E.

GO ON TO THE NEXT PAGE.

58. A circular running track is being built in a fenced-in athletic field 100 feet wide and 150 feet long. If a border of 10 feet is needed between the outside edge of the track and the fence, what is the radius of the largest track that can be built?

    F.   40
    G.   45
    H.   65
    J.   90
    K.   110

DO YOUR FIGURING HERE.

59. If a sphere is cut by two different planes, dividing it into sections, how many sections is it possible to end up with?

    A. 2 only
    B. 2 or 4 only
    C. 3 only
    D. 3 or 4 only
    E. 2, 3, or 4 only

60. For all real values of a and b, the equation $|a - b| = 5$ can be interpreted as "the positive difference of a and b is 5." What is the positive difference between the 2 solutions for a ?

    F. b

    G. $b + 5$

    H. $2b$

    J. $\sqrt{b^2 - 25}$

    K. 10

END OF TEST 2

STOP! DO NOT TURN THE PAGE UNTIL TOLD TO DO SO.

DO NOT RETURN TO A PREVIOUS TEST.

READING TEST

35 Minutes—40 Questions

DIRECTIONS: There are four passages in this test. Each passage is followed by several questions. After reading a passage, choose the best answer to each question and fill in the corresponding oval on your answer document. You may refer to the passages as often as necessary.

Passage I

PROSE FICTION: The following passage is excerpted from the coming-of-age novel *The Year of the Unicorn* by Krista Prouty (©2008 by Krista Prouty).

It was always the same, every Christmas. My sister and I would wake up early, my parents would send us back to bed, and we would instead huddle in my room, discussing which gifts might be waiting for us downstairs. One year it was a bicycle
5 that I wanted, and I can still remember telling my sister exactly what it would look like: pink, with silver streamers and a sparkly silver seat. Eventually we would hear our parents moving around downstairs and we would know that it was almost time. Once the scent of coffee made it to our rooms, we would hurl
10 ourselves downstairs since that signified that our parents were not only awake but caffeinated and ready for gift-giving.

The year that I was nine, and Lily was six, the gift that I had been craving was the Barbie Dream House. Another girl from my school had one and I had been lucky enough to be allowed
15 a glimpse of it after school one day. She was like a princess bestowing largesse; allowing one or two people over after school most days, demonstrating the various clever mechanisms, then sitting quietly, contentedly, while we gazed in wonder for a few minutes. Then, she sent us on our way. I knew that if I could only
20 have a Dream House of my own, my life would be complete. It was a bigger gift than I usually requested but, logically, I felt, that meant I was all the more likely to have my wish granted.

One night I overheard my parents, after they thought Lily and I had gone to bed.

25 "Bill, what are we going to do about Christmas this year?" My mother's voice, quiet and unsettlingly uncertain, came from the kitchen.

"I don't know yet, Mel, but we'll figure something out. We always do, honey."

30 "I know. I just can't help but worry." Whatever my mother said next was drowned out by the running water—she must have been washing up after dinner. I crept back to my bedroom, a little bit troubled by what I had heard but, as is the way of children, soon forgot and went back to Barbie Dream House dreaming.

35 On the Christmas morning in question, Lily and I huddled in my room, waiting for the signal to appear. She wanted a new bike and kept asking me if Santa would get it for her, but all I could think about was my Dream House. Somehow, I had convinced myself that I was certain to get it, that life and the fates
40 could not possibly be cruel enough to deny me this. I could see the wallpaper that was printed on the plastic walls, the darling matching furniture, and the ingenious hand-operated elevator. It would smell like new plastic. I inhaled deeply, imagining myself showing my gift off to friends and foes alike. Instead of
45 new plastic, however, my nostrils quivered to the odor of freshly brewed coffee. It was time.

My eyes still full of the glories I expected, I barreled down the stairs, almost knocking Lily down in my haste. Both of my parents were standing in the kitchen, sipping coffee. I tore past
50 them, even though I knew that they would expect me to stop and wait for them to walk into the living room with me. My longing was simply too exquisite to wait any longer. I burst through the double doors into our living room, words of joy and gratitude ready on my lips, only to find—there was no Dream House. Fran-
55 tically, I began to paw through the boxes under the tree, certain that it had to be there, somewhere, blind to the movement of my parents and sister entering the room behind me, nervous smiles on both my parents' faces. Eventually I was forced to concede that the tree was not somehow harboring a Dream House under
60 its limbs. I looked up at my parents, grief and confusion painted large on my features.

"Hold up a minute, honey. Santa brought you one more gift that wouldn't quite fit under the tree. Bill, go ahead—show her."

As I watched my father head towards a corner where a
65 large blanket was draped over some bulky object, hope flickered back to life a bit. But the size was all wrong, as was the shape. Still smiling anxiously, my father pulled the blanket away from what appeared to be a huge dollhouse. If Barbie's Dream House was sleek and modern, this was awkward and old-fashioned. It
70 had a peaked roof and a patio, with what looked like handmade furniture and wallpaper that looked suspiciously like the paper my parents had hung in Lily's room last fall. Slowly, realization dawned—my father had made it for me.

GO ON TO THE NEXT PAGE.

Looking back, I can only recall the rest of that day hazily,
75 even though the events up until that moment are as clear today
as they were at the time. I remember the feeling of devastation
that I felt, as I realized that the other girls from school would
not, in fact, be blown away by my Christmas gift. I tried to be as
grateful as I could, understanding even then that my father had
80 probably spent countless hours working on the house, but my
disappointment was only too evident. I just couldn't understand
why they had given me this crude approximation instead of my
heart's desire. As an adult, I wish I could go back in time, whis-
per the reason to my younger self, try to be more appreciative
85 of my father's efforts, but that is not the way of the world. I still
have the house, though, and when I have children of my own, I
will tell them the whole story, and I hope they will understand
better than I did.

1. Which of the following statements does NOT describe one of
the narrator's reactions to her Christmas gift?

   A. She is devastated by the realization that the other children
at school will not be impressed by this gift.

   B. She wishes that her parents had bought her a real Barbie
Dream House instead of a handmade one.

   C. She despises the house for its old-fashioned appearance
and lack of modern conveniences, such as an elevator.

   D. She appreciates all the effort her father went to in order to
give her this gift and tries to convey a sense of gratitude.

2. According to the passage, when the narrator smells coffee on
Christmas morning, it means that:

   F. her parents are ready to proceed with the Christmas festivities.

   G. she and her sister should hurry to the kitchen for breakfast.

   H. her father has finally finished preparing her Christmas gift.

   J. it is time to burst into the living room in front of her parents.

3. The narrator would most likely agree with which of the
following statements about owning a Barbie Dream House?

   A. She would become a princess able to bestow largesse on
other children.

   B. She would, at least for the moment, be content with her
life.

   C. It would allow her to appreciate her parents' hard work
and sacrifices.

   D. She would then be able to pass it on to her own children
someday.

4. What is the main point of the first paragraph?

   F. The smell of coffee still reminds the narrator of the Christ-
mases of her childhood.

   G. The narrator's family had a specific ritual that was
followed every Christmas morning.

   H. Most years, the narrator and her sister would hurl themselves into their gifts without warning.

   J. The narrator had once desperately wanted a pink and silver
bicycle.

5. Which of the following statements most accurately expresses
the narrator's feelings when she first sees the gift that her father
made for her?

   A. She is disappointed that it is not the exact gift that she had
hoped to receive.

   B. She gratefully acknowledges the long hours her father
must have put into the gift.

   C. She admires the traditional architecture of the house and
its attractive wallpaper.

   D. She looks forward to showing her new house off to all of
the other girls at school.

6. The narrator's father can most accurately be characterized as:

   F. ignorant and cruel.

   G. thoughtful but lazy.

   H. concerned and hardworking.

   J. caring but inaccessible.

7. It can logically be inferred from the passage that the reason
the narrator was not given the official Barbie Dream House
for Christmas is because:

   A. it is too costly a gift for her parents to buy that year.

   B. she had already been given the pink and silver bicycle that
she wanted.

   C. her father had always wanted to make his daughter a dollhouse.

   D. her parents do not wish for their daughter to be happy.

8. According to the passage, the reason the narrator hopes to
someday tell the children the story of her dollhouse is that she:

   F. wants them to be able to impress the other children at
school as she once did.

   G. knows that, by that time, it is likely to be worth a great
deal of money.

   H. remembers how much she appreciated the gift when it was
given to her.

   J. hopes that they will be better able to understand the meaning behind the gift than she was.

GO ON TO THE NEXT PAGE.

9. A reasonable conclusion that the narrator draws regarding her dollhouse is that:

A. it is far more beautiful than was the plastic Barbie Dream House that she had initially desired.

B. without an elevator, it is less valuable than it would otherwise have been.

C. it was given to her with the intention that she keep it to pass on to her own children someday.

D. constructing it must have been time-consuming and labor-intensive.

10. The main point of the last paragraph is that:

F. the narrator would have been much happier if she had been given a Barbie Dream House.

G. it is not fair to give one child a long-desired gift and not give the same to another child.

H. the disappointments suffered in childhood affect people well into adulthood.

J. the passage of time can alter the way events from the past are viewed.

Passage II

SOCIAL SCIENCE: This passage is adapted from T. H. Watkins' *The Great Depression* (©1993, Little, Brown and Co.; Blackside Inc.).

One of the most durable and well regarded of all the New Deal's programs came from President Roosevelt himself, who had his own share of inventiveness. If the president cared about the fate of people, he also cared about the fate of trees, having
5 practiced the art of silviculture on his Hyde Park estate with such enthusiasm that on various official forms he was fond of listing his occupation as "tree farmer." It was in early March, 1933, that he proceeded to bring the two concerns together—enlisting young unemployed men in a kind of volunteer "army" to be put to
10 work in the national forests, national parks, and on other federal public lands. When he went to Congress for authorization of the program, he called the new agency the Civilian Corps Reforestation Youth Rehabilitation Movement, but before sinking under the weight of an acronym like CCRYRM, it was soon changed
15 to the Civilian Conservation Corps (known forever after as the CCC). Congress chose not to handle the details itself. It simply authorized the president to create the program and structure it as he saw fit by executive order; it was to last two years. Responsibility was divided up among the Labor Department, which was
20 to screen and select the enrollees, the War Department, which would house and feed them in their nonworking hours, and the Departments of Agriculture and Interior, which would design and supervise projects in regional and national forests, national parks, and other public lands. The men would be paid $30 a
25 month, anywhere from $23 to $25 of it to be sent to their families.

The CCC officially began on April 5, 1933, calling for an enrollment of 250,000 to be housed in 1,468 camps around the country. The cost for the first year was estimated at $500 million. The men had to be US citizens between the ages of seventeen
30 and twenty-seven (later, twenty-four), out of school, out of work, capable of physical labor, over 60 inches but under 78 inches in height, more than 107 pounds in weight, and had to possess no fewer than "three serviceable natural masticating teeth above and below." They would serve terms of no more than nine months
35 so that as many as possible could be accommodated over the course of time.

Among the earliest enrollees were some veterans who had returned to Washington, setting up camp and demanding payment of their bonuses for service during the war. While making
40 it clear that he opposed the payments on economic grounds, FDR provided tents, showers, mess halls, and latrines, and, waiving the age restriction for them, invited the members of this new Bonus Army to join his new agency. What was more, Eleanor Roosevelt dropped by one rainy day for a visit, slogging through
45 ankle-deep mud to meet and talk with the men. "Hoover sent the army," said one veteran of the previous summer's BEF disaster, "Roosevelt sent his wife." When it became clear that no bonus would be forthcoming, about twenty-five hundred of the men took Roosevelt up on his offer and joined the CCC.

50 In the summer of 1934, Roosevelt expanded the size of the CCC to 350,000 and would raise it to 500,000 in 1935. Congress continued to reauthorize it faithfully over the next seven years, and by the time it was closed out in 1942, the CCC had put more than three million young "soil soldiers" to work. In the national
55 forests alone they built 3,470 fire towers, installed 65,100 miles of telephone lines, scraped and graded thousands of fire breaks, roads, and trails, and built 97,000 miles of truck trails and roads, spent 4.1 million man-hours fighting fires, and cut down and hauled out millions of diseased trees and planted more than 1.3
60 billion young trees in the first major reforestation campaign in the country's history. For the National Park Service, they built roads, campgrounds, bridges, and recreation and administration facilities; for the Biological Survey (a predecessor of today's Fish and Wildlife Service), they conducted wildlife surveys
65 and improved wildlife refuge lands; and for the Army Corps of Engineers, they built flood control projects in West Virginia, Vermont, and New York State.

In return, the CCC, at its best, took at least some young men out of the urban tangle of hopelessness where so many resided,
70 introduced them to the intricacies and healing joy of the outdoors, and clothed and fed them better than many had been for years. Moreover, the program taught more than a hundred thousand to read and write, passed out twenty-five thousand eighth-grade diplomas and five thousand high-school diplomas, gave struc-
75 ture and discipline to lives that had experienced little of either, strengthened bodies and minds, and for many provided a dose of self-esteem they had never known.

GO ON TO THE NEXT PAGE.

11. The main idea of the passage is that:

   A. the CCC forced unemployed young men to work in the national forests, national parks, and on other federal public lands for no payment or bonus.

   B. it was only after President Roosevelt created the CCC that veterans had suitable employment during the Great Depression.

   C. research into the history of the New Deal shows that the idea for the CCC came from Congress.

   D. among the programs of the New Deal, the CCC employed young men to build public works projects on public lands in return for modest wages, food, clothing, and some education.

12. The main idea of the third paragraph (lines 37–49) is that:

   F. President Hoover had dispatched the army to meet with disgruntled veterans, but President Roosevelt sent his wife, Eleanor, to meet with the Bonus Army.

   G. when they realized President Roosevelt would not pay the bonus, many veterans abandoned the Bonus Army and accepted his invitation to join the CCC.

   H. President Roosevelt supplied shelter and food to the veterans before paying the bonus the veterans demanded.

   J. many of the veterans were above the age requirement of the CCC.

13. As it is used in line 7 to describe President Roosevelt, the term *tree farmer* most nearly means that Roosevelt:

   A. had supported his family by growing trees before he entered politics.

   B. believed in an agrarian economy over urban industrialization.

   C. continued his successful business selling trees while in office.

   D. had a great interest in trees and knew a good deal about them.

14. According to the passage, which of the following was a project the CCC performed for the National Park Service?

   F. Building fire towers

   G. Building campground facilities

   H. Installing telephone lines

   J. Conducting wildlife surveys

15. According to the passage, which of the following statements is true about the CCC?

   A. The agency provided enrollees with academic instruction.

   B. The agency provided enrollees with urban job training.

   C. The agency accepted only men with six teeth.

   D. The agency offered courses in nutrition and self-esteem.

16. Information in the fourth paragraph (lines 50–67) makes it clear that the CCC:

   F. was voluntary and therefore did not pay members anything.

   G. ran for more years and employed more men than was originally intended.

   H. employed 4.1 million men.

   J. battled fires in West Virginia, Vermont, and New York.

17. The passage most strongly suggests that before the 1930s, the national forests:

   A. received no federal support or aid for projects to clear diseased trees.

   B. included land reserved for wildlife refuges.

   C. had never undergone a major reforestation campaign.

   D. experienced more floods than forest fires.

18. According to the passage, when did the CCC change its name?

   F. After President Roosevelt received authorization from Congress

   G. After Congress protested that CCRYRM was too difficult to say

   H. In the same year the size expanded to 500,000 men

   J. After the Bonus Army disbanded

19. The passage states that the same year the CCC was authorized enrollees had to be:

   A. over 78 inches in height.

   B. in school.

   C. between the ages of seventeen and twenty-seven.

   D. between the ages of seventeen and twenty-four.

20. According to the passage, CCC programs in national parks and forests were:

   F. conducted far from where the members were fed and housed.

   G. under the control of the Departments of Agriculture and the Interior.

   H. supervised by the Labor Department.

   J. minimum-wage jobs.

GO ON TO THE NEXT PAGE.

Passage III

HUMANITIES: This passage is adapted from John Gattuso, ed., *Native America* (©1993, Houghton Mifflin Co.).

Northwest natives are carvers by tradition, but it was the natives of the far north, in what is now British Columbia and Alaska, who first carved totem poles. The history of these fascinating works is surprisingly brief, for it wasn't until the mid-18th
5 century, when European explorers first encountered these remote tribes, that the unique sculptures began to appear. Although the natives were already expert carvers of canoes, tools, longhouses, and furniture, they lacked the iron tools necessary to fell a massive tree in one piece and carve its entire length.

10 With the iron axes they got in trade for their baskets, boxes, and pelts, the coastal tribes of the far north could take advantage of the trees that grew so tall and straight in their wet climate. Initially, the poles were made to stand against the front of a house, with figures facing out and a door cut through the base, so all
15 would enter the house through the pole. In this case, the totem pole functioned as a family crest, recounting genealogies, stories, or legends that in some way identified the owner. Towards the end of the 19th century, the poles stood free on the beach or in the village outside the carvers' homes. Some villages were virtual
20 forests of dozens, sometimes hundreds, of poles.

The family that carved the pole gave a potlatch with feasting, games, and much gift-giving. The guests, in return, raised the pole. These gatherings were costly and required a great deal of preparation and participation. The custom frustrated whites
25 trying to "civilize" the Indians, especially missionaries who solved the problem by knocking the poles down. Employers, too, complained that their Indian workers were unreliable when a pole was being carved or a potlatch planned. Eventually, both the Canadian and United States governments banned potlatches,
30 and pole carving nearly died out. The ban was lifted in the 1950s.

The Tlingit, on the southeastern coast of Alaska, and the Haidas and Tsimshian of western Canada are known for their pole carving. On a tour in 1899, a group of Seattle businessmen visited the Tlingit village of Tongas and, finding no one there, took
35 one of the poles. They erected it in Seattle where, at a towering 50 ft., it became one of the city's most distinctive monuments. In 1938, Tlingit carvers copied the pole after the original was destroyed by fire, and it remains in Pioneer Square today.

Poles serve the important purpose of recording the lore of
40 a clan, much as a book would. The top figure on the pole identifies the owner's clan, and succeeding characters (read from top to bottom) tell their stories. Raven, the trickster, might tell the story of how he fooled the Creator into giving him the sun, or Frog might tell how he wooed a human woman. With slight
45 variations between villages, everyone knew these stories, and

potlatch guests dramatized them at the pole-raising with masks, drumming, and songs. And so the legends were preserved from one generation to the next.

There is a story behind almost every image on the pole. For
50 example, if an animal had the power to transform itself into other beings, the carver would portray it in all its forms. If Raven were sometimes bird, sometimes human, he would be carved with both wings and limbs, or have a human face with a raven's beak. Other images are used to describe the spirits' special abilities.
55 Eyes are frequently used to suggest acuteness or skill. So, for example, if an eye appears in an animal's ear, it might indicate that that animal has a sharp sense of hearing. And human figures in unexpected places, like an ear or nose, might mean that the animal has great powers.

60 Learning to read totem poles is like learning to read a language. They speak of history, mythology, social structure, and spirituality. They serve many purposes and continue to be carved by the descendants of the original carvers.

Today, Haida, Tlingit, Tsimshian, Kwakiutl and other na-
65 tive craftsmen carve, predominantly for the tourist trade, small "souvenir" totem poles in wood and black slate (or argillite). They also carve extraordinarily beautiful masks, effigies, boxes, house posts, and fixtures….

21. Which of the following statements best expresses the main idea of the passage?

A. Many Native American tribes created totem poles with meaningful symbols, but these poles were less important than the canoes carved before the mid-18th century.

B. Although the Tlingit village was deserted, the Seattle businessmen who took the totem pole were not right to take it without permission.

C. The history of totem pole carving dates back to only the mid-18th-century, but these poles have played an important role in Native American culture since that time.

D. The ban issued by the Canadian and United States governments against potlatches was lifted in the 1950s, but interest in totem-pole carving had diminished by that time.

22. Which of the following questions is NOT answered in the passage?

F. In terms of geographical region, which were the first groups to carve totem poles?

G. What is the tallest totem pole in North America?

H. What is the predominant use of the small totem poles carved today?

J. What prevented Native American tribes from carving totem poles before the 18th century?

GO ON TO THE NEXT PAGE.

23. The passage suggests that one of the main purposes of totem poles is the way in which they:

A. demonstrate the artistic skill of the carvers.
B. function as landmarks in major North American cities.
C. document the history and mythology of various clans.
D. complement the festivities of the potlatch.

24. The main function of the sixth paragraph (lines 49–59) is to:

F. identify the origins of the stories behind every image on a totem pole.
G. describe and explain some of the images that might appear on a totem pole.
H. contrast the images on the totem poles of the Northwest natives with those of British Columbia and Alaska.
J. explain the role of the Raven in Native American mythology.

25. All of the following are used in the passage as illustrations of the role totem poles play in Native American culture EXCEPT the:

A. function of the top figure on the pole.
B. descriptions of the Raven and Frog as characters on the pole.
C. reference to the popularity of totem poles in the tourist industries of many tribes.
D. placement of the Tlingit totem pole in Seattle's Pioneer Square.

26. The second paragraph (lines 10–20) establishes all of the following about the totem poles carved by the coastal tribes of the far north EXCEPT that they were:

F. initially used as the entryways of houses.
G. fashioned from tall, straight trees.
H. used to identify the owners of the poles.
J. produced only by clans with family crests.

27. One of the main points of the fifth paragraph (lines 39–48) is that the various characters on a totem pole are meant to represent:

A. the owner of the totem pole.
B. the lore of the owner's clan.
C. Raven, the trickster, fooling the Creator.
D. Frog wooing a human woman.

28. According to the passage, which of the following places is home to the Tlingit?

F. Seattle
G. Western Canada
H. Pioneer Square
J. Alaska

29. The author most likely includes the information in lines 60–63 to suggest that:

A. totem poles are notable for reasons beyond physical beauty.
B. totem poles have replaced books for Native American tribes.
C. Native American tribes have no spoken or written language.
D. the descendants of the original carvers of totem poles carve copies of older poles.

30. Which of the following words best describes the attitude of the employers referred to in the third paragraph (lines 21–30) in reaction to potlatches?

F. Patient
G. Accepting
H. Irritated
J. Civilized

GO ON TO THE NEXT PAGE.

Passage IV

NATURAL SCIENCE: This passage is adapted from the article "The Pioneer Mission to Venus" by Janet G. Luhmann, James B. Pollack, and Lawrence Colin (©1994, Scientific American).

Venus is sometimes referred to as the Earth's "twin" because it resembles the Earth in size and in distance from the sun. Over its 14 years of operation, the National Aeronautics and Space Administration's *Pioneer Venus* mission revealed that the rela-
5 tion between the two worlds is more analogous to Dr. Jekyll and Mr. Hyde. The surface of Venus bakes under a dense carbon dioxide atmosphere, the overlying clouds consist of noxious sulfuric acid, and the planet's lack of a magnetic field exposes the upper atmosphere to the continuous hail of charged particles
10 from the sun. Our opportunity to explore the hostile Venusian environment came to an abrupt close in October 1992, when the *Pioneer Venus Orbiter* burned up like a meteor in the thick Venusian atmosphere. The craft's demise marked the end of an era for the U.S. space program; in the present climate of fiscal
15 austerity, there is no telling when humans will next get a good look at the earth's nearest planetary neighbor.

The information gleaned by *Pioneer Venus* complements the well-publicized radar images recently sent back by the *Magellan* spacecraft. *Magellan* concentrated on studies of Venus's surface
20 geology and interior structure. *Pioneer Venus*, in comparison, gathered data on the composition and dynamics of the planet's atmosphere and interplanetary surroundings. These findings illustrate how seemingly small differences in physical conditions have sent Venus and the Earth hurtling down very different evo-
25 lutionary paths. Such knowledge will help scientists intelligently evaluate how human activity may be changing the environment on the Earth.

Well before the arrival of *Pioneer Venus*, astronomers had learned that Venus does not live up to its image as Earth's near-
30 twin. Whereas Earth maintains conditions ideal for liquid water and life, Venus's surface temperature of 450 degrees Celsius is hotter than the melting point of lead. Atmospheric pressure at the ground is some 93 times that at sea level on Earth.

Even aside from the heat and the pressure, the air on Venus
35 would be utterly unbreathable to humans. The Earth's atmosphere is about 78 percent nitrogen and 21 percent oxygen. Venus's much thicker atmosphere, in contrast, is composed almost entirely of carbon dioxide. Nitrogen, the next most abundant gas makes up only about 3.5 percent of the gas molecules. Both planets
40 possess about the same amount of gaseous nitrogen, but Venus's atmosphere contains some 30,000 times as much carbon dioxide as does Earth's. In fact, Earth does hold a quantity of carbon dioxide comparable to that in the Venusian atmosphere. On Earth, however, the carbon dioxide is locked away in carbonate
45 rocks, not in gaseous form in the air. The crucial distinction is responsible for many of the drastic environmental differences that exist between the two planets.

The large *Pioneer Venus* atmospheric probe carried a mass spectrometer and gas chromatograph, devices that measured
50 the exact composition of the atmosphere of Venus. One of the most stunning aspects of the Venusian atmosphere is that it is extremely dry. It possesses only a hundred thousandth as much water as Earth has in its oceans. If all of Venus's water could somehow be condensed onto the surface, it would make a global
55 puddle only a couple of centimeters deep.

Unlike Earth, Venus harbors little if any molecular oxygen in its lower atmosphere. The abundant oxygen in the earth's atmosphere is a by-product of photosynthesis by plants; if not for the activity of living things, Earth's atmosphere also would
60 be oxygen poor. The atmosphere of Venus is far richer than the earth's in sulfur-containing gases, primarily sulfur dioxide. On Earth, rain efficiently removes similar sulfur gases from the atmosphere.

Pioneer Venus revealed other ways in which Venus is more
65 primordial than Earth. Venus's atmosphere contains higher concentrations of inert, or noble, gases—especially neon and isotopes of argon—that have been present since the time the planets were born. This difference suggests that Venus has held on to a far greater fraction of its earliest atmosphere. Much of
70 Earth's primitive atmosphere may have been stripped away and lost into space when our world was struck by a Mars-size body. Many planetary scientists now think the moon formed out of the cloud of debris that resulted from such a gigantic impact.

31. With regard to the possibility of returning to the planet Venus, information presented in the passage makes it clear that the author is:

A. cheerful and optimistic.
B. sarcastic and contentious.
C. doubtful and pragmatic.
D. uncertain and withdrawn.

32. Which of the following statements most accurately summarizes how the passage characterizes the state of scientific knowledge about Venus before the *Pioneer* mission?

F. The scientific community was hesitant to return to Venus after an earlier mission had ended in disaster.
G. Scientists saw Earth and Venus as near polar opposites in atmospheric conditions.
H. The common belief that Earth and Venus were "twins" had been eroding under the weight of scientific evidence.
J. Scientists knew little about the planet Venus because they were more interested in other planets.

GO ON TO THE NEXT PAGE.

33. Based on the passage, discoveries made in which two areas of study have caused scientists to re-evaluate their theories about Earth and Venus?

    A. Water content and bedrock composition
    B. Sulfuric gases and photosynthesis
    C. Carbon dioxide and climate change
    D. Atmosphere and surface temperature

34. The main point of the second paragraph (lines 17–27) is to:

    F. account for the failure of the *Magellan* mission and to show the superiority of the *Pioneer* mission.
    G. suggest that information from both the *Magellan* and *Pioneer* missions can bring the scientific community to a deeper understanding of Venus.
    H. show that the *Magellan* had sent back information regarding the physical characteristics while the *Pioneer* had not.
    J. hypothesize that the findings of the *Pioneer* mission will help scientists to approach problems more intelligently.

35. The passage indicates that if humans were to attempt to live on the planet Venus, survival would not be possible because:

    A. of the mistaken belief that Venus and Earth are "twin" planets.
    B. carbon dioxide is locked away in bicarbonate rocks, not in gaseous form.
    C. the atmospheric pressure, heat, and air are not suitable for human life.
    D. all of the water on Venus is condensed onto the surface.

36. According to the passage, some evidence gained before the *Pioneer Venus* mission suggesting that Earth and Venus are not near-twins stated that:

    F. Venus produces no lead on or underneath its surface.
    G. Earth was found to be much farther from the sun than was previously thought.
    H. the atmosphere of Venus contains 78 percent nitrogen and 21 percent oxygen.
    J. the surface temperature of Venus is 450 degrees Celsius and thus unlivable for humans.

37. As it is used in line 56, the word *harbors* most nearly means:

    A. sails.
    B. hides.
    C. holds.
    D. soaks.

38. According to the passage, "primordial" describes planets that:

    F. are oxygen-poor due to a lack of activity by living things.
    G. are not hospitable to humans because they have thick atmospheres and high surface temperatures.
    H. have preserved many of the characteristics present when the planets were formed.
    J. have been struck by large bodies which have altered the planets' atmospheres.

39. It can reasonably be inferred that the "activity of living things" described in line 59 directly refers to organisms on Earth that:

    A. produce oxygen by their own natural processes and influence the contents of Earth's atmosphere.
    B. remove sulfur gases from the atmosphere during heavy rainfall.
    C. lock away carbon dioxide in carbonate rocks and maintain a reserve of the gas.
    D. could easily live in oppressive atmospheres similar to the atmosphere of Venus.

40. According to the passage, the *Pioneer Venus* mission to Venus involved investigating details relating to the planet's:

    F. surface geology and interior structure.
    G. atmosphere as it has been changed by the influence of photosynthesis.
    H. similarities to the planet Earth.
    J. atmospheric contents.

END OF TEST 3

STOP! DO NOT TURN THE PAGE UNTIL TOLD TO DO SO.

DO NOT RETURN TO A PREVIOUS TEST.

SCIENCE TEST

35 Minutes–40 Questions

DIRECTIONS: There are seven passages in this test. Each passage is followed by several questions. After reading a passage, choose the best answer to each question and fill in the corresponding oval on your answer document. You may refer to the passages as often as necessary.

You are NOT permitted to use a calculator on this test.

Passage I

Metallic *alloys*, solid mixtures of metal, are useful for coin production when they contain a high percentage of zinc. When electric current is applied to zinc in the presence of precious metal solutions of *silver nitrate*, *copper sulfate*, or *potassium gold cyanide*, the precious metals *plate* (form a coating) on the zinc surface.

*   Silver nitrate, formed when silver dissolves in *nitric acid*, reacts with zinc to form solid silver and *zinc nitrate*.
*   Copper sulfate, formed when copper dissolves in *sulfuric acid*, reacts with zinc to form solid copper and *zinc sulfate*.
*   Potassium gold cyanide contains reactive gold ions.

A chemist performed experiments on precious metal plating.

Experiment 1

The chemist obtained 4 coin-like samples of a high percentage zinc alloy. All samples were circular, had a radius of 1 cm, and had the same thickness. The mass of each coin was recorded. Each coin was wired via a battery to a strip of either pure silver or copper metal. Coins wired to silver were placed in dilute nitric acid and coins wired to copper were placed in dilute sulfuric acid. Electric current of either 1,000 milliamperes (mA) or 2,000 mA was applied for 30 minutes to each sample. The coins were removed and the increase in mass from precious metal plating was recorded in milligrams. Results of the experiment are shown in Table 1.

	Table 1		
	Precious metal solution		Increased mass from plating (mg)
Coin sample	Identity	Electric current (mA)	
I	silver nitrate	1,000	2.0
II	silver nitrate	2,000	4.0
III	copper sulfate	1,000	1.2
IV	copper sulfate	2,000	2.4

Experiment 2

The chemist completely dissolved equal amounts of pure silver in 4 beakers of nitric acid. He then placed equivalent coin-like samples of zinc into the beakers for different lengths of time measured in minutes (min). The coin surfaces developed a silver metal coating without any electric current applied. The concentrations of silver coating on the coin and zinc nitrate in the surrounding solution were determined in parts per billion (ppb) and recorded in Table 2.

	Table 2		
Coin sample	Time (min)	Silver coating concentration (ppb)	Zinc nitrate concentration (ppb)
V	5	75	30
VI	15	125	55
VII	30	200	75
VIII	60	500	85

1. A comparison of the results for coin samples II and IV supports the hypothesis that zinc is plated more extensively when exposed to:

    A. silver nitrate and a current of 1,000 mA than silver nitrate and a current of 2,000 mA.
    B. copper sulfate and a current of 1,000 mA than copper sulfate and a current of 2,000 mA.
    C. silver nitrate than when exposed to copper sulfate.
    D. copper sulfate than when exposed to silver nitrate.

GO ON TO THE NEXT PAGE.

2. If the chemist were to repeat Experiment 1, but compress each coin sample to a radius of 0.5 cm to decrease the surface area exposed to the surrounding solution, how would the mass of precious metal plated most likely be affected?

F. The mass of precious metal plated would decrease for all coin samples.
G. The mass of precious metal plated would decrease for coin samples I and III and increase for coin samples II and IV.
H. The mass of precious metal plated would remain constant for all coin samples.
J. The mass of precious metal plated would increase for all coin samples.

3. According to the information in the passage, a zinc alloy coin sample exposed to which of the following conditions would result in the greatest concentration of zinc nitrate?

A. 10 minutes in a solution with a high initial concentration of silver nitrate
B. 10 minutes in a solution with a low initial concentration of silver nitrate
C. 6 minutes in a solution with a high initial concentration of silver nitrate
D. 6 minutes in a solution with a low initial concentration of silver nitrate

4. In Experiment 1, if the chemist had applied 1,580 mA to a 1 cm radius zinc alloy coin sample in a copper sulfate solution, approximately how much copper would have plated after 30 minutes?

F. 0.6 mg
G. 1.1 mg
H. 1.9 mg
J. 4.6 mg

5. In Experiment 1, which of the following variables was the same for all 4 zinc alloy coin sample trials?

A. Change in mass from plating
B. Electric current applied
C. Type of precious metal solution used
D. Initial radius of the sample

6. According to the passage, if a chemist wants to study the effect of plating zinc alloys with silver, the chemist should monitor the concentration of which of the following substances in the surrounding solution?

F. Potassium gold cyanide
G. Zinc nitrate
H. Copper sulfate
J. Sulfuric acid

GO ON TO THE NEXT PAGE.

Passage II

Organic compounds are molecules that frequently contain carbon (C), hydrogen (H), and oxygen (O) joined together by covalent bonds (symbolized by straight lines in chemical notation). As the number of bonds to oxygen atoms increases in a carbon chain, the overall molecule is increasingly oxidized. For example, aldehydes are more oxidized than alcohols, which are more oxidized than alkanes as shown in Table 1. The melting points of these compounds are listed in Table 2, and their *viscosities* (resistance to flow, or "stickiness,") are listed in Table 3.

Table 1

Carbons in the chain	Name prefix	Structure		
		alkane (suffix -ane)	alcohol (suffix -anol)	aldehyde (suffix -analdehyde)
4	but-	[structure]	[structure]	[structure]
5	pent-	[structure]	[structure]	[structure]
6	hex-	[structure]	[structure]	[structure]
7	hept-	[structure]	[structure]	[structure]
8	oct-	[structure]	[structure]	[structure]

Table 2

Carbons in the chain	Melting point (K)		
	alkane	alcohol	aldehyde
4	135	183	174
5	143	194	213
6	178	221	217
7	182	239	231
8	216	257	285

Table 3

Carbons in the chain	Viscosity (cP)		
	alkane	alcohol	aldehyde
4	0.01	3.0	0.4
5	0.24	5.1	0.5
6	0.29	5.4	0.8
7	0.39	5.8	1.0
8	0.54	8.4	1.2

GO ON TO THE NEXT PAGE.

7. Which organic compounds in Table 2 are solids at 215 K ?

   A. All alkanes, alcohols, and aldehydes with 5 carbons or fewer.
   B. Alcohols and aldehydes with 6 or more carbons and octane.
   C. The 4- and 5-carbon alcohols and aldehydes, and all alkanes with 7 or fewer carbons.
   D. The 5-carbon pentane and pentanol compounds and the 4-carbon butane, butanol, and butanaldehyde.

8. According to Tables 1 and 3, which organic compound has the highest viscosity?

   F. Octanol
   G. Octanaldehyde
   H. Hexanol
   J. Butane

9. According to Table 3, how do the different types of 5-carbon molecules differ with respect to their viscosity?

   A. The alkane has a higher viscosity than the aldehyde, and the aldehyde has a higher viscosity than the alcohol.
   B. The alkane has a higher viscosity than the alcohol, and the alcohol has a higher viscosity than the aldehyde.
   C. The alcohol has a higher viscosity than the alkane, and the alkane has a higher viscosity than the aldehyde.
   D. The alcohol has a higher viscosity than the aldehyde, and the aldehyde has a higher viscosity than the alkane.

10. For each type of organic compound, what is the relationship between the length of the carbon chain to the melting point and viscosity? As the number of carbons in the chain increases, the melting point:

    F. decreases, and the viscosity decreases.
    G. increases, and the viscosity increases.
    H. increases, but the viscosity decreases.
    J. decreases, but the viscosity increases.

11. According to Table 2, the difference in melting point between an alkane and an alcohol with the same number of carbons is approximately how much?

    A. 25 K
    B. 35 K
    C. 45 K
    D. 65 K

GO ON TO THE NEXT PAGE.

Passage III

A mass suspended by a lightweight thread and swinging back and forth approximates the motion of a *simple gravity pendulum*, a system in which gravity is the only force acting on the mass, causing an acceleration of 9.8 m/sec². The time to complete one cycle of swinging back and forth is the *period* and is inversely related to gravitational acceleration.

Using the same type and length of thread, 2 cubes were suspended, lifted to the same starting angle, and let go. The amount of time required for each pendulum to complete one swinging cycle (1 period) was recorded with a timer capable of reading to the nearest 0.01 sec. The measured times were used to calculate acceleration.

Experiment 1

A cube of lead (11.3 grams) and a cube of tin (7.4 grams) were suspended from a 0.5 m length of thread. Both cubes had the same length. (Note: A cube's volume is proportional to its length cubed; its surface area is proportional to its length squared.) The cubes were set in motion from a fixed starting angle, and the period for each was recorded.

Table 1		
Trial	Measured period (sec)	
	lead cube	tin cube
1	1.48	1.51
2	1.45	1.47
3	1.46	1.42
4	1.49	1.45
5	1.39	1.53

The average periods were 1.46 sec and 1.48 sec for the lead and tin cubes, respectively. The average accelerations were 9.3 m/sec² for lead and 9.1 m/sec² for tin.

Experiment 2

The same procedures used in Experiment 1 were repeated using a thread length of 1.0 m and the same fixed starting angle. Results were recorded in Table 2.

Table 2		
Trial	Measured period (sec)	
	lead cube	tin cube
6	2.10	2.12
7	2.04	2.06
8	2.05	2.07
9	2.12	2.11
10	2.00	2.10

The average periods were 2.06 sec and 2.09 sec for the lead and tin cubes, respectively. The average accelerations were 9.3 m/sec² for lead and 9.0 m/sec² for tin.

Experiment 3

Given the results of the first 2 experiments, the accuracy of the timer was tested. The procedures of Experiment 1 were repeated using only the lead cube. The trials were recorded on digital video at 100 frames per second. The video was then reviewed to obtain precise measurements of the period for each trial and results are shown in Table 3.

Table 3	
Trial	Measured period (sec)
11	1.47
12	1.42
13	1.49
14	1.50
15	1.46

The average period recorded in Table 3 was 1.47 sec.

12. To demonstrate that a pendulum's acceleration is reduced by drag force from air resistance, which additional experiment can be performed in addition to those in the passage?

   F. The cubes are suspended by 0.5 m and 1 m springs and set in motion by extending the spring 9.8 cm and letting go in a vacuum chamber with no air pressure.
   G. The cubes are suspended by 0.5 m and 1 m threads and set in motion from the same starting angle in a vacuum chamber with no air pressure.
   H. The cubes are suspended by 0.5 m and 1 m springs and set in motion by extending the spring 9.8 cm and letting go in a vacuum chamber at 1 atmosphere of pressure.
   J. The cubes are suspended by 0.5 m and 1 m threads and set in motion from the same starting angle in a vacuum chamber at 1 atmosphere of pressure.

GO ON TO THE NEXT PAGE.

13. In Experiment 1, could a timer that reads to the nearest second be used to obtain similar results, and why?

   A. No, because the period of both pendulums was between 1 and 2 seconds.
   B. No, because the pendulums would have traveled farther in 1 second than they did in 1 period.
   C. Yes, because the period of both pendulums was approximately 1.5 seconds.
   D. Yes, because the pendulums would not have traveled as far in 1 second as they did in 1 period.

14. The results of the experiments indicate that forces other than gravity are acting on the pendulums because the calculated values of acceleration were:

   F. the same for pendulums of different lengths.
   G. the same for cubes of different mass.
   H. lower than the expected 9.8 m/sec^2 from gravity alone.
   J. greater than the expected 9.8 m/sec^2 from gravity alone.

15. Based on the passage, if a tin cube is suspended from a 2.0 m thread and set in motion multiple times from the same starting angle, the average measured period will most likely be:

   A. less than 1.48 sec.
   B. approximately 1.48 sec.
   C. approximately 2.09 sec.
   D. greater than 2.09 sec.

16. In Experiment 2, if an additional trial were conducted using the lead cube, the cube's measured period would most likely be nearest:

   F. 1.90 sec.
   G. 2.05 sec.
   H. 2.15 sec.
   J. 2.20 sec.

17. Experiments 1 and 2 were conducted using lead and tin cubes most likely to determine whether a pendulum's period was altered by the material attached to the string and the cube's:

   A. length.
   B. surface area.
   C. starting angle.
   D. mass.

GO ON TO THE NEXT PAGE.

Passage IV

Accepted classification systems of life do not include *viruses*. Although viruses possess certain features of cellular organisms, including genetic material that codes for making new viral particles, they cannot *replicate* (make copies of) themselves without first infecting a living cell. Biologists agree that viruses originated from genetic material called *nucleic acid*, but it is difficult to prove any single theory regarding how this occurred. Three hypotheses of viral origin are presented here.

Coevolution Hypothesis

Some biologists argue that viruses evolved alongside other organisms over billions of years. They suggest that simple molecules of *ribonucleic acid* (RNA), a *nucleotide* that forms the genetic code for proteins, joined to form more complex sequences. These RNA sequences developed enzyme-like abilities including the ability to self-replicate and insert themselves into other nucleotide sequences. While some RNA sequences became incorporated into membrane-bound cells, others were packaged inside proteins as the first viral particles that could replicate after infecting cellular organisms (see Figure 1).

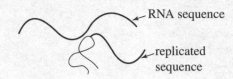

ancestral self-replicating RNA

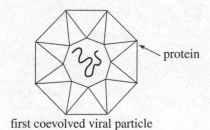

first coevolved viral particle

Figure 1

Cellular Origin Hypothesis

Some biologists claim that nucleotide sequences within *prokaryotic* (non-nucleated) and *eukaryotic* (nucleated) cellular organisms incorporated into a protein coating and escaped from the cell as a viral particle. Initially, DNA or RNA nucleotide sequences gained the code required for other cells to replicate them. Next, these sequences associated with proteins to form an outer *capsid*. Finally, the *virion* (viral particle) became capable of passing through the cell membrane and infecting other cells where it could be replicated. After the initial escape, viruses evolved independently from their initial host and ultimately could infect either prokaryotic or eukaryotic cells.

Regressive Evolution Hypothesis

An alternative explanation of viral origin is that viruses evolved from cellular organisms. Some cellular organisms, particularly certain bacteria, are *obligate intracellular parasites* because they must infect a host cell in order to reproduce. Regressive evolution suggests that some bacterial parasites gradually lost the structures required for survival outside of a cell. The result was a virus particle containing only nucleotides, a capsid (protein coating), and at times an outer membrane or envelope. This would account readily for viruses that contain complex *deoxyribonucleic acid* (DNA) similar to that found in bacteria and other cellular organisms (see Figure 2).

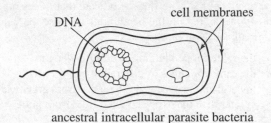

ancestral intracellular parasite bacteria

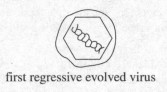

first regressive evolved virus

Figure 2

18. The development of which of the following is addressed in the passage by the Coevolution Hypothesis, but NOT by the Regressive Evolution Hypothesis?

- **F.** Self-replication
- **G.** Capsid
- **H.** Deoxyribonucleic acid
- **J.** Cell membrane transit

19. Supporters of all of the theories presented in the passage would agree with the conclusion that the first viruses:

- **A.** evolved from bacteria.
- **B.** could self-replicate outside a cell.
- **C.** were enclosed within a membrane.
- **D.** contained nucleic acid.

20. The Coevolution Hypothesis does NOT provide an explanation for the earliest virus particles possessing:

- **F.** protein.
- **G.** enzyme-like activity.
- **H.** nucleotides.
- **J.** DNA.

GO ON TO THE NEXT PAGE.

21. If the Cellular Origin Hypothesis is correct, which of the following conclusions can be made about modern T4 DNA viruses, which infect *Escherichia coli* bacteria, and modern PP7 RNA viruses, which infect *Pseudomonas aeruginosa* bacteria?

A. T4 and PP7 are more closely related to each other than to bacteria genetically.

B. T4 and PP7 are only distantly related genetically through a cellular organism.

C. T4 and PP7 both evolved from prokaryotic organisms.

D. T4 and PP7 both evolved from eukaryotic organisms.

22. The discovery of which of the following living organisms would provide the most support for the Regressive Evolution Hypothesis?

F. Extracellular parasites with DNA resembling a known virus

G. Extracellular parasites with unique RNA nucleotide sequences

H. Intracellular parasites with DNA resembling a known virus

J. Intracellular parasites with unique RNA nucleotide sequences

23. Supporters of all the theories presented would agree with which of the following conclusions about the origin of viruses?

A. Viral capsids contain a protein structure similar to the cell walls of modern bacteria.

B. The first viruses did not originate before the first cellular organisms.

C. RNA viruses are more advanced than DNA viruses.

D. The first virus contained DNA and was surrounded by an envelope similar to a cell membrane.

24. Which of the following questions is raised by the Coevolution Hypothesis, but is NOT answered in the passage?

F. Why were some RNA sequences packaged into protein structures and others incorporated into cell structures?

G. Why did obligate intracellular parasites lose their ability to survive outside of cells?

H. How could two different types of cellular organisms account for the origin of viruses?

J. How did virions develop the ability to pass through the cell membrane out of the cell?

GO ON TO THE NEXT PAGE.

Passage V

Wind causes *topsoil deflation*, a type of erosion that is affected by plant and organic cover as well as water content of the soil. Scientists performed 2 experiments using equal-sized fields containing the same volume of soil. The soil samples were primarily a mixture of sand and silt, but differed in the percentage of clay they contained. Soil X was composed of 5% clay and soil Y was composed of 40% clay. Large fans were used to simulate wind. Topsoil deflation was measured in kilograms per hectare (kg/ha) following 10 hours of wind.

Experiment 1

A mixture of compost and straw was used to represent plant and organic cover. The percentage of soil covered with the mixture was considered to approximate an equivalent percentage of natural vegetative cover. One field remained uncovered, and the other fields were covered with different percentages of compost and straw. The topsoil deflation from each field was recorded in Table 1.

Table 1				
Soil	Topsoil deflation (kg/ha) by percentage of organic cover			
	0%	25%	50%	75%
X	105,000	68,000	46,000	20,000
Y	65,000	42,000	28,500	12,000

Experiment 2

Rainfall was simulated using a sprinkler system. Sprinklers were turned on for either 4 hours or 8 hours for fields of each kind of soil. Two additional fields composed of each type of soil were left unwatered. Afterward, soil samples were taken from all of the fields to determine their water content percentage, which was recorded in Table 2. Wind was applied as in Experiment 1 and topsoil deflation for all fields was recorded in Table 3.

Table 2			
Soil	Water content of soil following various sprinkler times		
	0 hours	4 hours	8 hours
X	10%	13%	16%
Y	10%	14%	22%

Table 3			
Soil	Topsoil deflation (kg/ha) following various sprinkler times		
	0 hours	4 hours	8 hours
X	89,250	66,000	14,000
Y	53,400	40,100	10,300

25. According to the results of Experiments 1 and 2, topsoil deflation will be minimized by:

A. decreased organic cover, increased amount of rainfall, and the use of either Soil X or Y as topsoil.
B. decreased organic cover, decreased amount of rainfall, and the use of Soil Y as topsoil.
C. increased organic cover, increased amount of rainfall, and the use of Soil Y as topsoil.
D. increased organic cover, increased amount of rainfall, and the use of Soil X as topsoil.

26. If Experiment 1 were repeated using a soil containing 10% clay with 0% organic cover, which of the following would be the most likely topsoil deflation amount?

F. 110,200 kg/ha
G. 99,800 kg/ha
H. 70,700 kg/ha
J. 60,200 kg/ha

27. To further investigate the effect of water content on erosion from topsoil deflation, the scientists should repeat Experiment:

A. 1, using a different type of topsoil.
B. 1, using plastic covers over the fields.
C. 2, using no sprinklers.
D. 2, using fields exposed to various amounts of rainfall.

28. What assumption in experimental design is most important to consider when applying the findings of Experiment 1 to a practical situation?

F. The quantity of topsoil deflation is independent of the percentage of clay present in the soil.
G. The presence of straw on the soil does not accurately simulate vegetation and organic cover.
H. Air movement from fans provides an accurate simulation of the wind responsible for topsoil deflation.
J. Compost is more effective than water content in the prevention of topsoil erosion.

GO ON TO THE NEXT PAGE.

29. In Experiment 2, the water content in the two soil types was similar after 4 hours of sprinkling, yet the topsoil deflation was significantly different. Which of the following statements provides the best explanation for these findings?

A. Topsoil erosion is independent of the water content found in the soil.

B. Fields are susceptible to topsoil deflation only when water completely evaporates from the topsoil.

C. Soil with a lower percentage of clay is more prone to erosion from topsoil deflation than one with a higher percentage of clay.

D. Water is trapped in the topsoil by wind and this increases the rate of topsoil deflation.

30. If Experiment 2 were repeated with soil containing 10% clay, which of the following values would be expected for water content and topsoil deflation in a field following 8 hours of water sprinkling?

F. Water content of 17%; topsoil deflation of 13,400 kg/ha

G. Water content of 21%; topsoil deflation of 9,700 kg/ha

H. Water content of 15%; topsoil deflation of 10,900 kg/ha

J. Water content of 14%; topsoil deflation of 101,000 kg/ha

GO ON TO THE NEXT PAGE.

Passage VI

The oceans of Earth are exposed to various climates and consequently have different physical properties. Deep oceans can be divided into zones based on temperature gradient and penetration of sunlight. Figure 1 shows the zones of a typical deep-water ocean, the depth of the zone boundaries in meters (m), and the overall pressure at those depths in kilopascals (kPa). Figure 2 shows the water temperature in degrees Celsius (°C) in warmer tropical oceans and cooler temperate oceans at varying depths. Sound waves are used to measure water temperature at depth, and readings from two different ocean regions are recorded in Table 1.

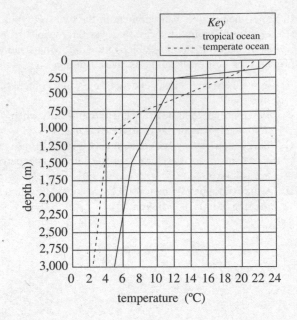

Figure 2

Zone of Ocean			Depth (m)	Total pressure (kPa)
surface			0	101
epipelagic	continental shelf	mixed	100	1,107
			140	1,509
			200	2,112
mesopelagic	thermocline			
	continental rise		1,000	10,153
bathypelagic				
			4,000	4.0×10^4
abyssopelagic	deep water			
	abyss		6,000	6.0×10^4
hadopelagic				

Figure 1

(Note: Figure is NOT drawn to scale)

Table 1			
Total pressure (kPa)	Depth (m)	Ocean temperature (°C)	
		Region 1	Region 2
101	0	24	21
200	9.8	22	20
300	19.8	14	11
400	29.7	11	9
500	39.7	10	8
600	49.6	9	8
700	59.6	7	6
800	69.5	5	3
900	79.5	4	2

GO ON TO THE NEXT PAGE.

31. According to Figure 1, the regions of several ocean zones overlap. Which of the following pairs of ocean zones share part of a common depth range?

A. Bathypelagic and mesopelagic
B. Bathypelagic and epipelagic
C. Epipelagic and thermocline
D. Epipelagic and mesopelagic

32. According to Figure 1, an oceanographic reading taken at a total pressure of 1,200 kPa is most likely from which of the following zones?

F. Abyss
G. Continental rise
H. Mixed
J. Continental shelf

33. According to Figure 2, a sonographic measurement of temperature would be unable to distinguish the difference between tropical and temperate oceans at which of the following depths?

A. 250 m
B. 500 m
C. 625 m
D. 750 m

34. According to Table 1, the relationship between depth and ocean temperature is best described by which of the following statements?

F. The water temperature increased with increasing depth in Region 1 only.
G. The water temperature decreased with increasing depth in Region 1 only.
H. The water temperature increased with increasing depth in Region 2 only.
J. The water temperature decreased with increasing depth in Region 2 only.

35. According to Figure 1 and Table 1, if water temperature measurements were taken at depths greater than 79.5, the total pressure at those depths would most likely:

A. decrease to less than 101 kPa.
B. increase to more than 900 kPa.
C. stay at 900 kPa.
D. increase to 101 kPa.

GO ON TO THE NEXT PAGE.

Passage VII

Although many forms of bacteria are helpful for human health, they can also cause illness and even death from severe infections. *Antibiotics* are a class of medicines used to combat bacterial infections. *Bacteriostatic* activity inhibits bacteria cell division and *bactericidal* activity kills bacterial cells. Both actions eliminate populations of bacteria over time. Several classes of bacteriostatic and bactericidal antibiotics are described in Table 1.

The effectiveness of several antibiotics against a bacterium known to cause common skin infections was tested. Drugs were introduced to the bacterial culture by themselves or in combination with sulfamethoxazole (forming SMX compounds). The effectiveness of these antibiotics at eliminating the responsible bacterium is shown in Figure 1.

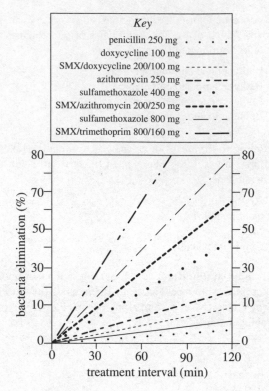

Key

penicillin 250 mg	· · · ·
doxycycline 100 mg	——
SMX/doxycycline 200/100 mg	- - - -
azithromycin 250 mg	▬ ▬ ▬
sulfamethoxazole 400 mg	· · ·
SMX/azithromycin 200/250 mg	▬ · ▬ ·
sulfamethoxazole 800 mg	- · - ·
SMX/trimethoprim 800/160 mg	· ▬ · ▬

Figure 1

Table 1				
Class	Example	Active against	Mechanism	Common uses
β-lactams	ampicillin	some gram-positive and gram-negative bacteria	disrupt cell wall synthesis; bactericidal	respiratory and skin infections
Tetracyclines	doxycycline	atypical gram-indeterminate bacteria	disrupt bacterial mRNA synthesis; mostly bacteriostatic	respiratory and genitourinary infections
Macrolides	azithromycin	gram-positive and atypical bacteria	disrupt bacterial protein synthesis; mostly bacteriostatic	atypical and respiratory infections
Aminoglycosides	gentamicin, streptomycin	gram-negative bacteria	disrupt bacterial protein synthesis; bactericidal	severe systemic infections
Quinolones	ofloxacin, gatifloxacin	broad spectrum of bacteria	disrupt bacterial DNA replication; bactericidal	respiratory, genitourinary, and gastrointestinal infections
Antifolates	sulfamethoxazole, trimethoprim	some gram-positive and gram-negative bacteria	disrupt bacterial DNA and RNA synthesis; mostly bacteriostatic	genitourinary and skin infections

GO ON TO THE NEXT PAGE.

36. According to the information in Table 1 and Figure 1, what can be concluded about the use of sulfamethoxazole as an antibiotic for common skin infections?

 F. Using sulfamethoxazole 800 mg is ineffective as an antibiotic.
 G. Increasing the dosage of sulfamethoxazole decreases its overall effectiveness as an antibiotic.
 H. As an antibiotic, the mechanism of action of sulfamethoxazole is unknown.
 J. Compounding antibiotics with sulfamethoxazole increases their effectiveness against common skin infections.

37. According to Figure 1, if an investigator administered a sulfamethoxazole dose of 600 mg, 20% of the original bacteria would remain after a treatment interval:

 A. greater than 120 min.
 B. between 90 and 120 min.
 C. between 60 and 90 min.
 D. between 30 and 60 min.

38. After treatment of a bacterial culture similar to that in the passage with 250 mg of penicillin for 2 hours, the culture will probably contain:

 F. less bacteria overall, but most will have survived.
 G. less bacteria overall, and most will have been killed.
 H. the same amount of bacteria overall, and most will have survived.
 J. the same amount of bacteria overall, and most will have been killed.

39. Is the statement "antibiotics compounded with sulfamethoxazole are more effective against common skin infections than when administered alone" supported by the information shown in Figure 1, and why?

 A. No, because penicillin is more effective against a common skin infection bacterium than sulfamethoxazole 400 mg.
 B. No, because azithromycin is more effective against a common skin infection bacterium than SMX/azithromycin.
 C. Yes, because sulfamethoxazole 800 mg is more effective against a common skin infection bacterium than SMX/azithromycin.
 D. Yes, because SMX/doxycycline is more effective against a common skin infection bacterium than doxycycline.

40. According to the passage, the most effective antibiotic against bacteria is one that results in the:

 F. lowest percentage of bacterial elimination in the shortest treatment interval.
 G. lowest percentage of bacterial elimination in the longest treatment interval.
 H. greatest percentage of bacterial elimination in the shortest treatment interval.
 J. greatest percentage of bacterial elimination in the longest treatment interval.

END OF TEST 4

STOP! DO NOT RETURN TO ANY OTHER TEST.

DIRECTIONS

This is a test of your writing skills. You will have forty (40) minutes to write an essay. Before you begin planning and writing your essay, read the writing prompt carefully to understand exactly what you are being asked to do. Your essay will be evaluated on the evidence it provides of your ability to express judgments by taking a position on the issue in the writing prompt; to maintain a focus on the topic throughout your essay; to develop a position by using logical reasoning and by supporting your ideas; to organize ideas in a logical way; and to use language clearly and effectively according to the conventions of standard written English.

You may use the unlined pages in this test booklet to plan your essay. These pages will not be scored. *You must write your essay on the lined pages in the answer folder.* Your writing on those lined pages will be scored. You may not need all the lined pages, but to ensure you have enough room to finish, do NOT skip lines. You may write corrections or additions neatly between the lines of your essay, but do NOT write in the margins of the lined pages. *Illegible essays cannot be scored, so you must write (or print) clearly.*

If you finish before time is called, you may review your work. Lay your pencil down immediately when time is called.

DO NOT OPEN THIS BOOK UNTIL YOU ARE TOLD TO DO SO.

Population Growth

Since the Industrial Revolution, the growth rate of Earth's human population has increased dramatically. It took mankind until the 1800s to reach one billion, but only 120 years after that to reach two billion, and less than 40 years after that to reach three billion. We continue to increase our numbers, currently measuring in at 7.3 billion in 2015. Some express a great deal of concern about this trend, arguing that the increasing population uses more resources than the planet can provide and encourages harmful practices such as deforestation and industrial pollution. Others say that while our population is at higher numbers than ever before and the subsequent problems are very real, the issues are caused less by the actual number of people and more by the unequal distribution of resources.

Read and carefully consider these perspectives. Each suggests a particular way of thinking about human population growth.

Perspective One	Perspective Two	Perspective Three
Overpopulation is one of the most serious environmental issues humans face. Our increasing numbers are causing myriad problems from loss of fresh water to extinction of species to lowered life expectancy in developing countries.	The number of people on earth is not a problem. We only have 7 billion, while scientists predict our planet can support up to 10 billion. The real problem is the unequal distribution of resources. A more equitable use of water, land, food, and fuel would eliminate many of the problems we currently face.	Though our population numbers are higher than they've ever been, this is not a cause for alarm. Our growth rate is already beginning to slow. As we approach critical mass, that decrease in rate will continue until we're at "replacement" levels of reproduction, allowing the human race to continue without drastically increasing the overall numbers.

Essay Task

Write a unified, coherent essay in which you evaluate multiple perspectives on the issues connected with population growth. In your essay, be sure to:

- analyze and evaluate the perspectives given
- state and develop your own perspective on the issue
- explain the relationship between your perspective and those given

Your perspective may be in full agreement with any of the others, in partial agreement, or wholly different. Whatever the case, support your ideas with logical reasoning and detailed, persuasive examples.

Chapter 28
Practice Exam 2:
Answers
and Explanations

English		Math		Reading		Science	
1. D	39. D	1. A	31. E	1. C	21. C	1. C	21. B
2. F	40. J	2. H	32. J	2. F	22. G	2. F	22. H
3. C	41. A	3. C	33. C	3. B	23. C	3. A	23. B
4. F	42. G	4. J	34. K	4. G	24. G	4. H	24. F
5. C	43. C	5. C	35. E	5. A	25. D	5. D	25. C
6. H	44. G	6. K	36. K	6. H	26. J	6. G	26. G
7. D	45. B	7. A	37. E	7. A	27. B	7. B	27. D
8. F	46. J	8. K	38. J	8. J	28. J	8. F	28. H
9. A	47. C	9. E	39. B	9. D	29. A	9. D	29. C
10. G	48. F	10. J	40. H	10. J	30. H	10. G	30. F
11. C	49. C	11. C	41. C	11. D	31. C	11. C	31. C
12. H	50. J	12. K	42. F	12. G	32. H	12. G	32. J
13. D	51. C	13. D	43. B	13. D	33. D	13. A	33. C
14. F	52. F	14. G	44. G	14. G	34. G	14. H	34. G
15. C	53. A	15. A	45. B	15. A	35. C	15. D	35. B
16. G	54. H	16. H	46. H	16. G	36. J	16. G	36. J
17. D	55. A	17. A	47. D	17. C	37. C	17. D	37. A
18. H	56. H	18. K	48. J	18. F	38. H	18. F	38. F
19. A	57. D	19. C	49. B	19. C	39. A	19. D	39. D
20. G	58. G	20. H	50. J	20. G	40. J	20. J	40. H
21. D	59. D	21. C	51. D				
22. F	60. H	22. F	52. K				
23. A	61. B	23. C	53. C				
24. F	62. J	24. G	54. H				
25. C	63. C	25. E	55. C				
26. G	64. J	26. G	56. G				
27. D	65. C	27. D	57. A				
28. H	66. H	28. F	58. F				
29. D	67. D	29. C	59. D				
30. J	68. F	30. H	60. K				
31. A	69. A						
32. F	70. G						
33. C	71. A						
34. F	72. G						
35. C	73. B						
36. J	74. F						
37. C	75. D						
38. J							

ENGLISH TEST

1. **D** The verb *associate* requires the preposition *with*. None of the other choices are idiomatically correct.

2. **F** All the proposed substitutions essentially expand upon the word *genders* without adding any new information to the sentence. As a result, you can eliminate (G), (H), and (J) because they are all unnecessarily wordy.

3. **C** You can eliminate (A) and (B) right away because the proposed sentence is totally out of context with what you've read so far. Only (C) gives the correct reason why you shouldn't include the proposed sentence: the content of the sentence is irrelevant to the passage as a whole.

4. **F** Eliminate (H) and (J) immediately because these will not be correct under any circumstances. Only (F) uses the correct form of the past participle.

5. **C** Choices (A) and (B) contain punctuation that is used to separate complete ideas. Since *Once you've learned a few basic stitches* is not a complete idea, neither answer choice can work. Instead, *once you've learned a few basic stitches* operates more as an introductory idea, which must be set off with a comma, as in (C).

6. **H** In this situation, (H) is the most concise answer that makes sense in the context. Notice all the other choices contain redundant words and phrases.

7. **D** This sentence is talking about the *completion of several projects*. Only (D) has the appropriate plural pronoun. If you picked (B), be careful: Pronouns must agree in number.

8. **F** Since you can count the starter kits (there are three, as the passage says), use *fewer* rather than *less*. With that, you can eliminate (H) and (J). Next, you need to use *than*, which is a comparison word, rather than *then*, which is a word used to describe a sequence of events in time. Only (F) works in this sentence.

9. **A** No change is necessary here because no pause is needed after the word *types*. Choices (B) and (C) in particular use punctuation that is much too strong in this context.

10. **G** Use Process Of Elimination aggressively here. The idiomatic phrase *ranging from* should not be split up with a comma, so eliminate (F) and (J). Then eliminate (H) because *ranging from very small to very large, with everything in between* is not a complete idea. Only (G) works in the context.

11. **C** This sentence talks about hooks that are *so big that you need to use two strands of yarn*, so it must be moved closer to other sentences that do the same. Only Sentence 3 works, because it talks about large hooks.

12. **H** Choices (F) and (G) don't make sense in the context. These are actually ideas with a negative slant and would be more appropriate in a sentence that was talking about some negative aspect of crocheting. Choice (J) might have worked better in the first paragraph. In this paragraph, however, (H) provides the most effective lead-in.

13. **D** As written, this sentence contains a comma error in its use of a comma to separate two complete ideas, so eliminate (A). Choices (C) and (D) both contain words that make the first part of the sentence incomplete, but (C) suggests a contrast where none exists. Choice (D) is the best answer because it fixes the complete problem and contains the appropriate transition word.

14. **F** Only (F) gives the idiomatically correct preposition. The others change the meaning of the sentence or use incorrect idioms.

15. **C** The essay is clearly in favor of crocheting, but it has not discussed the commercial potential of crocheting at all, so you can eliminate (A) and (B). Neither has it talked about the commercial potential of any other hobby, so you can eliminate (D).

16. **G** The verbs in this sentence are fairly complex, so use Process of Elimination aggressively. You can eliminate (F), (H), and (J) because all would be used in a situation in which the author *had seen* the painting. In the context of this sentence, however, the author is trying to suggest that she never believed that she *would see* the painting, so only (G) can work.

17. **D** This sentence may sound correct as written, but be careful. If you're going to use the *chance to* construction, you must complete the infinitive. In other words, in this situation, the sentence would have to read, *I finally got my chance to see the painting*. In this case, the only possible solution is to delete the underlined portion. Note that this is the most concise answer that works. Always give these deletions and omissions special consideration—they can often get some of the tangled logic out of the sentences as written.

18. **H** This sentence refers to the *grandeur* of the *painting*. In other words, you need the possessive pronoun *its* when describing the painting's grandeur. Only (H) works.

19. **A** The verbs in this sentence form a kind of list, so make sure all the verbs in the sentence are consistent (or "parallel") with one another. The verbs should read *packed*, *jumped*, and *headed*. Only (A) keeps all three verbs consistent with one another.

20. **G** The proposed insertion has the word *her* right at the beginning, which means that you need to find the sentence that contains its antecedent. Notice the clause in Sentence 3, *I met someone else who loved the painting as much as I did*. This *someone else* is the best available antecedent for *her* in the paragraph.

21. **D** There are incomplete ideas on either side of this sentence, so you can't use either a colon or a semicolon. Even a comma gives the sentence a pause where none is necessary. Only (D) gives the sentence its appropriate flow and does not break up the subject and its verb.

22. **F** Notice the word *impossible* directly before the underlined portion. Since this word is not underlined, it can't be changed, thus making (G), (H), and (J) redundant.

23. **A** Sentence 1 does talk about the size of the canvas, but Sentence 2 is out of context in this paragraph. This paragraph is about the author's impressions of the painting; the kind of technical detail presented in Sentence 2 is not part of these impressions.

24. F Remember that transitions are used to connect the ideas in paragraphs. The previous paragraph is about the author's impression of the painting, particularly relating to the size of the painting. The new paragraph goes on to present the author's impression of another element of the painting, which she finds *even more impressive*, as in (F). Choices (G), (H), and (J) might work in a different context, but they don't connect these paragraphs as well as (F).

25. C Notice that (A), (B), (D), and the underlined portion of the original sentence all contain the conjunctions *as* and *When*. The absence of any of these conjunctions in (C) creates a comma error, and (C) is therefore NOT an acceptable substitution.

26. G *From a distance* is the first part of the contrast in this sentence, the second part of which is *up close*. If you were to delete the prepositional phrase *from a distance*, this contrast would be unclear.

27. D The subjects of these paragraphs have been the author and her friend, so of all the answer choices, only (D), which contains the first-person plural pronoun *we*, could work here.

28. H This essay has been about the author's love of a single painting, so there is no need to mention other paintings at this point in the essay; eliminate (F) and (G). You can also eliminate (J) because this information is not contradicted elsewhere in the passage.

29. D No pause is necessary between *sights* and *on our trip*, so eliminate all answer choices that suggest this pause with unnecessary punctuation.

30. J The only clear placement for the underlined portion is after the word *bought*, completing the phrase *bought at the museum gift shop*. The other answer choices make the sentence unclear.

31. A The idea *cats have developed* is not complete, so a semicolon can't be used after it. Eliminate (D). In fact, no pause is needed anywhere in this sentence, so any of the choices that introduce unnecessary commas can be deleted. Choice (A) is the only choice that does not contain unnecessary pauses.

32. F Make sure you read the question carefully. It's asking for something that expresses the *ownership* relationship between people and cats. Choice (H) can be eliminated because it talks about dogs, and (G) and (J) can be eliminated because they don't express the ownership relationship for which the question is asking.

33. C In this sentence, the phrase *When communicating with each other* is a misplaced modifier. As written it sounds like the "*talk*" is somehow *communicating with each other*. It is of course the *cats* that are communicating with each other, which means that only (C) fixes the misplaced modifier.

34. F First, since this question is testing changes in verb tense, identify the subject of the verb. In this case, the subject is the plural noun *tails*, which requires a plural verb. You can eliminate (H) immediately, and (G) makes the sentence incomplete. Choice (J) changes the meaning of the sentence and uses a wordy passive construction. Given the new mistakes in all the proposed substitutions, the best answer is (F).

35. **C** The paragraph has been discussing the ways that cats communicate nonverbally. The sentence gives an exception to this rule, which only (C) adequately describes.

36. **J** You'll want to begin a new paragraph here because the focus of the essay changes with the introduction of the word *human*. Because this sentence is not describing a step in a process, and there's no first idea for which this can be the *next*, you can eliminate (H). Only (J) works.

37. **C** Use context. The previous sentence is describing plural cats, so this sentence should do the same. Only (C) gives the correct possessive form of the plural, *cats'*.

38. **J** Choices (F) and (G) are redundant. The word *logical* alone gets the point across here. Choice (H) modifies *logical*, but it does so unnecessarily—*to a startling degree* is not specific. Only (J) is concise while preserving the meaning of the sentence.

39. **D** *Clear* is an adjective, which modifies a noun; *clearly* is an adverb, which can modify a verb, an adjective, or another adverb. The word being modified here is *demonstrated*, which is a verb, so you'll need the adverb *clearly* and can eliminate (A) and (B). Choice (C) can't work because the conjunction *since* is not the appropriate transition between ideas in the sentence. Only (D) contains the correct adverb with the proper transition *when*.

40. **J** The information given is true and may be interesting, but in the context of this passage, it would be out of context. Remember, this is a passage about cats, so it is not at all likely that a sentence about birds will contribute to the main idea of the passage.

41. **A** The structure of this sentence is clumsy, but you can change only what appears in the underlined portion. In this instance, your most important clue is the comma after the word *examples*. This comma suggests that the infinitive phrase *to name only a few examples* is being set off as unnecessary to the meaning of the sentence. The sentence as written is the only choice that does not contain a grammatical error.

42. **G** Of all the possibilities listed here, only (G) establishes any kind of link between *cats* and *their owners*. Other answer choices talk about *mammals*, but this question asks specifically about *cats*.

43. **C** The underlined portion must be parallel with the rest of the sentence. Early in the sentence, the author speaks of *communicating as every bit as important as forging good relationships*. A second *as* will be needed to complete the comparison, and any verb used will need the same conjugation as *forging*. Choices (B) and (C) both meet these criteria, but of the two, (C) is more concise.

44. **G** Choice (G) is the most concise substitution that maintains the meaning of the sentence. Choices (F), (H), and (J) are redundant because they contain some form of the word *senseless* and other words that mean the same thing.

45. **B** Some of the transition words offered in the answer choices may seem similar, so it is best in this situation to compare what comes after those transition words. Again, you need an answer that expresses the relationship between *cats* and their *owners*. Although the word *human* does not appear in it, (B) is the only one of the answer choices that talks about a relationship between cats and humans.

46. **J** Choices (F), (G), and (H) all give redundant constructions. Only (J) gives a concise construction and maintains the meaning of the sentence.

47. **C** The *houses* described here are not in possession of anything, so you can eliminate (A) and (B). You can also eliminate (D) because it introduces an unnecessary pause after the word *houses*.

48. **F** Only (F) maintains the meaning of the subject without introducing new, unnecessary information. Choice (J) might look appealing, but (F) is still more concise. Think of it this way: To say the same thing, (F) takes one word and (J) takes two. Go with the most concise choice that works.

49. **C** *Michigan island* is a compound noun in this case, so the adjective *isolated* should not be set off from *Michigan* with a comma. Eliminate (A) and (D). Notice *so*, one of the FANBOYS, directly after the underlined portion. FANBOYS need a comma to link two complete ideas. Only (C) works.

50. **J** All items in a list must be consistent. In this sentence, the list should read *by horse, carriage, or bicycle*. Choices (F), (G), and (H) are not consistent.

51. **C** As written, this sentence creates a comma error. The idea that ends with the word *necessary* and the idea that begins with the word *Mackinac* are both complete, so of the different possible punctuation marks in the answer choices, only a period can be used to separate them.

52. **F** If the end of this sentence were deleted, the meaning of the sentence would not fundamentally change, but you would lose an interesting detail about Arch Rock, as (F) suggests. Choice (G) is misleading in that it suggests the geological descriptions of multiple tourist attractions, while the underlined portion gives the geological description of only one attraction. There is no contrast with the governor's mansion, so eliminate (H); the information is not detailed elsewhere in the passage, so eliminate (J).

53. **A** The next sentence discusses *fudge*, and only (A) contains any mention of stores that might sell this product.

54. **H** This question is testing the idiom *for sale*. The only viable alternative to this would be *on sale*, but that doesn't appear in the answer choices. Choices (F), (G), and (J) all suggest incorrect idioms.

55. **A** Choices (B), (C), and (D) are all grammatically correct while preserving the basic meaning of the sentence. Choice (A), *which*, is neither grammatically correct nor consistent with the meaning of the sentence. Therefore, (A) would NOT be an acceptable alternative.

56.   **H**   Only (H) removes the redundancy problem and maintains the meaning of the sentence.

57.   **D**   The pronoun in this portion of the sentence should refer back to the *local residents*. As such, it should be a third-person plural. Only (D) has the appropriate pronoun, *they*.

58.   **G**   Of all the answer choices, only (G) reduces the wordiness of the sentence while clarifying its meaning.

59.   **D**   The subject of this sentence is *privacy*, so the verb in the underlined portion must agree with a singular noun. Eliminate (A). Choices (B) and (C) change the meaning of the sentence by changing the tense of the helping verbs. Only (D) maintains the meaning of the sentence and fixes the verb-conjugation problem.

60.   **H**   This passage discusses Mackinac Island as a tourist destination and mentions cars only in the beginning of this essay. If the writer's intention is to show the difficulties residents have with cars, this essay has not succeeded; its subject has been the island itself and its many tourist attractions.

61.   **B**   The two nouns *friends* and *peers* are not part of a list or separate ideas. Instead, they are both the objects of the prepositional phrase *in front of*, and they should thus not be separated with any punctuation.

62.   **J**   Choice (J) is grammatically incorrect because it makes the sentence unable to stand on its own (i.e., it changes the sentence from a complete idea to an incomplete idea). It is therefore NOT an acceptable alternative to the underlined portion.

63.   **C**   Sentence 2 refers to something that *defies understanding*, and the word *though* suggests that something in a previous sentence does not defy understanding. Sentence 4 reads, *It is understandable that people would enjoy singing in the privacy of their homes*. Sentence 2 should follow this sentence because it describes, by way of a contrast, something that is not so understandable.

64.   **J**   Notice the other verb in this sentence, *see*. These verbs should be consistent; the basic subjects and verbs of each part of the sentence should read *look and you'll see*. Only (J) contains the consistent verb and maintains the meaning of the sentence.

65.   **C**   The *Even though* at the beginning of this sentence operates as a conjunction, thus making everything up to *busy restaurants* part of a single incomplete idea. Choices (A) and (C) set this idea off with a comma correctly, but (A) has the FANBOYS *but*. A coordinating conjunction preceded by a comma can be used only to separate two complete ideas.

66.   **H**   The phrase *such staples as* should not be divided with any punctuation. Only (H) gives the appropriate absence of punctuation. In order to use a colon, the idea before the colon must be complete. This one is not, so you can eliminate (G).

67. **D** The verb in the underlined portion must be consistent with the other major verb in this sentence, *responds*. Only choice (D) establishes this consistency. Choices (A) and (C) are in the wrong tense, and choice (B) makes for an awkward construction.

68. **F** The beginning of the next paragraph speaks of *another, more obvious reason*. The underlined portion, therefore, must contain a reason of some kind. Only (F) contains anything close, particularly in the final idea, *this is not the only reason for its enduring popularity*. The other answer choices do not link these two paragraphs, nor do they make sense in the larger context of the passage.

69. **A** This sentence should be in contrast with the previous sentence, and the sentence as written signals this contrast. The others give adverbs that suggest a comparison rather than a contrast.

70. **G** This sentence needs something that will suggest that the quality of people's voices doesn't matter. Only (G) does this with the word *regardless*. The prepositional phrase *in lieu of* suggests a substitution, but nothing is being substituted here; rather, the poor singing of many of karaoke's participants is being disregarded in consideration of other, more important things.

71. **A** Choice (D) gives the contraction *who is*, which does not work here, so you can eliminate that immediately. Choices (B) and (C) are not grammatically correct in this situation. The sentence as written contains the appropriate possessive pronoun and should therefore not be changed.

72. **G** The clause *who are ordinarily shy* is important in its modification of the word *people*. It would be incorrect to say that in general, karaoke brings people out of their shells. The clause is necessary because it clarifies that the sentence is talking about people not normally inclined to perform in public.

73. **B** The word *first* indicates that the underlined portion will need to have something to do with time. Choice (D) suggests a place, so you can eliminate it. Choices (A) and (C) suggest a cause and effect that is not substantiated in the rest of the sentence. Only (B), *when*, gives the appropriate time word.

74. **F** If you are not sure how to use *less* and *fewer*, look at the second word in each underlined portion. *Then* refers to a sequence of events; *than* is a comparison word. In this sentence, the author is making a comparison, so you need *than*. Eliminate (H). Now (F) is the only choice that makes the sentence grammatically correct. As a general note, *less* is used with general quantities (e.g., less money) and *fewer* is used with quantities that can be counted (e.g., fewer dollars). This question actually tests an exception to the rule in which both adjectives can work depending on the context; if were you to expand this sentence, it would read *less money than $7 billion* rather than *fewer than 7 billion dollars*.

75. **D** This passage deals with the international popularity of karaoke. At no point does the passage discuss specific regions. Therefore, the proposed insertion would not be appropriate at any point in the passage.

MATHEMATICS TEST

1. **A** The midpoint of segment XY is the average of X and Y, so add them up and divide by 2: $\frac{-15-11}{2} = \frac{-26}{2} = -13$.

2. **H** Use the Pythagorean theorem $(a^2 + b^2 = c^2)$ to find the length of DE: $8^2 + (DE)^2 = 10^2$, so $64 + (DE)^2 = 100$, $(DE)^2 = 36$, and $DE = \sqrt{36} = 6$. Also note that this is a Pythagorean triple with sides of 6, 8, and 10.

3. **C** The phrase *double the volume of the ant farm* means your equation must contain the expression $2V$, so eliminate (A), (B), and (E). The second sentence also says that the number of ants *is close to 50 more*, so your expression will have to contain the expression $2V + 50$; (C) is correct because it adds 50. Choice (D) is incorrect because, when the 2 is distributed, it becomes $2V + 100$.

4. **J** The probability that Lisa will take a fiction book can be defined as a fraction: The number of fiction books divided by the total number of books. Therefore, the probability of Lisa taking a fiction book is $\frac{5}{5+7} = \frac{5}{12}$, (J). Choice (K) is the probability that she will take a nonfiction book; (G) is the ratio of fiction books to nonfiction books.

5. **C** To find the average, add up all the test scores and divide by the number of tests: $\frac{108+81+79+99+85+82}{6} = \frac{534}{6} = 89$, choice (C). You can eliminate (A) and (B) because the average must be less than the highest test score.

6. **K** Angles 3 and 5 are alternate interior angles and therefore congruent. Angles 1 and 3 look congruent only because the triangle appears to be isosceles—the problem does not give any indication that it is, so eliminate (G).

7. **A** If p is Gregor's monthly pay, write an equation that represents Gregor's deposit. He spends 20% and deposits the rest, so $p - (0.2)p = 3,200$ or $(0.8)p = 3,200$. Divide through by the (0.8) to find that $p = 4,000$. If you're not sure how to set up the equation, you could also try out the answer choices as possibilities for Gregor's monthly pay to see which gives a deposit value of $3,200.

8. **K** By definition, similar polygons have equal corresponding angles, making (K) the correct response. Two similar polygons are really the same figure on different scales: smaller or larger versions of each other. Therefore, their dimensions are not necessarily the same, making (F), (G), (H), and (J) incorrect.

9. **E** Work through this word problem one step at a time. $60 × .30 = $18, so the dress is discounted $18. $60 − $18 = $42, the sale price. Now calculate Victoria's second discount: $42 × .10 = $4.20. $42 − $4.20 = $37.80, the price Victoria pays. Choice (D) incorrectly discounts the dress 40%; this is wrong because Victoria gets 10% off the *reduced price*, not the original price.

10.   **J**   Erin begins with x chips, which means (according to the second sentence of the question) Amy has $x - 3$. When Erin wins 4 of Amy's chips, Erin's total increases to $x + 4$, while Amy's drops to $x - 7$. Subtract $(x + 4) - (x - 7) = 11$, the difference in their chip totals.

11.   **C**   Since absolute value must always be greater than or equal to zero, you can eliminate (A) and (B). Substitute $y = 4$ into the expression $|1 - y| = |1 - 4| = |-3| = 3$.

12.   **K**   FOIL: multiply the First terms $3a \times a = 3a^2$, the Outer terms $3a \times (- b^2) = (-3ab^2)$, the Inner terms $2b \times a = 2ab$, and the Last terms $2b \times (-b^2) = -2b^3$. Add these terms to get $3a^2 - 3ab^2 + 2ab - 2b^3$, (K).

13.   **D**   Simplify the expression: $3 - 2(4 - y) = 3 - 8 + 2y = -5 + 2y$, which is the same as (D). Be careful when you multiply two negative values, such as $(-2) \times (-y)$: you should get a positive value.

14.   **G**   When raising a number with an exponent to another power, you multiply the exponents; therefore, $(y^3)^8 = y^{3 \times 8} = y^{24}$.

15.   **A**   Sketch out a little calendar until you see a pattern: Day 1 is Monday, 2 is Tuesday, 3 Wednesday, 4 Thursday, 5 Friday, 6 Saturday, 7 Sunday, 8 Monday, and so on. Notice that Sundays are always multiples of 7. Pick a multiple of 7 close to 260, such as 259. That means Day 259 is a Sunday, so Day 260 is a Monday.

16.   **H**   Draw a figure to see the relationship between the two shapes. Since the formula for area of a square is $A = s^2$ (where s is the side length of the square), you can find that a square with area 64 has side length 8, which would also be the diameter of the circle inscribed in this square, meaning the circle's radius would be 4. The formula for the area of a circle is $A = \pi r^2$, so $A = \pi(4)^2 = 16\pi$.

17.   **A**   Factor $x^2 - 5x - 14 = 0$ to $(x - 7)(x + 2) = 0$; therefore, the solutions (the values of x that make this true) are 7 and -2. Their product: $7 \times -2 = -14$. Also, note than in the standard formula $ax^2 + bx + c$, the product of the solutions will always be $\dfrac{c}{a}$.

18.   **K**   Factor $x^{12} - 9$ to $(x^6 - 3)(x^6 + 3)$; eliminate (F) and (G). Factor $(x^6 - 3)$ to $(x^3 - \sqrt{3})(x^3 + \sqrt{3})$; eliminate (H) and (J).

19.   **C**   Plug $x = \dfrac{1}{6}$ into the expression: $\dfrac{2x + 4}{3x} = \dfrac{2 \times \frac{1}{6} + 4}{3 \times \frac{1}{6}} = \dfrac{\frac{2}{6} + \frac{24}{6}}{\frac{3}{6}} = \dfrac{\frac{26}{6}}{\frac{3}{6}} = \dfrac{26}{3}$.

20.   **H**   Use the formula Distance = Rate × Time. Substitute the values from the problem: $60 = 90 \times t$. Therefore, $t = \dfrac{60}{90} = \dfrac{2}{3}$ hours. To convert from hours into minutes, multiply 60 minutes by $\dfrac{2}{3}$ hours: $60 \times \dfrac{2}{3} = 40$ minutes.

21.   **C**   Begin by drawing a perpendicular height by drawing vertical lines from the top vertices straight down to the base: These segments are the height of the trapezoid, and your figure should now look like a rectangle and two right triangles. Since the bottom base of the trapezoid is 11" and the top

base is 5", the difference is 6". Assume the two triangles you've created are the same size, which means the base of each is 3" (and the base of your rectangle is 5"). Use the Pythagorean theorem $(a^2 + b^2 = c^2)$ to find the height (which we'll call h) of one of the triangles: $h^2 + 3^2 = (3\sqrt{2})^2$, so $h^2 + 9 = 18$, $h^2 = 9$, and $h = 3$. This is also the height of the trapezoid, so plug these values (height and two bases) into the formula in the question: $A = h\left(\dfrac{b_1 + b_2}{2}\right) = 3\left(\dfrac{5+11}{2}\right) = 3\left(\dfrac{16}{2}\right) = 3(8) = 24$. If you hadn't been given the formula for the area of a trapezoid, or if you just find the formula too confusing, notice that the vertical heights split this figure into three familiar shapes: two triangles and a rectangle. You can find the area of each of these smaller pieces and add them together.

22. **F** By definition, the roots of a quadratic equation are the values for the variable that cause the equation to equal zero. Starting with the first answer choice, set each factor equal to zero and solve for x: $3x + 2 = 0$ yields $x = -\dfrac{2}{3}$, and $4x - 1 = 0$ yields $x = \dfrac{1}{4}$. None of the other answer choices yields both roots given in the problem.

23. **C** Draw the line segments $\overline{AC}$ and $\overline{BD}$; these are the diagonals. By definition, the diagonals of a rhombus bisect each other; therefore, the two halves of $\overline{AC}$ are 3 each and the two halves of $\overline{BD}$ are 4 each. The diagonals of a rhombus also (by definition) are perpendicular; this means that each of the four triangles inside this rhombus are right triangles. Use the Pythagorean theorem to find the length of the side of the rhombus: $3^2 + 4^2 = s^2$, so $9 + 16 = s^2$, $25 = s^2$, and $5 = s$. Note that these sides create a 3:4:5 Pythagorean triple.

24. **G** Underline the question and work the problem in bite-sized pieces. PITA (Plug In the Answers) is a good option. Start with choice (H). If the length is 16, the width is 14. The formula for area of a rectangle is, and the area with these dimensions would be 224, far bigger than the 80 the question provides. Eliminate (H), (J), and (K), and try (G). If the length is 10, the width is 8, and the area is 80. Choice (F) is the width and is therefore a possible trap answer.

25. **E** Don't be intimidated by the Cartesian plane: It's the same (x,y) coordinate plane you're used to. Slope is defined as $\dfrac{rise}{run}$, so use the two points given in the slope formula:

$$\dfrac{y_2 - y_1}{x_2 - x_1} = \dfrac{10 - (-5)}{5 - 1} = \dfrac{10 + 5}{4} = \dfrac{15}{4}.$$

26. **G** The equation of a circle is $(x - h)^2 + (y - k)^2 = r^2$, where (h,k) is the center of the circle, and r is the radius. The first part of the equation tells you that the x-coordinate of the center is -5, since $(x + 5)^2 = (x - [-5])^2$, so $h = -5$. The second part more clearly matches the formula, so it's easier to see that the y-coordinate of the center is 5. Therefore, the center of the circle is $(-5,5)$.

27. **D** The open circles at $x = 0$ and $x = 4$ mean that $x \neq 0$ and $x \neq 4$; therefore, eliminate (A), (B), and (E). The solid line between $x = 0$ and $x = 4$ means that x can be any value between 0 and 4, so eliminate (C). Make sure you read the question carefully. If you selected (C), you may have mistaken it for the range.

28. **F** The *point exactly halfway between* is another way to describe the midpoint, so plug the two points into the midpoint formula: $\left(\dfrac{x_1 + x_2}{2}, \dfrac{y_1 + y_2}{2}\right)$. This gives you $\left(\dfrac{-1+3}{2}, \dfrac{-5+3}{2}\right)$, which simplifies to $\left(\dfrac{2}{2}, \dfrac{-2}{2}\right)$, or $(1, -1)$.

29. **C** To find the *average rate of change*, begin by finding the total change: the liquid begins at $0°$ and eventually reaches $80°$, so the total change is the difference, $80°$. The question asks for the rate of change *during the times in which Sanjay is applying* heat to the container. Sanjay applies heat from minutes 0 to 5, $7\dfrac{1}{2}$ to 10, and 15 to $17\dfrac{1}{2}$. Find the difference in each of these pairs of numbers to see that Sanjay applied heat for 5 minutes, then 2.5 minutes, then another 2.5 minutes, or 10 minutes total. Therefore, the average rate of change in degrees per minute is $\dfrac{80°}{10\,\text{min}} = 8$ degrees/min.

30. **H** When you divide exponentials with the same base, you subtract the exponents, so $\dfrac{a^x}{a^y} = a^{x-y}$; therefore, $a^{x-y} = a^5$ and $x - y = 5$.

31. **E** Rearrange the equation into slope-intercept form ($y = mx + b$). $8 - 3y = 5x$ becomes $3y = 5x + 8$, or $y = \dfrac{5}{3}x + \dfrac{8}{3}$. In slope-intercept form, m is the slope; in this case, $\dfrac{5}{3}$.

32. **J** The least common denominator (LCD) must be a multiple of the denominator of each of the three given fractions. Take the factors of each denominator (3, 5, 7, 11) to the highest powers they appear: 3^2 (first fraction), 5^2 (second fraction), 7 (second fraction), and 11^3 (third fraction). This results in $3^2 \times 5^2 \times 7 \times 11^3$, choice (J). Choice (K) is the product of all three denominators and is wrong because choice (J) is smaller and still a multiple of all three denominators; in other words, both are common denominators but (J) is the "least."

33. **C** To multiply fractions, you multiply all the numbers on top of the fractions and all the numbers on the bottom of the fractions: $\dfrac{1}{4} \times \dfrac{2}{5} \times \dfrac{3}{6} \times \dfrac{4}{7} \times \dfrac{5}{8} \times \dfrac{6}{9} \times \dfrac{7}{10} = \dfrac{1 \times 2 \times 3 \times 4 \times 5 \times 6 \times 7}{4 \times 5 \times 6 \times 7 \times 8 \times 9 \times 10}$. Now, before you pull out the calculator, you can cancel out numbers that appear on both the top and bottom (4, 5, 6, and 7) because a number divided by itself (such as $\dfrac{4}{4}$) is 1, which doesn't affect the final product. After canceling, you get $\dfrac{1 \times 2 \times 3}{8 \times 9 \times 10} = \dfrac{6}{720}$, which reduces to $\dfrac{1}{120}$.

34. **K** The figure provided is a right triangle, so use the Pythagorean theorem ($a^2 + b^2 = c^2$) to find the distance asked for. $110^2 + 200^2 = c^2$, so $12{,}100 + 40{,}000 = c^2$, $52{,}100 = c^2$, and $\sqrt{52{,}100} = c$.

35. **E** The key phrase in this question is *at most*. It's possible that the second pentagon is the same size and is laid directly over the original pentagon. Because all points of one pentagon are the same as the other, select (E).

36. **K** When assigning employees to duties, there are 10 available to reserve a venue (the first duty). That leaves 9 remaining to arrange catering (because no one can be assigned more than one duty) and then 8 to plan activities. Then multiply $10 \times 9 \times 8$ to find how many different ways these duties can be assigned. Note the format of the answer choices—don't do more work than you have to.

37. **E** The easiest way to work this problem is to sketch it out. Draw $\overline{PQ}$, then draw the line perpendicular to $\overline{PQ}$ at Q; R is somewhere on this line. All of the answer choices have x-values greater than 1 and you can see the line rising to the right of Q (1,4) in your sketch. This means that the y-value of R must be greater than 4, which leaves only (E). Alternatively, you could find the slope of $\overline{PQ}$: The slope formula is $\frac{y_2 - y_1}{x_2 - x_1}$, so $\frac{2-4}{6-1} = \frac{-2}{5}$. Since $\angle PQR$ is a right angle, $\overline{PQ} \perp \overline{QR}$. In the coordinate plane, the slopes of perpendicular lines are negative reciprocals, so the slope of $\overline{QR}$ is $\frac{5}{2}$. Then use the points given in each answer choice to see which gives you the correct slope. It's (E): $\frac{9-4}{3-1} = \frac{5}{2}$.

38. **J** Solve the given equation for y. Start with $y = 0.25(100 - y)$. You can either distribute the 0.25 or divide both sides by the 0.25. In this case, it is easier to divide by 0.25. After doing this your equation becomes: $4y = 100 - y$. Add y to both sides to get $5y = 100$. Divide both sides by 5 to get $y = 20$. If you chose to begin the problem by distributing the 0.25, you should have gotten the same answer.

39. **B** Since $4\cos^2 x = 1$, $\cos^2 x = 0.25$ and $\cos x = 0.5$. You want to know x, the degree measure whose cosine is 0.5. A scientific/graphing calculator can help you calculate that: the $\cos^{-1}$ key will tell you the degree measure that yields the cosine you give it. $\cos^{-1}(0.5) = 60°$, so (B) is correct. If you prefer, you can try each of the answers in your scientific/graphing calculator. When you plug in (B), you can find that $\cos 60° = 0.5$, so $\cos^2 60° = 0.25$, and $4\cos^2 60° = 1$. Make sure your calculator is in degree mode!

40. **H** Sketch the rug over the floor to help you visualize the situation. The area of the exposed floor is the difference between the area of the entire floor and the area of the rug. First, find the area of the entire floor: area of a rectangle formula is $A = lw$, so $A = 16 \times 18 = 288$. Area of a circle formula is $A = \pi r^2$, where r is the radius. The diameter is 12, so $r = 6$. Therefore, $A = \pi \times 6^2 = \pi \times 36$, which is approximately 113. Calculate the difference: $288 - 113 = 175$. If you got a negative number when you did the calculation, you may have used the diameter of the circle in the area of a circle formula rather than the radius.

41. **C** The equation of the given line is in slope-intercept form: $y = mx + b$, where m is the slope, and b is the y-intercept. That tells you the slope of this line is -2. Since the slopes of perpendicular lines are negative reciprocals, the slope of the line in the credited answer choice must be $\frac{1}{2}$; eliminate (A), (B), and (E). The question says that the line you're looking for passes through the point $(0,-3)$: that makes the y-intercept (by definition) -3, so eliminate (D).

42. **F** Draw a vertical line from the point $\left(2\sqrt{3},2\right)$ straight down to the x-axis; this creates a right triangle with base $2\sqrt{3}$ and height 2. Use the Pythagorean theorem ($a^2 + b^2 = c^2$) to find the hypotenuse: $(2\sqrt{3})^2 + 2^2 = c^2$, so $4 \times 3 + 4 = c^2$, $12 + 4 = c^2$, $16 = c^2$, so $4 = c$. (A shortcut is to recognize that this is a 30°-60°-90° triangle. Such a triangle has a ratio of side lengths $1:\sqrt{3}:2$, which means this triangle's sides are 2, $2\sqrt{3}$, and 4.) Since sine is the ratio of the opposite side to the hypotenuse, $\sin\theta = \frac{2}{4} = \frac{1}{2}$.

43. **B** Substitute $a = 5$ and $b = -\frac{1}{4}$ into the answer choices. Before you actually work each out, you can eliminate (C) and (D) because the product and quotient of a positive and a negative number will be negative. Now try (A): $5 + \left(-\frac{1}{4}\right) = 4\frac{3}{4}$. Choice (B): $5 - \left(-\frac{1}{4}\right) = 5\frac{1}{4}$. Choice (E): $\left|5 \times \left(-\frac{1}{4}\right)\right| = \left|-\frac{5}{4}\right| = \frac{5}{4}$. Choice (B) is the greatest.

44. **G** Solve for x: add 1 to both sides to get $\frac{x}{3} = -\frac{13}{12} + 1$, or $\frac{x}{3} = -\frac{13}{12} + \frac{12}{12}$. Simplify to $\frac{x}{3} = -\frac{1}{12}$. Multiply both sides by 3 to get $x = -\frac{1}{4}$. Only (G) is true.

45. **B** Because the statement includes an absolute value, you'll need to solve it twice: once assuming the expression inside is positive, once assuming it's negative. First, the positive assumption: $2z - 3 \geq 7$, so $2z \geq 10$ and $z \geq 5$. Eliminate (C), (D), and (E). Now, assume the expression is negative: you'd multiply a negative number by -1 to make it positive, so $-(2z - 3) \geq 7$. Solve by multiplying both sides by -1 (remember to flip the sign): $2z - 3 \leq -7$, so $2z \leq -4$ and $z \leq -2$. Eliminate choice (A). Alternatively, you could try substituting in values for z. Try $z = 4$: $|2 \times 4 - 3| = |8 - 3| = |5| = 5$. This expression is supposed to be ≥ 7; since it isn't, you can eliminate any answer choices that include $z = 4$, so eliminate (C), (D), and (E). Try $z = -3$: $|2 \times (-3) - 3| = |-6 - 3| = |-9| = 9$. This is ≥ 7, so z could be equal to -3; therefore, eliminate (A).

46. **H** To simplify this expression, recall the identity $\tan x = \frac{\sin x}{\cos x}$. Now $\frac{\sin^2 x}{\cos x \tan x} = \frac{\sin^2 x}{\cos x \left(\dfrac{\sin x}{\cos x}\right)}$. Simplify: $\dfrac{\sin^2 x}{\cos x \left(\dfrac{\sin x}{\cos x}\right)} = \frac{\sin^2 x}{\sin x} = \sin x$.

47. **D** Try plugging the values of x given into the answer choices in the expression. Try $x = -4$:

$$\frac{a(-4)-b(-4)}{4a-4b}=\frac{-4a-(-4b)}{4a-4b}=\frac{-4a+4b}{4a-4b}=\frac{-(4a-4b)}{4a-4b}.\quad \text{Since}\quad \frac{4a-4b}{4a-4b}=1,\quad \frac{-(4a-4b)}{4a-4b}$$

simplifies to -1. Since $-1 < 0$, $x = -4$ is valid: eliminate (B), (C), and (E). Now try $x = -\dfrac{1}{4}$:

$$\frac{a\left(-\frac{1}{4}\right)-b\left(-\frac{1}{4}\right)}{4a-4b}=\frac{-\frac{1}{4}a-\left(-\frac{1}{4}b\right)}{4a-4b}=\frac{-\frac{1}{4}a+\frac{1}{4}b}{4a-4b}=\frac{-\frac{1}{4}(a-b)}{4(a-b)}=\frac{-\frac{1}{4}}{4}=-\frac{1}{16}.\ \text{This is also less than}$$

0, so eliminate (A).

48. **J** The original volume of the figure is described by the equation $V=\dfrac{1}{3}\pi r^2 h$. The new cylin-

der has had its radius halved and its height doubled, so the volume of the new cylinder will be

$V=\dfrac{1}{3}\pi\left(\dfrac{r}{2}\right)^2(2h)=\left(\dfrac{1}{3}\right)\pi\left(\dfrac{r^2}{4}\right)(2h)=\dfrac{1}{6}\pi r^2 h$. This volume is then one-half of the earlier volume,

and the ratio is 1:2. If you selected (H), be careful—you may have forgotten to square the new

radius value.

49. **B** Al's biking time going up the hill was m minutes, and because he went down the hill twice as fast,

his time going down was $\dfrac{1}{2}m$. His total time going up and down the hill was therefore $m+\dfrac{1}{2}m$

or $\dfrac{3}{2}m$. If you pick (D), be careful—you're not done here! The variable m represents the time in

minutes, and the question asks for the time in hours; therefore, you need to divide the total value

by 60: $\dfrac{\left(\dfrac{3}{2}m\right)}{60}=\dfrac{3}{120}m=\dfrac{m}{40}$.

50. **J** Since the wheel's diameter is 10, you can find the circumference ($C = \pi d$) of Pippin's wheel: $C = \pi d = 10\pi$. This means Pippin's wheel travels 10π inches in one rotation. Since her wheel rotated 15 times, multiply $10\pi \times 15 = 150\pi$.

51. **D** Draw a horizontal line, which is also the radius of the circle, from the center of the circle to the

right side of the square: this creates a 45°-45°-90° triangle. Recall that the ratio of sides in this type

of triangle is $s{:}s{:}s\sqrt{2}$. To find the length of the sides, and hence the radius, divide the hypotenuse

(x) by $\sqrt{2}$, giving $\dfrac{x}{\sqrt{2}}$, which, after multiplying by $\dfrac{\sqrt{2}}{\sqrt{2}}$ to rationalize the denominator, becomes

$\dfrac{x\sqrt{2}}{2}$, (D). You just found the radius, so (E) is wrong.

52. **K** No restrictions are needed because $f_{(x,y)} = f_{(y,x)}$ in all cases. Follow the same rules as the original function, just switch x and y. Because $-2yx = -2xy$, this is the same result that $f_{(x,y)}$ produced in the question and $f_{(y,x)} = -2yx + x + y - 4$. Therefore, all values of x and y will result in $f_{(x,y)} = f_{(y,x)}$, so (K) is correct. If you don't see this relationship immediately, you can use real numbers to test each of the answer choices. The question has already told you that $f_{(2,3)} = -11$, so see if $f_{(3,2)} = -11$ also. According to the original definition, $f_{(3,2)} = -2 \times 3 \times 2 + 2 + 3 - 4 = -12 + 1 = -11$. This means that $x = 2$ and $y = 3$ satisfy the goal $f_{(x,y)} = f_{(y,x)}$; therefore, eliminate (G), (H), and (J). Now you need to find out whether both variables must be positive, so try negative values: $x = -2$ and $y = -3$. $f_{(-2,-3)} = -2 \times -2 \times -3 + (-3) + (-2) - 4 = -12 - 3 - 2 - 4 = -21$ and $f_{(-3,-2)} = -2 \times -3 \times -2 + (-2) + (-3) - 4 = -12 - 2 - 3 - 4 = -21$. Since both are equal to -21, x and y don't have to be positive, so eliminate (F).

53. **C** *Each of the smaller pipes can handle exactly half as much water as the large pipe* means that the area of the cross-section of the small pipe is one-half the area of the cross-section of the large pipe. So start by finding the area of the circular cross-section of the large pipe: $A = \pi r^2$, so $A = \pi(4)^2 = 16\pi$. Therefore, the area of the cross-section of the smaller pipe is one-half that, or 8π. So for the smaller pipe's circular area $8\pi = \pi r^2$, $8 = r^2$, and $r = \sqrt{8} = \sqrt{4} \times \sqrt{2} = 2\sqrt{2}$.

54. **H** The height (which we'll call h) divides this figure into two right triangles, each with base length of 3 feet. Tangent is the ratio of the opposite side to the adjacent side, so $\tan 40° = \dfrac{3}{h}$. Solve for h by multiplying both sides by h: $h(\tan 40°) = 3$, so $h = \dfrac{3}{\tan 40°}$.

55. **C** Sketch the girls' paths out on the coordinate plane. They start at school $(0,0)$, then Susan walks to $(-8,2)$ and Cindy walks to $(3,-1)$. Connect the two points with a straight line, make a right triangle, and use the Pythagorean theorem: $a^2 + b^2 = c^2$. Side $a = 3$ (the difference in the y-points), and side $b = 11$ (the difference in the x-points). $3^2 + 11^2 = c^2$; $c^2 = 130$; $c = \sqrt{130}$, which is ≈ 11.4.

56. **G** If a is a positive integer and b is a negative integer, the only answer choice that will never yield a negative exponent (and therefore a fraction) is (G). If you're unsure, try substituting values for a and b. Let's say $a = 2$ and $b = -3$. Choice (F) becomes $3^{2-3} = 3^{-1} = \dfrac{1}{3}$; that's not an integer, so you can eliminate (F). Likewise, for (H), $3^{2(-3)} = 3^{-6} = \dfrac{1}{3^6} = \dfrac{1}{729}$, (J), $3^{-2} = \dfrac{1}{3^2} = \dfrac{1}{9}$, and (K), $3^{\frac{2}{-3}} = \dfrac{1}{3^{\frac{2}{3}}} = \dfrac{1}{\sqrt[3]{3^2}} = \dfrac{1}{\sqrt[3]{9}}$. Only (G) gives you an integer: $3^{2-(-3)} = 3^{2+3} = 3^5 = 243$.

57. **A** The question tells you that $0 < \dfrac{y}{x}$, which means $\dfrac{y}{x} \neq 0$, so eliminate (D) and (E). The only way $\dfrac{y}{x}$ could be larger than y itself is if $x < 1$ and $y \geq 1$. In other words, y could be 1 in this situation, and since we are told that $\dfrac{y}{x} > y$, $\dfrac{y}{x}$ must be greater than 1. This is a tough problem, and if you're not sure how to come up with these relationships, try to find numbers that make the initial

relationship true and try them out on the number line. If $x = 0.5$ and $y = 1$, then $\frac{y}{x} = 2$, for example, so you can eliminate (C) [and (D) and (E), which you've already eliminated]. You'll find that you can't get a number less than 1 for $\frac{y}{x}$.

58. F   Sketch out the rectangular 100 feet by 150 feet field described in the question. The 10 foot border within the field creates a new, smaller rectangle, 80 feet by 130 feet. The largest circle that can fit in this rectangle has a diameter of 80 feet, so it has a radius of 40 feet. If you picked (G), be careful—you may have forgotten to subtract 10 feet on both sides of the track.

59. D   Imagine cutting an orange: The first slice (one plane) cuts it into two pieces. If you hold those two pieces together and make another slice (the second plane), you cut both of those pieces, thereby creating 4 sections. Eliminate (A) and (C). Now, if you repeat this orange-slicing experiment, but your second slice is parallel to the first slice, it cuts a circular slice off only one piece, thereby creating 3 sections, so eliminate (B). The only way to keep the orange in two pieces after the first slice is for the second slice to repeat the first exactly. Since the question said the sphere was to be cut by two *different* planes, this cannot happen; therefore, it's impossible to get only 2 pieces, so eliminate (E).

60. K   "Positive difference" means that when you subtract $a - b$ you can get $+5$ or -5. (That's also what the absolute value indicates.) Solve for a in both cases: $a - b = 5$, so $a = b + 5$; and $a - b = -5$, so $a = b - 5$. Now subtract these two values: $(b + 5) - (b - 5) = b + 5 - b + 5 = 10$, choice (K). Alternatively, you could substitute a number for b: let's say $b = 2$, so $|a - 2| = 5$. Then solve: $a - 2 = 5$, so $a = 7$; and $a - 2 = -5$, so $a = -3$. The positive difference is $7 - (-3) = 7 + 3 = 10$.

READING TEST

1. C   When the narrator first sees her gift, her first response is confusion, followed by devastation that she won't be able to show her gift off to the other girls at school. Eliminate (A). She then recognizes that her father put a lot of effort into her gift and tries to be grateful. Eliminate (D). She then returns to being confused as to why they made her this house instead of buying her the real Barbie Dream House. Eliminate (B). That leaves (C), the correct answer. Disappointed and upset as the narrator is, the passage does not state that she hates the house.

2. F   The narrator of the story explains that only when she and her sister could smell coffee were they allowed to go downstairs to start Christmas. Therefore, choice (F) is the best answer. Choice (G) incorrectly refers to breakfast, which is not mentioned in the passage. Choice (H) incorrectly refers to the narrator's father's preparation of a gift instead of general morning readiness. Choice (J) is incorrect because the passage explicitly states that the narrator was expected to wait in the kitchen for her parents; she just burst in ahead of them one year because she was too excited to wait.

3. **B** The narrator talks about her dream of owning the Dream House in the second paragraph, when she says *I knew that if I could only have a Dream House of my own, my life would be complete.* Therefore, (B) is the best answer, as it is a good paraphrase of that statement. Choice (A) incorrectly refers to the other girl who owns the house and is not meant to be taken literally. Choice (C) confuses the actual result, based on her parents' hard work, with the narrator's dream, based on buying a particular toy. Choice (D) refers to the narrator's eventual comment that she will pass her gift on to her children someday, but that refers not to the Dream House but to her father's actual gift.

4. **G** The first paragraph describes the family's tradition of waiting until the parents have had a chance to wake up and make coffee before beginning to open the presents. Choice (G) is the best paraphrase of that summary and is the best answer. Choice (F) might be true but it is not mentioned in the passage and is not the best summary of the entire paragraph. Choice (H) states the opposite of what the passage says. Choice (J) is true, but is not the main point of the paragraph.

5. **A** When the narrator first sees her handmade doll house, she is confused and upset as she compares her house to her idealized Barbie Dream House. Choice (A) is the best paraphrase of her reaction. Choice (B) is incorrect because although the narrator does eventually try to be grateful, that is not her first response and she is not immediately successful in her attempt. Choice (C) goes against the passage—she compares the old-fashioned style of her house with the modern Barbie house and finds her house lacking. Choice (D) is incorrect because that was her goal before she saw her house, when she believed she would receive the official Barbie Dream House.

6. **H** The narrator's father is described in a few different places in the passage. First, he is overheard reassuring Mel, the mother, regarding Christmas. Then, when he is preparing to present his daughter with her gift, he is described as *smiling anxiously.* Finally, the narrator eventually realizes that her father had "spent countless hours working on the house." Therefore, (H) is the best characterization of the father in the story.

7. **A** In lines 25–30, the narrator overhears her parents discussing Christmas, wondering what they will do. This implies that there is some kind of problem. Her father then proceeds to make a homemade version of the Dream House that his daughter wants, implying that for some reason, he cannot give her the gift she wants but is willing to work very hard to give her something similar. Therefore, (A) is the best answer because it explains what problem might cause him to act in such a manner. Choice (B) is incorrect because it refers to an early comment regarding a previous Christmas, not the one being described. Choice (C) is incorrect because there is no evidence that the father made the dollhouse because he had always wanted to do so. Choice (D) is incorrect because the fact that the father put so much time and effort into making the dollhouse implies that they do in fact want their daughter to be happy.

8. **J** At the end of the passage, the narrator comments that she still has the dollhouse and that she hopes to someday tell her own children the story of how she got it. Therefore, (J) is the best answer since it refers only to her hopes of passing on the story. Choice (F) incorrectly refers to the narrator's

initial hopes of impressing other children with an official Barbie Dream House. Choice (G) focuses on the possible value of the house, which is not discussed in the passage. Choice (H) is incorrect because the narrator did not in fact appreciate the gift initially.

9. D   The narrator concludes, at the time of the gifting, that although she does not like her dollhouse as much as she would have liked a Barbie Dream House, it must have taken her father a lot of time and effort to build. Therefore, (D) is the best answer. Choice (A) is incorrect because she refers to the dollhouse as a crude approximation of what she wanted. Choice (B) is incorrect because the absence of an elevator is not mentioned in the passage. Choice (C) is incorrect because there is no evidence that her eventual decision to pass the house on to her children was anticipated by her *or* her parents at the time when it was given to her.

10. J   The last paragraph is written as if the narrator is looking back on her childhood and having trouble remembering the events that followed the previous part of the passage. She reflects that she now more fully understands her parents' actions and wishes she could go back in time and explain things to her younger self. Therefore, the best answer is (J). Choice (F) might be true, but the focus of the last paragraph is on the narrator as an adult, not as a child. Choice (G) is incorrect because the passage does not discuss the narrator's sister's gift. Choice (H) is too negative—the narrator is looking back on the events with greater wisdom and understanding, not bitterness.

11. D   This passage describes the formation and activities of the CCC. No one was "forced" to work in the CCC, so you can eliminate (A). The CCC did employ many veterans, but nothing in the passage supports the claim that veterans had suitable employment "only after" the creation of the CCC.

12. G   While (F) is true, it isn't the main idea of the paragraph. Choice (H) is incorrect because the bonuses were never paid. For (J), the paragraph says that the age restriction was waived, but at no point does it say how many of these veterans were over the age limit. Only (G) gives a reasonable summation of the content of the paragraph.

13. D   The passage states that Roosevelt *also cared about the fate of trees, having practiced the art of silviculture on his Hyde Park estate with such enthusiasm that on various official forms he was fond of listing his occupation as 'tree farmer.'* Choice (A) makes an assumption that is not supported in the passage; there is nothing to suggest that his interest in silviculture predated his political life. Choices (B) and (C) are not supported in the passage. Only (D) is supported by the sentence cited above.

14. G   Read this question carefully. The lines you need are 61–63: *For the National Park Service, they built roads, campgrounds, bridges, and recreation and administration facilities.* This clearly supports (G). The other activities in the answer choices are mentioned in the passage, but not as things the CCC did *for the National Park Service.*

15. **A** Starting on line 72, the passage reads, *the program taught more than a hundred thousand to read and write, passed out twenty-five thousand eighth-grade diplomas and five-thousand high-school diplomas.* This line most clearly supports (A). Choices (B) and (D) contain deceptive language from elsewhere in the passage, but they do not describe the CCC. Choice (C) is a trap because of the placement of the word *only*. As written, (C) means that all men the CCC accepted were those with six teeth.

16. **G** Lines 24–25 describe the terms of payment in the CCC, so eliminate (F). Line 58 describes the *4.1 million man-hours* spent fighting forest fires; it does NOT say that the CCC employed 4.1 million men, so eliminate (H). The states referred to in (J) are described in the passage as the sites of *flood control projects*, not firefighting projects. Only (G) has support in the passage.

17. **C** Lines 60–61 describe the *first major reforestation campaign in the country's history.* Although the specific years during which this reforestation campaign took place are unclear, the campaign must have taken place after the establishment of the CCC in 1933. It can therefore be inferred, because this was the "first," that the nation had not undergone a major reforestation campaign before, as (C) suggests.

18. **F** Lines 11–16 state the following: *When he went to Congress for authorization of the program, he called the new agency the Civilian Corps Reforestation Youth Rehabilitation Movement, but before sinking under the weight of an acronym like CCRYRM, it was soon changed to the Civilian Conservation Corps (known forever after as the CCC).* These lines describe the change, and only (F) is supported by the time of these events. The only other answer that might work chronologically would be (G), but nothing in the passage supports the claim that Congress complained about the length of the name.

19. **C** Lines 29–30 state that the *men had to be US citizens between the ages of seventeen and twenty-seven (later twenty-four).* Since the question asks about enrollees when the CCC was founded, you can disregard the "later" age; (C) gives the correct age range.

20. **G** Lines 21–24 state that *the Departments of Agriculture and Interior...would design and supervise projects in regional and national forests, national parks, and other public lands.* These lines give direct support to (G), and they show that the others are incorrect or inadequate responses to the question.

21. **C** This passage deals with the importance of the totem pole and the role the totem pole plays in Native American culture. Even with this very general overview of the passage, the only answer that fits is (C). The others are too specific or suggest incorrectly that the tone of the passage is negative.

22. **G** The question in (F) is answered in lines 2–3. The question in (H) is answered in lines 65–66. The question in (J) is answered in lines 8–9. Only the question posed in (G) goes unanswered in the passage. The discussion in the fourth paragraph is distracting, but notice this paragraph does not claim that the pole in Pioneer Square is the largest.

23. **C** Note the opening sentence of the fifth paragraph on line 39: *Poles serve the important purpose of recording the lore of a clan, much as a book would.* The other choices describe some minor functions of totem poles, but only the function described in (C) is described as *important*.

24. **G**   This paragraph describes the meanings of some of the symbols used on totem poles. Choice (F) would be fine if it did not contain the word *every*. Clearly, a short paragraph cannot describe every possible symbol. There are no regional comparisons, so you can eliminate (H). Choice (J) is too limited. Think in terms of the larger point of this paragraph; it describes figures other than the Raven. Only (G) adequately describes the main idea of the paragraph.

25. **D**   Choice (A) is addressed in lines 40–41. Choice (B) is addressed just after this in lines 42–44. Choice (C) is addressed in lines 64–66. Choice (D) may seem like it is addressed in the passage, but read this part of the passage carefully. There is no reference to the importance of this pole in Native American culture; after all, the group that took it, according to line 33, were *Seattle businessmen*, not the Tlingit.

26. **J**   Choice (F) is addressed in lines 13–15. Choice (G) is addressed in line 12. Choice (H) is addressed in line 17. Choice (J) is not addressed in the passage; the *family crest* is mentioned in line 16, but there is no evidence in the passage that the poles were constructed exclusively by clans who had family crests.

27. **B**   As lines 39–41 indicate, one of the main functions of the poles is to identify the lore of a clan. The points referred to in (A), (C), and (D) are mentioned, but none could be described as a "main point." Only (B) is general enough to be described as a "main point."

28. **J**   When the Tlingit are introduced in line 31, they are described as coming from *the southeastern coast of Alaska*. Only (J) could work. Don't be distracted by the other places mentioned in this paragraph; those places may have some significance for the Tlingit, but could not be described as the *home of the Tlingit*.

29. **A**   This paragraph is used to conclude some of the ideas in the preceding paragraphs and to suggest the broader importance of totem poles beyond their physical beauty. Choices (B), (C), and (D) all use words from the passage, but they use those words in misleading ways. Only (A) can be supported by evidence from the passage.

30. **H**   All we know about the employers is that they *complained that their Indian workers were unreliable when a pole was being carved or a potlatch planned* (lines 27–28). Because this is the only reference the author gives to these employers, we can only infer that the employers were *irritated*, as (H) suggests.

31. **C**   Lines 14–16 state: *… in the present climate of fiscal austerity, there is no telling when humans will next get a good look at the earth's nearest planetary neighbor*. Choice (A) can be eliminated because the author is clearly not cheerful and optimistic. Choice (B) can be eliminated because the author's tone does not suggest sarcasm or condescension. Choice (D) can be eliminated because of the word *withdrawn*. Only (C) is supported by the lines quoted above: He is doubtful (*there is no telling*) and pragmatic (*in the present climate of fiscal austerity*).

32. **H** Lines 28–33 discuss the state of scientific knowledge before the arrival of *Pioneer Venus*. The paragraph discusses in detail the differences in surface temperatures and atmospheric pressures. Choice (G) is too strong: The two planets are not *twins*, but the passage does not say that they are anything like *polar opposites*. The best answer is (H) because the paragraph details the objections to the term *twins*.

33. **D** This question asks about the same portion of the passage as question 32. Lines 28–33 detail some of the ways in which the "twin" characterization of Earth and Venus was reconsidered. The main evidence in this paragraph relates to surface temperature and atmosphere.

34. **G** The paragraph in question concerns the *Magellan* and *Pioneer Venus* missions. Each mission studied different elements of Venus's physical composition, and the information from each can be used in tandem with the other. The missions are contrasted, but neither is cast in a negative light, so you can eliminate (F) and (H), and (J) is too narrow in that it does not include the findings of the *Magellan*. Only (G) adequately summarizes the paragraph.

35. **C** Lines 34–35 state, *Even aside from the heat and the pressure, the air of Venus would be utterly unbreathable to humans.* It then goes on to discuss the atmospheric conditions in more detail. Choice (C) is the only one of the answer choices that addresses these issues. Choices (B) and (D) describe the physical properties of the planet, but they do not give any indication why human survival would not be possible. Eliminate (A) because it is not the mistaken belief that makes survival impossible—the belief is mistaken because survival would be impossible.

36. **J** Choice (J) is supported in lines 31–32, which say that Venus's *surface temperature of 450 degrees Celsius is hotter than the melting point of lead.* Choice (H) is misleading; these physical properties describe Earth. Choice (F) can be eliminated because "lead" is introduced as a point of comparison, not as one of the constitutive elements of Venus's surface. Choice (G) can be eliminated because it does not contain any mention of Venus.

37. **C** The full sentence in lines 56–57 reads as follows: *Unlike Earth, Venus harbors little if any molecular oxygen in its lower atmosphere.* In other words, Venus contains or holds or has little if any molecular oxygen in its lower atmosphere.

38. **H** The word *primordial* appears in line 65. The lines that follow state that Venus is *more primordial* than Earth because it *has held on to a far greater fraction of its earliest atmosphere.* Only (H) contains the appropriate reference to these early formations.

39. **A** The full sentence starting on line 57 establishes a clear link between the activity of these plants (i.e., living things) and the composition of the earth's atmosphere. The only answer that even mentions the earth is (A), and this choice provides a reasonable paraphrase of the passage.

40. **J** Choice (J) is the only answer that accurately paraphrases lines 20–22.

SCIENCE TEST

1. **C**   Table 1 shows that coin samples II and IV have an electric current of 2,000 mA. The current does not change, eliminating (A) and (B). The variable that does change is the identity of precious metal solution. For coin sample II exposed to silver nitrate, 4.0 mg of precious metal plates. For coin sample IV exposed to copper sulfate, only 2.4 mg of precious metal plates. Therefore, (D) is eliminated, and (C) is correct.

2. **F**   The precious metal solutions react with zinc to form a coating of pure precious metal on the coin samples. If the available surface area exposed to the solutions decreased, the amount of precious metal coating is expected to decrease. There is no specific evidence in the passage to support the plating amount remaining constant or increasing.

3. **A**   Table 2 shows that increasing the exposure time of a zinc coin to silver nitrate results in higher concentrations of zinc nitrate in the surrounding solution. Therefore, (C) and (D) are eliminated. The passage states that *Silver nitrate, formed when silver dissolves in nitric acid, reacts with zinc to form solid silver and zinc nitrate*. Therefore, increasing the amount of silver nitrate available to react with zinc is expected to result in higher concentrations of zinc nitrate. This eliminates (B) and makes (A) the best answer.

4. **H**   The question describes using the same sized sample of zinc and same exposure time as Experiment 1. Table 1 shows that when electric current is increased from 1,000 to 2,000 mA for zinc coins exposed to copper sulfate for 30 minutes, the plated copper increases from 1.2 to 2.4 mg. 1,580 mA is between 1,000 and 2,000 mA, so the amount of plated copper should fall between 1.2 and 2.4 mg.

5. **D**   In the description of Experiment 1, all coin samples were stated to have a radius of 1 cm. Table 1 shows that the change in mass from precious metal plating, electric current applied, and identity of precious metal solution used were not constant for samples I–IV.

6. **G**   The passage states that *Silver nitrate, formed when silver dissolves in nitric acid, reacts with zinc to form solid silver and zinc nitrate*. Therefore, when zinc is plated with solid silver, zinc nitrate is also formed as a product. Choices (F), (H), and (J) are not involved in this reaction.

7. **B**   Melting point is the temperature at which a substance changes from a solid to a liquid. Any compound with a melting point above 215 K will still be a solid at that temperature. For alkanes, according to Table 2, only octane will still be a solid at 215 K. Octane must be in the answer, and on this basis alone, choices (A), (C), and (D) can all be eliminated, leaving only choice (B). The remaining data in choice (B) are supported in Table 2 as well.

8. **F**   According to Table 3, the 8-carbon alcohol has the highest value for viscosity. Refer to Table 1 for the prefix and suffix of the compound's name: The structure is called octanol.

9. **D** Read across any single row of Table 3 to see that for a fixed number of carbons in the molecule, the alcohol has the highest viscosity. This eliminates (A) and (B). Further, for any given row, the alkane has the lowest viscosity, eliminating (C).

10. **G** Read down any single column in Table 2 to see that as the number of carbons in the molecule increases, the melting point increases. Therefore, (F) and (J) are eliminated. Read down any single column in Table 3 to see that as the number of carbons in the molecule increases, the viscosity increases as well, eliminating (H) and making (G) the correct answer.

11. **C** Compare the melting points of the alkanes and alcohols in Table 2. For any given number of carbons in the molecule, the melting points between these two types of compounds differ by varying but similar amounts between 41 and 57 K. Of the possible answers, (C) is the best approximation of the average of these differences.

12. **G** When testing the effects of different variables, all variables must be held constant except those being tested. To determine the effects of drag force or air resistance, therefore, all variables except drag force and air resistance must be held constant. Altering the apparatus to use a spring makes this into a completely different experiment, so (F) and (H) are eliminated. To negate the effects of air resistance, using a vacuum with no air pressure would be best, making (G) the best answer.

13. **A** In experiments, more precision is nearly always better. A timer that reads to the nearest second can give only whole number results. Therefore, it would read either "1" or "2" for each trial. This would not greatly alter the results for the tin cube (Trials 1 and 5 would be 2 seconds, and Trials 2–4 would be 1 second for an average of 1.4 seconds). However, all of the trials for the lead cube would round down to 1 second for an average of 1 second. This is significantly different from the 1.46 seconds obtained with the more precise timer, eliminating (C) and (D). Choice (B) is eliminated because the period of both pendulums is greater than 1 second, meaning they would travel a shorter distance in 1 second than they would in the time it takes them to complete a cycle.

14. **H** Choices (F) and (G) are true statements, but they do not explain why forces other than gravity must be acting on the pendulums. The passage states that for a *simple gravity pendulum, gravity is the only force acting on the mass causing an acceleration of 9.8 m/sec²*. The times obtained in Experiments 1 and 2 resulted in acceleration calculations less than this, indicating some other force was slowing the pendulum down (air resistance and friction). This eliminates (J) and makes (H) the best answer.

15. **D** Read if and when you can't answer a question from the figures. The length of the string isn't provided in the figures, so read the descriptions of the experiments to find the lengths of 0.5m for Experiment 1 and 1.0m for Experiment 2. The measured periods for all values for the tin cubes are greater in Table 2 than they are in Table 1. If the string increases to 2.0m, the measured periods will also increase and therefore must be greater than 2.09 seconds.

16. **G** Table 2 shows no consistent trend in the measured period among the various trials for the lead cube. All values, however, fall between 2.00 and 2.12 seconds. Only (G) offers a value in this range.

17. **D** Read if and when you can't answer a question from the figures. For questions that ask why something was done, the introduction and the experiments will offer more information. The experiments provide the different masses and also clarify that the lengths (and therefore surface area) and the starting angle were the same. This information eliminates (A), (B), and (C) and identifies (D) as the correct answer.

18. **F** In the description of the Coevolution Hypothesis, the passage states that *RNA sequences developed enzyme-like abilities including the ability to self-replicate*. Development of capsids was mentioned in the Regressive Evolution Hypothesis, but not in Coevolution, eliminating (G). DNA was not mentioned in the Coevolution Hypothesis, eliminating (H). Cell membrane transit was mentioned only in the Cellular Origin Hypothesis, eliminating (J).

19. **D** The first paragraph states that biologists agree that viruses originated from nucleic acid. Choice (A) is eliminated because the Coevolution Hypothesis does not provide an explanation for viruses evolving from bacteria. Choice (B) is eliminated because according to the passage, viruses cannot replicate unless they first infect a cell. Choice (C) is eliminated because only the Regressive Evolution Hypothesis and Coevolution Hypothesis mentions anything about viruses having membranes or envelopes.

20. **J** The Coevolution Hypothesis specifically mentions that the first virus particles were RNA nucleotides with enzyme-like activity that incorporated into protein structures. Therefore, (F), (G), and (H) are all eliminated. DNA is not mentioned as a component of the earliest virus particles in this hypothesis.

21. **B** The Cellular Origin Hypothesis states that viruses originated from cellular-organism ancestors. They could have come from prokaryotic or eukaryotic organisms, and the type of ancestor cell does not necessarily determine what type of cell they will evolve to infect. Therefore, (C) and (D) are eliminated because they cannot necessarily be determined from the information given. Given that both T4 and PP7 infect bacteria, they likely contain genetic material similar to the bacteria they infect. However, given that one is a DNA virus and one is an RNA virus, if they are related at all it is likely through a very distant ancestor virus that escaped a cellular organism long ago. This eliminates (A) and makes (B) the best answer.

22. **H** Since the Regressive Evolution Hypothesis suggests that viruses originated from obligate intracellular parasites, one would expect that they would share features of these ancestors. The hypothesis specifically states that intracellular parasites evolved into viruses, eliminating choices (F) and (G). Between the remaining choices, finding a parasite with DNA similar to a known virus could suggest that this organism and the known virus evolved from a common ancestor, making choice (H) the best answer.

23. **B** The passage states that viruses cannot replicate unless they first infect a cell. Therefore, the first viruses were unlikely to originate before cells, making (B) the best answer. There is nothing in the passage to support that viral capsids are similar to bacterial cell walls, and the word *capsid* does not even appear in the first hypothesis, eliminating (A). Choice (C) is eliminated because the differences in RNA and DNA viruses are not elaborated in the passage. Moreover, given that RNA viruses are mentioned in the Coevolution Hypothesis and DNA viruses are mentioned in the hypotheses that relate to more complex cellular organisms, it seems unlikely that RNA viruses would be considered more advanced than DNA viruses. Choice (D) is eliminated because the Coevolution Hypothesis specifically states that the first viruses contained RNA.

24. **F** The incorporation of RNA sequences into protein structures versus cell structures is specifically mentioned in the Coevolution Hypothesis. Choices (G) and (J) relate to the Regressive Evolution Hypothesis, and (H) relates to the Cellular Origin Hypothesis.

25. **C** Table 1 shows that as organic cover percentage increases, erosion from topsoil deflation decreases, eliminating (A) and (B). Choices (C) and (D) both state that increased rainfall will reduce erosion as shown in Table 3. The choice comes down to the type of topsoil. Tables 1 and 3 consistently show that Soil Y resists erosion more than Soil X does, eliminating (D).

26. **G** Soil X contains 5% clay, and Soil Y contains 40% clay. A soil with 10% clay should have topsoil deflation between the values for X and Y with 0% organic cover in Table 1, eliminating (F) and (J). Since 10% clay is most similar to the 5% clay found in Soil X, the topsoil deflation value is expected to be closer to 105,000 kg/ha than to 65,000 kg/ha, eliminating (H) and making (G) the best answer.

27. **D** Only Experiment 2 involved a variation in water content, eliminating (A) and (B). Between (C) and (D), only (D) provides a clear manner of comparing soils with different water contents.

28. **H** Experiment 1 investigates wind erosion of different types of topsoil with varying amounts of organic cover. If the fans did not adequately simulate the effects of real wind, it would be difficult to apply the findings to any practical situation, making (H) the best answer. Choice (F) is not an assumption but a variable being tested by the experiment. Choice (G) is the opposite of an assumption made in the experiment, that compost and straw do adequately simulate vegetation and organic cover. Choice (J) is not addressed in Experiment 1 because water content is not varied.

29. **C** Table 3 demonstrates that regardless of the water content, Soil X with the smaller clay percentage is more prone to topsoil deflation, making (C) the correct answer. Table 3 shows that erosion is related to water content for both soils, eliminating (A). Further, erosion takes place in the presence of water content, eliminating (B). Finally, Table 3 demonstrates that increased water content tends to decrease topsoil deflation, eliminating (D).

30. F Soil X contains 5% clay, and Soil Y contains 40% clay. A soil with 10% clay should have water content and topsoil deflation in Tables 2 and 3 that are between the values for Soils X and Y after 8 hours of sprinkling. Choices (H) and (J) have water contents that are too low, and (G) has an erosion value that is too low. Therefore, only (F) can be correct.

31. C According to Figure 1, bathypelagic, mesopelagic, and epipelagic zones are all within mutually exclusive depth ranges. In other words, none of them overlap, so (A), (B), and (D) are all eliminated and only (C) is possible. Depths between 100 and 200 m can be categorized in either the epipelagic or thermocline zone according to Figure 1.

32. J According to Figure 1, when total pressure is 1,200kPa, the ocean zone can be classified as epipelagic, continental shelf, or thermocline. Therefore, (J) is the best answer. Choices (F) and (G) are at higher pressures, and (H) is at a lower pressure.

33. C The points on Figure 2 where the two oceans would be indistinguishable for any temperature and depth combination would be where the two lines intersect. The tropical and temperate lines on Figure 2 intersect at two points, at depths of approximately 125 m and 625 m. This makes (C) the best answer. All other answer choices give depths where the two lines would yield different values of temperature and would thus be distinguishable from one another.

34. G The general trend for both regions in Table 1 is a decrease in ocean temperature with an increase in depth. This eliminates (F) and (H). However, Region 2 had a temperature of 8°C at a depth of both 39.7 m and 49.6 m, whereas Region 1 showed a decrease in temperature for every increased depth. Therefore, only Region 1 showed a consistent decrease in ocean temperature with increasing depth.

35. B Both Figure 1 and Table 1 demonstrate that as depth increases, total pressure increases. If the pressure at 79.5 m is 900kPa, it would be expected to increase beyond 900kPa at greater depth. Only (B) is possible. Note that (D) is eliminated because it is impossible to increase from 900 to 101kPa.

36. J Figure 1 shows that 800 mg of sulfamethoxazole results in greater bacterial elimination than 400 mg over time; (F) and (G) are both eliminated. Table 1 provides insight to the mechanism of action of sulfamethoxazole, so (H) is also eliminated. According to Figure 1, combining sulfamethoxazole (SMX) with either doxycycline or azithromycin increases overall elimination of a common skin infection bacterium, making (J) the best answer.

37. A According to Figure 1, it takes 120 minutes for an 800 mg dose of sulfamethoxazole to achieve 80% bacterial elimination and hence 20% original bacterial survival. At the same time, the 400 mg dose only achieves between 40–50% elimination. A 600 mg dose would be expected to give results between these two values at the 120 minute mark. Therefore, only (A) is possible because the time required to reach 20% survival would be greater than 120 minutes for a 600 mg dose.

38. **F** According to the passage and the data in Figure 1, penicillin is not very effective against the bacterium studied, but it does eliminate some bacteria, eliminating choices (H) and (J). In the experiment in the passage, less than 10% of the bacteria are eliminated by penicillin after 120 minutes (2 hours), meaning most survived. Therefore, (F) is better than (G).

39. **D** Figure 1 shows greater bacterial elimination by doxycycline and azithromycin when compounded with sulfamethoxazole (SMX). This eliminates (A) and (B). Choice (C) is a true statement. However, even though sulfamethoxazole 800 mg is more effective than SMX/azithromycin according to the figure, this does not answer the question of whether or not azithromycin is more effective when *combined with* sulfamethoxazole. Therefore, (D) is the best answer.

40. **H** The passage describes the goal of antibiotics as eliminating bacteria, so (F) and (G) are incorrect. From the data in Figure 1, it can be inferred that antibiotics that eliminate a large amount of bacteria in a short amount of time are most effective. This eliminates (J) and makes (H) the best answer.

WRITING TEST

To grade your essay, see the Essay Checklist on the following page. The following is an example of a top-scoring essay for the prompt given in this test. Note that it's not perfect, but it still follows an organized outline and has a strong introductory paragraph, a concluding paragraph, and transitions throughout.

The effects of population growth are very real issues for humans. As advances in medical technology increase our life expectancy and reproductive abilities, we find ourselves in the position of making lots more humans who in turn make lots more humans who then make even more humans, and the next thing we know, we're measuring our increases in billions. Our planet has a finite number of resources that are already challenged, and continuing to increase the number of humans on the planet will do nothing but further strain those resources. In order to alleviate the stresses of an overburdened planet, we need a more equitable and "green" distribution of resources and better global reproductive education.

Our planet provides all our resources for us, but we aren't using them responsibly. In some countries, people throw away tons of uneaten food while in other countries people hardly even get food to begin with. In some countries, people run clean water straight down the drain, simply waiting for it to warm up, while in other countries families walk several hours to collect a large jug or two of water for the whole day. Some countries, like Singapore and Hong Kong, have more than 18,000 people for every square mile, while in Alaska, the population averages out to just over one person per square mile. Although Perspective 2 fails to factor in the very real problem of increasing human numbers, the idea that problems are compounded by unequal distribution of resources is quite true. Perspective 1 places the blame squarely on the numbers themselves, but that's only part of the problem. Even such sustainable resources as oil and wind power have limits on how much can be harnessed in a given time. We have geographical limits on the number of oil wells we can dig, the number of wind turbines we can erect, how much potable water is available on our planet, and how much livestock can be produced for goods like food, leather, and wool. In order to ease the strain we place on our planet, we must consider ways to use the resources we have in a more responsible, sustainable, and equitable way.

The second thing we need to do is make sure our populations worldwide are educated about reproductive rates. Perspective 3 says that our population growth rate will naturally level off as we approach critical mass, but that seems a little idealistic. With increases in medical technology, humans in developed countries are living much longer than before. Our life expectancy in the United States has nearly doubled in the past two hundred years. In addition to folks living longer, advances in reproductive technology have allowed couples and individuals to reproduce who would not have had that ability a hundred years ago. While these advances are exciting and beneficial, they also skew the numbers higher than they would be otherwise. In order to maintain the human race without drastically increasing our numbers, we need to aim for the "replacement level" of reproduction, a level that aims for a one-to-one ratio between adult and child while also factoring in mortality rates. Ideally, the human race would sustain a population growth rate of zero. Though families such as the Duggars may make for entertaining television and dramatic magazine covers, giant families are no longer beneficial for the sustainability of the human race as a whole. It's not necessary to eliminate people or cease to care for the elderly or sick. We can support the number we have. As Perspective 2 points out, we have some time. We simply need to take advantage of that time to do something now rather than later.

The perpetuation of the human race is a good goal. We need to be aware of how we're growing, though, and make decided efforts to use our resources wisely and equitably, and educate everyone about ways to slow our growth rate so we don't run the danger of reaching the point of critical mass.

WRITING TEST

Essay Checklist

1. The Introduction
   Did you
   - start with a topic sentence that paraphrases or restates the prompt?
   - clearly state your position on the issue?

2. Body Paragraph 1
   Did you
   - start with a transition/topic sentence that discusses the opposing side of the argument?
   - give an example of a reason that one might agree with the opposing side of the argument?
   - clearly state that the opposing side of the argument is wrong or flawed?
   - show what is wrong with the opposing side's example or position?

3. Body Paragraphs 2 and 3
   Did you
   - start with a transition/topic sentence that discusses your position on the prompt?
   - give one example or reason to support your position?
   - show the grader how your example supports your position?
   - end the paragraph by restating your thesis?

4. Conclusion
   Did you
   - restate your position on the issue?
   - end with a flourish?

5. Overall
   Did you
   - write neatly?
   - avoid multiple spelling and grammar mistakes?
   - try to vary your sentence structure?
   - use a few impressive-sounding words?

SCORING YOUR PRACTICE EXAM

Step A

Count the number of correct answers for each section and record the number in the space provided for your raw score on the Score Conversion Worksheet below.

Step B

Using the Score Conversion Chart on the next page, convert your raw scores on each section to scaled scores. Then compute your composite ACT score by averaging the four subject scores. Add them up and divide by four. Don't worry about the essay score; it is not included in your composite score.

Score Conversion Worksheet		
Section	Raw Score	Scaled Score
1	_____/75	_____
2	_____/60	_____
3	_____/40	_____
4	_____/40	_____

SCORE CONVERSION CHART

Scaled Score	Raw Scores			
	Test 1 English	Test 2 Math	Test 3 Reading	Test 4 Science
36	75	60	40	40
35	73–74	59	39	39
34	72	58	38	—
33	71	57	37	38
32	70	54–56	36	37
31	69	52–53	35	36
30	68	50–51	34	—
29	66–67	48–49	33	35
28	65	46–47	32	33–34
27	63–64	44–45	30–31	32
26	61–62	42–43	29	31
25	59–60	40–41	28	29–30
24	57–58	37–39	26–27	28
23	55–56	35–36	25	26–27
22	52–54	33–34	24	24–25
21	49–51	31–32	23	23
20	46–48	29–30	21–22	21–22
19	44–45	26–28	20	19–20
18	41–43	23–25	19	17–18
17	39–40	20–22	18	14–16
16	36–38	17–19	16–17	13
15	33–35	14–16	15	11–12
14	31–32	12–13	14	09–10
13	29–30	10–11	12–13	08
12	27–28	08–09	10–11	06–07
11	25–26	06–07	09	05
10	23–24	05	07–08	—
09	22	04	06	04
08	18–21	—	—	03
07	15–17	03	05	02
06	12–14	02	04	—
05	09–11	—	03	—
04	07	—	—	01
03	05–06	01	02	—
02	03–04	—	01	—
01	00–02	00	00	00

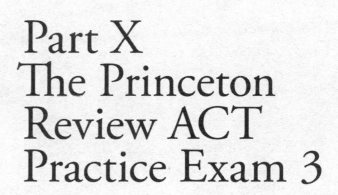

Part X
The Princeton Review ACT Practice Exam 3

Chapter 29
Practice Exam 3

ACT Diagnostic Test Form

Use a No. 2 pencil only. Be sure each mark is dark and completely fills the intended oval. Completely erase any errors or stray marks.

1. **YOUR NAME:** _____
(Print)　　　　　　　　　Last　　　　　　　　　First　　　　　　　　　M.I.

SIGNATURE: _____　**DATE:** _____ / _____ / _____

HOME ADDRESS: _____
(Print)　　　　　　　　　Number and Street

_____
City　　　　　　　　　State　　　　　　　Zip

E-MAIL: _____

PHONE NO.: _____
(Print)

SCHOOL: _____

CLASS OF: _____

IMPORTANT: Please fill in these boxes exactly as shown on the back cover of your tests book.

2. TEST FORM

_____

3. TEST CODE

⓪	⓪	⓪	⓪
①	①	①	①
②	②	②	②
③	③	③	③
④	④	④	④
⑤	⑤	⑤	⑤
⑥	⑥	⑥	⑥
⑦	⑦	⑦	⑦
⑧	⑧	⑧	⑧
⑨	⑨	⑨	⑨

4. PHONE NUMBER

⓪	⓪	⓪	⓪	⓪	⓪	⓪
①	①	①	①	①	①	①
②	②	②	②	②	②	②
③	③	③	③	③	③	③
④	④	④	④	④	④	④
⑤	⑤	⑤	⑤	⑤	⑤	⑤
⑥	⑥	⑥	⑥	⑥	⑥	⑥
⑦	⑦	⑦	⑦	⑦	⑦	⑦
⑧	⑧	⑧	⑧	⑧	⑧	⑧
⑨	⑨	⑨	⑨	⑨	⑨	⑨

5. YOUR NAME

First 4 letters of last name | FIRST INIT | MID INIT

Ⓐ	Ⓐ	Ⓐ	Ⓐ	Ⓐ	Ⓐ
Ⓑ	Ⓑ	Ⓑ	Ⓑ	Ⓑ	Ⓑ
Ⓒ	Ⓒ	Ⓒ	Ⓒ	Ⓒ	Ⓒ
Ⓓ	Ⓓ	Ⓓ	Ⓓ	Ⓓ	Ⓓ
Ⓔ	Ⓔ	Ⓔ	Ⓔ	Ⓔ	Ⓔ
Ⓕ	Ⓕ	Ⓕ	Ⓕ	Ⓕ	Ⓕ
Ⓖ	Ⓖ	Ⓖ	Ⓖ	Ⓖ	Ⓖ
Ⓗ	Ⓗ	Ⓗ	Ⓗ	Ⓗ	Ⓗ
Ⓘ	Ⓘ	Ⓘ	Ⓘ	Ⓘ	Ⓘ
Ⓙ	Ⓙ	Ⓙ	Ⓙ	Ⓙ	Ⓙ
Ⓚ	Ⓚ	Ⓚ	Ⓚ	Ⓚ	Ⓚ
Ⓛ	Ⓛ	Ⓛ	Ⓛ	Ⓛ	Ⓛ
Ⓜ	Ⓜ	Ⓜ	Ⓜ	Ⓜ	Ⓜ
Ⓝ	Ⓝ	Ⓝ	Ⓝ	Ⓝ	Ⓝ
Ⓞ	Ⓞ	Ⓞ	Ⓞ	Ⓞ	Ⓞ
Ⓟ	Ⓟ	Ⓟ	Ⓟ	Ⓟ	Ⓟ
Ⓠ	Ⓠ	Ⓠ	Ⓠ	Ⓠ	Ⓠ
Ⓡ	Ⓡ	Ⓡ	Ⓡ	Ⓡ	Ⓡ
Ⓢ	Ⓢ	Ⓢ	Ⓢ	Ⓢ	Ⓢ
Ⓣ	Ⓣ	Ⓣ	Ⓣ	Ⓣ	Ⓣ
Ⓤ	Ⓤ	Ⓤ	Ⓤ	Ⓤ	Ⓤ
Ⓥ	Ⓥ	Ⓥ	Ⓥ	Ⓥ	Ⓥ
Ⓦ	Ⓦ	Ⓦ	Ⓦ	Ⓦ	Ⓦ
Ⓧ	Ⓧ	Ⓧ	Ⓧ	Ⓧ	Ⓧ
Ⓨ	Ⓨ	Ⓨ	Ⓨ	Ⓨ	Ⓨ
Ⓩ	Ⓩ	Ⓩ	Ⓩ	Ⓩ	Ⓩ

6. DATE OF BIRTH

MONTH	DAY		YEAR	
◯ JAN				
◯ FEB				
◯ MAR	⓪	⓪	⓪	⓪
◯ APR	①	①	①	①
◯ MAY	②	②	②	②
◯ JUN	③	③	③	③
◯ JUL		④	④	④
◯ AUG		⑤	⑤	⑤
◯ SEP		⑥	⑥	⑥
◯ OCT		⑦	⑦	⑦
◯ NOV		⑧	⑧	⑧
◯ DEC		⑨	⑨	⑨

7. SEX

◯ MALE
◯ FEMALE

8. OTHER

1　Ⓐ Ⓑ Ⓒ Ⓓ Ⓔ
2　Ⓐ Ⓑ Ⓒ Ⓓ Ⓔ
3　Ⓐ Ⓑ Ⓒ Ⓓ Ⓔ

OpScan iNSIGHT™ forms by Pearson NCS EM-255315-1:654321　　　Printed in U.S.A.

THIS PAGE INTENTIONALLY LEFT BLANK

The Princeton Review
Diagnostic ACT Form

ENGLISH

1 Ⓐ Ⓑ Ⓒ Ⓓ	21 Ⓐ Ⓑ Ⓒ Ⓓ	41 Ⓐ Ⓑ Ⓒ Ⓓ	61 Ⓐ Ⓑ Ⓒ Ⓓ
2 Ⓕ Ⓖ Ⓗ Ⓙ	22 Ⓕ Ⓖ Ⓗ Ⓙ	42 Ⓕ Ⓖ Ⓗ Ⓙ	62 Ⓕ Ⓖ Ⓗ Ⓙ
3 Ⓐ Ⓑ Ⓒ Ⓓ	23 Ⓐ Ⓑ Ⓒ Ⓓ	43 Ⓐ Ⓑ Ⓒ Ⓓ	63 Ⓐ Ⓑ Ⓒ Ⓓ
4 Ⓕ Ⓖ Ⓗ Ⓙ	24 Ⓕ Ⓖ Ⓗ Ⓙ	44 Ⓕ Ⓖ Ⓗ Ⓙ	64 Ⓕ Ⓖ Ⓗ Ⓙ
5 Ⓐ Ⓑ Ⓒ Ⓓ	25 Ⓐ Ⓑ Ⓒ Ⓓ	45 Ⓐ Ⓑ Ⓒ Ⓓ	65 Ⓐ Ⓑ Ⓒ Ⓓ
6 Ⓕ Ⓖ Ⓗ Ⓙ	26 Ⓕ Ⓖ Ⓗ Ⓙ	46 Ⓕ Ⓖ Ⓗ Ⓙ	66 Ⓕ Ⓖ Ⓗ Ⓙ
7 Ⓐ Ⓑ Ⓒ Ⓓ	27 Ⓐ Ⓑ Ⓒ Ⓓ	47 Ⓐ Ⓑ Ⓒ Ⓓ	67 Ⓐ Ⓑ Ⓒ Ⓓ
8 Ⓕ Ⓖ Ⓗ Ⓙ	28 Ⓕ Ⓖ Ⓗ Ⓙ	48 Ⓕ Ⓖ Ⓗ Ⓙ	68 Ⓕ Ⓖ Ⓗ Ⓙ
9 Ⓐ Ⓑ Ⓒ Ⓓ	29 Ⓐ Ⓑ Ⓒ Ⓓ	49 Ⓐ Ⓑ Ⓒ Ⓓ	69 Ⓐ Ⓑ Ⓒ Ⓓ
10 Ⓕ Ⓖ Ⓗ Ⓙ	30 Ⓕ Ⓖ Ⓗ Ⓙ	50 Ⓕ Ⓖ Ⓗ Ⓙ	70 Ⓕ Ⓖ Ⓗ Ⓙ
11 Ⓐ Ⓑ Ⓒ Ⓓ	31 Ⓐ Ⓑ Ⓒ Ⓓ	51 Ⓐ Ⓑ Ⓒ Ⓓ	71 Ⓐ Ⓑ Ⓒ Ⓓ
12 Ⓕ Ⓖ Ⓗ Ⓙ	32 Ⓕ Ⓖ Ⓗ Ⓙ	52 Ⓕ Ⓖ Ⓗ Ⓙ	72 Ⓕ Ⓖ Ⓗ Ⓙ
13 Ⓐ Ⓑ Ⓒ Ⓓ	33 Ⓐ Ⓑ Ⓒ Ⓓ	53 Ⓐ Ⓑ Ⓒ Ⓓ	73 Ⓐ Ⓑ Ⓒ Ⓓ
14 Ⓕ Ⓖ Ⓗ Ⓙ	34 Ⓕ Ⓖ Ⓗ Ⓙ	54 Ⓕ Ⓖ Ⓗ Ⓙ	74 Ⓕ Ⓖ Ⓗ Ⓙ
15 Ⓐ Ⓑ Ⓒ Ⓓ	35 Ⓐ Ⓑ Ⓒ Ⓓ	55 Ⓐ Ⓑ Ⓒ Ⓓ	75 Ⓐ Ⓑ Ⓒ Ⓓ
16 Ⓕ Ⓖ Ⓗ Ⓙ	36 Ⓕ Ⓖ Ⓗ Ⓙ	56 Ⓕ Ⓖ Ⓗ Ⓙ	
17 Ⓐ Ⓑ Ⓒ Ⓓ	37 Ⓐ Ⓑ Ⓒ Ⓓ	57 Ⓐ Ⓑ Ⓒ Ⓓ	
18 Ⓕ Ⓖ Ⓗ Ⓙ	38 Ⓕ Ⓖ Ⓗ Ⓙ	58 Ⓕ Ⓖ Ⓗ Ⓙ	
19 Ⓐ Ⓑ Ⓒ Ⓓ	39 Ⓐ Ⓑ Ⓒ Ⓓ	59 Ⓐ Ⓑ Ⓒ Ⓓ	
20 Ⓕ Ⓖ Ⓗ Ⓙ	40 Ⓕ Ⓖ Ⓗ Ⓙ	60 Ⓕ Ⓖ Ⓗ Ⓙ	

MATHEMATICS

1 Ⓐ Ⓑ Ⓒ Ⓓ Ⓔ	16 Ⓕ Ⓖ Ⓗ Ⓙ Ⓚ	31 Ⓐ Ⓑ Ⓒ Ⓓ Ⓔ	46 Ⓕ Ⓖ Ⓗ Ⓙ Ⓚ
2 Ⓕ Ⓖ Ⓗ Ⓙ Ⓚ	17 Ⓐ Ⓑ Ⓒ Ⓓ Ⓔ	32 Ⓕ Ⓖ Ⓗ Ⓙ Ⓚ	47 Ⓐ Ⓑ Ⓒ Ⓓ Ⓔ
3 Ⓐ Ⓑ Ⓒ Ⓓ Ⓔ	18 Ⓕ Ⓖ Ⓗ Ⓙ Ⓚ	33 Ⓐ Ⓑ Ⓒ Ⓓ Ⓔ	48 Ⓕ Ⓖ Ⓗ Ⓙ Ⓚ
4 Ⓕ Ⓖ Ⓗ Ⓙ Ⓚ	19 Ⓐ Ⓑ Ⓒ Ⓓ Ⓔ	34 Ⓕ Ⓖ Ⓗ Ⓙ Ⓚ	49 Ⓐ Ⓑ Ⓒ Ⓓ Ⓔ
5 Ⓐ Ⓑ Ⓒ Ⓓ Ⓔ	20 Ⓕ Ⓖ Ⓗ Ⓙ Ⓚ	35 Ⓐ Ⓑ Ⓒ Ⓓ Ⓔ	50 Ⓕ Ⓖ Ⓗ Ⓙ Ⓚ
6 Ⓕ Ⓖ Ⓗ Ⓙ Ⓚ	21 Ⓐ Ⓑ Ⓒ Ⓓ Ⓔ	36 Ⓕ Ⓖ Ⓗ Ⓙ Ⓚ	51 Ⓐ Ⓑ Ⓒ Ⓓ Ⓔ
7 Ⓐ Ⓑ Ⓒ Ⓓ Ⓔ	22 Ⓕ Ⓖ Ⓗ Ⓙ Ⓚ	37 Ⓐ Ⓑ Ⓒ Ⓓ Ⓔ	52 Ⓕ Ⓖ Ⓗ Ⓙ Ⓚ
8 Ⓕ Ⓖ Ⓗ Ⓙ Ⓚ	23 Ⓐ Ⓑ Ⓒ Ⓓ Ⓔ	38 Ⓕ Ⓖ Ⓗ Ⓙ Ⓚ	53 Ⓐ Ⓑ Ⓒ Ⓓ Ⓔ
9 Ⓐ Ⓑ Ⓒ Ⓓ Ⓔ	24 Ⓕ Ⓖ Ⓗ Ⓙ Ⓚ	39 Ⓐ Ⓑ Ⓒ Ⓓ Ⓔ	54 Ⓕ Ⓖ Ⓗ Ⓙ Ⓚ
10 Ⓕ Ⓖ Ⓗ Ⓙ Ⓚ	25 Ⓐ Ⓑ Ⓒ Ⓓ Ⓔ	40 Ⓕ Ⓖ Ⓗ Ⓙ Ⓚ	55 Ⓐ Ⓑ Ⓒ Ⓓ Ⓔ
11 Ⓐ Ⓑ Ⓒ Ⓓ Ⓔ	26 Ⓕ Ⓖ Ⓗ Ⓙ Ⓚ	41 Ⓐ Ⓑ Ⓒ Ⓓ Ⓔ	56 Ⓕ Ⓖ Ⓗ Ⓙ Ⓚ
12 Ⓕ Ⓖ Ⓗ Ⓙ Ⓚ	27 Ⓐ Ⓑ Ⓒ Ⓓ Ⓔ	42 Ⓕ Ⓖ Ⓗ Ⓙ Ⓚ	57 Ⓐ Ⓑ Ⓒ Ⓓ Ⓔ
13 Ⓐ Ⓑ Ⓒ Ⓓ Ⓔ	28 Ⓕ Ⓖ Ⓗ Ⓙ Ⓚ	43 Ⓐ Ⓑ Ⓒ Ⓓ Ⓔ	58 Ⓕ Ⓖ Ⓗ Ⓙ Ⓚ
14 Ⓕ Ⓖ Ⓗ Ⓙ Ⓚ	29 Ⓐ Ⓑ Ⓒ Ⓓ Ⓔ	44 Ⓕ Ⓖ Ⓗ Ⓙ Ⓚ	59 Ⓐ Ⓑ Ⓒ Ⓓ Ⓔ
15 Ⓐ Ⓑ Ⓒ Ⓓ Ⓔ	30 Ⓕ Ⓖ Ⓗ Ⓙ Ⓚ	45 Ⓐ Ⓑ Ⓒ Ⓓ Ⓔ	60 Ⓕ Ⓖ Ⓗ Ⓙ Ⓚ

The Princeton Review
Diagnostic ACT Form

READING

1 Ⓐ Ⓑ Ⓒ Ⓓ		11 Ⓐ Ⓑ Ⓒ Ⓓ		21 Ⓐ Ⓑ Ⓒ Ⓓ		31 Ⓐ Ⓑ Ⓒ Ⓓ
2 Ⓕ Ⓖ Ⓗ Ⓙ		12 Ⓕ Ⓖ Ⓗ Ⓙ		22 Ⓕ Ⓖ Ⓗ Ⓙ		32 Ⓕ Ⓖ Ⓗ Ⓙ
3 Ⓐ Ⓑ Ⓒ Ⓓ		13 Ⓐ Ⓑ Ⓒ Ⓓ		23 Ⓐ Ⓑ Ⓒ Ⓓ		33 Ⓐ Ⓑ Ⓒ Ⓓ
4 Ⓕ Ⓖ Ⓗ Ⓙ		14 Ⓕ Ⓖ Ⓗ Ⓙ		24 Ⓕ Ⓖ Ⓗ Ⓙ		34 Ⓕ Ⓖ Ⓗ Ⓙ
5 Ⓐ Ⓑ Ⓒ Ⓓ		15 Ⓐ Ⓑ Ⓒ Ⓓ		25 Ⓐ Ⓑ Ⓒ Ⓓ		35 Ⓐ Ⓑ Ⓒ Ⓓ
6 Ⓕ Ⓖ Ⓗ Ⓙ		16 Ⓕ Ⓖ Ⓗ Ⓙ		26 Ⓕ Ⓖ Ⓗ Ⓙ		36 Ⓕ Ⓖ Ⓗ Ⓙ
7 Ⓐ Ⓑ Ⓒ Ⓓ		17 Ⓐ Ⓑ Ⓒ Ⓓ		27 Ⓐ Ⓑ Ⓒ Ⓓ		37 Ⓐ Ⓑ Ⓒ Ⓓ
8 Ⓕ Ⓖ Ⓗ Ⓙ		18 Ⓕ Ⓖ Ⓗ Ⓙ		28 Ⓕ Ⓖ Ⓗ Ⓙ		38 Ⓕ Ⓖ Ⓗ Ⓙ
9 Ⓐ Ⓑ Ⓒ Ⓓ		19 Ⓐ Ⓑ Ⓒ Ⓓ		29 Ⓐ Ⓑ Ⓒ Ⓓ		39 Ⓐ Ⓑ Ⓒ Ⓓ
10 Ⓕ Ⓖ Ⓗ Ⓙ		20 Ⓕ Ⓖ Ⓗ Ⓙ		30 Ⓕ Ⓖ Ⓗ Ⓙ		40 Ⓕ Ⓖ Ⓗ Ⓙ

SCIENCE REASONING

1 Ⓐ Ⓑ Ⓒ Ⓓ		11 Ⓐ Ⓑ Ⓒ Ⓓ		21 Ⓐ Ⓑ Ⓒ Ⓓ		31 Ⓐ Ⓑ Ⓒ Ⓓ
2 Ⓕ Ⓖ Ⓗ Ⓙ		12 Ⓕ Ⓖ Ⓗ Ⓙ		22 Ⓕ Ⓖ Ⓗ Ⓙ		32 Ⓕ Ⓖ Ⓗ Ⓙ
3 Ⓐ Ⓑ Ⓒ Ⓓ		13 Ⓐ Ⓑ Ⓒ Ⓓ		23 Ⓐ Ⓑ Ⓒ Ⓓ		33 Ⓐ Ⓑ Ⓒ Ⓓ
4 Ⓕ Ⓖ Ⓗ Ⓙ		14 Ⓕ Ⓖ Ⓗ Ⓙ		24 Ⓕ Ⓖ Ⓗ Ⓙ		34 Ⓕ Ⓖ Ⓗ Ⓙ
5 Ⓐ Ⓑ Ⓒ Ⓓ		15 Ⓐ Ⓑ Ⓒ Ⓓ		25 Ⓐ Ⓑ Ⓒ Ⓓ		35 Ⓐ Ⓑ Ⓒ Ⓓ
6 Ⓕ Ⓖ Ⓗ Ⓙ		16 Ⓕ Ⓖ Ⓗ Ⓙ		26 Ⓕ Ⓖ Ⓗ Ⓙ		36 Ⓕ Ⓖ Ⓗ Ⓙ
7 Ⓐ Ⓑ Ⓒ Ⓓ		17 Ⓐ Ⓑ Ⓒ Ⓓ		27 Ⓐ Ⓑ Ⓒ Ⓓ		37 Ⓐ Ⓑ Ⓒ Ⓓ
8 Ⓕ Ⓖ Ⓗ Ⓙ		18 Ⓕ Ⓖ Ⓗ Ⓙ		28 Ⓕ Ⓖ Ⓗ Ⓙ		38 Ⓕ Ⓖ Ⓗ Ⓙ
9 Ⓐ Ⓑ Ⓒ Ⓓ		19 Ⓐ Ⓑ Ⓒ Ⓓ		29 Ⓐ Ⓑ Ⓒ Ⓓ		39 Ⓐ Ⓑ Ⓒ Ⓓ
10 Ⓕ Ⓖ Ⓗ Ⓙ		20 Ⓕ Ⓖ Ⓗ Ⓙ		30 Ⓕ Ⓖ Ⓗ Ⓙ		40 Ⓕ Ⓖ Ⓗ Ⓙ

THIS PAGE INTENTIONALLY LEFT BLANK

ENGLISH TEST
45 Minutes—75 Questions

DIRECTIONS: In the five passages that follow, certain words and phrases are underlined and numbered. In the right-hand column, you will find alternatives for each underlined part. In most cases, you are to choose the one that best expresses the idea, makes the statement appropriate for standard written English, or is worded most consistently with the style and tone of the passage as a whole. If you think the original version is best, choose "NO CHANGE." In some cases, you will find in the right-hand column a question about the underlined part of the passage. You are to choose the best answer to the question.

You will also find questions about a section of the passage or the passage as a whole. These questions do not refer to an underlined portion of the passage, but rather are identified by a number or numbers in a box.

For each question, choose the alternative you consider best and blacken the corresponding oval on your answer document. Read each passage through once before you begin to answer the questions that accompany it. For many of the questions, you must read several sentences beyond the question to determine the answer. Be sure that you have read far enough ahead each time you choose an alternative.

PASSAGE I

The Rat Race

When I was a little girl, my family was deciding to move
from suburban Southern California to rural Northern California.
All of my friends lived in the neighborhood where I had grown

up but I didn't want to move. Classes starting in the fall and

unfamiliar faces looked at me with curiosity scared me stiff.

For example, I asked my parents why they were doing

this to me. I pleaded; begging to be allowed to stay behind
and live with my grandparents. My mother, trying to explain to
me, said, "Daddy needs to get away from the rat race." I
imagined my father in his car, surrounded by giant rats racing

1. **A.** NO CHANGE
    B. were deciding and moving
    C. were deciding to move
    D. decided to move

2. **F.** NO CHANGE
    G. up, because
    H. up, so
    J. up, but

3. **A.** NO CHANGE
    B. having looked
    C. looking
    D. DELETE the underlined portion.

4. **F.** NO CHANGE
    G. Nevertheless, I
    H. I, however,
    J. I

5. **A.** NO CHANGE
    B. pleaded, begging to be allowed
    C. pleaded, begging to be allowed,
    D. pleaded begging to be allowed

GO ON TO THE NEXT PAGE.

him home and <u>was blocking</u> his way. In my imagination
₆

<u>he didn't look scared so much as frustrated.</u>
₇

<u>I finally asked my father why he wanted us to move so far</u>
₈
<u>away from home.</u> One of his main reasons, he said, was the long
₈

drive home after work. For him, <u>the worst and most terrible thing,</u>
₉
about living in Southern California was having no time to go

fishing, one of his favorite hobbies.

[1] My parents eventually picked Redding for our new home,

partly because there were two lakes within an hour's drive, and

we made the move. [2] Since my father's new commute was

only fifteen minutes, he would be able to go fishing after work

sometimes. [3] I was sad to say goodbye to my friends when we

finally did move. [4] However, I had to admit that my father

looked <u>happier than</u> he had in years. [5] Before the move, he
₁₀
used to complain about crazy drivers while eating reheated

leftovers. [6] After the move, we had <u>dinner and, talked</u> about
₁₁

the weekend calmly as a family. [12]

6. **F.** NO CHANGE
   G. blocking
   H. were blocking
   J. DELETE the underlined portion.

7. At this point, the author would like to give the reader a better idea of how she thought her father felt. Given that all the choices are true, which one best accomplishes this purpose?

   A. NO CHANGE
   B. he was stuck on the highway for hours and hours.
   C. he couldn't see the rats even though I could.
   D. he looked so small compared to the giant rats.

8. Given that all the choices are true, which one provides the best opening to this paragraph?

   F. NO CHANGE
   G. The rats seemed like more of an annoyance than a danger.
   H. I didn't really understand what my mom meant by the "rat race" until years later.
   J. During holidays and long weekends, my father loved to go fishing.

9. **A.** NO CHANGE
   B. the most awfully terrible part
   C. the worst, most terrible thing
   D. the worst part

10. **F.** NO CHANGE
    G. more happier then
    H. happier then
    J. the happiest than

11. **A.** NO CHANGE
    B. dinner and talked,
    C. dinner, and talked
    D. dinner and talked

12. For the sake of the logic and coherence of this paragraph, Sentence 5 should be placed:

    F. where it is now.
    G. after Sentence 1.
    H. after Sentence 2.
    J. after Sentence 3.

GO ON TO THE NEXT PAGE.

As I got older, when we visited family and friends in Southern <u>California. I could</u> see the difference from the traffic at home in Redding. There weren't any huge rats on the highway,
₁₃

but as I sat in the car watching <u>the endless lines</u> of cars, I got a glimpse of what my parents had meant. Redding might have
₁₄
been unpleasantly empty of familiar associations for me but that same emptiness was more pleasant for my parents, because it included empty roads, empty skies, and empty days to fill as they pleased.

13. **A.** NO CHANGE
    B. California; I
    C. California, I
    D. California and I

14. **F.** NO CHANGE
    G. the unending and interminable lines
    H. the endlessly, continuing forever, lines
    J. the lines, going on into eternity without end

Question 15 asks about the preceding passage as a whole

---

15. Suppose the writer's goal had been to write a short essay telling the reader why, in her opinion, her family moved to Redding. Would this essay successfully fulfill that goal?

    A. Yes, because it describes her father's reasons for wanting to move, as the author understands them.
    B. Yes, because it demonstrates that children sometimes have misconceptions about the reasons for a move.
    C. No, because it fails to explain why the author was frightened by the prospect of the move.
    D. No, because it focuses more heavily on the feelings of a party other than the author.

PASSAGE II

The Latino Murals of Los Angeles

The Mexican-American artist Judith Baca credits her family for her artistic inspiration. She was raised by her mother and <u>grandmother, themselves</u> in a vibrant Latino community in East
₁₆
Los Angeles. Her art is thus a tribute to her family's past as well

as to her cultural <u>heritage, which she believes</u> her art embodies
₁₇
the spirit of Los Angeles.

Baca studied art both in Los Angeles and Cuernavaca, Mexico. Her chosen field of <u>art, the mural,</u> has long been a part
₁₈
of Mexican artistic culture, and has experienced a popular

16. **F.** NO CHANGE
    G. grandmother, themselves,
    H. grandmother related to her
    J. grandmother

17. **A.** NO CHANGE
    B. heritage; she
    C. heritage, she
    D. heritage, but she

18. **F.** NO CHANGE
    G. art, the mural—
    H. art the mural—
    J. art the mural,

GO ON TO THE NEXT PAGE.

revival in Los Angeles in recent years. She has gained fame for
her colorful murals depicting episodes from Latino history, many
                                                              19

of which can be found in the Los Angeles area. [20]

Moreover, the recent popularity of the mural as a form of
          21
art is often linked to the prevalence of graffiti in urban areas.
Some of the earliest examples of modern murals, such as

Willie Herrón's *The Wall That Cracked Open*, was treated
                                                       22
as graffiti, rather than art. Many muralists remain
anonymous, and their works tend to be in public places.

Some murals political messages also made people uneasy
     23
about this art form in the early days of its resurgence.

Today, however, city officials often hire known
muralists such as Baca to create masterpieces on
government property. Because of their size, murals often
require the assistance of other artists and, as evidence,
                                              24
sometimes become community efforts. Murals are also

a way for people to connect their cultural past with their present
                                                          25
reality, by using traditional figures to tell modern stories.
                                    25
It is this community involvement that has helped sway the
minds of officials, as well as the realization that many
murals convey positive messages. Some depict scenes

19. The underlined phrase could be placed in all the following locations EXCEPT:

   A. where it is now.
   B. after the word *revival*.
   C. after the word *popular*.
   D. before the word *experienced*.

20. If the writer were to delete the preceding sentence, the essay would primarily lose:

   F. an artistic evaluation of Baca's techniques compared to traditional techniques.
   G. an explanation of the historical circumstances that led to the development of murals as an art form.
   H. an analysis of Baca's place in the rebirth of murals with themes from Latino history.
   J. a piece of information regarding Baca's success and one region in which her work is popular.

21. A. NO CHANGE
    B. However, the
    C. The
    D. Therefore, the

22. F. NO CHANGE
    G. was mistakenly treated
    H. were treated
    J. was treated, by mistake,

23. A. NO CHANGE
    B. murals political messages,
    C. mural's political messages
    D. murals' political messages

24. F. NO CHANGE
    G. stated
    H. a result
    J. imagined

25. Given that all the choices are true, which one provides the most relevant information at this point in the essay?

    A. NO CHANGE
    B. more accessible to members of the public than most art is, because they are located in the heart of the community.
    C. often funded by government agencies that want to cover up abandoned factories and warehouses.
    D. particularly effective for telling allegorical stories, in part because their large size gives artists so much room.

GO ON TO THE NEXT PAGE.

of multicultural harmony, they are inspired by the
26
neighborhoods in which they are situated. Others show

scenes of past successes by members of the community. Still
27
others strive to depict the historic achievements of the generations
past.

By creating beautiful murals in her neighborhood,
Baca is working to create a sense of community pride. The bright
28

faces of the people, she paints signal the bright possibilities
29

available to the viewer. They're successes, Baca suggests, can be
30
yours.

26. **F.** NO CHANGE
    G. harmony, it was prompted
    H. harmony, that was inspired
    J. harmony, inspired

27. **A.** NO CHANGE
    B. by members of the community of past successes
    C. of past successes of the community by members
    D. of the community by members of past successes

28. **F.** NO CHANGE
    G. a sense of community pride is being created by Baca.
    H. the community is developing a sense of pride.
    J. a sense of community pride, which Baca is working to create.

29. **A.** NO CHANGE
    B. people she paints:
    C. people; she paints
    D. people she paints

30. **F.** NO CHANGE
    G. Its
    H. Their
    J. It's

PASSAGE III

The Birth of the Video Game

The last decade had saw increasingly sophisticated video
31
gaming consoles that allow players to compete at great distances,
control characters through body movements, and much more. The
possibilities of video gaming, taken for granted today, were
mind-blowing in 1972 when Nolan Bushnell and Ted Dabney
32
introduced the public to their new creation: *Pong*.

There had been other video games before *Pong*, of course. The
necessary technology had been developed as early as 1952, and
Pong were preceded by several other games, such as *Tennis for*
33

31. **A.** NO CHANGE
    B. has seen
    C. has saw
    D. would of seen

32. **F.** NO CHANGE
    G. 1972, where
    H. 1972, in which
    J. 1972, that

33. **A.** NO CHANGE
    B. precede
    C. was preceding
    D. was preceded

GO ON TO THE NEXT PAGE.

Two, Spacewar!, and *Computer Science.* However, it was not
until *Pong*, with its simple interface and addictive nature, that
the concept of home video gaming systems really took off.

[34]

[1] Looking back on *Pong* today, it seems ridiculously
old-fashioned, so it's easy to contrast it with modern games. [2]
It's not that *Pong* was the most advanced game of the

era: Several earlier games, in fact; were actually more
technologically advanced. [3] *Pong*'s strength was its

combination of novelty and accessibility. [4] The other games,
sophisticated as they were, simply proved too difficult for

the average consumer or person considering making a purchase.

[5] However, it was groundbreaking in its day, in it's own way. [40]

34. The writer is considering deleting the preceding sentence from the essay. The sentence should NOT be deleted because it:

F. serves as a transition from the more general discussion about *Pong* to the more specific description of what made *Pong* successful.

G. describes the technical skill required to play *Pong*, which is important to understanding the essay.

H. demonstrates which elements of *Pong* led to its ultimate ascendance over other, more technologically sophisticated games.

J. shows that those who claim that *Pong* was the first modern video game are basing their claim on insufficient information.

35. Given that all the choices are true, which one would best complete the sentence so that it most clearly explains the writer's reasons for calling *Pong* "old-fashioned"?

A. NO CHANGE

B. with its basic graphics, simplistic game play, and repetition.

C. and some people like for things to stay that way.

D. because of the lack of technological development and complex game-play.

36. F. NO CHANGE

G. games in fact,

H. games, in fact,

J. games, in fact

37. Which of the following alternatives to the underlined word would be LEAST acceptable?

A. uniqueness

B. complexity

C. innovation

D. freshness

38. F. NO CHANGE

G. the average consumer or individual possibly purchasing it.

H. the average consumer or someone making a purchase, possibly.

J. the average consumer.

39. A. NO CHANGE

B. they're

C. their

D. its

40. For the sake of the logic and coherence of this paragraph, Sentence 5 should be placed:

F. where it is now.

G. after Sentence 1.

H. after Sentence 2.

J. after Sentence 3.

GO ON TO THE NEXT PAGE.

The history of the video game becomes more understandable when it is remembered that the creators of early games were primarily engineers and mathematicians, developing these games for their own amusement, they paid little attention to popular marketing. These pioneering developers saw the games they created as "doodling," more or less. Even when they introduced their products to the public, they usually did so as part of a showpiece, on a temporary basis.

So just think of how far video game technology has come, and don't forget that the technology continues to advance every day. In *Pong*, a player uses a single knob to send a "ball" back and forth across the screen, gaining points and trying to prevent the ball from slipping past the "paddle," a bar at the bottom of the screen. Compared to high complex games like *Super Mario Galaxy* and *Halo*, *Pong* may seem laughable.

But anyway, I still think *Pong* is fun to play sometimes.

41.
A. NO CHANGE
B. mathematicians only developing
C. mathematicians. Developing
D. mathematicians, only developing

42.
F. NO CHANGE
G. public, whom they met at special events,
H. public, who wouldn't normally see their products,
J, public, with whom they spoke at events,

43.
A. NO CHANGE
B. high complexity
C. highly complexity
D. highly complex

44. Given that all the choices are true, which one would most effectively express the writer's attitude towards the future of the video game industry?
F. NO CHANGE.
G. The men who created *Pong* are truly to be thanked for introducing the world to one of its most entertaining hobbies.
H. At its core, *Pong* represents the ultimate goal of all video games: just having a good time.
J. Still, it opened the door to all of the advances that have come since, and that will no doubt continue until the games of today seem just as ridiculous as *Pong*.

Question 45 asks about the preceding passage as a whole

45. Suppose the writer's goal had been to write an essay demonstrating the impact a single invention can have on the development of an industry. Would this essay fulfill that goal?
A. No, because the essay focuses too heavily on the other games that preceded *Pong* rather than its actual impact.
B. No, because the essay concludes that *Pong* was ultimately not as influential as some assert.
C. Yes, because the essay explains how *Pong* was able to gain widespread acceptance for video games.
D. Yes, because the essay demonstrates that *Pong* was the first video game released to the public.

GO ON TO THE NEXT PAGE.

PASSAGE IV

The Life of a Hero

During a weekend visit <u>a while back</u>, I decided to show my
₄₆
nephew, Paul, my old comic books. The pristine copies of
Superman, *Spider-Man*, and my favorite, *Green Lantern*, were
all stored neatly in a box. I thought it would be fun to introduce
him to my favorite handful of characters. I knew Superman and
Spider-Man were still popular, but I figured the Green Lantern of
my youth had <u>probably went</u> the way of other long-forgotten
₄₇
heroes.

John Stewart, the first African-American to serve
as the <u>Green Lantern was one</u> of the first African-
₄₈
American superheroes to become widely popular. A

former <u>Marine and a practiced</u> and fearsome warrior. With
₄₉

his ring, he was almost unstoppable. He was <u>a fighter,</u>
₅₀
leading, and, on top of everything else, acting cool. Stewart

seemed to embody everything <u>I could have wanted</u> for my
₅₁
future: the respect of others, the power to control himself,

and <u>he was known for having a great sense of style.</u>
₅₂

46. Which choice provides the most specific information?
   - F. NO CHANGE
   - G. a few years ago
   - H. last summer
   - J. some time ago

47. A. NO CHANGE
   - B. probably gone
   - C. probably had left
   - D. probably went out

48. F. NO CHANGE
   - G. Lantern, was one,
   - H. Lantern, was one
   - J. Lantern was one,

49. A. NO CHANGE
   - B. Marine, he practiced
   - C. Marine, he was a practiced
   - D. Marine, practicing

50. F. NO CHANGE
   - G. was good at fighting,
   - H. had an ability to fight,
   - J. could fight,

51. A. NO CHANGE
   - B. could of wanted
   - C. could of been wanting
   - D. DELETE the underlined portion

52. F. NO CHANGE
   - G. he dressed with great personal style.
   - H. the best sense of style ever.
   - J. his sense of personal style was really great.

GO ON TO THE NEXT PAGE.

Growing up in the 1970s, I idolized Stewart. ⬚53 I devoured the comics featuring Stewart, not just because he was a true superhero but because of his back-story. Unlike Superman, Stewart seemed like a hero I could understand.

His life had its ups and its downs; his problems were real life
_____
                                              54
problems that I could relate to. He got in trouble sometimes and
_____
         54
fought with his friends and family. He came from a bad neighborhood and hadn't always been on the road to superhero status.

For a little while in the early 1990s, there was a series that focused solely on Stewart as the Green Lantern, but after
                                                          _____
                                                           55
it ended, Stewart was replaced and seemed likely to be

forgotten. Much to my surprise, however, Paul knew exactly
                                 _____
                                    56
who Stewart was. He was just as big a fan as I had been, but

for different reasons. For me, Stewart's rocky, life story was
                               _____
                                      57
central to his appeal. For Paul, however, Stewart's past didn't matter as much as did his actions; Paul admired Stewart because he was such a strong role model.
           _____
                           58

When I was young, Stewart was a role model that I could identify with. I assumed Paul would either have his own role models or would share my feelings about my role models.

53. At this point, the writer is considering adding the following true statement:

> Each Green Lantern was chosen by a group called The Guardians, whose members took into consideration a number of personal qualities, including physical strength, moral fiber, and a strong sense of duty to all living beings.

Should the writer make this addition here?

A. Yes, because it provides important background information that helps the reader understand the essay.
B. Yes, because it contributes to the writer's discussion of Stewart's positive attributes.
C. No, because it undermines the author's claim that Stewart was a more realistic role model.
D. No, because it provides information that is irrelevant to the main point of the paragraph.

54. Given that all of the choices are true, which one best explains the author's belief that Stewart was a more understandable character and shows a more realistic image of Stewart?

F. NO CHANGE
G. Stewart was a more sympathetic character and I had an easier time imagining myself in his shoes.
H. The Green Lantern ring allowed Stewart to fly into space, create weapons out of thin air, and protect his friends.
J. Unlike Superman, Stewart couldn't fly without his ring because he didn't naturally have superpowers.

55. A. NO CHANGE
    B. after;
    C. after:
    D. after,

56. Which of the following alternatives to the underlined portion would be LEAST acceptable?

F. though,
G. furthermore,
H. on the contrary
J. DELETE the underlined portion

57. A. NO CHANGE
    B. Stewarts rocky
    C. Stewarts' rocky,
    D. Stewart's rocky

58. Which choice most effectively supports the point being made in the first part of this sentence?

F. NO CHANGE
G. of what he did, not who he was.
H. of what he represented.
J. he was able to overcome his past.

GO ON TO THE NEXT PAGE.

Instead, he shared my role models but not my reasons. To him, Stewart was simply a superhero, just like Superman. He admired them both without worrying about that. In Paul's worldview, all ₅₉

superheroes are simply superheroes they're heroes, regardless of ₆₀ their pasts, not because of them.

59. **A.** NO CHANGE
B. their back-stories.
C. all that.
D. those.

60. **F.** NO CHANGE
G. superheroes; they're
H. superheroes, they're
J. superheroes being

PASSAGE V

Into the Trenches

It has often been suggested that, contrary to the worn-out time saying, the ocean, rather than space, is the true ₆₁

final frontier. There is the immense pressure that poses a serious ₆₂ danger to unknown geography that can injure people and vessel alike, various factors make sending human explorers very risky. Deep-sea expeditions also tend to incur prohibitive costs, with ₆₃ the cost increasing as the expedition ventures into deeper regions. The deepest section of the ocean is the *Marianas Trench*. [64] Due primarily to its depth and the potential for danger, the *Marianas Trench* remains largely unexplored to this day.

61. **A.** NO CHANGE
B. timeworn
C. timed out
D. out of time

62. **F.** NO CHANGE
G. From
H. Just like
J. Between

63. Given that all the choices are true, which one is the most relevant to the statement that follows in this sentence?

A. NO CHANGE
B. are known for being rather difficult,
C. are dangerous to diver and sea-life alike,
D. often cause damage to human life and to equipment,

64. The writer is considering adding the following true information to the end of the preceding sentence (placing a comma after the word *Trench*):

> which begins at 20,000 feet, has points where the depth approaches seven miles, and pressure reaching eight tons per square inch.

Should the writer make this addition?

F. Yes, because it provides specific information about the *Marianas Trench* that explains why the author included this sentence.
G. Yes, because it demonstrates how valuable human-led explorations of the depths of the ocean and likely to be.
H. No, because it detracts from the writer's discussion of the potential dangers of deep-sea exploration.
J. No, because it weakens the writer's point about the correlation between increasing depth and increasing cost.

GO ON TO THE NEXT PAGE.

The shallow portions of the oceans also hold many
fascinating species of plants and animals. The environment,
hostile though it may be to man, is hospitable to others,

65. Given that all the choices are true, which one best leads from the preceding paragraph to the subject of this paragraph?
A. NO CHANGE
B. One danger of deep-sea diving is a medical condition caused by an abrupt change in outside pressure.
C. Some argue that the bottom of the ocean isn't truly any more dangerous than the deep rainforest or highest mountain peaks.
D. Even knowing about all of the obstacles, however, some scientists feel the draw of the ocean's depths.

allowing for the development of creatures not found anywhere
else on the planet. The first and last exploration of the *Marianas*

66. F. NO CHANGE
G. to which development has been allowed
H. which allows for the developing of
J. development has been allowed

Trench's floor took place in 1960. Therefore, the cost of sending
people back has been seen as too great, the danger as too serious.

67. A. NO CHANGE
B. Nevertheless,
C. In contrast,
D. Since then,

The goal, then, has been to find a way to learn about this
frontier without risking the lives of scientist-explorers. One way
that scientists had discovered new information is through the use

68. F. NO CHANGE
G. could of discovered
H. were discovering
J. have discovered

of sonar. As sonar—which is far less expensive than a human-led
diving expedition is—capabilities have improved, scientists have
been able to get more accurate maps of the ocean's floor based
on sound-imaging.

69. Given that all the choices are true, which one most effectively describes what sonar is?
A. NO CHANGE
B. initially developed during World War I—
C. a sound-based method of determining surroundings—
D. not completely unlike the echolocation used by certain animals—

Another method of exploration that has become more
common in recent years, as technology has advanced revolves
around the use of unmanned submersibles. These include devices

70. F. NO CHANGE
G. advanced,
H. advanced—
J. advanced:

as simple for cameras and as advanced as underwater robots able
to perform a wide-range of functions. The latter have become
increasingly common in recent years as they have become ever
more advanced.

71. A. NO CHANGE
B. as
C. than
D. DELETE the underlined portion

The question faced today is why these underwater robots
will be sufficient, eliminating the need to send humans back

72. F. NO CHANGE
G. what
H. whether
J. DELETE the underlined portion

GO ON TO THE NEXT PAGE.

into the depths. Most of the robots used thus far have been
<u>73</u>
"tethered," or attached in some way to a larger device with

people aboard, the day when the robots can move independently

may not be far off. Given the extreme depths of some locations,

however, it seems likely that self-propelled robots will become

more useful and handy. If that is the case, one is forced to
<u>74</u>
wonder: Are more complex robots truly the key, or will humans

need to venture back into the ocean's inky depths? [75]

73. A. NO CHANGE
    B. Most, if not all,
    C. Although most
    D. All or most

74. F. NO CHANGE
    G. practically useful.
    H. useful.
    J. effectively useful.

75. The writer is considering ending the essay with the following sentence:

> Perhaps one day humans will be able to create a robot able to simulate the emotional responses of a human, or even a robot with the ability to experience feelings.

Should the writer add this sentence here?

A. Yes, because it expands the essay to encompass the ethical concerns raised by the development of artificial intelligence.
B. Yes, because it explains one reason for continued reliance on robots in deep-sea explorations.
C. No, because it fails to consider the usefulness of robots in present and future deep-sea exploration, as well as whether their use is cost-effective.
D. No, because it distracts from the essay's central topic of deep-sea exploration and the issues preventing humans from leading expeditions.

END OF TEST 1

STOP! DO NOT TURN THE PAGE UNTIL TOLD TO DO SO.

MATHEMATICS TEST

60 Minutes—60 Questions

DIRECTIONS: Solve each problem, choose the correct answer, and then darken the corresponding oval on your answer sheet.

Do not linger over problems that take too much time. Solve as many as you can; then return to the others in the time you have left for this test.

You are permitted to use a calculator on this test. You may use your calculator for any problems you choose,

but some of the problems may best be done without using a calculator.

Note: Unless otherwise stated, all of the following should be assumed:

1. Illustrative figures are NOT necessarily drawn to scale.
2. Geometric figures lie in a plane.
3. The word *line* indicates a straight line.
4. The word *average* indicates arithmetic mean.

DO YOUR FIGURING HERE.

1. If $\dfrac{5y-1}{3} = -6$, then which of the following must be true?

   A. $y = -18$

   B. $y = -\dfrac{19}{5}$

   C. $y = -\dfrac{17}{5}$

   D. $y = -1$

   E. $y = \dfrac{17}{5}$

2. The expression $\dfrac{12z^{10}}{4z^2}$ is equivalent to:

   F. $3z^5$
   G. $8z^5$
   H. $3z^8$
   J. $8z^8$
   K. $8z^{12}$

3. If $f(x) = \dfrac{x^2 - 18}{x + 2}$, then $f(12) = ?$

   A. -4
   B. 3
   C. 9
   D. 12
   E. 126

GO ON TO THE NEXT PAGE.

4. In one month, Rebecca, an entertainment journalist, recorded how many movies she watched and how many articles she wrote. She plotted this data in the graphs below: Graph 1 shows the relationship between the time elapsed and the number of movies watched; Graph 2 shows the relationship between the number of movies watched and the number of articles written. According to this data, how many articles did she write in the first 3 weeks of this month?

DO YOUR FIGURING HERE.

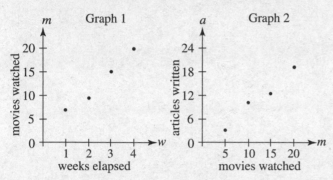

F. 3
G. 5
H. 8
J. 12
K. 15

5. What is the value of $117 - 54 + 6$, rounded to the nearest ten?

A. 40
B. 50
C. 60
D. 70
E. 80

6. A restaurant has 4 napkins at each table, plus 20 extra napkins held in reserve. If the restaurant has a total of 100 napkins, how many tables are in the restaurant?

F. 15
G. 20
H. 25
J. 30
K. 35

7. If $4(w-2) - w = 46$, then $w = ?$

A. 8
B. 10
C. 16
D. 18
E. 20

GO ON TO THE NEXT PAGE.

8. Six points (U, V, W, X, Y, Z) appear on a number line in that order, as shown in the figure below. Which of the following rays does NOT contain $\overline{WX}$?

$$\underset{\underset{U}{\bullet} \; \underset{V}{\bullet} \; \underset{W}{\bullet} \; \underset{X}{\bullet} \; \underset{Y}{\bullet} \; \underset{Z}{\bullet}}{\vphantom{x}}$$

F. $\overrightarrow{UY}$

G. $\overrightarrow{VZ}$

H. $\overrightarrow{YV}$

J. $\overrightarrow{YZ}$

K. $\overrightarrow{ZV}$

9. If $ab = 32$, $bc = 40$, and $c = 5$, then which of the following could be the value of a ?

A. 4

B. 6

C. 8

D. 10

E. 12

10. Yunyun swam 4 laps, and her coach recorded her time for each as 43.4 seconds, 44.1 seconds, 42.9 seconds, and 45.4 seconds, respectively, for a total of 175.8 seconds. If Yunyun must swim her 5th lap in x seconds in order to make her average time for all 5 laps 43 seconds, then which of the following equations could be solved for the correct value of x ?

F. $\dfrac{175.8 + x}{5} = \dfrac{43}{60}$

G. $\dfrac{175.8 + x}{5} = 43$

H. $\dfrac{175.8 + x}{4} = 43$

J. $\dfrac{175.8}{5} + x = 43$

K. $\dfrac{175.8}{4} + x = 43$

11. For how many integers from 123 to 132 is the tens digit greater than the ones digit?

A. 2

B. 3

C. 4

D. 9

E. 10

GO ON TO THE NEXT PAGE.

12. The number of points Julie scores in a basketball game is proportional to the amount of time she practiced that week. Last week, Julie scored 20 points after practicing for 12 hours. How many hours should Julie practice this week if she wants to score 35 points?

F. 7
G. 14
H. 16
J. 20
K. 21

DO YOUR FIGURING HERE.

13. Rectangle *ABCD* is graphed in the (x, y) coordinate plane below. What fraction of rectangle *ABCD* lies in Quadrant IV ?

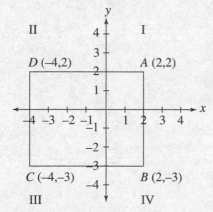

A. $\dfrac{2}{15}$

B. $\dfrac{1}{5}$

C. $\dfrac{4}{15}$

D. $\dfrac{1}{3}$

E. $\dfrac{2}{5}$

GO ON TO THE NEXT PAGE.

14. Which of the following is equivalent to the expression $\dfrac{2(z+3)-9}{5+4(z+3)}$?

    F. $-\dfrac{9}{5}$

    G. $-\dfrac{9}{10}$

    H. $-\dfrac{7}{9}$

    J. $\dfrac{-7z-21}{9z+15}$

    K. $\dfrac{2z-3}{4z+17}$

15. A circle with the equation $x^2 + y^2 = 49$ is graphed in the standard (x, y) coordinate plane. At which 2 points does this circle intersect the x-axis?

    A. $(-1,0)$ and $(1,0)$
    B. $(-7,0)$ and $(7,0)$
    C. $(-14,0)$ and $(14,0)$
    D. $(-21,0)$ and $(21,0)$
    E. $(-49,0)$ and $(49,0)$

16. Four actors (Jessica, Kevin, Lisa, and Michael) stand around a circular stage of circumference 19 feet. Kevin stands 5 feet counterclockwise from Jessica. Lisa stands 9 feet clockwise from Jessica. Michael stands 6 feet clockwise from Jessica and 13 feet counterclockwise from Jessica. In what order do the actors stand, starting with Jessica and going clockwise around the stage?

    F.   Jessica, Kevin, Lisa, Michael
    G.   Jessica, Kevin, Michael, Lisa
    H.   Jessica, Lisa, Kevin, Michael
    J.   Jessica, Michael, Kevin, Lisa
    K.   Jessica, Michael, Lisa, Kevin

17. In 1905, the distance between the edge of a lake and Marker X was 75 meters. In 2005, the distance between the edge of this lake and Marker X was 825 meters. If the edge of this lake withdrew from Marker X at a linear rate, then what was the distance, in meters, between the edge of the lake and Marker X in 1985 ?

    A.   675
    B.   682.5
    C.   690
    D.   705
    E.   750

GO ON TO THE NEXT PAGE.

DO YOUR FIGURING HERE.

18. For a decorating project, Beatrice found the area and perimeter of a drawing she made of a beach scene. She found that the area of her rectangular drawing was 144 square inches and that the perimeter was 80 inches. When she arrived at the craft store to purchase a frame for her drawing, she discovered that she had forgotten to write down the dimensions of her drawing. What are the dimensions of Beatrice's drawing, in inches?

   F. 4 by 36
   G. 6 by 24
   H. 8 by 18
   J. 9 by 16
   K. 12 by 12

19. Which of the following is equivalent to 5.046×10^{-3} ?

   A. 5,046
   B.   504.6
   C.   5.046
   D.   0.05046
   E.   0.005046

20. If the values of s and t are directly proportional and $s = 8$ when $t = 10$, then what is the value of s when $t = 15$?

   F. $\dfrac{4}{5}$

   G. $\dfrac{3}{2}$

   H. 12

   J. 13

   K. 18

21. The cost to rent headphones at the listening library is $3.50 for the first hour (or any fraction thereof), $2.50 for the second hour (or any fraction thereof), and $1.25 for each additional hour (or any fraction thereof) beyond the first two. If you rent headphones at 2:12 P.M. and are charged $9.75 when you return them, then which of the following could be the time you return the headphones?

   (Note: Assume that this listening library does not charge additional taxes or fees.)

   A. 5:30 P.M.
   B. 6:30 P.M.
   C. 7:30 P.M.
   D. 8:00 P.M.
   E. 8:30 P.M.

GO ON TO THE NEXT PAGE.

22. The degree measures of the 4 angles of quadrilateral *LMNO*, shown below, form a geometric sequence with a common ratio of 2. What is the last term of the sequence?

DO YOUR FIGURING HERE.

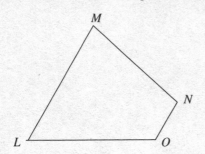

    F.   24°
    G. 96°
    H. 160°
    J.   192°
    K. 216°

23. Points *E*, *F*, and *G* are collinear. Point *H* is a point not on $\overline{EG}$. If the measure of $\angle GFH$ is 64°, then what is the measure of $\angle EFH$?

    A.   26°
    B.   58°
    C.   64°
    D. 116°
    E. 296°

24. If $6x + 10y = 14$ and $3x + 4y = 2$, then what is the value of $5x + 7y$?

    F.   5
    G.   2
    H. −5
    J.   −7
    K. −12

GO ON TO THE NEXT PAGE.

25. Which of the following correctly solves the equation $\frac{a-b}{2} = 6$

for any b?

A. $b = 12a$
B. $b = 12 - a$
C. $b = 3 - a$
D. $b = a - 3$
E. $b = a - 12$

DO YOUR FIGURING HERE.

26. The product of which of the following results in a negative odd number?

F. A positive even number and a negative even number
G. Two negative odd numbers
H. A positive even number and a negative odd number
J. A negative even number and a negative odd number
K. A positive odd number and a negative odd number

27. A bag contains 11 purple marbles, 11 yellow marbles, 11 red marbles, and 11 black marbles. John begins removing marbles at random from the bag, and the first 4 marbles removed are all purple. What is the probability that the fifth marble removed will also be purple?

A. $\frac{7}{44}$

B. $\frac{7}{40}$

C. $\frac{1}{4}$

D. $\frac{5}{11}$

E. $\frac{7}{11}$

GO ON TO THE NEXT PAGE.

DO YOUR FIGURING HERE.

28. A student in Miss Ruane's class must repeat a test if that student earns less than 70% of the points available on that test. There were 30 points available on the first test of this semester. If Oliver scored p points on this test and therefore must repeat it, then which of the following is true?

F. $p < 20$
G. $p > 20$
H. $p < 21$
J. $p = 21$
K. $p > 21$

29. A work crew paints a broken yellow line down the middle of a straight road $16\frac{1}{9}$ miles long over the course of 3 days. On Day 1, the crew records $5\frac{8}{27}$ miles of road painted. On Day 2, the crew forgets to measure how much road was painted, but on Day 3, the crew records $3\frac{2}{3}$ miles painted to finish the job. According to the measurements available, how many miles of road did the crew paint on Day 2 ?

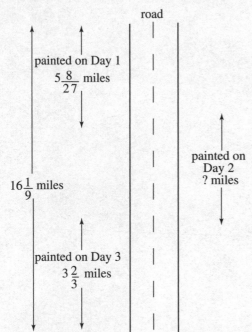

A. $7\frac{7}{27}$

B. $7\frac{4}{27}$

C. 7

D. $6\frac{7}{27}$

E. $6\frac{4}{27}$

GO ON TO THE NEXT PAGE.

30. The owners of the Movie Palace use the *Illuminator 100* light bulb in their projectors, but are now considering switching to the *Illuminator 100 Plus*, a more powerful light bulb that projects movies onto larger screens farther away. The *Illuminator 100 Plus* projects movies onto screens 108 feet wide and 180 feet from the projector, while the *Illuminator 100* projects movies onto screens only 81 feet wide, as shown in the figure below. How much farther from the projector, in feet, is the screen for the *Illuminator 100 Plus* than the screen for the *Illuminator 100* ?

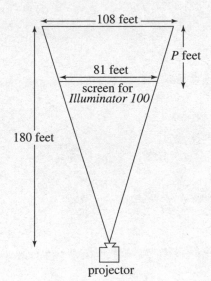

F. 27
G. 40
H. 45
J. 50
K. 55

31. What is the distance, in coordinate units, between points $J(-5,4)$ and $K(6,-2)$ in the standard (x, y) coordinate plane?

A. $\sqrt{15}$
B. $\sqrt{17}$
C. $\sqrt{157}$
D. 10
E. 17

GO ON TO THE NEXT PAGE.

32. Cynthia decorates the ceiling of her bedroom with stars that glow in the dark. She puts 1 star on the ceiling on the 1st day of decorating, 2 stars on the ceiling on the 2nd day of decorating, 3 stars on the 3rd day, and so on. If she puts stars on the ceiling in this pattern for 30 days (so she puts 30 stars on the ceiling on the 30th day), then what will be the total number of stars on the ceiling at the end of the 30 days?

   F. 155
   G. 435
   H. 450
   J. 465
   K. 480

DO YOUR FIGURING HERE.

33. In $\triangle PQR$, side $\overline{PQ}$ is 12 inches long and side $\overline{QR}$ is 41 inches long. Which of the following CANNOT be the length, in inches, of side $\overline{PR}$?

   A. 17
   B. 30
   C. 38
   D. 44
   E. 52

34. Which of the following is equivalent to the expression $\dfrac{5d^2 - 2}{20d}$?

   F. $\dfrac{3}{20}$

   G. $\dfrac{1}{5d^2}$

   H. d

   J. $\dfrac{d}{4} - \dfrac{1}{10d}$

   K. $\dfrac{d^2 - 1}{10d}$

GO ON TO THE NEXT PAGE.

Use the following information to answer
questions 35–37.

Merav's school has an Olympic-size pool that is 50 meters long, 25
meters wide, and 2 meters deep. The pool is surrounded by special
non-slip tiles, as shown in the figure below.

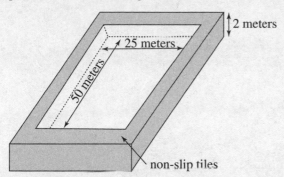

35. Merav's school laid non-slip tiles on the floor around its pool to
    reduce injuries among its athletes. These non-slip tiles extend 5
    meters beyond the pool on all sides. What is the area, in square
    meters, of the floor space that has the non-slip tiles?

    A.   800
    B.   850
    C.   900
    D.   950
    E.   1,000

36. For the synchronized swimming team, each swimmer needs an
    area within the pool to perform her routine without colliding
    with a teammate. Each area is 5 meters wide and 5 meters long.
    What is the maximum number of synchronized swimmers in
    the pool who can perform the routine without any collisions?

    F.   75
    G.   50
    H.   25
    J.   15
    K.   10

37. Merav pays $4.00 for a ticket to her school's first swim meet to
    watch her classmates compete. While there, Merav buys a slice
    of pizza and a soda. She pays $3.75 for the pizza and $1.75 for
    the soda, plus 10% sales tax for both of these items. What is
    the total amount Merav pays for her ticket, pizza, and soda?

    A. $ 3.75
    B. $ 9.50
    C. $10.05
    D. $10.45
    E. $10.75

GO ON TO THE NEXT PAGE.

38. Points G and H lie on circle F as shown below. If the measure of $\angle FGH$ is 40°, then what is the measure of central angle $\angle GFH$?

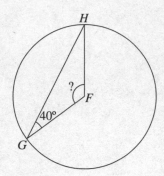

   F.   60°
   G.   80°
   H.   100°
   J.   120°
   K.   Cannot be determined from the information given

39. The pie chart below shows the operating expenses of Stephanie's office for the month of July, during which time the expenses totaled $10,000.

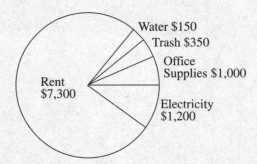

Stephanie tries to reduce her operating expenses for August by making her office more energy efficient and asking her landlord to lower her rent. She hopes to reduce her electricity expenses by $700 and her rent by $1,300. If she is successful in both of these goals and the rest of her expenses are unchanged, then what percent of her August expenses will be for office supplies?

   A.   5.0%
   B.   7.5%
   C.   10.0%
   D.   12.5%
   E.   15.0%

40. Assuming q is a positive integer, then the difference between $14q$ and $5q$ is always divisible by:

   F.   5
   G.   9
   H.   14
   J.   19
   K.   70

GO ON TO THE NEXT PAGE.

41. Ron earns $1,800 for a 6-week assignment. While working a 6-week assignment, Ron works a minimum of 20 hours each week. Ron's hourly rate of pay, therefore, depends upon how many hours he works. If r is Ron's average hourly pay, in dollars, for a 6-week assignment, then which of the following best describes r ?

A. $r \leq$ $15.00
B. $r \geq$ $15.00
C. $r \leq$ $90.00
D. $r \geq$ $90.00
E. $r \geq$ $180.00

42. In the standard (x, y) coordinate plane, the endpoints of $\overline{EF}$ lie at $(-5,9)$ and $(3,-3)$. What is the y-coordinate of the midpoint of $\overline{EF}$?

F. -6
G. -3
H. -1
J. 3
K. 6

43. Two wires connect the top of a flagpole to the ground, as shown below. Each wire makes a 75° angle with the ground at a point 8 feet from the flagpole. Which of the following expressions gives the height, in feet, of the flagpole?

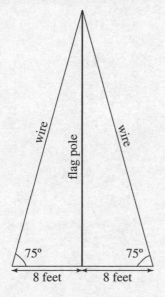

A. $8\cos 75°$

B. $8\sin 75°$

C. $8\tan 75°$

D. $\dfrac{8}{\cos 75°}$

E. $\dfrac{8}{\sin 75°}$

DO YOUR FIGURING HERE.

GO ON TO THE NEXT PAGE.

Use the following information to answer questions 44–46.

As shown in the figure below, $\triangle XYZ$ is a right triangle with legs of length x units and y units and hypotenuse of z units, such that $0 < x < y$. Quadrilaterals $ABYX$, $CDZY$, and $EFXZ$ are squares.

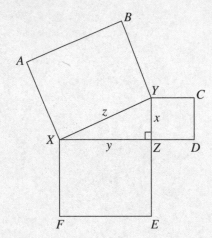

44. What is the perimeter, in units, of polygon $CDZXY$?

   F. $3x + y + z$
   G. $3x + 2y + z$
   H. $3x + 3y + 3z$
   J. $4x + y + z$
   K. $4x + 4y + 4z$

45. Given that $0 < x < y$, which of the following correctly lists the angles $\angle BYC$, $\angle AXF$, and $\angle EZD$ in order of their measures from least to greatest?

   A. $\angle AXF, \angle EZD, \angle BYC$
   B. $\angle BYC, \angle EZD, \angle AXF$
   C. $\angle BYC, \angle AXF, \angle EZD$
   D. $\angle EZD, \angle AXF, \angle BYC$
   E. $\angle EZD, \angle BYC, \angle AXF$

46. If $2x = z$, then what is the value of $\cos(\angle XYZ)$?

   F. $\dfrac{1}{2}$

   G. $\dfrac{\sqrt{3}}{2}$

   H. $\dfrac{2\sqrt{3}}{3}$

   J. $\sqrt{3}$

   K. 2

GO ON TO THE NEXT PAGE.

47. The sum of 4 consecutive even integers is t. What is the sum, in terms of t, of the 2 larger of these integers?

DO YOUR FIGURING HERE.

- **A.** $\dfrac{t}{2} - 4$

- **B.** $\dfrac{t}{2}$

- **C.** $\dfrac{t}{2} + 4$

- **D.** $t + 2$

- **E.** $t + 4$

48. Figure 1 below shows the graph of $y = x^2$ in the standard (x, y) coordinate plane. Which of the following is the equation for the graph in Figure 2 ?

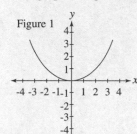 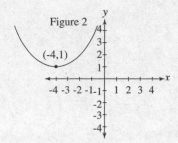

- **F.** $y = (x - 4)^2 - 1$
- **G.** $y = (x - 4)^2 + 1$
- **H.** $y = (x + 1)^2 - 4$
- **J.** $y = (x + 4)^2 - 1$
- **K.** $y = (x + 4)^2 + 1$

49. In a piggy bank, there are pennies, nickels, dimes, and quarters that total $5.29 in value. If there are 3 times as many dimes as there are pennies, 1 more dime than nickels, and 2 more quarters than dimes, then how many nickels are in the piggy bank?

- **A.** 11
- **B.** 13
- **C.** 17
- **D.** 21
- **E.** 23

50. The mean of 5 numbers is 87. The smallest of the 5 numbers is 75. What is the mean of the other 4 numbers?

- **F.** 72
- **G.** 87
- **H.** $88\dfrac{2}{5}$
- **J.** 90
- **K.** $108\dfrac{3}{4}$

GO ON TO THE NEXT PAGE.

51. "If Jenny is home, then her car is in the driveway." If the previous statement is true, then which of the following must also be true?

   A. "If Jenny's car is in the driveway, then she is home."
   B. "If Jenny is not home, then her car is in the driveway."
   C. "If Jenny is not home, then her car is not in the driveway."
   D. "If Jenny's car is not in the driveway, then she is home."
   E. "If Jenny's car is not in the driveway, then she is not home."

DO YOUR FIGURING HERE.

52. If $\left(y^{0.2}\right)^{a^2-20} = y$ and $y \neq 0$, then what is the solution set of a ?

   F. $\{1\}$
   G. $\{-\sqrt{10}, \sqrt{10}\}$
   H. $\{5\}$
   J. $\{-5, 5\}$
   K. $\{25\}$

53. If $g(x) = \csc x \tan x$, then which of the following trigonometric functions is equivalent to $g(x)$?

   (Note: $\csc x = \dfrac{1}{\sin x}$, $\sec x = \dfrac{1}{\cos x}$, and $\cot x = \dfrac{1}{\tan x}$)

   A. $g(x) = \sin x$
   B. $g(x) = \cos x$
   C. $g(x) = \tan x$
   D. $g(x) = \csc x$
   E. $g(x) = \sec x$

GO ON TO THE NEXT PAGE.

54. A particular linear equation includes the (x, y) pairs below. What is the value of b?

x	y
1	1
–2	b
3	–3
–3	9

- **F.** –8
- **G.** –5
- **H.** –1
- **J.** 0
- **K.** 7

55. If the volume of a sphere is 288π cubic inches, then which of the following is the surface area, in square inches, of the same sphere?

(Note: For a sphere with radius r, the volume is $\frac{4}{3}\pi r^3$ and the surface area is $4\pi r^2$.)

- **A.** 6π
- **B.** 8π
- **C.** 24π
- **D.** 36π
- **E.** 144π

56. When $x > 1$, $3\log_x x^{-2} = ?$

- **F.** –6
- **G.** $-\dfrac{2}{3}$
- **H.** $\dfrac{2}{3}$
- **J.** 1
- **K.** $\dfrac{3}{2}$

GO ON TO THE NEXT PAGE.

57. Jamie drew a triangle bounded by the lines $y = -x$, $x = -2$, and $y = 8$ and shaded the interior, as shown in the figure below. Then Jamie decided to reflect this triangle across the y-axis and shade the interior of the new triangle. Which of the following would describe the shaded region of Jamie's new triangle?

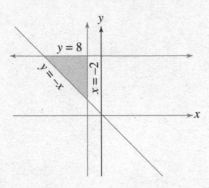

A. $x \geq 2$, $y \leq 8$, $y \leq x$
B. $x \geq 2$, $y \leq 8$, $y \geq x$
C. $x \geq 2$, $y \leq -8$, $y \leq x$
D. $x \geq -2$, $y \leq 8$, $y \geq x$
E. $x \leq -2$, $y \leq -8$, $y \leq x$

58. An angle with vertex at the origin and measure θ is shown in the standard (x, y) coordinate plane below. If one side of the angle includes the positive x-axis and the other side passes through $(-12, -5)$, then what is the sine of θ ?

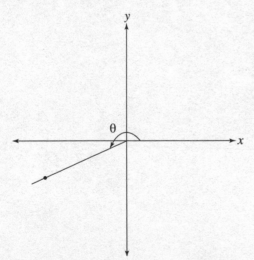

F. $-\dfrac{12}{5}$

G. $-\dfrac{12}{13}$

H. $-\dfrac{5}{13}$

J. $\dfrac{5}{12}$

K. $\dfrac{13}{12}$

GO ON TO THE NEXT PAGE.

59. Side $\overline{AB}$ of parallelogram $ABCD$ is shown in the figure below. If the coordinates of A are $(7,6)$ and those of B are $(5,1)$, then $\overline{CD}$ could lie on which of the following lines?

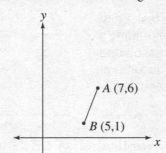

A. $y = \dfrac{5}{2}x + 9$

B. $y = x + 5$

C. $y = \dfrac{2}{5}x - 4$

D. $y = -\dfrac{2}{5}x + 4$

E. $y = -\dfrac{5}{2}x - 9$

60. If the function $f(x,y)$ is defined as $f(x,y) = (x-y)^2 + (x+y)^2$, then, for all values of c and d, $f(c^2, d^2) = ?$

F. $4c^2d^2$

G. $2c^4 + 2d^4$

H. $2c^4 - 2d^4$

J. 1

K. $-4c^2d^2$

END OF TEST 2

STOP! DO NOT TURN THE PAGE UNTIL TOLD TO DO SO.

DO NOT RETURN TO A PREVIOUS TEST.

READING TEST

35 Minutes—40 Questions

DIRECTIONS: There are four passages in this test. Each passage is followed by several questions. After reading a passage, choose the best answer to each question and fill in the corresponding oval on your answer document. You may refer to the passages as often as necessary.

Passage I

PROSE FICTION: This passage is adapted from the novel *Thick Skinned* by Grace McCloud, (©2005 by Grace McCloud). The setting is a forest in Oregon in 1935.

The dusk descends upon the earth like a series of linens slowly tucking a child into bed. The first sheet is just a soft lens that dampens the harsh glow of sunlight and reveals the untainted essence of the landscape. Colors seem richer, and subtle details
5 are easier to perceive. The final layer of dusk comes on thick like a quilt, burrowing the world in darkness and allowing all the daytime creatures the glorious serenity in letting go.

As my father and I gathered twigs and leaves for our campfire, it was still the earliest stage of evening. The vibrant forms
10 of daytime—flowers, trees, and radiant water—still flooded our eyes, but all the earth's activity took on the falling action of a story that had passed its climax. The tension had been resolved; the expectations now clear; the progression calm. My mother was playing her role, setting up tents and laying out pillows and
15 sleeping bags inside of them. Here, amid these familiar habits, the possibility of Dad losing his job at the plant, as so many of his friends had, began to evaporate with the disappearing sunlight.

The Wood River rolled by our campsite with a gentle gurgle. My father taught me to look at the river as he does: a metaphor
20 for the human body. "The shape of it basically stays the same," he said, "even though the underlying substance is always changing."

My father was now attempting to start the fire with the first load of kindling. As he teased bits of leaves, sticks, and dry pine needles into a stack underneath the firewood, I went to look a
25 second time for more of the same. Whenever you're trying to ignite damp, untreated wood, you need to keep some tiny flame alive by finding a steady supply of easier things to burn.

I set off from the campsite in the opposite direction from the one I had gone before, just as a fisherman would sail down-
30 stream after catching the first load of fish. The snaps and pops of the burning tinder started to come with greater frequency. Then, without even turning to look towards the campsite, I knew things were under way.

Just like the grand finale of a 4th of July fireworks display, the
35 sound of a blazing fire is a conversation of too many individual sparks to hear each of them speak.

"Honey, do you want me to start boiling some water?" my father yelled.

Even though it sounded like a question, it was really a re-
40 quest for my mother to hand him the pot. We always boil some water for the sake of the hot cocoa we would eventually sip by the fire, once all the work had been done to prepare the campsite for sleeping and the campfire for burning.

"Are you ready for your sandwich?" responded my mother,
45 as she began pulling the water pot and other food supplies out of a paper bag.

I sometimes marveled at the well-grooved partnership my parents had carved out. It seemed so familiar to both of them. Often, I considered it a sign that the once-heaving seas of young
50 love had quieted within them to something more like the standing water of a pond. However, right now the familiar habit of camping with my family was a welcome reprieve from the strange new presence at home: fear of the uncertain future. What sort of job would Dad get if he needed to find work? Would we have to
55 move away from Eugene or back into the dusty basements of my aunts' and uncles' houses where I had spent my earliest years?

"Myra, do you want your usual two?" my mom asked as she measured the amount of water we would need for our cocoa into the cooking pot. I used to sigh so mournfully at the end of
60 my cup that my mom would offer me the rest of hers. Soon, she realized she could just make me extra so that she didn't have to sacrifice her own.

"Yes, please," I replied.

After my mom had set the pot down on the flames, she stood
65 up, handed a sandwich to my father and leaned in with the same motion to get a kiss on the lips.

"Nice fire," she complimented.

GO ON TO THE NEXT PAGE.

My dad smiled in return, his face illuminated by firelight but projecting its own warmth. This time, the familiarity exchanged
70 between my parents seemed like a wonderful gift they had earned by being together for so long. Like a river, their relationship maintained a constant appearance while the substance that flowed through it continually changed.

The river next to our campsite began to disappear into thicker
75 darkness, while its sound continued throughout the night. Drifting off to sleep, I felt some peace knowing my worries would be carried away by the current.

1. As it is used in line 3, the word *untainted* can reasonably be said to mean all of the following EXCEPT:

   A. natural.
   B. non-toxic.
   C. undistorted.
   D. true.

2. The passage does NOT mention which of the following as something that at least one member of the family is doing?

   F. Wading in the Wood River
   G. Setting up a tent
   H. Gathering pine needles
   J. Igniting damp wood

3. The narrator describes her father as doing all of the following EXCEPT:

   A. sharing his hot cocoa with Myra during past camping excursions.
   B. exuding a sense of warmth once the campfire is ignited.
   C. describing to Myra a similarity between a river and a human body.
   D. helping to gather materials for use with starting the campfire.

4. The point of view from which the passage is told is best described as an adolescent girl who:

   F. knows her father only has a limited amount of time left at his job and worries that her life will fall apart once his job ends.
   G. hopes that her father's unemployment situation will have the upside of allowing her parents to repair their troubled marriage.
   H. realizes that her father's job is in jeopardy but feels like he worries too much about things that are beyond his control.
   J. recognizes the possibility of her father's unemployment and speculates about the effects it may have on the family.

5. In order to help light a fire, the passage most strongly suggests that the family has gathered:

   A. dry pine needles only.
   B. dry pine needles and sticks only.
   C. dry pine needles, sticks, and leaves only.
   D. dry pine needles, sticks, leaves, and twigs.

6. Which of the following does the narrator NOT directly mention as something seen during the earliest stages of dusk?

   F. Shining water
   G. Fish
   H. Flowers
   J. Trees

7. When the narrator's mother hands her husband a sandwich and compliments him on the fire, the narrator reacts to this interaction with a feeling of familiarity that:

   A. she often finds depressing.
   B. distracts her from the river.
   C. she worries will not last.
   D. thoroughly comforts her.

8. As it is used in line 33, the word *things* most precisely refers to the sound of:

   F. 4th of July fireworks.
   G. water boiling.
   H. the campfire fully igniting.
   J. the snaps and pops of kindling.

9. As it is used in line 10, the word *flooded* most nearly means:

   A. spilled.
   B. devastated.
   C. filled.
   D. soaked.

10. The narrator's statement in lines 49–51 most nearly means she believes her parents' relationship has:

    F. not been the same since the threat of her father losing his job began to put a strain on their marriage.
    G. become more stable and predictable than it was in the earlier part of their relationship.
    H. degraded into something disease ridden and murky, like a mosquito infested pond.
    J. somehow managed to grow more passionate and spontaneous with each passing year.

GO ON TO THE NEXT PAGE.

Passage II

SOCIAL SCIENCE: This passage is adapted from the article, "When Charities Need Help" by Ellen Wurtner, (©2009 by Ellen Wurtner).

Traditionally, when people think of charitable giving, there are only a few images that spring to mind. They probably envision dropping change into the Salvation Army basket outside retail stores around the holidays, or into a basket passed around at their

5 places of worship, or even into the hands of a homeless person whose pitiable appearance and humble request for "anything you can spare" is hard to deny. But can't we do better?

Religious institutions have typically been the societal force that drives philanthropy. This is most likely because religion
10 is vitally intertwined with morality, and charitable generosity has forever been exalted as one of the highest forms of moral behavior. Typically, churches collect alms for the poor at their church services and organize such hunger relief activities as soup kitchens.

15 Ted Stumbacher, head of the Global Empowerment Initiative, believes that truly effective philanthropy will need to have at its roots a more economic mindset. He feels religious organizations often provide only a temporary reprieve from suffering related to food, clothing, or shelter. While a noble end, this type of
20 charity succeeds more in establishing a life-long commitment to philanthropy among the churchgoing public than it does in remedying any of the systemic problems that face the world's impoverished masses.

Stumbacher points to several transformations taking place
25 over the past two decades as harbingers of the new paradigm of philanthropic organizations. Some organizations are devoting increased attention to their marketing images, using meticulous branding and celebrity endorsements to solidify consumer awareness. Despite the fact that charities are nonprofit entities, they
30 can still approach the task of maximizing their "market share" the way that other big corporations do. More commonly, nonprofits are finding non-monetary forms of assistance to tap, such as stationing clothing-recycling drop boxes around dense cities. These drop boxes not only allow used clothing to be funneled
35 to those in need but also prevent needless environmental stress by keeping these textiles out of the world's trash.

Similarly, Stumbacher notes the way charities are looking to increase the consumer choice aspect of giving. Rather than using the traditional model of citizens simply dropping money
40 into a basket intended for some generic form of relief to the poor, organizations like Donors Choose are giving philanthropists much more decision-making power in how their money is used. The website for Donors Choose allows donors to sift through a list of charitable projects, enabling them to fund the cause they find most
45 worthy. This model has proven to motivate giving by providing the giver with concrete imagery of where his money is going.

Other philanthropists, such as Karen Pitts, founder of Taste of Giving, say they are, "seeking to engage donors by merging their charitable giving with other activities they enjoy." Ms. Pitts
50 has organized wine tastings that successfully raise tens of thousands of dollars for charities. This is essentially a win-win-win situation. The wineries receive the excellent promotional context of a charitable event, the affluent wine drinkers are delighted to help others while enjoying themselves, and the charities enjoy
55 a healthy slice of the financial proceeds.

Perhaps the most forward-minded approach is that of Jacqueline Novogratz, founder of the Acumen Fund. Endeavoring to extinguish poverty at its roots, the Acumen Fund collects donations in a typical way but then treats its pool of resources
60 as investment capital. Instead of providing immediate relief of suffering, the Acumen Fund provides micro-loans to small businesses throughout third-world countries. Novogratz believes that this capitalistic approach is a more tenable form of long-term aid.

The old Chinese proverb, "give a man a fish and you'll
65 feed him for a day; teach a man to fish and you'll feed him for a lifetime" seems to be at the root of Novogratz's philosophy. By providing poor people with investment capital rather than food or clothing, she hopes to nourish and sustain them economically so that they can provide for themselves. Moreover, the Acumen
70 Fund is a very hands-on enterprise, making regular inspections of the businesses they fund to verify that money is being spent shrewdly, efficiently, and honestly.

Unfortunately, what makes so many of these innovative philanthropic approaches inspiring and effective is their adapta-
75 tion to the specific needs of their locales. Naysayers are quick to point out that these progressive business models will not be tenable on a large scale. As these ambitious charities grow with success, they may ultimately become lumbering organizational giants, such as UNICEF and the Rockefeller Foundation, and lose
80 the flexibility, creativity, and personality that made them great.

However, even if these new tactics cannot be used in all contexts, they are still very valuable. By redefining what forms charity can take, these new approaches are widening the base of donors. By employing innovative methods, these philanthropic
85 entrepreneurs are helping larger charitable organizations to reexamine and refine their own approach.

11. The passage indicates that in their attempt to promote philanthropy, religious institutions provide all of the benefits or services EXCEPT:

   A. instructing homeless people on how to live moral lives.
   B. collecting alms for the poor from churchgoers.
   C. organizing events that feed those who are hungry.
   D. providing temporary relief from suffering related to lack of shelter.

GO ON TO THE NEXT PAGE.

12. The author mentions clothing-recycling drop boxes and celebrity endorsements as two examples of:

F. philanthropic approaches that are gaining popularity.
G. problems Stumbacher cites with modern philanthropy.
H. ways Karen Pitts has raised money for the needy.
J. the best way to reverse environmental problems.

13. The main function of the first paragraph is to:

A. urge people to feel sympathy for and generosity towards homeless people.
B. cause the reader to picture himself in a charitable giving context.
C. discuss typical methods of charity and imply an alternative.
D. argue that the traditional methods of charity do nothing.

14. As the author describes it, when the churchgoing public performs charity through its religious organizations, it feels:

F. severe guilt.
G. moral superiority.
H. reluctant shame.
J. augmented pride.

15. When Karen Pitts talks about "other activities they enjoy" (line 49), she is most likely referring to:

A. finding positive promotional contexts for wineries in their community.
B. partaking in social events such as that of a wine tasting.
C. giving tens of thousands of dollars to charities that Pitts represents.
D. finding win-win opportunities with other donors in the wine industry.

16. The author most likely places the words "market share" in quotation marks in (line 30) to:

F. suggest that only big corporations understand how to build a successful business model.
G. imply a different sense of market share from that of corporations seeking to maximize their profits.
H. emphasize that nonprofit entities must learn to coexist with each other to avoid collective failure.
J. caution readers that nonprofits can also sometimes attain a monopoly in their markets.

17. Stumbacher feels that "religious organizations often provide only a temporary reprieve from suffering" (line 17–18) due to their:

A. inability to boost the self-esteem of the impoverished.
B. failure to address the systemic roots of poverty.
C. overemphasis on noble ends.
D. lack of branding and celebrity endorsements.

18. According to the passage, which of the following is true about the practices of the Acumen Fund?

F. Its method of distributing funds is less typical than its method of collecting funds.
G. It attempts but fails to treat the systemic roots of poverty.
H. It endeavors to temporarily relieve impoverished people of their suffering.
J. It collects most of its donations from small third-world businesses.

19. The passage mentions which of the following as a reason some innovative philanthropic approaches are effective?

A. They integrate charity with activities the recipients enjoy.
B. They do not temporarily relieve suffering.
C. They are less expensive than traditional methods.
D. They can adapt to specific local needs.

20. In the context of the tenth paragraph (lines 81–86), the statement in lines 75–77 most nearly means that:

F. new modes of providing charity will succeed only in large measures.
G. philanthropists do not have a realistic sense of the scale of some problems.
H. some ways of doing business locally may not work similarly globally.
J. large communities tend to have similar needs to those of smaller communities.

GO ON TO THE NEXT PAGE.

Passage III

HUMANITIES: This passage is adapted from the article "The Ascension of Reggaeton" by Eric Delgado, (©2008 by Eric Delgado).

Reggaeton music made its grand entrance onto mainstream U.S. radio with Daddy Yankee's 2004 crossover hit, "Gasolina." By that time, reggaeton's infectious and innovative blend of Jamaican dancehall reggae, Latin American salsa and merengue,
5 and North American hip-hop and electronic music had already been well established and widespread throughout Latin American countries. Reggaeton, pronounced "reggae-TONE," is thought to have originated in Panama, although the cultivation and popularity of its signature style took place in Puerto Rico. Puerto Ricans,
10 inspired by the blend of Spanish rap music and dancehall reggae coming out of Panama in the 1970s and 80s, perfected the genre of reggaeton during the early 1990s.

Like that of most hybrid musical forms, the evolution of reggaeton can be understood as the effect of underlying ethnic
15 migrations and the resulting cultural overlaps. Such a movement will inevitably create new combinations that are more than the sum of their parts. In the first half of the 20th century, Jamaican laborers migrated to Panama to assist with construction of the Panama Canal. Panamanians became exposed to and enamored
20 with Jamaican reggae, ultimately recording Spanish-language versions of Jamaican reggae songs. In the second half of the 20th century, the modern, more electronic form of Jamaican dancehall reggae was infiltrating Puerto Rico through attentive and interested DJs who imported music from their Caribbean neighbor.

25 The reggaeton genre was solidified with the release of a 1991 single by Jamaican dancehall star Shabba Ranks, "Dem Bow." Rerecorded in Spanish by Panamanian artist El General as "Son Bow," the track proved to be such an influential success that the beat of the song, referred to even now as simply "Dem
30 Bow," is the underlying rhythm of almost every reggaeton song. The bass drum accents the downbeat (1st beat) of each measure while a snare accents the syncopated offbeat of the 2nd and onbeat of the 4th beat of each measure.

Ethan Perry, a musicologist who studies emerging genres,
35 somewhat derisively explains, "Not only is it ironic that one song ["Dem Bow"] can so easily be pinpointed as the catalyst for a new genre, but it is also rare that a musical genre can be so easily defined by such a simple, recurring musical pattern. For this reason, it is hard to take reggaeton seriously as a genre when
40 it seems doomed by its own lack of imagination."

Although it may be true that reggaeton has predictable musical features, reggaeton artist Felipe Noche explains that attempts to belittle the genre will only strengthen its core appeal. "Reggaeton is a subversive, underground style. If mainstream
45 critics try to marginalize it, they will only solidify its street credibility, just like someone telling you they don't like your

girlfriend only makes you defend her even more passionately." Furthermore, reggaeton is not the only musical genre with very stable defining characteristics. Blues music, for example, is
50 characterized by a common type of chord progression known as "12-bar," and reggae almost universally features guitar or keyboard accents on all the off beats and kick-drum accents on the 3rd beat of each measure.

The syncopated rhythm found in "Dem Bow" and most
55 reggaeton is fundamental to Latin music. However, the fact that the reggaeton beat is recorded with bold, electronic, dancehall sounds instead of acoustic percussive instruments sets this style of music apart from the music Latino youths associate with their parents. When added to the aggressive, dance-friendly, urban rap
60 lyrics that typify reggaeton songs, it is not difficult to see how the genre offers Latino youth a provocative mixture of something culturally familiar but brashly individualistic.

The dissemination of reggaeton throughout the U.S. during the late 1990s was predictably strongest in areas with vibrant
65 Puerto Rican communities, such as New York, Miami, and Los Angeles. The work of influential Puerto Rican DJ Playero in the 90s helped to introduce these communities to eventual reggaeton stars like Daddy Yankee, Don Chezina, Master Joe, and O.G. Black. The popularity of reggaeton has extended internationally,
70 finding audiences throughout the Caribbean, as well as in Europe and Asia. These latter successes suggest the undeniable appeal of the genre is not limited to the Latino youth who first embraced it.

"At first when I got requests to play shows in Japan, I was truly stunned," says reggaeton artist Dos Cabezas, "but I think
75 there's an energy to this music that makes it exciting to everyone. It's got a gritty sound that evokes the rough attitude of street cultures everywhere, and the beat just makes people want to move."

Despite the negative feedback from some music critics who find the music too repetitive and from some parents who
80 find the lyrics too violent and sexually suggestive, reggaeton at least deserves the recognition of being a distinct art form that has achieved global prevalence in the early part of this century.

GO ON TO THE NEXT PAGE.

21. In the passage, who most directly expresses the idea that fans will respond to criticisms of reggaeton by embracing the music even more?

  A. Ethan Perry
  B. Felipe Noche
  C. Dos Cabezas
  D. DJ Playero

22. Viewed in the context of the passage, the words *ironic*, *easily*, *rare*, and *simple* (lines 35–38), are most likely intended by the speaker to convey a tone of:

  F. disparagement.
  G. neutrality.
  H. puzzlement.
  J. admiration.

23. The passage claims that reggaeton solidified itself as a genre:

  A. in 2004, when Daddy Yankee's "Gasolina" became a massive hit.
  B. no earlier than 1991, and sometime in the aftermath of the success of "Dem Bow."
  C. during the 1970s and 1980s when Puerto Ricans combined rap with reggae.
  D. in the late 1990s when it spread through New York, Miami, and Los Angeles.

24. In describing the Latino youth who listen to and relate to reggaeton, the author characterizes their parents' musical tastes as being:

  F. typified by syncopated rhythms and acoustic instruments.
  G. primarily centered on simple, recurring musical patterns.
  H. characterized by bold, electronic, dancehall sounds.
  J. a provocative cocktail of many different Latin styles.

25. Which of the following developments does the passage indicate occurred first chronologically?

  A. Shabba Ranks releases his version of "Dem Bow."
  B. Panamanians combine Spanish rap music with dancehall reggae.
  C. Jamaican laborers travel to Panama to help construct the Panama Canal.
  D. Daddy Yankee's single "Gasolina" attains widespread popularity.

26. The passage states that the song "Dem Bow" was:

  F. the last song that Shabba Ranks ever recorded as a dancehall artist.
  G. the reason El General became an international success.
  H. the first song to ever attempt the signature reggaeton beat.
  J. rerecorded by a Panamanian artist in a different language.

27. The quotation in (lines 73–77) most strongly emphasizes the aspects of reggaeton that:

  A. make it the toughest style of music to perform.
  B. borrow from traditional Japanese forms of music.
  C. help it to have such international, universal appeal.
  D. cause it to be so popular among Latino youth.

28. The passage identifies early 20th-century Panamanians as being both:

  F. increasingly familiar with and fond of Jamaican reggae music.
  G. diligent laborers and resentful of foreigners brought in to assist them.
  H. impressed by Jamaican music and helpful in teaching them the Spanish language.
  J. absorbed with dancehall reggae and undervalued by modern musicologists.

29. The passage devotes the LEAST attention to which of the following topics?

  A. The musical structure and characteristics that typify much reggaeton music
  B. The specific lyrics of reggaeton songs that some parents and critics find objectionable
  C. The areas in the United States in which reggaeton initially rose to prominence
  D. The historical roots of reggaeton and the various groups that helped to create it

30. Information and quotations about reggaeton in the passage best support the conclusion that it:

  F. is globally popular because it features many different underlying rhythmic structures as well as varied lyrical themes.
  G. would probably not have caught on in Miami during the 1990s without a strong Panamanian population there.
  H. is frequently characterized by certain musical and lyrical tendencies that are endearing to some listeners but disconcerting to others.
  J. was traditionally recorded with acoustic, percussive instruments until "Dem Bow" was released and became popular.

GO ON TO THE NEXT PAGE.

Passage IV

NATURAL SCIENCE: This passage is adapted from the article "Unearthing the Greatest Fossil Ever Found" by Stanley Walsh, (©2009 by Stanley Walsh).

Evolutionary biologists can finally breathe a sigh of relief. Those who have been bursting at the seams to blurt out the "big secret" can finally shout it from the mountaintops, and those who have been hunting tirelessly for a "missing link" to solidify the
5 Darwinian theory of evolution can finally rest easily.

The "big secret" and "missing link" are one and the same: a 47-million-year-old, uncannily preserved fossil of an ancient ancestor of the primate family, nicknamed Ida. After two years of secretly performing research on the fossil, experts are ready
10 to present their findings to the world. They firmly believe that the lemur monkey they have preserved in polyester resin is conclusive evidence of a transitional species, a fork in the road where the genetic tree branches off in the direction that eventually gives rise to such simian species as monkeys, apes, and humans.

15 Two things make this particular specimen so valuable. It is older than any previously found primate fossil, vastly predating the previous record-holder, Lucy, which is a 3.18-million-year-old fossil. Furthermore, it is one of the most complete fossils ever found, with 95% of the skeleton preserved. In fact, the fos-
20 silization conditions were so perfect in Ida's case that scientists could actually still analyze the last meal Ida had before apparently falling into a crater and dying of carbon dioxide poisoning. By contrast, Lucy's remains were only 40% complete, lacking a skull among other important features.

25 Ironically, for such a monumentally important fossil, Ida has actually been flying under the radar for the past 25 years. An amateur fossil hunter first discovered her in 1983, in a volcanic crater-lake called the Messel Pit, just outside of Frankfurt, Germany. Because the Messel Pit was already considered a bounti-
30 ful source of fossils, Ida's discoverer did not assume there was anything distinctive about the discovery and hung Ida on his wall as a display piece for the next 20 years. He revered it as a piece of natural art, not recognizing its exceedingly old age as a fossil.

Eventually, the piece made its way to a display in the 2006
35 Hamburg Fossil and Mineral Fair in Germany. A researcher from Norway's National History Museum, Professor Jorn Hurum, was immediately entranced upon seeing Ida. Unfortunately, his enthusiasm meant that the fossil dealer could charge an outlandish price of roughly 1 million dollars. Determined to secure this
40 landmark specimen for the sake of scientific inquiry, Professor Hurum quickly raised the needed bounty and brought Ida home to Oslo, Norway.

For the next two years, a team of top scientists studied Ida's features and attempted to integrate the information into the
45 genetic tree of the primates. All the while, the scientists knew they were on the cusp of providing the most conclusive evidence yet of the accuracy of Darwin's theory of evolution. However, they had all signed non-disclosure agreements that prevented them from discussing these tentative findings with others in the
50 field or the media.

Charles Darwin's revolutionary book *The Origin of Species*, published in 1859, first detailed the theory of natural selection. It was extremely controversial in its time, and its contention that humans evolved from a lineage of monkeys remains an
55 uncomfortable idea to many even to this day. Despite the 98.4% genetic similarity that humans have to chimpanzees, many of Darwin's skeptics have routinely rested their cases on the fact that there was a gigantic hole in the fossil evidence that relates to where the branch of higher primates begins.

60 Around 50 million years ago, the first primates are thought to have emerged, two different species called *tarsidae* and *adapidae*. Scientists have been unsure which species ultimately led to the higher primates (monkeys and humans). The discovery of Ida, an *adapid* with several human-like features, suggests that
65 *adapidae* are the ancestors of modern humans.

With so many anatomical features vividly preserved in Ida's fossilized remains, scientists have been able to identify several telltale similarities Ida has to modern humans. One feature that distinguishes Ida's species from non-anthropoid primates is
70 the talus bone, a bone that turns the corner between the leg and the foot. Her eyes face forward, which makes her visual fields overlap, a requirement for accurate depth perception. Her hands and feet have nails, rather than claws, and opposable thumbs. Both characteristics allow for the use of appendages in a more
75 refined way, whether it be peeling fruit, climbing, or, in the case of humans and their closer ancestors, using tools.

The debate over evolution is likely to continue for many years. However, the discovery of Ida has given evolutionary scientists a stronger supporting piece of evidence than they
80 ever dreamed was possible. As Harold Zemeckels, a professor of evolutionary biology at Emerson University, puts it, "This fossil is essentially a prayer answered, a perfect time capsule that's been miraculously gift-wrapped for posterity."

31. The language of the first paragraph is most likely intended to convey a sense of:

A. warning that a secret will be revealed.
B. anguish for an ongoing scientific struggle.
C. reluctance to accept a theory of evolution.
D. anticipation for the topic the passage will discuss.

GO ON TO THE NEXT PAGE.

32. According to the passage, "the big secret" and the "missing link" refer to:

F. Ida only.
G. Lucy only.
H. Ida, and the more recently discovered Lucy.
J. Lucy, and the more recently discovered Ida.

33. The passage characterizes the idea that Ida was a transitional species which later resulted in simians as:

A. a conclusion that results from an extended period of studying the fossil.
B. a conclusion that stems from analyzing the polyester resin.
C. a speculation based on ruling out *tarsidae* as simian ancestors.
D. a speculation that springs from scientists' desire to find a "missing link."

34. The passage implies that the price that was paid to obtain Ida's fossil from the private collector was:

F. outlandish because Lucy, an even older fossil, was cheaper.
G. higher than is customary due to the buyer's obvious interest.
H. unusual given how little the private collector valued it.
J. high due to its being discovered in a rare site for fossils.

35. In the passage, the amateur fossil hunter who found Ida in the Messel Pit is said to have:

A. not immediately assumed Ida was special and so kept it for himself.
B. not immediately assumed Ida was special and so showed it to fellow scientists.
C. immediately assumed Ida was special and so brought it to the Fossil and Mineral Fair.
D. immediately assumed Ida was special and so brought it to Oslo, Norway.

36. Which of the following best summarizes the objection of those who remain skeptical of Darwin's theory of evolution?

F. 98.4% is not a close enough genetic similarity to suggest genetic relation.
G. They are uncomfortable with the idea that chimpanzees evolved from lemurs.
H. There are not enough fossils available that date before 1859.
J. There is some explanation missing as to how and when higher primates evolved.

37. The passage states that Lucy was not:

A. at one point the oldest fossil known to man.
B. found in worse condition than was Ida.
C. found with a well preserved head.
D. only 40% complete as a fossil.

38. It can most reasonably be inferred that the word *enthusiasm* in line 38 refers to Professor Hurum's enthusiasm for:

F. the fossil dealer.
G. the specimen.
H. his home in Oslo.
J. the Fossil and Mineral Fair.

39. The author points out that scientists "could actually still analyze the last meal Ida had" (line 21) primarily to:

A. foreshadow the valuable clues scientists derived from her last meal.
B. explain why comparatively little was learned from Lucy's fossil.
C. underscore how well preserved Ida's fossil was by its environment.
D. argue for a new theory on the diets of early primates.

40. As it relates to the passage, the eighth paragraph (lines 60–65) serves mainly to:

F. explain the misconceptions that led some to doubt Darwin's theory.
G. demonstrate the confusion that results from classifying ancient fossils.
H. illustrate a scientific context in which Ida's fossil has proven helpful.
J. argue against the prevailing theory that humans came from *tarsidae*.

END OF TEST 3
STOP! DO NOT TURN THE PAGE UNTIL TOLD TO DO SO.
DO NOT RETURN TO A PREVIOUS TEST.

SCIENCE TEST

35 Minutes—40 Questions

DIRECTIONS: There are seven passages in this test. Each passage is followed by several questions. After reading a passage, choose the best answer to each question and fill in the corresponding oval on your answer document. You may refer to the passages as often as necessary.

You are NOT permitted to use a calculator on this test.

Passage I

When introduced into H_2O, many solid substances are able to dissolve, or disperse evenly throughout the solvent. Salts have been found to dissolve easily when introduced into H_2O, since they readily dissociate to yield ions that may interact directly with H_2O. Molecular compounds, on the other hand, do not dissolve as easily, since their interactions with water typically do not permit *ionization*, the physical process of converting an atom or molecule into an ion by adding or removing charged particles such as electrons or other ions. Two experiments were conducted to better understand the solubility of salts and molecules in water at various temperatures. The *solubility*, S, was measured as follows:

$$S = (m_{sub}) / (m_{H_2O})$$

where m_{sub} was the mass of the substance dissolved in water, and m_{H_2O} was the mass of the water itself. ΔS, or the change in solubility (from 0° C), was calculated in the experiments for three salts and three molecules with increasing temperature. The mass of water was held constant at 100g for each of these experiments.

Figure 1 shows the results of comparing the solubilities of three salts with increasing temperature, while Figure 2 shows the results of comparing the solubilities of three molecules with increasing temperature. Molecular masses (MM) are shown for each substance.

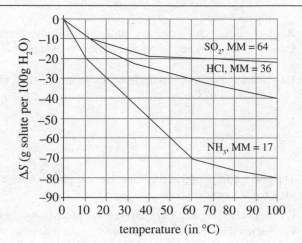

Figure 2

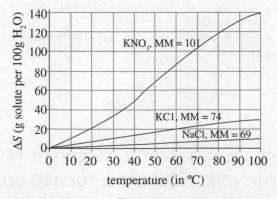

Figure 1

1. Based on Figure 1, at 40°C as the molecular masses of the salts increase, the ΔS:

A. decreases, because a greater mass of substance dissolves in the same mass of water.

B. decreases, because a smaller mass of substance dissolves in the same mass of water.

C. increases, because a greater mass of substance dissolves in the same mass of water.

D. increases, because a smaller mass of substance dissolves in the same mass of water.

GO ON TO THE NEXT PAGE.

2. Consider the trials represented in Figure 1 that occurred at 60°C. As the molecular mass of the substance decreased, the observed ΔS:

    F. increased only.
    G. increased, then decreased.
    H. decreased only.
    J. decreased, then increased.

3. If an additional trial had been done in which KCl dissolved in H_2O at 102°C, while it was still in aqueous form, the ΔS most likely would have been:

    A. less than 25.
    B. between 25 and 35.
    C. between 35 and 45.
    D. greater than 45.

4. According to Figure 2, when NH_3 was added to water at 20°C, the solubility of the resulting solution:

    F. increased, because ΔS was positive.
    G. increased, because ΔS was negative.
    H. decreased, because ΔS was positive.
    J. decreased, because ΔS was negative.

5. Based on Figures 1 and 2, which of the following combinations of solute and temperature at a known m_{H_2O} would produce the greatest increase in solubility?

    A. CH_4 (molecular compound, MM = 16) at 40°C
    B. NaF (salt, MM = 42) at 40°C
    C. CH_4 (molecular compound, MM = 16) at 80°C
    D. NaF (salt, MM = 42) at 80°C

GO ON TO THE NEXT PAGE.

Passage II

Recombination of genes is usually associated with the sexual reproduction of cells, or meiosis. However, it can also occur when cells that undergo asexual reproduction, or mitosis, need to be repaired, such as after radiation exposure. This repair process, known as *homologous recombination*, aligns two copies of the same double strand of DNA, one with the error and one without. As seen in Figure 1, correct genes are transplanted from the correct strand to the one with errors (genes with errors are represented with a *).

The activities of some genes have been found to promote homologous recombination (HR). In an experiment to quantify the genetic control over HR, 4 scientists measured the frequency of HR per hour over a 24-hour period in isolated connective tissue cells from rats placed in growth media. They then lysed the cells, separated out the entire protein content, and used gel electrophoresis to count the amount of protein present in the cells (see Figure 2).

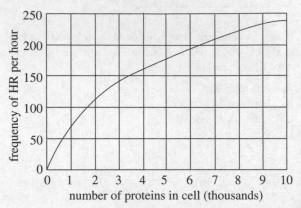

Figure 2

These scientists noticed that only a few specific proteins appeared to be responsible for promoting HR, and labeled the genes encoding them as W, X, Y, and Z. They engineered cells to express combinations of two active genes and recorded the HR. They then analyzed the DNA content of the lysed cells and calculated distances between four genes that encoded the relevant proteins (see Table 1).

Table 1		
Genes	HR (events per hour)	Distance between genes (centimorgans)
W and X	75	20
X and Y	125	30
W and Z	60	15

Each of the 4 scientists then proposed individual models for the positions of the genes they studied, taking into account the findings in Table 1. Each model shows where genes may be located along a strand of DNA (see Figure 3). Each model correctly assumes that the lengths of the genes are insignificant compared to the length of the DNA.

Scientist	Model			
1	Z	W	X	Y
2	W	Z X	Y	
3	ZY	W	X	
4	Y	W	ZX	

Figure 3

A final experiment showed that rat connective tissue cells in which genes W and Y were active had an HR frequency of 45 times per hour.

region with gene errors (A*B*)

A*B*
A*B*
A B
A B

A*B* removed
A*B* removed

region with corrected genes (AB)

A B
A B
A*B* regions have been swapped with A B regions
A*B*
A*B*

Figure 1

GO ON TO THE NEXT PAGE.

6. All 4 models agree on the distance between which of the following pairs of genes?

    F. Genes W and X
    G. Genes W and Y
    H. Genes X and Z
    J. Genes Y and Z

7. According to Figure 2, if some of the connective tissue cells had a protein content of 3,500 molecules per cell, the HR of these cells is most likely closest to which of the following?

    A. 50 events per hour
    B. 100 events per hour
    C. 150 events per hour
    D. 200 events per hour

8. If Scientist 2's model is correct and an additional gene, Gene V, is 10 centimorgans from Gene X and 15 centimorgans from Gene Z, then Gene V is most likely between:

    F. Genes W and X.
    G. Genes W and Z.
    H. Genes X and Y.
    J. Genes X and Z.

9. The result of the final experiment studying the distance between Genes W and Y is consistent with models proposed by which of the following scientists?

    A. Scientists 1 and 3
    B. Scientists 1 and 4
    C. Scientists 2 and 3
    D. Scientists 3 and 4

10. Based on the information provided, HR would occur when connective tissue cells are exposed to:

    F. growth media.
    G. sexual reproduction.
    H. asexual reproduction.
    J. X-rays.

11. Which scientist's model proposes that Genes Y and Z are separated by 65 centimorgans?

    A. Scientist 1's
    B. Scientist 2's
    C. Scientist 3's
    D. Scientist 4's

12. Genes A and B are separated by 10 centimorgans on a chromosome. An organism has alleles A and B* on 1 chromosome and alleles A* and B on the homologous chromosome. If a single HR event occurred between these 2 genes as shown in Figure 1, the genotype of Genes A and B for the 2 chromatids involved in the crossover would be:

    F. AB and AB.
    G. AB and A*B*.
    H. A*B and AB*.
    J. A*B* and A*B*.

GO ON TO THE NEXT PAGE.

Passage III

Groundwater is water stored beneath the surface of the Earth. Groundwater chemistry in 2 bodies of water—drawn from an *aquifer* and from beneath a *wetland*—was studied during a 2000 summer drought and again during the next summer, which had normal rainfall. Figure 1 shows the methane (CH_4) gas concentration in the groundwater at various depths in the aquifer and wetland. Figures 2 and 3 show the groundwater *conductivity* (directly proportional to the concentration of the dissolved ions) and pH at various depths in the aquifer and wetland, respectively. Also shown are the locations of the water table and the depths of the aquifer and wetland below this level.

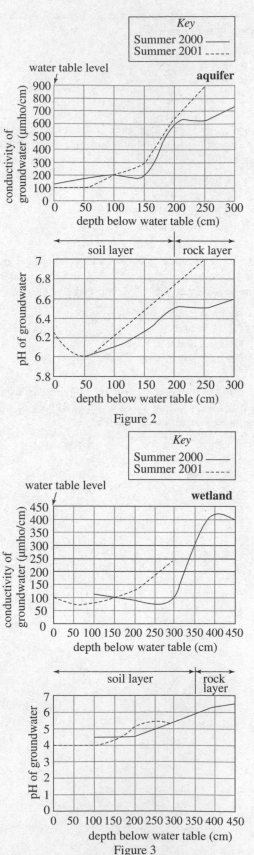

Figure 2

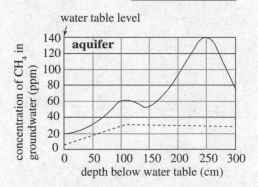

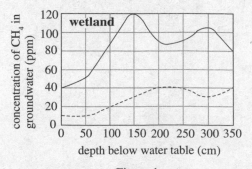

Figure 1

Figure 3

GO ON TO THE NEXT PAGE.

13. According to Figure 2, the conductivity of aquifer ground-water in 2000 at a depth of 250 cm was closest to which of the following?

    A. 350 µmho/cm
    B. 475 µmho/cm
    C. 625 µmho/cm
    D. 725 µmho/cm

14. Based on Figure 2, if the pH of aquifer groundwater at a depth of 260 cm had been measured in the summer of 2001, it would most likely have been closest to which of the following?

    F. 4.2
    G. 5.5
    H. 7.2
    J. 8.5

15. Which of the following is the most likely explanation for the difference in the depth of wetland groundwater in the 2 years?

    A. The amount of groundwater discharged to the wetland was higher during the drought, so the wetland received more water than normal.
    B. The amount of groundwater discharged to the wetland was higher during the drought, so the wetland received less water than normal.
    C. The amount of rainfall received by the wetland was higher during the drought, so the wetland received more water than normal.
    D. The amount of rainfall received by the wetland was lower during the drought, so the wetland received less water than normal.

16. If the data in Figures 2 and 3 are typical of aquifers and wetlands in general, one would most likely make which of the following conclusions about the soil layer in an aquifer and in a wetland?

    F. The soil layer in both an aquifer and a wetland is completely above the water table at all times.
    G. The soil layer in both an aquifer and a wetland is completely below the water table at all times.
    H. The soil layer in an aquifer is thicker than the soil layer in a wetland.
    J. The soil layer in an aquifer is thinner than the soil layer in a wetland.

17. According to Figure 1, the average concentration of CH_4 over the depths of 0 to 300 cm was higher during the summer of:

    A. normal rainfall than during the summer of drought in both the aquifer and the wetland.
    B. normal rainfall than during the summer of drought in the aquifer only.
    C. drought than during the summer of normal rainfall in both the aquifer and the wetland.
    D. drought than during the summer of normal rainfall in the wetland only.

GO ON TO THE NEXT PAGE.

Passage IV

Polyatomic ions can be represented by the combination of symbols

$$(X_aZ_b)^n$$

where a is the number of atoms of Element X, b is the number of atoms of Element Z, and n is the total positive or negative charge for the entire polyatomic ion. If a or b is equal to 1, then the number 1 is omitted. If n is equal to 0, indicating a net neutral charge, then the number 0 is also omitted. For example, $(NH_4)^{+1}$ represents an ammonium ion, which contains 1 nitrogen atom (the number 1 is omitted), 4 hydrogen atoms, and a net polyatomic ion charge of +1. Since polyatomic ions carry a charge, they are very soluble in water, as opposed to neutral molecules.

Some atoms that comprise polyatomic ions are able to donate or accept different numbers of electrons, depending on the atoms with which they interact. In these different situations, they are said to have different *oxidation states*. For instance, while oxygen (O) typically has a constant oxidation state of –2, meaning it typically only accepts 2 extra electrons, chlorine (Cl) can have oxidation states of –1, +1, +3, +5, and +7, meaning that it has the ability to either accept 1 extra electron (–1) or donate either 1, 3, 5, or 7 electrons. The specific ions that feature the different oxidation states of chlorine are listed below.

The energy required to remove an electron from an atom, thereby giving that atom a more positive oxidation state, is known as an *ionization energy*. The ionization energies for removing each of the first four electrons from elements with atomic numbers 11–15, as measured in electron-volts (eV), are shown in Figure 1.

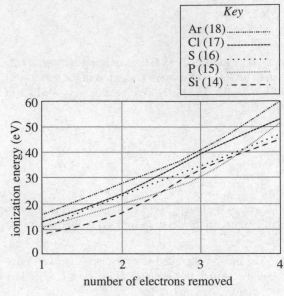

Figure 1

Table 1		
Name	Ion	Oxidation state of chlorine atom
Chloride	$(Cl)^{-1}$	–1
Hypochlorite	$(ClO)^{-1}$	+1
Chlorite	$(ClO_2)^{-1}$	+3
Chlorate	$(ClO_3)^{-1}$	+5
Perchlorate	$(ClO_4)^{-1}$	+7

18. Which of the following symbols correctly represents the negatively charged polyatomic ion containing seven oxygen atoms and two chromium (Cr) atoms?

   F. $(CrO_4)^{-1}$
   G. $(Cr_2O_2)^{-7}$
   H. $(Cr_7O_2)^{-2}$
   J. $(Cr_2O_7)^{-2}$

19. According to Table 1, what is the total charge for the polyatomic ion chlorite?

   A. –1
   B. +1
   C. +2
   D. +3

20. Based on Figure 1, the ionization energy required to remove 4 electrons from P (atomic number 15) is approximately twice the ionization energy required for which of the following?

   F. Removing 1 electron from S
   G. Removing 2 electrons from Ar
   H. Removing 3 electrons from Si
   J. Removing 4 electrons from Cl

GO ON TO THE NEXT PAGE.

21. A sample of bleach contains a mixture of chlorite and hypo-chlorite. Based on Table 1 and Figure 1, what is the ionization energy for the chlorine atom in each of these polyatomic ions?

A. Chlorite: IE of chlorine = 24 eV, Hypochlorite: IE of chlorine = 53 eV

B. Chlorite: IE of chlorine = 53 eV, Hypochlorite: IE of chlorine = 24 eV

C. Chlorite: IE of chlorine = 13 eV, Hypochlorite: IE of chlorine = 40 eV

D. Chlorite: IE of chlorine = 40 eV, Hypochlorite: IE of chlorine = 13 eV

22. Suppose a chloride ion is isolated and accelerated at a constant rate. How would the net force acting on the chloride ion compare with the net force acting on a perchlorate ion that is accelerated at the same constant rate?

F. It would be smaller, because chloride is more massive than perchlorate.

G. It would be smaller, because chloride is less massive than perchlorate.

H. It would be larger, because chloride is more massive than perchlorate.

J. It would be larger, because chloride is less massive than perchlorate.

GO ON TO THE NEXT PAGE.

Passage V

Simple diffusion (SD) is the process by which an uncharged solute in water migrates directly across an uncharged membrane, while *facilitated diffusion* (FD) is the process by which a charged or polar solute travels through a channel or transporter that crosses the membrane. Figure 1 illustrates how two solutes can diffuse, one by SD and one by FD.

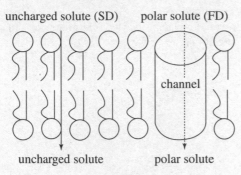

Figure 1

Solutes that cross a membrane by SD or by FD show different rates of flow across a membrane, also known as *flux*. As a solute crosses a membrane by SD, the flux follows a linear pattern over time, with smaller solutes having the greatest increase in flux over time. As a solute crosses a membrane by FD, the flux follows a logarithmic pattern, leveling off at a maximum flux since there are only a limited number of channels or transporters through which the solute can travel.

Experiment 1

One scientist introduced five different solutes of the same concentration to similar membranes at a constant temperature. The molecular masses of these solutes are shown in Table 1.

Table 1	
Solute	Molecular mass (amu)
#1	160
#2	800
#3	2,000
#4	10,000
#5	40,000

This scientist then measured the time it took for the solute to reach *equilibrium*, which is a state of equal concentration of the solute on both sides of the membrane. The results are shown in Figure 2.

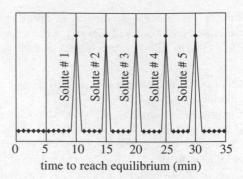

Figure 2

Experiment 2

Mixtures of solutes are subsequently introduced near three different membranes with different properties. The results of these three trials are presented in Figure 3.

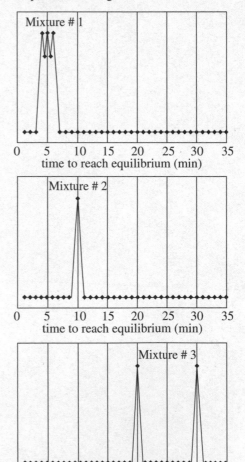

Figure 3

GO ON TO THE NEXT PAGE.

23. Based on the results of Experiments 1 and 2, Mixture #3 is likely to consist of which solutes from Experiment 1 ?

   A. Solute #1 only
   B. Solutes #1 and #3 only
   C. Solutes #3 and #5 only
   D. Solutes #2, #4, and #5 only

24. In Experiment 1, which solute spends the least amount of time flowing across the membrane before reaching equilibrium?

   F. Solute #1
   G. Solute #2
   H. Solute #3
   J. Solute #4

25. Based on the results of Experiments 1 and 2, which of the following ranks Solute #3, Solute #4, and Mixture #2 in order of smallest to largest average molecular mass?

   A. Solute #3, Solute #4, Mixture #2
   B. Solute #4, Mixture #2, Solute #3
   C. Mixture #2, Solute #3, Solute #4
   D. Mixture #2, Solute #4, Solute #3

26. In Experiment 1, on average, did molecules of Solute #3 or molecules of Solute #4 more easily diffuse across the membrane?

   F. Solute #3, because it has a larger molecular mass.
   G. Solute #3, because it has a smaller molecular mass
   H. Solute #4, because it has a larger molecular mass.
   J. Solute #4, because it has a smaller molecular mass.

27. In which mixture is the molecular mass most likely less than 160 amu ?

   A. Mixture 1
   B. Mixture 2
   C. Mixture 3
   D. Neither Mixture 1, 2, or 3

28. How does the number of molecules in 1 gram of Solute #1 compare with the number of molecules in 1 gram of Solute #5 ? The number of molecules in 1 gram of Solute #1 is:

   F. less, because Solute #1 has a larger molecular mass than Solute #5.
   G. less, because Solute #1 has a smaller molecular mass than Solute #5.
   H. more, because Solute #1 has a larger molecular mass than Solute #5.
   J. more, because Solute #1 has a smaller molecular mass than Solute #5.

GO ON TO THE NEXT PAGE.

Passage VI

The term "evolution" is often used in the context of biological changes in organism populations over time, but it can also be applied to the change in the chemical composition of the Earth's atmosphere. The hypotheses of two studies claim that this *chemical evolution* has altered the types of chemicals found in the atmosphere between the early stages of Earth's existence and the present day.

Study 1

Based on the hypothesis that volcanic eruptions were the source of gases in the early Earth's atmosphere, scientists recreated four model volcanic eruptions in closed chambers, each containing different percentages of the same volcanic particulate matter. They then observed the gases in the air above this model over time. The percent composition of this air after 1 day, when the air achieved a *steady state* of constant gas concentrations, is represented in Table 1.

Since the experiment provided only a suggestion of the gas levels in the early Earth's atmosphere, the scientists then analyzed the amount of trapped gases in sediment layers, which indicate the changing atmospheric levels of gases over billions of years. The data collected on O_2 and H_2O vapor are presented in Figure 1.

Table 1						
Volcanic eruption models		Percent composition of gas				
		1	2	3	4
Study 1 (low H_2 atmosphere)	H_2	3	2	1	0
	H_2O vapor	85	80	75	70
	CO_2	10	10	10	15
	H_2S	2	5	7	8
	N_2	0.5	1	2	2
	CH_4	0.3	0.3	0.3	0.3
	CO	0.05	0.05	0.05	0.05
Study 2 (high H_2 atmosphere)	H_2	45	40	35	30
	H_2O vapor	40	40	35	35
	CO_2	10	10	10	15
	H_2S	2	5	7	8
	N_2	0.5	1	2	2
	CH_4	0.3	0.3	0.3	0.3
	CO	0.05	0.05	0.05	0.05

Study 2

A separate study used the same volcanic models as in Study 1, but it hypothesized that the scientists in Study 1 underestimated the amount of H_2 in the early Earth atmosphere. They proposed a different composition of gases, highlighting an increased H_2 level in the atmosphere, also represented in Table 1. Based on these new data, the scientists proposed an alternative graph for the changing atmospheric levels of O_2 and H_2O vapor, also shown in Figure 1.

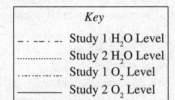

Key
- · –– · Study 1 H_2O Level
- ········· Study 2 H_2O Level
- · – · – Study 1 O_2 Level
- ———— Study 2 O_2 Level

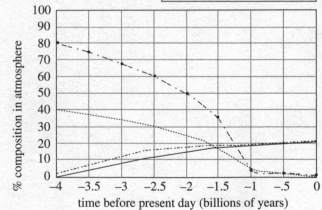

Figure 1

GO ON TO THE NEXT PAGE.

29. According to the results of Study 2, between 4 and 3 billion years before the present day, the percent composition of O_2 in the atmosphere:

   A. increased only.
   B. increased, then decreased.
   C. decreased only.
   D. decreased, then increased.

30. According to the results of Study 1, the percent composition of H_2O vapor in the atmosphere decreased most rapidly over what period of time?

   F. Between 2.5 and 2 billion years ago
   G. Between 2 and 1.5 billion years ago
   H. Between 1.5 and 1 billion years ago
   J. Between 1 and 0.5 billion years ago

31. Suppose that the actual early Earth atmosphere had a high H_2 composition of 42%. Based on Study 2, is it likely that the corresponding H_2S and N_2 compositions of this atmosphere were each 3%?

	3% H_2S	3% N_2
A.	Yes	Yes
B.	Yes	No
C.	No	Yes
D.	No	No

32. Suppose that in a new trial in Study 2, the percent composition of H_2 in the atmosphere was set at 33%, and the percent composition of N_2 was found to be 2%. The percent composition of H_2O vapor in this trial would most likely be:

   F. greater than 40%.
   G. greater than 35% and less than 40%.
   H. exactly 35%.
   J. greater than 30% and less than 35%.

33. Consider an early Earth environment that featured micro-organisms. Based on the results of Study 2, is it more likely that *aerobic organisms* (those that require O_2 to survive) or *anaerobic organisms* (those that do not require O_2 to survive) would have existed on Earth 4 billion years ago?

   A. Aerobic organisms, because of the high H_2O level 4 billion years ago
   B. Aerobic organisms, because of the low O_2 level 4 billion years ago
   C. Anaerobic organisms, because of the high H_2O level 4 billion years ago
   D. Anaerobic organisms, because of the low O_2 level 4 billion years ago

34. According to Study 2, how long did it take the H_2O vapor level to decrease to 75% of its composition 4 billion years before the present day?

   F. 500 million years
   G. 1 billion years
   H. 1.5 billion years
   J. 2 billion years

GO ON TO THE NEXT PAGE.

Passage VII

Engineers studied the trajectories of a cannonball launched from a cannon under various conditions.

Study 1

On a level surface during a mild day, engineers launched a cannonball from a cannon as shown in Figure 1.

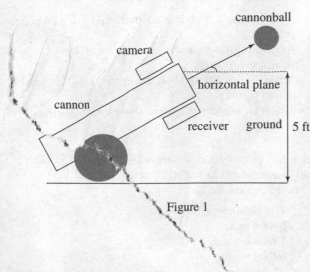

Figure 1

A camera was fixed atop the cannon so that it would point in the direction of the cannonball's launch. A receiver was also fixed to the cannon to record the cannonball's position as recorded by the camera.

As the cannonball traveled through the air, angle θ, which is defined in Figure 1, consistently changed. The change in θ was captured by the camera every 0.25 seconds after launch until the cannonball landed. For each recorded image, θ was measured (Figure 2).

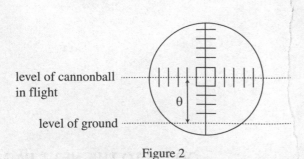

Figure 2

Furthermore, every 0.25 sec after launch, the receiver sent out a radar pulse, part of which was reflected by the cannonball to the receiver. The roundtrip travel time of each pulse was recorded to determine the distance, d, between the receiver and the ball at any given time (see Figure 3).

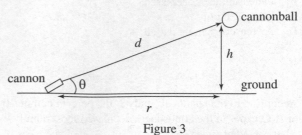

Figure 3

Using d and θ, the engineers determined the ball's height, h, and distance, r, at the end of each 0.25 sec interval. A curve plotting h versus r was constructed.

This procedure was followed using cannonball launch starting speeds of 135 ft/sec, 150 ft/sec, and 180 ft/sec. For each launch speed, the ball was launched at θ = 30 . The curves representing h and r for each of the launch speeds were connected by lines for time, t = 2 sec, 3 sec, 4 sec, and 5 sec after launch (see Figure 4).

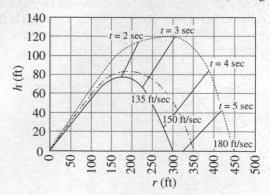

Figure 4

Study 2

Using an algorithm, the engineers calculated h and r at 0.25 sec intervals for the same cannonball launched in a vacuum in otherwise similar conditions to those in Study 1. The results are plotted in Figure 5.

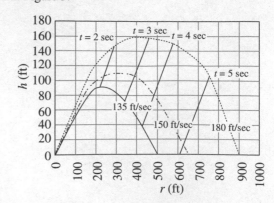

Figure 5

GO ON TO THE NEXT PAGE.

35. Suppose the cannonball were launched at 30° in a vacuum from a height of 5 ft. Based on Figure 5, the cannonball would land approximately how many feet farther from the cannon if it were launched at 150 ft/sec than if it were launched at 135 ft/sec?

A. 50 ft
B. 150 ft
C. 500 ft
D. 650 ft

36. While the cannonball was in flight, how often did the camera record the position of the ball?

F. Once per second
G. Twice per second
H. Three times per second
J. Four times per second

37. The cannon was an instrumental weapon used during the Ottoman invasion of the city of Constantinople in 1453. Assume that cannonballs identical to those used in Study 1 were launched on a windless day with a starting height of 5 ft above the ground and an angle of θ = 30°. If the launch speed of each cannonball were 180 ft/sec, how close would the cannon have needed to be to the 40-ft-tall wall surrounding Constantinople in order to travel over it?

A. 425 ft
B. 575 ft
C. 700 ft
D. 850 ft

38. Based on Figure 4, as the initial speed of the launched cannonball was increased, how did the values of h and r change at $t = 4$ sec?

	h	r
F.	decreased	decreased
G.	decreased	increased
H.	increased	decreased
J.	increased	increased

39. Based on Figure 5, if the ball were launched in a vacuum from a height of 5 ft at 135 ft/sec and 0 = 30°, how long would the cannonball most likely be in flight from launch to landing?

A. Between 4 sec and 5 sec
B. Between 5 sec and 6 sec
C. Between 6 sec and 7 sec
D. Between 7 sec and 8 sec

40. Based on Figure 3, if c represents the speed of light, which of the following represents the time taken by each radar pulse to make the roundtrip between the receiver and the ball?

F. $2c/d$
G. $2d/c$
H. c/r
J. r/c

END OF TEST 4

STOP! DO NOT RETURN TO ANY OTHER TEST.

Chapter 30
Practice Exam 3:
Answers
and Explanations

English		Math		Reading		Science	
1. D	39. D	1. C	31. C	1. B	21. B	1. C	21. D
2. H	40. G	2. H	32. J	2. F	22. F	2. H	22. G
3. C	41. C	3. C	33. A	3. A	23. B	3. B	23. C
4. J	42. F	4. J	34. J	4. J	24. F	4. J	24. F
5. B	43. D	5. D	35. B	5. D	25. C	5. D	25. C
6. G	44. J	6. G	36. G	6. G	26. J	6. F	26. G
7. A	45. C	7. D	37. C	7. D	27. C	7. C	27. A
8. F	46. H	8. J	38. H	8. H	28. F	8. H	28. J
9. D	47. B	9. A	39. D	9. C	29. B	9. D	29. A
10. F	48. H	10. G	40. G	10. G	30. H	10. J	30. H
11. D	49. C	11. B	41. A	11. A	31. D	11. A	31. B
12. F	50. G	12. K	42. J	12. F	32. F	12. G	32. H
13. C	51. A	13. B	43. C	13. C	33. A	13. C	33. D
14. F	52. H	14. K	44. F	14. J	34. G	14. H	34. H
15. A	53. D	15. B	45. E	15. B	35. A	15. D	35. B
16. J	54. F	16. K	46. F	16. G	36. J	16. J	36. J
17. B	55. A	17. A	47. C	17. B	37. C	17. C	37. A
18. F	56. G	18. F	48. K	18. F	38. G	18. J	38. J
19. C	57. D	19. E	49. A	19. A	39. C	19. A	39. A
20. J	58. G	20. H	50. J	20. H	40. H	20. G	40. G
21. C	59. B	21. B	51. E				
22. H	60. G	22. J	52. J				
23. D	61. B	23. D	53. E				
24. H	62. G	24. F	54. K				
25. B	63. A	25. E	55. E				
26. J	64. F	26. K	56. F				
27. A	65. D	27. B	57. B				
28. F	66. F	28. H	58. H				
29. D	67. D	29. B	59. A				
30. H	68. J	30. H	60. G				
31. B	69. C						
32. F	70. G						
33. D	71. B						
34. F	72. H						
35. B	73. C						
36. H	74. H						
37. B	75. D						
38. J							

ENGLISH TEST

1. **D**   The subject of the sentence is the collective noun *family*: Collective nouns are always singular, so eliminate (B) and (C) because both use the plural form *were*. Choice (A) makes the sentence wordier by complicating the tense for no reason.

2. **H**   *So* as a transition word appropriately follows a reason and then introduces a conclusion. *Because* would work if the conclusion were first and the reason followed the transition word. *But* does not work as a transition, and since both it and *so* are FANBOYS, it would need a comma because both ideas on either side are complete.

3. **C**   Choice (C) is consistent with the non-underlined *Classes starting in the fall.* Deleting the underlined portion would create an error.

4. **J**   Choice (J) is the most concise choice, free of any errors. If you don't need a transition word, don't use it.

5. **B**   Use the Vertical Line Test whenever you see STOP punctuation in the text or answers. The idea to the left of the Vertical Line (*I pleaded*) is a complete idea, but the idea to the right (*begging to be allowed to stay behind...*) is incomplete, eliminating (A). Something is needed, however, in between the ideas, and (B) correctly uses a comma. Choice (C) uses a pair of commas that would incorrectly make *begging to be allowed* unnecessary.

6. **G**   Choice (G) is consistent with the non-underlined *racing*, which like *blocking*, describes the rats. Deleting the underlined portion would create an error.

7. **A**   Choice (A) correctly fulfills the purpose stated in the question of giving the *reader a better idea of how she thought her father felt* because it offers the narrator's description of the emotion on her father's face.

8. **F**   Choice (F) correctly fulfills the purpose stated in the question by providing *the best opening* to the paragraph because the following sentences are the father's explanations of why he wants to move.

9. **D**   Choice (D) is the most concise choice, free of any errors.

10. **F**   Use *than* when you make a comparison; use *then* when you mean *next*. Choice (J) uses the superlative form *happiest*, but *than* would not be used in that construction.

11. **D**   Draw two vertical lines whenever you spot FANBOYS in the answers. The idea before *and* is complete, but the idea after *and* is incomplete, eliminating (C). There is no reason to use a comma after *and* nor after *talked*, eliminating (A) and (B).

12. **F**   Sentence 5 works best where it is now. The transition phrase *Before the move* works best right before Sentence 6's *After the move.*

13. **C**   Use the Vertical Line Test whenever you see STOP punctuation in the text or among the answers. The idea to the left is incomplete, which eliminates (A) and (B). Choice (C) correctly uses a comma to follow an introductory incomplete idea.

14. **F**   Choice (F) is the most concise choice, free of any errors.

15. **A**   Choice (A) addresses the purpose stated in the question of *telling the reader why, in her opinion, her family moved to Redding*, and the reason provided in (A) describes the passage accurately. The reasons given in (B), (C), and (D) do not describe the passage accurately.

16. **J**   Choice (J) is the most concise choice, free of any errors.

17. **B**   Use the Vertical Line Test whenever you see STOP punctuation in the text or among the answers. Be careful when both the wording and the punctuation change. Without the *which*, both ideas on either side are complete, making the semicolon correct. Choice (D) is also STOP, using a comma with FANBOYS. However, the *but* does not work as a transition word in between two ideas that agree with each other.

18. **F**   *The mural* is unnecessary, so either a pair of commas or a pair of dashes should surround it. Choice (G) incorrectly mixes one comma and one dash, while (H) and (J) incorrectly use only one of the two options.

19. **C**   Be careful with EXCEPT/LEAST/NOT questions. Choice (C) is correct because the underlined portion CANNOT go after the word *popular*: *Popular* needs to come right before *revival*.

20. **J**   Choice (J) is the best description of the preceding sentence, which specifically mentions the *fame* she has earned for her work in *Los Angeles*.

21. **C**   Choice (C) is the most concise choice, free of any errors. If you don't need a transition word, don't use it.

22. **H**   The subject of the sentence is the pronoun *some*, here used as a plural because it refers to *earliest examples*. Choice (H) is the only choice with the plural form of the verb.

23. **D**   The *murals* "possess" the *political messages*, so an apostrophe is needed. Since possession can be a tricky concept to think of for inanimate objects, try rewording the sentence. If *the political messages of the murals* works, then the apostrophe is needed. Choice (C) incorrectly uses the singular *mural*.

24. **H**   Choice (H) provides the correct transition from the reason (*Because of their immense size...require the assistance of other artists*) to a conclusion (*become community efforts*).

25. **B**   Choice (B) correctly fulfills the purpose stated in the question of providing *the most relevant information* because it links to the descriptions in the prior and following sentences of *community efforts* and *community involvement*.

26. J Choice (J) is the most concise choice, making clear that the *murals* are *inspired by the neighbor-hoods*. The pronoun *they* in (F) is ambiguous, and the pronouns *it* and *that* in (G) and (H) don't match in number any preceding noun in the sentence. Choices (F) and (G) also incorrectly use GO punctuation in between two complete ideas.

27. A Each choice changes the order of words and phrases, making it difficult to identify the intended meaning. Use the non-underlined portion beginning of the sentence and the following sentence to help as context, and lean on POE. In terms of order of ideas, *successes by members of the community* is consistent with *historic achievements of the generations past*.

28. F The non-underlined phrase at the beginning of the sentence describes Baca, so the correct choice must begin with *Baca*, which only (F) does.

29. D Use the Vertical Line Test whenever you see STOP punctuation in the text or among the answers. The ideas on either side of the vertical line are incomplete, eliminating (C), and there is no reason to use a comma in between them, eliminating (A). A colon can be used only after a complete idea, which eliminates (B).

30. H Choose a pronoun that matches in number with the plural *people* and that shows possession. *They're* is a contraction of *They are*.

31. B. Choice (B) offers the right tense of the helping verb *to have* and the right past participle of the ir-regular verb *to see*. Don't mistake the made-up *would of* in (D) with *would've*, the contraction of *would have*, even though *would've*, ahem, would've been the wrong tense here anyway.

32. F Use *when* to refer to a time, such as *1972*.

33. D The singular *technology* is the subject, making the plural verbs *were* and *precede* incorrect in (A) and (B). Choice (C) uses the participle *preceding*, which changes the meaning of the sentence in terms of which games came first, and it also does not work with the preposition *by* needed for the passive voice.

34. F Choice (F) is the best description of the sentence. Choice (H) is tempting, but the sentence never mentions other games.

35. B Choice (B) correctly fulfills the purpose stated in the question of explaining *the writer's reasons for calling* Pong *"old-fashioned"* because it lists the specific features that made the game old school.

36. H Use the Vertical Line Test whenever you see STOP punctuation in the text or among the answers. Both ideas on either side of the semicolon are incomplete, eliminating (F). *In fact* is unnecessary and therefore needs two commas around it, making (H) correct.

37. B Be careful with EXCEPT/LEAST/NOT questions. The correct choice is the word that does NOT mean the same as *novelty*.

38. **J** Choice (J) is the most concise choice, free of any errors.

39. **D** Choose the correct, singular possessive pronoun *its*, since the pronoun refers to the game *Pong*, a singular noun. The non-underlined portion of the sentence also helps. Just as *its* showed possession of *day*, so too does *its* show possession of *own way*. *It's* is a contraction of *it is*.

40. **G** Use the transition word *However* at the beginning of Sentence 5 to help place the sentence: It should follow a sentence that describes the opposite of *groundbreaking*, as Sentence 1 does describing *Pong* as *old-fashioned*.

41. **C** Use the Vertical Line Test whenever you see STOP punctuation in the text or among the answers. When the wording and the punctuation change, use the wording of the STOP choice. Without the word *only*, both ideas on either side of the vertical line are complete, making the period the correct choice.

42. **F** Choice (F) is the most concise choice, free of any errors.

43. **D** Choose the right form of the two modifiers. *Highly* describes *complex*, and *complex* describes games. Choice (C) changes the adjective *complex* into a noun, *complexity*, but the adjective is needed.

44. **J** Choice (J) correctly fulfills the purpose stated in the question of expressing *the writer's attitude toward the future of the video game industry*.

45. **C** Choice (C) correctly fulfills the purpose stated in the question of *demonstrating the impact a single invention can have on the development of an industry* by offering an accurate description of the passage and its emphasis on *Pong's* impact on video games.

46. **H** Choice (H) correctly provides *the most specific information* by offering a specific time.

47. **B** With the irregular verb *to go*, *gone* is the correct past participle, used with the helping verb *to have*. In this case, *had* is in the non-underlined portion and makes (B) correct. *Went* is the simple past tense of *to go*, used without *to have*.

48. **H** One comma is needed to close the unnecessary information *the first African-American to serve as the Green Lantern* because the first comma is in the non-underlined portion.

49. **C** The sentence is incomplete without a subject and a verb, which both (A) and (D) lack. Choices (B) and (C) both use a comma after the introductory incomplete idea and add a subject and verb to make the second idea complete. But the verb *practiced* in (B) does not work with the rest of the sentence. Choice (C) uses the verb *was* and makes *practiced* an adjective that is consistent with *fearsome* to describe *warrior*.

50. **G** Make all items on a list consistent in form; in this case, the non-underlined portion of the sentence provides the rest of the list with *leading* and *acting*, making *fighting* correct.

51. **A**   Do not mistake the sound-alikes *could of* with *could've*. The former is made up while the latter is the contraction of the verb phrase *could have*. Deleting the underlined portion would create an error, leaving (A) as the only option.

52. **H**   Choice (H) is the most concise choice, free of any errors.

53. **D**   Consider the reasons carefully in questions that ask if new text should be added or deleted. Because the proposed insertion offers tangential information, (D) is correct.

54. **F**   Choice (F) correctly fulfills the purpose stated in the question of explaining the *author's belief that Stewart was a more understandable character and shows a more realistic image of Stewart* by stating that the author *related to* the character's *ups* and *downs*.

55. **A**   Use the Vertical Line Test whenever you see STOP punctuation in the text or among the answers. From the beginning of the sentence until *but after* is incomplete, which eliminates both (B) and (C). Semicolons are STOP and can be used only in between two complete ideas, and colons can be used only after complete ideas. There is no reason to slow down the ideas, no reason to use a comma.

56. **G**   Be careful with EXCEPT/LEAST/NOT questions. A transition word, *furthermore* connects ideas that agree with each other, but *however* connects ideas that are different. Thus, (G) is the correct answer because it does NOT work. Deleting the underlined portion would not create an error, and *though* and *on the contrary* both work the same way as *however*.

57. **D**   The *rocky life story* belongs to *Stewart*, so the apostrophe is needed. Choice (C) incorrectly makes his name plural, and (A) adds a comma after *rocky* that is not needed and therefore wrong.

58. **G**   Choice (G) correctly fulfills the purpose stated in the question of supporting *the point being made in the first part of this sentence* by reaffirming it was *actions* (*what he did*) not his *past* (*not who he was*).

59. **B**   The pronouns *that* and *those* are both ambiguous, and only (B) offers a noun to make the point clear.

60. **G**   Use the Vertical Line Test whenever you see STOP punctuation in the text or among the answers. Choice (J) changes the wording, but the rest of the choices all use the same wording and change only the punctuation. In (F), (G), and (H), the two ideas on either side of the vertical line are complete, making the semicolon correct. Choice (J) makes the second idea incomplete, but it changes the meaning of the sentence.

61. **B**   The correct modifier is *timeworn*. All of the other choices are incorrect idioms, or idioms that do not work with the non-underlined *saying*.

62. **G** Choice (F) makes two complete ideas, linked incorrectly with a comma, something GO punctuation can't do. *Just like* and *between* are both conjunctions, which make the first idea incomplete, but neither is the correct idiom that works with the *to* in the sentence and make it sound as if *pressure* is a threat *to unknown geography*. Instead, the idiom *from...to* offers a range: *From the immense pressure that poses...to unknown geography that can injure....*

63. **A** Choice (A) correctly fulfills the purpose stated in the question of providing information that is *the most relevant to the statement that follows* by specifically mentioning *costs*.

64. **F** Consider the reasons carefully in questions that ask if new text should be added or deleted. Because the proposed insertion offers necessary information about the *Marianas Trench*, it clarifies what would otherwise be a confusing reference, and (F) is correct.

65. **D** Choice (D) correctly fulfills the purpose stated in the question of connecting the *preceding paragraph to the subject* of the next. The prior paragraph listed reasons why scientists would not explore the ocean's depths, but the new paragraph offers the reasons to do so.

66. **F** Choice (F) is concise and uses the correct idiom *development of* to make the meaning clear.

67. **D** Choice (D) offers a transition that shows a contrast to the last exploration but also references the time that has past since *1960*.

68. **J** Present tense is needed to be consistent with the non-underlined verbs *has been* and *is*, eliminating (F) and (H). Do not mistake the sound-alikes *could of* with *could've*. The former is made up, while the latter is the contraction of the verb phrase *could have*.

69. **C** Choice (C) correctly fulfills the purpose stated in the question of describing *what sonar is* by providing a definition.

70. **G** A comma is needed after *advanced* to close the unnecessary information begun with the non-underlined portion, *as technology has advanced*.

71. **B** The word *as* is needed to make the comparison. Deleting the underlined portion would create an error.

72. **H** The correct transition *whether* is needed to make the meaning clear it is uncertain if the robots will work. Deleting the underlined portion would create an error.

73. **C** While (A) is the most concise, it creates an error by making the idea complete. After the unnecessary information (the definition of *tethered*), a comma precedes another complete idea. GO punctuation can't link two complete ideas, but the comma isn't underlined. Thus, a conjunction is needed to make the first idea incomplete, and only (C) offers a conjunction.

74. **H** Choice (H) is the most concise choice, free of any errors.

75. **D** Consider the reasons carefully in questions that ask if new text should be added or deleted. Because the proposed insertion opens a new topic about *emotional responses of a human*, it digresses from the subject of the passage, as (D) states.

MATHEMATICS TEST

1. **C** Isolate the variable. First, multiply each side by 3 to get $5y - 1 = -18$. Next, add 1 to each side to get $5y = -17$. Last, divide each side by 5 to get $y = \dfrac{-17}{5}$. Choices (B) and (E) are trap answers and result from mistakes with the negative sign.

2. **H** Simplify the expression by reducing the integers and following the rules for exponents (MAD-SPM): $\dfrac{12}{4} = 3$. When **D**ividing like bases, **S**ubtract the exponents. $\dfrac{z^{10}}{z^2} = z^8$. Choices (F), (G), (J), and (K) are trap answers and result from swapping or mistaking some or all of the operations for the integers and exponents.

3. **C** Input 12 into the function given. $\dfrac{12^2 - 18}{12 + 2} = 9$. Use parentheses in your calculator when there are operations in the numerator and denominator of a fraction.

4. **J** Underline the question. *Articles written* are in Graph 2, but *weeks* are in Graph 1. The link between the two figures is *movies watched*. When *weeks elapsed* equals 3 on Graph 1, *movies watched* equals 15. When *movies watched* equals 15 on Graph 2, *articles written* equals 12 on Graph 2.

5. **D** First, perform the calculations to find that $117 - 54 + 6 = 69$. Next, round this value to the nearest ten, 70.

6. **G** Underline the question. Read the bite-sized pieces carefully and translate the English into math to write an equation. The *number of tables* is the unknown, so $4x + 20 = 100$. Isolate the variable by subtracting 20 from both sides and then dividing each side by 4 to find that $x = 20$. PITA (Plug In the Answer) is an alternative to writing the equation. Choice (H) is wrong because it doesn't include the extra 20 napkins. Choice (J) is wrong because it adds 20 to 100 instead of subtracting.

7. **D** Before you can isolate the variable, you have to collect like things, and the only way to collect the variables together is to first distribute. $4(w - 2) - w = 46$ becomes $4w - 8 - w = 46$ then $3w - 8 = 46$. Add 8 to both sides and then divide both sides by 3 to find that $w = 18$. Choice (C) is wrong because the 4 wasn't distributed to the 2 as well as the variable.

8.　**J**　Be careful with the NOT in the question and use the answers to see which contain $\overline{WX}$. Only (J) does not.

9.　**A**　Start with $bc = 40$ and replace c with 5. If $5b = 40$, then $b = 8$. Now replace b with 8 in $ab = 32$ and solve for a: $8a = 32$, and $a = 4$.

10.　**G**　Underline the question and work the problem in bite-sized pieces. Don't waste time adding up the times for the first 4 laps: The total of 178.5 is provided in the next bite-sized piece. Moreover, the answers make clear that the goal is to write the expression to solve for the 5th time without calculating the actual number. Use the Average Pie: Divide the total by the number of things to find the average. The total of all 5 laps will be the total of the first 4 (178.5) plus the 5th. Divide this total by 5 to get an average of 43: $\dfrac{175.8 + x}{5} = 43$.

11.　**B**　List all the integers from 123 to 132: 123, 124, 125, 126, 127, 128, 129, 130, 131, 132. Circle all the integers whose tens digit (the 2 or the 3 in this case) is greater than the ones (or units) digit. Only 130, 131, and 132 satisfy the condition, since 0, 1, and 2 are all less than 3.

12.　**K**　Set up a proportion. $\dfrac{20 \text{ points}}{12 \text{ hours}} = \dfrac{35 \text{ points}}{x \text{ hours}}$. Cross-multiply to solve for x. $20x = 420$, $x = 21$.

13.　**B**　Count the hash marks to determine the length and width of rectangle $ABCD$. Since the sides are horizontal and vertical, there is no need to use the distance formula. The width is 5 (the distance from the y-point −3 to the y-point 2), and the length is 6 (the distance from the x-point −4 to the x-point 2). The formula for area of a rectangle is $A = lw$, so $6 \times 5 = 30$. The rectangle formed in Quadrant IV is bounded by the x-axis and the y-point −3 and by the y-axis and the x-point 2. Thus, it makes a rectangle with sides 2 and 3 and an area of 6, $\dfrac{6}{30}$ of the whole, or $\dfrac{1}{5}$.

14.　**K**　Choice (H) is a trap answer that illustrates a basic rule of math: You can't reduce terms in the numerator and denominator if the terms are connected to other terms by addition or subtraction. You can't cancel $(z + 3)$ in the numerator and denominator. Instead, distribute and combine like things. $2(z + 3) − 9 = 2z + 6 − 9 = 2z − 3$. In the denominator, $5 + 4(z + 3) = 5 + 4z + 12 = 4z + 17$.

15.　**B**　The equation for a circle graphed in the standard (x,y) plane is $(x − h)^2 + (y − k)^2 = r^2$, where (h,k) are the coordinates of the center. If the circle is centered at the origin, both h and k are 0, and the equation simplifies to $x^2 + y^2 = r^2$. This circle is centered at the origin and has a radius of 7. Thus, the coordinates for the intersection with the x-axis are (−7, 0) and (7,0).

16.　**K**　When no figure is provided, draw your own. On a circle, make 19 evenly-spaced hash marks. Place Jessica first at the top, then Kevin (5 marks to the left, or counterclockwise) then Lisa (9 marks to the right, or clockwise). The exact distance between them is less important than the order, as the answers make clear. Use the first part of the last clue to place Michael in between Jessica and Lisa. The second part of the clue isn't necessary, but you can confirm that you've placed all correctly.

17. **A** Underline the question and work the problem in bite-sized pieces. The phrase *linear rate* means proportionally, so set up a proportion of the number of years' difference between 1905 and 2005 (100) and the meters the lake withdrew over those 100 years (825 − 75 = 750 meters). Since the lake withdrew at the same rate, use the proportion to solve for the meters the lake withdrew from 1905 to 1985. $\dfrac{750\ m}{100\ y} = \dfrac{x\ m}{80\ y}$. Cross-multiply to solve for *x*, and the lake increased by 600 meters. Note that the question, however, asks for the distance from the edge to Marker X in 1985, so add the 600 meters to 75 to find the correct answer of 675, (A).

18. **F** Underline the question and work the problem in bite-sized pieces. It also helps to draw a figure when none is provided. Use the area formula $A = lw$ and perimeter formula $P = 2l + 2w$ and use the answers. Only (F) provides dimensions that yield an area of 144 square inches and a perimeter of 80 inches.

19. **E** Use your calculator, or write the value out and use your pencil to move the decimal 3 spaces to the left. If you chose (A), you missed the negative exponent and moved the decimal 3 spaces to the right.

20. **H** Use the known proportion of *s* and *t* and solve for *s* when *t* is 15. $\dfrac{8}{10} = \dfrac{s}{15}$. Cross-multiply to solve for *s* is 12, (H). Choice (F) is the ratio of *s* to *t*, not the value of *s* when *t* is 15. Choice (G) is a ratio of *t* to *t*. Choice (K) is the sum of *s* and *t*.

21. **B** Underline the question and work the problem in bite-sized pieces. A good option here is to PITA (Plug In the Answers). Start in the middle with (C) and work the bite-sized pieces, keeping your work neatly organized.

From	To	Cost
2:12 P.M.	3:12 P.M.	$3.50
3:13 P.M.	4:12 P.M.	$2.50
4:13 P.M.	5:12 P.M.	$1.25
5:13 P.M.	6:12 P.M.	$1.25
6:13 P.M.	7:12 P.M.	$1.25
7:13 P.M.	7:30 P.M.	$1.25
	Total	$11.00

$11 is too high, so eliminate (C) as well as (D) and (E). Since $11.00 is $1.25 over the $9.75 charged, the answer must be choice (B), 6:30 P.M. $1.25 is charged from 6:13 P.M. until 6:30 P.M. Choice (C) is incorrect because the $1.25 is charged for every hour *or any fraction thereof*, tricky phrasing easy to miss if you solve it algebraically.

22. **J** *Geometric sequence* means a pattern of multiplication, in which each term is multiplied by the same amount to determine the next term. In a geometric sequence, each term divided by the prior term yields a constant, or *common*, *ratio*. Since the sum of the 4 angles of a quadrilateral equals 360°, $x + 2x + 4x + 8x = 360$. Thus, $x = 24$, and the fourth angle equals 192°. Choice (F) is the value of the common ratio. Choice (G) is the value of the third term.

23. **D** Draw a figure if none is provided.

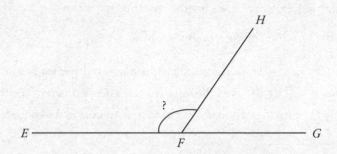

A straight line equals 180°, so the two angles formed by $\overline{FH}$ are supplementary, and $\angle EFH$ equals 116°.

24. **F** With a system of equations, elimination is almost always faster than substitution. First, multiply one equation by a common factor to make the coefficients of one of the variables the same in both equations. Multiply $3x + 4y = 2$ by 2 to get $6x + 8y = 4$. Now the coefficients for x are the same in both equations. Subtract $6x + 8y = 4$ from $6x + 10y = 14$: The two x-terms cancel out, and $2y = 10$, and $y = 5$. Replace y with 5 in either equation to solve for x: $6x + 10(5) = 14$, so $6x + 50 = 14$, $6x = -36$, and $x = -6$. Use both values to find that $5(-6) + 7(5) = -30 + 35 = 5$.

25. **E** Solve for b by first multiplying both sides by 2 to get $a - b = 12$. Subtract a from both sides, and $-b = 12 - a$. Choice (B) is incorrect because this is the value for $-b$, not b. The last step is to multiply both sides by -1 to find that $b = -12 + a$, or $b = a - 12$, choice (E). Choices (C) and (D) are both incorrect because the two sides of the equation were not multiplied by 2.

26. **K** Plug In your own numbers and try them on each answer to find a negative odd number. Use 2 and -4, 2 and -3, and 3 and -2 to find only (K) works. The product of two negative numbers is positive, so (G) and (J) won't work. The product of two even numbers or the product of an even and an odd is even, so (F) and (H) will not work either.

27. **B** Underline the question and work the problem in bite-sized pieces. Probability is a $\frac{part}{whole}$ relationship, in which the *part* is what you want, and the *whole* is what you've got. There are 44 total marbles to begin with, but after drawing four purples out of the bag, there are 40 marbles total, seven of which are purple. The probability of drawing a purple marble next is $\frac{7}{40}$, (B). Choice (A) is wrong because the four purple marbles already drawn isn't subtracted from the total; (C) is wrong

because this is the probability of drawing purple before the first four draws. Choice (E) is wrong because it's a ratio of the purple marbles left after four draws and the number of purple marbles at the start.

28. **H** Underline the question and work the problem in bite-sized pieces. Oliver must repeat the test if he scores *less than 70% of the points available*. 70% of $30 = \dfrac{70}{100} \times 30 = 21$. Oliver will repeat the test if his points, p, is less than 21, or if $p < 21$, (H).

29. **B** Underline the question and work the problem in bite-sized pieces. The miles of road painted on Day 2 will be the number of miles left after subtracting the Day 1 and Day 3 miles from the total. Use your calculator, or write out the conversions from mixed to compound fractions before finding a common denominator among the three fractions. $16\dfrac{1}{9} = \dfrac{9 \times 16 + 1}{9} = \dfrac{145}{9}$. $5\dfrac{8}{27} = \dfrac{27 \times 5 + 8}{27} = \dfrac{143}{27}$. $3\dfrac{2}{3} = \dfrac{3 \times 3 + 2}{3} = \dfrac{11}{3}$. The common denominator for these three fractions is 27. To convert $\dfrac{145}{9}$, multiply the numerator and denominator by 3 to get $\dfrac{435}{27}$. To convert $\dfrac{11}{3}$, multiply the numerator and denominator by 9 to get $\dfrac{99}{27}$. Last step, subtract Days 1 and 3 from the total: $\dfrac{435}{27} - \dfrac{143}{27} - \dfrac{99}{27} = \dfrac{193}{27}$, or $7\dfrac{4}{27}$. If you used your calculator to add the three fractions but then were uncertain what to do with a compound fraction as a result and mixed fractions in the answers, use the decimal value instead of the fraction. The decimal answer is $7.\overline{148}$. Eliminate (D) and (E), and then use your calculator to convert (A) and (B) to find which has the same decimal.

30. **H** Underline the question and work the problem in bite-sized pieces. Use a proportion of the 180-ft distance the *Illuminator 100 Plus* must be back from its 108-ft screen to find the distance the *Illuminator 100* must be back from its 81-ft screen. $\dfrac{180\text{-ft screen}}{180\text{-ft distance}} = \dfrac{81\text{-ft screen}}{x\text{-ft distance}}$, so x equals 135 feet. Last step, subtract 135 from 180 to solve for P, the number of feet *farther* the screen must be placed.

31. C Use the distance formula if you have memorized it or have it programmed into your calculator. If you don't have it memorized, draw the axes, plot the points, connect them with a line, make a right triangle, and use the Pythagorean theorem, $a^2 + b^2 = c^2$. See below.

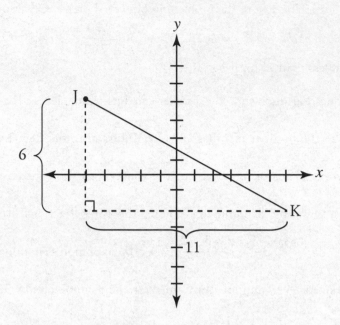

$11^2 + 6^2 = c^2$, and $c^2 = 157$. Thus, $c = \sqrt{157}$, (C). Both (B) and (E) are trap answers because a and b must be squared before they are added.

32. J Underline the question and work the problem in bite-sized pieces. You can use your calculator to add $1 + 2 + 3 + 4 + ...30 = 465$. If you identified this as an arithmetic series, you can use the simplified formula $S = (a_1 + a_n) \times \dfrac{n}{2}$, where n is the number of terms (30), a_1 is the first term (1), a_n is the nth term (30). $(1 + 30) \times \dfrac{30}{2} = 465$.

33. A Draw the figure if none is provided. This question tests the third-side rule of triangles: The third side must be less than the sum of the other two sides and greater than the difference of the other two sides. Choice (A) is correct because this is the only value that *CANNOT* be the third side because it falls out of the range of 29 and 53.

34. J Plug In your own number for d, find the value of the expression, and then find the same value in the answers, substituting your number for each d. If d is 2, then $\dfrac{5(2)^2 - 2}{20(2)} = \dfrac{18}{40}$, or $\dfrac{9}{20}$. Choices (F) and (H) can be eliminated right away. Choice (G) equals $\dfrac{1}{20}$, and (K) equals $\dfrac{3}{20}$.

Choice (J) is the equivalent value, $\dfrac{2}{4} - \dfrac{1}{10(2)} = \dfrac{1}{2} - \dfrac{1}{20} = \dfrac{9}{20}$. The rest of the choices are all trap answers for solving it algebraically because they represent errors in cancelation. Terms in the numerator and denominator can't be reduced if the terms are connected to other terms by addition or subtraction.

35. **B**   Underline the question and work the problem in bite-sized pieces. With a series of questions, some of the information needed may be in the introduction. To find the surface area of just the non-stick tiles, find the surface area of the pool and the non-stick tiles, and then subtract the surface area of the pool. The non-stick tiles extend by 5 meters on *all* sides for a total of 10 meters added to the length and 10 meters added to the width. $A = lw$, so $(50 + 10)(25 + 10) = (60)(35) = 2{,}100$. Subtract from this total the surface area of the pool: $2{,}100 - (50)(25) = 2{,}100 - 1{,}250 = 850$, (B).

36. **G**   Underline the question and work the problem in bite-sized pieces. With a series of questions, some of the information needed may be in the introduction. Find the number of swimmers by dividing the surface area of the pool by the individual area each swimmer needs. The surface area of the pool is $A = lw$, $(50)(25) = 1{,}250$. The individual area for each swimmer is $(5)(5) = 25$. $1{,}250 \div 25 = 50$, (G). Choices (H), (J), and (K) could all fit, but the question asks for the *maximum* number of swimmers who can fit.

37. **C**   Underline the question, and work the problem in bite-sized pieces. Add the cost of the pizza and soda, and calculate the tax first. $\$3.75 + \$1.75 = \$5.50$. Multiply the food subtotal by $\dfrac{10}{100}$, or .10, to get a tax of $\$0.55$. Add the tax to the food subtotal ($\$5.50 + \$0.55 = \$6.05$), and then add the cost of the ticket ($\$4$) for a total of $\$10.05$, (C). Choice (B) is wrong because it is the total of all three items without the tax on the food. Choice (D) is wrong because it includes the ticket in the tax calculation.

38. **H**   The three angles of a triangle equal 180°. The triangle formed in the circle is isosceles because sides $\overline{FG}$ and $\overline{FH}$ are each a radius of the circle. The sides are equal and therefore the angles opposite them are equal. $180° - 2(40°) = 100°$, (H).

39. **D**   Underline the question and work the problem in bite-sized pieces. Subtract the $\$700$ and $\$1{,}300$ from the given July total of $\$10{,}000$ to find the August total of $\$8{,}000$. To find the percent of the August total spent on office supplies, divide the part ($\$1{,}000$) by the whole ($\$8{,}000$). $\dfrac{x}{100} = \dfrac{1{,}000}{8{,}000} = 12.5\%$, (D). Choice (C) is wrong because it is the percent of office supplies out of July's total.

40.   **G**   Plug In your own number for q. If q is 2, then the difference between (14)(2) and (5)(2) is 28 − 10 = 18. Only (G) is a factor of 18.

41.   **A**   Underline the question and work the problem in bite-sized pieces. Divide the total amount earned ($1,800) by the number of weeks of the assignment (6) to find that Ron earned an average of $300/week. Divide the average week total by the *minimum* number of hours worked (20) to find that Ron's hourly wage, r, for those 20 hours is $15.00/hr. Ron will be paid $1,800 for 6 weeks of work whether he works as few as 20 hours or if he works more than 20 hours. If he works more than 20 hours in any given week, his hourly rate will drop, or be *less than* $15.00/hr. Thus, $r \le$ $15.00, (A). Choice (B) is wrong because his rate will decrease with more hours, not increase. Choices (C) and (D) are both wrong because $1,800 must be divided by 6, and then that quotient must be divided by 20.

42.   **J**   The midpoint is the average of the x-coordinates and the average of the y-coordinates: $\left(\dfrac{9 + -3}{2}\right) = \dfrac{6}{2} = 3$, (J). Choice (H) is wrong because it's the x-coordinate of the midpoint. Choice (K) is wrong because it either is the result from adding the y-coordinates but forgetting to divide them or from dividing the difference between the y-coordinates.

43.   **C**   Underline the question and work the problem in bite-sized pieces. The answers help by making it clear to use trigonometry, specifically SOHCAHTOA, to solve for the height of the flagpole in terms of the angle 75°. The figure provides the length of the ground (the side adjacent to the angle) but not the length of the wire (the hypotenuse). The only trig ratio that will work is tangent, found only in (C). TOA stands for Tangent = $\dfrac{opposite}{adjacent}$, so $\tan 75° = \dfrac{x}{8}$. Solve for x by multiplying both sides by 8, so $8\tan 75° = x$.

44.   **F**   With a series of questions, some of the information needed may be in the introduction. The lengths of the sides are provided on the figure as variables. The polygon $CDZXY$ is made up of the smaller square and the triangle: sides x, x, x, z, and y, or $3x + y + z$, (F). The perimeter, however, will not include the interior side $\overline{YZ}$, as (J) does.

45.   **E**   With a series of questions, some of the information needed may be in the introduction or on the figure. $\angle EZD$ is a vertical angle to $\angle YZX$, which is marked as 90°. Thus, $\angle EZD$ is 90° as well. The introduction confirms what the figures look like: $ABYX$, $CDZY$, and $EFXZ$ are squares, and each angle of a square is 90°. The question adds that $x < y$, which means $\angle YXZ < \angle XYZ$. Since $\angle YZX$ is 90°, $\angle YXZ$ and $\angle XYZ$ are complementary; that is, they add up to 90°. $\angle BYC + 2(90°) + \angle XYZ = 360°$: $\angle AXF + 2(90°) + \angle YXZ = 360°$. Since $\angle YXZ < \angle XYZ$, $\angle AXF$ must be $> \angle BYC$, and both must be $> \angle EZD$. Choice (E) provides the correct order.

46. **F** With the provided information that $2x = z$, this triangle is a 30°-60°-90° triangle, whose ratio of sides is $s : s\sqrt{3} : 2s$, and $\cos 30° = \frac{1}{2}$, (F). Alternatively, use the information given in the question and SOHCAHTOA. If $2x = z$, then $\cos \angle XYZ = \frac{adjacent}{hypotenuse} = \frac{x}{z}$ or $\frac{x}{2x}$, which reduces to $\frac{1}{2}$.

47. **C** Plug In your own number. But don't Plug In for the variable. Instead, Plug In four consecutive even integers and add to find t. For example, $2 + 4 + 6 + 8 = 20$, so use 20 for t. Add $6 + 8$ to get 14, and answer the question. Replace t with 20 in each answer choice, and (C) gives you 14.

48. **K** The graph of the function in Figure 2 has been moved to the left by 4 and up by 1. Choice (K) provides the correct function. If you don't know the rules of how parabolas move, graph each function in the answer choices in a graphing calculator to find the match for Figure 2.

49. **A** Underline the question and work the problem in bite-sized pieces. The algebra is complicated, and PITA (Plug In the Answers) is a great option. Start with (C). If there are 17 nickels, then the bite-sized pieces show that there must be 18 dimes, 6 pennies, and 20 quarters. Multiply the number of coins by their values to see if the total equals $5.29: 17($0.05) + 18($0.10) + 6($0.01) + 20($0.25) = 7.71. Eliminate (C), (D), and (E) because they are all too high. Choice (B), 13 nickels, would mean there are 14 dimes. But if the number of dimes has to be three times the number of pennies, 14 dimes would leave a fraction for number of pennies, which is impossible. The answer must be (A). 11 nickels, 12 dimes, 4 pennies, and 14 quarters. $11($0.05) + 12($0.10) + 4($0.01) + 16($0.25) = 5.29.

50. **J** Use the Average Pie. See below.

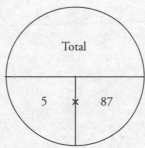

Since the total of all five numbers equals 435, subtracting the smallest number, 75, leaves a total of 360. Divide the total by the number of things to find the average, or mean. See below.

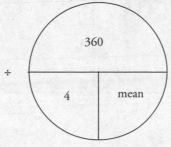

Choice (F) is wrong because it divides 360 by 5. Choice (K) is wrong because it divides 435 by 4.

51. **E** For an *If, Then* statement, the only fact that must be true is the contra-positive. Flip the two terms then negate them. *If A, then B* means that *if −B, then −A*. Choice (E) is the contrapositive of the original statement. All of the other choices *could* be true, but only (E) *must* be true.

52. **J** Use PITA (Plug In the Answers) and your calculator, or follow the MADSPM rules of exponents to simplify and solve for a. If you raise an exponential expression by a **P**ower, **M**ultiply the exponents. $(y^{0.2})^{a^2 - 20} = y$ becomes $y^{.2a^2 - 4} = y^1$. Now solve for a: $.2a^2 - 4 = 1$, so $.2a^2 = 5$, and $a^2 = 25$. Thus, $a = \pm5$.

53. **E** The note provides the reciprocal trig ratios if you don't remember them. Use the reciprocals plus $\tan x = \dfrac{\sin x}{\cos x}$ to rewrite the expression. $\csc x \tan x = \dfrac{1}{\sin x} \times \dfrac{\sin x}{\cos x} = \dfrac{1}{\cos x} = \sec x$, (E).

54. **K** The values in the chart of (x,y) values are points on a linear equation. The fastest way to do this question is to draw the axes and plot the three ordered pairs provided. For the the the (x,y) pair $(-2, b)$, b must be a positive value, which eliminates all answers except for (K).

55. **E** Use the provided formula for volume of a sphere to find the radius. $\dfrac{4}{3}\pi r^3 = 288\pi$. Solve for the radius by canceling π on both sides and multiplying both sides by $\dfrac{3}{4}$ to find that $r^3 = 216$. Take the cube root of both sides to find that the radius equals 6. Solve for the surface area using the provided formula. $4\pi r^2 = 4(6)^2\pi = 144$. Choice (C) is wrong because the radius isn't squared. Choice (D) is wrong because the square of the radius isn't multiplied by 4.

56. **F** Simplify the log first from $3 \log_x x^{-2}$ to $\log_x x^{-6}$. Since logs are the inverse of exponents, think the inverse of MADSPM: a **M**ultiplier outside the log becomes a **P**ower inside. $\log_b n = x$ can be rewritten in exponential form as $b^x = n$. That would mean that $x^x = x^{-6}$, so the solution to the log is −6, choice (F).

57. **B** Draw the translated triangle on the figure. See below.

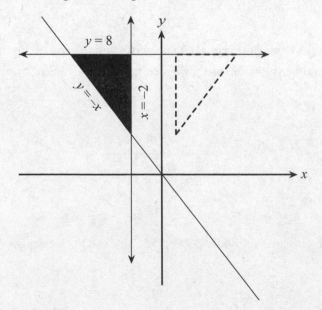

The translated triangle is still bordered by $y = 8$, so eliminate (C) and (E). The translation over the y-axis means the slope will be positive, so eliminate (D), and the triangle will be bordered by the line $x \geq 2$, so eliminate (A).

58. **H** Sine in Quadrant III is negative, so eliminate (J) and (K). Draw a line from the x-axis to the side of the angle that passes through $(-12,-5)$ to make a right triangle; $\sin = \dfrac{opposite}{hypotenuse} = \dfrac{-5}{13}$. Choice (G) is the cosine of θ.

59. **A** Use the ordered pairs given to solve for the slope of $\overline{AB}$: $\dfrac{y_2 - y_1}{x_2 - x_1} = \dfrac{6-1}{7-5} = \dfrac{5}{2}$. Since $\overline{CD}$ does not include either point A or B, it must be the line parallel to $\overline{AB}$. Parallel lines have the same slope, and only choice (A) has a slope of $\dfrac{5}{2}$. Choice (C) is wrong because it's the reciprocal of the slope, with the change in x-values in the numerator and the change in y-values in the denominator by mistake.

60. **G** Use the inputs (c^2, d^2) for the (x,y) pair in the defined function. $(c^2 - d^2)^2 + (c^2 + d^2)^2 = (c^4 - 2c^2d^2 + d^4) + (c^4 + 2c^2d^2 + d^4) = 2c^4 + 2d^4$. The remaining answers reflect errors in the order of operations or in FOILing.

READING TEST

1. **B** Be careful with negative questions. In this vocabulary-in-context question, *untainted* means something like "untouched," and (A), (C), and (D) could all work the same way as *untainted*, leaving (B) as the odd one out.

2. **F** This is a negative question with no line reference and no great lead words, so do this question Later, maybe Never. Line 14 supports (G); lines 22–27 support (H) and (J), and thus (F) is the correct answer because it's NOT done by any family member.

3. **A** A third negative question in a row is a third question to mark for Later or Never. Lines 68–69 support (B); lines 19–21 support (C), and lines 8–9 support (D). Lines 59–60 *disprove* (A), helping to confirm it is the correct answer.

4. **J** Do this question last. The work done on all the other questions will help disprove the wrong answers and help prove (J).

5. **D** The narrator and her father gather materials for the fire in line 8, and the narrator gathers more in lines 23–24. Note that this question can help with questions 2 and 3.

6. **G**   This is another negative question, but the narrator describes the scene at dusk in just one part of the passage, the beginning of the second paragraph. Choices (F), (H), and (J) are all found on line 10, leaving (G) as the only item not described.

7. **D**   Use the lead words in the question to find the right window to read in lines 64–77, and use POE to eliminate the wrong answers. There is no proof the narrator finds the scene *depressing* or that she is *distracted* or *worried*. In the last paragraph, the narrator *felt some peace*, supporting (D).

8. **H**   Read the sentence before the line reference to determine what *things* refers to. The narrator describes the *snaps and pops of the burning tinder* and therefore doesn't need to turn around to *look towards the campfire*.

9. **C**   Read the sentence and try to come up with your own word for *flooded*, and *filled* would be a good match.

10. **G**   Read the entire paragraph to place the statement in lines 49–51 in context. POE works well to eliminate the wrong answers. The relationship of the parents has neither *degraded,* [choice (H)], nor grown *more passionate and spontaneous,* [choice (J)], nor is the threat of the father's job loss described as changing the parents' relationship, [choice (F)]. Choice (G) is a good paraphrase of the narrator's metaphorical language describing her parents' relationship having *quieted* from the *once-heaving seas.*

11. **A**   Be careful with negative questions. Cross off answers that can be found in the passage. Choice (B) can be found in lines 12–13, (C) can be found in lines 13–14, and (D) can be found in lines 18–20.

12. **F**   Use the lead words in the question to find the right window of text to read. Lines 24–36 feature Stumbacher's identification of several alternative methods of philanthropy that have been introduced in the *past two decades* and thus are *gaining popularity* as (F) states. Be careful of the trap of (J): *clothing-recycling drop boxes* may offer an additional environmental benefit, but to claim that they are the *best way to reverse environmental problems* is too extreme and not supported by the passage.

13. **C**   The paragraph ends with the question *But can't we do better?* that implies *an alternative* to the various methods of charity described in the paragraph, making (C) the best choice.

14. **J**   The transition phrase *While a noble end* supports the idea that the author views the efforts of the churchgoing public positively. Thus (F), (G), and (H) can be eliminated because they are all negative.

15. **B**   Read the window of 5–10 lines to find the answer. The quote is followed by the example of *wine-tastings* in line 50. Choices (A), (C), and (D) all feature trap language, using the words *promotional context, tens of thousands of dollars,* and *win-win* right out of the passage but saying garbage with them.

16. **G**   The author writes that *Despite the fact that charities are nonprofit entities.* The transition phrase establishes that charities don't act like a for-profit business, so a business term like *market share* wouldn't normally be used to describe a charity's efforts.

17. **B** Read the full paragraph for the context of the quote. The author contrasts the *temporary reprieve* with the correction of the *systemic problems*, which (B) paraphrases.

18. **F** The lead words *Acumen Fund* can be found in the seventh paragraph, lines 56–63. Lines 59–60 establish that its method of collection is *typical* but that its distribution of the funds differs. Choice (J) uses trap language from the passage but says garbage with them. Choices (G) and (H) use trap language from an entirely different part of the passage.

19. **A** This question works well to do Later, as the answers to several prior questions help, particularly question 15.

20. **H** The statement in lines 75–77 offers a criticism from *Naysayers* on innovative philanthropic techniques. The transition word *However* at the start of the tenth paragraph reaffirms their value, eliminating (F) and (G), which are negative. Choice (J) does not show the contrast that the transition words reveal.

21. **B** Use the answers to look up each name in the passage and determine which person believes any criticism will only embolden reggaeton fans. Choice (B) (*Felipe Noche*) defends reggaeton in lines 42–43 and is the correct answer. Question 22 can help with this question if you do question 21 Later. If you selected (A) but got question 22 correct, remember that your answers should agree with each other.

22. **F** This question can help with question 21. The modifier *derisively* indicates Ethan Perry is critical, which matches (F).

23. **B** The lead word *solidified* appears in line 25, and lines 25–27 describe the role of *"Dem Bow"* as the important milestone in reggaeton history, making (B) the correct answer. The great lead words of proper nouns and dates in the other answers are easy to find in the passage, and each can be eliminated for being too soon or too late in reggaeton development. Question 26 can also help with this question if you do question 26 Now and question 23 Later.

24. **F** The lead word *parents* can be found in line 59. Read the paragraph for context, and use the transition word *However* to avoid the trap of (H). Lines 54–55 establish reggaeton's rhythmic similarities to Latin music, and lines 58–59 connect that style to *the music Latino youths associate with their parents*.

25. **C** Do this question Later since the chronology is likely to be given throughout the whole passage. However, it is likely that an event that occurred *first* will be in the beginning of the passage. Lines 17–19 support (C) as the correct answer, but the answers to questions 23 and 28 can also help.

26. **J** With its great lead word (*"Dem Bow"*), this is a good Now question. Choice (J) is somewhat paraphrased from lines 27–28.

27. **C** Within the window of the whole paragraph, the words *Japan* (line 73), *everyone* (line 75), and *everywhere* (line 77) provide proof for (C).

28. **F** The great lead words *20th-century* and *Panamanians* can be found in lines 17–19. Read the window of 5–10 lines, and the proof for (F) is found in lines 19–21.

29. **B** This negative question should be marked for Later or Never. Use the work on the rest of the questions and POE to eliminate (A) (third and fifth paragraphs (lines 25–33 and lines 41–53) and question 24), (C) (lines 63–66), and (D) (second paragraph (lines 13–24) and question 23, 25, and 28).

30. **H** Do this question Later, let the answers to the other questions help, and use POE. Choice (F) is tempting, but the discussion of the universal appeal in lines 73–77 doesn't offer any credit to the *rhythmic structures*. Choice (G) can be eliminated because lines 64–65 credit the *Puerto Rican communities* in *Miami*. Choice (J) can be eliminated because the lines discussing *"Dem Bow"* (lines 25–40) don't indicate a change in type of *instruments*. Choice (H) is supported best by the last paragraph, lines 78–82), but the answers to questions 21, 22, and 24 could also help support (H).

31. **D** Use the modifying phrase *bursting at the seams to blurt out the "big secret"* (lines 2–3) to help identify the sense of *anticipation,* [choice (D)], and eliminate the negative words in (B) and (C). Choice (A) is a trap with *secret*, but no language in the paragraph indicates a *warning*.

32. **F** While the lead words *"big secret"* and *"missing link"* first appear in lines 2–4, paragraph one, the answer is found in the second paragraph in lines 6–8.

33. **A** The phrase *conclusive evidence* in line 12 eliminates (C) and (D). Between choices (A) and (B), *extended period of studying* is a good paraphrase of *After two years of...research* in lines 8–9.

34. **G** The lead words in the question can be found in the fifth paragraph (lines 34–42). In lines 37–39, the modifiers *Unfortunately* and *outlandish* together with the professor's *enthusiasm* all support (G) as the best paraphrase. Choice (H) states almost the exact opposite. Choice (F) is a trap with the recycled *outlandish*, but nowhere does the paragraph make a comparison to the price paid for Lucy. Choice (J) cites the site of discovery, but the paragraph doesn't support that.

35. **A** Use the lead words *Messel Pit* to locate the right window of lines 25–33 to read for the answer. Choice (A) paraphrases correctly that the fossil hunter *did not assume there was anything distinctive* about Ida and hanging the fossil as a display (lines 30–32).

36. **J** The lead words *Darwin's theory of evolution* are found in several places throughout the passage. This question lacks a line reference, so use the other lead word *skeptical* to locate which window to read to find the answer. The word *skeptics* can be found in line 57 and identifies the third mention of *Darwin* as the right window. Choice (J) states that *there is some information missing* and is a good paraphrase of *gigantic hole in the fossil evidence* in line 58. Choice (F) is wrong because the transition word *Despite* in line 55 means the skeptics have other reasons to object other than the *98.4% genetic similarity*. Choice (G) is wrong because *chimpanzees* are linked to *humans*, not *lemurs*, in line 56. Choice (H) is wrong because *1859* in line 52 refers to the date of publication of the theory, not fossils.

37. **C** The *not* in the question is not capitalized or italicized to draw your attention and could therefore be easy to miss and make (D) a tempting trap. Choice (C) is correct because lines 22–24 state that Lucy was found *lacking a skull*.

38. **G** Read a window of 5–10 lines to find the answer. In line 37, the professor was *immediately entranced upon seeing Ida,* which identifies (G) as the correct answer.

39. **C** Use the modifying phrase *so perfect* in line 20 to help identify (C) as the correct answer with its match of *well-preserved*. The transition phrase *By contrast* and the description of Lucy's *only 40% complete* remains in lines 22–23 also identify Ida as well-preserved.

40. **H** Use POE. Choice (F) is wrong because the statement in line 62 that scientists have been *unsure* doesn't mean that they were wrong or had a *misconception*. Choice (G) is wrong because the passage doesn't state that the scientists' lack of certainty resulted from *classifying* the fossils. Lines 64–65 state that Ida's remains support the idea that humans evolved from "*adapidae*." This supports (II). Choice (J) is close, but there is no proof in the paragraph that a different theory prevailed before Ida's discovery.

SCIENCE TEST

1. **C** Consider the slopes of the three curves on Figure 1. As MM increases, the slope increases. KNO_3 has the greatest MM (101) and has the steepest slope.

2. **H** Consider the slopes of the three curves on Figure 1. As MM increases, the slope increases. Choice (F) is a trap answer and is wrong because the question asks about the direction of ΔS when the molecular mass (MM) *decreases*.

3. **B** Find KCl on Figure 1. At 100°, the ΔS of KCl is approximately 30. Continue the trend to make the prediction: at 102°, the ΔS of KCl will be just slightly greater than 30. Choices (C) and (D) are wrong because the slope of KCl is gradual. With only an increase of 2°, the ΔS will not increase by 5 or more.

4. **J** Look up the value on Figure 2. At 20°, the ΔS of NH_3 is –30. Choices (F) and (H) are wrong because each states that the ΔS was positive. Choice (H) is wrong because if the ΔS is negative, the solubility decreased.

5. **D** Use the trends in the figures. Both figures show that the greater the MM, the greater the ΔS, which eliminates (A) and (C). Choice (B) is wrong because salts are shown in Figure 1, which reveals a direct relationship between temperature and ΔS, not an inverse relationship.

6. **F** Table 1 lists the distances in between Genes W and X, X and Y, and W and Z. Only (F) features one of these pairs.

7. **C** Look up the values on Figure 2. When the number of proteins is 3,500 molecules per cell, the frequency of HR is 150 events.

8. **H** Look up Scientist 2 on Figure 3. Gene V is closer to Gene X and farther from Gene Z, so it will be between Genes X and Y. Choice (J) is a trap answer and is wrong because based on the values in Table 1 and Scientist 2's model, the distance in between Genes Z and Y is 5 centimorgans.

9. **D** Use the distances established in Table 1 to calculate each Scientists' distance between Genes W and Y. Scientist 1's model would make the distance 50 centimorgans; Scientist 2's model would make the distance 60 centimorgans; Scientist 3's model would make the distance 10 centimorgans; and Scientist 4's model would make the distance 10 centimorgans. Only Scientist 3 and 4 have values consistent with each other.

10. **J** The introduction lists situations for which recombination can occur outside of sexual reproduction, including when repair is necessary after exposure to radiation.

11. **A** Use the distances established in Table 1. The work done for question 9 shows that the distance between Genes Y and Z in Scientist 1's model is 65 centimorgans.

12. **G** Use the information in Figure 1. In regions with corrected genes, A*B* regions have been swapped with AB regions.

13. **C** Look up the value on Figure 2. Conductivity of aquifer groundwater is the top graph of Figure 2, and 2000 is the solid-line curve.

14. **H** Continue the trend shown in Figure 2: The pH of groundwater is the bottom of the two graphs, and 2001 is the dashed-line curve. Choice (J) is a trap answer and is wrong because 260 is barely above 250 when pH is 7. The pH will not increase in 10 cm to 8.5.

15. **D** Common sense and outside knowledge are often the solutions for "why" questions. A drought means a lower amount of rainfall, and a lower amount of rainfall means the wetland would receive less water.

16. **J** Use POE. Choices (F) and (G) are disproven by the data in Figures 2 and 3 because the soil layer for an aquifer is from the water table (0 cm below) to 200 cm below, and the soil layer for a wetland is shown from the water table (0 cm below) to 350 cm below. Choice (H) is wrong because the soil layer is thinner in an aquifer.

17. **C** The introduction clarifies that the drought occurred in 2000, the solid-line curve, which is greater at 0 to 300 cm than is the dashed-line curve in both the aquifer and wetland.

18. **J** Read if and only when you can't answer a question from the figures. The information needed is found in the beginning of the introduction, with an explanation of what the symbols represent. Choice (J) provides the correct representation of the values given in the question. The rest of the choices mix up the symbols and the numbers provided.

19. **A**   The question directs you to Table 1, but some information from the introduction is needed. The work done for question 18 can help. The total charge for a polyatomic ion is represented by n in the symbols $(X_a Z_b)^n$. Look up chlorite on Table 1 to find n is –1. Choice (D) is a trap answer and is wrong because +3 is the oxidation state of the chlorine atom.

20. **G**   Look up the ionization energy when 4 electrons are removed from P, using the key to correctly identify the P curve. Approximately 52 (eV) is required to remove 4 electrons and thus twice an ionization energy of approximately 26. Use POE to look up each answer choice. Choice (G) is correct because removing 2 electrons from Ar requires approximately 26–28 eV. Choice (F) is too small at barely 10 eV; (H) is too big at over 30 eV; and choice (J) is wrong because it is almost equal to the amount of ionization energy required to remove 4 electrons from P. The question, however, asks for a value half of that ionization energy.

21. **D**   Read if and only when you can't answer a question from the figures. The question directs you to both Table 1 and Figure 1, but the introduction clarifies that the *oxidation state of the chlorine atom* on Table 1 is the *number of electrons* removed on Figure 1. The oxidation state for chlorite is +3 and for hypochlorite is +1. Look up both values on Figure 1, using the key to correctly identify the curve for chlorine (Cl), to find ionization energy (IE) of approximately 40 eV and 13 eV, respectively. Choice (C) is wrong because the values of eV have been swapped for the polyatomic ions. Choices (A) and (B) are wrong because the eV values are the ionization energy needed to remove 2 and 4 electrons.

22. **G**   Enough of the prior questions for this passage required reading the introduction, and no information was provided about mass or net force. This is an outside knowledge question, but common sense can often be used to find the correct answer. Reading the introduction and working the prior questions have established that the subscript numbers represent the number of atoms. Chloride has 1 atom: When a or b is equal to 1, the number is omitted. Perchlorate has 4 atoms and is thus more massive than chloride. Choices (F) and (H) are wrong because they both state that chloride is more massive. Choice (J) is wrong because less force is needed to move something with less mass.

23. **C**   Find the common variable between the figures: *time to reach equilibrium* is on Figures 2 and 3. On Figure 3, Mixture #3 has peaks at 20 and 30 minutes, as do Solute #3 and Solute #5 on Figure 2. Choice (A) is a trap answer and is wrong because the time to reach equilibrium (10 min) matches Mixture #2, not Mixture #3.

24. **F**   Look up the value on Figure 2. Solute #1 has the smallest molecular mass, therefore the shortest amount of travel to attain equilibrium, which is supported by the quickest time in Figure 2.

25. **C**   Use the values from Table 1 to identify the molecular masses of Solute #3 (2,000) and Solute #4 (10,000). Eliminate (B) and (D). To identify the molecular mass of Mixture #2, use the common variable between Experiments 1 and 2: *time to reach equilibrium*. Since Mixture #2 takes 10 minutes, it must have a smaller molecular mass than both Solute #3 and Solute #4. The trends in Table 1 and Figure 1 show that as molecular mass increases, the time to reach equilibrium also increases.

26. **G** Read if and when you can't answer a question from the figures. However, even without reading, you can use POE to eliminate (F) and (J) because Table 1 disproves each choice's statement about the molecular mass. The introduction clarifies that solutes migrate *across* a membrane in *simple diffusion*. Use common sense to connect *diffuse easily* with the time to reach equilibrium. Figure 2 shows that Solute #3 reached equilibrium more quickly than did Solute #4.

27. **A** Use the molecular masses provided in Table 1: Solute #1 has a molecular mass of 160 amu. The common variable between the solutes and mixtures of *time to reach equilibrium* shows that Mixture #1 takes less time to reach equilibrium (5 min) than Solute #1 takes (10 min). Mixture #1 will likely have a smaller molecular mass than 160 amu. Mixtures #2 and #3 take the same time or more time than Solute #1 and will have the same or greater molecular mass. Choice (D) is wrong because both the text in the introduction and the data provided in the figures establishes the relationship between molecular mass and time to reach equilibrium.

28. **J** Read the question carefully: Compare the number of molecules in two equal weights. The molecular mass in amu and weight in grams for Solute #1 is less than the molecular mass in amu and weight in grams for Solute #5. Therefore, when the weights are equal, there must be far more molecules of Solute #1 than molecules of Solute #5. Imagine if you compared a teaspoon of sugar with a teaspoon of Quaker's oatmeal. There would be many more grains of sugar than grains of oatmeal. If time doesn't allow the reasoned logic to arrive at the correct answer, at least use POE to eliminate (F) and (H) because the reasons given are disproven by Table 1.

29. **A** Look up the values on Figure 1, which features the variables *billions of years before present day* and *% composition in atmosphere*. As the number of years increases from 4 billion to 3 billion years ago, the percent composition of O_2 in Study 2 (solid-line curve) increases. Choice (C) is a trap answer and is wrong because the percent composition decreases for H_2O. Use the key to confirm the correct curve.

30. **H** Look up the values on Figure 1, and use the key to confirm the correct curve for Study 1 H_2O vapor (dash-dash-dot). The steepest part of the curve is from 1.5 and 1 billion years ago.

31. **B** Look up H_2S and N_2 for Study 2 on Table 1. For volcanic eruption models 2–4, the percent of H_2S is greater than 3. Even though the percent is only 2 for volcanic eruption model 1, it is likely that H_2S would be 3%. None of the volcanic eruption models has a percentage greater than 2 for N_2, so it is unlikely that N_2 would be 3%. Choice (B) provides the correct order of *Yes* for H_2S and *No* for N_2. Choice (C) is a trap answer and is wrong because it swaps the order of *Yes* and *No* for the two gases.

32. **H** Look up the values for Study 2 on Table 1. H_2 is 35% in volcanic eruption model 3 and 30% in volcanic eruption model 4. N_2 is 2% in both models, and H_2O vapor is 35% in both models. In a new trial with H_2 at 33%, the results for H_2O vapor would be 35%, the same as in volcanic eruption models 3 and 4.

33. **D** The question defines *aerobic* and *anaerobic*. Use this information to find a correct answer that matches the correct term with level of O_2, (D). The level of H_2O is irrelevant to the level of O_2, which means both (A) and (C) can be eliminated. Choice (B) is wrong because aerobic organisms need O_2 to survive.

34. **H** Look up the values on Figure 1. 4 billion years ago, Study 2 (dashed-line curve) shows that H_2O was 40%. H_2O was 30% 2.5 billion years before the present day, 75% of its 4-billion year level, a time lapse of 1.5 billion years.

35. **B** Look up the values on Figure 5. When the cannonball is launched at 150 ft/sec, the cannonball lands at 650 feet. When the cannonball is launched at 135 ft/sec, the cannonball lands at 500 feet. Choices (C) and (D) are both trap answers, wrong because they are the values for the two different launch speeds. Choice (B) is correct because the cannonball lands 150 feet farther. Note that the values given in the question of 5 feet and 30° are the constants used; Figure 1 and the information in Study 1 clarify that these were the values used for all the speeds.

36. **J** Read if and when you can't answer a question from the figures. The information in Study 1 states that the change in θ was photographed every 0.25 seconds, or 4 times per second.

37. **A** Look up the values on Figure 4. When the cannonball is launched at 180 ft/sec, it reached a maximum height of 120 feet and traveled 450 feet. Choices (B), (C), and (D) are all wrong because the distances are too far away to travel over the 40-ft wall. Note that the values given in the question of 5 feet and 30° are the constants used; Figure 1 and the information in Study 1 clarify that these were the values used for all the speeds.

38. **J** Look up the trends on Figure 4. As speed increases, both the h and the r increase.

39. **A** Look up the values on Figure 5. When the cannonball is launched at 135 ft/sec, it lands (a h of 0) in between 4 and 5 seconds. Note that the values given in the question of 5 feet and 30° are the constants used; Figure 1 and the information in Study 1 clarify that these were the values used for all the speeds.

40. **G** Time $= \dfrac{distance}{speed}$. The distance the radar pulse travels is represented by d on Figure 3. A roundtrip would equal $2d$. Time $= \dfrac{2d}{c}$, (G). Choice (F) is wrong because it divides the speed by twice the distance. Choices (H) and (J) are wrong because r represents the distance of the ball, not the radar pulse.

SCORING YOUR PRACTICE EXAM

Step A

Count the number of correct answers for each section and record the number in the space provided for your raw score on the Score Conversion Worksheet below.

Step B

Using the Score Conversion Chart on the next page, convert your raw scores on each section to scaled scores. Then compute your composite ACT score by averaging the four subject scores. Add them up and divide by four. Don't worry about the essay score; it is not included in your composite score.

Score Conversion Worksheet		
Section	Raw Score	Scaled Score
1	_____/75	_____
2	_____/60	_____
3	_____/40	_____
4	_____/40	_____

SCORE CONVERSION CHART

Scaled Score	Raw Scores			
	Test 1 English	Test 2 Math	Test 3 Reading	Test 4 Science
36	75	58–60	40	38–40
35	74–73	56–57	––	37
34	72	54–55	39	36
33	71	52–53	38	35
32	70	51	37	34
31	69	50	36	33
30	68	49	34–35	32
29	66–67	47–48	33	31
28	65	45–46	32	30
27	63–64	43–44	31	29
26	61–62	41–42	30	28
25	58–60	39–40	29	26–27
24	56–57	37–38	28	24–25
23	53–55	35–36	26–27	23
22	50–52	34	25	21–22
21	47–49	32–33	23–24	20
20	44–46	31	22	18–19
19	42–43	29–30	20–21	16–17
18	40–41	26–28	19	15
17	37–39	23–25	18	14
16	35–36	18–22	16–17	13
15	32–34	14–17	15	12
14	30–31	11–13	13–14	11
13	28–29	9–10	12	10
12	26–27	07–08	10–11	09
11	24–25	06	08–09	08
10	22–23	05	07	07
09	19–21	04	06	05–06
08	16–18	03	05	04
07	13–15	––	––	––
06	11–12	02	04	03
05	08–10	––	03	02
04	06–07	01	02	––
03	04–05	––	––	01
02	03	––	01	––
01	00–02	00	00	00

Part XI
The Princeton
Review ACT
Practice Exam 4

Chapter 31
Practice Exam 4

ACT Diagnostic Test Form

1. YOUR NAME: _____
(Print)   Last   First   M.I.

SIGNATURE: _____ **DATE:** ____ / ____ / ____

HOME ADDRESS: _____
(Print)   Number and Street

_____
City   State   Zip

E-MAIL: _____

PHONE NO.: _____
(Print)

SCHOOL: _____

CLASS OF: _____

IMPORTANT: Please fill in these boxes exactly as shown on the back cover of your tests book.

2. TEST FORM

_____

3. TEST CODE

⓪	⓪	⓪	⓪
①	①	①	①
②	②	②	②
③	③	③	③
④	④	④	④
⑤	⑤	⑤	⑤
⑥	⑥	⑥	⑥
⑦	⑦	⑦	⑦
⑧	⑧	⑧	⑧
⑨	⑨	⑨	⑨

4. PHONE NUMBER

⓪	⓪	⓪	⓪	⓪	⓪	⓪
①	①	①	①	①	①	①
②	②	②	②	②	②	②
③	③	③	③	③	③	③
④	④	④	④	④	④	④
⑤	⑤	⑤	⑤	⑤	⑤	⑤
⑥	⑥	⑥	⑥	⑥	⑥	⑥
⑦	⑦	⑦	⑦	⑦	⑦	⑦
⑧	⑧	⑧	⑧	⑧	⑧	⑧
⑨	⑨	⑨	⑨	⑨	⑨	⑨

5. YOUR NAME

First 4 letters of last name				FIRST INIT	MID INIT
Ⓐ	Ⓐ	Ⓐ	Ⓐ	Ⓐ	Ⓐ
Ⓑ	Ⓑ	Ⓑ	Ⓑ	Ⓑ	Ⓑ
Ⓒ	Ⓒ	Ⓒ	Ⓒ	Ⓒ	Ⓒ
Ⓓ	Ⓓ	Ⓓ	Ⓓ	Ⓓ	Ⓓ
Ⓔ	Ⓔ	Ⓔ	Ⓔ	Ⓔ	Ⓔ
Ⓕ	Ⓕ	Ⓕ	Ⓕ	Ⓕ	Ⓕ
Ⓖ	Ⓖ	Ⓖ	Ⓖ	Ⓖ	Ⓖ
Ⓗ	Ⓗ	Ⓗ	Ⓗ	Ⓗ	Ⓗ
Ⓘ	Ⓘ	Ⓘ	Ⓘ	Ⓘ	Ⓘ
Ⓙ	Ⓙ	Ⓙ	Ⓙ	Ⓙ	Ⓙ
Ⓚ	Ⓚ	Ⓚ	Ⓚ	Ⓚ	Ⓚ
Ⓛ	Ⓛ	Ⓛ	Ⓛ	Ⓛ	Ⓛ
Ⓜ	Ⓜ	Ⓜ	Ⓜ	Ⓜ	Ⓜ
Ⓝ	Ⓝ	Ⓝ	Ⓝ	Ⓝ	Ⓝ
Ⓞ	Ⓞ	Ⓞ	Ⓞ	Ⓞ	Ⓞ
Ⓟ	Ⓟ	Ⓟ	Ⓟ	Ⓟ	Ⓟ
Ⓠ	Ⓠ	Ⓠ	Ⓠ	Ⓠ	Ⓠ
Ⓡ	Ⓡ	Ⓡ	Ⓡ	Ⓡ	Ⓡ
Ⓢ	Ⓢ	Ⓢ	Ⓢ	Ⓢ	Ⓢ
Ⓣ	Ⓣ	Ⓣ	Ⓣ	Ⓣ	Ⓣ
Ⓤ	Ⓤ	Ⓤ	Ⓤ	Ⓤ	Ⓤ
Ⓥ	Ⓥ	Ⓥ	Ⓥ	Ⓥ	Ⓥ
Ⓦ	Ⓦ	Ⓦ	Ⓦ	Ⓦ	Ⓦ
Ⓧ	Ⓧ	Ⓧ	Ⓧ	Ⓧ	Ⓧ
Ⓨ	Ⓨ	Ⓨ	Ⓨ	Ⓨ	Ⓨ
Ⓩ	Ⓩ	Ⓩ	Ⓩ	Ⓩ	Ⓩ

6. DATE OF BIRTH

MONTH	DAY		YEAR	
◯ JAN				
◯ FEB				
◯ MAR	⓪	⓪	⓪	⓪
◯ APR	①	①	①	①
◯ MAY	②	②	②	②
◯ JUN	③	③	③	③
◯ JUL		④	④	④
◯ AUG		⑤	⑤	⑤
◯ SEP		⑥	⑥	⑥
◯ OCT		⑦	⑦	⑦
◯ NOV		⑧	⑧	⑧
◯ DEC		⑨	⑨	⑨

7. SEX

◯ MALE
◯ FEMALE

8. OTHER

1 Ⓐ Ⓑ Ⓒ Ⓓ Ⓔ
2 Ⓐ Ⓑ Ⓒ Ⓓ Ⓔ
3 Ⓐ Ⓑ Ⓒ Ⓓ Ⓔ

OpScan iNSIGHT™ forms by Pearson NCS EM-255315-1:654321   Printed In U.S.A.

THIS PAGE INTENTIONALLY LEFT BLANK

The Princeton Review
Diagnostic ACT Form

ENGLISH

#					#					#					#				
1	Ⓐ	Ⓑ	Ⓒ	Ⓓ	21	Ⓐ	Ⓑ	Ⓒ	Ⓓ	41	Ⓐ	Ⓑ	Ⓒ	Ⓓ	61	Ⓐ	Ⓑ	Ⓒ	Ⓓ
2	Ⓕ	Ⓖ	Ⓗ	Ⓙ	22	Ⓕ	Ⓖ	Ⓗ	Ⓙ	42	Ⓕ	Ⓖ	Ⓗ	Ⓙ	62	Ⓕ	Ⓖ	Ⓗ	Ⓙ
3	Ⓐ	Ⓑ	Ⓒ	Ⓓ	23	Ⓐ	Ⓑ	Ⓒ	Ⓓ	43	Ⓐ	Ⓑ	Ⓒ	Ⓓ	63	Ⓐ	Ⓑ	Ⓒ	Ⓓ
4	Ⓕ	Ⓖ	Ⓗ	Ⓙ	24	Ⓕ	Ⓖ	Ⓗ	Ⓙ	44	Ⓕ	Ⓖ	Ⓗ	Ⓙ	64	Ⓕ	Ⓖ	Ⓗ	Ⓙ
5	Ⓐ	Ⓑ	Ⓒ	Ⓓ	25	Ⓐ	Ⓑ	Ⓒ	Ⓓ	45	Ⓐ	Ⓑ	Ⓒ	Ⓓ	65	Ⓐ	Ⓑ	Ⓒ	Ⓓ
6	Ⓕ	Ⓖ	Ⓗ	Ⓙ	26	Ⓕ	Ⓖ	Ⓗ	Ⓙ	46	Ⓕ	Ⓖ	Ⓗ	Ⓙ	66	Ⓕ	Ⓖ	Ⓗ	Ⓙ
7	Ⓐ	Ⓑ	Ⓒ	Ⓓ	27	Ⓐ	Ⓑ	Ⓒ	Ⓓ	47	Ⓐ	Ⓑ	Ⓒ	Ⓓ	67	Ⓐ	Ⓑ	Ⓒ	Ⓓ
8	Ⓕ	Ⓖ	Ⓗ	Ⓙ	28	Ⓕ	Ⓖ	Ⓗ	Ⓙ	48	Ⓕ	Ⓖ	Ⓗ	Ⓙ	68	Ⓕ	Ⓖ	Ⓗ	Ⓙ
9	Ⓐ	Ⓑ	Ⓒ	Ⓓ	29	Ⓐ	Ⓑ	Ⓒ	Ⓓ	49	Ⓐ	Ⓑ	Ⓒ	Ⓓ	69	Ⓐ	Ⓑ	Ⓒ	Ⓓ
10	Ⓕ	Ⓖ	Ⓗ	Ⓙ	30	Ⓕ	Ⓖ	Ⓗ	Ⓙ	50	Ⓕ	Ⓖ	Ⓗ	Ⓙ	70	Ⓕ	Ⓖ	Ⓗ	Ⓙ
11	Ⓐ	Ⓑ	Ⓒ	Ⓓ	31	Ⓐ	Ⓑ	Ⓒ	Ⓓ	51	Ⓐ	Ⓑ	Ⓒ	Ⓓ	71	Ⓐ	Ⓑ	Ⓒ	Ⓓ
12	Ⓕ	Ⓖ	Ⓗ	Ⓙ	32	Ⓕ	Ⓖ	Ⓗ	Ⓙ	52	Ⓕ	Ⓖ	Ⓗ	Ⓙ	72	Ⓕ	Ⓖ	Ⓗ	Ⓙ
13	Ⓐ	Ⓑ	Ⓒ	Ⓓ	33	Ⓐ	Ⓑ	Ⓒ	Ⓓ	53	Ⓐ	Ⓑ	Ⓒ	Ⓓ	73	Ⓐ	Ⓑ	Ⓒ	Ⓓ
14	Ⓕ	Ⓖ	Ⓗ	Ⓙ	34	Ⓕ	Ⓖ	Ⓗ	Ⓙ	54	Ⓕ	Ⓖ	Ⓗ	Ⓙ	74	Ⓕ	Ⓖ	Ⓗ	Ⓙ
15	Ⓐ	Ⓑ	Ⓒ	Ⓓ	35	Ⓐ	Ⓑ	Ⓒ	Ⓓ	55	Ⓐ	Ⓑ	Ⓒ	Ⓓ	75	Ⓐ	Ⓑ	Ⓒ	Ⓓ
16	Ⓕ	Ⓖ	Ⓗ	Ⓙ	36	Ⓕ	Ⓖ	Ⓗ	Ⓙ	56	Ⓕ	Ⓖ	Ⓗ	Ⓙ					
17	Ⓐ	Ⓑ	Ⓒ	Ⓓ	37	Ⓐ	Ⓑ	Ⓒ	Ⓓ	57	Ⓐ	Ⓑ	Ⓒ	Ⓓ					
18	Ⓕ	Ⓖ	Ⓗ	Ⓙ	38	Ⓕ	Ⓖ	Ⓗ	Ⓙ	58	Ⓕ	Ⓖ	Ⓗ	Ⓙ					
19	Ⓐ	Ⓑ	Ⓒ	Ⓓ	39	Ⓐ	Ⓑ	Ⓒ	Ⓓ	59	Ⓐ	Ⓑ	Ⓒ	Ⓓ					
20	Ⓕ	Ⓖ	Ⓗ	Ⓙ	40	Ⓕ	Ⓖ	Ⓗ	Ⓙ	60	Ⓕ	Ⓖ	Ⓗ	Ⓙ					

MATHEMATICS

#						#						#						#					
1	Ⓐ	Ⓑ	Ⓒ	Ⓓ	Ⓔ	16	Ⓕ	Ⓖ	Ⓗ	Ⓙ	Ⓚ	31	Ⓐ	Ⓑ	Ⓒ	Ⓓ	Ⓔ	46	Ⓕ	Ⓖ	Ⓗ	Ⓙ	Ⓚ
2	Ⓕ	Ⓖ	Ⓗ	Ⓙ	Ⓚ	17	Ⓐ	Ⓑ	Ⓒ	Ⓓ	Ⓔ	32	Ⓕ	Ⓖ	Ⓗ	Ⓙ	Ⓚ	47	Ⓐ	Ⓑ	Ⓒ	Ⓓ	Ⓔ
3	Ⓐ	Ⓑ	Ⓒ	Ⓓ	Ⓔ	18	Ⓕ	Ⓖ	Ⓗ	Ⓙ	Ⓚ	33	Ⓐ	Ⓑ	Ⓒ	Ⓓ	Ⓔ	48	Ⓕ	Ⓖ	Ⓗ	Ⓙ	Ⓚ
4	Ⓕ	Ⓖ	Ⓗ	Ⓙ	Ⓚ	19	Ⓐ	Ⓑ	Ⓒ	Ⓓ	Ⓔ	34	Ⓕ	Ⓖ	Ⓗ	Ⓙ	Ⓚ	49	Ⓐ	Ⓑ	Ⓒ	Ⓓ	Ⓔ
5	Ⓐ	Ⓑ	Ⓒ	Ⓓ	Ⓔ	20	Ⓕ	Ⓖ	Ⓗ	Ⓙ	Ⓚ	35	Ⓐ	Ⓑ	Ⓒ	Ⓓ	Ⓔ	50	Ⓕ	Ⓖ	Ⓗ	Ⓙ	Ⓚ
6	Ⓕ	Ⓖ	Ⓗ	Ⓙ	Ⓚ	21	Ⓐ	Ⓑ	Ⓒ	Ⓓ	Ⓔ	36	Ⓕ	Ⓖ	Ⓗ	Ⓙ	Ⓚ	51	Ⓐ	Ⓑ	Ⓒ	Ⓓ	Ⓔ
7	Ⓐ	Ⓑ	Ⓒ	Ⓓ	Ⓔ	22	Ⓕ	Ⓖ	Ⓗ	Ⓙ	Ⓚ	37	Ⓐ	Ⓑ	Ⓒ	Ⓓ	Ⓔ	52	Ⓕ	Ⓖ	Ⓗ	Ⓙ	Ⓚ
8	Ⓕ	Ⓖ	Ⓗ	Ⓙ	Ⓚ	23	Ⓐ	Ⓑ	Ⓒ	Ⓓ	Ⓔ	38	Ⓕ	Ⓖ	Ⓗ	Ⓙ	Ⓚ	53	Ⓐ	Ⓑ	Ⓒ	Ⓓ	Ⓔ
9	Ⓐ	Ⓑ	Ⓒ	Ⓓ	Ⓔ	24	Ⓕ	Ⓖ	Ⓗ	Ⓙ	Ⓚ	39	Ⓐ	Ⓑ	Ⓒ	Ⓓ	Ⓔ	54	Ⓕ	Ⓖ	Ⓗ	Ⓙ	Ⓚ
10	Ⓕ	Ⓖ	Ⓗ	Ⓙ	Ⓚ	25	Ⓐ	Ⓑ	Ⓒ	Ⓓ	Ⓔ	40	Ⓕ	Ⓖ	Ⓗ	Ⓙ	Ⓚ	55	Ⓐ	Ⓑ	Ⓒ	Ⓓ	Ⓔ
11	Ⓐ	Ⓑ	Ⓒ	Ⓓ	Ⓔ	26	Ⓕ	Ⓖ	Ⓗ	Ⓙ	Ⓚ	41	Ⓐ	Ⓑ	Ⓒ	Ⓓ	Ⓔ	56	Ⓕ	Ⓖ	Ⓗ	Ⓙ	Ⓚ
12	Ⓕ	Ⓖ	Ⓗ	Ⓙ	Ⓚ	27	Ⓐ	Ⓑ	Ⓒ	Ⓓ	Ⓔ	42	Ⓕ	Ⓖ	Ⓗ	Ⓙ	Ⓚ	57	Ⓐ	Ⓑ	Ⓒ	Ⓓ	Ⓔ
13	Ⓐ	Ⓑ	Ⓒ	Ⓓ	Ⓔ	28	Ⓕ	Ⓖ	Ⓗ	Ⓙ	Ⓚ	43	Ⓐ	Ⓑ	Ⓒ	Ⓓ	Ⓔ	58	Ⓕ	Ⓖ	Ⓗ	Ⓙ	Ⓚ
14	Ⓕ	Ⓖ	Ⓗ	Ⓙ	Ⓚ	29	Ⓐ	Ⓑ	Ⓒ	Ⓓ	Ⓔ	44	Ⓕ	Ⓖ	Ⓗ	Ⓙ	Ⓚ	59	Ⓐ	Ⓑ	Ⓒ	Ⓓ	Ⓔ
15	Ⓐ	Ⓑ	Ⓒ	Ⓓ	Ⓔ	30	Ⓕ	Ⓖ	Ⓗ	Ⓙ	Ⓚ	45	Ⓐ	Ⓑ	Ⓒ	Ⓓ	Ⓔ	60	Ⓕ	Ⓖ	Ⓗ	Ⓙ	Ⓚ

The Princeton Review
Diagnostic ACT Form

READING

1 Ⓐ Ⓑ Ⓒ Ⓓ	11 Ⓐ Ⓑ Ⓒ Ⓓ	21 Ⓐ Ⓑ Ⓒ Ⓓ	31 Ⓐ Ⓑ Ⓒ Ⓓ
2 Ⓕ Ⓖ Ⓗ Ⓙ	12 Ⓕ Ⓖ Ⓗ Ⓙ	22 Ⓕ Ⓖ Ⓗ Ⓙ	32 Ⓕ Ⓖ Ⓗ Ⓙ
3 Ⓐ Ⓑ Ⓒ Ⓓ	13 Ⓐ Ⓑ Ⓒ Ⓓ	23 Ⓐ Ⓑ Ⓒ Ⓓ	33 Ⓐ Ⓑ Ⓒ Ⓓ
4 Ⓕ Ⓖ Ⓗ Ⓙ	14 Ⓕ Ⓖ Ⓗ Ⓙ	24 Ⓕ Ⓖ Ⓗ Ⓙ	34 Ⓕ Ⓖ Ⓗ Ⓙ
5 Ⓐ Ⓑ Ⓒ Ⓓ	15 Ⓐ Ⓑ Ⓒ Ⓓ	25 Ⓐ Ⓑ Ⓒ Ⓓ	35 Ⓐ Ⓑ Ⓒ Ⓓ
6 Ⓕ Ⓖ Ⓗ Ⓙ	16 Ⓕ Ⓖ Ⓗ Ⓙ	26 Ⓕ Ⓖ Ⓗ Ⓙ	36 Ⓕ Ⓖ Ⓗ Ⓙ
7 Ⓐ Ⓑ Ⓒ Ⓓ	17 Ⓐ Ⓑ Ⓒ Ⓓ	27 Ⓐ Ⓑ Ⓒ Ⓓ	37 Ⓐ Ⓑ Ⓒ Ⓓ
8 Ⓕ Ⓖ Ⓗ Ⓙ	18 Ⓕ Ⓖ Ⓗ Ⓙ	28 Ⓕ Ⓖ Ⓗ Ⓙ	38 Ⓕ Ⓖ Ⓗ Ⓙ
9 Ⓐ Ⓑ Ⓒ Ⓓ	19 Ⓐ Ⓑ Ⓒ Ⓓ	29 Ⓐ Ⓑ Ⓒ Ⓓ	39 Ⓐ Ⓑ Ⓒ Ⓓ
10 Ⓕ Ⓖ Ⓗ Ⓙ	20 Ⓕ Ⓖ Ⓗ Ⓙ	30 Ⓕ Ⓖ Ⓗ Ⓙ	40 Ⓕ Ⓖ Ⓗ Ⓙ

SCIENCE REASONING

1 Ⓐ Ⓑ Ⓒ Ⓓ	11 Ⓐ Ⓑ Ⓒ Ⓓ	21 Ⓐ Ⓑ Ⓒ Ⓓ	31 Ⓐ Ⓑ Ⓒ Ⓓ
2 Ⓕ Ⓖ Ⓗ Ⓙ	12 Ⓕ Ⓖ Ⓗ Ⓙ	22 Ⓕ Ⓖ Ⓗ Ⓙ	32 Ⓕ Ⓖ Ⓗ Ⓙ
3 Ⓐ Ⓑ Ⓒ Ⓓ	13 Ⓐ Ⓑ Ⓒ Ⓓ	23 Ⓐ Ⓑ Ⓒ Ⓓ	33 Ⓐ Ⓑ Ⓒ Ⓓ
4 Ⓕ Ⓖ Ⓗ Ⓙ	14 Ⓕ Ⓖ Ⓗ Ⓙ	24 Ⓕ Ⓖ Ⓗ Ⓙ	34 Ⓕ Ⓖ Ⓗ Ⓙ
5 Ⓐ Ⓑ Ⓒ Ⓓ	15 Ⓐ Ⓑ Ⓒ Ⓓ	25 Ⓐ Ⓑ Ⓒ Ⓓ	35 Ⓐ Ⓑ Ⓒ Ⓓ
6 Ⓕ Ⓖ Ⓗ Ⓙ	16 Ⓕ Ⓖ Ⓗ Ⓙ	26 Ⓕ Ⓖ Ⓗ Ⓙ	36 Ⓕ Ⓖ Ⓗ Ⓙ
7 Ⓐ Ⓑ Ⓒ Ⓓ	17 Ⓐ Ⓑ Ⓒ Ⓓ	27 Ⓐ Ⓑ Ⓒ Ⓓ	37 Ⓐ Ⓑ Ⓒ Ⓓ
8 Ⓕ Ⓖ Ⓗ Ⓙ	18 Ⓕ Ⓖ Ⓗ Ⓙ	28 Ⓕ Ⓖ Ⓗ Ⓙ	38 Ⓕ Ⓖ Ⓗ Ⓙ
9 Ⓐ Ⓑ Ⓒ Ⓓ	19 Ⓐ Ⓑ Ⓒ Ⓓ	29 Ⓐ Ⓑ Ⓒ Ⓓ	39 Ⓐ Ⓑ Ⓒ Ⓓ
10 Ⓕ Ⓖ Ⓗ Ⓙ	20 Ⓕ Ⓖ Ⓗ Ⓙ	30 Ⓕ Ⓖ Ⓗ Ⓙ	40 Ⓕ Ⓖ Ⓗ Ⓙ

THIS PAGE INTENTIONALLY LEFT BLANK

ENGLISH TEST

45 Minutes—75 Questions

DIRECTIONS: In the five passages that follow, certain words and phrases are underlined and numbered. In the right-hand column, you will find alternatives for each underlined part. In most cases, you are to choose the one that best expresses the idea, makes the statement appropriate for standard written English, or is worded most consistently with the style and tone of the passage as a whole. If you think the original version is best, choose "NO CHANGE." In some cases, you will find in the right-hand column a question about the underlined part of the passage. You are to choose the best answer to the question.

You will also find questions about a section of the passage or the passage as a whole. These questions do not refer to an underlined portion of the passage, but rather are identified by a number or numbers in a box.

For each question, choose the alternative you consider best and blacken the corresponding oval on your answer document. Read each passage through once before you begin to answer the questions that accompany it. For many of the questions, you must read several sentences beyond the question to determine the answer. Be sure that you have read far enough ahead each time you choose an alternative.

PASSAGE I

Lou Gehrig, All-American

Since their inception in 1913, the New York Yankees have long been regarded as a force in Major League Baseball. Love them or hate them, there is no denying the tradition of excellence that they have leveraged <u>in order</u> to win 26 World Series

——— 1

championships, a league record.

1. Which of the following alternatives to the underlined portion would NOT be acceptable?
   - **A.** so as
   - **B.** as a means
   - **C.** so that
   - **D.** DELETE the underlined portion.

The Yankees have had many great baseball <u>players</u> contribute

——— 2

to the team, but one man stands out for his fortitude and good spirit: Lou Gehrig. Born to poor German immigrants in 1903, Gehrig received no encouragement to pursue baseball as a career. <u>His mother considered business</u> a better line of work for

——— 3

her son, wanting him to excel academically, not physically. Gehrig followed her wishes, at least at first. He attended Columbia University, but after only two years, and without a degree, Gehrig left school.

2. **F.** NO CHANGE
   G. players;
   H. players,
   J. players and

3. **A.** NO CHANGE
   B. His mother, considering business
   C. Business was considered by his mother to be
   D. Business considered his mother

GO ON TO THE NEXT PAGE.

However, he did have a job lined up before he withdrew from college. A Yankee scout had seen an intercollegiate game Gehrig played in—coincidentally, on the very day Yankee Stadium first opened to the public in 1923—and immediately signed him to a contract. He played well in his first three years in the majors, but he did not become a true superstar until 1926.

He broke many, long-standing records, including those for runs batted in and extra-base hits, and even played in 2,130 consecutive games! His formidable skills and unflinching dedication to the sport interested his teammates and the fans alike.

[1] The prognosis was a veritable death sentence. [2] Then suddenly, Gehrig's amazing stamina and talent seemed to

dissipate, leading one sports reporter to speculate that something was physically wrong with the athlete. [3] Unfortunately, that reporter was right: Gehrig was diagnosed with amyotrophic lateral sclerosis, a degenerative disease that leads to paralysis of both voluntary muscles and involuntary muscles, like those needed to control breathing and swallowing. 9

Most people faced with such daunting news would of withdrawn from society and mourned their fates.

4. Which of the following alternatives to the underlined portion would be LEAST acceptable?
F. that featured Gehrig
G. that Gehrig played in
H. in which Gehrig played
J. and played Gehrig

5. A. NO CHANGE
B. broke many long-standing records,
C. broke many, long-standing, records
D. broke many long-standing records

6. Given that all the choices are true, which one most clearly communicates how positively Gehrig was viewed as a player?
F. NO CHANGE
G. impressed
H. offended
J. confused

7. A. NO CHANGE
B. suddenly Gehrig's
C. suddenly Gehrigs
D. suddenly, Gehrigs

8. Which of the following alternatives to the underlined portion would be LEAST acceptable?
F. writer to infer
G. sports reporter to infer
H. writer to speculate
J. sports reporter to imply

9. Which of the following sequences of sentences makes this paragraph most logical?
A. NO CHANGE
B. 1, 3, 2
C. 2, 1, 3
D. 2, 3, 1

10. F. NO CHANGE
G. of withdrew
H. have withdrawn
J. have withdrew

GO ON TO THE NEXT PAGE.

11 However, on the day of

Gehrig's retirement from baseball, he delivered one of
        —————————————
                12
the most famous speeches of the time. He acknowledged his

grim fate but paid tribute to the life-affirming support he'd

received from his fans: "The ballplayer who loses his head, who
                        ———————————————————————
                                        13
can't keep his cool, is worse than no ballplayer at all." He spoke
———————————————————————————————
            13
highly of the encouragement his fans always provided and

proudly proclaimed that, despite his fate, he didn't regret

anything in his life or career. He was a man who's eternal
                                    ——————————
                                        14
optimism and good spirit lived on as a legacy of hope and

kindness for fans everywhere. We would all do well to learn that

lesson.

11. At this point, the writer is thinking about adding the following true statement:

> I know when I had to put my dog to sleep when he got cancer, all I could do was cry in my room for days.

Should the writer make this addition here?

A. Yes, because it provides a personal example comparable to the experience Lou Gehrig faced.
B. Yes, because it helps clarify the concept of mourning mentioned in the previous sentence.
C. No, because it detracts from the overall flow of the paragraph by adding irrelevant information.
D. No, because Gehrig did not have cancer.

12. F. NO CHANGE
    G. Gehrig's retirement,
    H. Gehrigs retirement
    J. Gehrigs' retirement

13. Given that all the choices are quotations attributed to Gehrig, which one would most effectively support the preceding statement in this sentence?

A. NO CHANGE
B. "They're wishing me luck—and I'm dying."
C. "I don't know if we're going to be successful or not, but we're going to give her a go."
D. "Yet today I consider myself the luckiest man on the face of the earth."

14. F. NO CHANGE
    G. man whose
    H. man, who's
    J. man who

> Question 15 asks about the preceding passage as a whole.

15. After reviewing this essay, the writer is thinking about deleting its opening phrase—"Since their inception in 1913,"—and revising the capitalization accordingly. Should this phrase be kept or deleted?

A. Kept, because it explains why the New York Yankees have been so successful.
B. Kept, because it establishes when in Yankees' history Gehrig lived and played.
C. Deleted, because it provides information that is presented effectively later in the passage.
D. Deleted, because it does not provide the years in which the Yankees won the World Series.

GO ON TO THE NEXT PAGE.

PASSAGE II

A Quarter for Your Thoughts

Ever since I was a little girl, I could always count on my grandmother to initiate a wonderful field trip. We lived in Virginia and so had immediate access to hundreds of famous places. Nonetheless, she took me to Civil War battlefields,
<u>16</u>
historic homes, national monuments, anywhere that had a story

to tell. <u>Old lighthouses can be dangerous, with rickety stairs and</u>
<u>17</u>
<u>rotting floorboards.</u>
<u>17</u>

My love of history has only grown over the years. History
<u>18</u>
was always so real for me, not the dull, dusty stuff other people

seemed to think it was. My <u>trips'</u> with my grandmother made me
<u>19</u>
feel as if I were shivering with George Washington at Valley Forge, where the Revolutionary Army endured a brutal winter, or hearing the words to the Gettysburg Address from Abraham

16. F. NO CHANGE
G. She
H. However, she
J. On the contrary, she

17. Given that all the choices are true, which one best identifies a personal connection the narrator feels to the locations she visits?

A. NO CHANGE
B. National monuments are especially fun to visit, but the lines can be quite long.
C. Civil War battlefields feel so alive when you walk through them; you almost expect to see a soldier around every corner.
D. The historic homes we visited are so nice they have been featured in decorating magazines.

18. Given that all the choices are true, which one introduces the subject of this paragraph and reinforces the essay's presentation of the relationship between the narrator and her grandmother?

F. NO CHANGE
G. My grandmother never visited Washington, D.C. until she was in her twenties, even though she lived so close.
H. A proper understanding of history requires extensive reading.
J. My grandmother indulged my love of history and deepened my appreciation for all there is to learn from it.

19. A. NO CHANGE
B. trip's
C. trips,
D. trips

GO ON TO THE NEXT PAGE.

Lincoln himself. [20] How could that ever be boring?

One day when I was visiting her, my grandmother took out a big, flat box. "This is for you. I thought we could begin a new
<u>21</u>

project," she told me, handing me a pamphlet to read. The U.S.
<u>22</u>
Mint was starting a project, minting brand new quarters for each of the 50 states bearing images significant and unique to each state's history. The box contained a map of the country, and each
<u>23</u>
state had a space where we could insert its quarter.

My enthusiasm caused laughter for a "quarter collection"
<u>24</u>
project, my friends didn't understand my eagerness when I eagerly tromped to the bank every couple of months when a new quarter came out. I was so excited when the first three were released Delaware, Pennsylvania, and New Jersey. My
<u>25</u>
grandmother and I would insert each quarter in its proper place and look up the story behind each new image we

saw. Amusingly, as time progressed, even my friends liked to
<u>26</u>
look at the growing collection of quarters on my map, asking

---

20. The writer is considering deleting the phrase "where the Revolutionary Army endured a brutal winter" from the preceding sentence (deleting the comma following the phrase). Should the phrase be kept or deleted?

   F. Kept, because it maintains the passage's focus on history.

   G. Kept, because it explains the significance of Valley Forge, which might otherwise cause confusion.

   H. Deleted, because the narrator has already established her interest in history.

   J. Deleted, because the information overstates the severity of the weather during the Revolution.

21. Given that all the choices are true, which one best introduces the subject of this paragraph?

   A. NO CHANGE

   B. In my opinion, anything that has happened in the last century isn't history; it's current events.

   C. My grandmother originally wanted to be a history teacher.

   D. Studying history has really encouraged me in my other studies, too.

22. F. NO CHANGE

   G. she told me to hand her a pamphlet to read.

   H. she read a pamphlet, telling me to hold it.

   J. she handed me a pamphlet, holding it.

23. A. NO CHANGE

   B. and when each

   C. for which each

   D. each

24. F. NO CHANGE

   G. Laughing at my enthusiasm

   H. So as to laugh about my enthusiasm

   J. Finding humor

25. A. NO CHANGE

   B. released;

   C. released:

   D. released,

26. Which of the following alternatives to the underlined portion would NOT be acceptable?

   F. saw. I was amused to see that,

   G. saw. To my utter amusement,

   H. saw; amusingly,

   J. saw, amusingly,

GO ON TO THE NEXT PAGE.

questions and <u>appreciating with admiration</u> the pristine
₂₇

collection.

    When the final quarter came out last year, my grandmother,
my friends, and I had a small <u>party, we wanted to celebrate the</u>
₂₈

complete collection. I think it is safe to say that

<u>the party was a smashing success.</u> Now, my grandmother says
₂₉

we'll have to start planning to visit all 50 states. <u>I wonder where</u>
₃₀

we'll go first!

27.
  A. NO CHANGE
  B. admiring
  C. lauding the high estimation of
  D. adoring and praising

28.
  F. NO CHANGE
  G. party, everyone wanted to
  H. party to
  J. party, let's

29. Given that all the choices are true, which one best makes a connection between the narrator's view of history and that of her friends?

  A. NO CHANGE
  B. my friends enjoyed themselves at the party.
  C. my friends now firmly believe that history can be fun, just like me.
  D. my friends are a little less negative about the study of history.

30. Which of the following alternatives to the underlined portion would be LEAST acceptable?

  F. am curious
  G. am anxious to see
  H. am nervous about
  J. can't wait to know

PASSAGE III

Aviation Princess

    My daughter just turned nine last week. We went to the mall,
and I gave her the best gift I could imagine: free rein to pick out
anything she <u>wanted and desired to have.</u> I expected her to pick
₃₁

out some clothes, a new video game, maybe even a

<u>doll. However,</u> she insisted the only one thing she wanted was a
₃₂

model airplane.

    I guess <u>about her request</u> I shouldn't be surprised. My
₃₃

31.
  A. NO CHANGE
  B. wanted, so that she could pick out her desire.
  C. wanted.
  D. wanted and had come to desire.

32. Which of the following alternatives to the underlined portion would NOT be acceptable?

  F. doll; however, she
  G. doll, but she
  H. doll however she
  J. doll. She

33. The best placement for the underlined phrase would be:

  A. where it is now.
  B. before the word *shouldn't*.
  C. after the word *shouldn't*.
  D. after the word *surprised* (ending the sentence with a period).

GO ON TO THE NEXT PAGE.

daughter <u>has grown up</u> in a military household, the pride and joy
₃₄

of her overly doting father. He <u>finds it perfectly appropriate</u> that,
₃₅
from a very early age, she has shared his love of aviation. I'll
never forget my utter dismay when he taught her to jump off the

swing set in our <u>backyard, pretending</u> she was a pilot and
₃₆
shouting, "Airborne!" I believe she was four at the time, but even

then she would play pilot more than <u>play house.</u>
₃₇

   <u>Yet</u> soon stories and pictures of aircraft weren't enough;
₃₈
she wanted to see the real thing. So my husband started
taking her to the annual air show at the local military base
<u>that happens every year.</u> Most other children her age admired
₃₉
how fast the planes flew or how nicely they were painted, but not

my daughter. ☐⁴⁰ She would ask, "Daddy, when are they going
to upgrade the avionics system in that F-22 *Raptor*?" or "Do you
think unmanned drones will ever be as useful as manned
aircraft?" I once overhead her correcting an older gentleman

34. **F.** NO CHANGE
    G. has been growing up
    H. would have grown up
    J. had grown up

35. Which of the following alternatives to the underlined portion
    would NOT be acceptable?

    A. believes it appropriately
    B. believes it appropriate
    C. considers it entirely appropriate
    D. deems it perfectly appropriate

36. **F.** NO CHANGE
    G. backyard pretending,
    H. backyard; pretending
    J. backyard. Pretending

37. Which of the following alternatives to the underlined portion
    would NOT be acceptable?

    A. house.
    B. she would play house.
    C. house was.
    D. she played house.

38. **F.** NO CHANGE
    G. Therefore,
    H. Although
    J. Instead,

39. **A.** NO CHANGE
    B. that takes place each year.
    C. which occurs every twelve months.
    D. DELETE the underlined portion and end the sentence with
    a period.

40. The writer is considering deleting the phrase *other children
    her age* from the preceding sentence. Should this phrase be
    kept or deleted?

    F. Kept, because it clarifies the types of questions children
    should be asking at air shows.
    G. Kept, because it emphasizes how different the narrator's
    daughter is from other children her age.
    H. Deleted, because it introduces information about aircraft
    but does not provide enough specific details.
    J. Deleted, because it interrupts the flow of passage.

GO ON TO THE NEXT PAGE.

whom was mistaken about the planned retirement date of the
___
41
F-15 *Eagle*. I would have been embarrassed about her

presumption, if she hadn't been absolute and unequivocal right.
___
42

Of course, my husband has big dreams for his little
___
43
aviatrix. She is going to be a military pilot, graduating at the

top of her class from the Naval Academy. Then she's going

to be the individual who design the next-generation supersonic
___
44
fighter personally, while lecturing at Harvard about the history of

fixed-wing aircraft. Otherwise, how she's going to fit that in
___
45
between being a surgeon and the president, I'll never know!

41. **A.** NO CHANGE
    B. who
    C. which
    D. DELETE the underlined portion.

42. **F.** NO CHANGE
    G. absolute and unequivocally
    H. absolutely and unequivocal
    J. absolutely and unequivocally

43. Which of the following alternatives to the underlined portion would be LEAST acceptable?

    A. ambitious aims
    B. impossible hopes
    C. great aspirations
    D. impressive plans

44. **F.** NO CHANGE
    G. to
    H. to individually accept a task in order to
    J. to take the initiative to

45. **A.** NO CHANGE
    B. In contrast, how
    C. How
    D. Despite this, how

PASSAGE IV

Light Bright, Light Bright: Turn on the Magic of Colored Light

As a child, I used to catch fireflies at dusk when I was young. I
___
46
remember feeling a strange excitement which, looking into my
___
47
cupped hands, I would see the light grow brighter then dimmer

as the fly flitted from one side to the other, trying to find an

escape. What I should have felt, however, was amazement at the

biological wonder I saw before me: bioluminescence.

Bioluminescence literally means "living light," and it refers
___
48
to a strange adaptation found in some organisms. It allows these

organisms to create a chemical reaction that generates and emits

46. **F.** NO CHANGE
    G. when I was a youth.
    H. before I grew up.
    J. DELETE the underlined portion and end the sentence with a period.

47. **A.** NO CHANGE
    B. when,
    C. in which,
    D. DELETE the underlined portion.

48. **F.** NO CHANGE
    G. simultaneously,
    H. consider that
    J. in addition,

GO ON TO THE NEXT PAGE.

light. Even though scientists know that this light is not intended
<u>   </u>
                              49
to be a heat source, they're not totally certain what it is intended

to do, either. Theorists hypothesize that organisms use their

self-manufactured light <u>for camouflaging themselves, illuminate</u>
                                              50
their surroundings, attract mates and prey, repulse predators, and

even communicate. ☐51 How the same adaptation can be

designed to both attract and repulse, however, is still a matter of

contention.

    The number of <u>terrestrial or land-based,</u> organisms
                                   52
that exhibit bioluminescence is rather small, and many,

such as fireflies and spiders, are fairly small in stature. In

fact, the vast majority are single-cell organisms that cannot be

seen with the naked eye. Unlike these smaller organisms,

<u>researchers are puzzled as to why most animals</u> and humans did
                                   53
not evolve this unique trait. Apparently the adaptation was not

universally necessary, given the bright rays of the sun that bathed

the surface year-round.

    However, <u>sunlight clearly doesn't stop the development</u>
                                        54
<u>of bioluminescence.</u> In total, ninety percent of all deep-sea
     54
marine lifeforms experience some sort of bioluminescence. Fish,

sharks, eels, and octopi, to name only a few, have all been seen

to bioluminesce in the murky depths. The most commonly

emitted colors are blue and <u>green, but</u> red and yellow have also
                                    55
been observed. <u>Its</u> a veritable rainbow of color 1,800 meters
                56

49. A. NO CHANGE
**   B.** Scientists
**   C.** In fact, scientists
**   D.** Understand that scientists

50. F. NO CHANGE
**   G.** in camouflaging theirselves,
**   H.** to camouflage itself,
**   J.** to camouflage themselves,

51. The writer is considering deleting the phrase "repulse predators" from the preceding sentence (deleting the comma after
the phrase). Should the phrase be kept or deleted?

**   A.** Kept, because it is an essential detail referred to directly
in the next sentence.
**   B.** Kept, because the evolutionary trait of repulsing predators
is critical to survival of the fittest.
**   C.** Deleted, because it repeats information previously provided in the essay.
**   D.** Deleted, because it makes the sentence long and difficult
to understand.

52. F. NO CHANGE
**   G.** terrestrial or, land-based
**   H.** terrestrial, or land-based,
**   J.** terrestrial, or land-based

53. A. NO CHANGE
**   B.** most animals
**   C.** animal researchers seek to discover why most animals
**   D.** researchers do not know why most animals

54. Given that all the choices are true, which one best indicates
the focus of this paragraph?

**   F.** NO CHANGE
**   G.** conditions are quite different in the ocean.
**   H.** there is no evidence that bioluminescence has ever devel-
oped anywhere other than on planet Earth.
**   J.** humans do not need bioluminescence, because we can use
our intellect to manipulate our surroundings.

55. A. NO CHANGE
**   B.** green but
**   C.** green; but
**   D.** green but,

56. F. NO CHANGE
**   G.** In it's
**   H.** Its'
**   J.** It's

GO ON TO THE NEXT PAGE.

below the surface thanks of these <u>organism's lights</u>, even though
almost no visible light can penetrate to that level.

    The extreme depth at which most of these organisms exist
represents the biggest obstacle researchers face in determining
the primary function of bioluminescence. Undoubtedly, this will
slow the pace of exploration <u>more then lack of money</u>. For that
reason, it may be some time before this mysterious

adaptation is <u>clarified</u>.

PASSAGE V

Doctors Without Borders

    In America, we take many things for granted. If we don't feel
well, we see a doctor. If we're hungry, we eat something. If
we're thirsty, we drink some water. <u>These very basic actions can</u>
be amazingly difficult, if not impossible, in some parts of the

world. That is why a group of French <u>physicians, started</u> Doctors
Without Borders in 1971.

---

57. **A.** NO CHANGE
    B. organism's lights',
    C. organisms' lights,
    D. organisms lights,

58. **F.** NO CHANGE
    G. then lack of money will.
    H. than lack of money.
    J. as lack of money.

59. Which of the following alternatives to the underlined word
would be LEAST acceptable?

    A. fully explained.
    B. accounted for.
    C. transmitted.
    D. cleared up.

> Question 60 asks about the preceding passage
> as a whole.

60. Suppose the writer's goal had been to write a brief essay
focusing on a fascinating evolutionary adaptation that can be
found in multiple habitats. Would this essay accomplish this
goal?

    F. Yes, because fireflies exhibit the adaptation and live in
trees.
    G. Yes, because bioluminescence is described, and it occurs
in both marine and non-marine habitats.
    H. No, because fireflies cannot live in both air and water.
    J. No, because all the habitats described exist on the same
planet.

61. **A.** NO CHANGE
    B. (Do NOT begin new paragraph) Yet these
    C. (Begin new paragraph) These
    D. (Begin new paragraph) Yet these

62. **F.** NO CHANGE
    G. physicians started,
    H. physicians; started
    J. physicians started

GO ON TO THE NEXT PAGE.

1 ■ ■ ■ ■ ■ ■ ■ ■ 1

Doctors Without Borders started as a humanitarian aid
organization designed to reach out to the innocent victims of wars
in lesser-developed parts of the world. The doctors who first
started the organization had been working in Nigeria during the
country's very bloody civil war in the late 1960s. There, they saw

everything from starvation, and disease, to death and outright
murder happening in the streets, and neither the United Nations

nor the Red Cross seemed to do anything to stop these atrocities.

66 The doctors felt that, although they couldn't put an end to
the fighting itself, they could at least help to alleviate the

suffering, thus they declared themselves neutral in the conflict
and entered war-torn areas to provide aid to anyone who needed
it, regardless of which side of the conflict the person was on.

In contrast, the original mission was simply to provide health
care as well as medical training to up-and-coming doctors

63. Which choice most effectively introduces the basic goal
of Doctors Without Borders, as described elsewhere in the
essay?

A. NO CHANGE
B. tends to specialize in trauma treatment, which helps the
doctors in their personal medical practices when they
return home.
C. has never sought political support from the United States
or other countries, because it wants to remain completely
neutral.
D. has never operated within the United States, although
arguably there are many people here who could benefit
from its services.

64. F. NO CHANGE
G. starvation, and disease
H. starvation and disease
J. starvation and disease,

65. Which of the following alternatives to the underlined portion
would be LEAST acceptable?

A. horrors.
B. offenses.
C. wrongs.
D. alarms.

66. The writer is considering deleting the preceding sentence.
Should this sentence be kept or deleted?

F. Kept, because readers are used to hearing about murders
and starvation anyway.
G. Kept, because it provides a specific example of the type
of actions that provoked the doctors to take action.
H. Deleted, because it does not explain how the doctors actu-
ally stopped the fighting in Nigeria.
J. Deleted, because it detracts from the actual foundation of
Doctors Without Borders.

67. A. NO CHANGE
B. suffering thus
C. suffering. Thus
D. suffering and thus

68. F. NO CHANGE
G. The
H. Meanwhile, the
J. Finally, the

GO ON TO THE NEXT PAGE.

732 | Cracking the ACT

in the various regions. ⑥⑨ In desperate need of medical

attention suffering in war-torn regions certainly felt the aid
___
70
Doctors Without Borders supplied was important. When not in

the direct line of fire between two opposing military groups,
___
71
however, the organization puts special emphasis on the

preventative aspects of health care, especially vaccinations, good

nutrition, and sanitation. These seeming simple goals have made
___
72
substantial strides in the overall quality of health in Africa,

where most of the work of Doctors Without Borders has been

focused over the last 40 years.

    Sadly, the noble effort expended by these selfless doctors have
___
73
not met universal support. In some conflicts, the aid workers—

despite their political neutrality—have found themselves the

victims of kidnappings, arrests, even murder. Doctors who

volunteer to serve in Doctors Without Borders know the dangers
___
74

they face, yet they choose to try to help anyway. We can only hope
___
75
that eventually their dignified actions will become unnecessary.
___
75

69. The writer is considering deleting the phrase "to up-and-coming doctors" from the preceding sentence. Should the phrase be kept or deleted?

   A. Kept, because it clarifies to whom the medical training is being provided.
   B. Kept, because it is important to specify that there are doctors already practicing in the region.
   C. Deleted, because a person who has not successfully graduated from medical school cannot be considered a doctor.
   D. Deleted, because Doctors Without Borders should not take such a grandiose task on themselves without government sanction.

70. **F.** NO CHANGE
     G. attention who
     H. attention, and
     J. attention, individuals

71. **A.** NO CHANGE
     B. among
     C. across
     D. next

72. **F.** NO CHANGE
     G. more seemingly
     H. seemingly
     J. more seeming

73. **A.** NO CHANGE
     B. efforts expended by these selfless doctors have
     C. efforts expended by these selfless doctors has
     D. effort expended by these selfless doctors had

74. **F.** NO CHANGE
     G. distribute
     H. provide
     J. deliver

75. Given that all the choices are true, which one most clearly shows that the self-sacrifice of the doctors deserves praise?

   A. NO CHANGE
   B. I don't know if I would have that depth of conviction or level of courage.
   C. Such unsung courage truly speaks to the depth of human kindness, and should be a lesson to us all.
   D. It is truly a shame that they are put into dangerous positions.

END OF TEST 1

STOP! DO NOT TURN THE PAGE UNTIL TOLD TO DO SO.

MATHEMATICS TEST

60 Minutes—60 Questions

DIRECTIONS: Solve each problem, choose the correct answer, and then darken the corresponding oval on your answer sheet.

Do not linger over problems that take too much time. Solve as many as you can; then return to the others in the time you have left for this test.

You are permitted to use a calculator on this test. You may use your calculator for any problems you choose, but some of the problems may best be done without using a calculator.

Note: Unless otherwise stated, all of the following should be assumed:

1. Illustrative figures are NOT necessarily drawn to scale.
2. Geometric figures lie in a plane.
3. The word *line* indicates a straight line.
4. The word *average* indicates arithmetic mean.

---

1. In a geometric sequence, the quotient of any two consecutive terms is the same. If the third term of a geometric sequence is 8 and the fourth term is 16, then what is the second term?

   A. −8
   B. −4
   C. 2
   D. 4
   E. 8

2. If the function $f(a,b)$ is defined as $f(a,b) = 2ab - (a+b)$, then $f(3,4) = ?$

   F. 7
   G. 17
   H. 21
   J. 24
   K. 31

3. The Korean BBQ taco truck sells short rib tacos for 99¢. Christine has only pennies, nickels, dimes, and quarters in her purse. If she wants to pay with exact change, then what is the least number of coins Christine can use to buy a 99¢ taco?

   (Note: Assume any sales tax is included in the price.)

   A. 6
   B. 7
   C. 8
   D. 9
   E. 10

4. What is the area, in square inches, of a square with a side length of 8 inches?

   F. 8
   G. 16
   H. 24
   J. 32
   K. 64

DO YOUR FIGURING HERE.

GO ON TO THE NEXT PAGE.

DO YOUR FIGURING HERE.

5. If $x = 3$, then the expression $\dfrac{(x+1)^2}{x^2-1}$ is equal to:

   A. 2

   B. $\dfrac{1}{2}$

   C. 0

   D. $-\dfrac{1}{2}$

   E. -8

6. Which of the following is NOT a factor of 1,776 ?

   F. 12
   G. 16
   H. 18
   J. 24
   K. 37

7. Lauren's world history teacher needs to select one of his 19 students to lead the class in song. Lauren's teacher decides that the song leader, who will be chosen at random, CANNOT be any of the 4 seniors in the class. What is the probability that Lauren, who is NOT a senior, will be chosen?

   A. 0

   B. $\dfrac{1}{19}$

   C. $\dfrac{1}{15}$

   D. $\dfrac{4}{19}$

   E. $\dfrac{15}{19}$

8. If $4(x-5) + x = 45$, then $x = $?

   F. 5
   G. 8
   H. 9
   J. 10
   K. 13

9. Joe rents a car to drive across the state to visit his family for Thanksgiving. The car rental company charges Joe $112 for the weekend rental, plus $0.99 for each mile he drives. If Joe drives the rental car m miles, then which of the following expressions gives Joe's total cost, in dollars, for renting the car?

   A. $0.99m - 112$
   B. $0.99m + 112$
   C. $49.95m$
   D. $112m + 0.99$
   E. $112.99m$

GO ON TO THE NEXT PAGE.

10. Stella wants to buy a scooter for $4,800. A loan company offers to finance the purchase in return for payments of $130 a month for 4 years. If Stella were to finance the scooter, then how much more than the purchase price of the scooter will Stella have paid at the end of the 4-year period?

    F. $ 520
    G. $ 780
    H. $1,040
    J. $1,300
    K. $1,440

11. The expression $\dfrac{20y^8}{4y^2}$ is equivalent to:

    A. $5y^4$
    B. $5y^6$
    C. $5y^8$
    D. $16y^4$
    E. $16y^6$

12. Which of the following is equal to $\dfrac{3-\dfrac{1}{2}}{2+\dfrac{3}{4}}$?

    F. $\dfrac{10}{11}$
    G.   2
    H.   12
    J.   20
    K. $\dfrac{55}{2}$

13. Point C is at 3.5 on the real number line. If Point D is also on the real number line and is 8.5 units from C, then which of the following are the possible locations of D ?

    A.   −12 and −5
    B.   −12 and 5
    C.   −5 and 5
    D.   12 and −5
    E.   12 and 5

14. The mean of 4 numbers in a data set is 7. If 3 of these numbers are 2, 4, and 10, then which of the following is the fourth number?

    F.   4
    G.   7
    H.   8
    J.   10
    K.   12

DO YOUR FIGURING HERE.

GO ON TO THE NEXT PAGE.

DO YOUR FIGURING HERE.

15. Motorcars, Inc. made $1,489,000 in net profit in 2007. In 2009, Motorcars, Inc. made $1,725,000 in net profit. If the net profit increased linearly from 2007 through 2009, then what was the net profit earned in 2008 ?

   A. $1,607,000
   B. $1,698,000
   C. $1,724,000
   D. $1,779,000
   E. $1,842,000

16. The art teacher at Valley High School is decorating her classroom by reproducing famous pictures on her walls. She has a picture 8 inches wide and 10 inches tall that she wants to replicate to scale on the wall. If the painting on the wall will be 6 feet tall, then approximately how wide will the painting be, in feet?

   F. 5
   G. 7
   H. 9
   J. 11
   K. 13

17. The formula for line l in standard form is $5x - y = 2$. Which of the following gives the formula for line l in slope-intercept form?

   A. $y = 5x + 2$
   B. $y = 5x - 2$
   C. $y = 2x - 5$
   D. $y = -5x - 2$
   E. $y = -5x + 2$

18. The expression $|2 - 14| - |-25|$ is equal to:

   F. 41
   G. 37
   H. 13
   J. −13
   K. −37

19. In $\triangle JKL$ the measure of $\angle J$ is exactly 37°, and the measure of $\angle K$ is less than or equal to 63°. Which of the following phrases best describes the measure of $\angle L$?

   A. Exactly 120°
   B. Exactly 100°
   C. Exactly 80°
   D. Greater than or equal to 80°
   E. Less than or equal to 80°

GO ON TO THE NEXT PAGE.

DO YOUR FIGURING HERE.

20. If $3x - 1 > 26$, then which of the following is the smallest possible integer value of x ?

    F.   6
    G.   7
    H.   8
    J.   9
    K. 10

21. Paul is tying red and white ribbons around a gift box. He begins by tying the white ribbon and one red ribbon around the box. These two ribbons intersect on one face of the box at a 62° angle, as shown in the figure below. Now Paul wants to tie a second red ribbon onto the box so that the two red ribbons are parallel. What is the degree measure of the angle, indicated below, between the white ribbon and the bottom red ribbon?

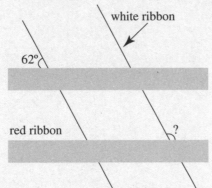

    A.   62°
    B.   76°
    C.   90°
    D. 104°
    E. 118°

22. In right triangle $\triangle PRS$ shown below, Q is the midpoint of $\overline{PR}$. What is the length of $\overline{QR}$, to the nearest inch?

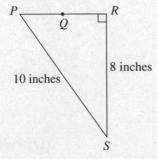

    F.   2
    G.   3
    H.   4
    J.   6
    K. 36

GO ON TO THE NEXT PAGE.

Use the following information to answer questions 23–24.

Katie notices that the textbooks for her past 3 math courses have the same length and width, but each year's textbook has more pages and weighs more than the previous year's textbook. Katie weighs the textbooks, to the nearest 0.1 ounce, for her past 3 math courses and wonders about the relationship between the number of pages in math textbooks and the weights of those textbooks. She graphs the number of pages and corresponding weights of her 3 math textbooks in the standard (x,y) coordinate plane, as shown below, and discovers a linear relationship among these 3 points. She concludes that the equation of the line that passes through these 3 points is $y = 0.1x + 2.2$.

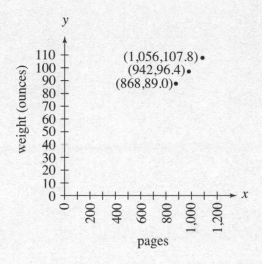

23. How much more, in ounces, does a math textbook with 1,056 pages weigh than one with 868 pages?

   A. 18.8
   B. 19.8
   C. 54.1
   D. 77.3
   E. 107.8

24. According to Katie's equation, how much would a math textbook with 1,338 pages weigh, in pounds?

   (Note: 16 ounces = 1 pound)

   F. 7.4
   G. 8.5
   H. 10.2
   J. 13.6
   K. 14.1

GO ON TO THE NEXT PAGE.

DO YOUR FIGURING HERE.

25. All line segments that intersect in the polygon below do so at right angles. If the dimensions given are in centimeters, then what is the area of the polygon, in square centimeters?

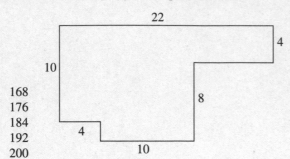

A. 168
B. 176
C. 184
D. 192
E. 200

26. Mr. Baylor spent 6 days grading 996 essays. He averaged 178 essays per day for the first 3 days. Which of the following is closest to his average speed, in essays graded per day, for the final 3 days?

F. 154
G. 157
H. 160
J. 163
K. 166

27. For all values of y, which of the following is equivalent to $(y+1)(y^2-3y+2)$?

A. $y^3 + y^2 - y - 2$
B. $y^3 + y^2 + 2y + 2$
C. $y^3 - 2y^2 - y + 2$
D. $y^3 - 2y^2 + y - 2$
E. $y^3 + 2y + 2$

28. For $\angle D$ in $\triangle DEF$ below, which of the following trigonometric expressions has value $\dfrac{4}{5}$?

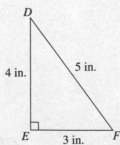

F. $\sin D$
G. $\tan D$
H. $\cos D$
J. $\sec D$
K. $\csc D$

GO ON TO THE NEXT PAGE.

29. Over the weekend, Shawn bought 22 songs from an online music store. He spent a total of $17.90 on contemporary and classical songs. If contemporary songs cost $0.95 each and classical songs cost $0.75 each, then how many contemporary songs did Shawn buy?

(Note: There is no sales tax charged on these songs because they were purchased online.)

- **A.** 7
- **B.** 9
- **C.** 10
- **D.** 13
- **E.** 15

30. If the operation # is defined as $x \# y = \dfrac{x^2 - y^2}{x + y}$, where x and y are real numbers such that $x \neq -y$, then what is the value of $(-3)\#(-7)$?

- **F.** 10
- **G.** 4
- **H.** 1
- **J.** −4
- **K.** −10

31. Esther is making $2\frac{1}{4}$ gallons of punch for a large party. While mixing the punch, she uses $\frac{1}{2}$ gallon of pineapple juice. What fraction of the punch consists of pineapple juice?

- **A.** $\dfrac{1}{9}$
- **B.** $\dfrac{1}{6}$
- **C.** $\dfrac{2}{9}$
- **D.** $\dfrac{1}{3}$
- **E.** $\dfrac{2}{3}$

32. Point O is the center of the circle shown below, and $\overline{XZ}$ is the diameter of the circle. If $\overline{XZ} = 8$ ft, Y lies on the circle, and $\overline{OX} = \overline{XY}$, then what is the area, in square feet, of $\triangle XYZ$?

- **F.** $4\sqrt{2}$
- **G.** $8\sqrt{3}$
- **H.** 16
- **J.** 32
- **K.** 64

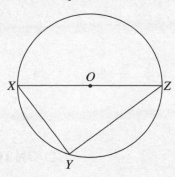

DO YOUR FIGURING HERE.

GO ON TO THE NEXT PAGE.

DO YOUR FIGURING HERE.

33. Which of the following values provides one of the roots for the equation $y^2 - 4y - 5 = 7$?

   A. −12
   B. −6
   C. −2
   D. −1
   E.   5

34. The plastic model house shown below consists of a right pyramid atop a right rectangular prism. The length and width of the prism and of the pyramid are 20 millimeters. The height of the prism is 16 millimeters, and the height of the pyramid is 12 millimeters. Which of the following is closest to the volume of the plastic model house, in cubic millimeters?

   (Note: The volume of a right pyramid is given by $\frac{1}{3}lwh$, where l is the length, w is the width, and h is the height. The volume of a right rectangular prism is given by lwh, where l is the length, w is the width, and h is the height.)

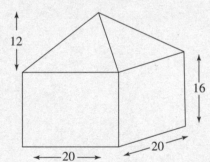

   F.   6,900
   G.   8,000
   H.   9,100
   J.   12,300
   K.   25,600

35. An isosceles trapezoid has bases of length 5 inches and 11 inches. The area of the trapezoid is 40 square inches. What is the height of the trapezoid, in inches?

   A.   4
   B.   5
   C.   7.5
   D.   17.5
   E.   35

GO ON TO THE NEXT PAGE.

36. What is the slope of the line that passes through the points (−2,6) and (3,−9) in the standard (*x,y*) coordinate plane?

F. $\dfrac{1}{15}$

G. $-\dfrac{1}{3}$

H. $-\dfrac{3}{5}$

J. -3

K. -5

DO YOUR FIGURING HERE.

37. Right triangle $\triangle WXY$ is isosceles and has its right angle at Point X. Point Z is collinear with points X and Y, with Y between X and Z. What is the measure of $\angle WYZ$?

A. 45°
B. 90°
C. 120°
D. 135°
E. 145°

38. The decimal construction of $\dfrac{5}{13}$ repeats and can be written as 0.384615384615⋯. What is the 99th digit to the right of the decimal point in this decimal construction?

F. 1
G. 3
H. 4
J. 5
K. 6

GO ON TO THE NEXT PAGE.

39. Points $W(-2,2)$, $X(2,2)$, and $Y(2,-2)$ lie in the standard (x,y) coordinate plane and are 3 of the vertices of square $WXYZ$. What is the length, in coordinate units, of $\overline{XZ}$?

A. 2
B. 4
C. 16
D. $2\sqrt{2}$
E. $4\sqrt{2}$

40. The equation $y = x^2$ is graphed in the standard (x,y) coordinate plane, then reflected across the x-axis. Which of the following is the equation of this reflection?

F. $y = x^2$
G. $y = -x^2$
H. $y = (-x)^2$
J. $y = |x|$
K. $|y| = |x|$

41. In the figure below, $\overline{JK} \parallel \overline{MN}$, and $\overline{JM}$ and $\overline{KN}$ intersect at L. Which of the following statements must be true?

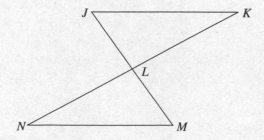

A. $\overline{JK} \cong \overline{MN}$
B. $\overline{JL} \cong \overline{LM}$
C. $\triangle JKL \cong \triangle MNL$
D. $\triangle JKL$ is similar to $\triangle MNL$
E. $\overline{JM}$ bisects $\overline{KN}$

GO ON TO THE NEXT PAGE.

Use the following information to answer questions 42–44.

The Wildcat athletic department at Wilson High School needs to raise $3,000.00 to fill a gap in its annual budget. The athletic department can choose 1 of the 2 options below to raise the needed funds.

Sell "Wildcat baseball caps" option: After paying a one-time fee of $23.00 to rent the necessary equipment, the athletic department can sell baseball caps featuring the school's logo. The athletic department will buy plain caps and print the school logo on each, at a cost of $3.50 per cap. The athletic department will sell each cap for $5.00.

Sell "Wildcat T-shirts" option: After paying a one-time fee of $19.00 to rent the necessary equipment, the athletic department can sell T-shirts featuring the school's logo. The athletic department will buy plain T-shirts and print the school logo on each, at a cost of $2.25 per T-shirt. The athletic department will sell each T-shirt for $4.00.

42. For the "Wildcat baseball caps" option, at least how many baseball caps must be sold in order to cover the one-time fee of renting the necessary equipment?

    F. 14
    G. 15
    H. 16
    J. 17
    K. 23

43. The Wildcat athletic department sold 540 tickets to Friday's football game. Of those tickets, 60% were adult tickets and the remainder were student tickets. The revenue from these ticket sales had already been factored into the annual budget. Jordan suggested raising the price of the adult tickets $2.00 to help fill the budget gap. If the athletic department had raised the price of each adult ticket $2.00, then by approximately what percent would the budget gap have been filled?

    A. 22%
    B. 23%
    C. 24%
    D. 25%
    E. 26%

GO ON TO THE NEXT PAGE.

44. The Wildcat athletic department chose the "Wildcat T-shirt" option and successfully filled the budget gap. What is the minimum number of T-shirts the athletic department must have sold?

F. 1,480
G. 1,664
H. 1,709
J. 1,726
K. 1,812

DO YOUR FIGURING HERE.

45. The graph of $y^2 = x$ is shown in the standard (x,y) coordinate plane below for values of x such that $0 \le x \le 4$. The x-coordinates of points D and E are both 4. What is the area of $\triangle DEO$, in square coordinate units?

A. $\dfrac{5}{2}$

B. 4

C. 8

D. 12

E. 16

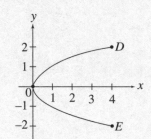

46. In $\triangle XYZ$ below, the length of $\overline{XY}$ is 12 centimeters. How long is $\overline{YZ}$, to the nearest tenth of a centimeter?

(Note: The law of sines states that in $\triangle ABC$ with sides length a, b, and c opposite $\angle A$, $\angle B$, and $\angle C$, respectively,

$$\frac{\sin A}{a} = \frac{\sin B}{b} = \frac{\sin C}{c}.)$$

(Note: $\sin 53° \approx 0.799$, $\sin 59° \approx 0.857$, $\sin 68° \approx 0.927$)

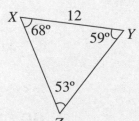

F. 9.6
G. 10.3
H. 11.1
J. 12.9
K. 13.9

GO ON TO THE NEXT PAGE.

DO YOUR FIGURING HERE.

47. Jacob used the quadratic equation to find that the solutions to an equation are $x = 3 \pm \sqrt{-16c^2}$, where c is a positive real number. Which of the following expressions gives these solutions as complex numbers?

   A. $3 \pm 1ci$
   B. $3 \pm 2ci$
   C. $3 \pm 4ci$
   D. $3 \pm 8ci$
   E. $3 \pm 16ci$

48. Points C and D are on the circle with center O as shown in the figure below. The length of $\overline{CD}$ is 12 millimeters and the measure of $\overset{\frown}{CD}$ is 60°. What is the length of the diameter of this circle?

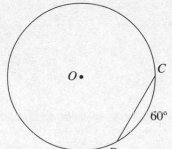

   F. 12
   G. 16
   H. 20
   J. 24
   K. 28

49. A nylon cord is stretched from the top of a playground pole to the ground. The cord is 25 feet long and makes a 19° angle with the ground. Which of the following expressions gives the horizontal distance, in feet, between the pole and the point where the cord touches the ground?

   A. $\dfrac{\sin 19°}{25}$

   B. $\dfrac{\cos 19°}{25}$

   C. $25\tan 19°$

   D. $25\sin 19°$

   E. $25\cos 19°$

50. What are the coordinates of the center of the circle with the equation $x^2 + 8x + y^2 - 2y + 8 = 0$ in the standard (x,y) coordinate plane?

   F. $(-4,\ 1)$
   G. $(-1,-4)$
   H. $(\ 1,-4)$
   J. $(\ 4,-1)$
   K. $(\ 4,\ 1)$

GO ON TO THE NEXT PAGE.

51. Scott's swimming pool has a depth of 8 feet and holds 13,000 gallons of water when full. Because of the warm weather, 10% of the water in the pool evaporates each day. Scott fills the pool with water and comes back the next day to measure the amount of water remaining in the pool. He considers this "Day 1" because it was taken 1 day after the pool was filled, and he labels his measurement as such. The next day, he measures the amount of water again, and he labels the results "Day 2" because it is now 2 days after he filled the pool. If Scott continues, on which day will he measure the pool that it is less than half full?

A. 5
B. 6
C. 7
D. 8
E. 9

52. If $\begin{vmatrix} a & b \\ c & d \end{vmatrix} = ad - bc$, then $\begin{vmatrix} 2d & 2c \\ 2a & 2b \end{vmatrix} = ?$

F. $2da - 2cb$
G. $2db - 2ca$
H. $4da - 4cb$
J. $4db - 4ca$
K. $ad - bc$

53. The figure below shows 4 congruent circles, each tangent to 2 other circles and to 2 sides of the square. If the length of a side of the square is 24 inches, then what is the area, in square inches, of 1 circle?

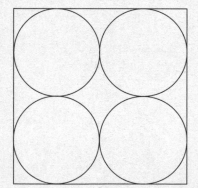

A. 9
B. 9π
C. 36
D. 36π
E. 144

54. Andy has 30 collectible comic books, which he bought in 2005 for $28.95 each. These comic books are currently valued at $34.35 each. Andy will sell these 30 comic books when their combined value is exactly $600.00 more than he paid for them. How much more will the average value per comic book have risen when Andy sells these 30 comic books?

F. $14.60
G. $12.72
H. $10.05
J. $7.84
K. $5.40

GO ON TO THE NEXT PAGE.

55. Circles with centers G and K intersect at points C and F, as shown below. Points B, G, H, J, K, and D are collinear. The lengths of $\overline{AC}$, $\overline{CE}$, and $\overline{HJ}$ are 18 cm, 10 cm, and 3 cm, respectively. What is the length, in centimeters, of $\overline{BD}$?

DO YOUR FIGURING HERE.

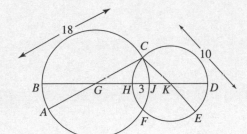

- **A.** 22
- **B.** 25
- **C.** 26
- **D.** 28
- **E.** 29

56. A parabola with vertex $(-3,-2)$ and axis of symmetry $y = -2$ crosses the y-axis at $\left(0, -2 + 3\sqrt{3}\right)$. At what other point does the parabola cross the y-axis?

- **F.** No other point
- **G.** $\left(0, 2 + 3\sqrt{3}\right)$
- **H.** $\left(0, 2 - 3\sqrt{3}\right)$
- **J.** $\left(0, -2 - 3\sqrt{3}\right)$
- **K.** Cannot be determined from the given information

57. If $z \neq 4$ and $z \neq -4$, then which of the following is equivalent to the expression $\dfrac{3z}{4-z} + \dfrac{3z}{z^2 - 16}$?

- **A.** $\dfrac{3z + 15z}{z^2 - 16}$
- **B.** $\dfrac{9z^2 - 12z}{z^2 - 16}$
- **C.** $\dfrac{-12z}{z^2 - 16}$
- **D.** $\dfrac{-3z^2}{z^2 - 16}$
- **E.** $\dfrac{-3z^2 - 9z}{z^2 - 16}$

GO ON TO THE NEXT PAGE.

58. The sides of the angle with measure θ are the positive x-axis and a portion of the line $y = -x$, as shown in the standard (x,y) coordinate plane below. What is the value of $\tan \theta$?

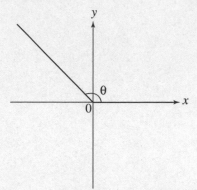

F. 1

G. $\dfrac{\sqrt{2}}{2}$

H. $\dfrac{1}{2}$

J. $-\dfrac{\sqrt{2}}{2}$

K. -1

59. The nth term of an arithmetic sequence, a_n, is given by $a_n = a_1 + dn - d$, where a_1 is the 1st term, and d is the common difference between terms. Which of the following expressions gives d in terms of a_n, a_1, and n ?

A. $\dfrac{a_n - a_1}{n - 1}$

B. $\dfrac{n - 1}{a_n - a_1}$

C. $\dfrac{a_n - a_1}{n}$

D. $\dfrac{a_n}{a_1 + n}$

E. $a_n - a_1 - n$

GO ON TO THE NEXT PAGE.

DO YOUR FIGURING HERE.

60. For all real positive values of x and y, $2\sqrt{x} \times 3\sqrt{y} = 12y$. What is x in terms of y ?

    F. $2y$
    G. $3y$
    H. $4y$
    J. $6y$
    K. **7y**

END OF TEST 2

STOP! DO NOT TURN THE PAGE UNTIL TOLD TO DO SO.

DO NOT RETURN TO A PREVIOUS TEST.

READING TEST

35 Minutes—40 Questions

DIRECTIONS: There are four passages in this test. Each passage is followed by several questions. After reading a passage, choose the best answer to each question and fill in the corresponding oval on your answer document. You may refer to the passages as often as necessary.

Passage I

PROSE FICTION: This passage is adapted from the novel *Oklahoma Sunrise* by Jack Elwyn Prouty (©2007 Jack Elwyn Prouty).

Rebecca stood and gazed out across the fields, into the unending horizon.

A warm breeze caressed the fields, causing the ears of the wheat to bend homeward, looking for all the world like they were
5 listening to a conversation none but they could hear. The ears bent and bobbed as the breeze eddied about them. She stood, inhaling the fresh and savory scent of the almost-ripe wheat, mixed with the rich scent of the earth. Someone had plowed nearby; the newly uncovered earth always smelled more alive. She could
10 hear bees—there was a hive somewhere not far away—and birds and men, all faintly but as much a part of the image in her mind as was the wheat itself. And underneath everything else, that slight tang in the air that said it would rain soon. Not even a tang, really—almost a feeling but somehow a smell, too.

15 The evening, just as dusk was falling, was always the best time to visit the fields alone. Earlier in the day there were too many people, and too many chores to do to justify standing silently in the middle of the field. Later it was too still, too quiet. It felt as if the field itself had gone to sleep; not an unpleasant feeling,
20 really, but not the feeling of being embraced by a living, breathing entity that she had wanted today. That she liked best of all.

Of course, the earth hadn't always been a friend to the people that cultivated it. Any farmer knows that there will be good years and bad years, and that sometimes one bad year will
25 follow another and then another, to the point where you wonder if a good year will ever come again. Growing up far away from the soil that had held her people for generations, Rebecca had known all of that. Known how the land had turned on her parents and driven them far from the only home they knew, seeking
30 work on a stranger's land, doing unfamiliar work. Still, she had felt the draw. Even as a child, she had known that someday, she would return. It was in her blood, really. Her great-grandparents had claimed the land as their own, poured their blood, sweat, and tears into it, and turned it from a wild tract of prairie into

35 productive fields of wheat and corn. Her grandparents had inherited the fields, and her parents in their turn had as well. They would have gone to Rebecca next, had her parents been able to hold on to what was theirs. Even when they had left, they had claimed the land as their own and had sworn that they'd return
40 to it someday. Both her mother and father had been prevented from returning home, but now Rebecca was here in their place, trying to reclaim her family's heritage.

She stood still, thinking about the past and the present, breathing in the heat and the life that surrounded her. The land
45 might not always be kind, but it is always good. She flinched a little bit as a bee landed on her cheek, inspecting this large thing that didn't seem to be a part of the field. She let it explore her face, knowing it would move on once it had ascertained that she was no flower. The feel of the bee's feet tramping across her nose
50 made her want to sneeze but she held her breath, not wanting to frighten it into stinging her.

When the bee ventured on in pursuit of more profitable discoveries, she opened her eyes and gazed out across her fields. They were hers, in truth if not writing, and would one day be
55 hers in every sense. For a moment, her stomach began to clench as her mind turned unwillingly but naturally to the realities of what lay ahead. The loans, the mortgage payments, the possibility of a bad crop ruining all her plans. Firmly, she pushed those thoughts aside. She had acknowledged them before and would
60 acknowledge them again, when she sat before her ledger or reviewed the accounts. This moment was for enjoying the sheer bounty of life, not for fears and numbers. Without the former, she could never face the latter. It was for the warm reality of the growing, breathing crops that she was determined to deal with
65 the men from the bank, to go without new things, and work until her back ached every day, only to get up and do the same the next morning, before the sun was up.

She breathed deeply, trying to take in the strength and life that surrounded her, trying to store it inside herself. This was her
70 people's land; she knew that in her bones. Whatever else might happen, that would not change.

GO ON TO THE NEXT PAGE.

1. Which of the following statements best expresses Rebecca's feelings during her visit to the fields, as expressed in lines 1–42 ?

   A. Overjoyed by the idea of ownership
   B. Connected with the land and her heritage
   C. Dismayed by her looming financial problems
   D. Exhausted and frustrated from hard work

2. The word *that* in line 28 most directly refers to:

   F. "someday, she would return " (lines 31–32).
   G. "far away from the soil" (lines 26–27).
   H. "it would move on once it had ascertained that she was no flower" (lines 48–49).
   J. "sometimes one bad year will follow another" (lines 24–25).

3. The main purpose of the information in lines 30–42 is to explain why Rebecca believes that the land is:

   A. her rightful heritage, passed down through her family, whose hard work forms the foundation for her claim.
   B. an entity unto itself, alive and free, and beyond the control of anyone.
   C. not worth the trouble that she and her predecessors have gone to in an attempt to claim it.
   D. beautiful, whether wild or cultivated, and filled with creatures that create a harmonious whole.

4. In the first four paragraphs (lines 1–42), the narrator describes all of the following aspects of Rebecca's surroundings EXCEPT the:

   F. different scents in the evening air.
   G. feel of freshly plowed earth.
   H. reason her family had left the area.
   J. best time of day to visit the fields.

5. The passage can best be described as a fictional depiction of a woman's impression of the land that:

   A. uses rich, suggestive detail to show that the land is a vital and cherished component of her personal life and family heritage.
   B. reveals a painful family history and explains why her ancestors had opted to give up all claims on the land.
   C. offers metaphors and similes to convey a deeper meaning than the one suggested by the events narrated in the story.
   D. explains exactly how one family can lose everything due to circumstances beyond the control of its members.

6. The narrator's statement in lines 62–63 ("Without the former, she could never face the latter") most directly refers back to Rebecca's:

   F. opinion about different times of the day and how that changes the atmosphere (lines 15–21).
   G. concern about the bee described in the fifth paragraph (lines 43–51).
   H. anxiety over financial matters being outweighed by her love of the land (lincs 54–61).
   J. enjoyment of the scents described in the second paragraph (lines 3–14).

7. One of the main purposes of the last two paragraphs (lines 52–71) is for the narrator to describe Rebecca's attitude towards the land in a way that:

   A. explains the importance of the stranger's land that is mentioned previously in the passage.
   B. purposefully identifies the mistakes made by Rebecca's parents, referenced earlier in the passage, which Rebecca cannot correct.
   C. deepens the reader's understanding of the challenges and rewards the land presents to Rebecca.
   D. invites the reader to draw a parallel between Rebecca and the land itself and perhaps the reader as well.

8. The point of view from which the passage is told can best be described as that of a narrator who:

   F. is aware of what Rebecca is thinking and feeling.
   G. suspects that Rebecca is not sincere in her plans.
   H. is personally involved in the events being described.
   J. is Rebecca's close relative who didn't move.

9. As it is used in line 34, the word *wild* most nearly means:

   A. unconquerable.
   B. unrestrained.
   C. uncultivated.
   D. irrepressible.

10. When Rebecca realized that "a bee landed on her cheek" (line 46), her first response is to:

   F. brush it away from her face.
   G. worry that it might sting her.
   H. hope that it will fly away.
   J. flinch, then try not to respond.

Passage II

SOCIAL SCIENCE: This passage is adapted from the article "Illuminating the Dark Ages" by Krista Correa (©2003 Krista Correa).

The period that began with the fall of the Roman Empire in the fifth century and ended with the Renaissance in the fourteenth century has been referred to by many names: the Medieval period, the Middle Ages, and the Dark Ages. The writer Petrarch
5 coined the latter name in the fourteenth century in an attempt to differentiate the culture of Medieval Europe from his own time. The popular conception at that time was that Europe was finally emerging from a cultural wasteland during which much of the ancient learning had been lost; Petrarch, like many other writers
10 and artists of his time, wanted to connect his studies with those of antiquity, rather than those of more recent years. The name stuck, as did the idea that very little of cultural or intellectual importance took place during the years so described.

Recent scholars have begun to challenge that idea, however,
15 asserting that while it is true that certain fields of study did go into decline during the Middle Ages (the term they prefer), other areas flourished. These historians advocate the more neutral term "Middle Ages" because they feel that it more accurately describes the centuries during which Europe began to transition slowly
20 from a Rome-based, empire-dominated system into the modern states that exist today. According to them, using a negative term like "Dark Ages" serves only to underscore misconceptions about the era. This argument represents a sharp break from the past.

Many scholars have used the term "Dark Ages" to identify
25 the lack of information available about the years between the fall of Rome and the Renaissance. Few written records exist from the early years and the documents that do exist don't always shed a great deal of light on the larger picture of what was happening in Europe. Some scholars, such as William Jordan in his new
30 edition of the *Dictionary of the Middle Ages*, have argued that the term "Dark Ages" needn't be negative—it simply refers to the darkness caused by this lack of information.

That view, however, has been largely discredited. Even when used in a seemingly neutral way, "Dark Ages" has an inherently
35 negative connotation in most people's minds. Moreover, other scholars point out that it is no longer accurate. Research continues to uncover information about the era that allows scholars to gain an ever more accurate idea of what life was like during the Middle Ages, while other research has helped historians gain
40 a better understanding of the evidence they already possessed.

Other scholars have preferred the term "Dark Ages" to describe the decline in learning that they believe to have taken place during this era. These scholars assumed that without the advances of Roman society, learning must have virtually halted.
45 Modern historians such as David Lindberg and Ronald Numbers, however, point out that this view is very far from the truth. Evidence abounds that, although some knowledge was indeed lost, much was retained and that intellectual studies continued throughout the Middle Ages. Their books, such as Lindberg's
50 *Science in the Middle Ages* and Numbers's *Galileo Goes to Jail and Other Myths about Science and Religion*, debunk many popular misconceptions about the Middle Ages, such as that people widely believed the Earth was flat (they didn't) and that they largely abandoned the field of mathematics (they didn't).

55 The goal of scholars such as Lindberg and Numbers is not to idealize the medieval world, or claim that it was filled with light and learning, but rather to balance the overly pessimistic views that are held by so many even today. No one would seriously dispute that, in some areas, learning did go into a decline
60 after the fall of Rome. What modern medievalists, or medieval scholars, would point out is that while some areas diminished, others were able to flourish. For example, three-dimensional, realistic art certainly became less common, and the ability to build a self-sustaining dome was lost for hundreds of years. However,
65 symbolic art developed to such a level that a skilled artist could convey an entire legend in a single picture. Architects in the Middle Ages developed the flying buttress along with some of the most intricate stonework ever seen before or since. The key to understanding the Middle Ages is to avoid making assumptions
70 based on prior assertions or possibly biased historians from the past, and to instead look at what was actually created.

Perhaps it is finally time, then, for the term "Dark Ages" to pass out of not only scholarly but also casual speech. If the goal of historical study is to illuminate, not judge, a descriptive
75 yet neutral term like "Middle Ages" might well serve more effectively. In the meantime, medievalists will continue studying the evidence they have in an attempt to understand the era that saw Western European culture transition into the modern era.

11. In the passage, which of the following scholars most directly contributed to the popularity of the term "Dark Ages"?

A. Jordan
B. Lindberg
C. Petrarch
D. Numbers

12. The passage most directly credits which of the following activities with the ability to flourish during the Middle Ages?

F. The construction of free-standing domes
G. Skilled and detailed stonework
H. Three-dimensional, realistic art
J. The field of mathematics

GO ON TO THE NEXT PAGE.

13. The passage indicates that, contrary to the historians with a traditional view of the Middle Ages, scholars today believe the Middle Ages were:

    A. a transitional period between the classical era and the modern.

    B. an era in which significant scientific discoveries were made.

    C. an epoch that suffered a decline in learning, art, and architecture.

    D. a time when much of the world lived in ignorance.

14. The passage states that an accurate picture of the Middle Ages will likely develop as a result of:

    F. reconsidering existing evidence and discovering new evidence.

    G. relying on written documents from the Renaissance.

    H. new excavations throughout the European countryside.

    J. disregarding all Renaissance accounts.

15. According to the passage, people during the Middle Ages did NOT:

    A. keep written documents.

    B. study advanced mathematics.

    C. know how to carve stone well.

    D. believe the world was flat.

16. The main purpose of the first paragraph (lines 1–13) is to:

    F. compare the advances of the Renaissance and the classical period with the failings of the Middle Ages.

    G. list all of the terms used to describe the period between the fifth and fourth century.

    H. demonstrate that Petrarch and other writers of the Renaissance lived in a cultural wasteland.

    J. introduce the era under discussion and some of the ways it has been described.

17. The passage identifies which of the following as two areas in which learning truly did go into decline during the Middle Ages?

    A. Symbolic art and architecture

    B. Astronomy and mathematics

    C. Dome-building and three-dimensional art

    D. Stonework and science

18. It can reasonably be inferred from the first paragraph (lines 1–13) that Renaissance writers such as Petrarch believed that their work would benefit from:

    F. association with the classical era.

    G. an in-depth study of science.

    H. the creation of a well-educated middle class.

    J. the new culture of the Renaissance.

19. As it is used in line 5, the word *coined* most nearly means:

    A. counterfeited.

    B. plagiarized.

    C. spent.

    D. created.

20. It can reasonably be inferred from the fourth and fifth paragraphs (lines 33–54) that before the work of modern scholars such as Numbers and Lindberg, most people tended to see educational pursuits during the Middle Ages as:

    F. insignificant.

    G. scientific.

    H. advanced.

    J. well-documented.

GO ON TO THE NEXT PAGE.

Passage III

HUMANITIES: This passage is adapted from the article "The Legend of Pocahontas" by Gehring Chester (©2005 Gehring Chester).

One of the most beloved figures from colonial lore, Pocahontas has been featured in countless movies and books. Almost any schoolchild knows her name, but for a variety of reasons, few know her true story. Many writers tend to latch onto false
5 versions of her story, choosing romantic adventure over political reality. Moreover, she didn't leave behind a personal written record, leaving modern historians no choice but to rely on the accounts of others. Whatever the cause, however, the result is the same: Pocahontas remains an enigmatic figure, known by
10 name to most but understood by few.

Many modern retellings of Pocahontas' story focus on her brave rescue of John Smith, the leader of the Jamestown colony. In these retellings, Pocahontas is depicted as an attractive young woman in her late teens or early twenties, involved in a romantic
15 relationship with Smith and defying her father to rescue Smith. This version of events makes for a gripping soap opera—unfortunately, it does not make for accurate history. Interestingly, the written accounts of Smith himself provide the basis for this version. Why he would have falsified the story remains unknown,
20 but few would dispute that he was not an unbiased observer.

Historians cite several reasons to question Smith's version of events. To begin with, most believe Pocahontas was likely a little girl when the rescue took place. The exact date of her birth is unknown, so some speculation is involved in any attempt to
25 specify her age. However, descriptions of her behavior, including cartwheels in the middle of the colonial fort, would indicate a younger child. A younger Pocahontas leads to the next problem: A little girl would hardly have entered into a romance with Smith. In fact, reliable written records indicate that she married another
30 Englishman, John Rolfe, seven years after Smith's rescue.

Perhaps the most problematic part of the legend is the rescue itself. Why would Pocahontas, whether a child or young woman, have risked her own life to save a stranger? If Pocahontas were not Smith's rescuer, why would Smith claim that she was? Most
35 historians today agree that some kind of rescue probably did take place; they disagree, however, as to what the event truly meant. Some argue that it was a literal rescue, while others claim that it was a staged "rescue" with a purely ceremonial meaning. In the end, either explanation still leaves many questions unanswered.

40 A number of recent books have sought to answer these questions and clarify the lives of the participants, with varying degrees of success. Camilla Townsend, author of *Pocahontas and the Powhatan Dilemma*, challenges many of the commonly held beliefs about Pocahontas in a valiant effort to uncover the truth
45 behind the story. Townsend does an admirable job of reviewing what little written evidence exists and paints an engaging portrait of an independent and spirited young woman acting as a bridge between two worlds. Unfortunately, Townsend's unwillingness to fabricate tales to fill in the gaps that inevitably exist leads
50 her to pepper her book liberally with open speculation. While her honesty with regard to her lack of information is preferable to the time-honored tendency to falsify or embrace apocryphal legends, the book leaves the reader wondering whether he or she has really learned anything other than the author's theories.

55 *Love and Hate in Jamestown*, by David A. Price, focuses not on Pocahontas but on John Smith. Price's careful scholarship and vivid writing create a picture of the Jamestown colony that allows the reader to see the characters as real people instead of just historical figures. His discussions of Pocahontas naturally
60 revolve around her encounters with Smith and are based on extensive research into accounts from the period as well as other biographies. Price is careful to note that there was no romance between Pocahontas and Smith but he does accept Smith's account of the rescue with fewer reservations than might be merited.

65 Another interesting take on the legend of Pocahontas can be found in *The True Story of Pocahontas*: *The Other Side of History* by two Native American authors, Dr. Linwood "Little Bear" Custalow and Angela L. Daniel "Silver Star." Rather than relying on European histories, Custalow takes the legend from
70 Powhatan oral traditions, passed down through generations. The historical truth of his version is more difficult to verify, relying as it does on spoken stories instead of written documents, but at the very least it gives a fascinating insight into these mythical figures and may prove to be the key to answering many of the
75 questions that still surround the story of Pocahontas.

21. The passage's author would most likely agree with which of the following statements about the recent books on Pocahontas?

   A. Although none of them is perfect, each adds its own informative perspective on the legend of Pocahontas.

   B. The recent books succeed in filling in the gaps that had previously existed in our knowledge of Pocahontas's life.

   C. The recent biographies only add to the excess of literature on a subject that is now well understood.

   D. The books suffer from a lack of primary sources that ultimately limit their historical usefulness.

22. It can reasonably be inferred that by the mention of "cartwheels" in line 26, the author means to express her:

   F. belief that John Smith's account of events is accurate.

   G. doubt that Pocahontas was as old as previous accounts have suggested.

   H. belief that different viewpoints on historical events can cause confusion.

   J. concern that Pocahontas was too young to understand the rescue of John Smith.

GO ON TO THE NEXT PAGE.

23. The author's comments about Townsend's "unwillingness to fabricate tales" (lines 48–49) about Pocahontas' life most likely indicates that in Townsend's view:

   A. those aspects of Pocahontas's life are less important than those that have been documented.

   B. historical accuracy is more important than is having a fully detailed but potentially inaccurate biography.

   C. the legend of Pocahontas is powerful enough to stand up to scrutiny without additional research.

   D. modern scholarship is too prone to rely on the secondary sources compiled by outside observers.

24. The passage indicates that an accurate account of Pocahontas' life would likely include all of the following EXCEPT:

   F. an encounter with Smith during her youth.

   G. her marriage to Rolfe.

   H. a visit to the colonial fort.

   J. a romantic relationship with Smith.

25. The passage best supports the conclusion that during her initial encounter with Smith, Pocahontas:

   A. was too young to have been involved in rescuing Smith.

   B. performed cartwheels as part of a ritual dance and religious ceremony.

   C. fell in love with Smith, even though he was significantly older than she was.

   D. was a young child who rescued Smith, either literally or ceremonially.

26. According to the passage, which of the following is true about *The True Story of Pocahontas: The Other Side of History*?

   F. It was coauthored by a Native American man and woman.

   G. It is Custalow's first book.

   H. It was applauded by Daniel and Townsend.

   J. It is Custalow's second book about Pocahontas.

27. The passage indicates that in an attempt to clarify the legend of Pocahontas, Custalow:

   A. questioned a number of tribal elders who had been present during Pocahontas's rescue of Smith.

   B. relied on Smith's firsthand accounts of meeting and being rescued by Pocahontas.

   C. analyzed a number of written documents held by the Powhatan people, unknown to European scholars.

   D. told Pocahontas's story as it has been passed down by the oral tradition of the Powhatan tribe.

28. It can most reasonably be inferred that the passage's author believes that, in a historical biography, the regular appearance of "open speculation" or reference to "the author's theories" (lines 50–54) is:

   F. uplifting.

   G. unfortunate.

   H. intelligent.

   J. inevitable.

29. The information in lines 22–30 deals primarily with:

   A. evidence for the author's belief that Smith's version of his rescue might not be entirely accurate.

   B. an attempt to disprove the commonly held theory that Pocahontas and Smith were romantically involved.

   C. the kind of behavior that would have been expected from a Native American girl during the colonial era.

   D. the analysis of an incident at the colonial fort during which Pocahontas performed cartwheels.

30. The passage indicates that scholars are still uncertain as to whether Smith:

   F. wrote about meeting Pocahontas.

   G. was literally rescued by Pocahontas.

   H. married Pocahontas.

   J. met Pocahontas.

GO ON TO THE NEXT PAGE.

Passage IV

NATURAL SCIENCE: This passage is adapted from the article "Does an Amoeba Have a Choice?" by Wilbur Stewart (©2007 Wilbur Stewart).

The question of how much freedom of choice humans exercise has long vexed scientists. Once the model of humans as the only thinking beings on the planet was abandoned, a new model of humans as higher-level animals took its place as the dominant
5 theory. According to the new theory, certain organisms, such as amoebas and plants, act unconsciously, according to almost mechanical impulses. Other organisms, such as dogs or horses, display a certain level of consciousness combined with instinct. Above them all stand humans—maybe not the only thinking
10 beings but still the most highly evolved, exercising "free will" when determining life choices.

Today, however, scientists are beginning to question that model as well. Could it be that much of what we take for conscious decision-making can actually be accounted for biologically? Are
15 we in truth not all that different from animals that act largely out of instinct? How separate are humans, really, from the rest of the natural world?

The human ability to form lasting romantic bonds is one of the primary proofs given in support of free will. Some theorists
20 argue that remaining with a single partner because of an emotional commitment is clearly unnatural and thus a sign of our higher development: social and emotional needs overpowering a base, animal instinct. Evolutionary biologists, however, have recently uncovered evidence that suggests that working as a
25 pair has many evolutionary advantages that may outweigh the disadvantages. Pair-bonding allows one party to remain behind and guard the offspring while the other seeks food and shelter; it increases the odds that an injured party will be cared for and thus survive; it even increases the chances that offspring will live
30 long enough to mature and become self-sufficient. Moreover, recent research seems to indicate that many of the feelings that humans experience when falling in love are in fact biologically motivated and that other animals finding a mate experience similar physical symptoms.

35 The truly staggering aspect of this new realization, however, is that it could extend not only to individuals but also to societies as a whole. If humans are instinctual animals, driven by biological imperatives much of the time, then the interplay between cities and even nations might also be open to biological
40 interpretation. After all, governments are composed of humans. The possible repercussions that such a discovery could have on international relations are truly astonishing. For example, perhaps in time scientists will determine which hormones cause humans to feel friendship, along with a way to administer those hormones
45 to a nation. Decade-long wars could be ended, amicably, in a matter of days.

Still other scientists, mainly chemists and physicists, have asserted that it's not so much that humans are like other animals as that all living things are relatively predictable on a cellular
50 level. Those scientists believe that all human interaction is, on some level, based in the laws of physics. Strange as that may sound at first, it's not as outrageous as it seems. Hormones and other natural chemicals are released in response to some kind of stimulus, causing biological impulses. In order for the body to
55 process those stimuli, however, a whole array of reactions has to take place. At the most basic level, those reactions are caused by cells sending out and responding to electrical impulses. Those electrical impulses become chemical impulses, or neurotransmitters, which eventually trigger biological impulses. All matter is
60 made up of protons, neutrons, and electrons, so by extension, all matter reacts to electrical impulses on some level. Advocates of the electro-chemical theory claim that studies involving large groups of people demonstrate their point most effectively. Human interaction can be compared to the interaction between differ-
65 ent particles—some are attracted to each other while others are repulsed, while the whole mass moves as a single entity. If it's true that group interactions can be compared to the mingling of different particles, then an entirely new background could be created against which national and international dynamics could
70 be newly considered.

One practical example of the convergence of scientific theory and human practice is the increasing involvement of scientists in the arena of criminal pursuit. Many police departments have realized that human behavior, even in flight, is startlingly pre-
75 dictable, if one knows how to find the patterns. That's where the academics come in; they're hired to look at the data accumulated by detectives and apply their knowledge of science to the case, trying to identify patterns. These academics consider the behavior of other animals, but they also compare the data to the movement
80 of particles and perform complex mathematical calculations. And, more often than might be expected, they help solve the cases.

31. According to the author of the passage, "free will" describes behavior such as:

   A. falling in love by a series of natural and biological processes.
   B. the study of pattern behavior to understand criminal behavior.
   C. the choice of one mate based on a mutual emotional connection.
   D. group efforts by all members of a city to improve that city.

GO ON TO THE NEXT PAGE.

32. Based on the passage, what relationship does the recent discovery described in the third paragraph (lines 30–34) have to the electro-chemical theory?

    F. It directly supports the electro-chemical theory.
    G. It supports another theory that is connected to the electro-chemical theory.
    H. It undermines the central claims of the electro-chemical theory.
    J. It is unrelated to the electro-chemical theory.

33. The author characterizes scientific contributions to police work as:

    A. charming but ultimately useless.
    B. mundane but logically unconvincing.
    C. alarming but theoretically persuasive.
    D. new and potentially helpful.

34. The supporters of the electro-chemical theory claim that humans are like particles in that both:

    F. are ultimately driven to action by biological impulses.
    G. are potentially capable of conscious decision-making.
    H. can more adequately be understood in groups than individually.
    J. respond to outside stimuli without intermediate thought.

35. In terms of where and how frequently they occur, electrical impulses are described by the author of the passage as:

    A. possible in humans and animals but not in other types of matter.
    B. common to humans, animals, and other types of matter.
    C. present in cellular interactions but absent from human interactions.
    D. the basis of a theory of group activity for non-human matter.

36. The chemists and physicists define biological impulses as:

    F. apparently unconnected to decisions based in free will.
    G. apparently central to whether humans exercise free will.
    H. the basis for chemical impulses, which in turn cause electrical impulses.
    J. caused by chemical impulses, which are caused by electrical impulses.

37. Lines 26–30 are best characterized as describing an explanation that:

    A. slowly developed as the primary method of childrearing among all higher-level organisms.
    B. rapidly emerged as the leading cause of the successful evolution of lower-level animals.
    C. alternatively offers a reason for behavior that had previously been attributed to free will.
    D. recently undermined the traditional belief that human behavior was biologically motivated.

38. The main point of the sixth paragraph (lines 71–81) is that:

    F. the new theories discussed in the passage have been put into practice effectively in at least one field.
    G. recent research has indicated that academic theories tend to be difficult to put into practice.
    H. academic theories can be evaluated more fully when they are put into practice.
    J. police work has relied on academic help since before the debates over free will.

39. The passage states that in response to the suggestion that the tendency to remain with a single mate demonstrates humanity's free will, evolutionary biologists:

    A. added several new elements to their theory.
    B. accepted that their initial idea was deeply flawed.
    C. redefined the term "free will" to fit their theory.
    D. suggested an alternative interpretation of pair-bonding.

40. Lines 12–17 mainly emphasize what quality?

    F. Confidence
    G. Uncertainty
    H. Ignorance
    J. Contentment

END OF TEST 3

STOP! DO NOT TURN THE PAGE UNTIL TOLD TO DO SO.

DO NOT RETURN TO A PREVIOUS TEST.

SCIENCE TEST

35 Minutes–40 Questions

DIRECTIONS: There are seven passages in this test. Each passage is followed by several questions. After reading a passage, choose the best answer to each question and fill in the corresponding oval on your answer document. You may refer to the passages as often as necessary.

You are NOT permitted to use a calculator on this test.

Passage I

The apoptotic index (*AI*) for a group of dividing cells is calculated as follows:

$$AI = \frac{\text{number of cells undergoing } apoptosis \text{ (cell death)}}{\text{total number of cells}}$$

Figure 1 shows the *AI* for a culture of fibroblast cells as a function of the surrounding concentration in parts per million (ppm) of a cell toxin.

One thousand actively dividing fibroblast cells in culture were studied. Figure 2 shows the distribution of the cells in each of the stages of the dividing cell cycle.

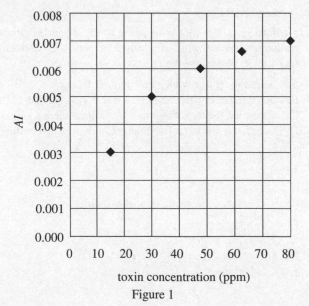

toxin concentration (ppm)

Figure 1

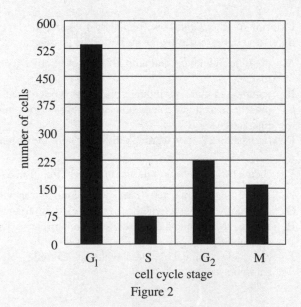

cell cycle stage

Figure 2

GO ON TO THE NEXT PAGE.

Electron micrographs were taken of the fibroblasts in culture. Figure 3 shows an example of cells in each of the 4 stages of the dividing cell cycle. Although the cells are not arranged in the sequence of the cell cycle, each stage is shown only once.

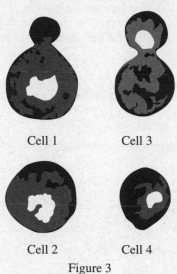

Cell 1   Cell 3

Cell 2   Cell 4

Figure 3

1. Which cell in Figure 3 is most likely in the stage of the cell cycle during which cytokinesis is occurring as mitosis nears completion?

   A. Cell 1
   B. Cell 2
   C. Cell 3
   D. Cell 4

2. Based on Figure 1, of the fibroblast cells that are surrounded by a toxin concentration of 90 ppm, the percent that are in apoptosis most likely is represented by which of the following ranges?

   F. Less than 0.5%
   G. Between 0.5% and 0.6%
   H. Between 0.6% and 0.7%
   J. Greater than 0.7%

3. Which of the following cells in Figure 3 is most likely in the first stage of the actively dividing cell cycle?

   A. Cell 1
   B. Cell 2
   C. Cell 3
   D. Cell 4

4. According to Figure 2, how did the number of fibroblast cells in stage G_2 compare with the number of cells in stage S? The number in G_2 was approximately:

   F. 2 times as great as the number in S.

   G. 3 times as great as the number in S.

   H. $\frac{1}{2}$ as great as the number in S.

   J. $\frac{1}{3}$ as great as the number in S.

5. Based on Figure 2, of the fibroblast cells that were in the actively dividing cell cycle, the proportion that were in G_1 is closest to which of the following?

   A. $\frac{540}{1000}$

   B. $\frac{300}{540}$

   C. $\frac{1000}{540}$

   D. $\frac{540}{300}$

GO ON TO THE NEXT PAGE.

Passage II

A *polymorphism* is the persistent occurrence of different appearances for a particular trait in a species. All humans have slight differences in their *genotypes* (genetic code) that result in different *phenotypes* (observable characteristics). Genetic polymorphisms are persistent variations in gene sequences at a particular location in chromosomes, such as those accounting for different blood types. Variations that cannot be observed with the naked eye require techniques such as *capillary electrophoresis* (the separation of genetic or protein material based on charge characteristics using an electric field).

The label on a vial of blood from a hospital patient was lost. The sample just tested positive for a disease of the blood protein hemoglobin that is very common in the hospital population. The sample was traced to a room with 4 patients who were subsequently tested to determine the source of the initial vial.

Tests and Results

Smears of the blood from the unidentified patient (P) and from the 4 newly tested patients (1–4) were observed under the microscope for the appearance of the blood cells. Results are shown in Table 1.

Table 1	
Patient	Blood smear findings
P	Sickle cells
1	Target cells
2	Sickle cells
3	Normal blood cells
4	Sickle cells

Serum was isolated from the blood of Patient P and from Patients 1–4 and placed in separate tubes. A buffer was added to each vial to establish a pH of 8.6. One at a time, samples from each tube were injected into the capillary electrophoresis device set at 7.5 kilovolts (kV) to separate the types of hemoglobin present into peaks. The hemoglobin proteins composing a peak had similar charge characteristics. Figure 1 shows the peaks that resulted from all 5 samples.

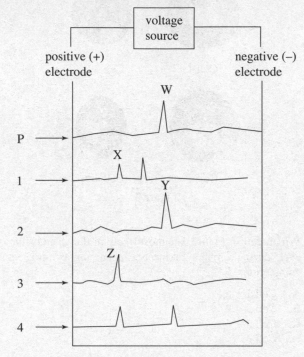

Note: Each peak is made up of hemoglobin proteins. W, X, Y, and Z are 4 specific peaks.

Figure 1

GO ON TO THE NEXT PAGE.

6. Are the data in Table 1 consistent with the hypothesis that Patient 4 and Patient P are the same person?

   F. Yes; Patient 4 has the same blood cell appearance as Patient P.
   G. Yes; Patient 4 has different blood cell appearance as Patient P.
   H. No; Patient 4 has the same blood cell appearance as Patient P.
   J. No; Patient 4 has different blood cell appearance as Patient P.

7. What is the most likely reason that the serum samples were treated with a buffer to bring pH to 8.6 ?

   A. Hemoglobin protein breaks down at that pH.
   B. All bacteria and viruses are destroyed at that pH.
   C. Capillary electrophoresis separation of hemoglobin functions best at that pH.
   D. Capillary electrophoresis separation of hemoglobin does not function at that pH.

8. Sickle cell anemia is caused by certain hemoglobin genotype combinations of 3 different alleles. The Hb^A allele is responsible for normal hemoglobin, the Hb^S allele is responsible for one variant that results in sickle cells, and the Hb^C allele is responsible for a different variant also resulting in sickle cells. Based on Table 1, the genotype of Patient 4 could be which of the following?

   I. $Hb^A\ Hb^A$
   II. $Hb^A\ Hb^S$
   III. $Hb^A\ Hb^C$

   F. II only
   G. I or III only
   H. II or III only
   J. I, II, or III

9. According to Figure 1, the pattern of protein peaks produced by serum from Patient P most closely resembles the pattern produced by the serum sample from:

   A. Patient 1.
   B. Patient 2.
   C. Patient 3.
   D. Patient 4.

10. Based on Figure 1, the hemoglobin proteins in which of the following 2 peaks were most likely closest in charge characteristic?

    F. W and X
    G. W and Z
    H. X and Y
    J. X and Z

11. During the capillary electrophoresis, all the hemoglobin proteins started with some quantity of charge before migrating from left to right in Figure 1. Therefore, the proteins resulting in peaks furthest to the left must have been the most:

    A. negative, as opposite charges attract each other.
    B. negative, as opposite charges repel each other.
    C. positive, as opposite charges attract each other.
    D. positive, as opposite charges repel each other.

GO ON TO THE NEXT PAGE.

Passage III

To help design a carnival game, bowling balls at rest on the ground are launched along a track by a constant force spring apparatus as shown in Figure 1.

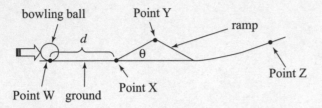

Figure 1

To win the game, the ball must pass Point Y but not Point Z. A total of 5 trials were done to determine the best design. For each combination of ball friction coefficient, μ, and ramp angle, θ, Point W was put at a distance, d, from Point X such that the ball will just barely reach Point Z before rolling back toward the ramp.

The ball's kinetic energy (KE) at Points X and Y along with its potential energy (PE) at Point Y are shown in joules (J) in Table 1 for each trial. The mechanical energy (ME) of the ball at any given point is the sum of its kinetic and potential energies. It should remain constant provided no energy is lost in the form of heat from friction or drag forces.

				Kinetic energy (J)		Potential energy (J) Point Y
Trial	μ	θ (°)	d (cm)	Point X	Point Y	
1	0.2	20	50	28.1	17.5	6.7
2	0.2	30	50	28.1	14.3	9.8
3	0.2	40	50	28.1	11.6	12.6
4	0.25	40	30	29.1	11.6	12.6
5	0.3	40	17	30.0	11.6	12.6

Table 1

GO ON TO THE NEXT PAGE.

12. Which of the following ranks Points X, Y, and Z from where the bowling ball had the slowest velocity to where the bowling ball had the fastest velocity during any trial?

- **F.** Point X, Point Y, Point Z
- **G.** Point X, Point Z, Point Y
- **H.** Point Z, Point X, Point Y
- **J.** Point Z, Point Y, Point X

13. In Trial 4, at the point immediately before climbing the ramp, the bowling ball's *ME* was closest to which of the following?

- **A.** 0 J
- **B.** 11.6 J
- **C.** 24.2 J
- **D.** 29.1 J

14. Based on the results of Trials 1–3, if an additional trial is performed with $\mu = 0.2$ and $\theta = 50°$, *PE* at Point Y will most likely be:

- **F.** greater than 12.6 J.
- **G.** between 9.8 J and 12.6 J.
- **H.** between 6.7 J and 9.8 J.
- **J.** less than 6.7 J.

15. The results of Trials 3–5 indicate that as the coefficient of friction increases, the minimum distance of Point W from Point X required for the bowling ball to barely reach Point Z:

- **A.** only increases.
- **B.** only decreases.
- **C.** remains the same.
- **D.** varies, but with no general trend.

16. The law of conservation of energy states that the total amount of energy in an isolated system remains constant. In which of the trials, if any, was mechanical energy transformed to heat energy?

- **F.** Only Trial 1
- **G.** Only Trial 5
- **H.** All trials had mechanical to heat energy transfers.
- **J.** No trials had mechanical to heat energy transfers.

GO ON TO THE NEXT PAGE.

Passage IV

Carboxylic acids are organic compounds containing a *carboxyl* (–COOH) group. These molecules are acidic since they are able to donate protons in solution. The acidity and other physical properties of carboxylic acids are affected by the composition of the atoms bound to the carboxyl group. Table 1 lists the freezing points and boiling points for several carboxylic acids.

Table 1			
Formula	Name	Freezing point (°C)	Boiling point (°C)
CHOOH	Formic acid	8.4	101
CH$_3$COOH	Acetic acid	16.6	118
CH$_3$CH$_2$COOH	Propionic acid	−20.8	141
CH$_3$(CH$_2$)$_2$COOH	Butyric acid	-5.5	164
CH$_3$(CH$_2$)$_3$COOH	Valeric acid	−34.5	186

Figure 1 shows how the vapor pressure (in mm Hg) of 3 carboxylic acids changes as a function of temperature.

Figure 2 shows how the vapor pressure of the same 3 carboxylic acids changes as a function of concentration when mixed with water at 20°C.

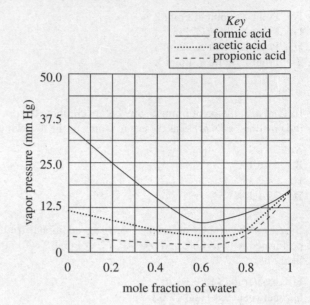

Figure 2

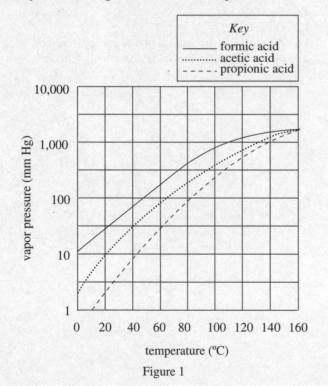

Figure 1

17. Which of the carboxylic acids listed in Table 1 has the *highest* melting point?

A. Propionic acid
B. Valeric acid
C. Acetic acid
D. Formic acid

GO ON TO THE NEXT PAGE.

18. According to Figure 2, the vapor pressure of a 0.5 mole fraction solution of water in formic acid is closest to the vapor pressure of which of the following water in formic acid solutions?

   F.   0.9 mole fraction
   G. 0.8 mole fraction
   H. 0.6 mole fraction
   J.   0.4 mole fraction

19. According to Figure 2, as the mole fraction of water in an acetic acid and water solution increases from 0 to 1, the vapor pressure:

   A. decreases, then increases.
   B. increases, then decreases.
   C. decreases only.
   D. increases only.

20. $CH_3(CH_2)_4COOH$ is the chemical formula for the carboxylic acid named hexanoic acid. Based on Table 1, this compound most likely boils at a temperature:

   F. lower than 160°C.
   G. between 200°C and 220°C.
   H. between 220°C and 240°C.
   J. higher than 240°C.

21. According to Figure 1, does acetic acid or formic acid resist vaporization more at 60°C ?

   A. Formic acid, because formic acid has the lower vapor pressure.
   B. Formic acid, because formic acid has the higher vapor pressure.
   C. Acetic acid, because acetic acid has the lower vapor pressure.
   D. Acetic acid, because acetic acid has the higher vapor pressure.

GO ON TO THE NEXT PAGE.

Passage V

A solenoid is a device that creates a magnetic field from electric current and can be used to exert a force on a nearby bar magnet to activate a mechanical device.

Scientists performed experiments on the solenoid apparatus shown in Figure 1.

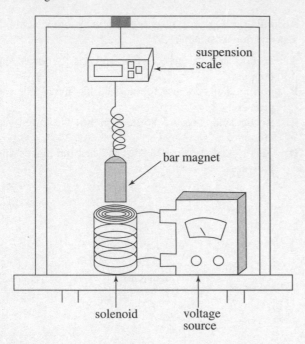

Figure 1

A wire carrying current from a voltage source was coiled into a hollow cylinder to form a solenoid with a length of XY. A solid cylinder bar magnet was suspended near the top of the solenoid as shown in Figure 2.

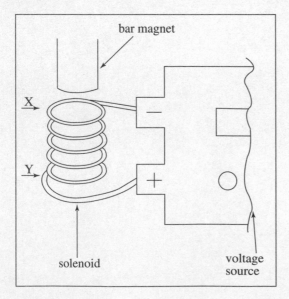

Figure 2

When the voltage source was turned on, the solenoid exerted a measurable force on the suspended bar magnet.

The bar magnet was attached to a digital suspension scale that measured weight in newtons (N). With the voltage source off, the scale read 4.7 N. Prior to the start of each experimental trial, the scale was adjusted to read 5.0000 N.

Experiment 1

The scientists applied various levels of voltage in volts (V) to the circuit and recorded the weight indicated by the suspension scale for each trial. Results were recorded in Table 1.

Table 1	
Voltage (V)	Weight (N)
7.25	5.0078
8.00	5.0095
8.75	5.0113

Experiment 2

The scientists removed the bar magnet, inverted it, and reattached it to the suspension scale so that the opposite end was now facing the solenoid. The procedures of Experiment 1 were repeated and results were recorded in Table 2.

Table 2	
Voltage (V)	Weight (N)
7.25	4.9922
8.00	4.9905
8.75	4.9887

Experiment 3

The bar magnet was returned to the original alignment it was in during Experiment 1. The length XY of the solenoid coil was varied while a voltage of 8.00 V was applied to the circuit. Weights were recorded in Table 3.

Table 3	
Solenoid length XY (cm)	Weight (N)
9.50	5.0105
8.50	5.0131
7.50	5.0169

GO ON TO THE NEXT PAGE.

22. Based on the results of Experiments 1 and 3, the length XY of the solenoid coil in Experiment 1 was most likely:

F. shorter than 7.50 cm.
G. between 7.50 cm and 8.50 cm.
H. between 8.50 cm and 9.50 cm.
J. longer than 9.50 cm.

23. In Experiments 1 and 2, the orientation of the bar magnet relative to the solenoid opening determined which of the following?

A. Solenoid length XY
B. Direction of the force exerted by the solenoid on the bar magnet
C. Density of the bar magnet
D. Magnetic field strength of the solenoid

24. Which of the following provides the best explanation for the results of Experiment 3 ? The force exerted on the bar magnet by the solenoid magnetic field:

F. decreased as the voltage applied to the circuit decreased.
G. increased as the voltage applied to the circuit decreased.
H. decreased as the length XY of the solenoid decreased.
J. increased as the length XY of the solenoid decreased.

25. Suppose the scientists maintained the same bar magnet orientation in Experiment 3 as in Experiment 2. Based on the results of Experiments 1 and 2, with the solenoid length XY equal to 9.50 cm, the weight on the scale would most likely have been:

A. 5.0169
B. 5.0105
C. 4.9895
D. 4.9831

26. Prior to all experiments, the suspension scale was calibrated to read exactly 0 N when nothing was attached. Once the bar magnet was attached, the scientists made which of the following adjustments to the scale reading for each of the experimental trials?

F. The displayed weight was adjusted downward by approximately 1.3 N.
G. The displayed weight was adjusted upward by approximately 1.3 N.
H. The displayed weight was adjusted downward by approximately 0.3 N.
J. The displayed weight was adjusted upward by approximately 0.3 N.

27. Which of the following graphs best depicts the results of Experiment 3 ?

A.
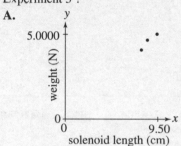

B.
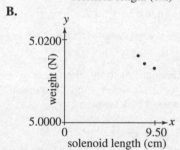

C.
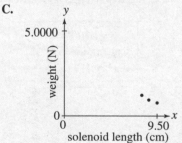

D.
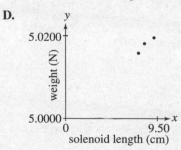

GO ON TO THE NEXT PAGE.

Passage VI

Average global temperature is influenced by multiple different factors and has gone through significant changes throughout the history of the earth.

Global temperature affects Earth's oceans. In general, as the average global temperature increases, glacial and continental ice coverage decreases from melting. This combined with the thermal expansion of the oceans results in rising sea levels. The sea level present at any given time over the past 150,000 years can be estimated from sedimentary rock layer analysis. Figure 1 shows for the years listed the difference in average global sea level compared to what has been the average temperature value from 1961 through 1990.

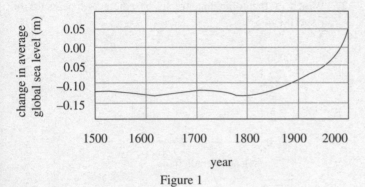

Figure 1

Figure 1 adapted from "Intergovernmental Panel on Climate Change Fourth Assessment Report 2007."

Figure 2 shows the change in both the average global temperature and average global sea level from the present. The change in average global sea level is determined by:

(average global sea level at a given time) –

(current average global sea level)

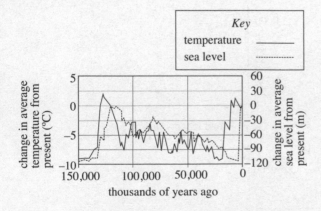

Figure 2

Figure 2 adapted from Petit et al. "Climate and atmospheric history of the past 420,000 years from the Vostok ice core," *Antarctica. Nature* 399: 429–436.

Two scientists discuss why the average global sea level has risen over the past 100 years.

Scientist 1

Rising sea levels are a direct result of widespread industrial burning of fossil fuels that started in the mid-19th century. This activity caused the release of greenhouse gases like carbon dioxide, which raised the average global temperature. This increase in temperature led to depleted ice coverage and rapid thermal expansion of oceans. Figure 1 shows that global sea level was essentially constant until approximately 1900 and has since risen to a level higher than at any time in the past 150,000 years. Between 1950 and 2000, global average sea level rose by 0.1 m as global temperature rose approximately 0.5°C. Since 2000 the change in global average sea level has increased at a rate of 2% per year.

Scientist 2

Rises and falls in the global average sea level occurred many times in the past 150,000 years and well before the industrial revolution of the mid-1800s. In general, global average sea level rises and falls with global average temperature, as shown in Figure 2. Industrial activity did not begin until the 1800s and could not have been responsible for the changes in average global temperature and sea level before that time. The recent rise in sea level in response to global temperature is not significantly different from those before 1800, so human activity does not by itself have a measurable effect on average global sea level.

28. According to Figure 2, over which of the following time intervals did the average global sea level increase more than 100 times as much as Scientist 1 claims it did between 1950 and 2000 ?

   F. Between 130,000 and 120,000 years ago
   G. Between 80,000 and 70,000 years ago
   H. Between 50,000 and 30,000 years ago
   J. Between 40,000 and 20,000 years ago

29. Which of the following statements about average global temperature would most likely be supported by Scientist 2 ?

   A. Average global temperature has remained essentially constant for the past 150,000 years.
   B. Average global temperature is changed only by widespread industrial activity.
   C. As the average global temperature decreases, average global sea level decreases.
   D. As the average global temperature decreases, average global sea level increases.

GO ON TO THE NEXT PAGE.

30. According to Scientist 1, the change in average global sea level has been increasing at a constant rate since 2000. Given the change in sea level given in Figure 1 for the year 2000, Scientist 1 would most likely conclude that the average global sea level change for the year 2003 was closest to which of the following?

    F. .046 m
    G. .048 m
    H. .051 m
    J. .053 m

31. Scientist 1 states that average global sea level is currently higher than at any point in the past 150,000 years. Does Figure 1 provide sufficient basis for this statement?

    A. No; Figure 1 shows the change in average global sea level for the past 500 years only.
    B. No; Figure 1 shows the change in average global sea level for the past 150,000 years.
    C. Yes; Figure 1 shows the change in average global sea level for the past 500 years only.
    D. Yes; Figure 1 shows the change in average global sea level for the past 150,000 years.

32. Assume that the current average sea level at a particular location is measured at 90 m above a fixed geographic landmark. Given Figure 2, the two scientists would most likely claim that 100,000 years ago, the average sea level above the same mark at that location was closest to which of the following?

    F. 120 m
    G. 100 m
    H. 60 m
    J. 30 m

33. Suppose Scientist 2 stated that there have been times over the past 150,000 years when average global sea level has been the same as what it is today. To support this claim, Scientist 2 would most likely cite the sea level data in Figure 2 for which of the following times?

    A. 50,000 years ago
    B. 65,000 years ago
    C. 115,000 years ago
    D. 130,000 years ago

34. Given Figure 1, Scientist 1 would most likely claim that from 1500 to 1800, average global temperature:

    F. varied by less than 1°C, remaining essentially constant.
    G. varied by 1°C.
    H. increased by more than 1°C.
    J. decreased by more than 1°C.

GO ON TO THE NEXT PAGE.

Passage VII

The force per unit area resulting from the separation of solutions of different concentrations by a selectively permeable membrane is called *osmotic pressure*. Molecules, including water, have a tendency to move from regions of high concentration to regions of low concentration. Selectively permeable membranes act as filters, only allowing molecules below a certain threshold size to pass through. Osmotic pressure is the pressure required to stop water from moving across such a membrane from a region of high to low water concentration.

Cupric ions (Cu_2+) and glucose were dissolved separately in equal volumes of water to make two solutions. The glucose solution was more dilute, meaning that it had a higher percentage of water molecules than the cupric ion solution. Of the three molecules used for the solutions, water is the smallest and glucose is the largest. Water and glucose solutions are colorless while cupric ion solutions are blue. However, mixing glucose and cupric ions results in a red solution.

Experiment 1

A U-shaped tube contains a selectively permeable membrane, dividing it into equal halves. Glucose solution is poured in the left and an equal volume of cupric ion solution is poured in the right. Over 2 hours, the water level fell on the left and rose on the right. At this time, the left-sided solution was red and the right-sided was blue.

Experiment 2

Cupric ion solution is poured in the left and an equal volume of pure water is poured in the right. Over 2 hours, the water level fell on the right and rose on the left. At this time, both sides of the tube contained blue-colored solutions.

Experiment 3

Glucose solution is poured in the left and an equal volume of pure water is poured in the right. Over 2 hours, the water level fell on the right and rose on the left. At this time, both sides of the tube contained colorless solutions.

35. Albumin molecules do not pass through the selectively permeable membrane used in Experiments 1–3 and form clear solutions in water. If Experiment 2 were repeated, but the left side was filled with an albumin solution, the solution levels would:

   A. fall on the left and rise on the right, resulting in a left-sided red solution and right-sided clear solution.
   B. fall on the right and rise on the left, resulting in red solutions on both sides.
   C. fall on the left and rise on the right, resulting in red solutions on both sides.
   D. fall on the right and rise on the left, resulting in clear solutions on both sides.

36. In Experiments 1 and 2, cupric ion particles were able to move:

   F. through the membrane into both the glucose solution and pure water.
   G. through neither membrane into neither the glucose solution nor the pure water.
   H. only through the membrane separating it from the glucose solution.
   J. only through the membrane separating it from pure water.

37. In Experiments 2 and 3, what did the left side of the U-tube contain at the start of the experiment?

	Experiment 2	Experiment 3
A.	Cupric ion solution	Pure water
B.	Glucose solution	Pure water
C.	Cupric ion solution	Glucose solution
D.	Glucose solution	Cupric ion solution

38. In Experiment 1, if the selectively permeable membrane allowed cupric ions, glucose, and water molecules all to pass, how would the results have differed, if at all?

   F. The water level would have fallen on the right and risen on the left.
   G. A red color would have appeared on both sides of the U-tube.
   H. A blue color would have appeared on both sides of the U-tube.
   J. The same results would have been observed.

GO ON TO THE NEXT PAGE.

39. After watching Experiment 1 only, an observer asserted that since the left-sided solution ended up red, cupric ions must be bigger than water molecules. Is this a valid assertion?

A. No; the results show only that cupric ions and water molecules are smaller than glucose molecules.

B. No; the results show only that cupric ions and water molecules are larger than glucose molecules.

C. Yes; the results show that water molecules but not cupric ions can pass through the selectively permeable membrane.

D. Yes; the results show that both water molecules and cupric ions can pass through the selectively permeable membrane.

40. In Experiment 1, before the molecules began to move relative to the semi-permeable membrane, the appearance of the right-sided solution in the U-tube was:

F. clear.

G. blue.

H. red.

J. purple.

END OF TEST 4

STOP! DO NOT RETURN TO ANY OTHER TEST.

Chapter 32
Practice Exam 4:
Answers
and Explanations

English		Math		Reading		Science	
1. C	39. D	1. D	31. C	1. B	21. A	1. C	21. C
2. F	40. G	2. G	32. G	2. J	22. G	2. J	22. J
3. A	41. B	3. D	33. C	3. A	23. B	3. D	23. B
4. J	42. J	4. K	34. G	4. G	24. J	4. G	24. J
5. B	43. B	5. A	35. B	5. A	25. D	5. A	25. C
6. G	44. G	6. H	36. J	6. H	26. F	6. F	26. J
7. A	45. C	7. C	37. D	7. C	27. D	7. C	27. B
8. J	46. J	8. K	38. H	8. F	28. G	8. H	28. F
9. D	47. B	9. B	39. E	9. C	29. A	9. B	29. C
10. H	48. F	10. K	40. G	10. J	30. G	10. J	30. J
11. C	49. A	11. B	41. D	11. C	31. C	11. A	31. A
12. F	50. J	12. F	42. H	12. G	32. G	12. J	32. J
13. D	51. A	13. D	43. A	13. A	33. D	13. D	33. C
14. G	52. H	14. K	44. J	14. F	34. F	14. F	34. F
15. B	53. B	15. A	45. C	15. D	35. B	15. B	35. D
16. G	54. G	16. F	46. K	16. J	36. J	16. H	36. F
17. C	55. A	17. B	47. C	17. C	37. C	17. C	37. C
18. J	56. J	18. J	48. J	18. F	38. F	18. G	38. G
19. D	57. C	19. D	49. E	19. D	39. D	19. A	39. A
20. G	58. H	20. K	50. F	20. F	40. G	20. G	40. G
21. A	59. C	21. E	51. C				
22. F	60. G	22. G	52. J				
23. A	61. B	23. A	53. D				
24. G	62. J	24. G	54. F				
25. C	63. A	25. D	55. B				
26. J	64. H	26. F	56. J				
27. B	65. D	27. C	57. E				
28. H	66. G	28. H	58. K				
29. C	67. C	29. A	59. A				
30. H	68. G	30. G	60. H				
31. C	69. A						
32. H	70. J						
33. D	71. A						
34. F	72. H						
35. A	73. B						
36. F	74. F						
37. C	75. C						
38. F							

ENGLISH TEST

1. **C** Read carefully! This question asks for the alternative that would NOT be acceptable. In this case, (C), *so that to win 26 World Series championships,* cannot work in the context, so (C) is the only possible answer.

2. **F** There is STOP punctuation in the answer choices, so use the Vertical Line Test! The idea before the line *The Yankees have had many great baseball players* is complete, but the idea after the line *contribute to the team, but one man stands out for his fortitude and good spirit: Lou Gehrig* is not. This eliminates (G). Then, if you can't cite a reason to use a comma, don't use one: In this case, no further punctuation or additional words are necessary, making (F) the best answer.

3. **A** Use POE. Choice (B) creates an incomplete idea, so it can be eliminated. Choice (C) switches to the passive voice and makes things unnecessarily wordy. Choice (D) changes the meaning of the sentence to nonsense. Only (A) works in the context.

4. **J** Read carefully! This question asks for the alternative that would be LEAST acceptable. In this case, (J), *A Yankee scout had seen an intercollegiate game and played Gehrig,* changes the meaning, so it would be the LEAST acceptable alternative in this context.

5. **B** If you cannot cite a reason to use a comma, don't use one. The only required comma comes at the end of the underlined portion as it sets off the unnecessary information *including those for runs batted in and extra-base hits.* Choice (B) is the only answer with the correct number of commas.

6. **G** Read the question carefully. It asks for a word that *most clearly communicates how positively Gehrig was viewed as a player.* The most positive word among the choices is *impressed,* so (G) must be the correct answer.

7. **A** Use a comma after an introductory idea. In this case, *Then suddenly* provides just such an introductory idea, so there should be a comma after the word *suddenly,* eliminating (B) and (C). Then, *Gehrig's* should be possessive because the *stamina* belongs to him, making (A) the correct answer.

8. **J** Pick the odd man out! The words *infer* and *speculate* mean essentially the same thing. The word *imply* cannot work as it changes the meaning, making (J) the LEAST acceptable alternative to the underlined portion. *Infer* means to deduce or interpret; *imply* means to suggest. This sports writer is *inferring* Gehrig's illness from Gehrig's slowed performance, but Gehrig's slowed performance *implies* that he is ill.

9. **D** *The prognosis* referred to in Sentence 1 must come after Sentence 3, which previews Gehrig's illness. Only (D) puts these two sentences in the appropriate order.

10. **H** Although *would of* and *would have* sound very similar, the correct form is *would have,* thus eliminating (F) and (G). Then, the past participle of *to withdraw* is *withdrawn.* If the word *have* were not there, *withdrew* would be acceptable, but this is not an option. The best answer is therefore (H).

11. **C** This entire passage is about Lou Gehrig, and the author's personal experience does not play a role at all. Therefore, this sentence about the narrator's experience with his dog does not contribute to the flow of the passage and should be eliminated. Choice (C) correctly states that the sentence should not be added and gives the correct reason it should not.

12. **F** The underlined portion refers to the *retirement* belonging to *Gehrig*, or *Gehrig's retirement*, eliminating (H) and (J). Then, if you can't cite a reason to use a comma, don't use one. There's no reason to use one here, so (G) can be eliminated, and the best answer is (F).

13. **D** Choose the quotation that supports the words in the first part of the sentence, *paid tribute to the life-affirming support he'd received from his fans.* Choice (D) acknowledges this support, whereas the others discuss other topics.

14. **G** The sentence could be rewritten to say *his eternal optimism. Whose* must therefore be the possessive, not the contraction *who's*, which can be expanded to *who is*. Choice (G) is the only one among the choices that gives the correct possessive form.

15. **B** The phrase comes at the beginning of the passage, which discusses the Yankees and the team's long tradition of success. The inclusion of the year *1913* helps to set the stage for the emergence of Lou Gehrig, who is the main subject of this essay, so the opening phrase should be kept.

16. **G** There is no contrast in this sentence, so there is no need for a word that suggests any such contrast. The best answer is therefore also the shortest, (G).

17. **C** Read the question carefully. It asks for a choice that *identifies a personal connection the narrator feels to the locations she visits.* Choice (C) is the best of the bunch: It has a positive tone and gives the narrator's personal spin on the places she visits.

18. **J** Read the question carefully. It asks for a choice that *reinforces...the relationship between the narrator and her grandmother.* Choice (J) is the only one among those listed that mentions both people, so it must be the correct answer.

19. **D** The narrator is discussing *her* trips. Nothing belongs to those trips, so there's no need for an apostrophe. Then, if you can't cite a reason to use a comma, don't use one. Choice (D), with no punctuation at all, is the best answer.

20. **G** The description of the cold weather conditions in this phrase helps to explain why the narrator was *shivering with George Washington*, so it should be kept. The passage as a whole is focused on travel, not history, so (G) gives a better reason the phrase should be kept.

21. **A** The second sentence of this paragraph states, *This is for you*, so some gift or item must be given in the first sentence. Choice (A) is the only one in which such a gift or item is given, so (A) is the only possible answer.

22. **F** Use POE on answers that don't have a clear meaning. Choice (G) is too wordy and changes the intended meaning of the sentence. Choices (H) and (J) don't make sense in the given context, so the sentence must be correct as written, as (F) suggests.

23. **A** If each answer says essentially the same thing, choose the shortest that makes sense in the context. In this case, (B) and (C) add unnecessary words, so they can be eliminated. Without the word *and*, however, the sentence becomes two complete ideas separated by a comma, which does not work either. Choice (A) is the shortest answer that preserves the grammatical correctness of the sentence.

24. **G** As written, the sentence creates a comma splice: a comma separating two complete ideas. The other choices correct this mistake, but only (G) makes sense in the given context.

25. **C** Whenever you see STOP punctuation, use the Vertical Line Test! The first idea, *I was so excited when the first three were released*, is complete, but the second, *Delaware, Pennsylvania, and New Jersey*, is not. Choice (B), which contains STOP punctuation, cannot work, but there must be some kind of punctuation between these ideas. The best comes in the form of the colon, as in (C), which is appropriate after a complete idea and before a list.

26. **J** Note the 3-1 split! Choices (F), (G), and (H) contain STOP punctuation. Choice (J) contains GO punctuation, so the odd man out must be correct. In addition, a comma would NOT be acceptable because the ideas surrounding it are both complete.

27. **B** All four answers say essentially the same thing and are grammatically correct, so choose the shortest that makes sense. In this case, the word *admiring* says everything the other answer choices do, and it does so in a single word, so (B) is the best answer.

28. **H** Choices (F), (G), and (J) all create comma splices in that they separate complete ideas with commas rather than some form of STOP punctuation. Only (H) fixes this error.

29. **C** Read the question carefully. It asks for a choice that *best makes a connection between the narrator's view of history and that of her friends*. The only answer that mentions both the narrator and her friends is (C). Choice (D) is close, but it doesn't mention the narrator at all.

30. **H** While *curious, anxious,* and *nervous* might mean the same thing in some contexts, in this context, *nervous* doesn't quite fit. *Curious* and *anxious* capture the largely positive tone of the essay, but *nervous* changes that tone to something negative or ambiguous. Choice (H) would therefore be the LEAST acceptable answer.

31. **C** All the answers say essentially the same thing and are grammatically correct, so choose the shortest that makes sense in the context. In this case, (C) contains all the information the other answers do, and it does so in the most concise way.

32. **H** Notice the 3-1 split! Choices (F), (G), and (J) all contain STOP punctuation (period, comma + FANBOYS, semicolon). Choice (H) is the only one that does not, so it must be the one that is NOT an acceptable alternative to the original sentence's STOP punctuation.

33.   **D**   The words cannot be where they currently are in the sentence because one can't *guess about* something. The only answer that could work is (D), which changes the end of the sentence to say *I shouldn't be surprised about her request.*

34.   **F**   The passage is in the present tense, so (H) and (J) can be eliminated for changing that tense. Then, (F) provides the most concise form of the verb in question, so it is the best answer.

35.   **A**   Notice the 3-1 split! Choices (B), (C), and (D) all use the adjective *appropriate*, while (A) uses the adverb *appropriately*. The adjective is preferable because it modifies the word *it*; the adverb in (A) would modify the verb *believes*, which would not make sense, thus making (A) the NOT acceptable alternative.

36.   **F**   There is STOP punctuation in the answer choices, so use the Vertical Line Test! The first idea, *I'll never forget my utter dismay when he taught her to jump off the swing set in our backyard,* is complete, but the second idea, *pretending she was a pilot and shouting, "Airborne!",* is not, so STOP punctuation is not acceptable, thus eliminating (H) and (J). A comma is acceptable in this situation, however, so (F) is correct. Choice (G) moves the comma to a place where there is no reason to have a comma.

37.   **C**   Each of the answer choices should refer to the daughter, or *she*, playing house. Choices (A), (B), and (D) all do so, but (C) changes the subject of this part of the sentence to *house*. Choice (C) creates an odd incomplete idea, so it is the alternative that would NOT be acceptable to the underlined portion.

38.   **F**   There is a semicolon in the middle of this sentence, so both parts of the sentence must be complete ideas. Choice (H) creates an incomplete idea, and (G) suggests a continuation where none exists. This leaves (F) and (J), which both provide contrasts, though (J) implies some kind of replacement or alternative where none exists.

39.   **D**   When DELETE shows up as an answer choice, there must be some very good reason NOT to pick it. In this case, there is no such reason: Each alternative gives information that is redundant with the word *annual*, so the phrase as a whole should be deleted, as (D) suggests.

40.   **G**   The sentence would be grammatically correct if the phrase *other children her age* could be removed, but such a removal would change the meaning of the sentence. The phrase should be kept because it clarifies the narrator's daughter's uniqueness among her peer group, as (G) suggests.

41.   **B**   When DELETE shows up as an answer choice, there must be some very good reason NOT to pick it. In this case, there is a reason—the sentence is incomplete without a word where the underlined portion is. The word *which* cannot be used with people, so that can be eliminated. Then, use the word *who* where you would use *he* and *whom* where you would use *him*. In this case, you'd say *he was mistaken*, which means the correct answer must be (B), *who*.

42. **J** Both words in the underlined portion modify the adjective *right*. Both words should therefore be adverbs, as both are in (J).

43. **B** Choices (A), (C), and (D) note the father's *big dreams*, but (B) claims those dreams are *impossible*, of which the passage gives no evidence. Choice (B) is therefore the LEAST acceptable alternative.

44. **G** The sentence is incorrect as written (because the subject *individual* and the verb *design* do not agree), so (F) can be eliminated. Then, all the remaining answers say essentially the same thing, so choose the shortest that makes sense in the context. In this case, (G) contains all the information the other answers do, and it does so in the most concise way.

45. **C** There is no contrast between this sentence and the last, so there is no need for the contrast words that appear in (A), (B), and (D). In this case, the best answer is also the shortest, (C), which gives the correct meaning and is grammatically sound.

46. **J** When DELETE shows up as an answer choice, there must be some very good reason NOT to pick it. In this case, there is no such reason: Each alternative gives information that is redundant with the phrase *as a child*, so the phrase as a whole should be deleted, as (J) suggests.

47. **B** When DELETE shows up as an answer choice, there must be some very good reason NOT to pick it. In this case, there is a reason: If a word is removed from this part of the sentence, this sentence has two complete ideas separated by only a comma. In this context, only (B) can work, as the sentences describes what happened *when* the author looked into his hands.

48. **F** The ideas on either side of the underlined portion are complete. These ideas should therefore be separated with STOP punctuation. Only (F) provides it in giving a comma plus *and*, one of the FANBOYS.

49. **A** There is a comma in the middle of this sentence, and the idea after the comma, *they're not totally certain what it is intended to do, either,* is complete. Because the second idea is complete and only a comma separates the two ideas, the first idea must be incomplete. Only (A) makes it incomplete, so it is the only possible answer.

50. **J** Because the pronoun refers back to *organisms*, it should be the plural *themselves*, eliminating (G) and (H). Then, note the other verbs in this sentence: *attract, repulse,* and *communicate*. The verb *camouflage* should be consistent with those, making (J) the only possible answer.

51. **A** The next sentence refers to how the *same adaptation can be used to both attract and repulse*, so the mention of how the adaptation can *repulse predators* in the previous sentence should be kept, and it should be kept for the reason that (A) gives. Although (B) may be true, (A) gives the better answer as it relates to the construction of this essay. Remember—this is English, not Science!

52. **H** The phrase *or land-based* is used to clarify the word *terrestrial*, but it could be removed with no change to the meaning or completeness of the sentence. The unnecessary phrase should therefore be set off with commas, as it is in (H).

53. **B** All the answers say essentially the same thing, so choose the shortest that makes sense in the context. In this case, (B) contains all the information the other answers do, and it does so in the most concise way. The mention of the *researchers* does not contribute anything to the meaning of the sentence and makes things overly wordy.

54. **G** The paragraph as a whole discusses the ocean and various sea creatures. The only choice that previews what is to come is (G), which mentions that things are *quite different in the ocean.*

55. **A** The two ideas in this sentence are complete: *the most commonly emitted colors are blue and green and red and yellow have also been observed.* There should therefore be STOP punctuation between them, eliminating (B) and (D). Choice (C) can also be eliminated because it incorrectly combines a semi-colon with a FANBOYS conjunction. Choice (A) provides the best available answer by combining a comma with one of the FANBOYS.

56. **J** The underlined portion can be expanded to read *It is a veritable rainbow of color,* making (J) the only possible answer. Choice (F) gives the possessive form; (G) does not make sense in the context; and (H) is never used.

57. **C** The word *these* suggests that the word *organisms* will be plural. Therefore, use the plural possessive *organisms',* which is contained only in (C).

58. **H** *Then* is used for time or sequence. *Than* is used for comparison. In this case, one thing is being described as *more than* another, so (H), which contains *than*, is the only possible answer.

59. **C** Choices (A), (B), and (D) are all synonyms for the underlined word, *clarified.* Choice (C) does not work in the context and changes the meaning, so it is the LEAST acceptable of the available alternatives.

60. **G** This essay describes bioluminescence as it exists in both marine and non-marine habitats, among animals on the earth and those in the ocean. The essay would therefore achieve the stated goal, and it would do so for the reason that (G) outlines.

61. **B** This sentence contrasts with the previous sentences, so it should begin with the word *yet*, thus eliminating (A) and (C). Then, because the idea continues from the ideas in the previous sentences, there is no need to begin a new paragraph, as (B) indicates.

62. **J** Whenever you see STOP punctuation in the answer choices, use the Vertical Line Test. In this case, both ideas are incomplete: *that is why a group of French physicians and started Doctors Without Borders in 1971.* Therefore, STOP punctuation cannot be used, so you can eliminate (H). There is no need for commas, so the best answer is the one with no punctuation, (J).

63. **A** Read the question carefully. It asks for a choice that *introduces the basic goal of Doctors Without Borders.* The only answer that does this is (A), which gives that basic goal: *to reach out to the innocent victims of wars in lesser-developed parts of the world.*

64. **H** If you cannot cite a reason to use a comma, don't use one. In this case, no comma is necessary, so choice (H), with no commas, is the correct answer.

65. **D** Choices (A), (B), and (C) each provide reasonable similes for the word *atrocities*. Choice (D) does not; furthermore, the UN and Red Cross are not raising sufficient *alarm* about these atrocities, though they are not trying to *stop these alarms* either. Choice (D) is therefore the LEAST acceptable alternative to the underlined portion.

66. **G** The sentence in question describes the state of things in Nigeria in the late 1960s and the international community's dismissive attitude toward it. The sentence provides some basis for why Doctors Without Borders formed when it did and the purpose that motivated that formation. The sentence should therefore be kept and for the reason that (G) states.

67. **C** The ideas on both sides of the punctuation are complete: *The doctors felt...alleviate the suffering* and *thus they declared...was on.* Because both ideas are complete, there must be STOP punctuation between them. Only (C) contains this type of punctuation.

68. **G** None of these introductory words is essential to the meaning of the sentence. There is no contrast, thus eliminating (F). There is no concurrent action, thus eliminating (H), and this is not a concluding thought, thus eliminating (J). Eliminate the introductory words altogether, and choose the most concise answer, (G).

69. **A** If the phrase in question were deleted, it would not be clear whom the medical training was being provided to, and readers might believe that Doctors With Borders had founded a medical school in the region. The sentence should therefore be kept and for the reason that (A) states.

70. **J** As written, this sentence does not contain a subject, unless the word *suffering* is the subject, but *suffering* cannot have *felt aid*. The only choice that provides an appropriate subject is (J), which completes the subject to be *individuals suffering in war-torn regions*.

71. **A** The word *between* is used for two things, so this sentence is correct as written. If there were three or more groups being discussed, the correct answer would be (B).

72. **H** The underlined word modifies the adjective *simple*, so it must be an adverb, thus eliminating (F) and (J). Then, because there is no reason to add the word *more*, the correct answer must be (H).

73. **B** First, match the subject in the beginning of the underlined portion to the verb at the end of it. Choice (A) says the *effort...have*, and (C) says the *efforts...has*, so both can be eliminated. Then, (D) changes the verb to make it sound like the action being described happened entirely in the past. Because the organization described continues into the present, only (B) can work appropriately in place of the underlined portion.

74. **F** Doctors Without Borders is a volunteer organization, and volunteers *serve* in this organization, making (F) the correct answer. Choices (G), (H), and (J) do not work in this context because they change the meaning, and each verb requires an object that the sentence does not provide.

75. **C** Read the question carefully. It asks for the choice that *most clearly shows that the self-sacrifice of the doctors deserves praise*. Only (C) does so. Although (A) praises Doctors Without Borders, it does not suggest that the doctors deserve praise.

MATHEMATICS TEST

1. **D** To find the quotient between terms in the geometric sequence, divide the fourth term by the third to find that $16 \div 8 = 2$. Then divide the third term by the quotient, 2, to find the second term: $8 \div 2 = 4$.

2. **G** To solve for $f(3,4)$, substitute 3 into the original equation for a and 4 for b: $f(3,4) = 2(3)(4) - (3 + 4) = 24 - 7 = 17$.

3. **D** To find the smallest number of coins Christine could use, start by counting the number of quarters she could use because they have the largest denomination. Because she wants to use exact change, she can only use three quarters, for a total of 75¢. This leaves 99¢ − 75¢ = 24¢. Next, count the number of dimes Christine could use, which is two, for a total of 20¢. The amount left is now 24¢ − 20¢ = 4¢, which must be paid in pennies. The total number of coins she will use is 3 quarters + 2 dimes + 4 pennies = 9 coins.

4. **K** The equation for the area of a square is $A = s^2$. Plug 8 into the equation for s: $A = 8^2 = 64$.

5. **A** Plug 3 into the equation for x: $\dfrac{(3+1)^2}{3^2 - 1} = \dfrac{4^2}{9-1} = \dfrac{16}{8} = 2$.

6. **H** When dealing with NOT questions, eliminate answer choices that work. Use your calculator and try out the answer choices. $1{,}776 \div 12 = 148$, and because 12 is a factor of 1,776, you can eliminate (F). The same is true of the numbers in (G), (J), and (K). However, $1{,}776 \div 18 = 98.\overline{66}$, so 18 is NOT a factor of 1,776 and is the correct answer.

7. **C** Be careful with the CANNOT and NOT in this problem. Probability equals $\dfrac{\text{Number of outcomes that fulfill your requirements}}{\text{Total number of possible outcomes}}$. In this case, only one person, Lauren, fulfills the requirements. There are 19 total students, but 4 of them cannot be the song leader, so the total number of students who could be the song leader is $19 - 4 = 15$. The probability that Lauren will be selected is therefore $\dfrac{1}{15}$. If you picked choice (B), you may have forgotten to subtract the 4 seniors from the total students.

8. **K** To solve for x, first distribute the 4 on the left side of the equation. Remember to watch your negatives! $4x - 20 + x = 45$. Next, combine like terms to get $5x - 20 = 45$. Then, add 20 to both sides: $5x = 65$, and finally divide both sides by 5 to find that $x = 13$.

9. **B** Read carefully to translate this word problem into a math function. The problem indicates that there is a charge of \$0.99 *for each mile*, which means that the final expression should include the term $.99m$. Eliminate (C), (D), and (E). The problem also states that the rental company charges \$112 *plus* the mileage fee, so the final expression should include addition, which makes (B) correct.

10. **K** Find the total amount that Stella would pay according to the finance plan. 4 years of 12 monthly payments per year makes a total of $4 \times 12 = 48$ payments. 48 payments $\times$ \$130 = \$6,240. The question asks how much *more* than the purchase price Stella would pay, so find the difference between the total price of the finance plan and the purchase price: \$6,240 − \$4,800 = \$1,440.

11. **B** Begin by reducing the number part of the fraction: $\dfrac{20y^8}{4y^2} = \dfrac{5y^8}{y^2}$. Next, remember the exponent rules: When dividing two numbers with exponents, subtract the exponents, so $\dfrac{5y^8}{y^2} = 5y^{8-2} = 5y^6$.

12. **F** To avoid making a careless error, be sure to write down all the steps in simplifying this fraction. First, do the subtraction in the numerator and the addition in the denominator: $\dfrac{3 - \frac{1}{2}}{2 + \frac{3}{4}} = \dfrac{\frac{6}{2} - \frac{1}{2}}{\frac{8}{4} + \frac{3}{4}} = \dfrac{\frac{5}{2}}{\frac{11}{4}}$.

To divide by a fraction, multiply by the reciprocal: $\dfrac{\frac{5}{2}}{\frac{11}{4}} = \dfrac{5}{2} \times \dfrac{4}{11} = \dfrac{20}{22} = \dfrac{10}{11}$.

13. **D** Point D could lie either to the right or to the left of point C. To find the point to the right, add the distance between the two points, 8.5, to point C: $8.5 + 3.5 = 12$. Eliminate (A), (B), and (C). To find the point to the left, subtract the distance between the points from point C: $3.5 - 8.5 = -5$, so (D) is correct.

14. **K** To find the mean, or average, of a group of numbers, add the numbers up, and then divide by the number of numbers. This can be written as an equation, $\text{Average} = \dfrac{\text{Total}}{\text{Number of numbers}}$. Since you don't know the total in this case, plug the information you have into the equation: $7 = \dfrac{\text{Total}}{4}$, then multiply both sides by 4 to find that Total = 28. Add the three numbers you are given to find that $2 + 4 + 10 = 16$. To find the value of the unknown number, subtract the total of the three known numbers from the total of all four numbers: $28 - 16 = 12$.

15. **A** Read carefully! The problem tells you that the *net profit increased linearly*, which means it increased by the same amount each year. This means that the answer should be the number that is exactly halfway between $1,489,000 and $1,725,000. You can eliminate (C) because it is much too close to $1,725,000 and (D) and (E) because they are bigger than $1,725,000. To solve, first find the difference between the 2009 profit and the 2007 profit: $1,725,000 − $1,489,000 = $236,000. To find the number in the middle, divide the difference by 2: $236,000 ÷ 2 = $118,000, then add that number to the 2007 profit: $1,489,000 + $118,000 = $1,607,000.

16. **F** Notice that the dimensions of the picture are given in inches, and the question asks for the dimensions of the finished painting in feet. Start by converting the dimensions of the original picture from inches to feet. To make the conversion, divide each measurement by 12. The width is $\frac{8}{12}$ = 0.67 feet, and the height is $\frac{10}{12}$ = 0.83 feet. Next, set up a proportion of the original measurements to the finished measurements: $\frac{0.67}{0.83} = \frac{x}{6}$. To solve for x, which is the width of the finished painting, first cross-multiply: $0.83x = (0.67)(6)$, or $0.83x = 4.02$. Then, divide both sides by 0.83: $x = 4.02 ÷ 0.83 = 4.84$. The question asks for the *approximate* width of the finished painting, so round 4.84 to 5.

17. **B** Slope-intercept form is $y = mx + b$, where m is the slope of the line, and b is its y-intercept. To put the given equation in that form, first subtract $5x$ from both sides: $-y = -5x + 2$. Next, divide both sides by -1, making sure to divide all three terms: $y = 5x - 2$. If you picked a different answer choice, you may have made a mistake with the negatives.

18. **J** Remember order of operations on this problem. First, do the subtraction within the first absolute value sign to get $|-12| - |-25|$. Next, apply the absolute value to each term to get $12 - 25$, and do the subtraction: $12 - 25 = -13$.

19. **D** All the angles in a triangle add up to 180°. Because the problem gives a range of possible values for the measure of $\angle K$, plug in a number that is less than 63°, such as 60°, then solve for $\angle L$:

$37° + 60° + \angle L = 180°$
$97° + \angle L = 180°$
$\angle L = 83°$

Only (D) describes this result.

20. **K** First, simplify the given inequality. Start by adding 1 to both sides: $3x > 27$. Next, divide both sides by 3: $x > 9$. Because x must be *greater* than 9, its smallest possible integer value is 10.

21.   **E**   This diagram of ribbons is essentially just parallel lines intersecting. The question states that the second red ribbon will be parallel to the first, and the two sides of the white ribbon are parallel to each other. The rule with intersecting parallel lines is that all big angles are equal, all small angles are equal, and any big angle plus any small angle equals 180°. The angle in question is a big angle, so to find its measurement, subtract the given small angle measurement from 180°: 180° − 62° = 118°.

22.   **G**   Begin by finding the measurement of $\overline{PR}$. If you recognize the side lengths of the triangle as a Pythagorean triple, you know that $\overline{PR} = 6$. Otherwise, use the Pythagorean theorem, $a^2 + b^2 = c^2$, where c is the hypotenuse. Make $\overline{PR}$ side a:

$a^2 + 8^2 = 10^2$
$a^2 + 64 = 100$
$a^2 = 36$
$a = 6$

Since the midpoint is the exact center of a line, $\overline{QR}$ is half the length of $\overline{PR}$: $\overline{QR} = 6 \div 2 = 3$.

23.   **A**   The three marked points on the graph show the weight (which is the given x-coordinate) for books of three different lengths (the y-coordinate gives the number of pages). The weight of a book with 1,056 pages is 107.8 ounces, and the weight of a book with 868 pages is 89.0 ounces. To find how much more the longer book weighs, subtract the two weights: 107.8 − 89 = 18.8.

24.   **G**   Katie's equation, $y = 0.1x + 2.2$, is given in the description of the graph. The number of pages is shown on the x-axis of the graph, so substitute 1,338 for x in the equation: $y = 0.1(1,338) + 2.2 = 133.8 + 2.2 = 136$. This gives you the weight of the book in ounces, but the question asks for its weight in pounds. Notice that the question tells you, in the note, how many ounces are in a pound, in case you don't know. To find the weight of the book in pounds, divide its weight in ounces by 16: 136 ÷ 16 = 8.5.

25.   **D**   First, divide the shape into smaller rectangles:

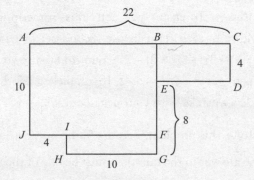

In this diagram, the points have been labeled for reference. Use the formula for the area of a rectangle, $A = lw$, to find the area of each smaller rectangle. Rectangle $BCDE$ has a length of 4. To find its width, note that $\overline{AC}$, which is equal to 22, will have the same measurement as $\overline{JI} + \overline{HG} + \overline{ED}$.

The measurements of two of those segments are given, so solve for $\overline{ED}$:

$$4 + 10 + \overline{ED} = 22$$
$$14 + \overline{ED} = 22$$
$$\overline{ED} = 8$$

The area of $BCDE = 4 \times 8 = 32$. Next, find the area of $IFGH$. The width is given, but you need to find the length. $\overline{AJ}$ plus $\overline{IH}$ must equal $\overline{CD}$ plus $\overline{EG}$, so fill in the values you know and solve for $\overline{IH}$:

$$10 + \overline{IH} = 4 + 8$$
$$10 + \overline{IH} = 12$$
$$\overline{IH} = 2$$

The area of $IFGH = 2 \times 10 = 20$. Now find the area of $ABFJ$. Its length is given, and the width is $\overline{JI} + \overline{IF}$. Since $\overline{IF} = \overline{HG}$, the width is $4 + 10 = 14$, and the area is $10 \times 14 = 140$. Finally, add up all the individual areas to find the area of the entire figure: $32 + 20 + 140 = 192$.

26. F To find the average speed of essay grading, divide the total essays graded by the number of days it took to grade them. This can be written as an equation, $\text{Average} = \dfrac{\text{Total essays}}{\text{Number of days}}$. If Mr. Baylor averaged 178 essays per day for the first 3 days, you can find the total number of essays he graded in those three days:

$$178 = \frac{\text{Total}}{3}$$

Total $= 178 \times 3 = 534$

In his last 3 days, he then had $996 - 534 = 462$ essays left to grade. Use the equation to find the average speed for the last 3 days: $\text{Average} = \dfrac{462}{3} = 154$.

27. C To correctly multiply, each term in the second set of parentheses must be multiplied by both terms in the first set of parentheses. To ensure you don't miss something, write out all six terms, then combine like terms. Multiply each term in the second set of parentheses first by y, then by 1: $(y + 1)(y^2 - 3y + 2) = y^3 + y^2 - 3y^2 - 3y + 2y + 2$. Count to be sure you have six terms before proceeding! Combine like terms to get $y^3 - 2y^2 - y + 2$. If you picked another answer, you may have either forgotten a term or made a mistake with your negatives.

28. H Use *SOHCAHTOA* to solve this problem. Because 5, the number in the denominator, is the hypotenuse of the triangle, the answer to the question must be one of the trig functions that has H in the denominator (that is, sine or cosine), so you can eliminate (G), (J), and (K). 4, the number in the numerator, is the side adjacent to $\angle D$. Since $\cos \theta = \dfrac{adj}{hyp}$, (H) is correct.

29. **A** Plug In the Answers! If Shawn bought 7 contemporary songs, he must have bought 15 classical songs because he bought 22 in all. This means that Shawn spent 7($0.95) + 15($0.75) on songs altogether. These numbers add up to $17.90, which is the number we want, making (A) the correct answer.

30. **G** To find the value of $(-3)\#(-7)$, substitute -3 for x and -7 for y throughout the equation: $\dfrac{(-3)^2 - (-7)^2}{(-3) + (-7)} = \dfrac{9 - 49}{-10} = \dfrac{-40}{-10} = 4$.

31. **C** A fraction is a $\dfrac{\text{part}}{\text{whole}}$ relationship, so create a fraction with the amount of pineapple juice in the numerator and the total amount of punch in the denominator, then simplify:

$$\dfrac{\frac{1}{2}}{2\frac{1}{4}} = \dfrac{\frac{1}{2}}{\frac{9}{4}} = \dfrac{1}{2} \times \dfrac{4}{9} = \dfrac{4}{18} = \dfrac{2}{9}.$$

32. **G** Label the figure first: You know that $\overline{XZ} = 8$. Because O is the center of the circle, $\overline{XO} = 4$, so $\overline{XY}$ is also 4. Any triangle formed with two vertices at the ends of the diameter of a circle and the third vertex also on the circle is a right triangle. Because the hypotenuse $(\overline{XZ})$ of triangle XYZ is twice as long as the short leg $(\overline{XY})$, this is a special 30-60-90 triangle, so the long side $(\overline{YZ})$ measures $4\sqrt{3}$ feet. If you forget this triangle, you can always use the Pythagorean theorem. The formula for the area of a triangle is $A = \dfrac{1}{2}bh$. Use $\overline{XY}$ and $\overline{YZ}$ as the base and height to find that $A = \dfrac{1}{2}(4)(4\sqrt{3}) = (2)(4\sqrt{3}) = 8\sqrt{3}$.

33. **C** The *roots* of a quadratic equation are the same as the solutions. Begin by subtracting 7 from both sides to set the equation equal to zero: $y^2 - 4y - 12 = 0$. Now you can factor. Since the y^2 coefficient is 1, each factor will begin with y, like this: $(y \quad)(y \quad) = 0$. Next, look for two numbers whose *sum* is -4 and whose *product* is -12. Those numbers are -6 and 2, so add them to your factors: $(y - 6)(y + 2) = 0$. To find the solutions for y, set each factor equal to zero and solve for y:

$$y - 6 = 0 \qquad\qquad y + 2 = 0$$
$$y = 6 \qquad\qquad\qquad y = -2$$

You could also plug in the answer choices into the original equation for y. You will find that only (C) makes the equation work.

34.   G   Start by finding the volume of the rectangular portion of the model house. The formula for volume of a rectangular prism is $V = lwh$, so the volume is $V = (20)(20)(16) = 6{,}400$. Next, use the formula given in the note to find the volume of the right pyramid: $V = \frac{1}{3}(20)(20)(12) = 1{,}600$. Finally, add the two volumes together to find the total volume of the model house: $6{,}400 + 1{,}600 = 8{,}000$.

35.   B   The formula for the area of a trapezoid is $A = \left(\dfrac{b_1 + b_2}{2}\right)h$. Plug the numbers you know into the formula, then solve for height:

$$40 = \left(\frac{5 + 11}{2}\right)h$$
$$40 = (8)h$$
$$h = 5$$

36.   J   The formula for slope is $slope = \dfrac{y_2 - y_1}{x_2 - x_1}$. Plug the values from the given points into the formula:
$slope = \dfrac{6 - (-9)}{-2 - 3} = \dfrac{15}{-5} = -3$.

37.   D   Draw the figure. Collinear means "in line with," so point Z is on the same line as points X and Y.

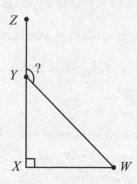

The problem states that $\triangle WXY$ is both a right triangle and isosceles, so $\angle XYW = 45°$. Angles on a straight line must add up to $180°$, so to find $\angle WYZ$, subtract $\angle XYW$ from $180°$: $180° - 45° = 135°$.

38.   H   Look for a pattern. This decimal repeats in 6-digit pattern. That means that the 6th digit is 5, and so is the 12th digit, the 18th digit, the 24th digit, and so on. Because 96 is a multiple of 6, the 96th digit is also 5. The 97th digit is therefore 3, the 98th is 8, and the 99th is 4.

39. E   For coordinate geometry problems, plot out the points. Plot the three points given, then draw the square, including the point not given in the problem.

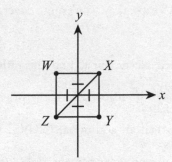

Once you have drawn the figure, you can count the hash marks to find that square *WXYZ* has sides of length 4. $\overline{XZ}$ is the diagonal of the square. Drawing the diagonal of a square divides it into two special 45-45-90 triangles, so the length of $\overline{XZ}$ is $4\sqrt{2}$.

40. G   First, draw the figure. If you have a graphing calculator you can use that to graph, or draw a picture.

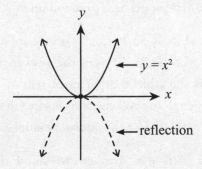

A reflection of a figure is a mirror image of it, in this case across the *x*-axis. Pick a value for *x* to try out in each answer choice. Since the *y*-coordinate of every point in the reflected figure is less than or equal to zero, eliminate any answer choice that would give a positive value for *y*, which leaves only (G). You could also try graphing each of the answer choices on your calculator, and pick the one that gives the reflection of the original.

41. D   Because $\overline{JM}$ and $\overline{KN}$ are parallel, you know something about the angles in this figure, but you are given no information about the lengths of any line segments. Therefore, you can eliminate any answer choices that have to do with the lengths of line segments rather than angles. $\angle KJM \cong \angle JMN$ and $\angle JKN \cong \angle KNM$ because they are opposite interior angles of a line that intersects parallel lines. $\angle JLK \cong \angle NLM$ because they are opposite angles of two intersecting lines. Therefore, (D) must be true because similar triangles have congruent angles. Choice (C) is incorrect because for the triangles to be congruent the sides would also have to be equal, and the problem does not include the measurements for any line segments.

42. **H** The printing cost of each cap is $3.50, and caps are sold for $5.00 each, so the profit on each cap is $5.00 − $3.50 = $1.50. The rental fee is $23.00, so to find the number of caps that must be sold to cover that fee, divide by the profit made on each cap: 23.00 ÷ 1.50 = 15.33. Be careful! If the athletic department only sells 15 caps, they won't quite cover the $23.00 rental charge, so round up to 16.

43. **A** Work this problem in bite-sized pieces. First, find the number of adult tickets sold by translating 60% of 540 into math: $\left(\dfrac{60}{100}\right)(540) = 324$. If the price of each ticket had been $2.00 more, the department would have earned an additional (324)($2.00) = $648.00. The budget deficit is $3,000.00, so the final step is to find what percent $648.00 is of $3,000.00. Translate into math, then solve:

$$\left(\dfrac{x}{100}\right)(3,000) = 648$$
$$(x)(30) = 648$$
$$x = 21.6$$

The question asks for the *approximate* percent, so round up to 22.

44. **J** The printing cost of each T-shirt is $2.25, and T-shirts are sold for $4.00 each, so the profit on each shirt is $4.00 − $2.25 = $1.75. Try out the answers to find the number of shirts that will cover the budget gap. If the athletic department sells 1,726 shirts, as in (J), it will make 1,726 × $1.75 = $3,020.25, enough to cover the budget gap. Choice (H) is too small, and while (K) would cover the gap, the question asks for the *minimum* number of shirts, so (J) is correct.

45. **C** The formula for the area of a triangle is $A = \dfrac{1}{2}bh$. Make $\overline{DE}$ the base of the triangle. Count the hash marks on the graph to find that $\overline{DE} = 4$. The height of the triangle is the perpendicular distance from point O to $\overline{DE}$, which in this case is along the *x*-axis. Again, count the hash marks on the graph to find that $h = 4$. Now plug the numbers into the area formula: $A = \dfrac{1}{2}(4)(4) = 8$.

46. **K** Use the formula for the law of sines given in the note. Because you know the length of $\overline{XY}$, designate that as side a, and make $\overline{YZ}$ side b: $\dfrac{\sin 53°}{12} = \dfrac{\sin 68°}{b}$. To find b, first cross multiply: $(b)(\sin 53°) = (12)(\sin 68°)$. Next, substitute the decimal values given in the second note for the sine expressions, then solve:

$$(b)(0.799) = (12)(0.927)$$
$$0.799b = 11.124$$
$$b = 13.9$$

47. C Factor the expression under the radical: $\sqrt{-16c^2} = \sqrt{(16)(c^2)(-1)} = \left(\sqrt{16}\right)\left(\sqrt{c^2}\right)\left(\sqrt{-1}\right) = 4c\sqrt{-1}$.

The imaginary number i is equal to $\sqrt{-1}$, so $4c\sqrt{-1} = 4ci$. Substitute $4ci$ into the original equa-

tion for $\sqrt{-16c^2}$ to find that $3 \pm \sqrt{-16c^2} = 3 \pm 4ci$.

48. J Draw two radii of the circle from the center to points C and D. Because the measure of an arc is proportional to the measure of the central angle it makes in a circle, $\angle COD = 60°$. Because $\overline{OC}$ and $\overline{OD}$ are both radii of the circle and therefore equal, $\angle C$ must also equal $\angle D$. All angles of a triangle add up to $180°$, so you can find the measurements of $\angle C$ and $\angle D$:

$\angle C + \angle D + 60° = 180$
$\angle C + \angle D = 120°$
$\angle C = \angle D = 60°$

Since all three angles are equal, triangle OCD is equilateral. That means that all three sides, as well as the radius of the circle, are equal to 12. The diameter of a circle is twice the radius, so $D = (2)(12) = 24$. If you picked (F), you picked the radius instead of the diameter!

49. E Draw a picture:

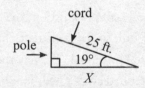

Use *SOHCAHTOA*. The distance between the pole and where the cord touches the ground is the side adjacent to the $19°$ angle, and you know the length of the hypotenuse, so use $\cos \theta = \dfrac{\text{adj}}{\text{hyp}}$:

$\cos 19° = \dfrac{x}{25}$

$x = 25\cos 19°$

50. F The formula for the graph of a circle is $(x - h)^2 + (y - k)^2 = r^2$, where (h,k) is the center of the circle, and r is the radius. If you multiply out the x and y expressions on the left side of the equation, you get an equation with two quadratics:

$(x - h)(x - h) + (y - k)(y - k) = r^2$
$x^2 - 2hx + h^2 + y^2 - 2ky + k^2 = r^2$

To find the center of the circle with the given equation, you need to put the equation into the standard format, which you do by completing the square for the two quadratics, then factoring. Start by subtracting 8 from both sides, and leave a space to complete each square: $x^2 + 8x$ ___ + $y^2 - 2y$ ___ = -8. Next, look at the x terms. $8x$ is equivalent to the middle term in the first quadratic in the example above:

$8x = -2hx$
$h = -4$

Since you need to add h^2, add $(-4)^2 = 16$ to the equation. Remember to add it to both sides: $x^2 + 8x + 16 + y^2 - 2y$ ___ = -8 + 16. Now repeat the process with the y terms:

$-2y = -2ky$
$k = 1$

Add $k^2 = 1^2 = 1$ to both sides of the equation: $x^2 + 8x + 16 + y^2 - 2y + 1 = 8 + 1$. Now you can factor:

$(x + 4)(x + 4) + (y - 1)(y - 1) = 9$
$(x + 4)^2 + (y - 1)^2 = 9$

The center of the circle is (-4,1).

51. C Read carefully, and work the problem in bite-sized pieces. When working with a series on the ACT, formulas are usually not necessary; just list out the terms. The question asks how long it took for the pool to be less than half full, so first calculate that half full is $13,000 \div 2 = 6,500$. Note that Day 1 is the day *after* the pool was filled. The day the pool was filled it held 13,000 gallons of water. On Day 1, 10% of the water had evaporated, so it had $13,000 - (13,000)(.1) = 11,700$ gallons. On Day 2, another 10% had evaporated, so the pool had $11,700 - (11,700)(.1) = 10,530$ gallons of water. Keep repeating the process until you get under 6,500 gallons:

Day 3: $10,530 - (10,530)(.1) = 9,477$
Day 4: $9,477 - \ \ (9,477)(.1) = 8,529$
Day 5: $8,529 - \ \ (8,529(.1) = 7,676$
Day 6: $7,676 - \ \ (7,676)(.1) = 6,909$
Day 7: $6,909 - \ \ (6,909)(.1) = 6,218$

52. J This is a matrix problem, but you don't need pre-calc to solve it. Just follow the directions! Note that the position of $2d$ in the second equation corresponds to the position of a in the first equation, $2c$ corresponds to b, $2a$ corresponds to c, and $2b$ corresponds to d. Make the appropriate substitutions into the right side of the first equation to get $(2d)(2b) - (2c)(2a) = 4db - 4ca$.

53. **D**   The length of one side of the square is equivalent to the diameter of two circles:

$$24 = 2d$$
$$d = 12$$

Next, find the radius:

$$d = 2r = 12$$
$$r = 6$$

The formula for the area of a circle is $A = \pi r^2$, so $A = \pi(6^2) = 36\pi$.

54. **F**   Read carefully, and work the problem in bite-sized pieces. First, calculate how much Andy paid for the 30 comic books: ($28.95)(30) = $868.50. The problem states that he will sell them when the combined value is $600 more than he paid for them, which means he will sell them when they are worth $868.50 + $600 = $1,468.50. To find how much each comic book will be worth when he sells them, divide the combined value by the number of comic books: $1,468.50 ÷ 30 = $48.95. To find how much more the value of each book will have risen when he sells them, subtract the current value per comic book from the value at sale time: $48.95 – $34.35 = $14.60.

55. **B** $\overline{AC}$ is a diameter of circle G, so it has the same measurement as $\overline{BJ}$, which is also a diameter. If the total length of $\overline{BJ}$ is 18, then $\overline{BH} = 18 – 3 = 15$. Similarly, $\overline{CE}$ is a diameter of circle K and therefore has the same measurement as $\overline{HD}$. If $\overline{HD} = 10$, then $\overline{JD} = 10 – 3 = 7$. To find the length of $\overline{BD}$, add up $\overline{BH}$, $\overline{HJ}$, and $\overline{JD}$: $15 + 3 + 7 = 25$.

56. **J**   Draw the figure. First plot the two points you are given, and draw in the axis of symmetry.

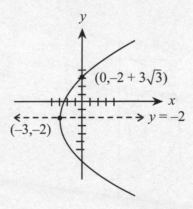

The parabola must be a mirror image across the line of symmetry, so you know it will open to the right, and must cross the y-axis below the line of symmetry at the same distance from it as the given y-intercept. You can then eliminate (F). Because the given y-intercept is $3\sqrt{3}$ units above the line of symmetry at $y = –2$, the other y-intercept will be $3\sqrt{3}$ units below $y = –2$, as specified in (J). You can also plot the points given in the answer choices, and you will find that only (J) comes close to being in the right position.

57.   E   The denominator of the second term in the expression is the common quadratic $x^2 - y^2$, which can

be factored as $(x + y)(x - y)$. So $z^2 - 16 = (z + 4)(z - 4)$. Start by multiplying the first term by $\dfrac{-1}{-1}$ to

make the z in the denominator positive: $\left(\dfrac{-1}{-1}\right)\left(\dfrac{3z}{4-z}\right) = \dfrac{-3z}{-4+z} = \dfrac{-3z}{z-4}$. Next, multiply the first

term by $\dfrac{(z+4)}{(z+4)}$ to get a common denominator, then add the fractions:

$$\frac{(z+4)(-3z)}{(z+4)(z-4)} + \frac{3z}{z^2-16} = \frac{-3z^2-12z}{z^2-16} + \frac{3z}{z^2-16} = \frac{-3z^2-12z+3z}{z^2-16} = \frac{-3z^2-9z}{z^2-16}.$$

You could also try plugging in a number for z. If you make $z = 2$, then

$$\frac{3z}{4-z} + \frac{3z}{z^2-16} = \frac{(3)(2)}{4-2} + \frac{(3)(2)}{2^2-16} = \frac{6}{2} + \frac{6}{-12} = 3 - \frac{1}{2} = 2\frac{1}{2}.$$

Plug $z = 2$ into the answer choices, and you will find that only (E) gives you the correct answer:

$$\frac{(-3)(2^2)-(9)(2)}{2^2-16} = \frac{-12-18}{-12} = \frac{-30}{-12} = \frac{5}{2} = 2\frac{1}{2}.$$

58.   K   In the second quadrant, tangent is always negative, so eliminate (F), (G), and (H). Draw a unit
circle around the origin on the figure:

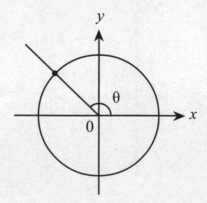

Because the equation for the line is $y = -x$, the coordinates of the point where the unit circle and

the line intersects will have the same absolute value, but x, or cosine, will be negative while y, or

sine, will be positive. Because $\tan \theta = \dfrac{\sin \theta}{\cos \theta}$, in this case $\tan \theta = -1$.

59. **A** Start by subtracting a_n from both sides to isolate the terms containing d: $a_n - a_1 = dn - d$. Now,

factor d out of the right side of the equation: $a_n - a_1 = d(n-1)$. Finally, divide both sides by $(n-1)$:

$$\frac{a_n - a_1}{n-1} = d .$$

You could also Plug In. If you use the arithmetic sequence 2, 4, 6, 8, 10,…, then $a_1 = 2$. Make

$n = 5$, and then $a_n = 10$. Because $d = 2$, the correct answer will be equal to 2 when you substitute

those numbers in. Only (A) works: $\frac{10-2}{5-1} = \frac{8}{4} = 2 .$

60. **H** Divide both sides by $3\sqrt{y}$ to isolate the x term:

$$2\sqrt{x} = \frac{12y}{3\sqrt{y}}$$

$$2\sqrt{x} = \frac{4y}{\sqrt{y}}$$

Now square both sides of the equation to get rid of the radicals:

$$\left(2\sqrt{x}\right)^2 = \left(\frac{4y}{\sqrt{y}}\right)^2$$

$$4x = \frac{16y^2}{y}$$

$$4x = 16y$$

$$x = 4y$$

You could also Plug In. Because y appears twice in the equation and x only appears once, pick a value for y first. Make $y = 9$, then solve for x:

$$2\sqrt{x} \times 3\sqrt{9} = (12)(9)$$

$$2\sqrt{x}(9) = 108$$

$$\sqrt{x} = 6$$

$$x = 36$$

Then plug $y = 9$ into the answer choices to find the one that gives the correct value for $x = 36$, which is (H): $(4)(9) = 36$.

READING TEST

1. **B** Choice (B) is correct because the fourth paragraph states that Rebecca *had felt the draw* of the fields. According to the first paragraph, she also enjoys the noises and smells of the field and can almost feel the atmosphere. Choice (A) may be tempting, but it is incorrect because Rebecca is not concerned with land ownership in those lines.

2. **J** Choice (J) is correct because the fourth paragraph mentions that Rebecca had *[k]nown how the land had turned on her parents,* who had left the farm and worked elsewhere as a result. Additionally, the paragraph mentions consecutive bad years of farming, so *that* must refer to poor farming conditions. Choices (F), (G), and (H) can all be eliminated because they do not address farming conditions.

3. **A** Choice (A) is correct because the fourth paragraph states that Rebecca wanted to *reclaim her family's heritage.* The paragraph also explains that her *great-grandparents had claimed the land as their own* and passed it down to Rebecca's parents. It may seem that (B) and (D) describe the land, but there is no support for the idea that the land is *beyond the control of anyone* or that it is *filled with creatures.*

4. **G** This question asks the reader to identify which aspect of Rebecca's surroundings is NOT mentioned within the first four paragraphs. Choice (G) is correct because there is no mention of how the earth feels. Choice (F) is incorrect because the scents are described in the second paragraph as Rebecca inhales *the fresh and savory scent of almost-ripe wheat* and the smell of the earth. Choice (H) is incorrect because the fourth paragraph states that *the land had turned on her parents and driven them far from the only home they knew.* Choice (J) is incorrect because the *best time to visit the fields alone* is described in the third paragraph.

5. **A** Choice (A) is correct because the question asks for Rebecca's impression of the land, and according to the fourth paragraph, she *felt the draw* of the fields. Later in the fourth paragraph, she is *trying to reclaim the family's heritage.* Choice (B) is incorrect because her family does not give up its claim on the land; rather, the fourth paragraph states that even when her parents left, *they had claimed the land as their own.* Choice (C) may seem plausible for a short story like this one, but there are not enough literary devices to believe the true meaning of the story lies beyond its narration. Choice (D) is incorrect because, though the passage briefly mentions why the family had to leave the land, (D) does not answer the question regarding Rebecca's impressions.

6. **H** The question asks what the lines *Without the former, she could never face the latter* refer to. In paragraph six, the author states *this moment was for enjoying the sheer bounty of life, not for fears and numbers,* so the *former* is enjoying life, while the *latter* is fears and numbers. Choice (H) mentions both of these and is the correct answer.

7. **C** Choice (C) is correct because in the last two paragraphs, Rebecca ponders *loans, mortgage payments,* and a *bad crop ruining all her plans.* However, she also focuses on the *warm reality* of owning the land. Choice (D) may be tempting because a story can do this, but there is no such parallel is drawn in the passage.

8. **F** This passage is narrated in the third person by an omniscient narrator, immediately eliminating (H) and (J). The narrator presents Rebecca's thoughts but does not judge them, eliminating (G). Thus (F) is correct because throughout the passage, the narrator explains what *she liked best of all,* that *she had felt the draw* to return to her land, and that *she knew that in her bones.*

9. **C** Choice (C) is correct because the fourth paragraph states that Rebecca's grandparents turned the wild prairie into *productive fields of wheat and corn.* Therefore, "wild" must mean fields not producing crops, which matches (C). The other choices offer synonyms for the word *wild,* but none of them work in this particular context.

10. **J** Choice (J) is correct because the fifth paragraph describes how as soon as the bee landed on her cheek, Rebecca first *flinched a little bit* and then *let it explore her face.* Be careful with the other choices—these may state what most of us would do if a bee landed on our faces, but the correct answer needs textual support!

11. **C** Choice (C) is correct because in the first paragraph, the author states that, *Petrarch coined* the name Dark Ages and that *the name stuck.* The other people are mentioned throughout the passage, but none of these is authors is described as having contributed to the popularity of the term as directly as Petrarch.

12. **G** Choice (G) is correct because the sixth paragraph states that architects from the Middle Ages developed *some of the most intricate stonework ever seen before or since.* Choices (F) and (H) are certainly old arts that flourished at some time, but the author states that both were either disappearing or uncommon in the Middle Ages.

13. **A** Choice (A) is correct because the last paragraph says that the Middle Ages are studied as a *transition into the modern era.* Make sure you are answering the right question! Choices (C) and (D) describe the beliefs of some, but this question asks about "scholars today."

14. **F** The question asks how the author believes an accurate picture of the Middle Ages will develop in the future. The author states in the last paragraph that *medievalists will continue studying the evidence* to try to understand the era. In the sixth paragraph, he also advises that historians *look at what was actually created.* These pieces of advice align best with (F), and the other choices are not quite sufficient.

15. **D** The question asks the reader to identify which answer was NOT characteristic of people during the Middle Ages. Choice (D) is correct because in the fifth paragraph, the author writes that, while there is a myth that people thought the Earth was flat, he states that *they didn't* believe that idea. Choice (A) is incorrect because the third paragraph states that *Few written records exist,* so

there were some written documents. Choice (B) is incorrect because the fifth paragraph states that mathematics was not abandoned in this time period. Choice (C) is incorrect because the sixth paragraph mentions the *intricate stonework* achieved in the Middle Ages.

16. **J**   Choice (J) is correct because the first paragraph introduces *The period that began with the fall of the Roman Empire* and goes on to call it the *Medieval Period* and the *Dark Ages*. Choice (G) overstates how many terms are given and narrows the field too much. Choice (H) is incorrect because, while the first paragraph did mention that some referred to the Middle Ages as a *cultural wasteland*, that was not the main point of the paragraph.

17. **C**   Choice (C) is correct because the sixth paragraph states that *three-dimensional, realistic art certainly became less common and the ability to build a self-sustaining dome was lost for hundreds of years.* Choices (A), (B), and (D) each refer to areas of study that developed or flourished, but this question asks for those that "truly did go into decline."

18. **F**   Choice (F) is correct because the first paragraph states that Petrarch *wanted to connect his studies with those of antiquity*, or the classical era. Choice (J) may be tempting, but it is incorrect because the paragraph states that Petrarch related his studies to older times, not newer times.

19. **D**   Choice (D) is correct because the paragraph gives some of the different names for the Middle Ages and states that Petrarch *coined* one of the terms. Therefore, *coined* must mean something like came up with or invented. Choice (D) fits this description. Choices (A) and (C) employ different meanings of the word *coin*, but those meanings do not apply in this context.

20. **F**   The question asks for how people viewed education in the Middle Ages before Numbers and Lindberg. The fifth paragraph states that scholars refer to the *decline in learning* that they believed was characteristic of this era. Choice (F) fits this description. The other choices are mentioned in the passage, but they are mentioned as coming *after* Numbers and Lindberg rather than before.

21. **A**   Choice (A) is correct because the books on Pocahontas were insightful. The fifth paragraph describes one as an *admirable job*, the sixth paragraph describes another as a *vivid writing*, and the seventh paragraph describes a third as an *interesting take*. The other choices may describe some of the books on Pocahontas, but choice (A) is the most comprehensive description.

22. **G**   Choice (G) is correct because the cartwheels are mentioned to *indicate a younger child*. Choice (F) is incorrect because there is no claim that John Smith's version is accurate. Choice (J) is incorrect because, while Pocahontas may have been a *younger child*, there is no indication that she was too young to understand John Smith's rescue.

23. **B**   Choice (B) is correct because Townsend is *unwilling to fabricate to fill in the gaps* and instead fills the book *liberally with open speculation*. Choices (A), (C), and (D) do not square with the author's description of Townsend's view.

24. **J** The question asks which of the answers would NOT be part of an accurate portrayal of Pocahontas' life. Choice (J) is correct because the third paragraph states that, at her young age, Pocahontas would *hardly have entered into a romance with Smith*. Choice (F) is incorrect because the fourth paragraph describes Pocahontas' rescue of John Smith. Choice (G) is incorrect because the third paragraph states that she did marry John Rolfe. Choice (H) is incorrect because the third paragraph describes her doing cartwheels at the fort.

25. **D** Choice (D) is correct because the third paragraph explains that Pocahontas was probably a *younger child*, and the fourth paragraph states that most scholars agree there was a rescue, either *literal* or staged with *purely ceremonial meaning*. Choices (A), (B), and (C) use words from the passage, but they use those words in ways not supported by the passage.

26. **F** Choice (F) is correct because the last paragraph states that the book had *two Native American authors*, Dr. Linwood Custalow and Angela L. Daniel. Choice (G) and (J) are incorrect because the paragraph does not mention whether Custalow had written a book before.

27. **D** Choice (D) is correct because the final paragraph states *Custalow takes the legend from Powhatan oral traditions*. Choice (A) is incorrect because Custalow did not question tribal elders. Choice (B) is incorrect because Custalow did not use Smith's account. Choice (C) is incorrect because Custalow did not analyze written documents.

28. **G** This question asks about the author's description of "open speculation." The fifth paragraph starts the discussion on the author's theories with the word *Unfortunately*. Choice (G) matches with the author's negative tone.

29. **A** Choice (A) is correct because the third paragraph states historians *have several reasons to question Smith's version of events* and goes on to explain several contradictions. Choice (B) is incorrect because, while there is some mention of the improbability that Smith and Pocahontas were romantically involved, this is not what the paragraph primarily deals with.

30. **G** Choice (G) is correct because the fourth paragraph reveals that scholars disagree about the rescue: *Some argue that it was a literal rescue, while others claim that it was a staged "rescue" with a purely ceremonial meaning.* None of these scholars argue any of the points made in (F), (H), or (J).

31. **C** Choice (C) is correct because the third paragraph states that forming *lasting romantic bonds is one of the primary proofs given in support of free will*. Choices (A), (B), and (D) give examples of things that contradict or complicate the idea of free will.

32. **G** Choice (G) is correct because the fifth paragraph states some scientists believe that *electrical impulses become chemical impulses, or neurotransmitters, which eventually trigger biological impulses.* The third paragraph describes the biological motivations that people have. Therefore, (G) is supported by the link between the two paragraphs. Choice (F) is incorrect because electro-chemical theory supports the third paragraph; the third paragraph does not support electro-chemical theory. Choice (H) is incorrect because the third paragraph does not undermine electro-chemical theory.

33. **D**   Choice (D) is correct because the last paragraph states that the scientific contributions can *help solve the cases*, which fits with (D)'s "helpful." The paragraph also indicates that incorporating the scientific methodologies into police work is *increasing* and is one example of *convergence*. This information, combined with the rest of the passage, fits with (D)'s "new." The other choices may be partially correct, but they have a negative or dismissive tone where no such tone exists in the passage.

34. **F**   Choice (F) is correct because the fifth paragraph states that *electrical impulses become chemical impulses, or neurotransmitters, which eventually trigger biological impulses*. The fifth paragraph uses this theory to suggest a link between humans and particles, as both respond to these electrical impulses with biological impulses.

35. **B**   Choice (B) is correct because the fifth paragraph states that *all matter is made up of protons, neutrons, and electrons*, each of which *reacts to electrical impulses*. Choices (A) and (C) are incorrect because electrical impulses are in all types of matter and in human interaction.

36. **J**   Choice (J) is correct because the fifth paragraph states that *electrical impulses become chemical impulses, which eventually trigger biological impulses*. Choice (H) is incorrect because it reverses this information. Choices (F) and (G) cannot work because these chemists do not focus on free will.

37. **C**   Choice (C) is correct because the paragraph addresses pair-bonding, which is typically seen as an example of free will. However, lines 26–30 and earlier indicate that pair-bonding *has many evolutionary advantages* that may signify its true motivation or origin. Choice (B) takes this mention of *evolutionary advantages* too literally.

38. **F**   Choice (F) is correct because the sixth paragraph mentions a *practical example of the convergence of scientific theory and human practice*. The paragraph describes police departments using these theories to solve crimes.

39. **D**   Choice (D) is correct because the third paragraph indicates that evolutionary biologists *uncovered evidence that suggests that working as a pair has many evolutionary advantages*. Pair-bonding had before been considered evidence of free will, because it does not seem to have a natural cause. This supports (D). Choice (C) misunderstands the role of pair-bonding: It was not used to redefine free will but to support an accepted definition of it.

40. **G**   Choice (G) is correct because the paragraph states that *scientists are beginning to question* previous ideas. The paragraph then asks *How separate are humans…from the rest of the natural world*? These questions show the uncertainty in the scientific world. Choices (F), (H), and (J) may describe other scientists, but these scientists are characterized by their uncertainty.

SCIENCE TEST

1. **C**   Use what you know from biology—*mitosis* refers to the splitting of a cell into two equal parts. If you weren't sure of this, use the blurb as a hint—it refers to *the dividing cell cycle*. This question is asking for the picture of what happens as *mitosis nears completion*, or in other words, the picture that shows the closest thing to two separate entities, which the picture for Cell 3 does.

2. **J**   The graph shows a direct relationship between toxin concentration and *AI*, the apoptotic index. Therefore, if the *AI* is approximately 0.007 (or 0.7%) at 80 ppm, it must be greater than that value at 90 ppm, making (J) the only possible answer.

3. **D**   As the actively dividing cell cycle progresses, the cell gets larger before its two halves split into equal parts. The first stage must therefore show the smallest and least divided picture, as (D), Cell 4, does.

4. **G**   According to Figure 2, there were 225 cells in cycle stage G_2, and there were 75 cells in stage S. There were therefore 3 times as many cells in cycle stage G_2 as there were in stage S, as (G) indicates.

5. **A**   The text above the graph indicates that the graph charts *one thousand actively dividing fibroblast cells*. There were just over 525 cells in cycle stage G_1. Therefore, the proportion of all the cells that were in cycle stage G_1 was approximately 525 of 1,000, or (A).

6. **F**   If you're unsure whether to answer Yes or No, use the reasons. Choices (G) and (J) can be eliminated because Patient 4 and Patient P do have the same blood-smear findings according to Table 1. Judging from Table 1 alone, we have all the necessary evidence to say that Patient 4 and Patient P are the same, thus making (F) the correct answer.

7. **C**   This question requires a bit of outside knowledge, *unless* you use POE aggressively! First, choice (A) suggests that hemoglobin breaks down at a pH of 8.6, but this experiment is measuring hemoglobin, so the scientists would not want it broken down. Always give special consideration to opposites—in this case, (C) and (D). Then, the scientists likely used this pH level because the process they were observing occurs *best* at this level, making (C) the correct answer.

8. **H**   Use POE. Table 1 indicates that Patient 4's blood contains sickle cells, which means that this patient must have at least one of the alleles that causes sickle cell anemia. As the question indicates, the alleles that cause sickle cell anemia are Hb^S and Hb^C. Pairs of alleles that contain only Hb^A will not have sickle cell anemia, thus eliminating (I), which contains only Hb^A, and therefore eliminating (G) and (J). The remaining two options, (II) and (III), both contain either Hb^S and Hb^C, so both are possibilities, making (H) the correct answer.

9. **B**   Match the peaks in the various lines. Patient P's single peak most closely resembles that of Patient 2, thus making (B) the only possible answer.

10.	J	The figure shows a positive electrode on the left side and a negative electrode on the right. Similar charge characteristics must therefore be similar positions relative to given electrodes. Of the choices listed, peaks X and Z seem to be a similar distance from the positive electrode, making (J) the best answer. Peaks W and Y are also similarly positioned, but no answer choice indicates this pair.

11.	A	Use POE. Opposite charges attract each other, eliminating (B) and (D). In addition, "the left" refers to the side of the positive electrode. Because opposite charges attract each other, the peaks closest to the positive electrode must be negative, as (A) indicates.

12.	J	The ball is moving at Points X and Y, but it stops at Point Z, meaning that its velocity at that point is 0, thus eliminating (F) and (G), which suggest that there is a slower velocity at Point X than at Point Z. Then, there are two ways to differentiate between Points X and Y. If you use the chart, you can see that Point X has a uniformly higher kinetic energy than Point Y, meaning its velocity is uniformly higher. If you use the figure, you can see that the velocity at Point X will be approximately the same as the ball's initial velocity, where its velocity on Point Y will be a bit slower after the ball has had to climb the ramp. In either case, the order of the velocities from slowest to fastest will be Point Z, Point Y, and Point X, as listed in (J).

13.	D	According to the text above Table 1, *ME* refers to the sum of the *PE* and *KE* at any given time. However, the question asks about *ME at the point immediately before climbing the ramp,* or Point X. According to the chart, the *KE* at Point X in this trial is 29.1 J. The sum of this number and any other cannot be less than 29.1 J, thus making (D) the only possible answer and suggesting that there is no *PE* at Point X.

14.	F	According to Table 1, the potential energy at Point Y increases as θ increases. Trials 1–3 vary only these two variables, so it can be inferred that if θ is 50°, the potential energy at Point Y will be greater than 12.6 J, (F).

15.	B	Use the text to translate this question. The *coefficient of friction* is listed in the table as μ, and the *minimum distance of Point W from Point X required for the bowling ball to barely reach Point Z* is listed in the table as *d*. Using Trials 3–5, then, we can see that as μ increases, *d* decreases, making (B) the only possible answer.

16.	H	Mechanical energy is described as *the sum of [the ball's] kinetic and potential energies* at any given point. Use the trials given in the chart. In Trial 1, the kinetic energy at Point X was 28.1 J, while the kinetic energy at Point Y was 17.5 J, and the potential energy at Point Y was 6.7 J. There is a change in the amount of energy from Point X (28.1 J) to that of Point Y (24.2 J), suggesting that some mechanical energy must have been lost. This same disparity can be seen in all five trials, as (H) suggests.

17. **C**   Freezing point is the temperature at which a liquid turns to a solid. Melting point is the tempera- ture at which a solid turns to a liquid. Freezing point and melting point therefore occur at the same temperature. According to Table 1, acetic acid has the highest freezing point, so it must also have the highest melting point, as (C) indicates.

18. **G**   According to Figure 2, the vapor pressure of formic acid in a 0.5 mole fraction of water is approxi- mately 11mm Hg. Draw a line straight across to see that formic acid has a solid vapor pressure at a 0.8 mole fraction of water, thus making (G) the correct answer.

19. **A**   According to Figure 2, the vapor pressure of acetic acid starts around 12.5mm Hg, decreases to ap- proximately 5mm Hg, then increases again to approximately 15mm Hg. It therefore decreases then increases, as (A) suggests.

20. **G**   Note the long molecular formulas in Table 1. Follow the coefficients: Butyric acid has subscripts 3, 2, and 2. Valeric acid has subscripts 3, 2, 3. As the final number increases, the boiling point increases as well, each time by approximately 20°. Therefore, since the new formula given in the problem has subscripts 3, 2, 4, it should have a boiling point approximately 20° higher than that of valeric acid, or approximately 206°. This number is contained in the range given in (G).

21. **C**   According to Figure 1, the vapor pressures for formic acid are uniformly higher than those for acetic acid at various temperatures. It can therefore be inferred that acetic acid is more resistant to these increases in vapor pressure, making (C) the correct answer. On questions like this one, if you are unsure how to answer, always use POE aggressively: It may reveal trends that you hadn't seen before. POE can also help to narrow down the choices: (A) and (D) can be eliminated right away, for instance, because they do not match the information in the graph.

22. **J**   According to Table 3, as the solenoid length of XY decreases, the weight increases. The text above the graph indicates that these weights were found at a voltage of 8.00 V. In Experiment 1, the weight at a voltage of 8.00 V is 5.0095 N, which is less than any given in Table 3. Because this weight is *less*, the solenoid coil in Experiment 1 must have had a *greater* length than any of those listed in Experiment 3, or greater than 9.50 cm, as (J) suggests.

23. **B**   Experiment 2 inverts the orientation of the bar magnet in Experiment 1. This variation caused a different trend. In Table 1, as voltage increased, weight increased. In Table 2, as voltage increased, weight decreased. The direction of the force must therefore have been different, as (B) suggests.

24. **J**   According to Table 3, as the solenoid length of XY decreases, the weight increases. The voltage is not be altered, thus eliminating (F) and (G). Choice (J) accurately describes the trends in the graph.

25. **C** Experiment 3's data is taken at 8.00 V. Compare the 8.00 V values in Experiments 1 and 2. In Experiment 1, the weight at 8.00 V is 5.0095 N, and in Experiment 2, the weight at 8.00 V is 4.9905 N. This is a decrease of approximately 0.02 N. Therefore, if the orientation of the magnet matches that of Experiment 2 rather than Experiment 1, the weight should be approximately 0.02 N less than the 5.0105 N value given in the chart. Choice (C) offers the closest value.

26. **J** According to the text above Experiment 1, before the start of each trial, *the scale read 4.7 N*. Then, *the scale was adjusted to read 5.0000 N*. The scale was therefore adjusted upward by approximately 0.3 N, as (J) suggests.

27. **B** According to Table 3, as the solenoid length of XY decreases, the weight increases. Choices (A) and (D) can be eliminated because they show direct relationships rather than inverse ones. Then, the weights in Table 3 are closer to 5.0200 N than they are to 0 N, so the data shown in (B) is more accurate.

28. **F** According to Scientist 1, *Between 1950 and 2000, global average sea level rose by 0.1m*. Choices (G), (H), and (J) show a general decrease in sea level, so all three can be eliminated. A jump 100 times more than 0.1m would be approximately 10, and only (F) shows an appropriately large jump in the sea level.

29. **C** Use POE! Scientist 2 draws heavily on Figure 2, and his basic argument is that *rises and falls in the global average sea level occurred many times in the last 150,000 years*. He would not say that the temperature has remained constant, eliminating (A), nor would he attribute global temperature change only to industrial activity, eliminating choice (B). Later in the passage, Scientist 2 states, *In general, global average sea level rises and falls with global average temperature*, which is paraphrased in (C).

30. **J** According to Figure 1, the change in average global sea level in 2000 was approximately 0.05 m. According to Scientist 1, *Since 2000 the change in global average sea level has increased at a rate of 2% per year*. Since you don't have a calculator, make the math easier for yourself—instead of 0.05 m, use 500. If the change in 2000 was 500, in 2001 it was 510, in 2002 it was approximately 520, and in 2003 it was approximately 530. Translate this back into the numbers you started with to find a change of approximately 0.053 m, (J). Even if you found this math a little tricky, you can certainly eliminate (F) and (G) because they are smaller, and you may have ballparked to see that (H) would not be quite high enough.

31. **A** If you're unsure how to answer the question, use POE on the reasons. Figure 1 shows data from the years 1500 to 2000. This eliminates (B) and (D). Then, because it is clear that Figure 1 does not address climate changes from 150,000 years ago, Figure 1 cannot be said to provide sufficient support Scientist 1's claim, making (A) the correct answer.

32. **J** According to Figure 2, 100,000 years ago, the change in average sea level from present was approximately −60 m. If the present location is fixed 90 m above a fixed landmark, then the level 100,000 years ago would be 60 m less than that or 30 m, (J).

33. **C** There are two major peaks in average global sea level according to Figure 2. One occurred recently, and the other occurred approximately 115,000 years ago. Scientist 2 would therefore cite the 115,000-year figure as evidence that sea levels have risen to present levels before. Choice (C) is therefore the best answer. If you chose (D), be careful! You may have been looking at the axis for air temperature rather than the one for global sea level.

34. **F** According to Figure 1, the change in average global sea level hovered between −0.15 m and −0.10 m from 1500 to 1800. Scientist 1 would likely consider this a negligible change, and because Scientist 1 sees a direct correlation between rising sea levels and rising temperatures, he would likely consider the rise in temperature to be negligible as well, as (F) suggests. Scientist 1's bigger point is that temperatures followed a natural course until 1800, when they began to rise dramatically.

35. **D** Use POE. If albumin molecules do not pass through the selectively permeable membrane, the albumin solution on the left side will not pass through to the right, meaning the solution levels on the left cannot fall, eliminating (A) and (C). Then, because there is no glucose-cupric combination, there is no reason for there to be a red solution, eliminating (B). Only (D) remains and is the correct answer.

36. **F** In Experiment 1, the cupric solution is able to pass through the membrane to produce a red color with the glucose solution. In Experiment 2, the cupric solution is able to pass through the membrane to form a blue-colored solution with the pure water. It can be inferred, then, that cupric was able to pass through the membrane in both experiments and into both glucose and pure water, as (F) suggests.

37. **C** Read the first lines of each experiment. Experiment 2 states that *Cupric ion solution is poured in the left*, and Experiment 3 states that *Glucose solution is poured in the left*. These statements match with the information in (C).

38. **G** Because *mixing glucose and cupric ions results in a red solution*, a membrane that allows all solutions to pass through would result in the mixing of all solutions. In Experiment 1, glucose is poured in the left and cupric in the right. With a membrane that allows both these solutions to pass through, the solutions will mix throughout the tube, creating a red solution in all parts of the tube.

39. **A** Because the solution on the left becomes red, cupric ions must be able to pass through the membrane, and because the water levels change, water must be passing through the membrane as well. If glucose were able to pass through the membrane, both sides of the tube would be filled with red-colored solution. Therefore, it can be inferred that glucose is larger than both cupric and pure water, but it is not possible to determine the relative sizes of cupric and pure water, as (A) suggests.

40.   **G**   Experiment 1 states, *cupric ion solution is poured on the right*. The information above Experiment 1 states, *Water and glucose solutions are colorless while cupric ion solutions are blue*. Therefore, before the experiment begins, the right side, containing only cupric ion solution, must have been blue, as (G) suggests.

SCORING YOUR PRACTICE EXAM

Step A

Count the number of correct answers for each section and record the number in the space provided for your raw score on the Score Conversion Worksheet below.

Step B

Using the Score Conversion Chart on the next page, convert your raw scores on each section to scaled scores. Then compute your composite ACT score by averaging the four subject scores. Add them up and divide by four. Don't worry about the essay score; it is not included in your composite score.

Score Conversion Worksheet		
Section	Raw Score	Scaled Score
1	_____/75	_____
2	_____/60	_____
3	_____/40	_____
4	_____/40	_____

SCORE CONVERSION CHART

Scaled Score	Raw Scores			
	Test 1 English	Test 2 Math	Test 3 Reading	Test 4 Science
36	75	58–60	40	38–40
35	74–73	56–57	––	37
34	72	54–55	39	36
33	71	52–53	38	35
32	70	51	37	34
31	69	50	36	33
30	68	49	34–35	32
29	66–67	47–48	33	31
28	65	45–46	32	30
27	63–64	43–44	31	29
26	61–62	41–42	30	28
25	58–60	39–40	29	26–27
24	56–57	37–38	28	24–25
23	53–55	35–36	26–27	23
22	50–52	34	25	21–22
21	47–49	32–33	23–24	20
20	44–46	31	22	18–19
19	42–43	29–30	20–21	16–17
18	40–41	26–28	19	15
17	37–39	23–25	18	14
16	35–36	18–22	16–17	13
15	32–34	14–17	15	12
14	30–31	11–13	13–14	11
13	28–29	9–10	12	10
12	26–27	07–08	10–11	09
11	24–25	06	08–09	08
10	22–23	05	07	07
09	19–21	04	06	05–06
08	16–18	03	05	04
07	13–15	––	––	––
06	11–12	02	04	03
05	08–10	––	03	02
04	06–07	01	02	––
03	04–05	––	––	01
02	03	––	01	––
01	00–02	00	00	00

NOTES

NOTES

NOTES

NOTES

NOTES

NOTES

NOTES

NOTES

NOTES

NOTES

International Offices Listing

China (Beijing)
1501 Building A,
Disanji Creative Zone,
No.66 West Section of North 4th Ring Road Beijing
Tel: +86-10-62684481/2/3
Email: tprkor01@chol.com
Website: www.tprbeijing.com

China (Shanghai)
1010 Kaixuan Road
Building B, 5/F
Changning District, Shanghai, China 200052
Sara Beattie, Owner: Email: sbeattie@sarabeattie.com
Tel: +86-21-5108-2798
Fax: +86-21-6386-1039
Website: www.princetonreviewshanghai.com

Hong Kong
5th Floor, Yardley Commercial Building
1-6 Connaught Road West, Sheung Wan, Hong Kong
(MTR Exit C)
Sara Beattie, Owner: Email: sbeattie@sarabeattie.com
Tel: +852-2507-9380
Fax: +852-2827-4630
Website: www.princetonreviewhk.com

India (Mumbai)
Score Plus Academy
Office No.15, Fifth Floor
Manek Mahal 90
Veer Nariman Road
Next to Hotel Ambassador
Churchgate, Mumbai 400020
Maharashtra, India
Ritu Kalwani: Email: director@score-plus.com
Tel: + 91 22 22846801 / 39 / 41
Website: www.score-plus.com

India (New Delhi)
South Extension
K-16, Upper Ground Floor
South Extension Part–1,
New Delhi-110049
Aradhana Mahna: aradhana@manyagroup.com
Monisha Banerjee: monisha@manyagroup.com
Ruchi Tomar: ruchi.tomar@manyagroup.com
Rishi Josan: Rishi.josan@manyagroup.com
Vishal Goswamy: vishal.goswamy@manyagroup.com
Tel: +91-11-64501603/ 4, +91-11-65028379
Website: www.manyagroup.com

Lebanon
463 Bliss Street
AlFarra Building - 2nd floor
Ras Beirut
Beirut, Lebanon
Hassan Coudsi: Email: hassan.coudsi@review.com
Tel: +961-1-367-688
Website: www.princetonreviewlebanon.com

Korea
945-25 Young Shin Building
25 Daechi-Dong, Kangnam-gu
Seoul, Korea 135-280
Yong-Hoon Lee: Email: TPRKor01@chollian.net
In-Woo Kim: Email: iwkim@tpr.co.kr
Tel: + 82-2-554-7762
Fax: +82-2-453-9466
Website: www.tpr.co.kr

Kuwait
ScorePlus Learning Center
Salmiyah Block 3, Street 2 Building 14
Post Box: 559, Zip 1306, Safat, Kuwait
Email: infokuwait@score-plus.com
Tel: +965-25-75-48-02 / 8
Fax: +965-25-75-46-02
Website: www.scorepluseducation.com

Malaysia
Sara Beattie MDC Sdn Bhd
Suites 18E & 18F
18th Floor
Gurney Tower, Persiaran Gurney
Penang, Malaysia
Email: tprkl.my@sarabeattie.com
Sara Beattie, Owner: Email: sbeattie@sarabeattie.com
Tel: +604-2104 333
Fax: +604-2104 330
Website: www.princetonreviewKL.com

Mexico
TPR México
Guanajuato No. 242 Piso 1 Interior 1
Col. Roma Norte
México D.F., C.P.06700
registro@princetonreviewmexico.com
Tel: +52-55-5255-4495
+52-55-5255-4440
+52-55-5255-4442
Website: www.princetonreviewmexico.com

Qatar
Score Plus
Office No: 1A, Al Kuwari (Damas)
Building near Merweb Hotel, Al Saad
Post Box: 2408, Doha, Qatar
Email: infoqatar@score-plus.com
Tel: +974 44 36 8580, +974 526 5032
Fax: +974 44 13 1995
Website: www.scorepluseducation.com

Taiwan
The Princeton Review Taiwan
2F, 169 Zhong Xiao East Road, Section 4
Taipei, Taiwan 10690
Lisa Bartle (Owner): lbartle@princetonreview.com.tw
Tel: +886-2-2751-1293
Fax: +886-2-2776-3201
Website: www.PrincetonReview.com.tw

Thailand
The Princeton Review Thailand
Sathorn Nakorn Tower, 28th floor
100 North Sathorn Road
Bangkok, Thailand 10500
Thavida Bijayendrayodhin (Chairman)
Email: thavida@princetonreviewthailand.com
Mitsara Bijayendrayodhin (Managing Director)
Email: mitsara@princetonreviewthailand.com
Tel: +662-636-6770
Fax: +662-636-6776
Website: www.princetonreviewthailand.com

Turkey
Yeni Sülün Sokak No. 28
Levent, Istanbul, 34330, Turkey
Nuri Ozgur: nuri@tprturkey.com
Rona Ozgur: rona@tprturkey.com
Iren Ozgur: iren@tprturkey.com
Tel: +90-212-324-4747
Fax: +90-212-324-3347
Website: www.tprturkey.com

UAE
Emirates Score Plus
Office No: 506, Fifth Floor
Sultan Business Center
Near Lamcy Plaza, 21 Oud Metha Road
Post Box: 44098, Dubai
United Arab Emirates
Hukumat Kalwani: skoreplus@gmail.com
Ritu Kalwani: director@score-plus.com
Email: info@score-plus.com
Tel: +971-4-334-0004
Fax: +971-4-334-0222
Website: www.princetonreviewuae.com

Our International Partners

The Princeton Review also runs courses with a variety of partners in Africa, Asia, Europe, and South America.

Georgia
LEAF American-Georgian Education Center
www.leaf.ge

Mongolia
English Academy of Mongolia
www.nyescm.org

Nigeria
The Know Place
www.knowplace.com.ng

Panama
Academia Interamericana de Panama
http://aip.edu.pa/

Switzerland
Institut Le Rosey
http://www.rosey.ch/

All other inquiries, please email us at
internationalsupport@review.com